Networking
ALL-IN-ONE DESK REFERENCE
FOR
DUMMIES®

by Doug Lowe

WILEY

Wiley Publishing, Inc.

Networking All-in-One Desk Reference For Dummies®

Published by
Wiley Publishing, Inc.
111 River Street
Hoboken, NJ 07030-5774

Copyright © 2004 by Wiley Publishing, Inc., Indianapolis, Indiana

Published by Wiley Publishing, Inc., Indianapolis, Indiana

Published simultaneously in Canada

For general information on our other products and services or to obtain technical support, please contact our Customer Care Department within the U.S. at 800-762-2974, outside the U.S. at 317-572-3993, or fax 317-572-4002.

Wiley also publishes its books in a variety of electronic formats. Some content that appears in print may not be available in electronic books.

Library of Congress Control Number: 2003114631

ISBN: 0-7645-4260-5

Manufactured in the United States of America

10 9 8 7 6 5 4 3 2 1

1O/RY/RR/QT/IN

About the Author

Doug Lowe has written a whole bunch of computer books, including more than 30 *For Dummies* books, such as *Networking For Dummies, 6th Edition, PowerPoint 2003 For Dummies, Internet Explorer 6 For Dummies,* and *Microsoft Office 2002 For Dummies Quick Reference.* He lives in that sunny All-American City Fresno, California, where the motto is, "Hi, I'm (your name here), and I'm running for governor!" with his wife and the youngest of his three daughters. He's one of those obsessive-compulsive decorating nuts who puts up tens of thousands of lights at Christmas and creates computer-controlled Halloween decorations that rival Disney's Haunted Mansion. Maybe his next book should be *Tacky Holiday Decorations For Dummies.*

Dedication

To Debbie, Rebecca, Sarah, and Bethany.

Author's Acknowledgments

I'd like to thank project editors Christine Berman and Kelly Ewing, who did a great job of overseeing all the editorial work that was required to put this book together in spite of a frantic schedule and oft-missed deadlines. I'd also like to thank Dan DiNicolo who gave the entire manuscript a thorough technical review and offered many excellent suggestions, and copy editor Rebekah Mancilla who made sure that the i's were crossed and the t's dotted (oops, reverse that!). And, as always, thanks to all the behind-the-scenes people who chipped in with help I'm not even aware of.

Table of Contents

Introduction

Welcome to *Networking All-in-One Desk Reference For Dummies,* the one networking book that's designed to replace an entire shelf full of the dull and tedious networking books you'd otherwise have to buy. This book contains all the basic and not-so-basic information you need to know to get a network up and running and to stay on top of the network as it grows, develops problems, and encounters trouble.

If you're just getting started as a network administrator, this book is ideal. As a network administrator, you have to know about a lot of different topics: installing and configuring network hardware, installing and configuring network operating systems, planning a network, working with TCP/IP, securing your network, working with wireless devices, backing up your data, and many others.

You can, and probably eventually will, buy separate books on each of these topics. It won't take long before your bookshelf is bulging with 10,000 or more pages of detailed information about every imaginable nuance of networking. But before you're ready to tackle each of those topics in depth, you need to get a birds-eye picture. This book is the ideal way to do that.

And if you already own 10,000 pages or more of network information, you may be overwhelmed by the amount of detail and wonder, "Do I really need to read 1,000 pages about Bind to set up a simple DNS server?" or "Do I really need a six-pound book to show me how to install Linux?" Truth is, most 1,000-page networking books have about a hundred or so pages of really useful information — the kind you use every day — and about 900 pages of excruciating details that apply mostly to networks at places like NASA and the CIA.

The basic idea of this book is that I've tried to wring out the hundred or so most useful pages of information on nine different networking topics: network basics, building a network, network administration and security, trouble-shooting and disaster planning, working with TCP/IP, wireless and home networking, Windows server operating systems, NetWare, and Linux.

So whether you've just been put in charge of your first network or you're a seasoned pro, you've found the right book.

About This Book

Networking All-in-One Desk Reference For Dummies is intended to be a reference for all the great things (and maybe a few not-so-great things) that you may need to know when you're setting up and managing a network. You can, of course, buy a huge 1,000-page book on each of the networking topics covered in this book. But then, who would you get to carry them home from the bookstore for you? And where would you find the shelf space to store them? In this book, you get the information you need all conveniently packaged for you in between one set of covers.

Networking All-in-One Desk Reference For Dummies doesn't pretend to be a comprehensive reference for every detail of these topics. Instead, this book shows you how to get up and running fast so that you have more time to do the things you really want to do. Designed using the easy-to-follow *For Dummies* format, this book helps you get the information you need without laboring to find it.

Networking All-in-One Desk Reference For Dummies is a big book made up of several smaller books — books, if you will. Each of these books covers the basics of one key element of network management, such as setting up network hardware, installing a network operating system, or troubleshooting network problems. Whenever one big thing is made up of several smaller things, confusion is always a possibility. That's why *Networking All-in-One Desk Reference For Dummies* is designed to have multiple access points (I hear an acronym coming on — MAP!) to help you find what you want. At the beginning of the book is a detailed table of contents that covers the entire book. Then, each book begins with a minitable of contents that shows you at a glance what chapters are included in that book. Useful running heads appear at the top of each page to point out the topic discussed on that page. And handy thumb tabs run down the side of the pages to help you quickly find each book. Finally, a comprehensive index lets you find information anywhere in the entire book.

This isn't the kind of book you pick up and read from start to finish, as if it were a cheap novel. If I ever see you reading it at the beach, I'll kick sand in your face. This book is more like a reference, the kind of book you can pick up, turn to just about any page, and start reading. You don't have to memorize anything in this book. It's a "need-to-know" book: You pick it up when you need to know something. Need to know what how to set up a DHCP server in Windows? Pick up the book. Need to know how to create a user account in Linux? Pick up the book. Otherwise, put it down and get on with your life.

How to Use This Book

This book works like a reference. Start with the topic you want to find out about. Look for it in the table of contents or in the index to get going. The table of contents is detailed enough that you should be able to find most of the topics you're looking for. If not, turn to the index, where you can find even more detail.

Of course, the book is loaded with information, so if you want to take a brief excursion into your topic, you're more than welcome. If you want to know the big security picture, read the whole chapter on security. If you just want to know how to make a decent password, read just the section on passwords. You get the idea.

Whenever I describe a message or information that you see on the screen, I present it as follows:

```
A message from your friendly network
```

If you need to type something, you'll see the text you need to type like this: **Type this stuff**. In this example, you type **Type this stuff** at the keyboard and press Enter. An explanation usually follows, just in case you're scratching your head and grunting, "Huh?"

How This Book Is Organized

Each of the nine books contained in *Networking All-in-One Desk Reference For Dummies* can stand alone. The first book covers the networking basics you should know to help you understand the rest of the stuff in this book. Of course, if you've been managing a network for awhile already, you probably know all this stuff, so you can probably skip Book I or just skim it over quickly for laughs. The remaining books cover a variety of networking topics that you would normally find covered in separate books. Here is a brief description of what you find in each book.

Book 1: Networking Basics

This book covers the networking basics you need to get going. You find out what a network is, how networking standards work, what hardware components are required to make up a network, and what network operating systems do. You discover the difference between peer-to-peer networking and client-server networking. And you also get a comparison of the most popular network operating systems, including Windows NT Server, Windows 2000 Server, Windows Server 2003, Novell's NetWare, and Linux.

Book II: Building a Network

In this book, you find out the ins and outs of building a network. First, you see how to create a plan for your network. After all, planning is the first step of any great endeavor. Then, you discover how to install network hardware such as network interface cards and how to work with various types of networking cable. You receive some general pointers about installing a network server operating system. And finally, you gain insight into how to configure various versions of Windows to access a network.

Book III: Network Administration and Security

In this book, you discover what it means to be a network administrator, with an emphasis on how to secure your network so that it's safe from intruders, but at the same time allows your network's users access to everything they need. In the real world, this responsibility isn't as easy as it sounds. This book begins with an overview of what network administrators do. Then, it describes some of the basic practices of good network security, such as using strong passwords and providing physical security for your servers. Then, it presents an overview of setting up network user accounts. And it concludes with some additional security techniques, such as using virus scanners and setting up firewalls.

Book IV: Network Troubleshooting and Disaster Planning

When something goes wrong with your network, you can turn to this book for guidance on isolating the problem and determining how to correct it. This book covers not only major network problems ("my network's dead,") but also those insidious performance problems ("I can get to the server, but it's ess-el-oh-double-ewe"). And, you find help for one of the most common network complaints: e-mail that doesn't get through.

Before something goes wrong with your network, I hope you'll turn to this book for guidance on how to protect your network through a good, comprehensive backup scheme, and how to create a disaster plan (known now by the trendy term, *Business Continuity Planning*).

Book V: TCP/IP and the Internet

This book is devoted to the most popular network technology on the planet: TCP/IP. (Actually, it may be the most popular protocol in the universe. The aliens in *Independence Day* had a TCP/IP network on their spaceship, enabling Will Smith and Jeff Goldblum to hack their way in. The aliens should have read the section on firewalls in Book III.)

In this book, you discover the various protocols that make up the entire TCP/IP suite. You find out all about IP addresses, subnetting, routing, and all that good stuff. You encounter DHCP and DNS. And you discover how to use those handy TCP/IP trouble-shooting tools like Ping and Tracert.

Book VI: Wireless and Home Networking

This book covers two topics: wireless networking and home networking. I combined these two topics because wireless is fast becoming the most cost-effective way to install a home network.

Book VII: Windows 2000 and 2003 Server Reference

This book describes the basics of setting up and administering a server using the latest version of Windows Server 2003 and its predecessor, Windows 2000 Server. You find chapters on installing a Windows server, managing user accounts, setting up a file server, and securing a Windows server. Plus, you find a handy reference to the many Windows networking commands you can use from a command prompt.

Book VIII: NetWare 6 Reference

NetWare was once the most popular network operating system for local area networks, and it's still very popular. This book presents the basics of setting up and installing NetWare 6, the current version of NetWare. You find chapters on installing NetWare, managing user objects, setting up TCP/IP on a NetWare server, and creating NetWare login scripts. Plus, you find a reference to the most popular NetWare console commands.

Book IX: Linux Reference

Linux has fast become an inexpensive alternative to Windows or NetWare. In this book, you discover the basics of installing and managing Red Hat Linux 9, the current version of the most popular Linux distribution. You find out how to install Red Hat Linux, work with Linux commands and GNOME, a popular graphical interface for Linux, configure Linux for networking, set up a Windows-compatible file server using Samba, and run popular Internet servers such as DHCP, Bind, and SendMail. Plus, you get a concise Linux command reference that will turn you into a Linux command line junkie in no time.

Icons Used in This Book

Like any *For Dummies* book, this book is chock-full of helpful icons that draw your attention to items of particular importance. You find the following icons throughout this book:

Hold it — technical stuff is just around the corner. Read on only if you have your pocket protector.

Pay special attention to this icon; it lets you know that some particularly useful tidbit is at hand.

Did I tell you about the memory course I took?

Danger, Will Robinson! This icon highlights information that may help you avert disaster.

Where to Go from Here

Yes, you can get there from here. With this book in hand, you're ready to plow right through the rugged networking terrain. Browse through the table of contents and decide where you want to start. Be bold! Be courageous! Be adventurous! And above all, have fun!

Book I

Networking Basics

"I guess you could say this is the hub of our network."

Contents at a Glance

Chapter 1: Understanding Networks

In This Chapter

✓ Introducing computer networks

✓ Finding out all about clients, servers, and peers

✓ Understanding the various types of networks

✓ Figuring out the disadvantages of networking

*T*he first computer network was invented when ancient mathematicians connected their abacuses (or is it *abaci*?) together with string so they could instantly share their abacus answers with each other so they could get their work done faster. Over the years, computer networks became more and more sophisticated. Now, instead of string, networks use electrical cables, fiber-optic cables, or wireless radio signals to connect computers to each other. The purpose, however, has remained the same: sharing information and getting work done faster.

This chapter describes the basics of what computer networking is and how it works.

What Is a Network?

A *network* is nothing more than two or more computers connected to each other so that they can exchange information, such as e-mail messages or documents, or share resources, such as disk storage or printers. In most cases, this connection is made via electrical cables that carry the information in the form of electrical signals. But in some cases, other types of connections are used. For example, fiber-optic cables let computers communicate at extremely high speeds by using impulses of light. Wireless networks let computers communicate by using radio signals, so the computers aren't restricted by physical cables.

In addition to the hardware that comprises the network, a network also requires special software to enable communications. In the early days of networking, you had to add this software to each computer on the network. Nowadays, network support is built into all major operating systems, including all current versions of Windows, Macintosh operating systems, and Linux.

Network building blocks

All networks, large or small, require specialized network hardware to make them work. For small networks, the hardware may consist of nothing more than a network interface card in each computer, a cable for each computer, and a network hub that all the computers plug into. Larger networks proba- bly have additional components, such as switches, routers, and repeaters.

Small or large, all networks are built from the following basic building blocks:

✦ **Client computers:** The computers that end users use to access the resources of the network. Client computers are typically located on users' desks. They usually run a desktop version of Windows such as Windows XP Professional, along with application software such as Microsoft Office. Client computers are sometimes referred to as *workstations.*

✦ **Server computers:** Computers that provide shared resources, such as disk storage and printers, as well as network services, such as e-mail and Internet access. Server computers typically run a specialized net- work operating system such as Windows 2000 Server, NetWare, or Linux, along with special software to provide network services. For example, a server may run Microsoft Exchange to provide e-mail serv- ices for the network, or it may run Apache Web Server so that the com- puter can serve Web pages.

✦ **Network interface cards (NICs):** A card installed in a computer that enables the computer to communicate over a network. Almost all NICs implement a networking standard called *Ethernet.* Many newer comput- ers come with either Ethernet cards already installed or with Ethernet support built into the motherboard so a separate card is not required. Every client and every server computer must have a network interface card (or a built-in network port) in order to be a part of a network.

✦ **Cable:** Computers in a network are usually physically connected to each other using cable. Although several types of cable have been popular over the years, the most commonly used cable today is called *twisted pair,* also known by its official designation 10BaseT. Another type of cable commonly used is *coaxial,* also called 10Base2. For high-speed network connections, *fiber-optic cable* is used.

In many cases, the cables run through the walls and converge on a cen- tral room called a *wiring closet.* But for smaller networks, the cables are often just strung along the floor.

✦ **Hubs and switches:** Network cable usually doesn't connect computers directly to each other. Instead, each computer is connected by cable to a device known as a *hub* or a *switch.* The hub or switch, in turn, connects to the rest of the network. Each hub or switch contains a certain number of *ports*, typically 8 or 16. Thus, you can use an eight-port hub or switch to connect up to eight computers. Hubs and switches can be connected to each other to build larger networks. For more information about hubs and switches, see the section "Network Topology," later in this chapter.

✦ **Wireless networks:** In many networks, cables and hubs are making way for wireless network connections, which enable computers to communicate via radio signals. In a wireless network, radio transmitters and receivers take the place of cables. The main advantage of wireless networking is its flexibility. With a wireless network, you don't have to run cables through walls or ceilings, and your client computers can be located anywhere within range of the network broadcast. The main disadvantage of wireless networking is that it is inherently less secure than a cabled network.

✦ **Network software:** Although network hardware is essential, what really makes a network work is software. A whole bunch of software has to be set up just right in order to get a network working. Server computers typically use special *network operating systems* (also known as a *NOS*) in order to function efficiently, and client computers need to have their network settings configured properly in order to access the network.

One of the most important networking choices to make is which network operating system you'll use on the network's servers. That's because much of the task of building a new network and managing an existing one is setting up and maintaining the network operating system on the servers.

Why bother?

If the truth be told, computer networks are a pain to set up. So, why bother? Because the benefits of having a network make the difficulty of setting one up worthwhile. You don't have to be a Ph.D. to understand the benefits of networking. In fact, you learned everything you need to know about the benefits of networking in kindergarten: Networks are all about sharing. Specifically, networks are about sharing three things: information, resources, and applications.

✦ **Sharing information:** Networks allow users to share information in several different ways. The most common way of sharing information is to share individual files. For example, two or more people can work together on a single spreadsheet file or word-processing document. In most networks, a large hard drive on a central server computer is set up as a common storage area where users can store files to be shared with other users.

In addition to sharing files, networks allow users to communicate with each other in various ways. For example, messaging applications let network users exchange messages with each other using an e-mail application such as Microsoft Outlook. Users can also hold online meetings over the network. In fact, with inexpensive video cameras and the right software, users can hold videoconferences over the network.

✦ **Sharing resources:** Certain computer resources, such as printers or hard drives, can be set up so that network users can share them. Sharing these resources can result in significant cost savings. For example, it is cheaper to buy a single high-speed printer with advanced features such as collating, stapling, and duplex printing that can be shared by an entire workgroup than it is to buy separate printers for each user in the group.

Hard drives can also be shared resources. In fact, providing users with access to a shared hard drive is the most common method of sharing files on a network. A computer whose main purpose in life is to host shared hard drives is called a *file server*.

In actual practice, entire hard drives are not usually shared. Instead, individual folders on a networked hard drive are shared. This way, the network administrator can allow different network users to have access to different shared folders. For example, a company may set up shared folders for its sales department and accounting department. Then, sales personnel can access the sales department's folder and accounting personnel can access the accounting department's folder.

You can share other resources on a network. For example, a network can be used to share an Internet connection. In the early days of the Internet, it was common for each user who required access to the Internet to have his or her own modem connection. Nowadays, it's more common for the network to provide a shared high-speed Internet connection that everyone on the network can access.

✦ **Sharing applications:** One of the most common reasons for networking in many businesses is so that several users can work together on a single business application. For example, an accounting department may have accounting software that can be used from several computers at the same time. Or a sales-processing department may have an order-entry application that runs on several computers to handle a large volume of orders.

Of Clients and Servers

The network computer that contains the hard drives, printers, and other resources that are shared with other network computers is called a *server*. This term comes up repeatedly, so you have to remember it. Write it on the back of your left hand.

Any computer that's not a server is called a *client*. You have to remember this term, too. Write it on the back of your right hand.

Only two kinds of computers are on a network: servers and clients. Look at your left hand and then look at your right hand. Don't wash your hands until you have these terms memorized.

The distinction between servers and clients in a network would be somewhat fun to study in a sociology class because it's similar to the distinction between the haves and the have-nots in society.

✦ Usually, the most powerful and expensive computers in a network are the servers. This fact makes sense because every user on the network shares the server's resources.

✦ The cheaper and less powerful computers in a network are the clients. Clients are the computers used by individual users for everyday work. Because clients' resources don't have to be shared, they don't have to be as fancy.

✦ Most networks have more clients than servers. For example, a network with ten clients can probably get by with one server.

✦ In many networks, a clean line of segregation exists between servers and clients. In other words, a computer is either a server or a client, and not both. A server can't become a client, nor can a client become a server.

✦ Other networks are more progressive, allowing any computer in the network to be a server and allowing any computer to be both server and client at the same time. The network illustrated in Figure 1-1, later in this chapter, is this type of network.

Dedicated Servers and Peers

In some networks, a server computer is a server computer and nothing else. This server computer is dedicated solely to the task of providing shared resources, such as hard drives and printers, to be accessed by the network client computers. Such a server is referred to as a *dedicated server* because it can perform no other task besides network services. A network that relies on dedicated servers is sometimes called a *client/server network*.

Other networks take an alternative approach, enabling any computer on the network to function as both a client and a server. Thus, any computer can share its printers and hard drives with other computers on the network.

And while a computer is working as a server, you can still use that same computer for other functions such as word processing. This type of network is called a *peer-to-peer network* because all the computers are thought of as peers, or equals.

Here are some points to ponder concerning the difference between dedicated server networks and peer-to-peer networks while you're walking the dog tomorrow morning:

✦ Peer-to-peer networking features are built into all current versions of Windows since Windows 95. Thus, if your computer runs a current version of Windows, you don't have to buy any additional software to turn your computer into a server. All you have to do is enable the Windows server features.

✦ The network server features that are built into desktop versions of Windows (such as Windows XP) aren't very efficient because these versions of Windows were not designed primarily to be network servers. If you're going to dedicate a computer to the task of being a full-time server, you should use a full-fledged network operating system, such as Windows 2000 Server, instead.

Networks Big and Small

Networks come in all sizes and shapes. In fact, it is common to categorize networks based on the geographical size they cover, as described in the following paragraphs.

✦ **Local area networks:** A *local area network,* or *LAN,* is a network in which computers are relatively close together, such as within the same office or building.

Note that the term *LAN* doesn't imply that the network is small. A LAN can, in fact, contain hundreds of computers. What makes a network a LAN is that all those computers are located within close proximity to each other. Usually a LAN is contained within a single building, but a LAN can extend to several buildings on a campus — provided the buildings are close to each other.

✦ **Wide area networks:** A *wide area network,* or *WAN,* is a network that spans a large geographic territory, such as an entire city, region, or even an entire country. WANs are typically used to connect two or more LANs that are relatively far apart. For example, a WAN may connect an office in San Francisco with an office in New York.

Again, it is the geographic distance that makes a network a WAN, not the number of computers involved. If the office in San Francisco and the office in New York both have only one computer, the WAN will have a total of two computers but will span more than 3,000 miles.

✦ **Metropolitan area networks:** A *metropolitan area network,* or *MAN,* is a network that's smaller than a typical WAN but larger than a LAN. Typically, a MAN connects two or more LANs within a same city but are far enough apart that the networks can't be connected using a simple cable or wireless connection.

Network Topology

The term *network topology* refers to the shape of how the computers and other network components are connected to each other. There are several different types of network topologies, each with advantages and disadvantages.

In the following discussion of network topologies, I use two important terms:

✦ **Node:** A *node* is a device that is connected to the network. For our purposes here, a node is the same as a computer. Network topology deals with how the nodes of a network are connected to each other.

✦ **Packet:** A *packet* is a message that is sent over the network from one node to another node. The packet includes the address of the node that sent the packet, the address of the node the packet is being sent to, and data.

Bus topology

The first type of network topology is called a *bus,* in which nodes are strung together in a line, as shown in Figure 1-1. Bus topology is commonly used for LANs.

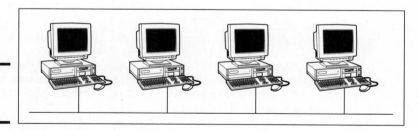

Figure 1-1:
Bus
topology.

The key to understanding how a bus topology works is to think of the entire network as a single cable, with each node "tapping" into the cable so that it can listen in on the packets being sent over that cable. If you're old enough to remember party lines, you get the idea.

In a bus topology, every node on the network can see every packet that's sent on the cable. Each node looks at each packet to determine whether the packet is intended for it. If so, the node claims the packet. If not, the node ignores the packet. This way, each computer can respond to data sent to it and ignore data sent to other computers on the network.

If the cable in a bus network breaks, the network is effectively divided into two networks. Nodes on either side of the break can continue to communicate with each other, but data can't span the gap between the networks, so nodes on opposite sides of the break can't communicate with each other.

Star topology

In a star topology, each network node is connected to a central device called a *hub* or a *switch,* as shown in Figure 1-2. Star topologies are also commonly used with LANs.

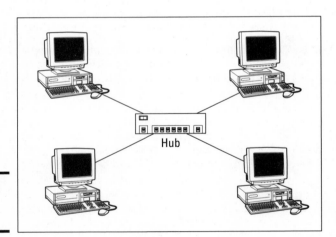

Hub

Figure 1-2:
Star
topology.

If a cable in a star network breaks, only the node connected to that cable is isolated from the network. The other nodes can continue to operate without interruption — unless, of course, the node that's isolated because of the break happens to be the file server.

You should be aware of the somewhat technical distinction between a hub and a switch. Simply put, a *hub* doesn't know anything about the computers that are connected to each of its ports. So when a computer connected to the hub sends a packet to a computer that's connected to another port, the hub sends a duplicate copy of the packet to all its ports. In contrast, a switch knows which computer is connected to each of its ports. As a result, when a switch receives a packet intended for a particular computer, it sends the packet only to the port that the recipient is connected to.

Strictly speaking, only networks that use switches have a true star topology. If the network uses a hub, the network topology has the physical appearance of a star, but is actually a bus. That's because when a hub is used, each computer on the network sees all the packets sent over the network, just like in a bus topology. In a true star topology, as when a switch is used, each computer sees only those packets that were sent specifically to it, as well as broadcast packets that were specifically sent to all computers on the network.

Expanding stars

Physicists tell us that the universe is expanding, and network administrators know they're right. A simple bus or star topology is suitable only for small networks, with a dozen or so computers, but small networks inevitably become large networks as more computers are added. For larger networks, it's common to create more complicated topologies that combine stars and buses.

For example, a bus can be used to connect several stars. In this case, two or more hubs or switches are connected to each other using a bus. Each of these hubs or switches is then the center of a star that connects two or more computers to the network. This type of arrangement is commonly used in buildings that have two or more distinct workgroups. The bus that connects the switches is sometimes called a *backbone*.

Another way to expand a star topology is to use a technique called *daisy-chaining*. When you use daisy-chaining, a hub or switch is connected to another hub or switch as if it were one of the nodes on the star. Then, this second hub or switch serves as the center of a second star.

Ring topology

A third type of network topology is called a *ring*, shown in Figure 1-3. In a ring topology, packets are sent around the circle from computer to computer. Each computer looks at each packet to decide whether the packet was intended for it. If not, the packet is passed on to the next computer in the ring.

Years ago, ring topologies were common in LANs, as two popular networking technologies used rings: ARCNET and Token Ring. ARCNET is still used for certain applications such as factory automation, but is rare in business networks. Token Ring is a popular network technology for IBM midrange computers. Although plenty of Token Ring networks are still in existence, not many new networks use Token Ring any more.

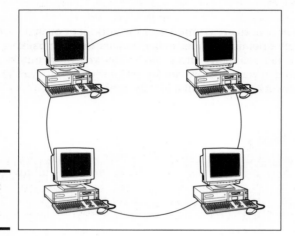

Figure 1-3:
Ring
topology.

Ring topology was also used by FDDI, one of the first types of fiber-optic network connections. FDDI has given way to more efficient fiber-optic techniques, however. So ring networks have all but vanished from business networks.

Mesh topology

A fourth type of network topology, known as *mesh,* has multiple connections between each of the nodes on the network, as shown in Figure 1-4. The advantage of a mesh topology is that if one cable breaks, the network can use an alternative route to deliver its packets.

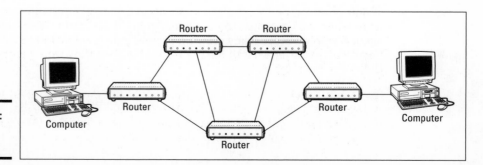

Figure 1-4:
Mesh
topology.

Mesh networks are not very practical in a LAN setting. For example, to network eight computers in a mesh topology, each computer would have to have seven network interface cards, and 28 cables would be required to connect each computer to the seven other computers in the network. Obviously, this scheme isn't very scalable.

However, mesh networks are common for metropolitan or wide area networks. These networks use devices called *routers* to route packets from network to network. For reliability and performance reasons, routers are usually arranged in a way that provides multiple paths between any two nodes on the network in a mesh-like arrangement.

The Downside of Networking

Although networks are one of the best things that ever happened to computers, not everything about networks is rosy. The following sections describe two of the disadvantages of using a network: the loss of user independence and the need for network management.

It's not a personal computer anymore!

One of the hardest lessons to learn about networking is this: After you hook your computer up to a network, it's not a *personal* computer anymore. You are now part of a network of computers, and in a way, you've given up one of the key things that made PCs so successful in the first place — independence.

I got my start in computers back in the days when mainframe computers ruled the roost. *Mainframe computers* are big, complex machines that used to fill entire rooms and had to be cooled with chilled water. My first computer was a water-cooled Binford Power-Proc Model 2000. Argh, argh, argh. (I'm not making up the part about the water. A plumber was frequently required to install a mainframe computer. In fact, the really big ones were cooled by liquid nitrogen.)

Mainframe computers required staffs of programmers and operators who wore white lab coats just to keep them going. They had to be carefully managed. A whole bureaucracy grew up around managing mainframes. But the beauty of mainframe computers was that because they were centralized, they were manageable.

Mainframe computers used to be the dominant computer in the workplace. Personal computers changed all that. Personal computers took the computing power out of the big computer room and put it on the user's desktop, where it belongs. PCs severed the tie to the centralized control of the mainframe computer. With a PC, a user could look at the computer and say, "This is mine . . . all mine!" Mainframes still exist, but they're not nearly as popular as they once were.

Networks are changing everything all over again. In a way, it's a change back to the mainframe computer way of thinking. Larger networks have staff dedicated to their maintenance, just like mainframe computers did. And the servers are often located in dedicated computer rooms, just like mainframe computers were.

With a network, you can no longer think of your PC as your own. You're part of a network, and like the mainframe, the network has to be carefully managed.

Here are a few ways in which a network robs you of your independence:

✦ You can't just indiscriminately delete files from the network. They may not be yours.

✦ The network forces you to be concerned about security. For example, a server computer has to know who you are before it will let you access its files. So you'll have to know your user ID and password to access the network. This security feature is to prevent some 15-year-old kid from hacking his way into your office network via its Internet connection and stealing all your computer games.

✦ Just because you send something to a printer doesn't mean it immediately starts to print. Someone else may have sent a big print job before you, so you'll just have to wait.

✦ You may try to retrieve an Excel spreadsheet file from a network drive, only to discover that someone else is using it. You'll just have to wait.

✦ If you find a really cool series of movies of astronauts walking on the moon at the NASA Web site and download them to the network server, you may get calls from angry coworkers complaining that no room is left on the server's drive for their important files.

✦ Someone may pass a virus to you over the network. You may then accidentally infect other network users.

✦ You have to be careful about saving sensitive files on the server. If you write an angry note about your boss and save it on the server's hard drive, your boss may find the memo and read it.

✦ If you want to access a file on a coworker's computer but that person hasn't yet arrived at work to turn on her computer, you have to go into her office and turn it on yourself. To add insult to injury, you have to know that person's password.

✦ If your computer is a server, you can't just turn it off when you're finished using it. Someone else may be accessing a file on your hard drive or printing on your printer.

Network administration: Someone has to do it

Because so much can go wrong, even with a simple network, even small networks need to be managed. As a result, at least one person should be designated as the *network manager* (sometimes also called the *network administrator*). This way, someone is responsible for making sure that the network doesn't fall apart or get out of control.

For a small network, the network administrator doesn't have to be a technical genius. In fact, some of the best network administrators are complete idiots when it comes to technical stuff. What's important is that the manager be organized. The manager's job is to make sure that plenty of space is available on the file server, that the file server is backed up regularly, that new employees can access the network, and so on.

The larger the network becomes, however, the more often the network administrator will be called upon to solve technical problems. So for larger networks, the administrator should be someone who knows what he or she is doing.

The network manager's job also includes solving basic problems that the users themselves can't solve and knowing when to call in an expert when something really bad happens.

For more information about network administration, see Book III.

Chapter 2: Understanding Network Protocols and Standards

In This Chapter

✔ Deciphering the layers of the OSI reference model

✔ Understanding an ethernet

✔ Getting the inside scoop on TCP/IP and IPX/SPX

✔ Finding out about other important protocols

*P*rotocols and standards are what make networks work together. Protocols make it possible for the various components of a network to communicate with each other. Standards also make it possible for network components manufactured by different companies to work together. This chapter introduces you to the protocols and standards that you're most likely to encounter when building and maintaining a network.

Understanding Protocols

A *protocol* is a set of rules that enable effective communications to occur. We encounter protocols every day. For example, when you pay for groceries with a check, the clerk first tells you how much the groceries cost. You then write a check, providing information such as the date, the name of the grocery store, the amount written with numerals and spelled out, and your signature, and you give the check to the clerk. The clerk accepts the check and asks to see your driver's license. You show the clerk your driver's license, and the clerk looks at it, looks at you, looks at your driver's license again, writes the driver's license number on the check, asks whether you've gained some weight since the picture was taken, and then accepts the check.

Here's another example of an everyday protocol: making a phone call. You probably take most of the details of the phone calling protocol for granted, but it's pretty complicated if you think about it:

✦ When you pick up a phone, you have to listen for a dial tone before dialing the number. If you don't hear a dial tone, you know that either (1) someone else in your family is talking on the phone, or (2) something is wrong with your phone.

✦ When you hear the dial tone, you initiate the call by dialing the number of the party you want to reach. If the person you want to call is in the same area code as you, most of the time you simply dial that person's seven-digit phone number. If the person is in a different area code, you dial a one, the three-digit area code, and the person's seven-digit phone number.

✦ If you hear a series of long ringing tones, you wait until the other person answers the phone. If the phone rings a certain number of times with no answer, you hang up and try again later. If you hear a voice say, "Hello," you can begin a conversation with the other party. If the person on the other end of the phone has never heard of you, you say, "Sorry, wrong number," hang up, and try again.

✦ If you hear a voice that rambles on about how they're not home but they want to return your call, you wait for a beep and leave a message.

✦ If you hear a series of short tones, you know the other person is talking to someone else on the phone. So you hang up and try again later.

✦ If you hear a sequence of three tones that increase in pitch, then a recorded voice that begins, "We're sorry . . .", you know that the number you dialed is invalid. Either you dialed the number incorrectly, or the number has been disconnected.

I can go on and on, but I think you probably get the point. Exchanges such as writing checks or making phone calls follow the same rules every time they happen.

Computer networks depend upon many different types of protocols in order to work. These protocols are very rigidly defined, and for good reason. Network cards must know how to talk to other network cards in order to exchange information, operating systems must know how to talk to network cards in order to send and receive data on the network, and application programs must know how to talk to operating systems in order to know how to retrieve a file from a network server.

Protocols come in many different types. At the lowest level, protocols define exactly what type of electrical signal represents a one and what type of signal represents a zero. At the highest level, protocols allow a computer user in the United States to send an e-mail message to another computer user in New Zealand. And in between are many other levels of protocols. You find out more about these levels of protocols (which are often called *layers*) in the section "The Seven Layers of the OSI Reference Model," later in this chapter.

Various protocols tend to be used together in matched sets called *protocol suites.* The two most popular protocol suites for networking are *TCP/IP* and *IPX/SPX.* TCP/IP was originally developed for UNIX networks and is the protocol of the Internet. IPX/SPX was originally developed for NetWare networks and is still widely used for Windows networks. A third important protocol is *Ethernet,* a low-level protocol that's used with both TCP/IP and IPX/SPX.

Understanding Standards

A *standard* is an agreed-upon definition of a protocol. In the early days of computer networking, each computer manufacturer developed its own networking protocols. As a result, you weren't able to easily mix equipment from different manufacturers on a single network.

Then along came standards to save the day. Standards are industry-wide protocol definitions that are not tied to a particular manufacturer. With standard protocols, you can mix and match equipment from different vendors. As long as the equipment implements the standard protocols, it should be able to coexist on the same network.

Many organizations are involved in setting standards for networking. The five most important organizations are

✦ **American National Standards Institute (ANSI):** The official standards organization in the United States. ANSI is pronounced *An-See.*

✦ **Institute of Electrical and Electronics Engineers (IEEE):** An international organization that publishes several key networking standards; in particular, the official standard for the Ethernet networking system (known officially as IEEE 802.3). IEEE is pronounced *Eye-triple-E.*

✦ **International Organization for Standardization (ISO):** A federation of more than 100 standards organizations from throughout the world. If I had studied French in high school, I'd probably understand why the acronym for International Organization for Standardization is ISO, and not IOS.

✦ **Internet Engineering Task Force (IETF):** The organization responsible for the protocols that drive the Internet.

✦ **World Wide Web Consortium (W3C):** An international organization that handles the development of standards for the World Wide Web.

Table 2-1 lists the Web sites for each of these standards organizations.

Table 2-1	Web Sites for Major Standards Organizations
Organization	*Web Site*
ANSI (American National Standards Institute)	www.ansi.org
IEEE (Institute of Electrical and Electronic Engineers)	www.ieee.org
ISO (International Organization for Standardization)	www.iso.org
IETF (Internet Engineering Task Force)	www.ietf.org
W3C (World Wide Web Consortium)	www.w3c.org

The Seven Layers of the OSI Reference Model

OSI sounds like the name of a top-secret government agency you hear about only in Tom Clancy novels. What it really stands for in the networking world is Open Systems Interconnection, as in the Open Systems Interconnection Reference Model, affectionately known as the OSI model.

The OSI model breaks the various aspects of a computer network into seven distinct layers. These layers are kind of like the layers of an onion: Each successive layer envelops the layer beneath it, hiding its details from the levels above. The OSI model is also like an onion in that if you start to peel it apart to have a look inside, you're bound to shed a few tears.

The OSI model is not a networking standard in the same sense that Ethernet and Token Ring are networking standards. Rather, the OSI model is a framework into which the various networking standards can fit. The OSI model specifies what aspects of a network's operation can be addressed by various network standards. So, in a sense, the OSI model is sort of a standard of standards.

Table 2-2 summarizes the seven layers of the OSI model.

Table 2-2		The Seven Layers of the OSI Model
Layer	*Name*	*Description*
1	Physical	Governs the layout of cables and devices such as repeaters and hubs.
2	Data Link	Provides MAC addresses to uniquely identify network nodes and a means for data to be sent over the Physical layer in the form of packets. Bridges and switches are layer 2 devices.
3	Network	Handles routing of data across network segments.

Layer	Name	Description
4	Transport	Provides for reliable delivery of packets.
5	Session	Establishes sessions between network applications.
6	Presentation	Converts data so that systems that use different data formats can exchange information.
7	Application	Allows applications to request network services.

The first three layers are sometimes called the *lower layers*. They deal with the mechanics of how information is sent from one computer to another over a network. Layers 4 through 7 are sometimes called the *upper layers*. They deal with how applications programs relate to the network through application programming interfaces.

The following sections describe each of these layers in greater detail.

The seven layers of the OSI model are a somewhat idealized view of how networking protocols should work. In the real world, actual networking protocols don't follow the OSI model to the letter. The real world is always messier than we'd like. Still, the OSI model provides a convenient — if not completely accurate — conceptual picture of how networking works.

The Physical Layer

The bottom layer of the OSI model is the *Physical layer*. It addresses the physical characteristics of the network, such as the types of cables used to connect devices, the types of connectors used, how long the cables can be, and so on. For example, the Ethernet standard for 10BaseT cable specifies the electrical characteristics of the twisted-pair cables, the size and shape of the connectors, the maximum length of the cables, and so on. The star, bus, ring, and mesh network topologies described in Book I, Chapter 1 apply to the Physical layer.

Another aspect of the Physical layer is the electrical characteristics of the signals used to transmit data over the cables from one network node to another. The Physical layer doesn't define any meaning to those signals other than the basic binary values of zero and one. The higher levels of the OSI model must assign meanings to the bits that are transmitted at the Physical layer.

One type of Physical layer device commonly used in networks is a *repeater*. A repeater is used to regenerate the signal whenever you need to exceed the cable length allowed by the Physical layer standard. 10BaseT hubs are also Physical layer devices. Technically, they're known as *multiport repeaters* because the purpose of a hub is to regenerate every packet received on any port on all of the hub's other ports. Repeaters and hubs don't examine the contents of the packets that they regenerate. If they did, they would be working at the Data Link layer, and not at the Physical layer.

The *network adapter* (also called a *network interface card* or *NIC*) that's installed in each computer on the network is a Physical layer device. You can display information about the network adapter (or adapters) installed in a Windows computer by displaying the adapter's Properties dialog box, as shown in Figure 2-1. To access this dialog box in Windows 2000 or XP, open the Control Panel and double-click the System icon, click the Hardware tab, and then click the Device Manager button. A list of all the devices on the computer appears. Double-click the network adapter to see its Properties dialog box.

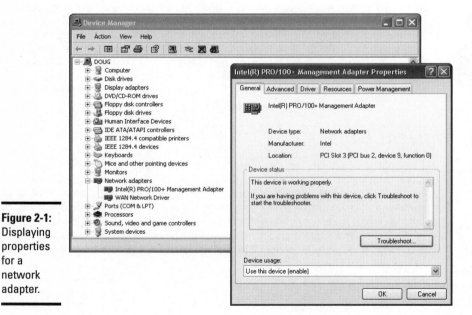

Figure 2-1:
Displaying properties for a network adapter.

The Data Link Layer

The *Data Link layer* is the lowest layer at which meaning is assigned to the bits that are transmitted over the network. Data link protocols address things such as the size of each packet of data to be sent, a means of addressing each packet so that it's delivered to the intended recipient, and a way to ensure that two or more nodes don't try to transmit data on the network at the same time.

The Data Link layer also provides basic error detection and correction to ensure that the data sent is the same as the data received. If an uncorrectable error occurs, the data link standard must specify how the node is to be informed of the error so that it can retransmit the data.

At the Data Link layer, each device on the network has an address known as the *Media Access Control address,* or *MAC address.* This address is actually hard-wired into every network device by the manufacturer. MAC addresses are unique; no two network devices made by any manufacturer anywhere in the world can have the same MAC address. And once a device has been manufactured, its MAC address can't be changed.

You can see the MAC address for a computer's network adapter by opening a command window and running the `ipconfig /all` command, as shown in Figure 2-2. In this example, the MAC address of the network card is 00-50-BA-84-39-11.

Figure 2-2:
Displaying the MAC address of your network adapter.

```
C:\WINDOWS\System32\command.com                            _ □ ×

C:\>ipconfig /all

Windows IP Configuration

        Host Name . . . . . . . . . . . . : doug
        Primary Dns Suffix . . . . . . . :
        Node Type . . . . . . . . . . . . : Unknown
        IP Routing Enabled. . . . . . . . : No
        WINS Proxy Enabled. . . . . . . . : No

Ethernet adapter Local Area Connection:

        Connection-specific DNS Suffix  . : ve1.client2.attbi.com
        Description . . . . . . . . . . . : D-Link DFE-530TX+ PCI Adapter
        Physical Address. . . . . . . . . : 00-50-BA-84-39-11
        Dhcp Enabled. . . . . . . . . . . : Yes
        Autoconfiguration Enabled . . . . : Yes
        IP Address. . . . . . . . . . . . : 192.168.1.100
        Subnet Mask . . . . . . . . . . . : 255.255.255.0
        Default Gateway . . . . . . . . . : 192.168.1.1
        DHCP Server . . . . . . . . . . . : 192.168.1.1
        DNS Servers . . . . . . . . . . . : 204.127.198.19
                                            63.240.76.19
        Lease Obtained. . . . . . . . . . : Monday, April 21, 2003 3:23:24 PM
        Lease Expires . . . . . . . . . . : Tuesday, April 22, 2003 3:23:24 PM

C:\>
```

One of the most import functions of the Data Link layer is to provide a way for packets to be sent safely over the physical media without interference from other nodes attempting to send packets at the same time. The two most popular ways to do this are CSMA/CD and token passing. Ethernet networks use CSMA/CD, and Token Ring networks use token passing. For an explanation of how CSMA/CD and Token Ring work, see the upcoming sections "How CSMA/CD works" and "How token passing works."

Two types of Data Link layer devices are commonly used on networks: bridges and switches. A *bridge* is an intelligent repeater that is aware of the MAC addresses of the nodes on either side of the bridge and can forward packets accordingly. A *switch* is an intelligent hub that examines the MAC address of arriving packets in order to determine which port to forward the packet to.

How CSMA/CD works

An important function of the Data Link layer is to make sure that two computers don't try to send packets over the network at the same time. If they do, the signals will collide with each other, and the transmission will be garbled. Ethernet accomplishes this feat by using a technique called *CSMA/CD*, which stands for "carrier sense multiple access with collision detection." This phrase is a mouthful, but if you take it apart piece by piece, you'll get an idea of how it works.

Carrier sense means that whenever a device wants to send a packet over the network media, it first listens to the network media to see whether anyone else is already sending a packet. If it doesn't hear any other signals on the media, the computer assumes that the network is free, so it sends the packet.

Multiple access means that nothing prevents two or more devices from trying to send a message at the same time. Sure, each device listens before sending. However, suppose that two devices listen, hear nothing, and then proceed to send their packets at the same time? Picture what happens when you and someone else arrive at a four-way stop sign at the same time. You wave the other driver on, he or she waves you on, you wave, he or she waves, you both wave, and then you both go at the same time.

Collision detection means that after a device sends a packet, it listens carefully to see whether the packet crashes into another packet. This is kind of like listening for the screeching of brakes at the four-way stop. If the device hears the screeching of brakes, it waits a random period of time and then tries to send the packet again. Because the delay is random, two packets that collide are sent again after different delay periods, so a second collision is unlikely.

CSMA/CD works pretty well for smaller networks. After a network hits about 30 computers, however, packets start to collide like crazy, and the network slows to a crawl. When that happens, the network should be divided into two or more separate sections that are sometimes called *collision domains*. This subdivision is accomplished at the next layer up in the OSI scheme, the Network layer.

How token passing works

An alternative to CSMA/CD is *token passing*, which is the technique used by IBM's once-popular Token Ring network. Token passing is a more orderly approach to handling the problem of packet collisions. Instead of sending a message whenever it determines that the network is silent, a device in a token ring network must wait for its turn. In a token passing network, a special type of packet called a *token* is constantly passed through the network from computer to computer. A computer can send a packet of data only when it has the token. In this way, token passing networks ensure that collisions never happen.

Sometimes, a defective network adapter accidentally swallows the token. When that happens, the token disappears from the network. When the token has been missing for a certain period of time, the network assumes that the token has been swallowed, and the network burps in order to generate a new token.

The advantage of token passing is that it has a predictable speed. Because the token moves around the network at pretty much the same speed whether or not it's carrying data, the performance of token passing networks tends to be pretty stable. In contrast, CSMA/CD can be very fast if network traffic is minimal, but it can grind to a halt if the network becomes overloaded. However, because the potential performance of CSMA/CD networks is higher than the performance of token passing networks, CSMA/CD is much more popular than token passing.

The Network Layer

The *Network layer* handles the task of routing network messages from one computer to another. The two most popular layer 3 protocols are IP (which is usually paired with TCP) and IPX (normally paired with SPX for use with Novell and Windows networks).

Network layer protocols provide two important functions: logical addressing and routing. The following sections describe these functions.

Logical addressing

As you know, every network device has a physical address called a MAC address, which is assigned to the device at the factory. When you buy a network interface card to install into a computer, the MAC address of that card is fixed and can't be changed. But what if you want to use some other addressing scheme to refer to the computers and other devices on your network? This is where the concept of *logical addressing* comes in; a logical address lets you access a network device by using an address that you assign.

Logical addresses are created and used by Network layer protocols such as IP or IPX. The Network layer protocol translates logical addresses to MAC addresses. For example, if you use IP as the Network layer protocol, devices on the network are assigned IP addresses such as 207.120.67.30. Because the IP protocol must use a Data Link layer protocol to actually send packets to devices, IP must know how to translate the IP address of a device to the device's MAC address.

Data Link layer addresses (or MAC addresses) are assigned at the factory and can't be changed. Network layer addresses (or IP addresses) are assigned in the field and can be changed.

You can use the `ipconfig` command that was shown in Figure 2-2 to see the IP address of your computer. The IP address shown in the figure is 192.168. 1.100. Another way to display this information is to use the System Information command, found on the Start menu under Start⇨Programs⇨ Accessories⇨System Tools⇨System Information. The IP address is highlighted in Figure 2-3. Notice that the System Information program displays a lot of other useful information about the network besides the IP address. For example, you can also see the MAC address, what protocols are being used, and other information.

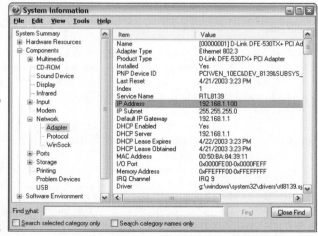

Figure 2-3: Using the System Information command to display network information.

Although the exact format of logical addresses varies depending on the protocol being used, most protocols divide the logical address into two parts: a network address and a device address. The network address identifies which network the device resides on, and the device address then identifies the device on that network. For example, in a typical IP address, such as 192.168.1.100, the network address is 192.168.1 and the device address (called a *host address* in IP) is 100.

Similarly, IPX addresses consist of two parts: a network address and a node address. In an IPX address, the node address is the same as the MAC address. As a result, IPX doesn't have to translate between layer 3 and layer 2 addresses.

Routing

Routing comes into play when a computer on one network needs to send a packet to a computer on another network. In this case, a device called a *router* is used to forward the packet to the destination network. In some cases, a packet may actually have to travel through several intermediate networks in order to reach its final destination network. You can find out more about routers in Book I, Chapter 3.

An important feature of routers is that you can use them to connect networks that use different layer 2 protocols. For example, a router can be used to send a packet from an Ethernet to a Token Ring network. As long as both networks support the same layer 3 protocol, it doesn't matter if their layer 1 and layer 2 protocols are different.

 A protocol is considered *routable* if it uses addresses that include a network part and a host part. Any protocol that uses physical addresses is not routable because physical addresses don't indicate to which network a device belongs.

The Transport Layer

The *Transport layer* is the layer where you'll find two of the most well-known networking protocols: TCP (normally paired with IP) and SPX (normally paired with IPX). As its name implies, the Transport layer is concerned with the transportation of information from one computer to another.

The main purpose of the Transport layer is to ensure that packets are transported reliably and without errors. The Transport layer does this task by establishing connections between network devices, acknowledging the receipt of packets, and resending packets that are not received or are corrupted when they arrive.

In many cases, the Transport layer protocol divides large messages into smaller packets that can be sent over the network efficiently. The Transport layer protocol reassembles the message on the receiving end, making sure that all of the packets that comprise a single transmission are received so that no data is lost.

For some applications, speed and efficiency are more important than reliability. In such cases, a *connectionless protocol* can be used. A connectionless protocol doesn't go to the trouble of establishing a connection before sending a packet. Instead, it simply sends the packet. TCP is a connection-oriented Transport layer protocol. The connectionless protocol that works alongside TCP is called UDP.

In Windows XP, you can view information about the status of TCP and UDP connections by running the NETSTAT command from a command window, as Figure 2-4 shows. Here, you can see that three TCP connections are established.

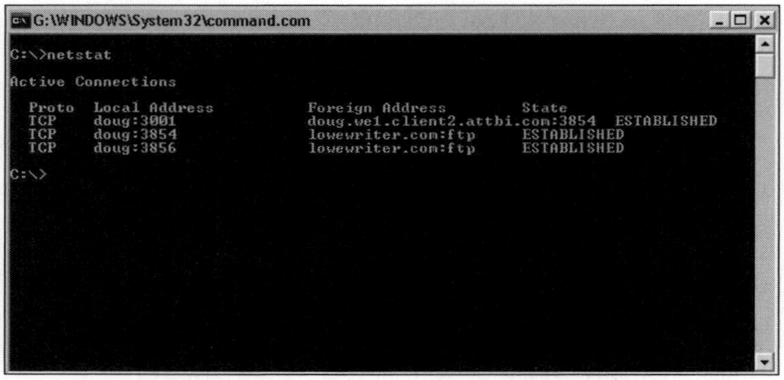

Figure 2-4: Displaying the status of TCP and UDP connections with the NETSTAT command.

```
G:\WINDOWS\System32\command.com                              _ □ ×

C:\>netstat

Active Connections

  Proto  Local Address          Foreign Address              State
  TCP    doug:3001              doug.we1.client2.attbi.com:3854  ESTABLISHED
  TCP    doug:3854              lowewriter.com:ftp           ESTABLISHED
  TCP    doug:3856              lowewriter.com:ftp           ESTABLISHED

C:\>
```

Another important feature of the Transport layer protocols is *name resolution*. The Transport layer allows network nodes to be identified by names rather than numbers. For example, in Figure 2-4 you can see that the Local Address and Foreign Address columns use names rather than numeric addresses. The Local Address column lists "doug" as the name for each connection. That's the Windows computer name assigned to my computer. The Foreign Address column lists `doug.we1.client2.attbi.com` and `lowewriter.com`. These names are mapped to numeric network addresses by Transport layer protocols.

In fact, you can use the command NETSTAT /N to see the numeric network addresses instead of the names. With the /N switch, the output in Figure 2-4 would look like this:

```
Active Connections

  Proto  Local Address            Foreign Address          State
  TCP    127.0.0.1:3001           192.168.1.100:3863
    ESTABLISHED
  TCP    192.168.1.100:3863       209.68.34.15:21
    ESTABLISHED
  TCP    192.168.1.100:3865       209.68.34.15:21
    ESTABLISHED
```

 TCP is a connection-oriented Transport layer protocol. UDP is a connection-less Transport layer protocol.

The Session Layer

The *Session layer* establishes conversations known as *sessions* between networked devices. A session is an exchange of connection-oriented transmissions between two network devices. Each of these transmissions is handled by the Transport layer protocol. The session itself is managed by the Session layer protocol.

A single session can include many exchanges of data between the two computers involved in the session. After a session between two computers has been established, it is maintained until the computers agree to terminate the session.

The session layer allows three types of transmission modes:

✦ *Simplex*, in which data flows in only one direction.

✦ *Half-duplex*, in which data flows in both directions, but only in one direction at a time.

✦ *Full-duplex*, in which data flows in both directions at the same time.

 In actual practice, the distinctions between the Session, Presentation, and Application layers are often blurred, and some commonly used protocols actually span all three layers. For example, SMB — the Server Manager Block protocol that is the basis of file sharing in Windows networks — functions at all three layers.

The Presentation Layer

The *Presentation layer* is responsible for how data is represented to applications. Most computers — including Windows, UNIX, and Macintosh computers — use the American Standard Code for Information Interchange (ASCII) to represent data. However, some computers (such as IBM mainframe computers) use a different code, known as Extended Binary Coded Decimal Interchange Code (EBCDIC). ASCII and EBCDIC are not compatible with each other. To exchange information between a mainframe computer and a Windows computer, the Presentation layer must convert the data from ASCII to EBCDIC and vice versa.

Besides simply converting data from one code to another, the Presentation layer can also apply sophisticated compression techniques so that fewer bytes of data are required to represent the information when it's sent over the network. At the other end of the transmission, the Presentation layer then uncompresses the data.

The Presentation layer can also scramble the data before it is transmitted and unscramble it at the other end by using a sophisticated encryption technique that even Sherlock Holmes would have trouble breaking.

The Application Layer

The highest layer of the OSI model, the *Application layer,* deals with the techniques that application programs use to communicate with the network. The name of this layer is a little confusing. Application programs such as Microsoft Office or QuickBooks aren't a part of the Application layer. Rather, the Application layer represents the programming interfaces that application programs such as Microsoft Office or QuickBooks use to request network services.

Some of the better-known Application layer protocols are

✦ DNS (Domain Name System) for resolving Internet domain names.

✦ FTP (File Transfer Protocol) for file transfers.

✦ SMTP (Simple Mail Transfer Protocol) for e-mail.

✦ SMB (Server Message Block) for file sharing in Windows networks.

✦ NFS (Network File System) for file sharing in UNIX networks.

✦ Telnet for terminal emulation.

Following a Packet through the Layers

Figure 2-5 shows how a packet of information flows through the seven layers as it travels from one computer to another on the network. The data begins its journey when an end-user application sends data to another network computer. The data enters the network through an Application layer interface, such as SMB. The data then works its way down through the protocol stack. Along the way, the protocol at each layer manipulates the data by adding header information, converting the data into different formats, combining packets to form larger packets, and so on. When the data reaches the Physical layer protocol, it is actually placed on the network media (in other words, the cable) and sent to the receiving computer.

When the receiving computer receives the data, the data works its way up through the protocol stack. Then, the protocol at each layer reverses the processing that was done by the corresponding layer on the sending computer. Headers are removed, data is converted back to its original format, packets that were split into smaller packets are recombined into larger messages, and so on. When the packet reaches the Application layer protocol, it is delivered to an application that can process the data.

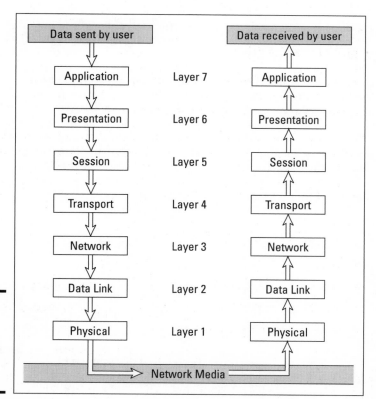

Figure 2-5:
How data
travels
through the
seven
layers.

The Ethernet Protocol

As you know, the first two layers of the OSI model deal with the physical structure of the network and the means by which network devices can send information from one device on a network to another. By far, the most popular set of protocols for the Physical and Data Link layers is *Ethernet*.

Ethernet has been around in various forms since the early 1970s. (For a brief history of Ethernet, see the sidebar "Ethernet folklore and mythology," later in this chapter.) The current incarnation of Ethernet is defined by the IEEE standard known as 802.3. Various flavors of Ethernet operate at different speeds and use different types of media. However, all the versions of Ethernet are compatible with each other, so you can mix and match them on the same network by using devices such as bridges, hubs, and switches to link network segments that use different types of media.

The actual transmission speed of Ethernet is measured in millions of bits per second, or Mbps. Ethernet comes in three different speed versions: 10Mbps, known as *Standard Ethernet;* 100Mbps, known as *Fast Ethernet;* and 1000Mbps, known as *Gigabit Ethernet.* Keep in mind, however, that network transmission speed refers to the maximum speed that can be achieved over the network under ideal conditions. In reality, the actual throughput of an Ethernet network rarely reaches this maximum speed.

Ethernet operates at the first two layers of the OSI model — the Physical and the Data Link layers. However, Ethernet divides the Data Link layer into two separate layers known as the Logical Link Control (LLC) layer and the Medium Access Control (MAC) layer. Figure 2-6 shows how the various elements of Ethernet match up to the OSI model.

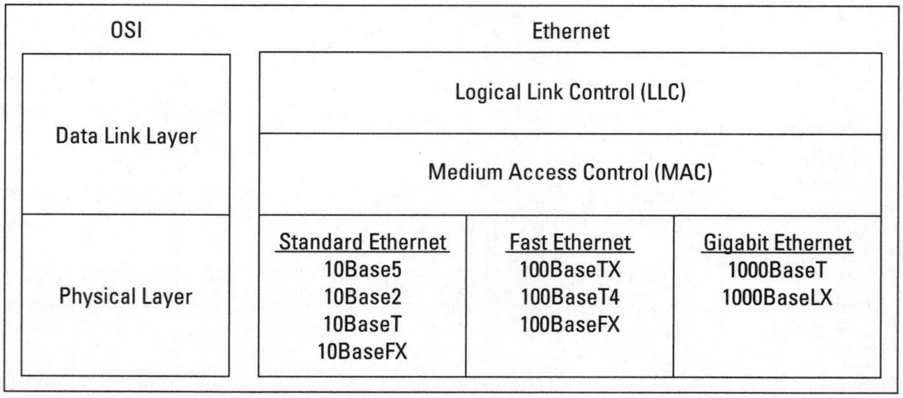

OSI	Ethernet		
Data Link Layer	Logical Link Control (LLC)		
	Medium Access Control (MAC)		
Physical Layer	Standard Ethernet 10Base5 10Base2 10BaseT 10BaseFX	Fast Ethernet 100BaseTX 100BaseT4 100BaseFX	Gigabit Ethernet 1000BaseT 1000BaseLX

Figure 2-6:
Ethernet
and the OSI
model.

Ethernet folklore and mythology

If you're a history buff, you may be interested in the story of how Ethernet came to be so popular. Here's how it happened: The original idea for the Ethernet was hatched in the mind of a graduate computer science student at Harvard University named Robert Metcalfe. Looking for a thesis idea in 1970, he refined a networking technique that was used in Hawaii called the AlohaNet (it was actually a wireless network) and developed a technique that would enable a network to efficiently use as much as 90 percent of its capacity. By 1973, he had his first Ethernet network up and running at the famous Xerox Palo Alto Research Center (PARC). Bob dubbed his network "Ethernet" in honor of the thick network cable, which he called "the ether." (Xerox PARC was busy in 1973. In addition to Ethernet, PARC developed the first personal computer that used a graphical user interface complete with icons, windows, and menus, and the world's first laser printer.)

In 1979, Xerox began working with Intel and DEC (a once popular computer company) to make Ethernet an industry standard networking product. Along the way, they enlisted the help of the IEEE, which formed committee number 802.3 and began the process of standardizing Ethernet in 1981. The 802.3 released the first official Ethernet standard in 1983.

Meanwhile, Bob Metcalfe left Xerox, turned down a job offer from Steve Jobs to work at Apple computers, and started a company called the Computer, Communication, and Compatibility Corporation — now known as 3Com. 3Com has since become one of the largest manufacturers of Ethernet equipment in the world.

The following sections describe Standard Ethernet, Fast Ethernet, and Gigabit Ethernet in more detail.

Standard Ethernet

Standard Ethernet is the original Ethernet. It runs at 10Mbps, which was considered fast in the 1970s but is pretty slow by today's standards. Because the cost of Fast Ethernet has dropped dramatically in the past few years, Fast Ethernet has pretty much replaced Standard Ethernet for most new networks. However, plenty of existing Standard Ethernet networks are still in use.

Standard Ethernet comes in four incarnations, depending on the type of cable used to string the network together:

✦ **10Base5:** The original Ethernet cable was thick (about as thick as your thumb), heavy, and difficult to work with. It is seen today only in museums.

✦ **10Base2:** This thinner type of coaxial cable (it resembles television cable) became popular in the 1980s and lingered into the early 1990s. Plenty of 10Base2 cable is still in use, but it's rarely installed in new networks. 10Base2 (like 10Base5) uses a bus topology, so wiring a 10Base2 network involves running cable from one computer to the next until all the computers are connected in a segment.

✦ **10BaseT:** *Unshielded twisted-pair* cable (also known as *UTP*) became popular in the 1990s because it's easier to install, lighter, more reliable, and offers more flexibility in how networks are designed. 10BaseT networks use a star topology with hubs at the center of each star. Although the maximum length of 10BaseT cable is only 100 meters, hubs can be chained together to extend networks well beyond the 100 meter limit.

   10BaseT cable has four pairs of wires that are twisted together throughout the entire span of the cable. However, 10BaseT uses only two of these wire pairs, so the unused pairs are spares.

✦ **10BaseFL:** Fiber-optic cables were originally supported at 10Mbps by the 10BaseFL standard. However, because faster fiber-optic versions of Ethernet now exist, 10BaseFL is rarely used.

Fast Ethernet

Fast Ethernet refers to Ethernet that runs at 100Mbps, which is ten times the speed of standard Ethernet. The following are the three varieties of fast Ethernet:

✦ **100BaseT4:** The 100BaseT4 protocol allows transmission speeds of 100Mbps over the same UTP cable as 10BaseT networks. To do this, it uses all four pairs of wire in the cable. 100BaseT4 simplifies the task of upgrading an existing 10BaseT network to 100Mbps.

✦ **100BaseTX:** The most commonly used standard for office networks today is 100BaseTX, which transmits at 100Mbps over just two pairs of a higher grade of UTP cable than the cable used by 10BaseT. The higher-grade cable is referred to as *Category 5*. Most new networks are wired with Category 5 or better cable.

✦ **100BaseFX:** The fiber-optic version of Ethernet running at 100Mbps is called 10BaseFX. Because fiber-optic cable is expensive and tricky to install, it isn't used much for individual computers in a network. However, it's commonly used as a network *backbone*. For example, a fiber backbone is often used to connect individual workgroup hubs to routers and servers.

Gigabit Ethernet

Gigabit Ethernet is Ethernet running at a whopping 1,000Mbps, which is 100 times faster than the original 10Mbps Ethernet. Gigabit Ethernet is considerably more expensive than Fast Ethernet, so it's typically used only when the improved performance justifies the extra cost. For example, you may find

Gigabit Ethernet used as the backbone for very large networks or to connect server computers to the network. And in some cases, Gigabit Ethernet is even used for desktop computers that require high-speed network connections.

Gigabit Ethernet comes in two flavors:

+ **1000BaseT:** Gigabit Ethernet can run on Category 5 UTP cable, but higher grades such as Category 5e or Category 6 is preferred because it is more reliable.

+ **1000BaseLX:** Several varieties of fiber cable are used with Gigabit Ethernet, but the most popular is called 1000BaseLX.

The TCP/IP Protocol Suite

TCP/IP, the protocol on which the Internet is built, is actually not a single protocol but rather an entire suite of related protocols. TCP is even older than Ethernet. It was first conceived in 1969 by the Department of Defense. For more on the history of TCP/IP, see the sidebar "The fascinating story of TCP/IP," later in this chapter. Currently, the Internet Engineering Task Force, or IETF, manages the TCP/IP protocol suite.

The TCP/IP suite is based on a four-layer model of networking that is similar to the seven-layer OSI model. Figure 2-7 shows how the TCP/IP model matches up with the OSI model and where some of the key TCP/IP protocols fit into the model. As you can see, the lowest layer of the model, the Network Interface layer, corresponds to the OSI model's Physical and Data Link layers. TCP/IP can run over a wide variety of Network Interface layer protocols, including Ethernet, as well as other protocols, such as Token Ring and FDDI (an older standard for fiber-optic networks).

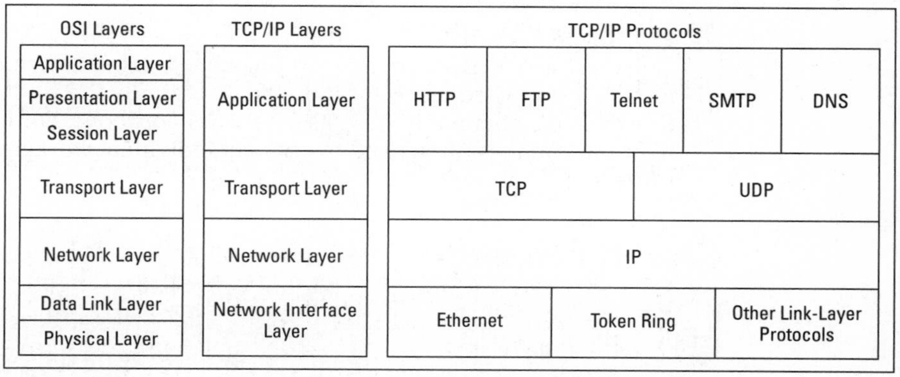

Figure 2-7:
TCP/IP and
the OSI
model.

OSI Layers	TCP/IP Layers	TCP/IP Protocols				
Application Layer						
Presentation Layer	Application Layer	HTTP	FTP	Telnet	SMTP	DNS
Session Layer						
Transport Layer	Transport Layer	TCP			UDP	
Network Layer	Network Layer	IP				
Data Link Layer	Network Interface Layer	Ethernet		Token Ring	Other Link-Layer Protocols	
Physical Layer						

The Application layer of the TCP/IP model corresponds to the upper three layers of the OSI model — that is, the Session, Presentation, and Application layers. Many protocols can be used at this level. A few of the most popular are HTTP, FTP, Telnet, SMTP, DNS, and SNMP.

You can find out about many of the details of these and other TCP/IP protocols in Book V. In the rest of this section, I just want to point out a few more details of the three most important protocols in the TCP/IP suite: IP, TCP, and UDP.

IP

IP, which stands for *Internet Protocol,* is a Network layer protocol that is responsible for delivering packets to network devices. The IP protocol uses logical IP addresses to refer to individual devices rather than physical (MAC) addresses. A protocol called ARP (for *Address Resolution Protocol*) handles the task of converting IP addresses to MAC addresses.

Because IP addresses consist of a network part and a host part, IP is a *routable protocol.* As a result, IP can forward a packet to another network if the host is not on the current network. (The ability to route packets across networks is where IP gets its name. An *internet* is a series of two or more connected TCP/IP networks that can be reached by routing.)

TCP

TCP, which stands for *Transmission Control Protocol*, is a connection-oriented Transport layer protocol. TCP lets a device reliably send a packet to another device on the same network or on a different network. TCP ensures that each packet is delivered if at all possible. It does so by establishing a connection with the receiving device and then sending the packets. If a packet doesn't arrive, TCP resends the packet. The connection is closed only after the packet has been successfully delivered or an unrecoverable error condition has occurred.

One key aspect of TCP is that it's always used for one-to-one communications. In other words, TCP allows a single network device to exchange data with another single network device. TCP is not used to broadcast messages to multiple network recipients. Instead, the User Datagram Protocol (UDP) is used for that purpose.

Many well-known Application layer protocols rely on TCP. For example, when a user running a Web browser requests a page, the browser uses HTTP to send a request via TCP to the Web server. When the Web server receives the request, it uses HTTP to send the requested Web page back to the browser, again via TCP. Other Application layer protocols that use TCP include Telnet (for terminal emulation), FTP (for file exchange), and SMTP (for e-mail).

TECHNICAL STUFF

10Base what?

The names of Ethernet cable standards resemble the audible signals a quarterback might shout at the line of scrimmage. In reality, the cable designations consist of three parts:

✔ The first number is the speed of the network in Mbps. So 10BaseT is for 10Mbps networks (Standard Ethernet), 100BaseTX is for 100Mbps networks (Fast Ethernet), and 1000BaseT is for 1,000Mbps networks (Gigabit Ethernet).

✔ The word *Base* indicates the type of network transmission that the cable uses. *Base* is short for *baseband*. Baseband transmissions carry one signal at a time and are relatively simple to implement. The alternative to baseband is *broadband*, which can carry more than one signal at a time but is more difficult to implement. At one time, broadband incarnations of the 802.x networking standards existed, but they have all but fizzled due to lack of use.

✔ The tail end of the designation indicates the cable type. For coaxial cables, a number is used that roughly indicates the maximum length of the cable in hundreds of meters. 10Base5 cables can run up to 500 meters. 10Base2 cables can run up to 185 meters. (The IEEE rounded 185 up to 200 to come up with the name 10Base2.) If the designation ends with a *T*, twisted pair cable is used. Other letters are used for other types of cables.

UDP

The *User Datagram Protocol* (or *UDP*) is a connectionless Transport layer protocol that is used when the overhead of a connection is not required. After UDP has placed a packet on the network (via the IP protocol), it forgets about it. UDP doesn't guarantee that the packet actually arrives at its destination. Most applications that use UDP simply wait for any replies expected as a result of packets sent via UDP. If a reply doesn't arrive within a certain period of time, the application either sends the packet again or gives up.

Probably the best known Application layer protocol that uses UDP is DNS, the Domain Name System. When an application needs to access a domain name such as www.wiley.com, DNS sends a UDP packet to a DNS server to look up the domain. When the server finds the domain, it returns the domain's IP address in another UDP packet. (Actually, the process is much more complicated than that. For a more detailed explanation, see Book V, Chapter 4.)

The fascinating story of TCP/IP

Some people are fascinated by history. They subscribe to cable TV just to get the History Channel. If you're one of those history buffs, you may be interested in the following chronicle of TCP/IP's humble origins. (For maximum effect, play some melancholy violin music in the background as you read the rest of this section.)

In the summer of 1969, the four mop-topped singers from Liverpool were breaking up. The war in Vietnam was escalating. Astronauts Neil Armstrong and Buzz Aldrin walked on the moon. And the Department of Defense built a computer network called ARPANET to link its defense installations with several major universities throughout the United States.

In the early 1970s, ARPANET was becoming difficult to manage, so it was split into two networks: one for military use, called MILNET, and the other for nonmilitary use. The nonmilitary network retained the name ARPANET. To link MILNET with ARPANET, a new method of connecting networks, called *Internet Protocol* or just *IP* for short, was invented.

The whole purpose of IP was to enable these two networks to communicate with each other.

Fortunately, the designers of IP realized that it wouldn't be too long before other networks wanted to join in the fun, so they designed IP to allow for more than two networks. In fact, their ingenious design allowed for tens of thousands of networks to communicate via IP.

The decision was a fortuitous one, as the Internet quickly began to grow. By the mid-1980s, the original ARPANET reached its limits. Just in time, the National Science Foundation (NSF) decided to get into the game. NSF had built a network called NSFNET to link its huge supercomputers. NSFNET replaced ARPANET as the new background for the Internet. Around that time, such magazines as *Time* and *Newsweek* began writing articles about this new phenomenon called the Internet, and the *Net* (as it became nicknamed) began to grow like wildfire. Soon NSFNET couldn't keep up with the growth, so several private commercial networks took over management of the Internet backbone. The Internet has grown at a dizzying rate ever since, and nobody knows how long this frenetic growth rate will continue. One thing is sure: TCP/IP is now the most popular networking protocol in the world.

The IPX/SPX Protocol Suite

Although TCP/IP has quickly become the protocol of choice for most networks, plenty of networks still use an alternative protocol suite called IPX/SPX. Novell originally developed the IPX/SPX suite in the 1980s for use with their NetWare servers. IPX/SPX also works with all Microsoft operating systems, with OS/2, and even with UNIX and Linux.

Microsoft's version of the IPX/SPX protocol goes by different names, depending on which version of Windows you're using. You may see it called NWLink, IPX/SPX Compatible Protocol, or NWLINK IPX/SPX/NetBIOS Compatible Transport Protocol.

NetWare versions 5.0 and later fully support TCP/IP, so you don't have to use IPX/SPX with Novell networks unless the network has a server that runs NetWare 4.*x* or (heaven forbid) 3.*x*. If your network doesn't have one of the older NetWare servers, you're better off using TCP/IP instead of IPX/SPX.

Here are a few other points to know about IPX/SPX:

✦ IPX stands for *Internetwork Package Exchange*. It's a Network layer protocol that's analogous to IP.

✦ SPX stands for *Sequenced Package Exchange*. It's a Transport layer protocol that's analogous to TCP.

✦ Unlike TCP/IP, IPX/SPX is not a standard protocol established by a standards group, such as IEEE. Instead, IPX/SPX is a proprietary standard developed and owned by Novell. Both IPX and IPX/SPX are registered trademarks of Novell, which is why Microsoft's versions of IPX/SPX aren't called simply "IPX/SPX."

Other Protocols Worth Knowing About

Other networks besides Ethernet, TCP/IP, and IPX/SPX are worth knowing about:

✦ **NetBIOS:** Short for Network Basic Input Output System, this is the basic application-programming interface for network services on Windows computers. It is installed automatically when you install TCP/IP, but doesn't show up as a separate protocol when you view the network connection properties (refer to Figure 2-1). NetBIOS is a Session layer protocol that can work with Transport layer protocols such as TCP, SPX, or NetBEUI.

✦ **NetBEUI:** Short for Network BIOS Extended User Interface, this is a Transport layer protocol that was designed for early IBM and Microsoft networks. NetBEUI is now considered obsolete.

✦ **AppleTalk:** Apple computers have their own suite of network protocols known as AppleTalk. The AppleTalk suite includes a Physical and Data Link layer protocol called LocalTalk, but can also work with standard lower level protocols, including Ethernet and Token Ring.

✦ **SNA:** *Systems Network Architecture* is an IBM networking architecture that dates back to the 1970s, when mainframe computers roamed the earth and PCs had barely emerged from the primordial computer soup. SNA was designed primarily to support huge terminals such as airline reservation and banking systems, with tens of thousands of terminals attached to central host computers. Now that IBM mainframes support TCP/IP and terminal systems have all but vanished, SNA is beginning to fade away. Still, many networks that incorporate mainframe computers have to contend with SNA.

Chapter 3: Understanding Network Hardware

In This Chapter

✓ Introducing servers

✓ Working with network interface cards

✓ Becoming familiar with network cable, network hubs, and switches

✓ Exploring repeaters, bridges, and routers

✓ Figuring out network storage

The building blocks of networks are network hardware devices such as servers, adapter cards, cables, hubs, switches, routers, and so on. This chapter provides an overview of these building blocks.

Servers

Server computers are the lifeblood of any network. Servers provide the shared resources that network users crave, such as file storage, databases, e-mail, Web services, and so on. Choosing the equipment you use for your network's servers is one of the key decisions you'll make when you set up a network. In this section, I describe some of the various ways you can equip your network's servers.

Right off the bat, I want to get one thing straight: Only the smallest networks can do without at least one dedicated server computer. For a home network or a small office network with only a few computers, you can get away with true peer-to-peer networking. That's where each client computer shares its resources such as file storage or printers, and a dedicated server computer is not needed. For a more detailed explanation of why this isn't a good idea for larger networks, see Book II, Chapter 1.

What's important in a server

Here are some general things to keep in mind when picking a server computer for your network:

✦ **Scalability:** *Scalability* refers to the ability to increase the size and capacity of the server computer without unreasonable hassle. It is a major mistake to purchase a server computer that just meets your current needs because, you can rest assured, your needs will double within a year. If at all possible, equip your servers with far more disk space, RAM, and processor power than you currently need.

✦ **Reliability:** The old adage "you get what you pay for" applies especially well to server computers. Why spend $3,000 on a server computer when you can buy one with similar specifications at a discount electronics store for $1,000? One reason is reliability. When a client computer fails, only the person who uses that computer is affected. When a server fails, however, everyone on the network is affected. The less expensive computer is probably made of inferior components that are more likely to fail.

✦ **Availability:** This concept of availability is closely related to reliability. When a server computer fails, how long does it take to correct the problem and get the server up and running again? Server computers are designed so that their components can be easily diagnosed and replaced, thus minimizing the downtime that results when a component fails. In some servers, components are *hot swappable,* which means that certain components can be replaced without shutting down the server. Some servers are designed to be *fault-tolerant* so that they can continue to operate even if a major component fails. For more information about fault-tolerant computers, see the sidebar "Tolerant to a fault."

✦ **Service and support:** Service and support are factors often overlooked when picking computers. If a component in a server computer fails, do you have someone on site qualified to repair the broken computer? If not, you should get an on-site maintenance contract for the computer. Don't settle for a maintenance contract that requires you to take the computer in to a repair shop or, worse, mail it to a repair facility. You can't afford to be without your server that long.

Components of a server computer

The hardware components that comprise a typical server computer are similar to the components used in less expensive client computers. However, server computers are usually built from higher grade components than client computers for several reasons. The following paragraphs describe the typical components of a server computer:

✦ **Motherboard:** The motherboard is a single, large electronic circuit board to which all the other components of your computer are connected. More than any other component, the motherboard *is* the computer. All other components attach to the motherboard.

Tolerant to a fault

For most networks, a server failure means that everyone is inconvenienced until the server is repaired. For some networks, though, server failures are devastating. For example, if an airline reservation system fails, the airline may potentially lose millions of dollars in revenue in just a few hours.

Fault tolerance refers to the ability of a computer system to recover from hardware failures. The two most common forms of fault tolerance are backup power supplies (also known as a *UPS*, for *Uninterruptible Power Supply*) and RAID disk subsystems. (UPS and RAID are explained in greater detail later in this chapter.) Together, these two features safeguard the server against the two most likely causes of failure: loss of power and a disk crash.

For most networks, Uninterruptible Power Supplies and RAID disk subsystems provide enough fault tolerance. For mission-critical systems that absolutely must operate without failure, you can provide complete fault tolerance by using redundant components for each part of the system. The redundant components include the processor, memory, disk subsystem, network interface card, power supply, and every other major system of the computer. These redundant components run in parallel; that is, they perform identical calculations and repeat the same processes.

Besides running systems in parallel, the fault-tolerant computer must constantly monitor each redundant component to check for errors. If a failure occurs in one of the components, the computer deactivates the failing component. The remaining system can continue to operate while you repair the failed component.

One widely recognized definition of *fault-tolerant* is that the computer should be up and running 99.999% of the time. This means that, on average, a fault-tolerant computer should have no more than five minutes of downtime per year.

Fault-resilient computers are up and running 99.99% of the time, which gives them more breathing room: They can be down 52 minutes each year.

Truly fault-tolerant computers are very expensive and are thus used only for mission-critical, people-will-die-or-we'll-all-go-broke kinds of applications, such as automated teller machines, stock market trading systems, air-traffic control systems, and the like. Fault-resilient systems are more expensive than regular servers, but are considerably less expensive than fault-tolerant systems, so they're used more often.

One of the oldest and best known manufacturers of fault-tolerant servers was Tandem. Tandem had been making fault-tolerant computers, called *NonStop Servers*, since 1974. Compaq acquired Tandem in 1997, and Compaq merged with Hewlett-Packard in 2002. So HP now manufactures the NonStop Servers. For more information, see www.tandem.com.

The major components on the motherboard include the processor (or CPU), supporting circuitry called the *chipset,* memory, expansion slots, a standard IDE hard drive controller, and I/O ports for devices such as keyboards, mice, and printers. Some motherboards also include additional built-in features such as a graphic adapter, SCSI disk controller, or a network interface.

✦ **Processor:** The processor, or CPU, is the brain of the computer. Although the processor isn't the only component that affects overall system performance, it is the one that most people think of first when deciding what type of server to purchase. At the time of this writing, Intel had four processor models, summarized in Table 3-1. Two of them — the Pentium 4 and Celeron — should be used only for desktop or notebook computers. Server computers should have an Itanium 2 or a Xeon processor, or a comparable processor from one of Intel's competitors, such as AMD.

Each motherboard is designed to support a particular type of processor. CPUs come in two basic mounting styles: slot or socket. However, you can choose from several types of slots and sockets, so you have to make sure that the motherboard supports the specific slot or socket style used by the CPU. Some server motherboards have two or more slots or sockets to hold two or more CPUs.

The term *clock speed* refers to how fast the basic clock that drives the processor's operation ticks. In theory, the faster the clock speed, the faster the processor. However, clock speed alone is reliable only for comparing processors within the same family. In fact, the Xeon is significantly faster than the Pentium 4 running at the same clock speed. That's because the Xeon contains more advanced circuitry than the Pentium 4, so it's able to accomplish more work than the Pentium 4 with each tick of the clock.

Table 3-1	Intel Processors	
Processor	*Clock Speed*	*Intended Usage*
Itanium 2	900Mhz or 1 GHz	Servers
Xeon	1.4–2.0GHz	Servers
Pentium 4	2–3GHz	Desktops
Celeron	850MHz–2.4GHz	Low-end desktops

✦ **Memory:** Don't scrimp on memory. People rarely complain about servers having too much memory. Many different types of memory are available, so you have to pick the right type of memory to match the memory supported by your motherboard. The total memory capacity of the server depends on the motherboard. Most new servers can support up to 12GB of memory.

✦ **Hard drives:** Most desktop computers use inexpensive hard drives called *IDE* drives. These drives are adequate for individual users, but because performance is more important for servers, another type of drive known as *SCSI* is usually used instead. For the best performance, use the SCSI drives along with a high-performance SCSI controller card.

✦ **Network connection:** The network connection is one of the most important parts of any server. Many servers have network adapters built into the motherboard. If your server isn't equipped as such, you'll need to add a separate network adapter card. See the section "Network Adapters," later in this chapter, for more information.

✦ **Video:** Fancy graphics aren't that important for a server computer. You can equip your servers with inexpensive generic video cards and monitors without affecting network performance. (This is one of the few areas where it's acceptable to cut costs on a server.)

✦ **Power supply:** Because a server usually has more devices than a typical desktop computer, it requires a larger power supply (300 watts is typical). If the server houses a large number of hard drives, it may require an even larger power supply.

Server form factors

The term *form factor* refers to the size, shape, and packaging of a hardware device. Server computers typically come in one of three form factors:

✦ **Tower case:** Most servers are housed in a traditional tower case, similar to the tower cases used for desktop computers. A typical server tower case is 18 inches high, 20 inches deep, and 9 inches wide and has room inside for a motherboard, five or more hard drives, and other components. Tower cases also come with built-in power supplies.

Some server cases include advanced features specially designed for servers, such as redundant power supplies (so both servers can continue operating if one of the power supplies fails), hot-swappable fans, and hot-swappable disk drive bays. (Hot-swappable components can be replaced without powering down the server.)

✦ **Rack mount:** If you only need a few servers, tower cases are fine. You can just place the servers next to each other on a table or in a cabinet that's specially designed to hold servers. If you need more than a few servers, though, space can quickly become an issue. For example, what if your departmental network requires a bank of ten file servers? You'd need a pretty long table.

Rack-mount servers are designed to save space when you need more than a few servers in a confined area. A rack-mount server is housed in a small chassis that's designed to fit into a standard 19-inch equipment rack. The rack allows you to vertically stack servers in order to save space.

Because of their small size, rack-mount servers are not as expandable as tower-style servers. A typical system includes built-in video and network connections, room for three hard drives, two empty expansion slots for additional adapters, and a SCSI port to connect additional external hard drives.

✦ **Blade servers:** Blade servers are designed to save even more space than rack-mount servers. A blade server is a server on a single card that can be mounted alongside other blade servers in a blade chassis, which itself fits into a standard 19-inch equipment rack. A typical blade chassis holds six or more servers, depending on the manufacturer.

One of the key benefits of blade servers is that you don't need a separate power supply for each server. Instead, the blade enclosure provides power for all its blade servers. Some blade server systems provide rack-mounted power supplies that can serve several blade enclosures mounted in a single rack.

In addition, the blade enclosure provides KVM switching so that you don't have to use a separate KVM switch. You can control any of the servers in a blade server network from a single keyboard, monitor, and mouse.

One of the biggest benefits of blade servers is that they drastically cut down the amount of cable clutter. With rack-mount servers, each server requires its own power cable, keyboard cable, video cable, mouse cable, and network cables. With blade servers, a single set of cables can service all the servers in a blade enclosure.

Saving space with a KVM switch

If you have more than two or three servers together in one location, you should consider getting a device called a *KVM switch* to save space. A KVM switch lets you connect several server computers to a single keyboard, monitor, and mouse. (KVM stands for *Keyboard, Video, and Mouse*.) Then, you can control any of the servers from a single keyboard, monitor, and mouse by turning a dial or by pressing a button on the KVM switch.

Simple KVM switches are mechanical affairs that let you choose from among 2 to 16 or more computers. More elaborate KVM switches can control more computers, using a pop-up menu or a special keyboard combination to switch among computers. Some advanced KVMs can even control a mix of PCs and Macintosh computers from a single keyboard, monitor, and mouse.

To find more information about KVM switches, go to a Web search engine such as Google and search for "KVM."

Network Interface Cards

Every computer on a network, both clients and servers, requires a network interface card (or NIC) in order to access the network. A NIC is usually a separate adapter card that slides into one of the server's motherboard expansion slots. However, some motherboards have a built-in network interface, so a separate card isn't needed.

For client computers, you can get away with using inexpensive NICs because client computers are used only to connect one user to the network. However, the NIC in a server computer connects many network users to the server. As a result, it makes sense to spend more money on a higher quality NIC for a heavily used server. Most network administrators prefer to use name-brand cards from manufacturers such as Intel, SMC, or 3Com.

The network interface cards that you use must have a connector that matches the type of cable that you use. If you plan on wiring your network with thinnet cable, make sure that the network cards have a BNC connector. For twisted-pair wiring, make sure that the cards have an RJ-45 connector.

Some network cards provide two or three connectors. I see them in every combination: BNC and AUI, RJ-45 and AUI, BNC and RJ-45, and all three. Selecting a card that has both BNC and RJ-45 connectors isn't a bad idea. This way, you can switch from thinnet cable to twisted-pair cable or vice versa without buying new network cards. You can get both types of connectors for a cost of only $5 to $10 more per card. Don't worry about the AUI connector, though. You'll probably never need it.

Most NICs made today work with both 10Mbps and 100Mbps UTP networks (that is, 10BaseT and 100BaseT) and are called *10/100 cards*. These cards automatically adjust their speed to match the speed of the network. So you can use a 10/100 card on a network that has older 10Mbps cards without trouble. You can find inexpensive 10/100 cards for as little as $15 each. Name-brand cards cost three or four times that much.

1000BaseT cards are considerably more expensive than 10/100 cards. Inexpensive 1000BaseT cards start at about $150, but the price can go up to $500 or more for cards with advanced features such as larger on-board buffers and embedded network I/O processors.

Here are a few other points to ponder concerning network interface cards:

✦ A NIC is a Physical layer and Data Link layer device. Because a NIC establishes a network node, it must have a physical network address, also known as a MAC address. The MAC address is burned into the NIC at the factory, so you can't change it. Every NIC ever manufactured has a unique MAC address.

✦ For server computers, it makes sense to use more than one NIC. That way, the server can handle more network traffic. Some server NICs have two or more network interfaces built into a single card.

✦ Fiber-optic networks also require NICs. Fiber-optic NICs are still too expensive for desktop use in most networks. Instead, they're used for high-speed backbones. If a server connects to a high-speed fiber backbone, it will need a fiber-optic NIC that matches the fiber-optic cable being used.

✦ Long ago and far away, Novell manufactured a network interface card known as the *NE2000*. The NE2000 card is no longer made, but NE2000 remains a standard of compatibility for network interface cards. If a card is NE2000-compatible, you can use it with just about any network. If you buy a card that is not NE2000-compatible, make sure that the card is compatible with the network operating system that you intend to use.

Network Cable

You can construct an Ethernet network by using one of two different types of cable: *coaxial cable,* which resembles TV cable, or *twisted-pair cable,* which looks like phone cable. Twisted-pair cable is sometimes called *UTP,* or *10BaseT cable,* for reasons I try hard not to explain later (in the section "Twisted-pair cable").

You may encounter other types of cable in an existing network: thick yellow cable that used to be the only type of cable used for Ethernet, fiber-optic cables that span long distances at high speeds, or thick twisted-pair bundles that carry multiple sets of twisted-pair cable between wiring closets in a large building. For all but the largest networks, the choice is between coaxial cable and twisted-pair cable.

 A third choice — one that's becoming more popular every day — is to forego network cable and instead build your network using wireless network components. Because Chapters 2, 3, and 4 of Book VI are devoted exclusively to wireless networking, I don't describe wireless network components in this chapter.

Coaxial cable

One type of cable that you can use for Ethernet networks is coaxial cable, usually called *thinnet* or sometimes *BNC cable* because of the type of connectors used on each end of the cable. Thinnet cable operates only at 10Mbps and is rarely used for new networks. However, you'll find plenty of existing thinnet networks still being used. Figure 3-1 shows a typical coaxial cable.

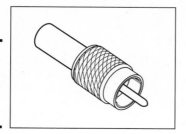

Figure 3-1:
A coaxial
cable with a
BNC
connector.

Here are some salient points about coaxial cable:

✦ You attach thinnet to the network interface card by using a goofy twist-on connector called a *BNC connector*. You can purchase pre-assembled cables with BNC connectors already attached in lengths of 25 or 50 feet, or you can buy bulk cable on a big spool and attach the connectors yourself by using a special tool. (I suggest buying pre-assembled cables. Attaching connectors to bulk cable can be tricky.)

✦ With coaxial cables, you connect your computers point-to-point in a bus topology. At each computer, a T connector is used to connect two cables to the network interface card.

✦ A special plug called a *terminator* is required at each end of a series of thinnet cables. The terminator prevents data from spilling out the end of the cable and staining the carpet.

✦ The cables strung end-to-end from one terminator to the other are collectively called a *segment*. The maximum length of a thinnet segment is about 200 meters (actually, 185 meters). You can connect as many as 30 computers on one segment. To span a distance greater than 185 meters or to connect more than 30 computers, you must use two or more segments with a device called a *repeater* to connect each segment.

✦ Although Ethernet coaxial cable resembles TV coaxial cable, the two types of cable are not interchangeable. Don't try to cut costs by wiring your network with cheap TV cable.

Twisted-pair cable

A popular alternative to thinnet cable is *twisted-pair cable,* or *UTP.* (The *U* stands for *unshielded,* but no one says *unshielded twisted pair.* Just *twisted pair* will do.) UTP cable is even cheaper than thin coaxial cable, and best of all, many modern buildings are already wired with twisted-pair cable because this type of wiring is often used with modern phone systems. Figure 3-2 shows a twisted-pair cable.

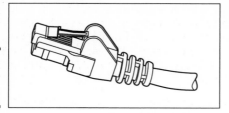

Figure 3-2:
Twisted-pair
cable.

When you use UTP cable to construct an Ethernet network, you connect the computers in a star arrangement. In the center of the star is a device called a *hub*. Depending on the model, Ethernet hubs enable you to connect from 4 to 24 computers using twisted-pair cable.

An advantage of UTP's star arrangement is that if one cable goes bad, only the computer attached to that cable is affected; the rest of the network continues to chug along. With coaxial cable, a bad cable affects the entire network, and not just the computer to which the bad cable is connected.

Here are a few other details that you should know about twisted-pair cabling:

✦ UTP cable consists of pairs of thin wire twisted around each other; several such pairs are gathered up inside an outer insulating jacket. Ethernet uses two pairs of wires, or four wires altogether. The number of pairs in a UTP cable varies, but it is often more than two.

✦ UTP cable comes in various grades called *Categories*. Don't use anything less than Category 5 cable for your network. Although cheaper, it may not be able to support faster networks.

   Although higher Category cables are more expensive than lower Category cables, the real cost of installing Ethernet cabling is the labor required to actually pull the cables through the walls. As a result, I recommend that you always spend the extra money to buy Category 5 cable.

✦ If you want to sound like you know what you're talking about, say "Cat 5" instead of "Category 5."

✦ Although Category 5 cable is fine for 100Mbps networks, the newer 1000Mbps networks require an even better cable. Category 5e cable (the *e* stands for *enhanced*), and Category 6 cable will support 1000Mbps networks.

✦ UTP cable connectors look like modular phone connectors but are a bit larger. UTP connectors are officially called *RJ-45 connectors*.

✦ Like thinnet cable, UTP cable is also sold in prefabricated lengths. However, RJ-45 connectors are much easier to attach to bulk UTP cable than BNC cables are to attach to bulk coaxial cable. As a result, I suggest that you buy bulk cable and connectors unless your network consists of just two or three computers. A basic crimp tool to attach the RJ-45 connectors costs about $50.

✦ The maximum allowable cable length between the hub and the computer is 100 meters (about 328 feet).

Hubs and Switches

The biggest difference between using coaxial cable and twisted-pair cable is that when you use twisted-pair cable, you also must use a separate device called a *hub*. Years ago, hubs were expensive devices — expensive enough that most do-it-yourself networkers who were building small networks opted for thinnet cable in order to avoid the expense and hassle of using hubs.

TECHNICAL STUFF

Hubs and switches demystified

Both hubs and switches let you connect multiple computers to a twisted-pair network. Switches are more efficient than hubs, but not just because they are faster. If you really want to know, here's the actual difference between a hub and a switch:

✔ In a hub, every packet that arrives at the hub on any of its ports is automatically sent out on every other port. The hub has to do this because it is a Physical layer device, so it has no way to keep track of which computer is connected to each port. For example, suppose that John's computer is connected to port 1 on an 8-port hub, and Andrea's computer is connected to port 5. If John's computer sends a packet of information to Andrea's computer, the hub receives the packet on port 1 and then sends it out on ports 2–8. All the computers connected to the hub get to see the packet so that they can determine whether the packet was intended for them.

✔ A switch is a Data Link layer device, which means it's able to look into the packets that pass through it to examine a critical piece of Data Link layer information: the MAC address. With this information in hand, a switch can keep track of which computer is connected to each of its ports. So if John's computer on port 1 sends a packet to Andrea's computer on port 5, the switch receives the packet on port 1 and then sends the packet out on port 5 only. This process is not only faster, but also improves the security of the system because other computers don't see packets that aren't meant for them.

Nowadays, the cost of hubs has dropped so much that the advantages of twisted-pair cabling outweigh the hassle and cost of using hubs. With twisted-pair cabling, you can more easily add new computers to the network, move computers, find and correct cable problems, and service the computers that you need to remove from the network temporarily.

A *switch* is simply a more sophisticated type of hub. Because the cost of switches has come down dramatically in the past few years, most new networks are built with switches rather than hubs. If you have an older network that uses hubs and seems to run slowly, you may be able to improve the network's speed by replacing the older hubs with newer switches. For more information, see the sidebar "Hubs and switches demystified," earlier in this chapter.

If you use twisted-pair cabling, you need to know some of the ins and outs of using hubs:

✦ Because you must run a cable from each computer to the hub or switch, find a central location for the hub or switch to which you can easily route the cables.

✦ The hub or switch requires electrical power, so make sure that an electrical outlet is handy.

✦ When you purchase a hub or switch, purchase one with at least twice as many connections as you need. Don't buy a four-port hub or switch if you want to network four computers because when (not *if*) you add the fifth computer, you have to buy another hub or switch.

✦ You can connect hubs or switches to one another, as shown in Figure 3-3; this is called *daisy-chaining.* When you daisy-chain hubs or switches, you connect a cable to a standard port on one of the hubs or switches and the daisy-chain port on the other hub or switch. Be sure to read the instructions that come with the hub or switch to make sure that you daisy-chain them properly.

✦ You can daisy-chain no more than three hubs or switches together. If you have more computers than three hubs can accommodate, don't panic. For a small additional cost, you can purchase hubs that have a BNC connection on the back. Then you can string the hubs together using thinnet cable. The three-hub limit doesn't apply when you use thinnet cable to connect the hubs. You can also get stackable hubs or switches that have high-speed direct connections that enable two or more hubs or switches to be counted as a single hub or switch.

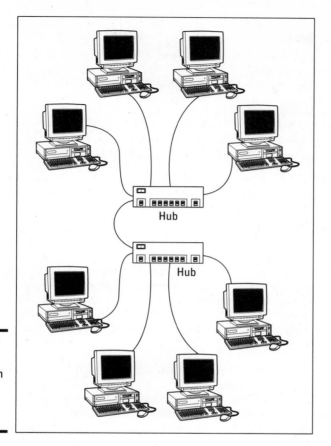

Figure 3-3:
You can
daisy-chain
hubs or
switches
together.

✦ When you shop for network hubs, you may notice that the expensive ones have network-management features that support something called *SNMP*. These hubs are called *managed hubs*. Unless your network is very large and you know what SNMP is, don't bother with the more expensive managed hubs. You'd be paying for a feature that you may never use.

✦ For large networks, you may want to consider using a *managed switch*. A managed switch allows you to monitor and control various aspects of the switch's operation from a remote computer. The switch can alert you when something goes wrong with the network, and it can keep performance statistics so that you can determine which parts of the network are heavily used and which are not. A managed switch costs two or three times as much as an unmanaged switch, but for larger networks, the benefits of managed switches are well worth the additional cost.

Repeaters

A *repeater* is a gizmo that gives your network signals a boost so that the signals can travel farther. It's kind of like the Gatorade stations in a marathon. As the signals travel past the repeater, they pick up a cup of Gatorade, take a sip, splash the rest of it on their heads, toss the cup, and hop in a cab when they're sure that no one is looking.

You need a repeater when the total length of a single span of network cable is larger than the maximum allowed for your cable type:

Cable	Maximum Length
10Base2 (Coaxial)	185 meters or 606 feet
10/100BaseT (Twisted Pair)	100 meters or 328 feet

For coaxial cable, the preceding cable lengths apply to cable segments — not individual lengths of cable. A segment is the entire run of cable from one terminator to another and may include more than one computer. In other words, if you have ten computers and you connect them all with 25-foot lengths of thin coaxial cable, the total length of the segment is 225 feet. (Made you look! Only nine cables are required to connect ten computers — that's why it's not 250 feet.)

For 10BaseT or 100BaseT cable, the 100-meter length limit applies to the cable that connects a computer to the hub or the cable that connects hubs to each other when hubs are daisy-chained with twisted-pair cable. In other words, you can connect each computer to the hub with no more than 100 meters of cable, and you can connect hubs to each other with no more than 100 meters of cable.

Figure 3-4 shows how you can use a repeater to connect two groups of computers that are too far apart to be strung on a single segment. When you use a repeater like this, the repeater divides the cable into two segments. The cable length limit still applies to the cable on each side of the repeater.

Here are some points to ponder when you lie awake tonight wondering about repeaters:

✦ Repeaters are used only with Ethernet networks wired with coaxial cable; 10/100BaseT networks don't use repeaters.

Actually, that's not quite true: 10/100BaseT does use repeaters. It's just that the repeater isn't a separate device. In a 10/100BaseT network, the hub is actually a multiport repeater. That's why the cable used to attach each computer to the hub is considered a separate segment.

✦ Some 10/100BaseT hubs have a BNC connector on the back. This BNC connector is a thinnet repeater that enables you to attach a full 185-meter thinnet segment. The segment can attach other computers, 10BaseT hubs, or a combination of both.

✦ A basic rule of Ethernet life is that a signal can't pass through more than three repeaters on its way from one node to another. That doesn't mean you can't have more than three repeaters or hubs, but if you do, you have to carefully plan the network cabling so that the three-repeater rule isn't violated.

✦ A two-port 10Base2 repeater costs about $200. Sheesh! I guess that's one of the reasons few people use coaxial cable anymore.

✦ Repeaters are legitimate components of a by-the-book Ethernet network. They don't extend the maximum length of a single segment; they just enable you to tie two segments together. Beware of the little black boxes that claim to extend the segment limit beyond the standard 185-meter limit for thinnet or the 100-meter limit for 10/100BaseT cable. These products usually work, but playing by the rules is better.

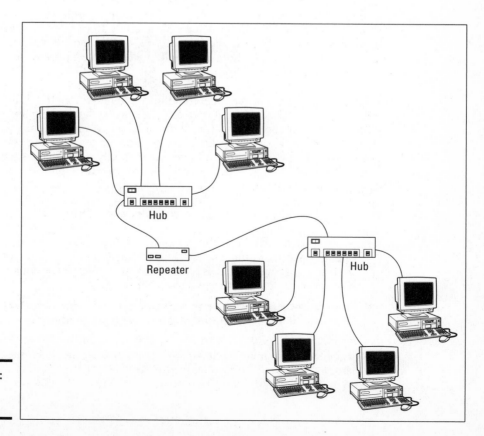

Figure 3-4:
Using a
repeater.

Hub

Repeater

Hub

Bridges

A *bridge* is a device that connects two networks so that they act as if they are one network. Bridges are used to partition one large network into two smaller networks for performance reasons. You can think of a bridge as a kind of smart repeater. Repeaters listen to signals coming down one network cable, amplify them, and send them down the other cable. They do this blindly, paying no attention to the content of the messages that they repeat.

In contrast, a bridge is a little smarter about the messages that come down the pike. For starters, most bridges have the capability to listen to the network and automatically figure out the address of each computer on both sides of the bridge. Then the bridge can inspect each message that comes from one side of the bridge and broadcast it on the other side of the bridge, but only if the message is intended for a computer that's on the other side.

This key feature enables bridges to partition a large network into two smaller, more efficient networks. Bridges work best in networks that are highly segregated. For example (humor me here — I'm a Dr. Seuss fan), suppose that the Sneetches networked all their computers and discovered that, although the Star-Bellied Sneetches' computers talked to each other frequently and the Plain-Bellied Sneetches' computers also talked to each other frequently, rarely did a Star-Bellied Sneetch computer talk to a Plain-Bellied Sneetch computer.

A bridge can partition the Sneetchnet into two networks: the Star-Bellied network and the Plain-Bellied network. The bridge automatically learns which computers are on the Star-Bellied network and which are on the Plain-Bellied network. The bridge forwards messages from the Star-Bellied side to the Plain-Bellied side (and vice versa) only when necessary. The overall performance of both networks improves, although the performance of any network operation that has to travel over the bridge slows down a bit.

Here are a few additional things to consider about bridges:

✦ Some bridges also have the capability to translate the messages from one format to another. For example, if the Star-Bellied Sneetches build their network with Ethernet and the Plain-Bellied Sneetches use Token Ring, a bridge can tie the two together.

✦ You can get a basic bridge to partition two Ethernet networks for about $500 from mail-order suppliers. More sophisticated bridges can cost as much as $5,000 or more.

✦ If you've never read Dr. Seuss's classic story of the Sneetches, you should.

Routers

A *router* is like a bridge, but with a key difference. Bridges are Data Link layer devices, so they can tell the MAC address of the network node to which each message is sent, and can forward the message to the appropriate segment. However, they can't peek into the message itself to see what type of information is being sent. In contrast, a router is a Network layer device, so it can work with the network packets at a higher level. In particular, a router can examine the IP address of the packets that pass through it. And because IP addresses have both a network and a host address, a router can determine what network a message is coming from and going to. Bridges are ignorant of this information.

One key difference between a bridge and a router is that a bridge is essentially transparent to the network. In contrast, a router is itself a node on the network, with its own MAC and IP addresses. This means that messages can be directed to a router, which can then examine the contents of the message to determine how it should handle the message.

You can configure a network with several routers that can work cooperatively together. For example, some routers are able to monitor the network to determine the most efficient path for sending a message to its ultimate destination. If a part of the network is extremely busy, a router can automatically route messages along a less-busy route. In this respect, the router is kind of like a traffic reporter up in a helicopter. The router knows that 101 is bumper-to-bumper all the way through Sunnyvale, so it sends the message on 280 instead.

Here is some additional information about routers:

✦ Routers aren't cheap. For big networks, though, they're worth it.

✦ The functional distinctions between bridges and routers — and switches and hubs, for that matter — get blurrier all the time. As bridges, hubs, and switches become more sophisticated, they're able to take on some of the chores that used to require a router, thus putting many routers out of work.

✦ Some routers are nothing more than computers with several network interface cards and special software to perform the router functions.

✦ Routers can also connect networks that are geographically distant from each other via a phone line (using modems) or ISDN.

✦ You can also use a router to join your LAN to the Internet. Figure 3-5 shows a router used for this purpose.

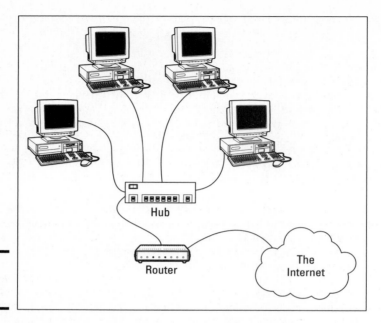

Figure 3-5:
Using a
repeater.

Network Attached Storage

Many network servers exist solely for the purpose of making disk space available to network users. As networks grow to support more users, and users require more disk space, network administrators are constantly finding ways to add more storage to their networks. One way to do that is to add additional file servers. However, a simpler and less expensive way is to use *network attached storage,* also known as *NAS.*

A NAS device is a self-contained file server that's preconfigured and ready to run. All you have to do to set it up is take it out of the box, plug it in, and turn it on. NAS devices are easy to set up and configure, easy to maintain, and less expensive than traditional file servers.

NAS should not be confused with a related technology called *storage area networks,* or *SAN.* SAN is a much more complicated and expensive technology that provides huge quantities of data storage for large networks. For more information on SAN, see the sidebar "SAN is NAS spelled backwards," later in this chapter.

A typical entry-level NAS device is the Dell 725N. This device is a self-contained file server built into a small rack-mount chassis. It supports up to four hard drives with a total capacity up to one terabyte (or 1,000 GB). The 475N has a dual-processor motherboard that can hold up to 3GB of memory, and two built-in 10/100/1000Mbps network ports. An LCD display on the front panel displays the device's IP address.

The Dell 725N runs a special version of Windows 2000 Server called the Windows 2000 Server Appliance Kit. This version of Windows is designed specifically for NAS devices. It allows you to configure the network storage from any computer on the network by using a Web browser.

Note that some NAS devices use customized versions of Linux rather than the Windows 2000 Server Appliance Kit. Also, in some systems, the operating system resides on a separate hard drive that's isolated from the shared disks. This prevents the user from inadvertently damaging the operating system.

SAN is NAS spelled backwards

It's easy to confuse the terms *storage area network* (SAN) and *network attached storage* (NAS). Both refer to relatively new network technologies that let you manage the disk storage on your network. However, NAS is a much simpler and less expensive technology. A NAS device is nothing more than an inexpensive self-contained file server. Using NAS devices actually simplifies the task of adding storage to a network because the NAT eliminates the chore of configuring a network operating system for routine file sharing tasks.

A storage area network is designed for managing very large amounts of network storage — sometimes downright huge amounts. A SAN consists of three components: storage devices (perhaps hundreds of them), a separate high-speed network (usually fiber-optic) that directly connects the storage devices to each other, and one or more SAN servers that connect the SAN to the local area network. The SAN server manages the storage devices attached to the SAN and allows users of the LAN to access the storage.

Setting up and managing a storage area network is a job for a SAN expert. For more information about storage area networks, see the home page of the Storage Networking Industry Association at www.snia.org.

Chapter 4: Understanding Network Operating Systems

In This Chapter

✔ Understanding what network operating systems do

✔ Figuring out the advantages of Windows Server 2003

✔ Analyzing Windows 2000 Server

✔ Taking a look at Windows NT Server

✔ Navigating NetWare

✔ Exploring other network operating systems

✔ Delving into peer-to-peer networking

*O*ne of the basic choices that you must make before you proceed any further is to decide which network operating system (NOS) to use as the foundation for your network. This chapter begins with a description of several important features found in all network operating systems. Next, it provides an overview of the advantages and disadvantages of the most popular network operating systems.

Network Operating System Features

All network operating systems, from the simplest (such as Windows XP Home Edition) to the most complex (such as Windows Server 2003 Datacenter Edition), must provide certain core functions, such as the ability to connect to other computers on the network, share files and other resources, provide for security, and so on. In the following sections, I describe some of these core NOS features in general terms.

Network support

It goes without saying that a network operating system should support networks. (I can picture Mike Myers in his classic Saturday Night Live role as Linda Richman, host of Coffee Talk, saying "I'm getting a little verklempt. . . . Talk amongst yourselves. . . . I'll give you a topic — network operating systems do not network, nor do they operate. Discuss.")

A network operating system must support a wide variety of networking protocols in order to meet the needs of its users. That's because a large network typically consists of a mixture of various versions of Windows, as well as Macintosh and possibly Linux computers. As a result, the server may need to simultaneously support TCP/IP, NetBIOS, and AppleTalk protocols.

Many servers have more than one network interface card installed. In that case, the NOS must be able to support multiple network connections. Ideally, the NOS should have the ability to balance the network load among its network interfaces. In addition, in the event that one of the connections fails, the NOS should be able to seamlessly switch to the other connection.

Finally, most network operating systems include a built-in ability to function as a router that connects two networks. The NOS router functions should also include firewall features in order to keep unauthorized packets from entering the local network.

File sharing services

One of the most important functions of a network operating system is its ability to share resources with other network users. The most common resource that's shared is the server's file system. A network server must be able to share some or all its disk space with other users so that those users can treat the server's disk space as an extension of their own computer's disk space.

The NOS allows the system administrator to determine which portions of the server's file system to share. Although an entire hard drive can be shared, it is not commonly done. Instead, individual directories or folders are shared. The administrator can control which users are allowed to access each shared folder.

Because file sharing is the reason many network servers exist, network operating systems have more sophisticated disk management features than are found in desktop operating systems. For example, most network operating systems have the ability to manage two or more hard drives as if they were a single drive. In addition, most can create mirrors, which automatically keeps a backup copy of a drive on a second drive.

Multitasking

Only one user at a time uses a desktop computer; however, multiple users simultaneously use server computers . As a result, a network operating system must provide support for multiple users who access the server remotely via the network.

At the heart of multiuser support is *multitasking,* which is the ability of an operating system to execute more than one program — called a *task* or a *process* — at a time. Multitasking operating systems are like the guy that used to spin plates balanced on sticks on the old Ed Sullivan show. He'd run from plate to plate, trying to keep them all spinning so they wouldn't fall off the sticks. To make it challenging, he'd do it blindfolded or riding on a unicycle.

Although multitasking creates the appearance that two or more programs are executing on the computer at one time, in reality, a computer with a single processor can execute only one program at a time. The operating system switches the CPU from one program to another to create the appearance that several programs are executing simultaneously, but at any given moment, only one of the programs is actually executing. The others are patiently waiting for their turns. (If the computer has more than one CPU, the CPUs *can* execute programs simultaneously, which is called *multiprocessing.*)

To see multitasking in operating on a Windows computer, press Ctrl+Alt+Delete to bring up the Windows Task Manager and then click the Processes tab. All the tasks currently active on the computer appear.

In order for multitasking to work reliably, the network operating system must completely isolate the executing programs from each other. Otherwise, one program may perform an operation that adversely affects another program. Multitasking operating systems do this by providing each task with its own unique *address space* that makes it almost impossible for one task to affect memory that belongs to another task.

In most cases, each program executes as a single task or process within the memory address space allocated to the task. However, a single program can also be split into several tasks. This technique is usually called *multithreading*, and the program's tasks are called *threads.*

The two approaches to multitasking are preemptive and non-preemptive. In preemptive multitasking, the operating system decides how long each task gets to execute before it should step aside so that another task can execute. When a task's time is up, the operating system's task manager interrupts the task and switches to the next task in line. All the network operating systems in widespread use today use preemptive multitasking.

The alternative to preemptive multitasking is non-preemptive multitasking. In non-preemptive multitasking, each task that gets control of the CPU is allowed to run until it voluntarily gives up control so that another task can run. Non-preemptive multitasking requires less operating system overhead because the operating system doesn't have to keep track of how long each task has run. However, programs have to be carefully written so that they don't hog the computer all to themselves.

Directory services

Directories are everywhere. When you need to make a phone call, you look up the number in a phone directory. When you need to find the address of a client, you look up him or her in your Rolodex. And when you need to find the Sam Goody store at a shopping mall, you look for the mall directory.

Networks have directories, too. Network directories provide information about the resources that are available on the network, such as users, computers, printers, shared folders, and files. Directories are an essential part of any network operating system.

In early network operating systems, such as Windows NT 3.1 and NetWare 3.x, each server computer maintained its own directory database of resources that were available just on that server. The problem with that approach was that network administrators had to maintain each directory database separately. That wasn't too bad for networks with just a few servers, but maintaining the directory on a network with dozens or even hundreds of servers was next to impossible.

In addition, early directory services were application-specific. For example, a server would have one directory database for user logins, another for file sharing, and yet another for e-mail addresses. Each directory had its own tools for adding, updating, and deleting directory entries.

Modern network operating systems provide global directory services that combine the directory information for an entire network and for all applications so that it can be treated as a single integrated database. These directory services are based on an ISO standard called X.500. In an X.500 directory, information is organized hierarchically. For example, a multinational company can divide its user directory into one or more countries, each country can have one or more regions, and, in turn, each region can have one or more departments.

Security services

All network operating systems must provide some measure of security to protect the network from unauthorized access. Hacking seems to be the national pastime these days. With most computer networks connected to the Internet, anyone anywhere in the world can and probably will try to break into your network.

The most basic type of security is handled through *user accounts,* which grant individual users the right to access the network resources and govern what resources the user can access. User accounts are secured by passwords;

therefore, good password policy is a cornerstone of any security system. Most network operating systems let you establish password policies, such as requiring that passwords have a minimum length and include a mix of letters and numerals. In addition, passwords can be set to expire after a certain number of days, so users can be forced to frequently change their passwords.

Most network operating systems also provide for data encryption, which scrambles data before it is sent over the network or saved on disk, and digital certificates, which are used to ensure that users are who they say they are and files are what they claim to be.

Microsoft's Server Operating Systems

Microsoft currently supports three versions of its flagship server operating system: Windows NT Server 4, Windows 2000 Server, and Windows Server 2003. Windows Server 2003 is the newest version. It's so new, in fact, that few people are using it. So Windows 2000 Server is the Windows server that you're most likely to find in the field. Although Microsoft still supports Windows NT Server 4, it no longer sells this operating system. Still, plenty of networks are chugging along just fine with NT.

Windows NT 4 Server

Windows NT Server was the last in a long series of Windows servers dubbed *NT,* which stood for *New Technology*. The "new technology" that got everyone so excited about Windows NT in the first place was 32-bit processing, a huge step up from the 16-bit processing of earlier versions of Windows. Windows NT was the first Microsoft operating system that was reliable enough to work as a network server on large networks. Version 4.0 shipped in July 1996, so it is now more than 7 years old. That's a lifetime in operating system years (which are kind of like dog years).

Probably the most important feature of Windows NT is its directory model, which is based on the concept of *domains*. A domain is a group of computers that are managed by a single directory database. To access shared resources within a domain, you must have a valid user account within the domain and be granted rights to access the resources in which you're interested. The domain system uses 15-character NetBIOS names to access individual computers within a domain and to name the domain itself.

NTFS drives

Windows NT Server introduced a new type of formatting for hard drives, different from the standard FAT system used by MS-DOS since the early 1980s. (*FAT* stands for *File Allocation Table,* in case you're interested.) The new system, called *NTFS* (for *NT File System*) offers many advantages over FAT drives:

✔ NTFS is much more efficient at using the space on your hard drive. As a result, NTFS can cram more data onto a given hard drive than FAT.

✔ NTFS drives provide better security features than FAT drives. NTFS stores security information on disk for each file and directory. In contrast, FAT has only rudimentary security features.

✔ NTFS drives are more reliable because NTFS keeps duplicate copies of important information, such as the location of each file on the hard drive. If a problem develops on an NTFS drive, Windows NT Server can probably correct the problem without losing any data. In contrast, FAT drives are prone to losing information.

Here's a summary of the other features of NT:

✦ Officially, Microsoft claims that NT Server will run on any 486 processor with at least 16MB of memory. But I wouldn't try it on anything less than a 200MHz Pentium with 64MB of RAM. Of course, these days, 200MHz Pentiums with 64MB of RAM are given away as prizes in Cracker Jack boxes.

✦ Windows NT 4 uses the same user interface that was designed for Windows 95. In fact, the main difference between NT 4 and its predecessor, Windows NT 3.51, was this new user interface.

✦ Some of the file system limits are

  • Max number of users: Unlimited

  • Number of disk volumes: 25

  • Max size of a volume: 17,000GB

  • Max hard drive space for server: 408,000GB

  • Largest file: 17 billion GB (Wow! That's more than the maximum hard drive space for a server, which is impossible!)

  • Max amount of RAM in server: 4GB

  • Max number of open files: Unlimited

✦ Microsoft began to officially phase out Windows NT 4 in 2002. Here are some of the important dates for Windows NT support:

- July 1, 2003: Windows NT is no longer available to system builders as of this date.

- January 1, 2004: Microsoft will stop publishing nonsecurity patches. Security-related patches will continue to be made available as security problems are detected.

- January 1, 2005: Security patches will no longer be available.

Windows 2000 Server

Although Windows Server 2003 is newer, Windows 2000 Server is currently the most popular server operating system from Microsoft. Windows 2000 Server built on the strengths of Windows NT Server 4 by adding new features that made Windows 2000 Server faster, easier to manage, more reliable, and easier to use for large and small networks alike.

The most significant new feature offered by Windows 2000 Server is called *Active Directory,* which provides a single directory of all network resources and enables program developers to incorporate the directory into their programs. Active Directory drops the 15-character domain and computer names in favor of Internet-style DNS names, such as Marketing.MyCompany.com or Sales.YourCompany.com. (However, it still supports the old-style names for older clients that don't deal well with DNS names.)

Windows 2000 Server comes in three versions:

✦ **Windows 2000 Server** is the basic server, designed for small- to medium-sized networks. It includes all the basic server features, including file and printer sharing, and acts as a Web and e-mail server.

✦ **Windows 2000 Advanced Server** is the next step up, designed for larger networks. Advanced Server can support server computers that have up to 8GB of memory (not hard drive — RAM!) and four integrated processors instead of the single processor that desktop computers and most server computers have.

✦ **Windows 2000 Datacenter Server** supports servers that have as many as 32 processors with up to 64GB of RAM and is specially designed for large database applications.

For small networks with 50 or fewer computers, Microsoft offers a special bundle called the Small Business Server, which includes the following components for one low, low price:

✦ Windows 2000 Server, the operating system for your network server.

✦ Exchange Server 2000, for e-mail and instant messaging.

✦ Internet Security and Acceleration Server 2000, which provides improved security and performance for your Web applications.

✦ SQL Server 2000, a database server.

✦ FrontPage 2000, for building Web sites.

✦ Outlook 2000, for reading e-mail.

The pricing for Windows 2000 Server is based on the number of clients that will use each server. Each server must have a server license and an appropriate number of client licenses. When you buy Windows 2000 Server, you get a server license and either 5, 10, or 25 client licenses. You can then purchase additional client licenses 5 or 20 at a time. Table 4-1 lists the prices for the various types of Windows 2000 Server and client licenses.

Table 4-1	Windows 2000 Server Pricing
Product	*Price*
Windows 2000 Server, 5 clients	$999
Windows 2000 Server, 10 clients	$1,199
Windows 2000 Server, 25 clients	$1,799
Windows 2000 Advanced Server, 25 clients	$3,999
Client license 5-pack	$199
Client license 20-pack	$799

Windows Server 2003

At the time of this writing, Microsoft had just released a new version of Windows Server called Windows Server 2003. For several years prior to its release, this new version was called Windows .NET Server. (*.NET* is pronounced *dot-net*.) Windows Server 2003 builds on Windows 2000 Server, with the following added features:

✦ A new and improved version of Active Directory with tighter security, an easier-to-use interface, and better performance.

✦ A better and easier-to-use system management interface, called the Manage My Server window. On the flip side, for those who prefer brute-force commands, Windows Server 2003 includes a more comprehensive set of command-line management tools than is offered by Windows 2000 Server. Of course, the familiar Microsoft Management Console tools from Windows 2000 Server are still there.

✦ A major change in the application-programming interface for Windows programs, known as the .NET Framework.

✦ Support for ever-larger clusters of computers. A *cluster* is a set of computers that work together as if they were a single server. Windows 2000 Server Datacenter Edition Previous versions supported clusters of four servers; Windows Server 2003 Enterprise and Datacenter Editions support clusters of eight servers. (Obviously, this is a benefit only for very large networks. The rest of us should just grin and say, "Cool!")

✦ An enhanced distributed file system that lets you combine drives on several servers to create one shared volume.

✦ Support for storage area networks.

✦ A built-in Internet firewall to secure your Internet connection.

✦ A new version of Microsoft's Web server, Internet Information Services (IIS) 6.0.

Like its predecessor, Windows Server 2003 comes in several versions. Four, to be specific:

✦ **Windows Server 2003, Standard Edition:** This is the basic version of Windows 2003. If you're using Windows Server 2003 as a file server or to provide other basic network services, this is the version you'll use. Standard Edition can support servers with up to four processors and 4GB of RAM.

✦ **Windows Server 2003, Web Edition:** A version of Windows 2003 optimized for use as a Web server.

✦ **Windows Server 2003, Enterprise Edition:** Designed for larger networks, this version can support servers with up to eight processors, 32GB of RAM, server clusters, and advanced features designed for high performance and reliability.

✦ **Windows Server 2003, Datacenter Edition:** The most powerful version of Windows 2003, with support for servers with 64 processors, 64GB of RAM, and server clusters, as well as advanced fault-tolerance features designed to keep the server running for mission-critical applications.

Table 4-2 lists the pricing for Windows Server 2003, which is similar to the pricing for Windows 2000 Server with the exception of the Web Edition.

Table 4-2	Windows 2003 Server Pricing
Product	*Price*
Windows Server 2003, 5 clients	$999
Windows Server 2003, 10 clients	$1,199
Windows Server 2003 Enterprise Edition, 25 clients	$3,999
Client license 5-pack	$199
Client license 20-pack	$799
Windows Server 2003, Web Edition	$399

Novell NetWare

NetWare is one of the most popular network operating systems, especially for large networks. NetWare has an excellent reputation for reliability. In fact, some network administrators swear that they have NetWare servers on their networks that have been running continuously, without a single reboot, since Teddy Roosevelt was president.

NetWare versions

NetWare released the first version of NetWare in 1983, two years before the first version of Windows and four years before Microsoft's first network operating system, the now defunct LAN Manager. Over the years, NetWare has gone through many versions. The versions you're most likely to encounter still in use today are

✦ NetWare version 3.*x*, the version that made NetWare famous. NetWare 3.*x* used a now outdated directory scheme called the *bindery*. Each NetWare 3.*x* server has a bindery file that contains information about the resources on that particular server. With the bindery, you had to log on separately to each server that contained resources you wanted to use.

✦ NetWare 4.*x*, in which NetWare Directory Service, or NDS, replaced the bindery. NDS is similar to Active Directory. It provides a single directory for the entire network rather than separate directories for each server.

✦ NetWare 5.*x* was the next step. It introduced a new user interface based on Java for easier administration, improved support for Internet protocols, multiprocessing with up to 32 processors, and many other features.

✦ The most popular version today is NetWare 6, which is described in more detail later in this section.

✦ Novell released its newest version, NetWare 6.5, in summer 2003.

NetWare 6 features

The most popular version of NetWare is version 6. Here are a few of the most important new features of NetWare 6:

+ An improved disk management system called Novell Storage Services that can manage billions of files on a single volume. Whether storing billions of files on a single volume is a good idea is a separate question; if you decide to do it, NetWare 6 will let you.

+ Web-based access to network folders and printers.

+ Built-in support for Windows, Linux, UNIX, and Macintosh file systems so that you can access data on the server from these operating systems without installing special client software.

+ iFolder, a feature that automatically keeps your files synchronized between your work computer and your home computer or a traveling laptop computer.

NetWare 6 is also available in a special Small Business edition, which includes the basic NetWare 6 operating system plus a collection of goodies designed to make networking easier for small businesses. Among the extras you get with NetWare for Small Business are the following:

+ GroupWise 6, an e-mail and group-scheduling program that is similar to Microsoft Outlook and Exchange.

+ ZENWorks, a tool for managing software and hardware on your network.

+ BorderManager, a suite of security programs for safeguarding your network's Internet access.

+ A basketful of programs for accessing the Internet and creating a Web server.

Unlike Windows Server 2003, NetWare's pricing is based only on the number of clients that the server supports. Novell doesn't charge for the basic server license. Table 4-3 summarizes the pricing structure for NetWare 6. Note that Novell offers competitive upgrade prices as an incentive for users to switch from Microsoft or other servers.

Table 4-3	NetWare 6 Server Pricing	
Product	*Full Price*	*Upgrade Price*
NetWare 6, 5 clients	$995	$530
NetWare 6, 10 clients	$1,840	$975
NetWare 6, 25 clients	$4,600	$2,440

NetWare 6.5

Novell's newest version of NetWare, version 6.5, builds on NetWare 6.0 with a number of new features. In particular:

✦ Improvements to the browser-based management tools.

✦ Built-in open-source components such as the Apache and Tomcat Web server, the MySql database manager, and PHP for dynamic Web applications.

✦ A virtual office feature that enables users to access their e-mail, files, and other network resources from any computer with a browser.

✦ Nterprise Branch Office, a feature that lets you easily integrate a server at a remote branch office with a central office network via the Internet.

Other Server Operating Systems

Although NetWare and Windows NT/2000 Server are the most popular choices for network operating systems, they're not the only available choices. The following sections briefly describe two other server choices: Linux and the Macintosh OS/X Server.

Linux

Perhaps the most interesting operating system available today is Linux. Linux is a free operating system that is based on UNIX, a powerful network operating system often used on large networks. Linux was started by Linus Torvalds, who thought it would be fun to write a version of UNIX in his free time — as a hobby. He enlisted help from hundreds of programmers throughout the world, who volunteered their time and efforts via the Internet. Today, Linux is a full-featured version of UNIX; its users consider it to be as good or better than Windows. In fact, almost as many people now use Linux as use Macintosh computers.

Linux offers the same networking benefits of UNIX and can be an excellent choice as a server operating system.

Apple Mac OS/X Server

All the other server operating systems I describe in this chapter run on Intel-based PCs with Pentium or Pentium-compatible processors. But what about Macintosh computers? After all, Macintosh users need networks, too.

For Macintosh networks, Apple offers a special network server operating system known as Mac OS/X server. Mac OS/X Server has all the features you'd expect in a server operating system: file and printer sharing, Internet features, e-mail, and so on.

Peer-to-Peer Networking with Windows

If you're not up to the complexity of dedicated network operating systems, you may want to opt for a simple peer-to-peer network based on a desktop version of Windows.

Advantages of peer-to-peer networks

The main advantage of a peer-to-peer network is that it is easier to set up and use than a network with a dedicated server. Peer-to-peer networks rely on the limited network server features that are built into Windows, such as the ability to share files and printers. Recent versions of Windows, such as Windows XP, come with a Networking Wizard that automatically configures a basic network for you so you don't have to manually configure any network settings.

Another advantage of peer-to-peer networks is that they can be less expensive than server-based networks. Here are some of the reasons that peer-to-peer networks are inexpensive:

✦ Peer-to-peer networks don't require you to use a dedicated server computer. Any computer on the network can function as both a network server and a user's workstation. (However, you can configure a computer as a dedicated server if you want to. Doing so results in better performance but negates the cost benefit of not having a dedicated server computer.)

✦ Peer-to-peer networks are easier to set up and use, which means that you can spend less time figuring out how to make the network work and keep it working. And, as Einstein proved, time is money (hence his famous equation, $E=M\$^2$).

✦ Then you must consider the cost of the server operating system itself. Both NetWare and Windows Server can cost as much as $200 per user. And the total cost increases as your network grows, although the cost per user drops. For a peer-to-peer Windows server, you pay for Windows once. You don't pay any additional charges based on the number of users on your network.

Workgroups versus domains

In a Windows network, a *domain* is a group of server computers that share a common user account database. A user at a client computer can log in to a domain to access shared resources for any server in the domain. Each domain must have one server designated as the *primary domain controller*, or *PDC*. This server is ultimately in charge of the domain.

A peer-to-peer network can't have a domain because it doesn't have a dedicated server computer to act as the PDC. Instead, computers in a peer-to-peer computer are grouped together in *workgroups*, which are simply groups of computers that can share resources with each other. Each computer in a workgroup keeps track of its own user accounts and security settings, so no single computer is in charge of the workgroup.

To create a domain, you have to designate a server computer as the primary domain controller and configure user accounts. Workgroups are much easier to administer. In fact, you don't have to do anything to create a workgroup except decide on the name you want to use. Although you can have as many workgroups as you want on a peer-to-peer network, most networks have just one workgroup. That way, any computers on the network can share resources with any other computer on the network.

One of the most common mistakes when setting up a peer-to-peer network is misspelling the workgroup name on one of the computers. For example, suppose you decide that all the computers should belong to a workgroup named MYGROUP. If you accidentally spell the workgroup name MYGRUOP for one of the computers, that computer will be isolated in its own workgroup. If you can't locate a computer on your network, the workgroup name is one of the first things to check.

Drawbacks of peer-to-peer networks

Yes, peer-to-peer networks are easier to install and manage than NetWare or NT, but they do have their drawbacks:

✦ Because peer-to-peer networks are Windows-based, they're subject to the inherent limitations of Windows. Windows is designed primarily to be an operating system for a single-user, desktop computer rather than function as part of a network, so Windows can't manage a file or printer server as efficiently as a real network operating system.

✦ If you don't set up a dedicated network server, someone (hopefully, not you) may have to live with the inconvenience of sharing his or her computer with the network. With NetWare or NT/2000 Server, the server computers are dedicated to network use so that no one has to put up with this inconvenience.

✦ Although a peer-to-peer network may have a lower cost per computer for smaller networks, the cost difference between peer-to-peer networks and NetWare or NT/2000 is less significant in larger networks (say, 10 or more clients).

✦ Peer-to-peer networks don't work well when your network starts to grow. Peer-to-peer servers just don't have the security or performance features required for a growing network.

Windows XP

The current version of Microsoft's desktop operating system, Windows XP, has powerful peer-to-peer networking features built in. Windows XP comes in two flavors: Home Edition and Professional Edition. As its name suggests, the Home Edition is designed for home users. It includes great multimedia features, such as a home movie editor called Windows Movie Maker and built-in support for CD-ROM burners, scanners, video cameras, and many other features. Windows XP Professional Edition is designed for users with more demanding network needs.

All Windows XP networking features are based on TCP/IP. NetBIOS is required only if the Windows XP client must exchange information with older Windows computers that don't support TCP/IP.

Windows XP provides the following networking features:

✦ Built-in file and printer sharing allows you to share files and printers with other network users.

✦ A Network Setup Wizard that automatically sets the most common configuration options. The wizard eliminates the need to work through multiple Properties dialog boxes to configure network settings.

✦ An Internet Connection Sharing feature (ICS) that allows a Windows XP computer to share an Internet connection with other users. The ICS feature includes firewall features that protect your network from unauthorized access via the Internet connection.

✦ Simple user account management that lets you create multiple users and assign passwords.

✦ Built-in support for wireless networking.

✦ A network bridge feature that lets you use a Windows XP computer to bridge two networks. The computer must have two network adapters, one for each network.

✦ Advanced network diagnostics and troubleshooting tools help you to find and correct networking problems.

Older Windows versions

Previous versions of Windows also offer peer-to-peer networking features. The following paragraphs summarize the networking features of the major Windows releases prior to Windows XP:

✦ **Windows Me:** Short for Windows Millenium Edition, this release was aimed at home users. It provided a Home Networking Wizard to simplify the task of configuring a network. It was the last version of Windows that was based on the old 16-bit MS-DOS code.

✦ **Windows 2000 Professional:** A desktop version of Windows 2000. It has powerful peer-to-peer networking features similar to those found in Windows XP, although they are a bit more difficult to set up. It was the first desktop version of Windows that integrated well with Active Directory.

✦ **Windows 98** and **Windows 98 Second Edition:** These were popular upgrades to Windows 95 that enhanced its basic networking features.

✦ **Windows 95:** Was the first 32-bit version of Windows. However, it still relied internally on 16-bit MS-DOS code, so it wasn't a true 32-bit operating system. It provided basic peer-to-peer network features, with built-in drivers for common network adapters and basic file and printer sharing features.

✦ **Windows for Workgroups:** Was the first version of Windows to support networking without requiring an add-on product. It simplified the task of creating NetBIOS-based networks for file and printer sharing. However, it had only weak support for TCP/IP.

Book II

Building a Network

"If it works, it works. I've just never seen network cabling connected with Chinese handcuffs before."

Contents at a Glance

Chapter 1: Planning a Network

In This Chapter

✔ Making a network plan

✔ Taking stock of your computer stock

✔ Making sure that you know why you need a network

✔ Making the three basic network decisions that you can't avoid

✔ Using a starter kit

✔ Looking at a sample network

Okay, so you're convinced that you need to network your computers. What now? Do you stop by Computers-R-Us on the way to work, install the network before morning coffee, and expect the network to be fully operational by noon?

I don't think so.

Networking your computers is just like any other worthwhile endeavor: To do it right requires a bit of planning. This chapter helps you to think through your network before you start spending money. It shows you how to come up with a networking plan that's every bit as good as the plan that a network consultant would charge $1,000 for. See? This book is already saving you money!

Making a Network Plan

Before you begin any networking project, whether it's a new network installation or an upgrade of an existing network, you should first make a detailed plan. If you make technical decisions too quickly, before studying all the issues that affect the project, you'll regret it. You'll discover too late that a key application won't run over the network, that the network has unacceptably slow performance, or that key components of the network don't work together.

Here are some general thoughts to keep in mind while you create your network plan:

✦ **Don't rush the plan.** The most costly networking mistakes are the ones that you make before you install the network. Think things through and consider alternatives.

✦ **Write down the network plan.** The plan doesn't have to be a fancy, 500-page document. If you want to make it look good, pick up a ½-inch three-ring binder. This binder will be big enough to hold your network plan with room to spare.

✦ **Ask someone else to read your network plan before you buy anything.** Preferably, ask someone who knows more about computers than you do.

✦ **Keep the plan up-to-date.** If you add to the network, dig up the plan, dust it off, and update it.

"The best laid schemes of mice and men gang oft agley, and leave us not but grief and pain for promised joy." Robert Burns lived a few hundred years before computer networks, but his famous words ring true. A network plan is not chiseled in stone. If you discover that something doesn't work the way you thought it would, that's okay. Just change your plan.

Being Purposeful

One of the first steps in planning your network is making sure that you understand why you want the network in the first place. Here are some of the more common reasons for needing a network, all of them quite valid:

✦ My coworker and I exchange files using a floppy disk just about every day. With a network, we could trade files without using the floppies.

✦ I don't want to buy everyone a laser printer when I know the one we have now just sits there taking up space most of the day. So wouldn't buying a network be better than buying a laser printer for every computer?

✦ I want to provide an Internet connection for all my computers. Many networks, especially smaller ones, exist solely for the purpose of sharing an Internet connection.

✦ Someone figured out that we're destroying seven trees a day by printing interoffice memos on paper, so we want to save the rainforest by setting up an e-mail system.

✦ Business is so good that one person typing in orders eight hours each day can't keep up. With a network, I can have two people entering orders, and I won't have to pay overtime to either person.

✦ My brother-in-law just put in a network at his office, and I don't want him to think that I'm behind the times.

Make sure that you identify all the reasons why you think you need a network and then write them down. Don't worry about winning the Pulitzer Prize for your stunning prose. Just make sure that you write down what you expect a network to do for you.

If you were making a 500-page networking proposal, you'd place the description of why a network is needed in a tabbed section labeled "Justification." In your ½-inch network binder, file the description under "Purpose."

As you consider the reasons why you need a network, you may conclude that you don't need a network after all. That's okay. You can always use the binder for your stamp collection.

Taking Stock

One of the most challenging parts of planning a network is figuring out how to work with the computers that you already have. In other words, how do you get from here to there? Before you can plan how to get "there," you have to know where "here" is. In other words, you have to take a thorough inventory of your current computers.

What you need to know

You need to know the following information about each of your computers:

✦ **The processor type and, if possible, its clock speed.** It would be nice if each of your computers had a shiny new 2GHz Pentium 4 processor. In most cases, though, you find a mixture of computers: some new, some old, some borrowed, some blue. You may even find a few archaic pre-Pentium computers.

You can't usually tell what kind of processor that a computer has just by looking at the computer's case. Most computers, however, display the processor type when you turn them on or reboot them. If the information on the startup screen scrolls too quickly for you to read it, try pressing the Pause key to freeze the information. After you finish reading it, press the Pause key again so that your computer can continue booting.

✦ **The size of the hard drive and the arrangement of its partitions.** To find out the size of your computer's hard drive in Windows, open the My Computer window, right-click the drive icon, and choose the Properties command from the shortcut menu that appears. Figure 1-1 shows the Properties dialog box for a 24.4GB hard drive that has about 4GB of free space.

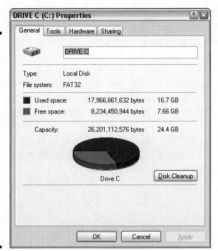

Figure 1-1:
The
Properties
dialog box
for a hard
drive shows
the drive's
total
capacity
and the
amount of
free space
available on
the drive.

If your computer has more than one hard drive, Windows lists an icon for each drive in the My Computer window. Jot down the size and amount of free space available on each drive.

✦ **The amount of memory.** To find this information in Windows, right-click the My Computer desktop icon and choose the Properties command. The amount of memory on your computer is shown in the dialog box that appears. For example, Figure 1-2 shows the System Properties dialog box for a computer running Windows XP Home Edition with 128MB of RAM.

✦ **The operating system version.** If you're running Windows 95 or later, you can determine the version by checking the System Properties dialog box. For example, Figure 1-2 shows the System Properties dialog box for a computer running Windows XP Home Edition.

✦ **What type of network card, if any, is installed in the computer.** To find out the exact name of the card, open the Control Panel and double-click the System icon. Click the Hardware tab and then click the Device Manager button, which brings up the Device Manager dialog box, as shown in Figure 1-3. In this case, you can see that the computer's network card is a D-Link DFE-530TX+ PCI adapter.

The Device Manager is also useful for tracking down other hardware devices attached to the computer.

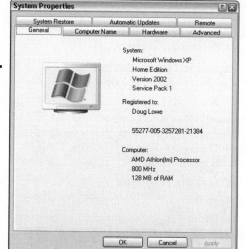

Figure 1-2: The System Properties dialog box for a computer running Windows XP Home Edition with 128MB of RAM.

✦ **What network protocols are in use.** To determine this in Windows XP, open the Control Panel, double-click the Network Connections icon to open the Network Connections dialog box, and then right-click the network connection and choose the Properties command. In previous versions of Windows, double-click Network in the Control Panel.

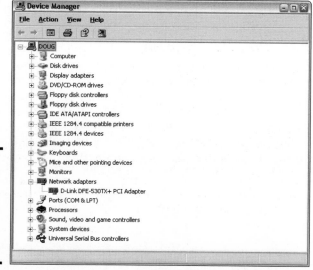

Figure 1-3: Using the Device Manager to probe for hardware devices.

+ **What kind of printer, if any, is attached to the computer.** Usually, you can tell just by looking at the printer. You can also tell by examining the Printers and Faxes folder. (In Windows XP, choose Start⇨Control Panel and then double-click Printers and Faxes.)

+ **Any other devices connected to the computer.** A CD, DVD, or CD-RW drive? Scanner? Zip or Jazz drive? Tape drive? Video camera? Battle droid? Hot tub?

+ **Which driver and installation disks are available?** Hopefully, you'll be able to locate the disks or CDs required by hardware devices such as the network card, printers, scanners, and so on. If not, you may be able to locate the drivers on the Internet.

+ **What software is used on the computer.** Microsoft Office? WordPerfect? QuickBooks? Make a complete list and include version numbers.

Programs that gather information for you

Gathering information about your computers is a lot of work if you have more than a few computers to network. Fortunately, several software programs are available that can automatically gather the information for you. These programs inspect various aspects of a computer, such as the CPU type and speed, amount of RAM, and the size of the computer's hard drives. Then they show the information on the screen and give you the option of saving the information to a hard drive file or printing it.

Windows 98 and later versions come with just such a program, called Microsoft System Information. Microsoft System Information gathers and prints information about your computer. You can start Microsoft System Information by choosing Start⇨Programs⇨Accessories⇨System Tools⇨ System Information.

When you fire up Microsoft System Information, you see a window similar to the one shown in Figure 1-4. Initially, Microsoft System Information displays basic information about your computer, such as your version of Microsoft Windows, the processor type, the amount of memory on the computer, and so on. You can obtain information that is more detailed by clicking Hardware Resources, Components, or other categories in the left side of the window.

If you have Windows 95, don't panic. You may also have Microsoft System Information: Microsoft includes it with Office. To start Microsoft System Information from any of the Office programs (Word, Excel, or PowerPoint), choose the Help⇨About command. When the About dialog box appears, click the System Info button.

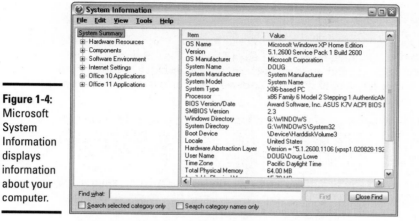

Figure 1-4:
Microsoft
System
Information
displays
information
about your
computer.

To Dedicate or Not to Dedicate: That Is the Question

One of the most basic questions that a network plan must answer is whether the network will have one or more dedicated servers or whether it will rely completely on peer-to-peer networking. If the only reason for purchasing your network is to share a printer and exchange an occasional file, then you may not need a dedicated server computer. In that case, you can create a peer-to-peer network by using the computers that you already have. However, all but the smallest networks will benefit from having a separate, dedicated server computer.

✦ Using a dedicated server computer makes the network faster, easier to work with, and more reliable. Consider what happens when the user of a server computer, which doubles as a workstation, decides to turn off the computer, not realizing that someone else is accessing files on his or her hard drive.

✦ You don't necessarily have to use your biggest and fastest computer as your server computer. I've seen networks where the slowest computer on the network is the server. This advice is especially true when the server is mostly used to share a printer or to store a small number of shared files. So if you need to buy a computer for your network, consider promoting one of your older computers to be the server and using the new computer as a client.

Types of Servers

Assuming that your network will require one or more dedicated servers, you should next consider what types of servers the network will need. In some cases, a single server computer can fill one or more of these roles. Whenever possible, it's best to limit each server computer to a single server function.

File servers

File servers provide centralized disk storage that can be conveniently shared by client computers on the network. The most common task of a file server is to store shared files and programs. For example, the members of a small workgroup can use disk space on a file server to store their Microsoft Office documents.

File servers must ensure that two users don't try to update the same file at the same time. The file servers do this by *locking* a file while a user updates the file so that other users can't access the file until the first user finishes. For document files (for example, word-processing or spreadsheet files), the whole file is locked. For database files, the lock can be applied just to the portion of the file that contains the record or records being updated.

Print servers

Sharing printers is one of the main reasons that many small networks exist. Although it isn't necessary, a server computer can be dedicated for use as a *print server,* whose sole purpose is to collect information being sent to a shared printer by client computers and print it in an orderly fashion.

✦ A single computer may double as both a file server and a print server, but performance is better if you use separate print and file server computers.

✦ With inexpensive ink-jet printers running about $100 each, just giving each user his or her own printer is tempting. However, you get what you pay for. Instead of buying $100 printers for 15 users, you may be better off buying one $1,500 laser printer and sharing it.

Web servers

A *Web server* is a server computer that runs software that enables the computer to host an Internet Web site. The two most popular Web server programs are Microsoft's IIS (Internet Information Services) and Apache, an open-source Web server managed by the Apache Software Foundation.

Mail servers

A *mail server* is a server that handles the network's e-mail needs. It is configured with e-mail server software, such as Microsoft Exchange Server. Exchange Server is designed to work with Microsoft Outlook, the e-mail client software that comes with Microsoft Office.

Most mail servers actually do much more than just send and receive electronic mail. For example, here are some of the features that Exchange Server 2000 offers beyond simple e-mail:

✦ Collaboration features that simplify the management of collaborative projects.

✦ Audio and video conferencing.

✦ Chat rooms and instant messaging (IM) services.

✦ Microsoft Exchange Forms Designer, which lets you develop customized forms for applications, such as vacation requests or purchase orders.

Database servers

A *database server* is a server computer that runs database software, such as Microsoft's SQL Server 2000. Database servers are usually used along with customized business applications, such as accounting or marketing systems.

Choosing a Server Operating System

If you determine that your network will require one or more dedicated servers, the next step is to determine what network operating system those servers should use. If possible, all the servers should use the same NOS so that you don't find yourself supporting different operating systems.

Although you can choose from many network operating systems, from a practical point of view, your choices are limited to the following:

✦ Windows 2000 Server or Windows Server 2003

✦ Novell NetWare

✦ Linux or another version of UNIX

For more information, refer to Book I, Chapter 4.

Using a network starter kit — networks to go

For me, one of the most fun parts of building a network is going to my local computer store and filling a shopping cart full of stuff. I love to wander the aisles and pick out a network switch, network interface cards, cables, connectors, a case of Diet Coke, and other goodies.

If shopping isn't your bag, you can buy a starter kit that comes with everything you need to network two computers. A typical network starter kit for two computers includes two Ethernet network interface cards, a small hub or switch, two twisted-pair cables with connectors already attached (so that you can connect both computers to the hub), and instructions for hooking everything up. A kit of this sort costs between $75 and $150, depending on where you purchase it, who manufactures the individual components in the kit, whether the kit includes a hub or a switch, and the capacity of the hub or switch.

The starter kit accommodates the first two computers in your network. For each additional computer that you want to connect, you need to purchase an add-on kit that contains a network interface card and a cable.

Here are a few additional points to ponder concerning network starter kits:

✔ The cable that comes with the starter kit is generally 25 feet long, which is usually enough cable to connect computers that are located in the same room. If the computers are in separate rooms, you probably need additional network cable.

✔ The hub that comes with twisted-pair starter kits usually has ports for connecting as many as four or five computers. If you know that you need to network more than that, you should probably purchase the hub and other network components separately.

✔ You can also purchase wireless starter kits that include everything you need to create a wireless network for two computers.

Planning the Infrastructure

You also need to plan the details of how you will connect the computers in the network. This includes determining which network topology that the network will use, what type of cable will be used, where the cable will be routed, and what other devices, such as repeaters, bridges, hubs, switches, and routers, will be needed.

Although you have many cabling options to choose from, you'll probably use Cat5 or better UTP for most — if not all — of the desktop client computers on the network. However, you have many decisions to make beyond this basic choice:

✦ Will you use hubs, which are cheaper, or switches, which are faster but more expensive?

✦ Where will you place workgroup hubs or switches — on a desktop somewhere within the group or in a central wiring closet?

✦ How many client computers will you place on each hub or switch, and how many hubs or switches will you need?

✦ If you need more than one hub or switch, what type of cabling will you use to connect the hubs and switches to one another?

For more information about network cabling, see Chapter 2 of this book and Book I, Chapter 3.

If you're installing new network cable, don't scrimp on the cable itself. Because installing network cable is a labor-intensive task, the cost of the cable itself is a small part of the total cable installation cost. And if you spend a little extra to install higher grade cable now, you won't have to replace the cable in a few years when it's time to upgrade the network.

Drawing Diagrams

One of the most helpful techniques for creating a network plan is to draw a picture of it. The diagram can be a detailed floor plan, showing the actual location of each network component. This type of diagram is sometimes called a *physical map.* If you prefer, the diagram can be a *logical map,* which is more abstract and Picasso-like. Any time you change the network layout, update the diagram. Also include a detailed description of the change, the date that the change was made, and the reason for the change.

You can diagram very small networks on the back of a napkin, but if the network has more than a few computers, you'll want to use a drawing program to help you create the diagram. One of the best programs for this purpose is Microsoft Visio, shown in Figure 1-5. Here is a rundown of some of the features that make Visio so useful:

✦ Smart shapes and connectors maintain the connections you've drawn between network components, even if you rearrange the layout of the components on the page.

✦ Stencils provide dozens of useful shapes for common network components — not just client and server computers, but routers, hubs, switches, and just about anything else you can imagine. If you're really picky about the diagrams, you can even purchase stencil sets that have accurate drawings of specific devices, such as Cisco routers or IBM mainframe computers.

✦ You can add information to each computer or device in the diagram, such as the serial number or physical location. Then, you can quickly print an inventory that lists this information for each device in the diagram.

✦ You can easily create large diagrams that span multiple pages.

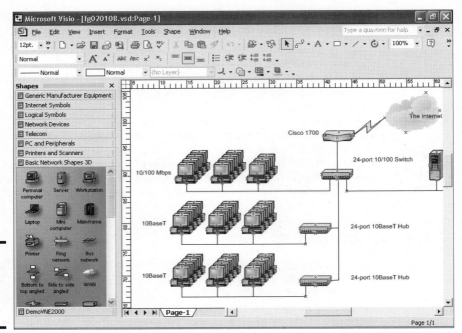

Figure 1-5:
Using Visio
to create a
network
diagram.

Sample Network Plans

In what's left of this chapter, I present some network plans that are drawn from real-life situations. These examples will illustrate many of the network design issues I've covered so far in this chapter. The stories you're about to read are true. The names have been changed to protect the innocent.

Building a small network: California Sport Surface, Inc.

California Sport Surface, Inc. (CSS) is a small company specializing in the installation of outdoor sports surfaces, such as tennis courts, running tracks, and football fields. CSS has an administrative staff of just four employees who work out of a home office. The company currently has three computers:

✦ A brand-new Dell desktop computer running Windows XP Home Edition, shared by the president (Mark) and vice president (Julie) to prepare proposals and marketing brochures, to handle correspondence, and to do other miscellaneous chores. This computer has a built-in 10/100Mbps Ethernet network port.

+ An older Gateway computer running Windows 98 Second Edition, used by the bookkeeper (Erin), who uses QuickBooks to handle the company's accounting needs. This computer doesn't have a network port.

+ A notebook that runs Windows 2000, used by the company's chief engineer (Daniel), who often takes it to job sites to help with engineering needs. This computer has a built-in 10Mbps Ethernet port.

The company owns just one printer, a moderately priced ink-jet printer that's connected to Erin's computer. The computers aren't networked, so whenever Mark, Julie, or Daniel need to print something, they must copy the file to a diskette and give it to Erin, who then prints the document. The computer shared by Mark and Julie is connected to the Internet via a residential DSL connection.

The company wants to install a network to support these three computers. Here are the primary goals of the network:

+ Provide shared access to the printer so that users don't have to exchange diskettes to print their documents.

+ Provide shared access to the Internet connection so that users can access the Internet from any of the computers.

+ Allow for the addition of another desktop computer, which the company expects to purchase within the next six months, and potentially another notebook computer. (If business is good, the company hopes to hire another engineer.)

+ The network should be intuitive to the users and should not require any extensive upkeep.

CSS's networking needs can be met with the simple peer-to-peer network diagrammed in Figure 1-6. Here's what the network will require:

+ A 10/100Mbps Ethernet adapter card for the Gateway computer, which is the only computer that doesn't currently have a network port.

+ A combination DSL router and four-port 10/100Mbps switch, such as the LinkSys BEFSR41W or the Belkin F5D5231-4. The company may outgrow this device when it adds an additional laptop, but if and when that happens, another 4- or 8-port 10/100Mbps switch can be added then.

+ The firewall features of the DSL router will need to be enabled to protect the network from Internet hackers.

+ File and printer sharing will need to be activated on Erin's computer, and the printer will need to be shared.

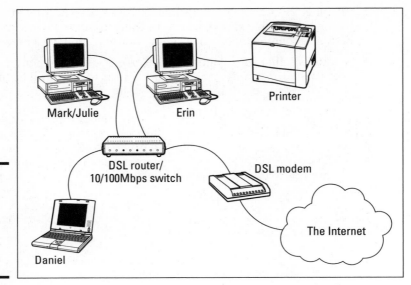

Figure 1-6:
California
Sport
Surface's
peer-to-
peer
network.

Connecting two networks: Creative Course Development, Inc.

Creative Course Development, Inc. (CCD) is a small educational publisher located in central California that specializes in integrated math and science curriculum for primary and secondary grades. They publish a variety of course materials, including textbooks, puzzle books, and CD-ROM software.

CCD leases two office buildings that are adjacent to each other, separated only by a small courtyard. The creative staff, which consists of a dozen writers and educators, works in Building A. The sales, marketing, and administrative staff, which consists of six employees, works in Building B.

The product development and marketing staff has 14 relatively new personal computers, all running Windows XP Professional, and a server computer running Windows 2000 Server. These computers are networked by a 100Mbps UTP network, which utilizes a single 24-port 100Mbps switch. A fractional T1 line that's connected to the network through a small Cisco router provides Internet access.

The administrative staff has a hodgepodge of computers, some running Windows 98 Second Edition, some running Windows XP, and one still running Windows 95. They have a small Windows NT server that meets their needs. The older computers have 10BaseT network cards; the newer ones have 10/100Mbps cards. However, the computers are all connected to a fairly old 10Mbps Ethernet hub with 12 ports. Internet access is provided by an ISDN connection.

Both groups are happy with their computers and networks. The problem is that the networks can't communicate with each other. For example, the marketing team in Building A relies on daily printed reports from the sales system in Building B to keep track of sales, and they frequently go to the other building to follow up on important sales or to look into sales trends.

Although several solutions to this problem exist, the easiest is to bridge the networks with a pair of wireless switches. To do this, CCD will purchase two wireless access points. One will be plugged into the 100Mbps switch in Building A, and the other will be plugged into the hub in Building B. After the access points are configured, the two networks will function as a single network. Figure 1-7 shows a logical diagram for the completed network.

**Book II
Chapter 1**

Although the wireless solution to this problem sounds simple, a number of complications still need to be dealt with. Specifically:

✦ Depending on the environment, the wireless access points may have trouble establishing a link between the buildings. It may be necessary to locate the devices on the roof. In that case, CCD will have to spend a little extra money for weatherproof enclosures.

✦ Because the wireless access point in Building A will be connected to a switch rather than a hub, the switch will provide some degree of isolation between the networks. As a result, overall network performance shouldn't be affected.

✦ Before the networks were connected, each network had its own DHCP server to assign IP addresses to users as needed. Unfortunately, both DHCP servers have the same local IP address (192.168.0.1). When the networks are combined, one of these DHCP servers will have to be disabled.

✦ In addition, both networks had their own Internet connections. With the networks bridged, CCD can eliminate the ISDN connection altogether. Users in both buildings can get their Internet access via the shared T1 connection.

✦ The network administrator will also have to determine how to handle directory services for the network. Previously, each network had its own domain. With the networks bridged, CCD may opt to keep these domains separate, or they may decide to merge them into a single domain. (Doing so will require considerable work, so they'll probably leave the domains separate.)

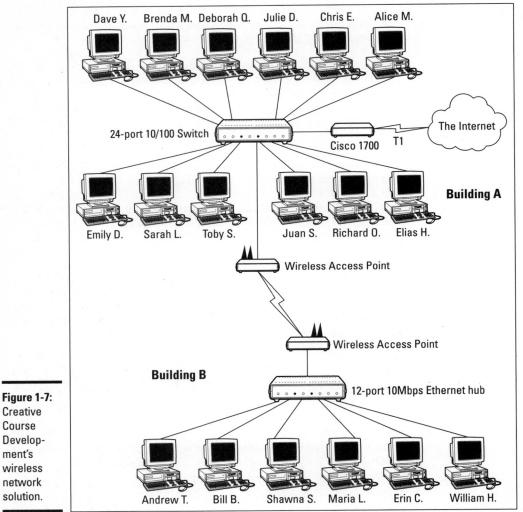

Figure 1-7: Creative Course Development's wireless network solution.

Improving network performance: DCH Accounting

DCH Accounting is an accounting firm that has grown in two years from 15 employees to 35, all located in one building. Here's the lowdown on the existing network:

✦ The network consists of 35 client computers and three servers running Windows 2000 Server.

✦ The 35 client computers run a variety of Windows operating systems. About a third (a total of 11) run Windows XP Professional. The rest run Windows 98 and a few still run Windows 95.

✦ The Windows XP computers all have 10/100Mbps Ethernet cards. The older computers have 10Mbps cards.

✦ The servers have 10Mbps cards.

✦ All the offices in the building are wired with Category 5 wiring to a central wiring closet, where a small equipment rack holds two 24-port 10BaseT hubs.

✦ Internet access is provided through a T1 connection with a Cisco 1700 router.

**Book II
Chapter 1**

**Planning a
Network**

Lately, network performance has been noticeably slow, particularly Internet access and large file transfers between client computers and the servers. Users have started to complain that sometimes the network seems to crawl.

The problem is most likely that the network has outgrown the old 10BaseT hubs. All network traffic must flow through them, and they're limited to the speed of 10Mbps. As a result, the new computers with the 10/100Mbps Ethernet cards are connecting to the network at 10Mbps, and not 100Mbps. In addition, the hubs treat the entire network as a single Ethernet segment. With 35 users, the network is saturated.

The performance of this network can be dramatically improved in two steps. The first step is to replace the 10Mbps network interface cards in the three servers with 10/100Mbps cards. Second, add a 24-port 10/100Mbps switch to the equipment rack. The equipment rack can be rewired, as shown in Figure 1-8.

✦ Connect the servers, the Cisco router, and the 100Mbps clients to the switch. This will use 15 of the 24 ports.

✦ Connect the two hubs to the switch. This will use two more ports, leaving 7 ports for future growth.

✦ Divide the remaining clients between the two hubs. Each hub will have 12 computers connected.

This arrangement connects all the 100Mbps clients to 100Mbps switch ports and groups the remaining 24 slower computers into two groups of 12, each with its own hub.

For even better performance, DCH can simply replace both hubs with 24-port switches.

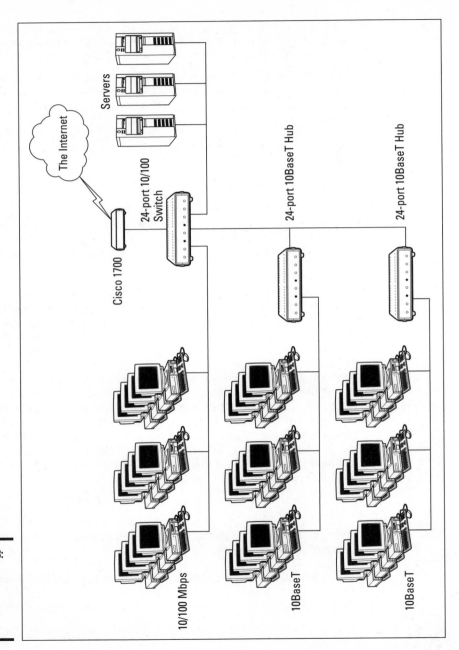

Figure 1-8:
DCH
Accounting's
switched
network.

Chapter 2: Installing Network Hardware

In This Chapter

- ✓ **Installing network interface cards**
- ✓ **Installing network cable**
- ✓ **Attaching cable connectors**
- ✓ **Figuring out pinouts for twisted-pair cabling**
- ✓ **Building a crossover cable**
- ✓ **Installing hubs and switches**

*A*fter you have your network planned out comes the fun of actually putting everything together. In this chapter, I describe some of the important details for installing network hardware, including cables, hubs and switches, network interface cards, and professional touches, such as patch panels.

Installing a Network Interface Card

You have to install a network interface card into each computer before you can connect the computers to the network cables. Installing a network interface card is a manageable task, but you have to be willing to roll up your sleeves.

If you've installed one adapter card, you've installed them all. In other words, installing a network interface card is just like installing a modem, a new video controller card, a sound card, or any other type of card. If you've ever installed one of these cards, you can probably install a network interface card blindfolded.

Here's a step-by-step procedure for installing a network interface card:

1. **Shut down Windows and then turn off the computer and unplug it.**

   Never work in your computer's insides with the power on or the power cord plugged in!

2. **Remove the cover from your computer.**

   Figure 2-1 shows the screws that you must typically remove in order to open the cover. Put the screws someplace where they won't wander off.

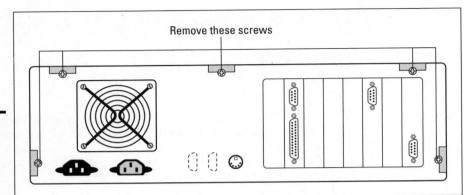

Figure 2-1:
Removing your computer's cover.

3. **Find an unused expansion slot inside the computer.**

The expansion slots are lined up in a neat row near the back of the computer; you can't miss 'em. Most newer computers have at least two or three slots known as *PCI slots*.

Many older computers also have several slots known as *ISA slots.* You can distinguish ISA slots from PCI slots by noting the size of the slots. PCI slots are smaller than ISA slots, so you can't accidentally insert a PCI card in an ISA slot or vice versa.

Some computers also have other types of slots — mainly VESA and EISA slots. Standard ISA or PCI networking cards won't fit into these types of slots, so don't try to force them.

4. **When you find the right type of slot that doesn't have a card in it, remove the metal slot protector from the back of the computer's chassis.**

If a small retaining screw holds the slot protector in place, remove the screw and keep it in a safe place. Then, pull the slot protector out and put the slot protector in a box with all your other old slot protectors. (After a while, you collect a whole bunch of slot protectors. Keep them as souvenirs or Christmas tree ornaments.)

5. **Insert the network interface card into the slot.**

Line up the connectors on the bottom of the card with the connectors in the expansion slot and then press the card straight down. Sometimes you have to press uncomfortably hard to get the card to slide into the slot.

6. **Secure the network interface card with the screw that you removed in Step 4.**

7. **Put the computer's case back together.**

   Watch out for the loose cables inside the computer; you don't want to pinch them with the case as you slide it back on. Secure the case with the screws that you removed in Step 2.

8. **Turn the computer back on.**

If you're using a Plug and Play card with Windows, the card is automatically configured after you start the computer again. If you're working with an older computer or an older network interface card, you may need to run an additional software installation program. See the installation instructions that come with the network interface card for details.

Installing Twisted-Pair Cable

Most Ethernet networks are built using twisted-pair cable, which resembles phone cable but isn't the same. Twisted-pair cable is sometimes called *UTP.* For more information about the general characteristics of twisted-pair cable, refer to Book I, Chapter 3.

You may encounter other types of cable in an existing network; for example, on older networks, you may encounter two types of coaxial cable. The first type resembles television cable and is known as RG-58 cable. The second type is a thick yellow cable that used to be the only type of cable used for Ethernet. You may also encounter fiber-optic cables that span long distances at high speeds or thick twisted-pair bundles that carry multiple sets of twisted-pair cable between wiring closets in a large building. Most networks, however, use simple twisted-pair cable.

In the following sections, you find out what you need to know in order to select and install twisted-pair cable.

Cable categories

Twisted-pair cable comes in various grades called *Categories.* These Categories are specified by the ANSI/EIA standard 568. (*ANSI* stands for *American National Standards Institute*; *ESA* stands for *Electronic Industries Association*). The standards indicate the data capacity, also known as the *bandwidth*, of the cable. Table 2-1 lists the various Categories of twisted-pair cable.

Although higher Category cables are more expensive than lower Category cables, the real cost of installing Ethernet cabling is the labor required to actually pull the cables through the walls. You should never install anything less than Category 5 cable. And if at all possible, you should invest in

Category 5e (the *e* stands for *enhanced*) or even Category 6 cable to allow for future upgrades to your network.

If you want to sound like you know what you're talking about, say "Cat 5" instead of saying "Category 5."

Table 2-1	Twisted-Pair Cable Categories	
Category	Maximum Data Rate	Intended Use
1	1Mbps	Voice only
2	4Mbps	4Mbps Token Ring
3	16Mbps	10BaseT Ethernet
4	20Mbps	16Mbps Token Ring
5	100Mbps (2 pair)	100BaseT Ethernet
	1000Mbps (4 pair)	1000BaseTX
5e	1000Mbps (2 pair)	1000BaseT
6	1000Mbps (2 pair)	1000BaseT

What's with the pairs?

Most twisted-pair cable has four pairs of wires, for a total of eight wires. Standard 10BaseT or 100BaseT Ethernet actually uses only two of the pairs, so the other two pairs are unused. You may be tempted to save money by purchasing cable with just two pairs of wires, but that's a bad idea. If a network cable develops a problem, you can sometimes fix it by switching over to one of the extra pairs. If you use two-pair cable, though, you won't have any spare pairs to use.

You may also be tempted to use the extra pairs for some other purpose, such as for a voice line. Don't. The electrical noise generated by voice signals in the extra wires can interfere with your network.

To shield or not to shield

Unshielded twisted-pair cable, or *UTP*, is designed for normal office environments. When you use UTP cable, you must be careful not to route cable close to fluorescent light fixtures, air conditioners, or electric motors (such as automatic door motors or elevator motors). UTP is the least expensive type of cable.

In environments that have a lot of electrical interference, such as factories, you may want to use *shielded twisted-pair* cable, also known as *STP*. Because STP can be as much as three times more expensive than regular UTP, you won't want to use STP unless you have to. With a little care, UTP can withstand the amount of electrical interference found in a normal office environment.

Most STP cable is shielded by a layer of aluminum foil. For buildings with unusually high amounts of electrical interference, you can use more expensive braided copper shielding for even more protection.

When to use plenum cable

The outer sheath of both shielded and unshielded twisted-pair cable comes in two varieties: PVC and Plenum. *PVC* cable is the most common and least expensive type. *Plenum cable* is a special type of fire-retardant cable that is designed for use in the plenum space of a building. Plenum cable has a special Teflon coating that not only resists heat, but also gives off fewer toxic fumes if it does burn. Unfortunately, plenum cable costs more than twice as much as ordinary PVC cable.

Book II
Chapter 2

Installing Network Hardware

Most local building codes require that you use plenum cable whenever the wiring is installed within the plenum space of the building. The *plenum space* is a compartment that is part of the building's air distribution system, and is usually the space above a suspended ceiling or under a raised floor.

Note that the area above a suspended ceiling is *not* a plenum space if both the delivery and return lines of the air-conditioning and heating system are ducted. Plenum cable is required only if the air-conditioning and heating system are not ducted. When in doubt, it's best to have the local inspector look at your facility before you install cable.

Sometimes solid, sometimes stranded

The actual copper wire that composes the cable comes in two varieties: solid and stranded. Your network will have some of each.

✦ In *stranded cable,* each conductor is made from a bunch of very small wires that are twisted together. Stranded cable is more flexible than solid cable, so it doesn't break as easily. However, stranded cable is more expensive than solid cable and isn't very good at transmitting signals over long distances. Stranded cable is best used for patch cables, such as the cable used to connect a computer to a wall jack or the cable used to connect patch panels to hubs and switches.

Strictly speaking, the cable that connects your computer to the wall jack is called a *station cable* — not a patch cable. Patch cables are used in the wiring closet, usually to connect patch panels to hubs or switches.

✦ In *solid cable,* each conductor is a single solid strand of wire. Solid cable is less expensive than stranded cable and carries signals farther, but it isn't very flexible. If you bend it too many times, it will break. Solid cable is usually used for permanent wiring within the walls and ceilings of a building.

Installation guidelines

The hardest part about installing network cable is the physical task of pulling the cable through ceilings, walls, and floors. This job is just tricky enough that I recommend that you don't attempt it yourself except for small offices. For large jobs, hire a professional cable installer. You may even want to hire a professional for small jobs if the ceiling and wall spaces are difficult to access.

Here are some general pointers to keep in mind if you decide to install cable yourself:

+ You can purchase twisted-pair cable in prefabricated lengths, such as 50 feet, 75 feet, or 100 feet. You can also special-order prefabricated cables in any length you need. However, attaching connectors to bulk cable isn't that difficult. I recommend that you use prefabricated cables only for very small networks and only when you don't need to route the cable through walls or ceilings.

+ Always use a bit more cable than you need, especially if you're running cable through walls. For example, when you run a cable up a wall, leave a few feet of slack in the ceiling above the wall. That way, you'll have plenty of cable if you need to make a repair later on.

+ When running cable, avoid sources of interference, such as fluorescent lights, big motors, X-ray machines, and so on. The most common source of interference for cables that are run behind fake ceiling panels are fluorescent lights; be sure to give light fixtures a wide berth as you run your cable. Three feet should do it.

+ The maximum allowable cable length between the hub and the computer is 100 meters (about 328 feet).

+ If you must run cable across the floor where people walk, cover the cable so that no one trips over it. Inexpensive cable protectors are available at most hardware stores.

+ When running cables through walls, label each cable at both ends. Most electrical supply stores carry pads of cable labels that are perfect for the job. These pads contain 50 sheets or so of precut labels with letters and numbers. They look much more professional than wrapping a loop of masking tape around the cable and writing on the tape with a marker.

  Or, if you want to scrimp, you can just buy a permanent marker and write directly on the cable.

+ When several cables come together, tie them with plastic cable ties. Avoid masking tape if you can; the tape doesn't last, but the sticky glue stuff does. It's a mess a year later. Cable ties are available at electrical supply stores.

Cable ties have all sorts of useful purposes. Once on a backpacking trip, I used a pair of cable ties to attach an unsuspecting buddy's hat to a high tree limb. He wasn't impressed with my innovative use of the cable ties, but my other hiking companions were.

✦ When you run cable above suspended ceiling panels, use cable ties, hooks, or clamps to secure the cable to the actual ceiling or to the metal frame that supports the ceiling tiles. Don't just lay the cable on top of the tiles.

Getting the tools that you need

Of course, to do a job right, you must have the right tools.

Start with a basic set of computer tools, which you can get for about $15 from any computer store or large office-supply store. These kits include the right screwdrivers and socket wrenches to open up your computers and insert adapter cards. (If you don't have a computer tool kit, make sure that you have several flat-head and Phillips screwdrivers of various sizes.)

If all your computers are in the same room, and you're going to run the cables along the floor, and you're using prefabricated cables, the computer tool kit should contain everything that you need.

If you're using bulk cable and plan on attaching your own connectors, you need the following tools in addition to the tools that come with the basic computer tool kit:

✦ **Wire cutters:** You need big ones for thinnet cable; smaller ones are okay for 10baseT cable. If you're using yellow cable, you need the Jaws of Life.

✦ **A crimp tool:** You need the crimp tool to attach the connectors to the cable. Don't use a cheap $25 crimp tool. A good one will cost $100 and will save you many headaches in the long run. Remember this adage: When you crimp, you mustn't scrimp.

✦ **Wire stripper:** You need this only if the crimp tool doesn't include a wire stripper.

If you plan on running cables through walls, you need these additional tools:

✦ **A hammer.**

✦ **A bell.**

✦ **A song to sing.** Just kidding about these last two.

✦ **A keyhole saw.** This is useful if you plan on cutting holes through walls to route your cable.

✦ **A flashlight.**

✦ **A ladder.**

✦ **Someone to hold the ladder.**

✦ **Possibly a *fish tape*.** A fish tape is a coiled-up length of stiff metal tape. To use it, you feed the tape into one wall opening and fish it toward the other opening, where a partner is ready to grab it when the tape arrives. Next, your partner attaches the cable to the fish tape and yells something like "Let 'er rip!" or "Bombs away!" Then you reel in the fish tape and the cable along with it. (You can find fish tape in the electrical section of most well-stocked hardware stores.)

If you plan on routing cable through a concrete subfloor, you need to rent a jackhammer and a backhoe and hire someone to hold a yellow flag while you work.

Pinouts for twisted-pair cables

Each pair of wires in a twisted pair cable is one of four colors: orange, green, blue, or brown. The two wires that make up each pair are complementary: One is white with a colored stripe; the other is colored with a white stripe. For example, the orange pair has a white wire with an orange stripe (called white/orange) and an orange wire with a white stripe (called orange/white). Likewise, the blue pair has a white wire with a blue stripe (white/blue) and a blue wire with a white stripe (blue/white).

When you attach a twisted-pair cable to a modular connector or jack, you must match up the right wires to the right pins. You can use several different standards to wire the connectors. To confuse matters, you can use one of the two popular standard ways of hooking up the wires. One is known as EIA/TIA 568A; the other is EIA/TIA 568B, also known as AT&T 258A. Table 2-2 shows both wiring schemes.

It doesn't matter which of these wiring schemes you use, but pick one and stick with it. If you use one wiring standard on one end of a cable and the other standard on the other end, the cable won't work.

Table 2-2	Pin Connections for Twisted-Pair Cable		
Pin Number	*Function*	*EIA/TIA 568A*	*EIA/TIA 568B* *AT&T 258A*
Pin 1	Transmit +	White/Green	White/orange wire
Pin 2	Transmit -	Green	Orange wire
Pin 3	Receive +	White/Orange	White/green wire
Pin 4	Unused	Blue	Blue wire
Pin 5	Unused	White/Blue	White/blue wire

Pin Number	Function	EIA/TIA 568A	EIA/TIA 568B AT&T 258A
Pin 6	Receive -	Orange	Green wire
Pin 7	Unused	White/Brown	White/brown wire
Pin 8	Unused	Brown	Brown wire

10BaseT and 100BaseT actually use only two of the four pairs, connected to pins 1, 2, 3, and 6. One pair is used to transmit data, and the other is used to receive data. The only difference between the two wiring standards is which pair is used for transmit and receive. In the EIA/TIA 568A standard, the green pair is used for transmit and the orange pair is used for receive. In the EIA/TIA 568B and AT&T 258A standards, the orange pair is used for transmit and the green pair for receive.

If you want, you can get away with connecting only pins 1, 2, 3, and 6. However, I suggest that you connect all four pairs as indicated in Table 2-2.

Attaching RJ-45 connectors

RJ-45 connectors for twisted-pair cables are not too difficult to attach if you have the right crimping tool. The only trick is making sure that you attach each wire to the correct pin and then pressing the tool hard enough to ensure a good connection.

Here's the procedure for attaching an RJ-45 connector:

1. **Cut the end of the cable to the desired length.**

Make sure that you make a square cut — not a diagonal cut.

2. **Insert the cable into the stripper portion of the crimp tool so that the end of the cable is against the stop.**

Squeeze the handles and slowly pull the cable out, keeping it square. This strips off the correct length of outer insulation without puncturing the insulation on the inner wires.

3. **Arrange the wires so that they lay flat and line up according to Table 2-2.**

You'll have to play with the wires a little bit to get them to lay out in the right sequence.

4. **Slide the wires into the pinholes on the connector.**

Double-check to make sure that all the wires slipped into the correct pinholes.

5. **Insert the plug and wire into the crimping portion of the tool and then squeeze the handles to crimp the plug.**

Squeeze it tight!

6. **Remove the plug from the tool and double-check the connection.**

You're done!

Here are a few other points to remember when dealing with RJ-45 connectors and twisted-pair cable:

✦ The pins on the RJ-45 connectors are not numbered, but you can tell which is pin 1 by holding the connector so that the metal conductors are facing up, as shown in Figure 2-2. Pin 1 is on the left.

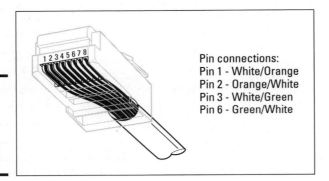

Figure 2-2:
Attaching an RJ-45 connector to twisted-pair cable.

Pin connections:
Pin 1 - White/Orange
Pin 2 - Orange/White
Pin 3 - White/Green
Pin 6 - Green/White

✦ Some people wire 10baseT cable differently — using the green and white pair for pins 1 and 2 and the orange and white pair for pins 3 and 6. This doesn't affect the operation of the network (the network is color-blind), *as long as the connectors on both ends of the cable are wired the same!*

✦ If you're installing cable for a Fast Ethernet system, you should be extra careful to follow the rules of Category-5 cabling. That means, among other things, making sure that you use Category-5 components throughout. The cable and all the connectors must be up to Category-5 specs. When you attach the connectors, don't untwist more than ½ inch of cable. And don't try to stretch the cable runs beyond the 100-meter maximum. When in doubt, have cable for a 100Mbps Ethernet system professionally installed.

Crossover cables

A *crossover cable* is a cable that can be used to directly connect two devices without a hub or switch. You can use a crossover cable to connect two computers directly to each other, but crossover cables are more often used to daisy-chain hubs and switches to each other.

If you want to create your own crossover cable, you have to reverse the wires on one end of the cable, as shown in Table 2-3. This table shows how you should wire both ends of the cable to create a crossover cable. Connect one of the ends according to the Connector A column and the other according to the Connector B column.

Note that you don't need to use a crossover cable if one of the switches or hubs that you want to connect has a crossover port, usually labeled *Uplink*. If the hub or switch has an Uplink port, you can daisy-chain it by using a normal network cable. For more information about daisy-chaining hubs and switches, see the section "Installing Hubs and Switches," later in this chapter.

Table 2-3	Creating a Crossover Cable	
Pin	*Connector A*	*Connector B*
Pin 1	White/Green	White/orange wire
Pin 2	Green/White	Orange/white wire
Pin 3	White/Orange	White/green wire
Pin 4	Blue/White	Blue/white wire
Pin 5	White/Blue	White/blue wire
Pin 6	Orange/White	Green/white wire
Pin 7	White/Brown	White/brown wire
Pin 8	Brown/White	Brown/white wire

Wall jacks and patch panels

If you want, you can run a single length of cable from a network hub or switch in a wiring closet through a hole in the wall, up the wall to the space above the ceiling, through the ceiling space to the wall in an office, down the wall, through a hole, and all the way to a desktop computer. That's not a good idea, however, for a variety of reasons. For one, every time someone moves the computer or even cleans behind it, the cable will get moved a little bit. Eventually, the connection will fail, and the RJ-45 plug will have to be replaced. Then the cables in the wiring closet will quickly become a tangled mess.

The alternative is to put a *wall jack* in the wall at the user's end of the cable and connect the other end of the cable to a *patch* panel. Then, the cable itself is completely contained within the walls and ceiling spaces. To connect a computer to the network, you plug one end of a patch cable (properly called a *station cable*) into the wall jack and plug the other end into the computer's network interface. In the wiring closet, you use a patch cable to connect the wall jack to the network hubs or switches. Figure 2-3 shows how this arrangement works.

Connecting a twisted-pair cable to a wall jack or a patch panel is similar to connecting it to an RJ-45 plug. However, you don't usually need any special tools. Instead, the back of the jack has a set of slots that you lay each wire across. You then snap a removable cap over the top of the slots and press it down. This forces the wires into the slots, where little metal blades pierce the insulation and establish the electrical contact.

When you connect the wire to a jack or patch panel, be sure to untwist as little of the wire as possible. If you untwist too much of the wire, the signals that pass through the wire may become unreliable.

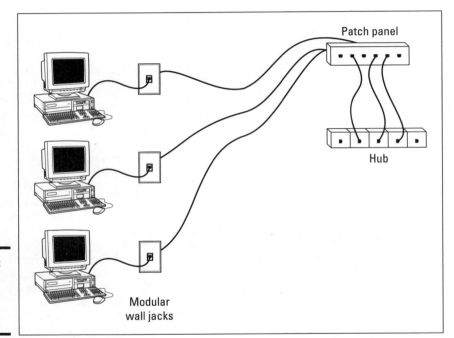

Figure 2-3:
Using wall
jacks and
patch
panels.

Installing Coaxial Cable

Although twisted-pair cable is by far the most commonly used type of networking cable, some networks still rely on old-fashioned coaxial cable, usually called *thinnet* or sometimes *BNC cable* because of the type of connectors used on each end of the cable.

Here are some salient points about working with coaxial cable:

✦ You attach thinnet to the network interface card by using a goofy twist-on connector called a *BNC connector.* You can purchase pre-assembled cables with BNC connectors already attached in lengths of 25 or 50 feet, or you can buy bulk cable on a big spool and attach the connectors yourself by using a special tool. (I suggest buying pre-assembled cables. Attaching connectors to bulk cable can be tricky.)

✦ With coaxial cables, you run cable from one computer to computer until all the computers are chained together. At each computer, a T connector is used to connect two cables to the network interface card.

✦ A special plug called a *terminator* is required at each end of a series of thinnet cables. The terminator prevents data from spilling out the end of the cable and staining the carpet.

✦ The cables strung end-to-end from one terminator to the other are collectively called a *segment*. The maximum length of a thinnet segment is about 200 meters (actually, 185 meters). You can connect as many as 30 computers on one segment. To span a distance greater than 185 meters or to connect more than 30 computers, you must use two or more segments with a funky device called a *repeater* to connect each segment.

✦ Although Ethernet coaxial cable resembles TV coaxial cable, the two types of cable are not interchangeable. Don't try to cut costs by wiring your network with cheap TV cable.

Book II
Chapter 2

Installing Network Hardware

Attaching a BNC connector to coaxial cable

Properly connecting a BNC connector to coaxial cable is an acquired skill. You need two tools — a wire stripper that can cut through the various layers of the coaxial cable at just the right location, and a crimping tool that crimps the connector tightly to the cable after you get the connector into position. BNC connectors have three separate pieces, as shown in Figure 2-4.

Here's the procedure, in case you ignore my advice and try to attach the connectors yourself:

1. **Slide the hollow tube portion of the connector (lovingly called the** *ferrule***) over the cable.**

Let it slide back a few feet to get it out of the way.

2. **Cut the end of the cable off cleanly.**

3. **Use the stripping tool to strip the cable.**

Strip the outer jacket back ½ inch from the end of the cable; strip the braided shield back ¼ inch from the end; and then strip the inner insulation back ³⁄₁₆ inch from the end.

4. **Insert the solid center conductor into the center pin.**

Slide the center pin down until it seats against the inner insulation.

5. **Use the crimping tool to crimp the center pin.**

6. **Slide the connector body over the center pin and inner insulation but under the braided shield.**

   After you push the body back far enough, the center pin clicks into place.

7. **Now slide the ferrule forward until it touches the connector body.**

   Crimp it with the crimping tool.

Don't get sucked into the trap of trying to use easy "screw-on" connectors. They aren't very reliable.

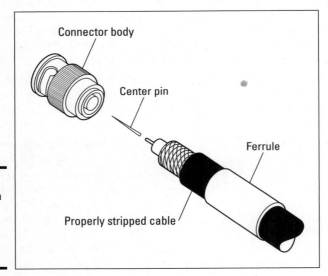

Figure 2-4: Attaching a BNC connector to coaxial cable.

Installing Hubs and Switches

The biggest difference between using coaxial cable and twisted-pair cable is that when you use twisted-pair cable, you also must use a separate device called a *hub* or a *switch*. Years ago, hubs were expensive devices — expensive enough that most do-it-yourself networkers who were building small networks opted for thinnet cable to avoid the expense and hassle of using hubs.

Nowadays, the cost of hubs has dropped so much that the advantages of using twisted-pair cabling outweigh the hassle and cost of using hubs. With twisted-pair cabling, you can more easily add new computers to the network, move computers, find and correct cable problems, and service the computers that you need to remove from the network temporarily.

A *switch* is simply a more sophisticated type of hub. Because the cost of switches has come down dramatically in the past few years, most new networks are built with switches rather than hubs. If you have an older network that uses hubs and seems to run slowly, you may be able to improve the network's speed by replacing the older hubs with newer switches.

You only need to know a few details when working with hubs and switches. Here they are, in no particular order:

✦ Installing a hub or switch is usually very simple. Just plug in the power cord and then plug in patch cables to connect the network.

✦ Each port on the hub or switch has an RJ-45 jack and a single LED indicator labeled *Link* that lights up when a connection has been established on the port. If you plug one end of a cable into the port and the other end into a computer or other network device, the Link light should come on. If it doesn't, something is wrong with the cable, the hub or switch port, or the device on the other end of the cable.

✦ Each port may also have an LED indicator that flashes to indicate network activity. If you stare at a hub or switch for awhile, you can find out who uses the network most by noting which activity indicators flash the most.

✦ The ports may also have a Collision indicator that flashes whenever a packet collision occurs on the port. It's perfectly acceptable for this light to flash now and then, but if it flashes a lot, you may have a problem with the network. Usually this just means that the network is overloaded and should be segmented with a switch to improve performance. But in some cases, a flashing Collision indicator may be caused by a faulty network node that clogs up the network with bad packets.

Daisy-chaining hubs or switches

If a single hub or switch doesn't have enough ports for your entire network, you can connect hubs or switches together by *daisy-chaining* them. If one of the hubs or switches has an uplink port, you can use a normal patch cable to connect the uplink port to one of the regular ports on the other hub or switch. If neither device has an uplink port, use a crossover cable to connect them. (For instructions on making a crossover cable, see the section "Crossover cables," earlier in this chapter.)

On some hubs and switches, a button is used to switch one of the ports between a normal port and an uplink port. This button is often labeled MDI/MDIX. To use the port as a normal port, switch the button to the MDI position. To use the port as an uplink port, switch the button to MDIX.

Some hubs and switches have a separate jack for the uplink port, but it turns out that the uplink port shares one of the normal ports internally. If that's the case, plugging a cable into the uplink port disables one of the normal ports. You shouldn't plug cables into both of these jacks. If you do, the hub or switch won't work properly.

Keep in mind these two simple rules when daisy-chaining hubs:

✦ The number of hubs that you can chain together is limited. For 10BaseT networks, you shouldn't connect more than three hubs to each other. For 100BaseT, you can chain only two hubs together.

✦ The cable you use to daisy-chain a 100BaseT hub can't be longer than 5 meters.

You can get around the first rule by using *stackable hubs*. Stackable hubs have a special type of cable connector that connects two or more hubs in a way that lets them function as if they were a single hub. Stackable hubs are a must for large networks.

Chapter 3: Setting Up a Network Server

In This Chapter

✔ Thinking about the different ways to install a network operating system

✔ Getting ready for installation

✔ Installing a network operating system

✔ Figuring out what to do after you install the network operating system

*A*fter you've installed the network cables and other devices, such as hubs and switches, the next step in building a network is usually setting up a server. After you've physically connected the server computer to the network, you can install the network operating system (NOS) on the server. Then, you can configure it to provide the network services that you expect and need from the server.

The Many Ways to Install a Network Operating System

Regardless of which network operating system you choose for your network servers, you can use any of several common ways to actually install the NOS software on the server computer. The following sections describe these alternatives.

Full install versus upgrade

One of the basic NOS installation choices is whether you want to perform a full installation or an upgrade installation. In some cases, you may be better off performing a full installation even if you're installing the NOS on a computer that already has an earlier version of the NOS installed.

✦ If you're installing the NOS on a brand-new server, you'll be performing a *full installation* that installs the operating system and configures it with default settings.

✦ If you're installing the NOS on a server computer that already has a server operating system installed, you can perform an *upgrade installation* that replaces the existing operating system with the new one but retains as many of the settings from the existing operating system as possible.

✦ You can also perform a full installation on a computer that already has an operating system installed. In that case, you have the option of deleting the existing operating system or performing a *multiboot installation* that installs the new server operating system alongside the existing operating system. Then, when you restart the computer, you can choose which operating system you want to run.

Although multiboot installation may sound like a good idea, it's fraught with peril. I suggest that you avoid multiboot unless you have a specific reason to use it. For more information about multiboot setups, see the sidebar "Giving multiboot the boot."

✦ You can't upgrade a client version of Windows to a server version. Instead, you must perform a full installation, which deletes the existing Windows operating system, or a multiboot installation, which leaves the existing client Windows intact. Either way, however, you can preserve existing data on the Windows computer when you install the server version.

Installing over the network

Normally, you'll install a NOS directly from the CD-ROM distribution disks on the server's CD-ROM drive. However, you can also install the operating system from a shared drive located on another computer, provided that the server computer already has access to the network. You can either use a shared CD-ROM drive, or you can copy the entire contents of the distribution CD-ROM disk onto a shared hard drive.

Obviously, the server computer must have network access in order for this technique to work. If the server already has an operating system installed, it probably already has access to the network. If not, you can boot the computer from a floppy that has basic network support.

If you're going to install the NOS onto more than one server, you can save time by first copying the distribution CD onto a shared hard drive. That's because even the fastest CD-ROM drives are slower than the network. Even with a basic 10Mbps network, access to hard drive data over the network is much faster than access to a local CD-ROM drive.

Giving multiboot the boot

Multiboot installations enable you to have more than one operating system on a single computer. Of course, only one of these operating systems can be running at any time. When you boot the computer, a menu appears with each of the installed operating systems listed. You can choose which operating system to boot from this menu.

Multiboot is most useful for software developers or network managers who want to make sure that software is compatible with a wide variety of operating systems. Rather than set up a bunch of separate computers with different operating system versions, you can install several operating systems on a single PC and use that one PC to test the software. For production network servers, however, you probably don't need to have more than one operating system installed.

If you still insist on loading two or more operating systems on a network server, be sure to install each operating system into its own disk partition. Although most network operating systems let you install two (or more) operating systems into a single partition, doing so is not a very good idea. To support two operating systems in a single partition, the operating systems have to play a risky shell game with key system files — moving or renaming them each time you restart the computer. Unfortunately, things can go wrong. For example, if lightning strikes and the power goes out just as the NOS is switching the startup files around, you may find yourself with a server that can't boot to any of its installed operating systems

The best way to set up a multiboot system is to install each operating system into its own partition. Then, you can use a boot manager program to choose the partition you want to boot from when you start the computer.

Automated and remote installations

In case you find yourself in the unenviable position of installing a NOS onto several servers, you can use a few tricks to streamline the process:

✦ *Automated setup* lets you create a setup script that provides answers to all the questions asked by the installation program. After you've created the script, you can start the automated setup, leave, and come back when the installation is finished. Creating the setup script is a bit of work, so automated setup makes sense only if you have more than a few servers to install.

✦ Microsoft has a feature called *Remote Installation Services* (RIS) that lets you install Windows 2000 Server or Windows Server 2003 from a remote network location without even going to the server computer. RIS is tricky to set up, however, so it's really only worth it if you have a lot of servers on which to install operating systems. (RIS can also install client operating systems.)

Gathering Your Stuff

Before you install a network operating system, you should gather everything you need so that you don't have to look for something in the middle of the setup. The following sections describe the items you're most likely to need.

A capable server computer

Obviously, you have to have a server computer on which to install the NOS. Each NOS has a list of the minimum hardware requirements supported by the operating system. For example, Table 3-1 summarizes the minimum requirements for Windows NT Server, Windows 2000 Server, and Windows Server 2003 Standard Edition.

My suggestion is that you take these minimums with a grain of salt. Windows Server 2003 will crawl like a snail on a 133MHz Pentium; you shouldn't try it on anything less than 550MHz. As for the memory requirement, consider 64KB to be the minimum for Windows NT and 256MB the minimum for Windows 2000 Server or Windows Server 2003.

Table 3-1	Minimum Hardware Requirements for Microsoft Server Operating Systems		
Item	*Windows NT Server*	*Windows 2000 Server*	*Windows Server 2003*
CPU	33MHz 486	133MHz Pentium	133MHz Pentium
RAM	16MB	128MB	128MB
Free disk space	125MB	1GB	1.5GB

You should also check your server hardware against the list of compatible hardware published by the maker of your NOS. For example, Microsoft publishes a list of hardware that it has tested and certified as compatible with Windows servers. This list is called the *Hardware Compatibility List*, or *HCL* for short. You can check the HCL for your specific server by going to Microsoft's Web site at www.microsoft.com/whdc/hcl/default.mspx. You can also test your computer's compatibility by running the Check System Compatibility option from the Windows distribution CD-ROM disk.

You can find more specific details on server computer recommendations in Book I, Chapter 3.

The server operating system

You also need a server operating system to install. You need either the distribution CD-ROM disks or access to a copy of them over the network. In addition to the disks, you should have the following:

✦ **The product key:** The installation program will ask you to enter the product key during the installation to prove that you have a legal copy of the software. If you have the actual CD-ROM disks, the product key should be on a sticker attached to the case.

✦ **Manuals:** If the operating system came with printed manuals, you should keep them handy.

✦ **A startup diskette:** If you're installing onto a brand-new server, you need some way to boot the computer. Depending on the NOS version you're installing and the capabilities of the server computer, you may be able to boot the computer directly from the CD-ROM distribution disk. If not, you need a floppy disk from which to boot the server.

✦ **Your license type:** You can purchase Microsoft operating systems on a per-server or a per-user basis. You need to know which plan you have when you install the NOS.

Book II
Chapter 3

Setting Up a
Network Server

TIP

Check the CD-ROM distribution disk for product documentation and additional last-minute information. For example, Windows servers have a \docs folder that contains several files that have useful setup information.

Other software

In most cases, the installation program should be able to automatically configure your server's hardware devices and install appropriate drivers. Just in case, though, you should dig out the driver disks that came with your devices, such as network interface cards, SCSI devices, CD-ROM drives, printers or scanners, and so on.

A working Internet connection

This isn't an absolute requirement, but the installation will go much smoother if you have a working Internet connection before you start. The installation process may use this Internet connection for several things:

✦ **Downloading late-breaking updates or fixes to the operating system.** This can eliminate the need to install a service pack after you finish installing the NOS.

✦ **Locating drivers for nonstandard devices.** This can be a big plus if you can't find the driver disk for your obscure SCSI card.

✦ **Activating the product after you complete the installation (for Microsoft operating systems).** For more information, see the section on product activation, later in this chapter.

A good book

You'll spend lots of time watching progress bars, so you may as well have something to do while you wait.

Making Informed Decisions

When you install a NOS, you have to make some decisions about how you want the operating system and its servers to be configured. Most of these decisions aren't cast in stone, so don't worry if you're not 100 percent sure how you want everything configured. You can always go back and reconfigure things. However, you'll save yourself time if you make the right decisions up front, rather than just guess when the Setup program starts asking you questions.

The following paragraphs list most of the decisions that you'll need to make. (This list is for Windows 2000 Server and Windows Server 2003 installations. For other network operating systems, the decisions may vary slightly.)

✦ **The existing operating system:** If you want to retain the existing operating system, the installation program can perform a multiboot setup, which will allow you to choose which operating system to boot to each time you start the computer. This is rarely a good idea for server computers, so I recommend that you elect to delete the existing operating system.

✦ **Partition structure:** Most of the time, you'll want to treat the entire server disk as a single partition. However, if you want to divide the disk into two or more partitions, you should do so during setup. (Unlike most of the other setup decisions, this one is hard to change later.)

✦ **File system:** Windows servers provide two choices for the file system to format the server's disk: FAT32 and NTFS. In almost all cases, you should elect to use NTFS. Use FAT32 only if you're installing a dual-boot system where the other operating system is Windows ME or 9*x*.

✦ **Computer name:** During the operating system setup, you'll be asked to provide the computer name used to identify the server on the network. If your network has only a few servers, you can just pick a name such as Server01 or MyServer. If your network has more than a few servers, you'll want to follow an established guideline for creating server names.

✦ **Administrator password:** Okay, this one is tough. You don't want to pick something obvious, like *Password*, *Administrator*, or your last name. On the other hand, you don't want to type in something random that you'll later forget, because you'll be in a big pickle if you forget the administrator password. I suggest that you make up a complex password consisting of a mix of uppercase and lowercase letters, some numerals, and a special symbol or two; then write it down and keep it in a secure location where you know it won't get lost.

✦ **Networking protocols:** You'll almost always need to install the TCP/IP protocol, the Microsoft network client protocol, and file and printer sharing. Depending on how the server will be used, you may want to install other protocols as well.

✦ **TCP/IP configuration:** You need to know what IP address to use for the server. Even if your network has a DHCP server to dynamically assign IP addresses to clients, most servers use static IP addresses.

✦ **Workgroup or domain:** You need to decide whether the server will join a domain or just be a member of a workgroup. In either case, you need to know the domain name or the workgroup name.

Final Preparations

Before you begin the actual installation, you should take a few more steps:

✦ Clean up the server's disk by uninstalling any software that you don't need and removing any old data that is no longer needed. This process is especially important if you're converting a computer that's been in use as a client computer to a server. You probably don't need Microsoft Office or a bunch of games on the computer after it becomes a server.

✦ Do a complete backup of the computer. Operating system setup programs are almost flawless, so the chances of losing data during installation are minimal. But you still face the chance that something may go wrong.

✦ If the computer is connected to an Uninterruptible Power Supply (UPS) that has a serial or USB connection to the computer, unplug the serial or USB connection. In some cases, this control connection can confuse the operating system's Setup program when it tries to determine which devices are attached to the computer.

✦ If the computer has hard drives compressed with DriveSpace or DoubleSpace, uncompress the drives before you begin.

✦ Light some votive candles, take two Tylenol, and put on a pot of coffee.

Installing a Network Operating System

The following sections present an overview of a typical installation of Windows Server 2003. Although the details vary, the overall installation process for other network operating systems is similar.

The method you use to begin the installation depends on whether the computer already has a working operating system:

✦ If the computer already has a working operating system, simply insert the Windows 2003 Setup disk in the computer's CD-ROM drive. After a moment, a dialog box appears, asking whether you want to install Windows Server 2003. Click Yes to proceed.

✦ If you're installing Windows Server 2003 from a network drive, open the My Network Places window, navigate to the shared folder that contains the distribution files, and run `Winnt32.exe`.

✦ If the computer doesn't already have a working operating system but can boot from a CD-ROM disk, insert the distribution disk into the CD-ROM drive and restart the computer.

✦ If the computer doesn't have a working operating system and can't boot from its CD-ROM drive, insert a bootable floppy disk that has CD-ROM support into the A drive and restart the computer. When the MS-DOS command prompt appears, type **d:** to switch to the CD-ROM drive (assuming drive D is the CD-ROM), type **cd \i386** and then type **winnt**.

As the Setup program proceeds, it leads you through five distinct installation phases: Collecting Information, Dynamic Update, Preparing Installation, Installing Windows, and Finalizing Installation. The following sections describe each of these installation phases in greater detail.

Phase 1: Collecting Information

In the first installation phase, the Setup program asks for the preliminary information that it needs to begin the installation. A wizard-like dialog box appears to gather the following information:

✦ **Setup Type:** You can choose to perform a new installation or an upgrade.

✦ **License Agreement:** The official license agreement is displayed. You have to agree to its terms in order to proceed.

✦ **Product Key:** Enter the 25-character product key that's printed on the sticker attached to the CD-ROM disk case. If Setup says you entered an invalid product key, double-check it carefully. You probably just typed the key incorrectly.

✦ **Setup Options:** You can click Advanced Options to change the file locations used for Setup, but you should stick to the defaults. If you need to use accessibility features, such as the Magnifier, during Setup, click Accessibility Options and enable the features you need. In addition, if you want to change the language setting, click Primary Language and make your selections.

✦ **Upgrade to NTFS:** If you want to upgrade a FAT32 system to NTFS, you need to say so now.

Phase 2: Dynamic Update

In the next installation phase, Setup connects to Microsoft's Web site via your Internet connection and checks to see whether any of the installation files have been changed. If so, the updated installation files are downloaded at this time. If you don't have a working Internet connection, you have to skip this phase.

Phase 3: Preparing Installation

In this phase, the computer is restarted and booted into a special text-mode Setup program. After the Welcome screen appears, Setup proceeds through the following steps:

✦ **Partition Setup:** Here, you're asked to choose the partition that you want to use for the installation. You can reconfigure your partitions from this screen by deleting existing partitions or creating new ones. In most cases, you'll want to install Windows into a single partition that uses all available space on the drive.

✦ **Delete Existing Windows installation:** This screen lets you choose whether you want to delete your existing Windows installation or leave it in place. You should choose to delete it unless you want a multiboot installation.

✦ **Convert to NTFS:** If you elected to convert an existing FAT32 partition to NTFS, the conversion will take awhile. This step is a good time to get a fresh cup of coffee.

✦ **Copying Files:** Now Windows copies its installation files onto your hard drive. This step also takes awhile.

Phase 4: Installing Windows

Now that the drive has been set up and the installation files copied, Windows Setup reboots your computer back into Windows mode and begins the actual process of installing Windows. You're taken through the following steps:

✦ **Installing Devices:** Windows automatically examines each and every device on the computer and installs and configures the appropriate device drivers. This step can take awhile.

✦ **Regional and Language Options:** In this step, you're asked to enter information about your region and language. If you're in the United States, you can accept the defaults. Otherwise, you can change the settings appropriately.

✦ **Personalize Your Software:** In this step, you can enter your name and your company name. Your name is required, but the company name is optional.

✦ **License Modes:** In this step, you choose whether you purchased per-server or per-device/per-user licensing. You can change this setting later, but you can change the setting only once. If you're not sure, double-check the invoice that Microsoft shipped along with the software.

**Book II
Chapter 3**

**Setting Up a
Network Server**

✦ **Computer Name and Administrator Name:** Enter the computer name and Administrator account password here. Be sure to write down the password and keep it in a secure location. You'll be in serious trouble if you forget it.

✦ **Date and Time Settings:** If the date and time information is incorrect, you can change it here.

✦ **Network Settings:** In most cases, you can select the Typical option in this step to install the network features that are used most often: Client for Microsoft Networks, Network Load Balancing, File and Printer Sharing for Microsoft Networks, and Internet Protocol (TCP/IP). If you don't want to use these defaults, you can select Custom Settings and then configure these features yourself.

✦ **Workgroup or Domain:** Next, you're asked whether the computer is part of a workgroup or a domain. Choose the appropriate option and enter the workgroup or domain name.

✦ **Copying Files:** Now Windows copies files, updates the registry, and ties up any loose ends. This step can take a long time, so you may want to go for a walk.

Phase 5: Finalizing Installation

To complete the installation, Setup saves your settings and reboots the computer one final time. When the computer restarts, press Ctrl+Alt+Delete to bring up the Log On dialog box. Enter the password you created for the Administrator account, click OK, and you're logged on. Now the real fun begins.

Life After Setup

After the Setup program completes its duty, you still have several tasks to complete before your server is ready to use. The following sections describe these post-installation chores.

Logging on

After the Setup program restarts your computer for the last time, you must log on to the server using the Administrator account. To do so, press Ctrl+Alt+Delete to bring up the Log On To Windows dialog box. Then, type the password you created for the Administrator account during setup and click OK to log on. Windows grinds and whirs for a moment while it starts up and then displays the familiar Windows desktop.

Activating Windows

Microsoft's Product Activation feature is designed to prevent you from installing an illegal copy of Windows or other Microsoft software products. After you install a product, you have 30 days to activate it. If you don't activate the product within 30 days, it stops working. To prevent that from happening, you should activate the software first thing after installing it.

Fortunately, activating a Windows server operating system is easy to do if you have a working Internet connection. Windows displays a pop-up reminder in the notification area (in the right corner of the taskbar). Just click this bubble to start the Activation Wizard, shown in Figure 3-1.

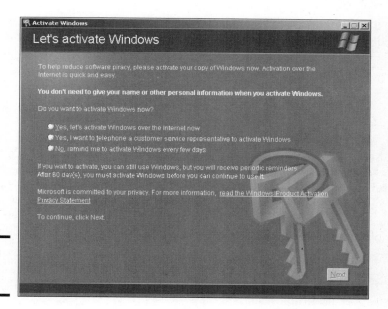

Figure 3-1:
Activating
Windows.

When you activate a Microsoft software product, a unique code is assigned to your system and sent to Microsoft, where the code is stored in a Product Activation database. The code includes information about the configuration of your computer, so Microsoft can tell if someone tries to install the same copy of the software on a different computer.

The activation code is based on ten hardware characteristics and allows for you to make certain changes to your computer without having to reactivate. Product Activation has a certain amount of built-in tolerance to hardware changes. As a result, you can add another hard drive or more memory to your server without having to reactivate. But if you change the computer too much, Product Activation will think you've stolen the software or are trying to install it on a second computer. In that case, you have to contact Microsoft and convince them that you've just done a major overhaul of the server computer and should be allowed to reactivate your software. Good luck. For the details about how Product Activation determines when you need to reactivate, see the sidebar "How much change is too much?"

You can activate your software in two ways. The easiest is to do it automatically over the Internet. If you don't have a working Internet connection, you can do it over the phone. However, you'll probably be put on hold for awhile until a customer service representative can answer. Then, you'll have to read a 50-digit number over the phone and then take down the long confirmation number that you'll be given to type into the Activation dialog box. Product Activation over the Internet is a lot easier.

If your company has a volume licensing agreement with Microsoft, you don't have to bother with Product Activation; it doesn't apply to products purchased under a volume licensing agreement.

How much change is too much?

Microsoft's Product Activation feature uses an activation code that is based in part on your computer's hardware configuration. In particular, the code includes information about the following ten hardware components of your system:

- The display adapter
- The SCSI disk adapter
- The IDE disk adapter
- The network adapter's MAC address
- The amount of RAM
- The processor type
- The processor's serial number
- The hard drive device type
- The hard drive's Volume Serial Number
- The CD-ROM, CD-RW, or DVD-ROM drive

To determine whether your computer's hardware has changed, Product Activation uses a voting system that compares the hardware that was present when the product was first installed with the current hardware. For each component that is the same, one vote is tallied — except for the network card's MAC address, which counts for three votes. If you get at least seven votes, you don't have to reactivate the product. However, if you get fewer than seven votes, you have to reactivate.

For example, suppose that you upgrade the computer's hard drive and add 128MB of memory. Because the network card is the same, it counts for three votes. The SCSI disk adapter, IDE disk adapter, processor type, serial number, and CD-ROM drive score an additional five votes for a total of nine votes. Because you exceeded seven votes, you don't have to reactivate.

However, suppose also that you then replace the network interface card. Now you don't get the three votes for the network card, so you have only six votes and will need to reactivate the product. (You may be able to thwart this setback by making sure that the new hard drive uses the same volume serial number as the old drive.)

Service packs

Service packs are maintenance updates to an operating system that contain minor enhancements and bug fixes. Most of the fixes in a service pack address security problems that have been discovered since the operating system was first released. The usual way to get service packs is by downloading them from the operating system vendor's Web site.

Depending on the operating system version you've installed, you may or may not need to apply a service pack immediately after installing the operating system. The Windows Server 2003 Setup program automatically checks for updates before it installs the operating system, so you shouldn't normally have to install a service pack after running Setup. However, you may need to do so with other operating systems.

Unfortunately, applying service packs is something you have to do throughout the life of the server. Microsoft and other operating system vendors periodically release new service packs to correct problems as they arise.

Testing the installation

After Setup finishes, you'll want to make sure that your server is up and running. Here are some simple checks that you can perform to make sure that your server has been properly installed:

✦ Check the Event Viewer to see whether it contains any error messages related to installation or startup. Depending on the Windows server version you're using, you can open the Event Viewer by choosing Start➪ Administrative Tools➪Event Viewer or Start➪Program Files➪ Administrative Tools➪Event Viewer. (Non-Windows server operating systems have similar features that allow you to view event logs.)

✦ Check your TCP/IP settings by running the command `ipconfig /all` from a command prompt. This test tells you whether TCP/IP is running and shows you the host name, IP address, and other useful TCP/IP information.

✦ To make sure that you can reach the server over the network, open a command prompt at a client computer and attempt to ping the server by entering the command `ping hostname` where *hostname* is the name displayed by the `ipconfig` command for the server.

Configuring Server Roles

After you've installed your server operating system and verified that the installation was successful, the next step is to configure the various services that you want the server to provide. You can find information about configuring services for specific network operating systems in later chapters throughout this book. For now, I want to show you the Configure Your Server Wizard that's built into Windows Server 2003. This wizard starts automatically the first time you log on to Windows Server 2003. You can get back into this wizard at any time by choosing Start➪All Programs➪Administrative Tools➪Configure Your Server.

After displaying some preliminary configuration information, the wizard lets you set up a default Typical configuration for a first server or a Custom configuration that lets you choose which services you want to enable. I suggest that you choose Custom configuration even if this server is the first on your network. That way, you can see which services are being set up and how they'll be configured.

Figure 3-2 shows the Server Role page of the Configure Your Server Wizard. This page lets you configure the various roles your server will play. You can use the wizard to configure one of these roles at a time by choosing one of the roles from the list and clicking Next. The wizard takes you through one or more pages that ask for configuration information for the server role you selected. You eventually come back to this page, where you can configure other server roles.

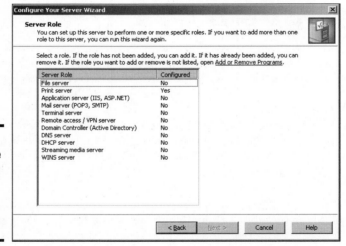

Figure 3-2:
You can use this page to configure the roles your server will play.

The following paragraphs describe the server roles you can configure:

✦ **File Server:** This role allows you to create shared folders that network users can access. You can set up disk quotas to limit the amount of storage available to each user, and you can set up an indexing service that helps users quickly find their files.

✦ **Print Server:** This role allows you to share printers connected to the server with network users.

✦ **Application Server:** This is a fancy name for Internet Information Services, Microsoft's Web server. If you want the server to host Web sites, you need to configure the application server role.

✦ **Mail Server:** This role provides basic e-mail features based on the standard Internet mail protocols (POP3 and SMTP).

✦ **Terminal Server:** This role lets other users run applications on the server computer as if they were working at the server.

✦ **Remote Access/VPN Server:** This role enables dialup connections and Virtual Private Network connections, which work like dialup connections but operate over the Internet rather than over a private phone line.

✦ **Domain Controller:** This role enables Activate Directory and designates the server as a domain controller so that it can manage user accounts, logon activity, and access privileges.

✦ **DNS Server:** This role configures the computer as a DNS server for the network so that it can resolve Internet names. For smaller networks, you'll probably use your ISP's DNS server. You probably need your own DNS server only for large networks.

✦ **DHCP Server:** A DHCP server assigns IP addresses to computers automatically so that you don't have to manually configure an IP address for each computer. On many networks, the router that provides the network's connection to the Internet doubles as a DHCP server. Unless your network is really large, you probably don't need two DCHP servers.

✦ **Streaming Media Server:** If you plan on using digital media (such as audio or video) over your network, you should set up the Streaming Media Server role. One common use of streaming media is for online conferencing using programs such as Microsoft NetMeeting.

✦ **WINS Server:** This role allows the server to translate NetBIOS names to IP addresses. All Windows networks should have at least one WINS server. However, you need two or more servers only for very large networks.

Chapter 4: Configuring Client Computers

In This Chapter

✔ **Configuring network connections for Windows clients**

✔ **Setting the computer name, description, and workgroup**

✔ **Joining a domain**

✔ **Configuring Windows logon options**

*B*efore your network setup is complete, you must configure the network's client computers. In particular, you have to configure each client's network interface card so that it works properly, and you have to install the right protocols so that the clients can communicate with other computers on the network.

Fortunately, the task of configuring client computers for the network is child's play with Windows. For starters, Windows automatically recognizes your network interface card when you start up your computer. All that remains to connect to the network in Windows is to make sure that Windows properly installed the network protocols and client software.

With each version of Windows, Microsoft has simplified the process of configuring client network support. In this chapter, I describe the steps for configuring networking for Windows XP Professional, Windows 2000, Windows 98, and Windows 95. I don't cover Windows XP Home Edition or Windows Millennium Edition because those versions are designed primarily for home use.

Configuring Network Connections

Windows automatically detects the presence of a network interface card, so you don't usually need to manually install device drivers for a NIC. When Windows detects a NIC, it automatically creates a network connection and configures it to support basic networking protocols. However, you may need to manually change the configuration of a network connection. The following sections show you how.

Windows XP and Windows 2000

To configure a network connection in Windows XP Professional or Windows 2000 Professional, follow these steps:

1. **Click Start⇨Control Panel to open the Control Panel.**

The Control Panel appears.

2. **Double-click the Network Connections icon.**

The Network Connections folder appears, as shown in Figure 4-1.

3. **Right-click the connection that you want to configure and then choose Properties from the menu that appears.**

In Windows XP, you can also select the network connection and click Change Settings Of This Connection from the task pane. Either way, the Properties dialog box for the network connection appears, as shown in Figure 4-2.

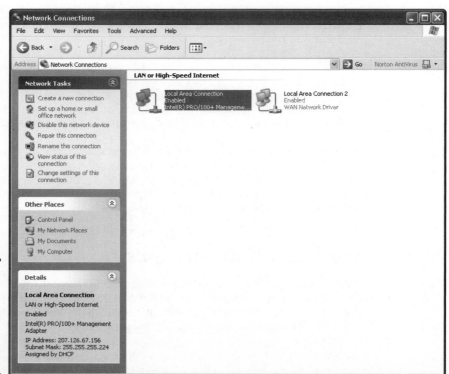

Figure 4-1:
The
Network
Connections
folder
(Windows
XP).

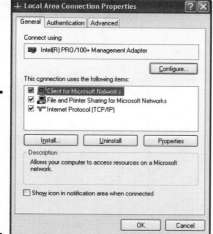

Figure 4-2:
The
Properties
dialog box
for a
network
connection
(Windows
XP).

4. To configure the network adapter card settings, click Configure.

This action summons the Properties dialog box for the network adapter, as shown in Figure 4-3. This dialog box has four tabs that let you configure the NIC:

- **General:** This tab shows basic information about the NIC, such as the device type and status. For example, the device shown in Figure 4-3 is an Intel(R) PRO/100+ Management Adapter. (It's installed in slot 3 of the computer's PCI bus.) If you're having trouble with the NIC, you can click the Troubleshoot button to call up the Windows XP Hardware Troubleshooter. You can also disable the device if it's preventing other components of the computer from working properly.

- **Advanced:** This tab lets you set a variety of device-specific parameters that affect the operation of the NIC. For example, some cards have a parameter that lets you set the card's speed (typically 10Mbps or 100Mbps) or the number of buffers the card should use. You should consult the manual that came with the card before you play with these settings.

- **Driver:** This tab displays information about the device driver that is bound to the NIC and lets you update the driver to a newer version, roll back the driver to a previously working version, or uninstall the driver.

- **Resources:** This tab lets you manually set the system resources used by the card, including the memory range, I/O range, IRQ, and DMA channels. In the old days, before Plug and Play cards, you had to configure these settings whenever you installed a card, and it was easy to create resource conflicts. Newer versions of Windows configure these settings automatically, so you should rarely need to fiddle with them.

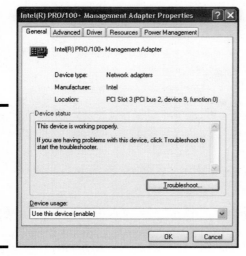

Figure 4-3:
The Properties dialog box for a network adapter (Windows XP).

- **Power Management:** This tab lets you set power management options. You can specify that the network card can be shut down when the computer goes into sleep mode and that the network card should be allowed to wake up the computer periodically in order to refresh the network state.

When you click OK to dismiss the network adapter Properties dialog box, the Network Connection Properties dialog box closes. You need to click Change Settings For This Connection again to continue the procedure.

5. **Make sure that the network items that your client requires are listed in the Network Connection Properties dialog box.**

   The following paragraphs describe the items you'll commonly see listed here. Note that not all networks need all these items.

   - **Client for Microsoft Networks:** This item is required to access a Microsoft Windows network. It should always be present.

   - **File And Printer Sharing For Microsoft Networks:** This item allows your computer to share its files or printers with other computers on the network. This option is usually used with peer-to-peer networks, but you can use it even if your network has dedicated servers.

- **Internet Protocol (TCP/IP):** This item enables the client computer to communicate via the TCP/IP protocol. If all the servers on the network support TCP/IP, this protocol should be the only one installed on the client.

- **NWLink IPX/SPX/NetBIOS Compatible Transport Protocol:** This protocol is required only if some of the servers on the network require it.

6. **If a protocol that you need isn't listed, click the Install button to add the protocol that you need.**

   A dialog box appears, asking whether you want to add a network client, adapter, protocol, or service, as shown in Figure 4-4. Click Protocol and then click Add. A list of available protocols appears. Select the one that you want to add and then click OK. (You may be asked to insert a disk or the Windows CD-ROM.)

7. **Make sure that the network client that you want to use appears in the list of network resources.**

   For a Windows-based network, make sure that Client For Microsoft Networks is listed. For a NetWare network, make sure that Client Service For NetWare appears. If your network uses both types of servers, you can choose both clients.

   If you have NetWare servers, use the NetWare client software that comes with NetWare rather than the client supplied by Microsoft with Windows.

8. **If the client that you need isn't listed, click the Install button to add the client that you need, click Client, and then click Add; choose the client that you want to add and click OK.**

   The client you selected is added to the Network Connection Properties dialog box.

**Book II
Chapter 4**

**Configuring Client
Computers**

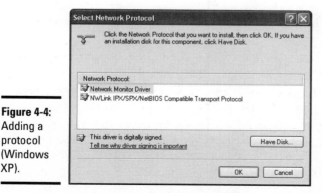

Figure 4-4:
Adding a
protocol
(Windows
XP).

9. **To remove a network item that you don't need (such as File And Printer Sharing For Microsoft Networks), select the item and click the Uninstall button.**

For security reasons, you should make it a point to remove any clients, protocols, or services that you don't need.

10. **To configure TCP/IP settings, click Internet Protocol (TCP/IP) and click Properties to display the TCP/IP Properties dialog box; adjust the settings and then click OK.**

The TCP/IP Properties dialog box, shown in Figure 4-5, lets you choose from the following options:

- **Obtain An IP Address Automatically:** Choose this option if your network has a DHCP server that assigns IP addresses automatically. Choosing this option drastically simplifies the task of administering TCP/IP on your network.

- **Use The Following IP Address:** If your computer must have a specific IP address, choose this option and then type in the computer's IP address, subnet mask, and default gateway address. For more information about these settings, see Book V, Chapter 2.

- **Obtain DNS Server Address Automatically:** The DHCP server can also provide the address of the Domain Name System (DNS) server that the computer should use. Choose this option if your network has a DHCP server.

- **Use The Following DNS Server Addresses:** Choose this option if a DHCP server is not available. Then, type the IP address of the primary and secondary DNS servers. For more information about DNS servers, refer to Book V, Chapter 4.

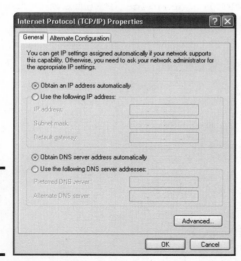

Figure 4-5:
Configuring
TCP/IP
(Windows
XP).

Windows 9x

To configure network settings in Windows 95 and Windows 98, you use a procedure similar to the one you use for Windows XP or Windows 2000. However, you should know a couple of important differences:

✦ To display the Network Properties dialog box, right-click Network Neighborhood on the Desktop and choose Properties. Or, open the Control Panel and double-click Network.

✦ Windows 95/98 doesn't have a Network Connections folder. Instead, network adapters are listed in the Network Properties dialog box along with network clients, services, and protocols. After you add a network client, service, or protocol to the Network Properties dialog box, you must bind it to the adapter that you want to use it with. To do that, bring up the Properties dialog box for the client, service, or protocol you want to bind, click the Bindings tab, and add the network adapter you want to bind to.

**Book II
Chapter 4**

Configuring Client
Computers

Configuring Client Computer Identification

Every client computer must identify itself in order to participate in the network. The computer identification consists of the computer's name, an optional description, and the name of either the workgroup or the domain to which the computer belongs.

The computer name must follow the rules for NetBIOS names; it may be from 1 to 15 characters long and may contain letters, numbers, or hyphens but no spaces or periods. For small networks, it's common to make the computer name the same as the user name. For larger networks, you may want to develop a naming scheme that identifies the computer's location. For example, a name such as C-305-1 may be assigned to the first computer in room 305 of building C. Or MKTG010 may be a computer in the marketing department.

If the computer will join a domain, you need to have access to an Administrator account on the domain unless the administrator has already created a computer account on the domain. Note that only Windows 2000, Windows XP, and Windows server (NT, 2000, and 2003) computers can join a domain. (Windows 98 or 95 users can still access domain resources by logging on to the domain as users, but domain computer accounts for Windows 9x clients aren't required.)

When you install Windows on the client system, the Setup program asks for the computer name and workstation or domain information. You can change this information later if you want. The exact procedure varies, depending on which version of Windows the client uses, as described in the following sections.

Windows XP and Windows 2000

To change the computer identification in Windows XP or Windows 2000, follow these steps:

1. **Open the Control Panel and double-click the System icon to bring up the System Properties dialog box.**

2. **Click the Computer Name tab.**

   The computer identification information appears, as shown in Figure 4-6.

Figure 4-6: The Computer Name tab of the System Properties dialog box (Windows XP).

3. **Click the Change button.**

   The Computer Name Changes dialog box appears, as shown in Figure 4-7.

4. **Type the new computer name and then specify the workgroup or domain information.**

   To join a domain, select the Domain radio button and type the domain name into the appropriate text box. To join a workgroup, select the Workgroup radio button and type the workgroup name in the corresponding text box.

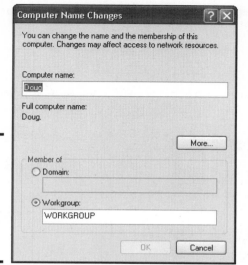

**Book II
Chapter 4**

Configuring Client
Computers

Figure 4-7:
The
Computer
Name
Changes
dialog box
(Windows
XP).

5. **Click OK.**

6. **If prompted, enter the user name and password for an Administrator account.**

You'll only be asked to provide this information if a computer account has not already been created for the client computer.

7. **When a dialog box appears, informing you that you need to restart the computer, click OK and then restart the computer.**

You're done!

Windows 9x

To change the computer identification for a Windows 98 or Windows 95 client, follow these steps:

1. **Right-click the Network Places icon on the desktop and choose Properties.**

The Network dialog box appears.

2. **Click the Identification tab.**

The computer identification information appears, as shown in Figure 4-8.

3. **Type the computer name, description, and workgroup name.**

   The computer name should be unique on the network, and all computers that you want to share resources with should have the same workgroup name.

4. **Click OK.**

   You're done!

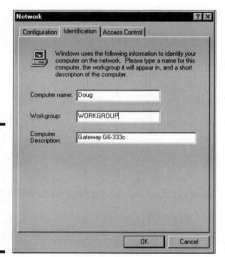

Figure 4-8: The Identification tab of the Network dialog box (Windows 98).

Configuring Network Domain Logon

Every user who wants to access a domain-based network must log on to the domain by using a valid user account. The user account is created on the domain controller — not on the client computer.

Network logon isn't required to access workgroup resources. Instead, workgroup resources can be password-protected in order to restrict access.

Windows XP and Windows 2000

When you start a Windows XP or Windows 2000 computer that has been configured to join a domain, as described in the section "Configuring Computer Identification," earlier in this chapter, the Log On To Windows dialog box appears. The user can use this dialog box to log on to a domain by entering a domain user name and password and selecting the domain that he or she wants to log on to from the Log On To drop-down list.

Windows 2000 and Windows XP allow you to create local user accounts that allow users to access resources on the local computer. To log on to the local computer, the user selects This Computer from the Log On To drop-down list and enters the user name and password for a local user account. When a user logs on by using a local account, he or she isn't connected to a network domain. To log on to a domain, the user must select the domain from the Log On To drop-down list.

If the computer is not part of a domain, Windows XP can display a friendly logon screen that displays an icon for each of the computer's local users. The user can log on simply by clicking the appropriate icon and entering a password. This feature is not available for computers that have joined a domain.

Note that if the user logs on by using a local computer account rather than a domain account, he or she can still access domain resources. A Connect To dialog box appears whenever the user attempts to access a domain resource. Then, the user can enter a domain user name and password to connect to the domain.

Windows 9x

Windows 9*x* doesn't show a logon screen unless you explicitly configure it to display a network logon screen. To do so, follow these steps:

1. **Call up the Network dialog box by opening the Control Panel and double-clicking the Network icon.**

   If you prefer, you can right-click the Network Neighborhood icon on the desktop and choose the Properties command.

2. **Click the Configuration tab if it isn't already selected.**

   The network configuration settings appear, as shown in Figure 4-9.

3. **Choose Client for Microsoft Networks in the Primary Network Logon drop-down list.**

   This step configures the computer to log on to the Windows network at startup.

4. **Select Client For Microsoft Networks in the list of installed Network Components and then click the Properties button.**

   The Client For Microsoft Networks Properties dialog box appears, as shown in Figure 4-10.

5. **Check the Log On To Windows NT Domain checkbox and enter the domain name in the text box.**

Book II
Chapter 4

Configuring Client
Computers

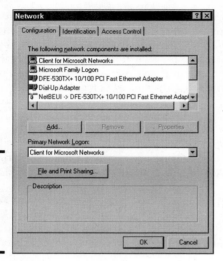

Figure 4-9:
The
Network
dialog box
(Windows
98).

6. **Select the type of network logon you want.**

   You have two choices:

   • Quick Logon, which logs you on to the domain but doesn't attempt to reconnect any mapped network drives.

   • Logon And Restore Network Connections, which attempts to reconnect to all mapped network drives when you log on. This option results in a slower logon, but all network drives are immediately available after the logon completes.

7. **Click OK.**

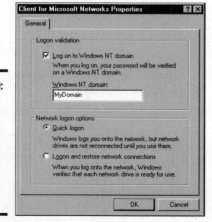

Figure 4-10:
The Client
for
Microsoft
Networks
Properties
dialog box
(Windows
98).

The next time you restart the computer, the Enter Network Password dialog box appears, as shown in Figure 4-11. Here, the user can enter a user name, password, and domain to log on to the network.

Figure 4-11:
The Enter
Network
Password
dialog box
(Windows
98).

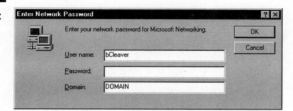

Chapter 5: Configuring Other Network Features

In This Chapter

✔ Setting up network printers

✔ Configuring your client computer's Internet connections

✔ Mapping network drives

*A*fter you have your network servers and clients up and running, you still have many details to attend to before you can pronounce your network "finished." In this chapter, you discover a few more configuration chores that have to be done: configuring Internet access, setting up network printers, configuring e-mail, and configuring mapped network drives.

Configuring Network Printers

Before network users can print on the network, the network's printers must be properly configured. For the most part, this is a simple task. All you have to do is configure each client that needs access to the printer.

Before you configure a network printer to work with network clients, read the client configuration section of the manual that came with the printer. Many printers come with special software that provides more advanced printing and networking features than the standard features provided by Windows. If so, you may want to install the printer manufacturer's software on your client computers rather than use the standard Windows network printer support.

Adding a network printer

The exact procedure for adding a network printer varies a bit, depending on the Windows version that the client runs. The following steps describe the procedure for Windows XP Professional:

1. **Choose Start➪Printers And Faxes.**

   The Printers And Faxes folder opens.

2. **Click Add A Printer in the task pane.**

   The Welcome page of the Add Printer Wizard appears.

3. **Click Next.**

   The wizard asks whether you want to set up a local printer or a network printer.

4. **Check A Network Printer and then click Next.**

   This brings up the page shown in Figure 5-1, which provides you with three ways to identify the printer you want to set up:

   - Browse for a printer. This option displays a list of all the printers that are available on the network.

   - Specify the server's name and the name of the printer; for example, \\MyServer\Printer1. This option is best if the printer is connected to a server and you know the name of the server and the printer.

   - Specify the URL of the printer, using a host name such as http://printer1.MyDomain.com or an IP address such as http://207.126.67.155. This option is best if the printer is connected directly to the network.

   If you don't know the host name or IP address, you can usually find out by printing a configuration page at the printer. You can usually print a configuration page by pressing or holding down one or more front panel keys in a certain way or by selecting a front-panel menu command. You'll have to consult the printer's documentation to find out how to print the configuration page for your printer.

5. **If you know the printer name or URL, select the appropriate option and enter the name or URL. Otherwise, select Browse For A Printer. Then click Next.**

   Assuming that you opted to browse for the printer, a list of available printers appears, as shown in Figure 5-2.

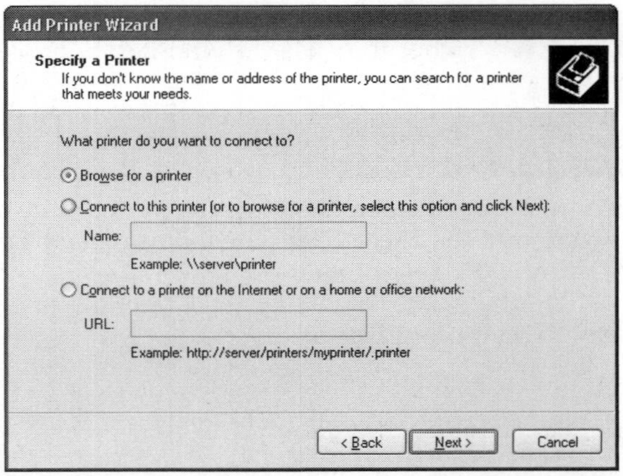

Add Printer Wizard

Specify a Printer
If you don't know the name or address of the printer, you can search for a printer that meets your needs.

What printer do you want to connect to?

◉ Browse for a printer

○ Connect to this printer (or to browse for a printer, select this option and click Next):

Name: [   ]

Example: \\server\printer

○ Connect to a printer on the Internet or on a home or office network:

URL: [   ]

Example: http://server/printers/myprinter/.printer

[< Back] [Next >] [Cancel]

Figure 5-1:
Three ways
to identify
the printer.

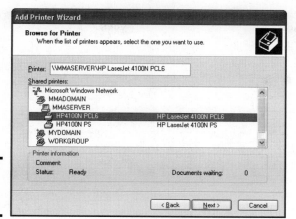

Figure 5-2:
Browsing
for a printer.

6. **Select the printer that you want to use and then click Next.**

   The next page of the wizard asks whether you want to specify the
   printer as the user's default printer.

7. **Choose Yes or No to indicate whether you want to designate the
   printer as the default printer and then click Next.**

   The wizard's final page appears, summarizing the settings you've
   chosen.

8. **Click Finish to complete the wizard and install the printer.**

   You may be asked to insert a Windows CD-ROM or the driver disk that
   came with the printer. In many cases, however, the wizard will be able to
   locate the correct printer drivers on the server computer to which the
   printer is attached.

Accessing a network printer using a Web interface

Printers that have a direct network connection often include a built-in Web
server that lets you manage the printer from any browser on the network.
For example, Figure 5-3 shows the home page for a Hewlett-Packard LaserJet
4100 Series printer. This Web interface lets you view status information
about the printer and check the printer's configuration. You can even view
error logs to find out how often the printer jams.

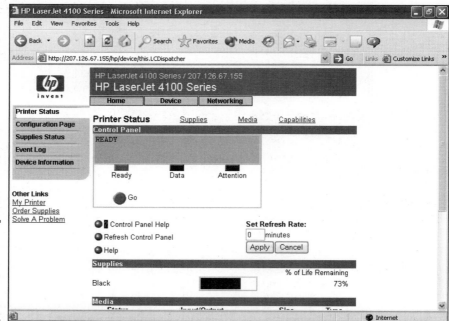

Figure 5-3:
The
browser
interface for
an HP 4100
printer.

To call up a printer's Web interface, enter its IP address or host name in the address bar of any Web browser.

In addition to simply displaying information about the printer, you can also adjust the printer's configuration from a Web browser. For example, Figure 5-4 shows the Network Settings page for an HP 4100 printer. Here, you can change the network configuration details, such as the TCP/IP hostname, IP address, subnet mask, domain name, and so on. Other configuration pages allow you to tell the printer to send an e-mail notification to an address that you specify whenever you encounter a problem with the printer.

As the network administrator, you may need to visit the printer's Web page frequently. I suggest that you add it to your browser's Favorites menu so that you can get to it easily. If you have several printers, add them under a folder named Network Printers.

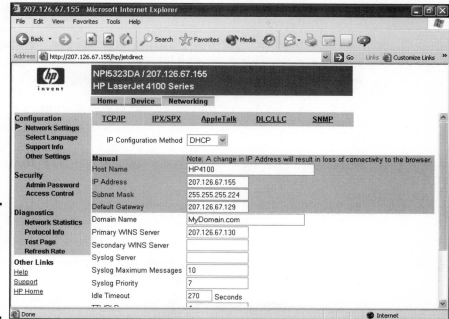

Figure 5-4:
The Network Settings page for an HP 4100 printer.

Configuring Internet Access

To enable the network users to access the Internet, you need to make sure that the TCP/IP configuration settings on each client computer are set correctly. If you have a high-speed Internet connection, such as T1, DSL, cable, or ISDN, connected to the Internet via a router, and your network uses DHCP for automatic TCP/IP configuration, you may not need to do anything special to get your clients connected to the Internet.

Configuring clients for DHCP

The easiest way to configure client computers to access the Internet via a shared high-speed connection is to use DHCP. DHCP automatically distributes the detailed TCP/IP configuration information to each client. Then, if your configuration changes, all you have to do is change the DHCP server's configuration. You don't have to manually change each client. Plus, the DHCP server avoids common manual configuration errors, such as assigning the same IP address to two computers.

Before you configure the clients to use DHCP, you should first set up the DHCP server. The DHCP server's configuration should include

✦ A scope that specifies the range of IP addresses and the subnet mask to be distributed to client computers.

✦ The IP address of the router that should be used as the default gateway for client computers to reach the Internet.

✦ The IP addresses of the DNS servers that clients should use.

Note that DCHP can be provided by a server computer or by an intelligent router that has built-in DHCP. For more information about configuring DHCP, see Book V, Chapter 3.

After the DHCP server is configured, setting up Windows clients to use it is a snap. Just follow these steps:

1. **Open the Control Panel and double-click the Network Connections icon.**

2. **Right-click the LAN connection icon and choose Properties.**

This brings up the connection Properties dialog box, as shown in Figure 5-5.

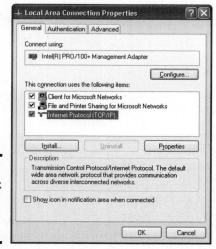

Figure 5-5:
The network connection Properties dialog box.

3. **Select Internet Protocol (TCP/IP) from the list of items used by the connection and then click Properties.**

This displays the Internet Protocol (TCP/IP) Properties dialog box, as shown in Figure 5-6.

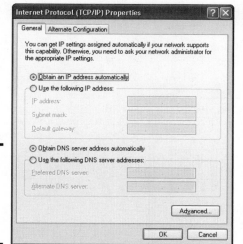

Figure 5-6:
Making
sure that
TCP/IP is
configured
for DHCP.

4. **Make sure that both the Obtain An IP Address Automatically and Obtain DNS Server Address Automatically options are selected.**

   These options enable DHCP for the client.

5. **Click OK to return to the network connection Properties dialog box and then click OK again.**

That's all there is to it. The computer is now configured to use DHCP. You should check to make sure that every computer on your network is configured for DHCP.

If your network doesn't have a DHCP server, you'll have to configure the TCP/IP configuration manually for each computer. Start by deciding the IP address that you want to assign to each computer. Then, follow the preceding procedure on every computer. When you get to Step 4, enter the computer's IP address as well as the IP address of the default gateway (your Internet router) and the IP addresses of your DNS servers.

Frankly, setting up a DHCP server is a lot easier than manually configuring each computer's TCP/IP information unless your network has only two or three computers. So unless your network is tiny, get a DHCP server.

Disabling dialup connections

If your client computers were previously configured to use dialup connections to access the Internet, you need to disable those connections so that the computer will access the Internet via your LAN connection. If you use Internet Explorer as your Web browser, follow these steps:

1. **Open the Control Panel, double-click the Internet Options icon, and then click the Connections tab.**

The connection options appear, as shown in Figure 5-7.

Figure 5-7:
The
Connections
tab of the
Internet
Options
dialog box.

2. **Choose the Never Dial A Connection option.**

The Never Dial A Connection option tells Windows to not automatically call the dialup connection to connect to the Internet. That way, Windows will use the LAN connection to reach the Internet.

If for some reason the network is down, the user can still call the dialup connection by opening the Network Connections folder, right-clicking the dialup connection, and choosing Connect.

If you prefer, you can choose the Dial Whenever a Network Connection Is Not Present option. When you select this option, Windows first tries to use an existing LAN connection to reach the Internet. If the LAN connection is not working, it automatically calls the dialup connection instead.

3. **Click OK to dismiss the Internet Options dialog box.**

If you have replaced your old dialup Internet connections with a faster shared LAN connection, you may want to remove the dialup connection altogether. To do so, call up the Internet Options dialog box, click the Connections tab, select the dialup connection that you want to delete, and click Remove.

Using Internet Connection Sharing

Actually, the title of this section is misleading. It should be "*Not* Using Internet Connection Sharing." Windows 2000 and XP come with a built-in feature called *Internet Connection Sharing (ICS)*, designed to let you share an Internet connection with several computers on a small network. However, this feature is designed to be used only on very small networks that don't have a separate router to enable the connection to be shared.

In Windows XP, ICS has a companion feature called the *Internet Connection Firewall* that provides basic firewall support for home networks. This feature keeps hackers from invading your home network.

I recommend that you use ICS and the firewall only for home networks with no more than three computers. Even then, you're better off purchasing an inexpensive connection sharing device. For more information, refer to Book VI, Chapter 4.

If ICS has been enabled and you don't need it, you should disable it. Otherwise, it will disrupt your network. To disable ICS, follow these steps:

1. **Open the Control Panel and double-click the Network Connections icon.**

This opens the Network Connections folder.

2. **Right-click the LAN connection, choose Properties, and then click Advanced.**

This reveals the Internet Connection Firewall and Internet Connection Sharing options, as shown in Figure 5-8.

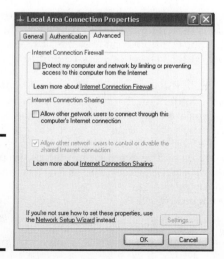

Figure 5-8:
The Advanced tab of the connection Properties dialog box.

3. **Uncheck all the options on this dialog box.**

Specifically, make sure that the Internet Connection Firewall is disabled by unchecking the Protect My Computer option and make sure that Internet Connection Sharing is disabled by unchecking the Allow Other Network Users option.

4. **Click OK and then close the Network Connections folder.**

You're done! Internet Connection Sharing and the Internet Connection Firewall are now disabled.

Mapping Network Drives

One of the main reasons that users want to use a network is to access shared disk storage located on network file servers. Although you can do this in several ways, the most common method is called *mapping*. Mapping assigns a drive letter to a shared folder on a network server. Then, the user can use the drive letter to access the shared folder as if it were a local drive.

Before you map network drives for your network's client computers, you should devise a strategy for how you'll share folders and map them to drives. Here are just two possibilities:

✦ For private storage, you can create a separate shared folder for each user on the file server and then map a drive letter on each user's computer to that user's shared folder. For example, you can create shares named jBrannan, dHodgson, and mCaldwell. Then, you can map Drive N to jBrannan on jBrannan's computer, dHodgson on dHodgson's computer, and mCaldwell on mCaldwell's computer.

✦ For shared storage for an entire department, you can create a share for the entire department and then map a drive to that share on each computer in the department. For example, you may map Drive M to a share named Marketing for the entire Marketing department to use.

After you've decided how to map the file server's shared folder, the next step is to create and share the folders on the server. For information about how to do that, refer to appropriate chapters on specific network operating systems later in this book.

When you're ready to map drives on the client computers, follow these steps:

1. **Open the My Computer window.**

2. **Choose Tool⇨Map Network Drive.**

The Map Network Drive dialog box appears, as shown in Figure 5-9.

Figure 5-9:
The Map
Network
Drive dialog
box.

3. **Select the drive letter that you want to map in the Drive drop-down list.**

4. **Type a valid path to the server and share that you want to map in the Folder text box.**

   For example, to map a folder named mCaldwell on a server named MKT-SERVER, type **\\MKTSERVER\mCaldwell**.

   If you don't know the server or share name, click the Browse button and browse your way to the folder that you want to map.

5. **To cause the network drive to be automatically mapped each time the user logs on, check the Reconnect At Logon option.**

   If you leave this option unchecked, the drive is mapped only until the next time you shut Windows down or log off.

6. **Click OK.**

   That's it! You're done.

If you're the type who prefers to do things through the command line, you can quickly map network drives by using the NET USE command at a command prompt. For example, here's a NET USE command that maps Drive M to \\MKTSERVER\mCaldwell:

```
net use m: \\MKTSERVER\mCaldwell /persistent:yes
```

Specifying /persistent:yes causes the drive to be remapped each time the user logs on. To remove a drive mapping via the command line, use a command like this:

```
net use m: /delete
```

Here, the mapping for Drive M is removed.

Manually setting up drive mappings as described here works well enough for small networks but not so well for large networks. If a server or share name changes, would you want to go to 200 computers in order to update drive mappings? How about 2,000 computers? For larger networks, you're more likely to use either login scripts or group policies to configure network storage for end users. You can find more information about login scripts and group policies in Book III, Chapter 2.

Chapter 6: Verifying Your Network Installation

In This Chapter

✔ Checking the network configuration settings

✔ Pinging yourself and others

✔ Making sure that you can log on

✔ Verifying mapped drives and checking network printers

You've installed all the network cards, plugged in all the cables, and configured all the software. However, one task remains before you can declare your network finished: You must verify that the network works as expected.

Verifying a network is not difficult. All you have to do is make sure that users can log on and access the network resources they need. If everything works the way it should, you can declare victory, give yourself a high five, and take the afternoon off. If not, you have to do some troubleshooting to determine the source of the problem.

In this short chapter, I describe some of the tests that you should perform to make sure that your network is functioning. Along the way, I suggest a few of the most common problems that may interrupt the network. However, the focus of this chapter is on verifying that your network is functioning — not on troubleshooting it if it isn't. For information about network troubleshooting, refer to Book IV.

Incidentally, most of the techniques described in this chapter work from an MS-DOS command prompt. You can open a command prompt by choosing Start⇨Run, typing **Command** as the name of the program to run, and then clicking OK.

Is the Computer Connected to the Network?

This one is easy to check. Just check the Link light on the computer's network interface card and the light on the network hub or switch port that the computer is connected to. If both are lit, the computer is connected to the network. If one or both are not lit, you have a connection problem. Several things may be wrong:

✦ The patch cable that connects the computer to the wall outlet or that connects to the hub or switch may be bad. Replace it with one that you know is good in order to verify this problem.

✦ The cable run between the wall outlet and the patch panel may be bad. The cable may be physically broken, or it may be routed right next to a 20,000-watt generator or an elevator motor.

✦ The computer's NIC may be bad or configured incorrectly. Check the configuration settings. If necessary, replace the card.

✦ The hub or switch may be bad.

Is the Network Configuration Working?

You can run three commands from a command window to verify the basic configuration of each computer. These commands are Net Config Workstation, Net Config Server, and Ipconfig.

The Net Config Workstation command displays basic information about the computer's network configuration. Here's a sample of the output it displays:

```
C:>net config workstation
Computer name                        \\DOUG
Full Computer name                   doug
User name                            Doug Lowe

Workstation active on
        NetbiosSmb (000000000000)
        NetBT_Tcpip_{FC6D2F39-FDDD-448E-9B3C-0C12847F2B61}
   (0050BA843911)

Software version                     Windows 2002

Workstation domain                   WORKGROUP
Workstation Domain DNS Name          (null)
Logon domain                         DOUG

COM Open Timeout (sec)               0
COM Send Count (byte)                16
COM Send Timeout (msec)              250
The command completed successfully.
```

The most important information to check in the Net Config Workstation command's output is the computer name and domain information.

If the computer is configured to enabled File and Print Sharing, you can also run net config server to display basic information about the server configuration. Here's a sample of its output:

```
C:>net config server
Server Name                       \\DOUG
Server Comment

Software version                  Windows 2002
Server is active on
      NetbiosSmb (000000000000)
      NetBT_Tcpip_{FB6D2F79-FDDF-418E-9B7C-0C82887F2A61}
  (0050ba843911)


Server hidden                     No
Maximum Logged On Users           5
Maximum open files per session    16384

Idle session time (min)           15
The command completed successfully.
```

The Ipconfig command displays information about the computer's TCP/IP
configuration. If you type ipconfig by itself, the computer's IP address,
subnet mask, and default gateway are displayed. If you type ipconfig
/all, you see more detailed information. Here's typical output from the
Ipconfig /All command:

```
C:>ipconfig /all
Windows IP Configuration

        Host Name . . . . . . . . . . . . . : doug
        Primary Dns Suffix  . . . . . . . :
        Node Type . . . . . . . . . . . . : Unknown
        IP Routing Enabled. . . . . . . . : No
        WINS Proxy Enabled. . . . . . . . : No

Ethernet adapter Local Area Connection:

        Connection-specific DNS Suffix  . :
    we1.client2.attbi.com
        Description . . . . . . . . . . . : D-Link DFE-530TX+
    PCI Adapter
        Physical Address. . . . . . . . . : 00-50-BA-84-39-11
        Dhcp Enabled. . . . . . . . . . . : Yes
        Autoconfiguration Enabled . . . . : Yes
        IP Address. . . . . . . . . . . . : 192.168.1.100
        Subnet Mask . . . . . . . . . . . : 255.255.255.0
        Default Gateway . . . . . . . . . : 192.168.1.1
        DHCP Server . . . . . . . . . . . : 192.168.1.1
        DNS Servers . . . . . . . . . . . : 204.127.198.19
                                            63.240.76.19
        Lease Obtained. . . . . . . . . . : Saturday, May 24,
    2003 6:28:49 PM
        Lease Expires . . . . . . . . . . : Sunday, May 25,
    2003 6:28:49 PM
```

The most important information to glean from this output is the computer's IP address. You should also verify that the default gateway matches the IP address of your Internet router, and that the IP address for the DHCP and DNS servers is correct.

Can the Computers Ping Each Other?

A basic test that you should perform to ensure that your network is functioning is to use the Ping command from a command prompt to make sure that the computers on the network can contact each other. The Ping command simply sends a packet to another computer and requests that the second computer send a packet back in reply. If the reply packet is received, Ping displays a message indicating how long it took to hear from the other computer. If the reply packet is not received, Ping displays an error message indicating that the computer could not be reached.

You should try several Ping tests. First, you can make sure that TCP/IP is up and running by having the computer try to ping itself. Open a command prompt and type **ping 127.0.0.1** (127.0.0.1 is the standard loop-back address that a computer can use to refer to itself). If you prefer, you can also type **ping localhost**.

Next, have the computer ping itself by using the IP address displayed by the Ipconfig command. For example, if Ipconfig says the computer's IP address is 192.168.0.100, type **ping 192.168.0.100** at the command prompt.

Now try to ping your servers. You'll have to run Ipconfig at each of the servers to determine their IP addresses. Or, you can just ping the computer's name.

A final test is to make sure that you can ping the workstation from other computers on the network. You don't have to try to ping every computer from every other computer on the network unless you've determined that you have a connectivity problem that you need to pinpoint. However, you should try to ping each workstation from each of the servers, just to make sure the servers can see the workstations. Make a list of the IP addresses of the workstations as you test them and then take that list to the servers and ping each IP address on the list.

Can You Log On?

After you've established that the basic network connections are working, the next step is to verify that network login works. This is as simple as attempting to log in from each computer by using the correct user account for the computer. If you can't log in, several things may be causing the problem. Here are the most common:

✦ You may not have the right user account information. Double-check the user name, password, and domain.

✦ Make sure that the domain name is correct.

✦ Passwords are case-sensitive. Make sure that you type the password correctly and that the Caps Lock key is not on.

✦ You may not have a computer account for the computer. Double-check the computer name and make sure that you have a valid computer account on the server.

✦ Double-check the user account policies to make sure that there isn't something that would prevent the user from logging in, such as a time of day restriction.

Are Network Drives Mapped Correctly?

After you know the user can log on, you should make sure that mapped network drives are available. To do so, type **net use** at a command prompt. You'll see a list of all the network mappings. For example:

```
C:>net use
New connections will be remembered.

Status  Local  Remote          Network

-------------------------------------------------------------
OK      M:     \\Doug\Prod      Microsoft Windows Network
OK      X:     \\Doug\admin     Microsoft Windows Network
OK      Z:     \\Doug\Marketing Microsoft Windows Network
The command completed successfully.
```

Here, you can see that three drives are mapped, and you can tell the server and share name for each mapped drive.

Next, try to display a directory list of each drive to make sure that you can actually reach it. For example, type **dir m:**. If everything is working, you see a directory of the shared folder you've mapped to Drive M.

Do Network Printers Work?

The final test I describe in this chapter is making sure that your network printers work. The easiest way to do this is to print a short document to the network printer and make sure that the document prints. I suggest that you open Notepad (Start⇨Accessories⇨NotePad), type a few words (like "Yo, Adrianne!"), and then choose File⇨Print to bring up the Print dialog box. Select the network printer and click OK.

If the network printer doesn't appear in the list of available printers, go to the Printers and Faxes folder and recheck the network printer. You may have incorrectly configured the printer. If the configuration looks okay, go to the printer itself and make sure that it is turned on and ready to print.

Book III

Network Administration and Security

The 5th Wave   By Rich Tennant

"We take network security very seriously here."

Contents at a Glance

Chapter 1: Help Wanted: Job Description for a Network Administrator

In This Chapter

- ✓ Deciphering the many jobs of the network administrator
- ✓ Documenting the network
- ✓ Dusting, vacuuming, and mopping
- ✓ Managing the network users
- ✓ Choosing the right tools
- ✓ Getting certified

*H*elp wanted. Network administrator to help small business get control of a network run amok. Must have sound organizational and management skills. Only moderate computer experience required. Part-time only.

Does this ad sound like one that your company should run? Every network needs a network administrator, whether the network has 2 computers or 200. Of course, managing a 200-computer network is a full-time job, whereas managing a 2-computer network isn't. At least, it shouldn't be.

This chapter introduces you to the boring job of network administration. Oops . . . you're probably reading this chapter because you've been elected to be the network manager, so I'd better rephrase that: This chapter introduces you to the wonderful, exciting world of network management! Oh, boy! This is going to be fun!

Figuring Out What Network Administrators Do

Simply put, network administrators administer networks, which means that they take care of the tasks of installing, configuring, expanding, protecting, upgrading, tuning, and repairing the network. Network administrators take care of the network hardware, such as cables, hubs, switches, routers, servers, and clients, as well as network software, such as network operating systems, e-mail servers, backup software, database servers, and application software. Most importantly, network administrators take care of network users by answering their questions, listening to their troubles, and solving their problems.

On a big network, these responsibilities constitute a full-time job. Large networks tend to be volatile: Users come and go, equipment fails, cables break, and life in general seems to be one crisis after another.

Smaller networks are much more stable. After you get your network up and running, you probably won't have to spend much time managing its hardware and software. An occasional problem may pop up, but with only a few computers on the network, problems should be few and far between.

Regardless of the network's size, all network administrators must attend to several common chores:

✦ The network administrator should be involved in every decision to purchase new computers, printers, or other equipment. In particular, the network administrator should be prepared to lobby for the most network-friendly equipment possible, such as new computers that already have network cards installed and configured and printers that are network-ready.

✦ The network administrator must put on the pocket protector whenever a new computer is added to the network. The network administrator's job includes considering what changes to make to the cabling configuration, what computer name to assign to the new computer, how to integrate the new user into the security system, what rights to grant the user, and so on.

✦ Every once in a while, your trusty operating system vendor (in other words, Microsoft and Novell) releases a new version of your network operating system. The network administrator must read about the new version and decide whether its new features are beneficial enough to warrant an upgrade. In most cases, the hardest part of upgrading to a new version of your network operating system is determining the *migration path* — that is, how to upgrade your entire network to the new version while disrupting the network or its users as little as possible. Upgrading to a new network operating system version is a major chore, so you need to carefully consider the advantages that the new version can bring.

✦ Between upgrades, Microsoft and Novell have a nasty habit of releasing patches and service packs that fix minor problems with their server operating systems. For more information, see the section "Patching Things Up," later in this chapter.

✦ One of the easiest traps that you can get sucked into is the quest for network speed. The network is never fast enough, and users always blame the hapless network manager. So the administrator spends hours and hours tuning and tweaking the network to squeeze out that last

2 percent of performance. You don't want to get caught in this trap, but in case you do, Book IV, Chapter 2 can help. It clues you in to the basics of tuning your network for best performance.

✦ Network administrators perform routine chores, such as backing up the servers, archiving old data, freeing up server hard drive space, and so on. Much of network administration is making sure that things keep working and finding and correcting problems before any users notice that something is wrong. In this sense, network administration can be a thankless job.

✦ Network administrators are also responsible for gathering, organizing, and tracking the entire network's software inventory. You never know when something is going to go haywire on Joe in Marketing's ancient Windows 95 computer and you're going to have to reinstall that old copy of Lotus Approach. Do you have any idea where the installation disks are?

Choosing the Part-Time Administrator

The larger the network, the more technical support it needs. Most small networks — with just a dozen or two computers — can get by with a part-time network administrator. Ideally, this person should be a closet computer geek: someone who has a secret interest in computers but doesn't like to admit it. Someone who will take books home with him or her and read them over the weekend. Someone who enjoys solving computer problems just for the sake of solving them.

The job of managing a network requires some computer skills, but it isn't entirely a technical job. Much of the work that the network administrator does is routine housework. Basically, the network administrator dusts, vacuums, and mops the network periodically to keep it from becoming a mess.

Here are some additional ideas on picking a part-time network administrator:

✦ The network administrator needs to be an organized person. Conduct a surprise office inspection and place the person with the neatest desk in charge of the network. (Don't warn them in advance, or everyone may mess up their desks intentionally the night before the inspection.)

✦ Allow enough time for network administration. For a small network (say, no more than 20 or so computers), an hour or two each week is enough. More time is needed upfront as the network administrator settles into the job and discovers the ins and outs of the network. After an initial settling-in period, though, network administration for a small office network doesn't take more than an hour or two per week. (Of course, larger networks take more time to manage.)

✦ Make sure that everyone knows who the network administrator is and that the network administrator has the authority to make decisions about the network, such as what access rights each user has, what files can and can't be stored on the server, how often backups are done, and so on.

✦ Pick someone who is assertive and willing to irritate people. A good network administrator should make sure that backups are working *before* a hard drive fails and make sure that everyone is following good anti-virus practices *before* a virus wipes out the entire network. This policing will irritate people, but it's for their own good.

✦ In most cases, the person who installs the network is also the network administrator. This is appropriate because no one understands the network better than the person who designs and installs it.

✦ The network administrator needs an understudy — someone who knows almost as much about the network, is eager to make a mark, and smiles when the worst network jobs are "delegated."

✦ The network manager has some sort of official title, such as Network Boss, Network Czar, Vice President in Charge of Network Operations, or Dr. Network. A badge, a personalized pocket protector, or a set of Spock ears helps, too.

Documenting the Network

One of the network administrator's main jobs is to keep the network documentation up-to-date. I suggest that you keep all the important information about your network in a three-ring binder. Give this binder a clever name, such as *The Network Bible* or *My Network and Welcome to It.* Here are some things that it should include:

✦ **An up-to-date diagram of the network.** This diagram can be a detailed floor plan, showing the actual location of each computer, or something more abstract and Picasso-like. Any time that you change the network layout, update the diagram. Also include a detailed description of the change, the date that the change was made, and the reason for the change.

Microsoft sells a program called *Visio* that is specially designed for creating network diagrams. I highly recommend it.

✦ **A detailed inventory of your computer equipment.** Table 1-1 provides a sample checklist that you can use to keep track of your computer equipment.

Table 1-1	Computer Equipment Checklist
Computer location:	
User:	
Manufacturer:	
Model number:	
Serial number:	
Date purchased:	
CPU type and speed:	
Memory:	
Hard drive size:	
Video type:	
Printer type:	
Other equipment:	
Operating system version:	
Application software & version:	
Network card type:	
MAC address:	

✦ A System Information printout from System Information for each computer. (Choose Start⇨All Programs⇨Accessories⇨System Tools⇨System Information.)

✦ A detailed list of network resources and drive assignments.

✦ Any other information that you think may be useful, such as details about how you must configure a particular application program to work with the network and copies of every network component's original invoice — just in case something breaks and you need to seek warranty service.

✦ Backup schedules.

✦ No passwords in the binder!

You may want to keep track of the information in your network binder by using a spreadsheet or a database program. However, make sure that you keep a printed copy of the information on hand.

If your network is large, you may want to invest in a *network discovery* program that can gather the network documentation automatically. This software scans the network carefully, looking for every computer, printer, router, and other device it can find and builds a database of information. It then automatically draws a pretty diagram and chugs out helpful reports.

Completing Routine Chores

Much of the network manager's job is routine stuff — the equivalent of vacuuming, dusting, and mopping. Or, if you prefer, changing the oil and rotating the tires every 3,000 miles. Yes, it's boring, but it has to be done.

✦ The network manager needs to make sure that the network is properly backed up. If something goes wrong and the network isn't backed up, guess who gets the blame? On the other hand, if disaster strikes, yet you're able to recover everything from yesterday's backup with only a small amount of work lost, guess who gets the pat on the back, the fat bonus, and the vacation in the Bahamas? Book IV, Chapter 3 describes the options for network backups. You'd better read it soon.

✦ Another major task for network administrators is sheltering your network from the evils of the outside world. These evils come in many forms, including hackers trying to break into your network and virus programs arriving through e-mail. Book III, Chapter 4 describes this task in more detail.

✦ Users think that the network server is like the attic: They want to throw files up there and leave them forever. No matter how much storage your network has, your users will fill it up sooner than you think. So the network manager gets the fun job of cleaning up the attic once in a while. Oh, joy. The best advice I can offer is to constantly complain about how messy it is up there and warn your users that spring-cleaning is coming up.

Managing Network Users

Managing network technology is the easiest part of network management. Computer technology can be confusing at first, but computers aren't nearly as confusing as people. The real challenge of managing a network is managing the network's users.

The difference between managing technology and managing users is obvious: You can figure out computers, but you can never really figure out people. The people who use the network are much less predictable than the network itself. Here are some tips for dealing with users:

✦ Training is a key part of the network manager's job. Make sure that everyone who uses the network understands it and knows how to use it. If the network users don't understand the network, they may unintentionally do all kinds of weird things to it.

✦ Never treat your network users like they are idiots. If they don't understand the network, it's not their fault. Explain it to them. Offer a class.

Buy them each a copy of *Networking All-in-One Desk Reference For Dummies* and tell them to read it during their lunch hour. Hold their hands. But don't treat them like idiots.

✦ Make up a network cheat sheet that contains everything that the users need to know about using the network on one page. Make sure that everyone gets a copy.

✦ Be as responsive as possible when a network user complains of a network problem. If you don't fix the problem soon, the user may try to fix it. You probably don't want that.

✦ The better you understand the psychology of network users, the more prepared you'll be for the strangeness they often serve up. Toward that end, I recommend that you read the *Diagnostic and Statistical Manual of Mental Disorders* (also known as *DSM-IV*) cover to cover.

Patching Things Up

One of the annoyances that every network manager faces is applying software patches to keep your operating system and other software up-to-date. A software *patch* is a minor update that fixes small glitches that crop up from time to time, such as minor security or performance issues. These glitches aren't significant enough to merit a new version of the software, but they are important enough to require fixing. Most of the patches correct security flaws that computer hackers have uncovered in their relentless attempts to prove that they are smarter than the security programmers at Microsoft or Novell.

Periodically, all the recently released patches are combined into a *service pack*. Although the most diligent network administrators apply all patches as they're released, many administrators just wait for the service packs.

For all versions of Windows, you can use the Windows Update Web site to apply patches to keep your operating system and other Microsoft software up-to-date. You can find Windows Update in the Start menu. If all else fails, just fire up Internet Explorer and go to windowsupdate.microsoft.com. Windows Update automatically scans your computer's software and creates a list of software patches and other components that you can download and install. You can also configure Windows Update to automatically notify you of updates so that you don't have to remember to check for new patches.

Novell periodically posts patches and updates to NetWare on its product support Web site (support.novell.com). You can subscribe to an e-mail notification service that automatically e-mails you to let you know of new patches and updates.

Discovering Software Tools for Network Administrators

Network managers need certain tools to get their jobs done. Managers of big, complicated, and expensive networks need big, complicated, and expensive tools. Managers of small networks need small tools.

Some of the tools that the manager needs are hardware tools, such as screwdrivers, cable crimpers, and hammers. The tools that I'm talking about here, however, are software tools. I've already mentioned a couple: Visio to help you draw network diagrams and a network discovery tool to help you map your network. Here are a few others:

✦ Many of the software tools that you need to manage a network come with the network itself. As the network manager, you should read through the manuals that come with your network software to see what management tools are available. For example, Windows includes a `net diag` command that you can use to make sure that all the computers on a network can communicate with each other. (You can run `net diag` from an MS-DOS prompt.) For TCP/IP networks, you can use the TCP/IP diagnostic commands summarized in Table 1-2. For more information about these commands, refer to Book V, Chapter 5.

Table 1-2	TCP/IP Diagnostic Commands
Command	*What It Does*
arp	Displays address resolution information used by the Address Resolution Protocol (ARP).
hostname	Displays your computer's host name.
ipconfig	Displays current TCP/IP settings.
nbtstat	Displays the status of NetBIOS over TCP/IP connections.
netstat	Displays statistics for TCP/IP.
nslookup	Displays DNS information.
ping	Verifies that a specified computer can be reached.
route	Displays the PC's routing tables.
tracert	Displays the route from your computer to a specified host.

✦ The System Information program that comes with Windows is a useful utility for network managers.

✦ Another handy tool available from Microsoft is the Hotfix Checker, which scans your computers to see what patches need to be applied. You can download the Hotfix Checker free of charge from Microsoft's Web site. Just go to `www.microsoft.com` and search for `hfnetchk.exe`.

✦ If you prefer GUI-based tools, check out Microsoft Baseline Security Analyzer. You can download it from Microsoft's Web site free of charge. To find it, go to `www.microsoft.com` and search for `Microsoft Baseline Security Analyzer`.

✦ I suggest that you get one of those 100-in-1 utility programs, such as Symantec's Norton Utilities. Norton Utilities includes invaluable utilities for repairing damaged hard drives, rearranging the directory structure of your hard drive, gathering information about your computer and its equipment, and so on.

Never use a hard drive repair program that was not designed to work with the operating system or version that your computer uses or the file system you've installed. Any time that you upgrade to a newer version of your operating system, you should also upgrade your hard drive repair programs to a version that supports the new operating system version.

✦ A *protocol analyzer* is a program that's designed to monitor and log the individual packets that travel along your network. (Protocol analyzers are also called *packet sniffers.*) You can configure the protocol analyzer to filter specific types of packets, watch for specific types of problems, and provide statistical analysis of the captured packets. Most network administrators agree that *Sniffer,* by Sniffer Technologies (`www.sniffer.com`) is the best protocol analyzer available. However, it's also one of the most expensive. If you prefer a free alternative, check out *Ethereal,* which you can download free from `www.ethereal.com`.

✦ Windows 2000 and XP, as well as Windows 2000 Server and Windows Server 2003, include a program called *Network Monitor* that provides basic protocol analysis and can often help solve pesky network problems.

Building a Library

One of Scotty's best lines in the original *Star Trek* series was when he refused to take shore leave, so he could get caught up on his technical journals. "Don't you ever relax?" asked Kirk. "I am relaxing!" Scotty replied.

To be a good network administrator, you need to read computer books. Lots of them. And you need to enjoy doing it. If you're the type who takes computer books with you to the beach, you'll make a great network administrator.

You need books on a variety of topics. I'm not going to recommend specific titles, but I do recommend that you get a good, comprehensive book on each of the following topics:

- ✦ Network cabling and hardware
- ✦ Ethernet
- ✦ Windows NT 4
- ✦ Windows 2000 Server
- ✦ Windows Server 2003
- ✦ NetWare 6
- ✦ Linux
- ✦ TCP/IP
- ✦ DNS and BIND
- ✦ SendMail
- ✦ Exchange Server
- ✦ Security and hacking
- ✦ Wireless networking

In addition to books, you may also want to subscribe to some magazines to keep up with what's happening in the networking industry. Here are a few you should probably consider, along with their Web addresses:

- ✦ *InformationWeek:* www.informationweek.com
- ✦ *InfoWorld:* www.infoworld.com
- ✦ *Network Computing:* www.networkcomputing.com
- ✦ *Network Magazine:* www.networkmagazine.com
- ✦ *Windows & .NET Magazine:* www.winntmag.com
- ✦ *2600 Magazine:* www.2600.com (a great magazine on computer hacking and security)

 The Internet is one of the best sources of technical information for network administrators. You'll want to stock your browser's Favorites menu with plenty of Web sites that contain useful networking information. In addition, you may want to subscribe to one of the many online newsletters that deliver fresh information on a regular basis via e-mail. You can find a list of my favorite picks in Appendix A.

Certification

Remember the scene near the end of *The Wizard of Oz,* when the Wizard grants the Scarecrow a diploma, the Cowardly Lion a medal, and the Tin Man a testimonial?

Network certifications are kind of like that. I can picture the scene now:

The Wizard: "And as for you, my network-burdened friend, any geek with thick glasses can administer a network. Back where I come from, there are people who do nothing but configure Cisco routers all day long. And they don't have any more brains than you do. But they do have one thing you don't have: certification. And so, by the authority vested in me by the Universita Committeeatum E Pluribus Unum, I hereby confer upon you the coveted certification of CND."

You: "CND?"

The Wizard: "Yes, that's, uh, *Certified Network Dummy.*"

You: "The Seven Layers of the OSI Reference Model are equal to the Sum of the Layers on the Opposite Side. Oh, rapture! I feel like a network administrator already!"

My point is that certification in and of itself doesn't guarantee that you really know how to administer a network. That ability comes from real-world experience — not exam crams.

Nevertheless, certification is becoming increasingly important in today's competitive job market. So you may want to pursue certification — not just to improve your skills, but also to improve your resume. Certification is an expensive proposition. Each test can cost several hundred dollars, and depending on your technical skills, you may need to buy books to study or enroll in training courses before you take the tests.

You can pursue two basic types of certification: vendor-specific certification and vendor-neutral certification. The major networking vendors such as Microsoft, Novell, and Cisco provide certification programs for their own equipment and software. CompTIA, a nonprofit industry trade association, provides the best-known vendor-neutral certification.

The following paragraphs describe some of the certifications offered by CompTIA, Microsoft, Novell, and Cisco.

CompTIA

www.comptia.org

✦ **A+** is a basic certification for an entry-level computer technician. To attain A+ certification, you have to pass two exams: one on computer hardware; the other on operating systems.

✦ **Network+** is a popular vendor-neutral networking certification. It covers four major topic areas: Media and Topologies, Protocols and Standards, Network Implementation, and Network Support.

✦ **Server+** covers network server hardware. It includes details such as installing and upgrading server hardware, installing and configuring a NOS, and so on.

✦ **Security+** is for security specialists. The exam topics include general security concepts, communication security, infrastructure security, basics of cryptography, and operational/organizational security.

Microsoft

www.microsoft.com/traincert

✦ **MCP,** or *Microsoft Certified Professional,* is a certification in a specific Microsoft technology or product.

✦ **MCSE,** or *Microsoft Certified Systems Engineer,* is a prestigious certification for networking professionals who design and implement networks. To gain this certification, you have to pass a total of seven exams. Microsoft offers a separate Windows 2000 Server and Windows Server 2003 certification tracks.

✦ **MCSA,** or *Microsoft Certified System Administrator,* is for networking professionals who administer existing networks.

Novell

www.novell.com/training/certinfo/

✦ **CNA,** or *Certified Novell Administrator,* is designed for professionals who will administer and maintain existing Novell networks.

✦ **CNE,** or *Certified Novell Engineer,* is for professionals who design, install, configure, support, and troubleshoot Novell networks.

Cisco

www.cisco.com/certification

✦ **CCNA,** or *Cisco Certified Network Associate,* is an entry-level apprentice certification. A CCNA should be able to install, configure, and operate Cisco equipment for small networks (under 100 nodes).

✦ **CCNP,** or *Cisco Certified Network Professional,* is a professional-level certification for Cisco equipment. A CCNP should be able to install, configure, and troubleshoot Cisco networks of virtually any size.

✦ **CCDA,** or *Cisco Certified Design Associate,* is an entry-level certification for network design.

+ **CCDP,** or *Cisco Certified Design Professional,* is for network design professionals. Both the CCDA and CCNA certifications are prerequisites for the CCDP.

+ **CCIP,** or *Cisco Certified Internetwork Professional,* is a professional-level certification that emphasizes advanced use of IP and related protocols to create intranetworks.

+ **CCIE,** or *Cisco Certified Internetwork Expert,* is the top dog of Cisco certifications.

Knowing When the Guru Needs a Guru, Too

No matter how much you know about computers, plenty of people know more than you do. This rule seems to apply at every rung of the ladder of computer experience. I'm sure that a top rung exists somewhere, occupied by the world's best computer guru. However, I'm not sitting on that rung, and neither are you. (Not even Bill Gates is sitting on that rung. In fact, Bill Gates got to where he is today by hiring people on higher rungs.)

As the local computer guru, one of your most valuable assets can be a knowledgeable friend who's a notch or two above you on the geek scale. That way, when you run into a real stumper, you have a friend to call for advice. Here are some tips for handling your own guru:

+ In dealing with your own guru, don't forget the Computer Geek's Golden Rule: "Do unto your guru as you would have your own users do unto you." Don't pester your guru with simple stuff that you just haven't spent the time to think through. If you have thought it through and can't come up with a solution, however, give your guru a call. Most computer experts welcome the opportunity to tackle an unusual computer problem. It's a genetic defect.

+ If you don't already know someone who knows more about computers than you do, consider joining your local PC users' group. The group may even have a subgroup that specializes in your networking software or may be devoted entirely to local folks who use the same networking software that you use. Odds are good that you're sure to make a friend or two at a users' group meeting. Also, you can probably convince your boss to pay any fees required to join the group.

+ If you can't find a real-life guru, try to find an online guru. Check out the various computing newsgroups on the Internet. Subscribe to online newsletters that are automatically delivered to you via e-mail.

**Book III
Chapter 1**

**Job Description for
a Network
Administrator**

Mastering Helpful Bluffs and Excuses

As network administrator, you just won't be able to solve a problem some-times, at least not immediately. You can do two things in this situation. The first is to explain that the problem is particularly difficult and that you'll have a solution as soon as possible. The second solution is to look the user in the eyes and, with a straight face, try one of these phony explanations:

✦ Blame it on the version of whatever software you're using. "Oh, they fixed that with version 39."

✦ Blame it on cheap, imported memory chips.

✦ Blame it on Democrats. Or Republicans. Or hanging chads. Whatever.

✦ Blame it on Enron executives.

✦ Hope that the problem wasn't caused by stray static electricity. Those types of problems are very difficult to track down. Tell your users that not properly discharging themselves before using their computers can cause all kinds of problems.

✦ You need more memory.

✦ You need a bigger hard drive.

✦ You need an Itanium to do that.

✦ Blame it on Jar-Jar Binks.

✦ You can't do that in Windows XP.

✦ You can only do that in Windows XP.

✦ You're not using Windows XP, are you?

✦ Could be a virus.

✦ Or sunspots.

✦ All work and no beer make Homer something something something. . . .

Chapter 2: Security 101

In This Chapter

✔ Assessing the risk for security

✔ Determining your basic security philosophy

✔ Physically securing your network equipment

✔ Figuring out user account security

✔ Using other network security techniques

*B*efore you had a network, computer security was easy. You simply locked your door when you left work for the day. You could rest easy, secure in the knowledge that the bad guys would have to break down the door to get to your computer.

The network changes all that. Now, anyone with access to any computer on the network can break into the network and steal *your* files. Not only do you have to lock your door, but you also have to make sure that other people lock their doors, too.

Fortunately, network operating systems have built-in provisions for network security. This situation makes it difficult for someone to steal your files, even if they do break down the door. All modern network operating systems have security features that are more than adequate for all but the most paranoid users.

When I say *more* than adequate, I mean it. Most networks have security features that would make even Maxwell Smart happy. Using all these security features is kind of like Smart insisting that the Chief lower the "Cone of Silence." The Cone of Silence worked so well that Max and the Chief couldn't hear each other! Don't make your system so secure that even the good guys can't get their work done.

If any of the computers on your network are connected to the Internet, you have to contend with a whole new world of security issues. For more information about Internet security, refer to Chapter 4 of this book. Also, if your network supports wireless devices, you have to contend with wireless security issues. For more information about security for wireless networks, see Book VI, Chapter 4.

Do You Need Security?

Most small networks are in small businesses or departments where everyone knows and trusts everyone else. Folks don't lock up their desks when they take a coffee break, and although everyone knows where the petty cash box is, money never disappears.

Network security isn't necessary in an idyllic setting like this one, is it? You bet it is. Here's why any network should be set up with at least some minimal concern for security:

+ Even in the friendliest office environment, some information is and should be confidential. If this information is stored on the network, you want to store it in a directory that's only available to authorized users.

+ Not all security breaches are malicious. A network user may be routinely scanning through his or her files and come across a filename that isn't familiar. The user may then call up the file, only to discover that it contains confidential personnel information, juicy office gossip, or your resume. Curiosity, rather than malice, is often the source of security breaches.

+ Sure, everyone at the office is trustworthy now. However, what if someone becomes disgruntled, a screw pops loose, and he or she decides to trash the network files before jumping out the window? What if someone decides to print a few $1,000 checks before packing off to Tahiti?

+ Sometimes the mere opportunity for fraud or theft can be too much for some people to resist. Give people free access to the payroll files, and they may decide to vote themselves a raise when no one is looking.

+ If you think that your network doesn't contain any data that would be worth stealing, think again. For example, your personnel records probably contain more than enough information for an identity thief: names, addresses, phone numbers, social security numbers, and so on. Also, your customer files may contain your customers' credit-card numbers.

+ Hackers who break into your network may not be interested in stealing your data. Instead, they may be looking to plant a *Trojan horse* program on your server, which enables them to use your server for their own purposes. For example, someone may use your server to send thousands of unsolicited spam e-mail messages. The spam won't be traced back to the hackers; it will be traced back to you.

+ Finally, remember that not everyone on the network knows enough about how Windows and the network work to be trusted with full access to your network's data and systems. One careless mouse click can wipe out an entire directory of network files. One of the best reasons for activating your network's security features is to protect the network from mistakes made by users who don't know what they're doing.

Two Approaches to Security

When you're planning how to implement security on your network, you should first consider which of two basic approaches to security you will take:

✦ An open-door type of security, in which you grant everyone access to everything by default and then place restrictions just on those resources to which you want to limit access.

✦ A closed-door type of security, in which you begin by denying access to everything and then grant specific users access to the specific resources that they need.

In most cases, the open-door policy is easier to implement. Typically, only a small portion of the data on a network really needs security, such as confidential employee records or secrets such as the Coke recipe. The rest of the information on a network can be safely made available to everyone who can access the network.

If you choose the closed-door approach, you set up each user so that he or she has access to nothing. Then, you grant each user access only to those specific files or folders that he or she needs.

The closed-door approach results in tighter security, but can lead to the Cone of Silence Syndrome: Like Max and the Chief who can't hear each other talk while they're under the Cone of Silence, your network users will constantly complain that they can't access the information that they need. As a result, you'll find yourself frequently adjusting users' access rights. Choose the closed-door approach only if your network contains a lot of information that is very sensitive, and only if you are willing to invest time administrating your network's security policy.

You can think of the open-door approach as an *entitlement model,* in which the basic assumption is that users are entitled to network access. In contrast, the closed-door policy is a *permissions model,* in which the basic assumption is that users aren't entitled to anything but must get permissions for every network resource that they access.

Book III
Chapter 2

Security 101

Physical Security: Locking Your Doors

The first level of security in any computer network is physical security. I'm amazed when I walk into the reception area of an accounting firm and see an unattended computer sitting on the receptionist's desk. As often as not, the receptionist has logged on to the system and then walked away from the desk, leaving the computer unattended.

Physical security is important for workstations but vital for servers. Any hacker worth his or her salt can quickly defeat all but the most paranoid security measures if they can gain physical access to a server. To protect the server, follow these guidelines:

✦ Lock the computer room.

✦ Give the key only to people you trust.

✦ Keep track of who has the keys.

✦ Mount the servers on cases or racks that have locks.

✦ Disable the floppy drive on the server. (A common hacking technique is to boot the server from a floppy, thus bypassing the carefully crafted security features of the network operating system.)

✦ Keep a trained guard dog in the computer room and feed it only enough to keep it hungry and mad. (Just kidding.)

There's a big difference between a locked door and a door with a lock. Locks are worthless if you don't use them.

Client computers should be physically secure as well. You should instruct users to not leave their computers unattended while they're logged on. In high-traffic areas (such as the receptionist's desk), users should secure their computers with the keylock. Additionally, users should lock their office doors when they leave.

Here are some other potential threats to physical security that you may not have considered:

✦ The nightly cleaning crew probably has complete access to your facility. How do you know that the person who vacuums your office every night doesn't really work for your chief competitor or doesn't consider computer hacking to be a sideline hobby? You don't, so you'd better consider the cleaning crew a threat.

✦ What about your trash? Paper shredders aren't just for Enron accountants. Your trash can contain all sorts of useful information: sales reports, security logs, printed copies of the company's security policy, even handwritten passwords. For the best security, every piece of paper that leaves your building via the trash bin should first go through a shredder.

✦ Where do you store your backup tapes? Don't just stack them up next to the server. Not only does that make them easy to steal, it also defeats one of the main purposes of backing up your data in the first place: securing your server from physical threats, such as fires. If a fire burns down your computer room and the backup tapes are sitting unprotected next to the server, your company may go out of business and you'll certainly be out of a job. Store the backup tapes securely in a fire-proof safe and keep a copy off-site, too.

✦ I've seen some networks in which the servers are in a locked computer room, but the hubs or switches are in an unsecured closet. Remember that every unused port on a hub or a switch represents an open door to your network. The hubs and switches should be secured just like the servers.

Securing User Accounts

Next to physical security, the careful use of user accounts is the most important type of security for your network. Properly configured user accounts can prevent unauthorized users from accessing the network, even if they gain physical access to the network. The following sections describe some of the steps that you can take to strengthen your network's use of user accounts.

Obfuscating your usernames

Huh? When it comes to security, *obfuscation* simply means picking obscure usernames. For example, most network administrators assign usernames based on some combination of the user's first and last name, such as BarnyM or baMiller. However, a hacker can easily guess such a user ID if he or she knows the name of at least one employee. After the hacker knows a username, he or she can focus on breaking the password.

You can slow down a hacker by using names that are more obscure. Here are some suggestions on how to do that:

✦ Add a random three-digit number to the end of the name. For example: BarnyM320 or baMiller977.

✦ Throw a number or two into the middle of the name. For example: Bar6nyM or ba9Miller2.

✦ Make sure that usernames are different from e-mail addresses. For example, if a user's e-mail address is `baMiller@Mydomain.com`, do *not* use baMiller as the user's account name. Use a more obscure name.

Do *not* rely on obfuscation to keep people out of your network! Security by obfuscation doesn't work. A resourceful hacker can discover even the most obscure names. The purpose of obfuscation is to slow intruders down — not to stop them. If you slow an intruder down, you're more likely to discover that he or she is trying to crack your network before he or she successfully gets in.

Using passwords wisely

One of the most important aspects of network security is the use of passwords. Usernames aren't usually considered secret. Even if you use obscure names, casual hackers will eventually figure them out.

Passwords, on the other hand, are top secret. Your network password is the one thing that keeps an impostor from logging on to the network by using your username and therefore receiving the same access rights that you ordinarily have. *Guard your password with your life.*

Here are some tips for creating good passwords:

+ Don't use obvious passwords, such as your last name, your kid's name, or your dog's name.

+ Don't pick passwords based on your hobbies, either. A friend of mine is into boating, and his password is the name of his boat. Anyone who knows him can guess his password after a few tries. Five lashes for naming your password after your boat.

+ Store your password in your head — not on paper. Especially bad: Writing down your password on a sticky note and sticking it on your computer's monitor. Ten lashes for that. (If you must write down your password, write it on digestible paper that you can swallow after you've memorized the password.)

+ Most network operating systems enable you to set an expiration time for passwords. For example, you can specify that passwords expire after 30 days. When a user's password expires, the user must change it. Your users may consider this process a hassle, but it helps to limit the risk of someone swiping a password and then trying to break into your computer system later.

+ You can also configure user accounts so that when they change passwords, they can't specify a password that they've used recently. For example, you can specify that the new password can't be identical to any of the user's past three passwords.

+ You can also configure security policies so that passwords must include a mixture of uppercase letters, lowercase letters, numerals, and special symbols. Thus, passwords like `DIMWIT` or `DUFUS` are out. Passwords like `87dIM@wit` or `duF39&US` are in.

+ Some administrators of small networks opt against passwords altogether because they feel that security is not an issue on their network. Or short of that, they choose obvious passwords, assign every user the same password, or print the passwords on giant posters and hang them throughout the building. In my opinion, ignoring basic password security is rarely a good idea, even in small networks. You should consider not using passwords only if your network is very small (say, two or three computers), if you don't keep sensitive data on a file server, or if the main reason for the network is to share access to a printer rather than sharing files. (Even if you don't use passwords, imposing basic security precautions like limiting access that certain users have to certain network directories is still possible. Just remember that if passwords aren't used, nothing prevents a user from signing on by using someone else's username.)

Generating Passwords For Dummies

How do you come up with passwords that no one can guess but that you can remember? Most security experts say that the best passwords don't correspond to any words in the English language but consist of a random sequence of letters, numbers, and special characters. Yet, how in the heck are you supposed to memorize a password like `Dks4%DJ2`? Especially when you have to change it three weeks later to something like `3pQ&X(d8`.

Here's a compromise solution that enables you to create passwords that consist of two four-letter words back to back. Take your favorite book (if it's this one, you need to get a life) and turn to any page at random. Find the first four- or five-letter words on the page. Suppose that word is `When`. Then repeat the process to find another four- or five-letter word; say you pick the word `Most` the second time. Now combine the words to make your password: `WhenMost`. I think you agree that `WhenMost` is easier to remember than `3PQ&X(D8` and is probably just about as hard to guess. I probably wouldn't want the folks at the Los Alamos Nuclear Laboratory using this scheme, but it's good enough for most of us.

**Book III
Chapter 2**

Security 101

Here are some additional thoughts on concocting passwords from your favorite book:

✦ If the words end up being the same, pick another word. And pick different words if the combination seems too commonplace, such as `WestWind` or `FootBall`.

✦ For an interesting variation, insert a couple of numerals or special characters between the words. You end up with passwords like `into#cat`, `ball3%and`, or `tree47wing`.

✦ To further confuse your friends and enemies, use medieval passwords by picking words from Chaucer's *Canterbury Tales*. Chaucer is a great source for passwords because he lived before the days of word processors with spell-checkers. He wrote *seyd* instead of *said, gret* instead of *great, welk* instead of *walked, litel* instead of *little*. And he used lots of seven-letter and eight-letter words suitable for passwords, such as *glotenye* (gluttony), *benygne* (benign), and *opynyoun* (opinion). And he got As in English.

If you use any of these password schemes and someone breaks into your network, don't blame me. You're the one who's too lazy to memorize D#Sc$h4@bb3xaz5.

✦ If you do decide to go with passwords such as KdI22UR3xdkL, you can find random password generators on the Internet. Just go to a search engine, such as Google (www.google.com), and search for Password Generator. You can find Web pages that generate random passwords based on criteria that you specify, such as how long the password should be, whether it should include letters, numbers, punctuation, uppercase and lowercase letters, and so on.

Securing the Administrator account

It stands to reason that at least one network user must have the authority to use the network without any of the restrictions imposed on other users. This user is called the *administrator*. The administrator is responsible for setting up the network's security system. To do that, the administrator must be exempt from all security restrictions.

Many networks automatically create an administrator user account when you install the network software. The username and password for this initial administrator are published in the network's documentation and are the same for all networks that use the same network operating system. One of the first things that you must do after getting your network up and running is to change the password for this standard administrator account. Otherwise, your elaborate security precautions will be a complete waste of time. Anyone who knows the default administrator username and password can access your system with full administrator rights and privileges, thus bypassing the security restrictions that you so carefully set up.

Don't forget the password for the administrator account! If a network user forgets his or her password, you can log in as the supervisor and change that user's password. If you forget the administrator's password, though, you're stuck.

Hardening Your Network

In addition to taking care of physical security and user account security, you should also take steps to protect your network from intruders by configuring the other security features of the network's servers and routers. The following sections describe the basics of hardening your network.

Using a firewall

A *firewall* is a security-conscious router that sits between your network and the outside world and prevents Internet users from wandering into your LAN and messing around. Firewalls are the first line of defense for any network that's connected to the Internet. You should *never* connect a network to the Internet without installing a carefully configured firewall. For more information about firewalls, refer to Chapter 4 of this book.

Disabling unnecessary services

A typical network operating system can support dozens of different types of network services: file and printer sharing, Web server, mail server, and many others. In many cases, these features are installed on servers that don't need or use them. When a server runs a network service that it doesn't really need, the service not only robs CPU cycles from other services that are needed, but also poses an unnecessary security threat.

When you first install a network operating system on a server, you should enable only those network services that you know the server will require. You can always enable services later if the needs of the server change.

Patching your servers

Hackers regularly find security holes in network operating systems. After those holes are discovered, the operating system vendors figure out how to plug the hole and release a software patch for the security fix. The trouble is that most network administrators don't stay up-to-date with these software patches. As a result, many networks are vulnerable because they have well-known holes in their security armor that should have been fixed but weren't.

Even though patches are a bit of a nuisance, they are well worth the effort for the protection that they afford. Fortunately, newer versions of the popular network operating systems have features that automatically check for updates and let you know when a patch should be applied.

Securing Your Users

Security techniques, such as physical security, user account security, server security, and locking down your servers are child's play compared to the most difficult job of network security: securing your network's users. All the best-laid security plans will go for naught if your users write down their passwords on sticky notes and post them on their computers.

The key to securing your network users is to create a written network security policy and stick to it. Have a meeting with everyone to go over the security policy to make sure that everyone understands the rules. Also, make sure to have consequences when violations occur.

Here are some suggestions for some basic security rules you can incorporate into your security policy:

✦ Never write down your password or give it to someone else.

✦ Accounts should not be shared. Never use someone else's account to access a resource that you can't access under your own account. If you need access to some network resource that isn't available to you, you should formally request access under your own account.

✦ Likewise, never give your account information to a coworker so that he or she can access a needed resource. Your coworker should instead formally request access under his or her own account.

✦ Do not install any software or hardware on your computer without first obtaining permission — especially wireless access devices or modems.

✦ Do not enable file and printer sharing on workstations without first getting permission.

✦ Never attempt to disable or bypass the network's security features.

Chapter 3: Managing User Accounts

In This Chapter

✔ Understanding user accounts

✔ Looking at the built-in accounts

✔ Using rights and permissions

✔ Working with groups and policies

✔ Running login scripts

*U*ser accounts are the backbone of network security administration. Through the use of user accounts, you can determine who can access your network, as well as what network resources each user can and cannot access. You can restrict access to the network to just specific computers or to certain hours of the day. In addition, you can lock out users who no longer need to access your network.

The specific details for managing user accounts are unique to each network operating system and are covered in separate chapters later in this book. The purpose of this chapter is simply to introduce you to the concepts of user account management, so you know what you can and can't do, regardless of which network operating system you use.

User Accounts

Every user who accesses a network must have a *user account*. User accounts allow the network administrator to determine who can access the network and what network resources each user can access. In addition, the user account can be customized to provide many convenience features for users, such as a personalized Start menu or a display of recently used documents.

Every user account is associated with a *username* (sometimes called a *user ID*), which the user must enter when logging in to the network. Each account also has other information associated with it. In particular:

✦ **The user's password:** This also includes the password policy, such as how often the user has to change his or her password, how complicated the password must be, and so on.

+ **The user's contact information:** This includes full name, phone number, e-mail address, mailing address, and other related information.

+ **Account restrictions:** This includes restrictions that allow the user to log on only during certain times of the day. This feature enables you to restrict your users to normal working hours so that they can't sneak in at 2 a.m. to do unauthorized work. This feature also discourages your users from working overtime because they can't access the network after hours, so use it judiciously. You can also specify that the user can log on only at certain computers.

+ **Account status:** You can temporarily disable a user account so that the user can't log on.

+ **Home directory:** This specifies a shared network folder where the user can store documents.

+ **Dial-in permissions:** These authorize the user to access the network remotely via a dialup connection.

+ **Group memberships:** These grant the user certain rights based on groups to which they belong. For more information, see the section "Group Therapy," later in this chapter.

Built-In Accounts

Most network operating systems come preconfigured with two built-in accounts, named "Administrator" and "Guest." In addition, some server services, such as Web or database servers, create their own user accounts under which to run. The following sections describe the characteristics of these accounts.

The Administrator account

The Administrator account is the King of the Network. This user account is not subject to any of the account restrictions to which other, mere mortal accounts must succumb. If you log in as the administrator, you can do anything.

Because the Administrator account has unlimited access to your network, it is imperative that you secure it immediately after you install the server. When the NOS Setup program asks for a password for the Administrator account, start off with a good random mix of uppercase and lowercase letters, numbers, and symbols. Don't pick some easy-to-remember password to get started, thinking you'll change it to something more cryptic later. You'll forget, and in the meantime, someone will break in and reformat the server's C: drive or steal your customer's credit-card numbers.

Here are a few additional things worth knowing about the Administrator account:

✦ You can't delete it. The system must always have an administrator.

✦ You can grant administrator status to other user accounts. However, you should do so only for users who really need to be administrators.

✦ You should use it only when you really need to do tasks that require administrative authority. Many network administrators grant administrative authority to their own user accounts. That's not a very good idea. If you're killing some time surfing the Web or reading your e-mail while logged in as an administrator, you're just inviting viruses or malicious scripts to take advantage of your administrator access. Instead, you should set yourself up with two accounts: a normal account that you use for day-to-day work, and an Administrator account that you use only when you need it.

✦ The default name for the Administrator account is usually simply "Administrator." You may want to consider changing this name. Better yet, change the name of the Administrator account to something more obscure and then create an ordinary user account that has few — if any — rights and give that account the name "Administrator." That way, hackers who spend weeks trying to crack your Administrator account password will discover that they've been duped, once they finally break the password. In the meantime, you'll have a chance to discover their attempts to breach your security and take appropriate action.

✦ Don't forget the password for the Administrator account! If a network user forgets his or her password, you can log on as the administrator and change that user's password. If you forget the administrator's password, though, you're stuck.

The Guest account

Another commonly created default account is called the *Guest account*. This account is set up with a blank password and few — if any — access rights. The Guest account is designed to allow anyone to step up to a computer and log on, but after they do, it then prevents them from doing anything. Sounds like a waste of time to me. I suggest you disable the Guest account.

Service accounts

Some network users aren't actual people. I don't mean that some of your users are subhuman. Rather, some users are actually software processors that require access to secure resources and therefore require user accounts. These user accounts are usually created automatically for you when you install or configure server software.

**Book III
Chapter 3**

**Managing User
Accounts**

For example, when you install Microsoft's Web server (IIS), an Internet user account called IUSR is created. The complete name for this account is `IUSR_<servername>`. So if the server is named WEB1, the account is named `IUSR_WEB1`. IIS uses this account to allow anonymous Internet users to access the files of your Web site.

As a general rule, you shouldn't mess with these accounts unless you know what you're doing. For example, if you delete or rename the IUSR account, you must reconfigure IIS to use the changed account. If you don't, IIS will deny access to anyone trying to reach your site. (Assuming that you *do* know what you're doing, renaming these accounts can increase your network's security. However, don't start playing with these accounts until you've researched the ramifications.)

User Rights

User accounts and passwords are only the front line of defense in the game of network security. After a user gains access to the network by typing a valid user ID and password, the second line of security defense — rights — comes into play.

In the harsh realities of network life, all users are created equal, but some users are more equal than others. The Preamble to the Declaration of Network Independence contains the statement, "We hold these truths to be self-evident, that *some* users are endowed by the network administrator with certain inalienable rights. . . ."

The specific rights that you can assign to network users depend on which network operating system you use. Here is a partial list of the user rights that are possible with Windows servers:

✦ **Log on locally:** The user can log on to the server computer directly from the server's keyboard.

✦ **Change system time:** The user can change the time and date registered by the server.

✦ **Shut down the system:** The user can perform an orderly shutdown of the server.

✦ **Back up files and directories:** The user can perform a backup of files and directories on the server.

✦ **Restore files and directories:** The user can restore backed-up files.

✦ **Take ownership of files and other objects:** The user can take over files and other network resources that belong to other users.

NetWare has a similar set of user rights.

Network rights I'd like to see

The network rights allowed by most network operating systems are pretty boring. Here are a few rights I wish would be allowed:

✔ **Cheat:** Provides a special option that enables you to see what cards the other players are holding when you're playing Hearts.

✔ **Spy:** Eavesdrops on other user's Internet sessions so that you can find out what Web sites they're viewing.

✔ **Complain:** Automatically sends e-mail messages to other users that explain how busy, tired, or upset you are.

✔ **Set pay:** Grants you special access to the payroll system so that you can give yourself a pay raise.

✔ **Sue:** In America, everyone has the right to sue. So this right should be automatically granted to all users.

Permissions (Who Gets What)

User rights control what a user can do on a network-wide basis. *Permissions* enable you to fine-tune your network security by controlling access to specific network resources, such as files or printers, for individual users or groups. For example, you can set up permissions to allow users into the accounting department to access files in the server's \ACCTG directory. Permissions can also enable some users to read certain files but not modify or delete them.

Each network operating system manages permissions in a different way. Whatever the details, the effect is that you can give permission to each user to access certain files, folders, or drives in certain ways.

Any permissions that you specify for a folder apply automatically to any of that folder's subfolders, unless you explicitly specify a different set of permissions for the subfolder.

In Novell's NetWare, file system rights are referred to as *trustee rights*. NetWare has eight different trustee rights, listed in Table 3-1. For every file or directory on a server, you can assign any combination of these eight rights to any individual user or group.

Table 3-1	NetWare Trustee Rights	
Trustee Right	*Abbreviation*	*What the User Can Do*
Read	R	The user can open and read the file.
Write	W	The user can open and write to the file.
Create	C	The user can create new files or directories.
Modify	M	The user can change the name or other properties of the file or directory.
File Scan	F	The user can list the contents of the directory.
Erase	E	The user can delete the file or directory.
Access Control	A	The user can set the permissions for the file or directory.
Supervisor	S	The user has all rights to the file.

Windows refers to file system rights as *permissions*. Windows servers have six basic permissions, listed in Table 3-2. As with NetWare trustee rights, you can assign any combination of Windows permissions to a user or group for a given file or folder.

Table 3-2	Windows Basic Permissions	
Permission	*Abbreviation*	*What the User Can Do*
Read	R	The user can open and read the file.
Write	W	The user can open and write to the file.
Execute	X	The user can run the file.
Delete	D	The user can delete the file.
Change	P	The user can change the permissions for the file.
Take Ownership	O	The user can take ownership of the file.

Note the last permission listed in Table 3-2. In Windows, the concept of file or folder ownership is important. Every file or folder on a Windows server system has an owner. The *owner* is usually the user who creates the file or folder. However, ownership can be transferred from one user to another. So why the Take Ownership permission? This permission prevents someone from creating a bogus file and giving ownership of it to you without your permission. Windows doesn't allow you to give ownership of a file to another user. Instead, you can give another user the right to take ownership of the file. That user must then explicitly take ownership of the file.

You can use Windows permissions only for files or folders that are created on drives formatted as NTFS volumes. If you insist on using FAT or FAT32 for your Windows shared drives, you can't protect individual files or folders on the drives. This is one of the main reasons for using NTFS for your Windows servers.

Group Therapy

A *group account* is an account that doesn't represent an individual user. Instead, it represents a group of users who use the network in a similar way. Instead of granting access rights to each of these users individually, you can grant the rights to the group and then assign individual users to the group. When you assign a user to a group, that user inherits the rights specified for the group.

For example, suppose that you create a group named "Accounting" for the accounting staff and then allow members of the Accounting group access to the network's accounting files and applications. Then, instead of granting each accounting user access to those files and applications, you simply make each accounting user a member of the Accounting group.

Here are a few additional details about groups:

✦ Groups are one of the keys to network management nirvana. As much as possible, you should avoid managing network users individually. Instead, clump them into groups and manage the groups. When all 50 users in the accounting department need access to a new file share, would you rather update 50 user accounts or just one group account?

✦ A user can belong to more than one group. Then, the user inherits the rights of each group. For example, suppose that you have groups set up for Accounting, Sales, Marketing, and Finance. A user who needs to access both Accounting and Finance information can be made a member of both the Accounting and Finance groups. Likewise, a user who needs access to both Sales and Marketing information can be made a member of both the Sales and Marketing groups.

✦ You can grant or revoke specific rights to individual users to override the group settings. For example, you may grant a few extra permissions for the manager of the accounting department. You may also impose a few extra restrictions on certain users.

User Profiles

User profiles are a Windows feature that keeps track of an individual user's preferences for his or her Windows configuration. For a non-networked computer, profiles enable two or more users to use the same computer, each with his or her own desktop settings, such as wallpaper, colors, Start menu options, and so on.

The real benefit of user profiles becomes apparent when profiles are used on a network. A user's profile can be stored on a server computer and accessed whenever that user logs on to the network from any Windows computer on the network.

The following are some of the elements of Windows that are governed by settings in the user profile:

✦ Desktop settings from the Display Properties dialog box, including wallpaper, screen savers, and color schemes.

✦ Start menu programs and Windows toolbar options.

✦ Favorites, which provide easy access to the files and folders that the user accesses frequently.

✦ Network settings, including drive mappings, network printers, and recently visited network locations.

✦ Application settings, such as option settings for Microsoft Word.

✦ The My Documents folder.

Logon Scripts

A *logon script* is a batch file that runs automatically whenever a user logs on. Logon scripts can perform several important logon tasks for you, such as mapping network drives, starting applications, synchronizing the client computer's time-of-day clock, and so on. Logon scripts reside on the server. Each user account can specify whether to use a logon script and which script to use.

Here's a sample logon script that maps a few network drives and synchronizes the time:

```
net use m: \\MYSERVER\Acct
net use n: \\MYSERVER\Admin
net use o: \\MYSERVER\Dev
net time \\MYSERVER /set /yes
```

Logon scripts are a little out of vogue because most of what a logon script does can be done via user profiles. Still, many administrators prefer the simplicity of logon scripts, so they're still used even on Windows Server 2003 systems.

Chapter 4: Firewalls and Virus Protection

In This Chapter

✔ Understanding what firewalls do

✔ Examining the different types of firewalls

✔ Looking at virus protection

*I*f your network is connected to the Internet, a whole host of security issues bubble to the surface. You probably connected your network to the Internet so that your network's users could get out to the Internet. Unfortunately, however, your Internet connection is a two-way street. Not only does it enable your network's users to step outside the bounds of your network to access the Internet, but it also enables others to step in and access your network.

And step in they will. The world is filled with hackers who are looking for networks like yours to break into. They may do it just for the fun of it, or they may do it to steal your customer's credit-card numbers or to coerce your mail server into sending thousands of spam messages on their behalf. Whatever their motive, rest assured that your network will be broken into if you leave it unprotected.

This chapter presents an overview of two basic techniques for securing your network's Internet connection: firewalls and virus protection.

Firewalls

A *firewall* is a security-conscious router that sits between the Internet and your network with a single-minded task: preventing *them* from getting to *us*. The firewall acts as a security guard between the Internet and your LAN. All network traffic into and out of the LAN must pass through the firewall, which prevents unauthorized access to the network.

Some type of firewall is a must-have if your network has a connection to the Internet, whether that connection is broadband (cable modem or DSL), T1, or some other high-speed connection. Without it, sooner or later a hacker will discover your unprotected network and tell his friends about it. Within a few hours your network will be toast.

You can set up a firewall using two basic ways. The easiest way is to purchase a *firewall appliance,* which is basically a self-contained router with built-in firewall features. Most firewall appliances include a Web-based interface that enables you to connect to the firewall from any computer on your network using a browser. You can then customize the firewall settings to suit your needs.

Alternatively, you can set up a server computer to function as a firewall computer. The server can run just about any network operating system, but most dedicated firewall systems run Linux.

Whether you use a firewall appliance or a firewall computer, the firewall must be located between your network and the Internet, as shown in Figure 4-1. Here, one end of the firewall is connected to a network hub, which is, in turn, connected to the other computers on the network. The other end of the firewall is connected to the Internet. As a result, all traffic from the LAN to the Internet and vice versa must travel through the firewall.

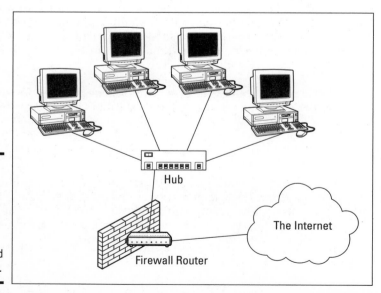

Figure 4-1:
A firewall router creates a secure link between a network and the Internet.

Hub

The Internet

Firewall Router

The term *perimeter* is sometimes used to describe the location of a firewall on your network. In short, a firewall is like a perimeter fence that completely surrounds your property and forces all visitors to enter through the front gate.

In large networks — especially campus-wide or even metropolitan networks — it's sometimes hard to figure out exactly where the perimeter is located. If your network has two or more WAN connections, make sure that every one of those connections connects to a firewall and not directly to the network. You can do this by providing a separate firewall for each WAN connection or by using a firewall with more than one WAN port.

The Many Types of Firewalls

Firewalls employ four basic techniques to keep unwelcome visitors out of your network. The following sections describe these basic firewall techniques.

Packet filtering

A *packet-filtering* firewall examines each packet that crosses the firewall and tests the packet according to a set of rules that you set up. If the packet passes the test, it's allowed to pass. If the packet doesn't pass, it's rejected.

Packet filters are the least expensive type of firewall. As a result, packet-filtering firewalls are very common. However, packet filtering has a number of flaws that knowledgeable hackers can exploit. As a result, packet filtering by itself doesn't make for a fully effective firewall.

Packet filters work by inspecting the source and destination IP and port addresses contained in each TCP/IP packet. TCP/IP *ports* are numbers that are assigned to specific services that help to identify for which service each packet is intended. For example, the port number for the HTTP protocol is 80. As a result, any incoming packets headed for an HTTP server will specify port 80 as the destination port.

Port numbers are often specified with a colon following an IP address. For example, the HTTP service on a server whose IP address is 192.168.10.133 would be 192.168.10.133:80.

Literally thousands of established ports are in use. Table 4-1 lists a few of the most popular ports.

Table 4-1	Some Well-Known TCP/IP Ports
Port	*Description*
20	File Transfer Protocol (FTP)
21	File Transfer Protocol (FTP)
22	Secure Shell Protocol (SSH)
23	Telnet
25	Simple Mail Transfer Protocol (SMTP)
53	Domain Name Server (DNS)
80	World Wide Web (HTTP)
110	Post Office Protocol (POP3)
119	Network News Transfer Protocol (NNTP)
137	NetBIOS Name Service
138	NetBIOS Datagram Service
139	NetBIOS Session Service
143	Internet Message Access Protocol (IMAP)
161	Simple Network Management Protocol (SNMP)
194	Internet Relay Chat (IRC)
389	Lightweight Directory Access Protocol (LDAP)
396	NetWare over IP
443	HTTP over TLS/SSL (HTTPS)

The rules that you set up for the packet filter either permit or deny packets that specify certain IP addresses or ports. For example, you may permit packets that are intended for your mail server or your Web server and deny all other packets. Or, you may set up a rule that specifically denies packets that are heading for the ports used by NetBIOS. This rule keeps Internet hackers from trying to access NetBIOS server resources, such as files or printers.

One of the biggest weaknesses of packet filtering is that it pretty much trusts that the packets themselves are telling the truth when they say who they're from and who they're going to. Hackers exploit this weakness by using a hacking technique called *IP spoofing,* in which they insert fake IP addresses in packets that they send to your network.

Another weakness of packet filtering is that it examines each packet in isolation, without considering what packets have gone through the firewall before and what packets may follow. In other words, packet filtering is *stateless*. Rest assured that hackers have figured out how to exploit the stateless nature of packet filtering to get through firewalls.

In spite of these weaknesses, packet filter firewalls have several advantages that explain why they are commonly used:

✦ **Packet filters are very efficient.** They hold up each inbound and outbound packet for only a few milliseconds while they look inside the packet to determine the destination and source ports and addresses. After these addresses and ports have been determined, the packet filter quickly applies its rules and either sends the packet along or rejects it. In contrast, other firewall techniques have a more noticeable performance overhead.

✦ **Packet filters are almost completely transparent to users.** The only time a user will be aware that a packet filter firewall is being used is when the firewall rejects packets. Other firewall techniques require that clients and/or servers be specially configured to work with the firewall.

✦ **Packet filters are inexpensive.** Most routers include built-in packet filtering.

Stateful packet inspection (SPI)

Stateful packet inspection, also known as *SPI,* is a step-up in intelligence from simple packet filtering. A firewall with stateful packet inspection looks at packets in groups rather than individually. It keeps track of which packets have passed through the firewall and can detect patterns that indicate unauthorized access. In some cases, the firewall may hold on to packets as they arrive until the firewall has gathered enough information to make a decision about whether the packets should be authorized or rejected.

Stateful packet inspection was once found only on expensive, enterprise-level routers. Now, however, SPI firewalls are affordable enough for small- or medium-sized networks to use.

Circuit-level gateway

A *circuit-level gateway* manages connections between clients and servers based on TCP/IP addresses and port numbers. After the connection is established, the gateway doesn't interfere with packets flowing between the systems.

For example, you could use a Telnet circuit-level gateway to allow Telnet connections (port 23) to a particular server and prohibit other types of connections to that server. After the connection is established, the circuit-level gateway allows packets to flow freely over the connection. As a result, the circuit-level gateway can't prevent a Telnet user from running specific programs or using specify commands.

Application gateway

An *application gateway* is a firewall system that is more intelligent than a packet-filtering, stateful packet inspection, or circuit-level gateway firewall. Packet filters treat all TCP/IP packets the same. In contrast, application gateways know the details about the applications that generate the packets that pass through the firewall. For example, a Web application gateway is aware of the details of HTTP packets. As a result, it can examine more than just the source and destination addresses and ports to determine whether the packets should be allowed to pass through the firewall.

In addition, application gateways work as *proxy servers.* Simply put, a proxy server is a server that sits between a client computer and a real server. The proxy server intercepts packets that are intended for the real server and processes them. The proxy server can examine the packet and decide to pass it on to the real server, or it can reject the packet. Or, the proxy server may be able to respond to the packet itself, without involving the real server at all.

For example, Web proxies often store copies of commonly used Web pages in a local cache. When a user requests a Web page from a remote Web server, the proxy server intercepts the request and checks to see whether it already has a copy of the page in its cache. If so, the Web proxy returns the page directly to the user. If not, the proxy passes the request on to the real server.

Application gateways are aware of the details of how various types of TCP/IP servers handle sequences of TCP/IP packets, so they can make more intelligent decisions about whether an incoming packet is legitimate or is part of an attack. As a result, application gateways are more secure than simple packet-filtering firewalls, which can deal with only one packet at a time.

The improved security of application gateways, however, comes at a price. Application gateways are more expensive than packet filters, both in terms of their purchase price and in the cost of configuring and maintaining them. In addition, application gateways slow the network performance down because they do more detailed checking of packets before allowing them to pass.

The Built-In Firewall in Windows XP

If you're using a Windows XP as a router to share an Internet connection for a small network, you can use the built-in firewall feature to provide basic packet-filtering firewall protection. Here are the steps to activate this feature in Windows XP:

1. **Choose Start⇨Control Panel.**

The Control Panel appears.

2. **Click the Network Connections link.**

If Control Panel appears in Classic view rather than Category view, you don't see a Network Connections link. Instead, just double-click the Network Connections icon.

3. **Double-click the Local Area Connection icon.**

A dialog box showing the connection's status appears.

4. **Click the Properties button.**

The Connection Properties dialog box appears.

5. **Click the Advanced Tab and then check the Protect My Computer option.**

This option enables the firewall.

6. **Click OK.**

That's all there is to it.

Do *not* enable the Windows Internet firewall if you're using a separate firewall router to protect your network. Because the other computers on the network are connected directly to the router and not to your computer, the firewall won't protect the rest of the network. Additionally, as an unwanted side effect, the rest of the network will lose the ability to access your computer.

Virus Protection

Viruses are one of the most misunderstood computer phenomena around these days. What is a virus? How does it work? How does it spread from computer to computer? I'm glad you asked.

What is a virus?

Make no mistake — viruses are real. Now that most people are connected to the Internet, viruses have really taken off. Every computer user is susceptible to attacks by computer viruses, and using a network increases your vulnerability because it exposes all network users to the risk of being infected by a virus that lands on any one network user's computer.

Viruses don't just spontaneously appear out of nowhere. Viruses are computer programs that are created by malicious programmers who've lost a few screws and should be locked up.

What makes a virus a virus is its capability to make copies of itself that can be spread to other computers. These copies, in turn, make still more copies that spread to still more computers, and so on, ad nauseam.

Then, the virus patiently waits until something triggers it — perhaps when you type a particular command or press a certain key, when a certain date arrives, or when the virus creator sends the virus a message. What the virus does when it strikes also depends on what the virus creator wants the virus to do. Some viruses harmlessly display a "gotcha" message. Some send e-mail to everyone it finds in your address book. Some wipe out all the data on your hard drive. Ouch.

A few years back, viruses moved from one computer to another by latching themselves onto floppy disks. Whenever you borrowed a floppy disk from a buddy, you ran the risk of infecting your own computer with a virus that may have stowed away on the disk.

Nowadays, virus programmers have discovered that e-mail is a much more efficient method to spread their viruses. Typically, a virus masquerades as a useful or interesting e-mail attachment, such as instructions on how to make $1,000,000 in your spare time, pictures of naked celebrities, or a Valentine's Day greeting from your long-lost sweetheart. When a curious but unsuspecting user double-clicks the attachment, the virus springs to life, copying itself onto the user's computer and, in some cases, sending copies of itself to all the names in the user's address book.

After the virus has worked its way onto a networked computer, the virus can then figure out how to spread itself to other computers on the network.

Here are some more tidbits about protecting your network from virus attacks:

✦ The term *virus* is often used to refer not only to true virus programs (which are able to replicate themselves) but also to any other type of program that's designed to harm your computer. These programs include so-called *Trojan horse* programs that usually look like games but are, in reality, hard drive formatters.

✦ A *worm* is similar to a virus, but it doesn't actually infect other files. Instead, it just copies itself onto other computers on a network. After a worm has copied itself onto your computer, there's no telling what it may do there. For example, a worm may scan your hard drive for interesting information, such as passwords or credit-card numbers, and then e-mail them to the worm's author.

✦ Computer virus experts have identified several thousand "strains" of viruses. Many of them have colorful names, such as the I Love You virus, the Stoned virus, and the Michelangelo virus.

✦ Antivirus programs can recognize known viruses and remove them from your system, and they can spot the telltale signs of unknown viruses. Unfortunately, the idiots who write viruses aren't idiots (in the intellectual sense), so they're constantly developing new techniques to evade detection by antivirus programs. New viruses are frequently discovered, and antivirus programs are periodically updated to detect and remove them.

Antivirus programs

The best way to protect your network from virus infection is to use an antivirus program. These programs have a catalog of several thousand known viruses that they can detect and remove. In addition, they can spot the types of changes that viruses typically make to your computer's files, thus decreasing the likelihood that some previously unknown virus will go undetected.

It would be nice if Windows came with built-in antivirus software, but alas, it does not. So you have to purchase a program on your own. The two best-known antivirus programs for Windows are Norton Antivirus by Symantec and McAfee's VirusScan.

The people who make antivirus programs have their finger on the pulse of the virus world and frequently release updates to their software to combat the latest viruses. Because virus writers are constantly developing new viruses, your antivirus software is next to worthless unless you keep it up-to-date by downloading the latest updates.

The following are several approaches to deploying antivirus protection on your network:

✦ You can install antivirus software on each network user's computer. This technique would be the most effective if you could count on all your users to keep their virus software up-to-date. Because that's an unlikely proposition, you may want to adopt a more reliable approach to virus protection.

✦ Managed antivirus services place antivirus client software on each client computer in your network. Then, an antivirus server automatically updates the clients on a regular basis to make sure that they're kept up-to-date.

✦ Server-based antivirus software protects your network servers from viruses. For example, you can install antivirus software on your mail server to scan all incoming mail for viruses and remove them before your network users ever see them.

✦ Some firewall appliances include antivirus enforcement checks that don't allow your users to access the Internet unless their antivirus software is up-to-date. This type of firewall provides the best antivirus protection available.

Safe computing

Besides using an antivirus program, you can take a few additional precautions to ensure virus-free computing. If you haven't talked to your kids about these safe-computing practices, you had better do so soon.

✦ Regularly back up your data. If a virus hits you and your antivirus software can't repair the damage, you may need the backup to recover your data. Make sure that you restore from a backup that was created before you were infected by the virus!

✦ If you buy software from a store and discover that the seal has been broken on the disk package, take the software back. Don't try to install it on your computer. You don't hear about tainted software as often as you hear about tainted beef, but if you buy software that's been opened, it may well be laced with a virus infection.

✦ Use your antivirus software to scan your disk for virus infection after your computer has been to a repair shop or worked on by a consultant. These guys don't intend harm, but they occasionally spread viruses accidentally, simply because they work on so many strange computers.

✦ Don't open e-mail attachments from people you don't know or attachments you weren't expecting.

✦ Use your antivirus software to scan any floppy disk or CD-ROM that doesn't belong to you before you access any of its files.

Book IV

Network Troubleshooting and Disaster Planning

The 5th Wave   By Rich Tennant

"You the guy having trouble staying connected to the network?"

Contents at a Glance

Chapter 1: Solving Network Problems

In This Chapter

- ✔ Checking the obvious things
- ✔ Fixing computers that have expired
- ✔ Pinpointing the cause of trouble
- ✔ Restarting client and server computers
- ✔ Reviewing network event logs
- ✔ Keeping a record of network woes

Face it: Networks are prone to breaking.

They have too many parts. Cables. Connectors. Cards. Hubs. Switches. Routers. All these parts must be held together in a delicate balance; the network equilibrium is all too easy to disturb. Even the best-designed computer networks sometimes act as if they're held together with baling wire, chewing gum, and duct tape.

To make matters worse, networks breed suspicion. After your computer is attached to a network, users begin to blame the network every time something goes wrong, regardless of whether the problem has anything to do with the network. You can't get columns to line up in a Word document? Must be the network. Your spreadsheet doesn't add up? The @@#$% network's acting up again. The stock market's down? Arghhh!!!!!!

The worst thing about network failures is that sometimes they can shut down an entire company. It's not so bad if just one user can't access a particular shared folder on a file server. If a critical server goes down, however, your network users may be locked out of their files, their applications, their e-mail, and everything else they need to conduct business as usual. When that happens, they'll be beating down your doors and won't stop until you get the network back up and running.

In this chapter, I review some of the most likely causes of network trouble and suggest some basic troubleshooting techniques that you can employ when your network goes on the fritz.

When Bad Things Happen to Good Computers

The following are some basic troubleshooting steps about what you should examine at the first sign of network trouble. In many (if not most) of the cases, one of the following steps can get your network back up and running.

1. **Make sure that your computer and everything attached to it is plugged in.**

   Computer geeks love it when a user calls for help, and they get to tell the user that the computer isn't plugged in. They write it down in their geek logs so that they can tell their geek friends about it later. They may even want to take your picture so that they can show it to their geek friends. (Most "accidents" involving computer geeks are a direct result of this kind of behavior. So try to be tactful when you ask a user whether he or she is sure the computer is actually turned on.)

2. **Make sure that your computer is properly connected to the network.**

3. **Note any error messages that appear on the screen.**

4. **Try the built-in Windows network troubleshooter.**

   For more information, see the section "Using the Windows Networking Troubleshooter," later in this chapter.

5. **Check the free disk space on the server.**

   When a server runs out of disk space, strange things can happen. Sometimes you get a clear error message indicating such a situation, but not always. Sometimes the network just grinds to a halt; operations that used to take a few seconds now take a few minutes.

6. **Do a little experimenting to find out whether the problem is indeed a network problem or just a problem with the computer itself.**

   See the section "Time to Experiment," later in this chapter, for some simple things that you can do to isolate a network problem.

7. **Try restarting the computer.**

   An amazing number of computer problems are cleared up by a simple restart of the computer. Of course, in many cases, the problem recurs, so you'll have to eventually isolate the cause and fix the problem. Some problems are only intermittent, and a simple reboot is all that's needed.

8. **Try restarting the network server.**

   See the section "How to Restart a Network Server," later in this chapter.

How to Fix Dead Computers

If a computer seems totally dead, here are some things to check:

✦ Is it plugged in?

✦ If the computer is plugged into a surge protector or a power strip, make sure that the surge protector or power strip is plugged in and turned on. If the surge protector or power strip has a light, it should be glowing.

✦ Make sure that the computer's On/Off switch is turned on. This advice sounds too basic to even include here, but many computers are set up so that the computer's actual power switch is always left in the On position and the computer is turned on or off by means of the switch on the surge protector or power strip. Many computer users are surprised to find out that their computers have On/Off switches on the back of the cases.

To complicate matters, newer computers have a Sleep feature, in which they appear to be turned off but really they're just sleeping. All you have to do to wake such a computer is jiggle the mouse a little. (I used to have an uncle like that.) It's easy to assume that the computer is turned off, press the power button, wonder why nothing happened, and then press the power button and hold it down, hoping it will take. If you hold down the power button long enough, the computer will actually turn itself off. Then, when you turn the computer back on, you get a message saying the computer wasn't shut down properly. Arghhh! The moral of the story is to jiggle the mouse if the computer seems to have nodded off.

✦ If you think the computer isn't plugged in but it looks like it is, listen for the fan. If the fan is running, the computer is getting power, and the problem is more serious than an unplugged power cord. (If the fan isn't running, but the computer is plugged in and the power is on, the fan may be out to lunch.)

✦ If the computer is plugged in, turned on, and still not running, plug a lamp into the outlet to make sure that power is getting to the outlet. You may need to reset a tripped circuit breaker or replace a bad surge protector. Or you may need to call the power company. (If you live in California, don't bother calling the power company. It probably won't do any good.)

Surge protectors have a limited life span. After a few years of use, many surge protectors continue to provide electrical power for your computer, but the components that protect your computer from power surges no longer work. If you're using a surge protector that is more than two or three years old, replace the old surge protector with a new one.

✦ The monitor has a separate power cord and switch. Make sure that the monitor is plugged in and turned on. (The monitor actually has two cables that must be plugged in. One runs from the back of the monitor to the back of the computer; the other is a power cord that comes from the back of the monitor and must be plugged into an electrical outlet.)

✦ Your keyboard, monitor, mouse, and printer are all connected to the back of your computer by cables. Make sure that these cables are all plugged in securely.

✦ Make sure that the other ends of the monitor and printer cables are plugged in properly, too.

✦ Some monitors have knobs that you can use to adjust the contrast and brightness of the monitor's display. If the computer is running but your display is dark, try adjusting these knobs. They may have been turned down all the way.

Ways to Check a Network Connection

Network gurus often say that 95 percent of all network problems are cable problems. The cables that connect client computers to the rest of the network are finicky beasts. They can break at a moment's notice, and by "break," I don't necessarily mean "to physically break in two." Sure, some broken cables look like someone got to the cable with pruning shears. However, cable problems aren't usually visible to the naked eye.

✦ If your network uses twisted-pair cable, you can quickly tell whether the cable connection to the network is good by looking at the back of your computer. Look for a small light located near where the cable plugs in; if this light is glowing steadily, the cable is good. If the light is dark or it's flashing intermittently, you have a cable problem (or a problem with the network card or the hub or switch that the other end of the cable is plugged in to).

If the light is not glowing steadily, try removing the cable from your computer and reinserting it. This action may cure the weak connection.

✦ Detecting a cable problem in a network that's wired with *coaxial cable,* the kind that looks like cable-TV cable, is more difficult. The connector on the back of the computer forms a T. The base end of the T plugs into your computer. One or two coaxial cables plug into the outer ends of the T. If you use only one coaxial cable, you must use a special plug called a *terminator* instead of a cable at the other end of the T. If you can't find a terminator, try conjuring one up from the twenty-first century. *Warning:* Do not do this if your name happens to be Sarah Connor.

Don't unplug a coaxial cable from the network while the network is running. Data travels around a coaxial network in the same way that a baton travels around the track in a relay race. If one person drops it, the race is over. The baton never gets to the next person. Likewise, if you unplug the network cable from your computer, the network data never gets to the computers that are "down the line" from your computer.

If you must disconnect the cable from your computer, make sure that you disconnect the T connector itself from the network card; don't disconnect the cable from the T connector itself.

✦ Hopefully, your network is wired so that each computer is connected to the network with a short (six feet or so) patch cable. One end of the patch cable plugs into the computer, and the other end plugs into a cable connector mounted on the wall. Try quickly disconnecting and reconnecting the patch cable. If that doesn't do the trick, try to find a spare patch cable that you can use.

✦ Hubs and switches are prone to having cable problems, too — especially those hubs that are wired in a "professional manner" involving a rat's nest of patch cables. Be careful whenever you enter the lair of the rat's nest. If you need to replace a patch cable, be very careful when you disconnect the suspected bad cable and reconnect the good cable in its place.

A Bunch of Error Messages Just Flew By!

Do error messages display when your computer boots? If so, they can provide invaluable clues to determine the source of the problem.

If you see error messages when you start up the computer, keep the following points in mind:

✦ Don't panic if you see a lot of error messages. Sometimes a simple problem that's easy to correct can cause a plethora of error messages when you start your computer. The messages may look as if your computer is falling to pieces, but the fix may be very simple.

✦ If the messages fly by so fast that you can't see them, press your computer's Pause key. Your computer comes to a screeching halt, giving you a chance to catch up on your error-message reading. After you've read enough, press the Pause key again to get things moving. (On computers that don't have a Pause key, pressing Ctrl+Num Lock or Ctrl+S does the same thing.)

✦ If you missed the error messages the first time, restart the computer and watch them again.

✦ Better yet, press F8 when you see the message `Starting Windows`. This displays a menu that allows you to select from several startup options, including one that processes each line of your `CONFIG.SYS` file separately so that you can see the messages displayed by each command before proceeding to the next command.

Double-Checking Your Network Settings

I swear that there are little green men who sneak into offices at night, turn on computers, and mess up TCP/IP configuration settings just for kicks. These little green men are affectionately known as *networchons*.

Remarkably, network configuration settings sometimes get inadvertently changed so that a computer, which enjoyed the network for months or even years, one day finds itself unable to access the network. So one of the first things you do, after making sure that the computers are actually on and that the cables aren't broken, is a basic review of the computer's network settings. Check the following:

✦ At a command prompt, run `ipconfig` to make sure that TCP/IP is up and running on the computer and that the IP addresses, subnet masks, and default gateway settings look right.

✦ Call up the network connection's Properties dialog box and make sure that the necessary protocols are installed correctly.

✦ Open the System Properties dialog box (double-click System in Control Panel) and check the Computer Name tab. Make sure that the computer name is unique and the domain or workgroup name is spelled properly.

✦ Double-check the user account to make sure that the user really has permission to access the resources they need.

For more information about network configuration settings, see Book II, Chapters 3 and 5.

Using the Windows Networking Troubleshooter

Windows comes with a built-in troubleshooter that can often help you to pin down the cause of a network problem. Figure 1-1 shows the Windows XP version. Answer the questions asked by the troubleshooter and click Next to move from screen to screen. The Networking Troubleshooter can't solve all networking problems, but it does point out the causes of the most common problems.

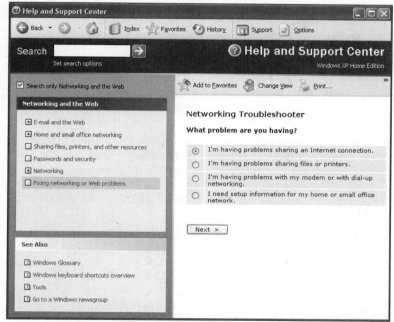

Figure 1-1:
The
Windows XP
Networking
Trouble-
shooter.

The procedure for starting the Networking Troubleshooter depends on which version of Windows you are using:

✦ For Windows XP, choose Start⇨Help And Support⇨Networking And The Web⇨Fixing Network Or Web problems and then click Home And Small Office Networking Troubleshooter.

✦ For Windows 98, click the Start button, then choose Help⇨Trouble-shooting⇨Windows 98 Troubleshooters, and finally click Networking.

✦ For Windows Me, choose Start⇨Help⇨Troubleshooting⇨Home Networking & Network Problems. Finally, click Home Networking Troubleshooter.

Windows 95 also came with a network troubleshooter, but it's not as thorough.

Time to Experiment

If you can't find some obvious explanation for your troubles — like the computer is unplugged — you need to do some experimenting to narrow down the possibilities. Design your experiments to answer one basic question: Is it a network problem or a local computer problem?

**Book IV
Chapter 1**

**Solving Network
Problems**

Here are some ways you can narrow down the cause of the problem:

✦ Try performing the same operation on someone else's computer. If no one on the network can access a network drive or printer, something is probably wrong with the network. On the other hand, if the error occurs on only one computer, the problem is likely with that computer. The wayward computer may not be reliably communicating with the network or configured properly for the network, or the problem may have nothing to do with the network at all.

✦ If you're able to perform the operation on another computer without problems, try logging on to the network with another computer using your own username. Then see whether you can perform the operation without error. If you can, the problem is probably on your computer. If you can't, the problem may be with the way your user account is configured.

✦ If you can't log on at another computer, try waiting for a bit. Your account may be temporarily locked out. This can happen for a variety of reasons — the most common of which is trying to log on with the wrong password several times in a row. If you're still locked out an hour later, call the network administrator and offer a doughnut.

Who's on First

When troubleshooting a networking problem, it's often useful to find out who is actually logged on to a network server. For example, if a user is unable to access a file on the server, you can check to see whether the user is logged on. If so, you know that the user's account is valid, but the user may not have permission to access the particular file or folder that he or she is attempting to access. On the other hand, if the user is not logged on, the problem may lie with the account itself or with the way the user is attempting to connect to the server.

It's also useful to find out who's logged on in the event that you need to restart the server. For more information about restarting a server, see the section "How to Restart a Network Server," later in this chapter.

The exact procedure of checking who is logged on depends on which server operating system you're using. The following paragraphs describe how to find out who's logged on to Windows NT 4 Server, Windows 2000 Server, or Windows Server 2003.

✦ For Windows NT 4 Server, choose Start⇨Program Files⇨Administrative Tools⇨Server Manager. Double-click the server in the list of available servers and then click the Users button to bring up the dialog box shown in Figure 1-2.

✦ For Windows 2000 Server, right-click the My Computer icon on the desktop and pick Manage from the menu that appears to bring up the Computer Management window. Open System Tools in the tree list and then open Shared Folders and select Sessions. A list of users who are logged on appears.

✦ For Windows Server 2003, you can bring up the Computer Management window by choosing Start➪Administrative Tools➪Computer Management.

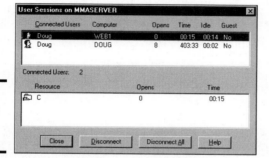

Figure 1-2:
Who's on a Windows NT server.

You can immediately disconnect all users in Windows NT Server by clicking Disconnect All. In Windows 2000 Server or Windows Server 2003, right-click Sessions in the Computer Management window and choose All Tasks➪ Disconnect All.

How to Restart a Client Computer

Sometimes trouble gets a computer so tied up in knots that the only thing you can do is reboot. In some cases, the computer just starts acting weird. Strange characters appear on the screen, or Windows goes haywire and doesn't let you exit a program. Sometimes the computer gets so confused that it can't even move. It just sits there, like a deer staring at oncoming headlights. It won't move, no matter how hard you press the Esc key or the Enter key. You can move the mouse all over your desktop, or you can even throw it across the room, but the mouse pointer on the screen stays perfectly still.

When a computer starts acting strange, you need to reboot. If you must reboot, you should do so as cleanly as possible. I know this procedure may seem elementary, but the technique for safely restarting a client computer is worth repeating, even if it is basic:

1. **Save your work if you can.**

Use the File⇨Save command, if you can, to save any documents or files that you were editing when things started to go haywire. If you can't use the menus, try clicking the Save button in the toolbar. If that doesn't work, try pressing Ctrl+S — the standard keyboard shortcut for the Save command.

2. **Close any running programs if you can.**

Use the File⇨Exit command or click the Close button in the upper-right corner of the program window. Or press Alt+F4.

3. **Choose the Start⇨Shut Down command from the taskbar.**

For Windows XP, choose Start⇨Turn Off Computer.

The Shut Down Windows dialog box appears.

4. **Select the Restart option and then click OK.**

Your computer restarts itself.

If restarting your computer doesn't seem to fix the problem, you may need to turn your computer all the way off and then turn it on again. To do so, follow the previous procedure until Step 4. Choose the Shut Down option instead of the Restart option and then click OK. Depending on your computer, Windows either turns off your computer or displays a message stating that you can now safely turn off your computer. If Windows doesn't turn the computer off for you, flip the On/Off switch to turn your computer off. Wait a minute or so and then turn the computer back on.

Most newer computers don't immediately shut themselves off when you press the Power button. Instead, you must hold the Power button down for a few seconds to actually turn off the power. This precaution is designed to prevent you from accidentally powering down your computer.

Here are a few things to try if you have trouble restarting your computer:

✦ If your computer refuses to respond to the Start⇨Shut Down command, try pressing Ctrl+Alt+Delete. This is called the "three-finger salute." It's appropriate to say "Queueue" as you do it.

When you press Ctrl+Alt+Delete, Windows 9*x* and later versions attempt to display a dialog box that enables you to close any running programs or shut down your computer entirely. Unfortunately, sometimes Windows 9*x* becomes so confused that it can't display the Restart dialog box, in which case pressing Ctrl+Alt+Delete may restart your computer.

✦ If Ctrl+Alt+Delete doesn't do anything, you've reached the last resort. The only thing left to do is press the Reset button on your computer.

Pressing the Reset button is a drastic action that you should take only after your computer becomes completely unresponsive. Any work you haven't yet saved to disk is lost. (Sniff.) (If your computer doesn't have a Reset button, turn the computer off, wait a few moments, and then turn the computer back on again.)

✦ If at all possible, save your work before restarting your computer. Any work you haven't saved is lost. Unfortunately, if your computer is totally tied up in knots, you probably can't save your work. In that case, you have no choice but to push your computer off the digital cliff.

Restarting Network Services

Once in awhile, the NOS service that supports the task that's causing you trouble inexplicably stops or gets stuck. If users can't access a server, it may be because one of the key network services has stopped or is stuck.

You can review the status of services by using the Services tool, as shown in Figure 1-3. To display it, choose Services from the Administrative Tools menu. Review this list to make sure that all key services are running. If a key service is paused or stopped, restart it.

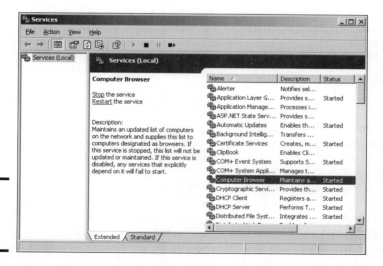

Figure 1-3:
The
Services
tool.

Which service qualifies as a *key* service depends on what roles you've defined for the server. Table 1-1 lists a few key services that are common to most Windows network operating systems. However, many servers require additional services besides these.

Table 1-1	Key Windows Services
Service	*Description*
Computer Browser	Maintains a list of computers on the network that can be accessed. If this service is disabled, the computer won't be able to use browsing services, such as My Network Places.
DHCP Client	Enables the computer to obtain its IP address from a DHCP server. If this service is disabled, the computer's IP address won't be configured properly.
DNS Client	Enables the computer to access a DNS server to resolve DNS names. If this service is disabled, the computer won't be able to handle DNS names, including Internet addresses and Active Directory names.
Server	Provides basic file and printer sharing services for the server. If this service is stopped, clients won't be able to connect to the server to access files or printers.
Workstation	Enables the computer to establish client connections with other servers. If this service is disabled, the computer won't be able to connect to other servers.

Key services usually stop for a reason, so simply restarting a stopped service probably won't solve your network's problem — at least, not for long. You should review the System log to look for any error messages that may explain why the service stopped in the first place.

If you're using Windows 2000 Server or Windows Server 2003, you can double-click a service to display a dialog box that describes the service. This information can come in handy if you're not certain what a particular service does.

How to Restart a Network Server

Sometimes, the only way to flush out a network problem is to restart the network server that's experiencing trouble.

Restarting a network server is something you should do only as a last resort. Network operating systems are designed to run for months or even years at a time without rebooting. Restarting a server invariably results in a temporary shutdown of the network. If you must restart a server, try to do it during off hours if possible.

Before you restart a server, check to see whether a specific service that is required has been paused or stopped. You may be able to just restart the individual service rather than the entire server. For more information, see the section "Restarting Network Services," earlier in this chapter.

Here is the basic procedure for restarting a network server. Keep in mind that for NetWare or Windows 2000 servers, you may need to take additional steps to get things going again. Check with your network administrator to be sure.

1. **Make sure that everyone is logged off the server.**

   The easiest way to do that is to restart the server after normal business hours, when everyone has gone home for the day. Then, you can just shut down the server and let the shutdown process forcibly log off any remaining users.

   To find out who's logged on, refer to the section "Who's On First?" earlier in this chapter.

2. **After you're sure the users have logged off, shut down the network server.**

   You want to do this step behaving like a good citizen if possible — decently and in order. If you use Novell NetWare, type **down** on the server's keyboard and then reboot the server. For Windows servers, use the Start⇨Shut Down command.

Windows Server 2003 won't let you shut down the server without providing a reason for the shutdown. When you press Ctrl+Alt+Delete, a dialog box appears, as shown in Figure 1-4. In this dialog box, you can select one of several predetermined reasons for planned or unplanned shutdowns from the drop-down list. You can also provide additional details about the shutdown if you want. This dialog box doesn't let you shut down until you select a reason and type at least one character in the Comment text box. The information you supply here is entered into the server's System log, which you can review by using the Event Viewer.

Book IV Chapter 1

Solving Network Problems

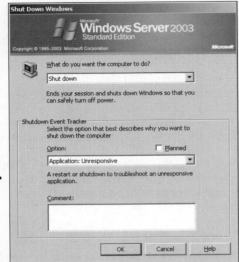

Figure 1-4:
Tracking
shutdowns
in Windows
Server 2003.

3. **Reboot the server computer or turn it off and then on again.**

   Watch the server start up to make sure that no error messages appear.

4. **Tell everyone to log back on and make sure that everyone can now access the network.**

Remember the following when you consider restarting the network:

✦ Restarting the network server is more drastic than restarting a client computer. Make sure that everyone saves his or her work and logs off the network before you do it! You can cause major problems if you blindly turn off the server computer while users are logged on.

✦ Obviously, restarting a network server is a major inconvenience to every network user. Better offer treats.

Looking at Event Logs

One of the most useful troubleshooting techniques for diagnosing network problems is to review the network operating system's built-in event logs. These logs contain information about interesting and potentially trouble-some events that occur during the daily operation of your network. Ordinarily, these logs run in the background, quietly gathering information about network events. When something goes wrong, you can check the logs to see whether the problem generated a noteworthy event. In many cases, the event logs contain an entry that pinpoints the exact cause of the problem and suggests a solution.

To display the event logs in a Windows server, use the Event Viewer available from the Administrative Tools menu. For example, Figure 1-5 shows an Event Viewer from a Windows Server 2003 system. The tree listing on the left side of the Event Viewer lists five categories of events that are tracked: Application events, Security events, System events, Directory Service events, and File Replication Service events. Select one of these options to see the log that you want to view. For details about a particular event, double-click the event; this action displays a dialog box that has detailed information about the event.

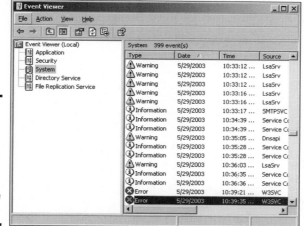

Figure 1-5:
Event logs keep track of interesting and potentially troublesome events.

Documenting Your Trials and Tribulations

For a large network, you'll probably want to invest in problem management software that tracks each problem through the entire process of troubleshooting, from initial report to final resolution. For small- and medium-sized networks, it's probably sufficient to put together a three-ring binder with preprinted forms. Or, record your log in a Word document or Excel spreadsheet.

Regardless of how you track your network problems, the tracking log should include the following information:

✦ The real name and the network username of the person reporting the problem.

✦ The date the problem was first reported.

✦ An indication of the severity of the problem. Is it merely an inconvenience, or is a user unable to complete his or her work because of the problem? Does a workaround exist?

✦ The name of the person assigned to resolve the problem.

✦ A description of the problem.

✦ A list of the software involved, including versions.

✦ A description of the steps taken to solve the problem.

✦ A description of any intermediate steps that were taken to try to solve the problem, along with an indication of whether those steps were "undone" when they didn't help solve the problem.

✦ The date the problem was finally resolved.

Chapter 2: Network Performance Anxiety

In This Chapter

✔ Understanding performance problems

✔ Looking at bottlenecks

✔ Developing a procedure for solving performance problems

✔ Monitoring performance

✔ Implementing other tips for speeding up your network

The term *network performance* refers to how efficiently the network responds to users' needs. It goes without saying that any access to resources that involves the network will be slower than similar access that doesn't involve the network. For example, it takes longer to open a Word document that resides on a network file server than it takes to open a similar document that resides on the user's local hard drive. However, it shouldn't take *much* longer. If it does, you have a network performance problem.

This chapter is a general introduction to the practice of tuning your network so that it performs as well as possible. Keep in mind that many specific bits of network tuning advice are scattered throughout this book. In this chapter, you can find some specific techniques for analyzing your network's performance, taking corrective action when a performance problem develops, and charting your progress.

Why Administrators Hate Performance Problems

Network performance problems are among the most difficult network problems to track down and solve. If a user simply can't access the network, it usually doesn't take long to figure out why: the cable is broken, a network card or hub is malfunctioning, the user doesn't have permission to access the resource, and so on. After a little investigation, the problem usually reveals itself, you fix it, and move on to the next problem.

Unfortunately, performance problems are messier. Here are just a few of the reasons that network administrators hate performance problems:

+ **Performance problems are difficult to quantify.** Exactly how much slower is the network now than it was a week ago, a month ago, or even a year ago? Sometimes the network just *feels* slow, but you can't quite define exactly how slow it really is.

+ **Performance problems usually develop gradually.** Sometimes a network slows down suddenly and drastically. More often, though, the network gradually gets slower, a little bit at a time, until one day the users notice that the network is slow.

+ **Performance problems often go unreported.** They gripe about the problem to each other around the water cooler, but they don't formally contact you to let you know that their network seems 10 percent slower than usual. As long as they can still access the network, they just assume that the problem is temporary, or that it's just their imaginations.

+ **Many performance problems are intermittent.** Sometimes a user calls you and complains that a certain network operation has become slower than molasses, and by the time you get to the user's desk, the operation performs like a snap. Sometimes you can find a pattern to the intermittent behavior, such as it's slower in the morning than in the afternoon, or it's only slow while backups are running or while the printer is working. Other times, you can't find a pattern. Sometimes the operation is slow; sometimes it isn't.

+ **Performance tuning is not an exact science.** Improving performance sometimes involves educated guesswork. Will upgrading all the users from 10Mbps to 100Mbps improve performance? Probably. Will segmenting the network improve performance? Maybe. Will adding another 512MB of RAM to the server improve performance? Hopefully.

+ **The solution to performance problems is sometimes a hard sell.** If a user is unable to access the network due to a malfunctioning component, there's usually not much question that the purchase of a replacement is justified. However, if the network is slow and you think you can fix it by upgrading all the network cards to 10/100Mbps cards and replacing all the hubs with 100Mbps switches, you may have trouble selling management on the upgrade.

What Exactly Is a Bottleneck?

The term *bottleneck* does not in any way refer to the physique of your typical computer geek. (Well, I guess it *could,* in some cases.) Rather, computer geeks coined the phrase when they discovered that the tapered shape of a bottle of Jolt Cola limited the rate at which they could consume the beverage. "Hey," a computer geek said one day, "the gently tapered narrowness of this bottle's neck imposes a distinct limiting effect upon the rate at which I can consume the tasty caffeine-laden beverage contained within. This draws to mind a hitherto undiscovered yet obvious analogy to the limiting effect that a single slow component of a computer system can have upon the performance of the system as a whole."

"Fascinating," replied all the other computer geeks, who were fortunate enough to be present at that historic moment.

The phrase stuck and is used to this day to draw attention to the simple fact that a computer system is only as fast as its slowest component. It's the computer equivalent of the old truism that a chain is only as strong as its weakest link.

For a simple demonstration of this concept, consider what happens when you print a word-processing document on a slow printer. Your word-processing program reads the data from disk and sends it to the printer. Then you sit and wait while the printer prints the document.

Would buying a faster CPU or adding more memory make the document print faster? No. The CPU is already much faster than the printer, and your computer already has more than enough memory to print the document. The printer itself is the bottleneck, so the only way to print the document faster is to replace the slow printer with a faster one.

Here are some other random thoughts about bottlenecks:

✦ **A computer system always has a bottleneck.** For example, suppose that you've decided that the bottleneck on your file server is a slow IDE hard drive, so you replace it with the fastest SCSI drive money can buy. Now, the hard drive is no longer the bottleneck: The drive can process information faster than the controller card to which the disk is connected. You haven't really eliminated the bottleneck; you've just moved it from the hard drive to the disk controller. No matter what you do, the computer will always have some component that limits the overall performance of the system.

✦ **One way to limit the effect of a bottleneck is to avoid waiting for the bottleneck.** For example, print spooling lets you avoid waiting for a slow printer. Spooling doesn't speed up the printer, but it does free you up to do other work while the printer chugs along. Similarly, disk caching lets you avoid waiting for a slow hard drive.

✦ **One of the reasons computer geeks are switching from Jolt Cola to Snapple is that Snapple bottles have wider necks.**

The Five Most Common Network Bottlenecks

Direct from the home office in sunny Fresno, California, here are the ten — oops, five — most common network bottlenecks, in no particular order.

The hardware inside your servers

Your servers should be powerful computers capable of handling all the work your network will throw at them. Don't cut corners by using a bottom-of-the-line computer that you bought at a discount computer store.

The following are the four most important components of your server hardware:

✦ **Processor:** Your server should have a powerful processor. As a general rule, any processor that is available in an $800 computer from a low-cost general appliance store is not a processor that you want to see in your file server. In other words, avoid processors that are designed for consumer-grade home computers.

✦ **Memory:** You can't have too much memory. Memory is cheap, so don't skimp. Don't even think about running a server with less than 512MB of RAM.

✦ **Disk:** Don't mess around with inexpensive IDE hard drives. To be respectable, you should have nothing but SCSI drives.

✦ **Network card:** Cheap $14.95 network cards are fine for home networks, but don't use one in a file server that supports 50 users and expect to be happy with the server's performance. Remember that the server computer uses the network a lot more than any of the clients. So equip your servers with good network cards.

The server's configuration options

All network operating systems have options that you can configure. Some of these options can make the difference between a pokey network and a zippy network. Unfortunately, no hard-and-fast rules exist for setting these options. Otherwise, you wouldn't have options.

The following are some of the more important tuning options available for most servers:

✦ **Virtual memory options:** *Virtual memory* refers to disk paging files that the server uses when it doesn't have enough real memory to do its work. Few servers ever have enough real memory, so virtual memory is always an important server feature. You can specify the size and location of the virtual memory paging files. For best performance, you should provide at least 1.5 times the amount of real memory. For example, if you have 1GB of real memory, allocate at least 1.5GB of virtual memory. If necessary, you can increase this size later.

✦ **Disk striping:** Use the disk defragmenter to optimize the data storage on your server's disks. If the server has more than one hard drive, you can increase performance by creating *striped volumes,* which allow disk I/O operations to run concurrently on each of the drives in the stripe set.

✦ **Network protocols:** Make sure that your network protocols are configured correctly and remove any protocols that aren't necessary.

✦ **Free disk space on the server:** Servers like to have plenty of breathing room on their disks. If the amount of free disk space on your server drops precipitously low, the server chokes up and slows to a crawl. Make sure that your server has plenty of space — a few GBs of unused disk space provides a healthy buffer.

Servers that do too much

One common source of network performance problems is servers that are overloaded with too many duties. Just because modern network operating systems come equipped with dozens of different types of services doesn't mean that you should enable and use them all on a single server. If a single server is bogged down because of too much work, add a second server to relieve the first server of some of its chores. Remember the old saying: "Many hands make light work."

For example, if your network needs more disk space, consider adding a second file server rather than adding another drive to the server that already has four drives that are nearly full. Or, better yet, purchase a file server appliance that is dedicated just to the task of serving files.

As a side benefit, your network will be easier to administer and more reliable if you place separate functions on separate servers. For example, if you have a single server that doubles as a file server and a mail server, you'll lose both services if you have to take the server down to perform an upgrade or repair a failed component. However, if you have separate file and mail server computers, only one of the services will be interrupted if you have to take down one of the servers.

**Book IV
Chapter 2**

**Network
Performance
Anxiety**

The network infrastructure

The infrastructure consists of the cables and any switches, hubs, routers, and other components that sit between your clients and your servers. The following network infrastructure items can slow down your network:

✦ **Hubs:** Because switches are so inexpensive now, you can affordably solve a lot of performance problems by replacing old, outdated hubs with switches. Using switches instead of hubs reduces the overall load on your network.

✦ **Segment sizes:** Keep the number of computers and other devices on each network segment to a reasonable number. About 20 devices is usually the right number. (Note that if you replace your hubs with switches, you instantly cut the size of each segment because each port on a switch constitutes a separate segment.)

✦ **The network's speed:** If you have an older network, you'll probably discover that many — if not all — of your users are still working at 10Mbps. Upgrading to 100Mbps will speed up the network dramatically.

✦ **The backbone speed:** If your network uses a backbone to connect segments, consider upgrading the backbone to 1Gbps.

The hardest part about improving the performance of a network is determining what the bottlenecks are. With sophisticated test equipment and years of experience, network gurus can make pretty good educated guesses. Without the equipment and experience, you can still make pretty good uneducated guesses. In the remaining sections in this chapter, I give you some pointers on how to discover your computer's bottlenecks and improve your computer's performance.

Malfunctioning components

Sometimes a malfunctioning network card or other component slows down the network. For example, a switch may malfunction intermittently, occasionally letting packets through but dropping enough of them to slow down the network. After you've identified the faulty component, replacing it will restore the network to its original speed.

Tuning Your Network the Compulsive Way

You have two ways to tune your network. The first is to think about it a bit, take a guess at what may improve performance, try it, and see whether the network seems to run faster. This approach is the way most people go about tuning the network.

Then you have the compulsive way, which is suitable for people who organize their sock drawers by color and their food cupboards alphabetically by food groups. The compulsive approach to tuning a network goes something like this:

1. **Establish a method for objectively testing the performance of some aspect of the network.**

   This method is called a *benchmark,* and the result of your benchmark is called a *baseline.*

2. **Change one variable of your network configuration and rerun the test.**

   For example, suppose that you think that increasing the size of the disk cache can improve performance. Change the cache size, restart the server, and run the benchmark test. Note whether the performance improves, stays the same, or becomes worse.

3. **Repeat Step 2 for each variable that you want to test.**

Here are some salient points to keep in mind if you decide to tune your network the compulsive way:

✦ If possible, test each variable separately — in other words, reverse the changes you've made to other network variables before proceeding.

✦ Write down the results of each test so that you have an accurate record of the impact that each change has made on your network's performance.

✦ Be sure to change only one aspect of the network each time you run the benchmark. If you make several changes, you won't know which one caused the change. One change may improve performance, but the other change may worsen performance so that the changes cancel each other out — kind of like offsetting penalties in a football game.

✦ If possible, conduct the baseline test during normal working hours, when the network is undergoing its normal workload.

✦ To establish your baseline performance, run your benchmark test two or three times to make sure that the results are repeatable.

Monitoring Network Performance

One way to monitor network performance is to use a stopwatch to see how long it actually takes to complete common network tasks, such as opening documents or printing reports. If you choose to monitor your network by using the stopwatch technique, you'll want to get a clipboard, baseball cap, and gray sweat suit to complete the ensemble.

A more high-tech approach to monitoring network performance is to use a monitor program that automatically gathers network statistics for you. After you've set up the monitor, it plugs away, silently spying on your network and recording what it sees in performance logs. You can then review the performance logs to see how your network is doing.

For large networks, you can purchase sophisticated monitoring programs that run on their own dedicated servers. For small- and medium-sized networks, you can probably get by with the built-in monitoring facilities that come with the network operating system. For example, Figure 2-1 shows the Performance Monitor tool that comes with Windows Server 2003. Other operating systems come with similar tools.

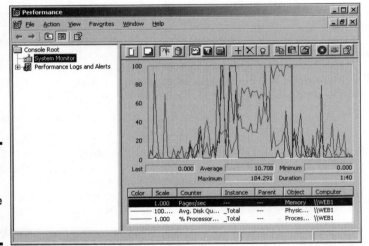

Figure 2-1:
Monitoring network performance in Windows Server 2003.

The Windows Performance Monitor lets you keep track of several different aspects of system performance at once. You track each performance aspect by setting up a *counter*. You can choose from dozens of different counters. Table 2-1 describes some of the most commonly used counters. Note that each counter refers to a server object, such as physical disk, memory, or the processor.

Table 2-1	Commonly Used Performance Counters	
Object	*Counter*	*Description*
Physical Disk	% Free Space	The percentage of free space on the server's physical disks. Should be at least 15 percent.
Physical Disk	Average Queue Length	Indicates how many disk operations are waiting while the disk is busy servicing other disk operations. Should be 2 or less.
Memory	Pages/second	The number of pages retrieved from the virtual memory page files per second. A typical threshold is about 2,500 pages per second.
Processor	% Processor Time	Indicates the percentage of the processor's time that it is busy doing work rather than sitting idle. Should be 85 percent or less.

Here are a few more things to consider about performance monitoring:

✦ The Performance Monitor enables you to view real-time data or to view data that you've saved in a log file. Real-time data gives you an idea about what's happening with the network at a particular moment, but the more useful information comes from the logs.

✦ You can schedule logging to occur at certain times of the day and for certain intervals. For example, you may schedule the log to gather data every 15 seconds from 9:00 to 9:30 every morning and then again from 3:00 to 3:30 every afternoon.

✦ Even if you don't have a performance problem now, you should set up performance logging and let it run for a few weeks to gather some baseline data. If you develop a problem later on the baseline data will prove invaluable as you research the problem.

✦ The act of gathering performance data slows down your server. So don't leave performance logging on all the time. Use it only occasionally to gather baseline data or when you're experiencing a performance problem.

More Performance Tips

Here are a few last-minute performance tips that barely made it in:

✦ You can often find the source of a slow network by staring at the network hubs or switches for a few minutes. These devices have colorful arrays of green and red lights. The green lights flash whenever data is transmitted; the red lights flash when a collision occurs. An occasional red flash is normal, but if one or more of the red lights is flashing repeatedly, the NIC connected to that port may be faulty.

✦ Check for scheduled tasks, such as backups, batched database updates, or report jobs. If at all possible, schedule these tasks to run after normal business hours, such as at night when no one is in the office. These jobs tend to slow down the network by hogging the server's hard drives.

✦ Sometimes faulty application programs can degrade performance. For example, some programs develop what is known as a *memory leak*: They use memory, but forget to release the memory after they finish. Programs with memory leaks can slowly eat up all the memory on a server, until the server runs out and grinds to a halt. If you think a program may have a memory leak, contact the manufacturer of the program to see whether a fix is available.

✦ A relatively new source of performance problems is so-called *spyware*. Spyware is software that installs itself into your computer, monitors what you do, and periodically reports your activities to a computer on the Internet. Spyware is often associated with advertising programs installed by music sharing software. If your users have been downloading music, they're probably infected by spyware. To find out more, use Google or another search engine to search for information about "spyware."

Chapter 3: Protecting Your Network

In This Chapter

✔ Understanding the need for backup

✔ Working with tape drives and other backup media

✔ Understandig the different types of backups

✔ Mastering tape rotation and other details

*I*f you're the hapless network manager, the safety of the data on your network is your responsibility. You get paid to lie awake at night worrying about your data. Will it be there tomorrow? If it's not, will *you* be able to get it back? And — most importantly — if you can't get it back, will *you* be there tomorrow?

This chapter covers the ins and outs of being a good, responsible, trustworthy network manager. They don't give out merit badges for this stuff, but they should.

Backing Up Your Data

Backups are the cornerstone of any disaster recovery plan. Without backups, a simple hard drive failure can set your company back days or even weeks as it tries to reconstruct lost data. In fact, without backups, your company's very existence is in jeopardy.

The main goal of backups is simple: Keep a spare copy of your network's critical data so that, no matter what happens, you never lose more than one day's work. The stock market may crash, hanging chads may factor into another presidential election, and Jar-Jar Binks may be in yet another *Star Wars* movie. However, you never lose more than one day's work if you stay on top of your backups.

The way to do this, naturally, is to make sure that data is backed up on a daily basis. In many networks, it's feasible to back up all the network hard drives every night. However, even if full nightly backups aren't possible, you can still use techniques that can ensure that every file on the network has a backup copy that's no more than one day old.

The goal of disaster planning — which is now called by the more trendy name *business continuity planning* (also known as *BCP*) — is to make sure that your company can resume operations shortly after a disaster occurs, such as a fire, earthquake, vandalism, flood, or any other imaginable calamity. Backups are a key component of any disaster recovery plan, but disaster planning entails much more than just backups. For more information about the larger context of disaster planning and BCP, skip ahead to the next chapter.

All About Tapes and Tape Drives

If you plan on backing up the data on your network server's hard drives, you need something to back up the data to. You can copy the data onto diskettes, but a 20GB hard drive would need about 14,000 diskettes to do a full backup. That's a few more diskettes than most people want to keep in the closet. Instead of diskettes, you want to back up your network data to tape. Depending on the make and model of the tape drive, you can copy as much as 80GB of data onto a single tape.

One of the benefits of tape backup is that you can run it unattended. In fact, you can schedule tape backup to run automatically during off hours, when no one is using the network. In order for unattended backups to work, you must ensure that you have enough tape capacity to back up your entire network server's hard drive without having to manually switch tapes. If your network server has only 10GB of data, you can easily back it up onto a single tape. However, if you have 100GB of data, you should invest in several tape drives that have a combined capacity of at least 100GB. That way, you can run your backups unattended.

Here are some additional thoughts concerning tape backups:

✦ The most popular style of tape backup for smallish networks is called *Travan drives*. Travan drives come in a variety of models with tape capacities ranging from 8GB to 20GB. You can purchase an 8GB drive for under $200 and a 20GB unit for about $300. (Travan drives used to be known as *QIC drives*.)

✦ For larger networks, you can get tape backup units that offer higher capacity and faster backup speed than Travan drives, but for more money, of course. DAT (digital audio tape) units can back up as much as 40GB on a single tape, and DLT (digital linear tape) drives can store up to 80GB on one tape. DAT and DLT drives can cost $1,000 or more, depending on the capacity.

✦ If you're really up the backup creek with hundreds of gigabytes to back up, you can get robotic tape backup units that automatically fetch and load tape cartridges from a library, so you can do complete backups without having to load tapes manually. Naturally, these units aren't cheap: The small ones, which have a library of eight tapes and a total backup capacity of over 300GB, start at about $5,000.

✦ An alternative to tape drives for backups is removable hard drives — these hard drives are housed in cartridges that you can insert or remove like a giant floppy disk. The best-known removable hard drives are made by Iomega. Iomega's Zip drives sell for about $175 and can back up 750MB of data on each cartridge.

✦ Another alternative to tape drives for backups is rewritable CD drives, known as *CD-RW* drives. A CD-RW drive can write about 600MB of data to each CD.

✦ Frankly, a 750MB Zip drive or a 600MB CD-RW drive doesn't really have enough capacity to do backups properly. If you fill up a 100GB disk, you'd need more than 130 Zip cartridges or 150 CDs to back it all up. As a result, Zip drives and CD-RW drives are a viable backup option for small networks only.

✦ Yet another alternative backup media is DVD recorders, which can write up to 4.7GB of data on a single disc.

Backup Software

All versions of Windows come with a built-in backup program. In addition, most tape drives come with backup programs that are often faster or more flexible than the standard Windows backup. You can also purchase sophisticated backup programs that are specially designed for large networks, which have multiple servers with data that must be backed up.

For a basic Windows file server, you can use the backup program that comes with Windows Server. Server versions of Windows come with a decent backup program that can run scheduled, unattended tape backups.

Backup programs do more than just copy data from your hard drive to tape. Backup programs use special compression techniques to squeeze your data so that you can cram more data onto fewer tapes. Compression factors of 2:1 are common, so you can usually squeeze 10GB of data onto a tape that would hold only 5GB of data without compression. (Tape drive manufacturers tend to state the capacity of their drives by using compressed data, assuming a 2:1 compression ratio. So a 20GB tape has an uncompressed capacity of 10GB.)

**Book IV
Chapter 3**

Protecting Your Network

Backup programs also help you to keep track of which data has been backed up and which hasn't, and they offer options such as incremental or differential backups that can streamline the backup process, as described in the next section.

Types of Backups

You can perform five different types of backups. Many backup schemes rely on full backups daily, but for some networks, it's more practical to use a scheme that relies on two or more of these backup types.

The differences among the fives types of backup involve a little technical detail known as the *archive bit*. The archive bit indicates whether a file has been modified since the last time it was backed up. The archive bit is a little flag that's stored along with the file's name, creation date, and other directory information. Any time that a program modifies a file, the archive bit is set to the On position. That way, backup programs know that the file has been modified and needs to be backed up.

The differences among the various types of backup center around whether they use the archive bit to determine which files to back up, and whether they flip the archive bit to the Off position after they back up a file. Table 3-1 summarizes these differences, and they're explained in the following sections.

Backup programs allow you to select any combination of drives and folders to back up. As a result, you can customize the file selection for a backup operation to suit your needs. For example, you can set up one backup plan that backs up all a server's shared folders and drives plus its mail server stores, but leaves out folders that rarely change, such as the operating system folders or installed program folders. You can then back up those folders on a less regular basis. The drives and folders that you select for a backup operation are collectively called the *backup selection*.

Table 3-1	How Backup Types Use the Archive Bit	
Backup Type	*Selects Files Based on Archive Bit?*	*Resets Archive Bits After Backing Up?*
Normal	No	Yes
Copy	No	No
Daily	No *	No
Incremental	Yes	Yes
Differential	Yes	No

* Selects files based on the Last Modified date.

The archive bit would have made a good Abbott and Costello routine. ("All right, I wanna know who modified the archive bit." "What." "Who?" "No, what." "Wait a minute . . . just tell me what's the name of the guy who modified the archive bit!" "Right.")

Normal backups

A *normal backup,* also called a *full backup,* is the most basic type of backup. In a normal backup, all files in the backup selection are backed up — regardless of whether the archive bit has been set. In other words, the files are backed up even if they haven't been modified since the last time they were backed up. As each file is backed up, its archive bit is reset, so backups that select files based on the archive bit setting won't back up the files.

When a normal backup finishes, none of the files in the backup selection will have their archive bits set. As a result, if you immediately follow a normal backup with an incremental backup or a differential backup, no files will be selected for backup by the incremental or differential backup because no files will have their archive bits set.

The easiest backup scheme is to simply schedule a normal backup every night. That way, all your data is backed up on a daily basis. So if the need arises, you can restore files from a single tape or set of tapes. Restoring files is more complicated when other types of backups are involved.

As a result, I recommend that you do normal backups nightly if you have the tape capacity to do them unattended — that is, without having to swap tapes. If you can't do an unattended normal backup because the amount of data to be backed up is greater than the capacity of your tape drive or drives, you'll have to use other types of backups in combination with normal backups.

If you aren't able to get a normal backup on a single tape and you can't afford a second tape drive, take a hard look at the data that's being included in the backup selection. I recently worked on a network that was having trouble backing up onto a single tape. When I examined the data that was being backed up, I discovered about 5GB of static data that was essentially an online archive of old projects. This data was necessary because network users needed it for research purposes, but the data was read-only. Even though the data never changed, it was being backed up to tape every night, and the backups required two tapes. After we removed this data from the cycle of nightly backups, the backups were able to squeeze onto a single tape again.

If you do remove static data from the nightly backup, make sure that you have a secure backup of the static data, either on tape, CD-RW, or some other media.

Copy backups

A *copy backup* is similar to a normal backup, except that the archive bit is not reset as each file is copied. As a result, copy backups don't disrupt the cycle of normal and incremental or differential backups.

Copy backups are usually not incorporated into regular, scheduled backups. Instead, you use a copy backup when you want to do an occasional one-shot backup. For example, if you're about to perform an operating system upgrade, you should back up the server before proceeding. If you do a full backup, the archive bits will be reset, and your regular backups will be disrupted. However, if you do a copy backup, the archive bits of any modified files will remain unchanged. As a result, your regular normal and incremental or differential backups will be unaffected.

Note that if you don't incorporate incremental or differential backups into your backup routine, the difference between a copy backup and a normal backup is moot.

Daily backups

A *daily backup* backs up just those files that have been changed the same day that the backup is performed. A daily backup examines the modification date stored with each file's directory entry to determine whether a file should be backed up. Daily backups don't reset the archive bit.

I'm not a big fan of this option because of the small possibility that some files may slip through the cracks. Someone may be working late one night and modify a file after the evening's backups have completed, but before midnight. Those files won't be included in the following night's backups. Incremental or differential backups, which rely on the archive bit rather than the modification date, are more reliable.

Incremental backups

An incremental backup backs up only those files that you've modified since the last time you did a backup. Incremental backups are a lot faster than full backups because your network users probably modify only a small portion of the files on the server in any given day. As a result, if a full backup takes three tapes, you can probably fit an entire week's worth of incremental backups on a single tape.

As an incremental backup copies each file, it resets the file's archive bit. That way, the file will be backed up again before your next normal backup only when a user modifies the file again.

Here are some thoughts about using incremental backups:

✦ The easiest way to use incremental backups is to do a normal backup every Monday and then do an incremental backup on Tuesday, Wednesday, Thursday, and Friday. (This assumes, of course, that you can do a full backup overnight on Monday. If your full backup takes more than 12 hours, you may want to do it on Friday instead so that it can run over the weekend.)

✦ When you use incremental backups, the complete backup consists of the full backup tapes and all the incremental backup tapes that you've made since you did the full backup. If the hard drive crashes and you have to restore the data onto a new drive, you first restore Monday's normal backup and then you restore each of the subsequent incremental backups.

✦ Incremental backups complicate the task of restoring individual files because the most recent copy of the file may be on the full backup tape or on any of the incremental backups. Fortunately, backup programs keep track of the location of the most recent version of each file in order to simplify the process.

✦ When you use incremental backups, you can choose whether you want to store each incremental backup on its own tape or append each backup to the end of an existing tape. In many cases, you can use a single tape for an entire week's worth of incremental backups.

Differential backups

A *differential backup* is similar to an incremental backup, except that it doesn't reset the archive bit as files are backed up. As a result, each differential backup represents the difference between the last normal backup and the current state of the hard drive. To do a full restore from a differential backup, you first restore the last normal backup, and then you restore the most recent differential backup.

For example, suppose that you do a normal backup on Monday and differential backups on Tuesday, Wednesday, and Thursday, and your hard drive crashes Friday morning. Friday afternoon, you install a new hard drive. Then, to restore the data, you first restore the normal backup from Monday. Then, you restore the differential backup from Thursday. The Tuesday and Wednesday differential backups aren't needed.

The main difference between incremental and differential backups is that incremental backups result in smaller and faster backups, but differential backups are easier to restore. If your users frequently ask you to restore individual files, you may want to consider differential backups.

**Book IV
Chapter 3**

**Protecting Your
Network**

Local versus Network Backups

When you back up network data, you have two basic approaches to running the backup software: You can perform a *local backup,* in which the backup software runs on the file server itself and backs up data to a tape drive that's installed in the server, or you can perform a *network backup,* in which you use one network computer to back up data from another network computer. In a network backup, the data has to travel over the network to get to the computer that's running the backup.

If you run the backups from the file server, you'll tie up the server while the backup is running. Your users will complain that their access to the server has slowed to a snail's pace. On the other hand, if you run the backup over the network from a client computer or a dedicated backup server, you'll flood the network with gigabytes of data being backed up. Your users will then complain that the entire network has slowed to a snail's pace.

Network performance is one of the main reasons you should try to run your backups during off hours, when other users are not accessing the network. Another reason to do this is so that you can perform a more thorough backup. If you run your backup while other users are accessing files, the backup program is likely to skip over any files that are being accessed by users at the time the backup runs. As a result, your backup won't include those files. Ironically, the files most likely to get left out of the backup are often the files that need backing up the most because they're the files that are being used and modified.

Here are some extra thoughts on client and server backups:

✦ You may think that backing up directly from the server would be more efficient than backing up from a client because data doesn't have to travel over the network. Actually, this assumption doesn't always hold, because the network may well be faster than the tape drive. The network probably won't slow down backups unless you back up during the busiest time of the day, when hordes of network users are storming the network gates.

✦ To improve network backup speed and to minimize the effect that network backups have on the rest of the network, consider using a 100Mbps switch rather than a normal hub to connect the servers and the backup client. That way, network traffic between the server and the backup client won't bog down the rest of the network.

✦ Any files that happen to be open while the backups are running won't get backed up. That's usually not a problem, because backups are run at off hours when people have gone home for the day. However, if someone leaves his or her computer on with a Word document open, that

Word document won't be backed up. One way to solve this problem is to set up the server so that it automatically logs everyone off the network before the backups begin.

✦ Some backup programs have special features that enable them to back up open files. For example, the Windows Server 2003 backup does this by creating a snapshot of the volume when it begins, thus making temporary copies of any files that are modified during the backup. The backup backs up the temporary copies rather than the versions being modified. When the backup finishes, the temporary copies are deleted.

How Many Sets of Backups Should You Keep?

Don't try to cut costs by purchasing one backup tape and reusing it every day. What happens if you accidentally delete an important file on Tuesday and don't discover your mistake until Thursday? Because the file didn't exist on Wednesday, it won't be on Wednesday's backup tape. If you have only one tape that's reused every day, you're outta luck.

The safest scheme is to use a new backup tape every day and keep all your old tapes in a vault. Pretty soon, though, your tape vault can start looking like the warehouse where they stored the Ark of the Covenant at the end of *Raiders of the Lost Ark.*

As a compromise between these two extremes, most users purchase several tapes and rotate them. That way, you always have several backup tapes to fall back on, just in case the file you need isn't on the most recent backup tape. This technique is called *tape rotation,* and several variations are commonly used:

✦ The simplest approach is to purchase three tapes and label them A, B, and C. You use the tapes on a daily basis in sequence: A the first day, B the second day, C the third day; then A the fourth day, B the fifth day, C the sixth day, and so on. On any given day, you have three *generations* of backups: today's, yesterday's, and the day-before-yesterday's. Computer geeks like to call these the *grandfather, father,* and *son* tapes.

✦ Another simple approach is to purchase five tapes and use one each day of the week.

✦ A variation of this scheme is to buy eight tapes. Take four of them and write *Monday* on one label, *Tuesday* on the second, *Wednesday* on the third, and *Thursday* on the fourth label. On the other four tapes, write *Friday 1, Friday 2, Friday 3,* and *Friday 4.* Now, tack a calendar up on the wall near the computer and number all the Fridays in the year: 1, 2, 3, 4, 1, 2, 3, 4, and so on.

On Monday through Thursday, you use the appropriate daily backup tape. When you do backups on Friday, you consult the calendar to decide which Friday tape to use. With this scheme, you always have four weeks' worth of Friday backup tapes, plus individual backup tapes for the past five days.

✦ If bookkeeping data lives on the network, it's a good idea to make a backup copy of all your files (or at least all your accounting files) imme- diately before closing the books each month; then retain those backups for each month of the year. Does that mean you should purchase 12 additional tapes? Not necessarily. If you back up just your accounting files, you can probably fit all 12 months on a single tape. Just make sure that you back up with the "append to tape" option rather than the "erase tape" option so that the previous contents of the tape aren't destroyed. Also, treat this accounting backup as completely separate from your normal daily backup routine.

You should also keep at least one recent full backup at another location. That way, if your office should fall victim to an errant Scud missile or a rogue asteroid, you can re-create your data from the backup copy that you stored offsite.

A Word About Tape Reliability

From experience, I've found that although tape drives are very reliable, they do run amok once in a while. Problem is, they don't always tell you they're not working. A tape drive — especially the less expensive Travan drives — can spin along for hours, pretending to back up your data, when in reality, your data isn't being written reliably to the tape. In other words, a tape drive can trick you into thinking that your backups are working just fine, but when disaster strikes and you need your backup tapes, you may just dis- cover that the tapes are worthless.

Don't panic! You have a simple way to assure yourself that your tape drive is working. Just activate the "compare after backup" feature of your backup software. Then, as soon as your backup program finishes backing up your data, it rewinds the tape, reads each backed-up file, and compares it with the original version on the hard drive. If all files compare, you know your backups are trustworthy.

Here are some additional thoughts about the reliability of tapes:

✦ The Compare After Backup feature doubles the time required to do a backup, but that doesn't matter if your entire backup fits on one tape. You can just run the backup after hours. Whether the backup and repair operation takes one hour or ten doesn't matter, as long as it's finished by the time you arrive at work the next morning.

✦ If your backups require more than one tape, you may not want to run the "compare after backup" feature every day. However, be sure to run it periodically to check that your tape drive is working.

✦ If your backup program reports errors, throw away the tape and use a new tape.

✦ Actually, you should ignore that last comment about waiting for your backup program to report errors. You should discard tapes *before* your backup program reports errors. Most experts recommend that you should use a tape only about 20 times before discarding it. If you use the same tape every day, replace it monthly. If you have tapes for each day of the week, replace them twice a year. If you have more tapes than that, figure out a cycle that replaces tapes after about 20 uses.

About Cleaning the Heads

An important aspect of backup reliability is proper maintenance of your tape drives. Every time you back up to tape, little bits and specs of the tape rub off onto the read and write heads inside the tape drive. Eventually, the heads become too dirty to reliably read or write data.

To counteract this problem, you should clean the tape heads regularly. The easiest way to clean them is to use a special tape-cleaning cartridge. To clean the heads with a tape-cleaning cartridge, you just insert the cartridge into the tape drive. The drive automatically recognizes that you've inserted a cleaning cartridge and performs a special routine that wipes the special cleaning tape back and forth over the heads to clean them. When the cleaning routine is done, the tape is ejected. The whole thing takes about 30 seconds.

Because the maintenance requirements of each drive differ, you should check the drive's user's manual to find out how and how often to clean the drive. As a general rule, clean the drives once a week.

The most annoying aspect of tape drive cleaning is that the cleaning cartridges have a limited lifespan. Unfortunately, if you insert a used-up cleaning cartridge, the drive accepts it and pretends to clean the drive. For this reason, you should keep track of the number of times you've used the cleaning cartridge and replace it when you've exceeded the number of uses recommended by the manufacturer.

Backup Security

Backups create an often-overlooked security exposure for your network. No matter how carefully you set up user accounts and enforce password policies, if any user (including a guest) can perform a backup of the system, that user may make an unauthorized backup. In addition, your backup tapes themselves are vulnerable to theft. As a result, you should make sure that your backup policies and procedures are secure by taking the following measures:

✦ Set up a user account for the user who does backups. Because this user account will have backup permission for the entire server, guard its password carefully. Anyone who knows the username and password of the backup account can log in and bypass any security restrictions that you've placed on that user's normal user ID.

✦ You can counter potential security problems by restricting the backup user ID to a certain client and a certain time of the day. If you're really clever (and paranoid), you can probably set up the backup user's account so that only the program it can run is the backup program.

✦ Use encryption to protect the contents of your backup tapes.

✦ Secure the backup tapes in a safe location, such as, um, a safe.

Chapter 4: Disaster Recovery and Business Continuity Planning

In This Chapter

↙ **Realizing the need for backups**

↙ **Making a plan**

↙ **Practicing disaster recovery**

↙ **Remembering tape rotation and other details**

On April Fool's Day about 15 years ago, my colleagues and I discovered that some loser had broken into the office the night before and pounded our computer equipment to death with a crowbar. (I'm not making this up.)

Sitting on a shelf right next to the mangled piles of what used to be a Wang minicomputer system was an undisturbed disk pack that contained the only complete backup of all the information that was on the destroyed computer. The vandal didn't realize that one more swing of the crowbar would have escalated this major inconvenience into a complete catastrophe. Sure, we were up a creek until we could get the computer replaced. And in those days, you couldn't just walk into your local Computer Depot and buy a new computer off the shelf — this was a Wang minicomputer system that had to be specially ordered. After we had the new computer, though, a simple restore from the backup disk brought us right back to where we were on March 31. Without that backup, getting back on track would have taken months.

I've been paranoid about disaster planning ever since. Before then, I thought that disaster planning meant doing good backups. That's a part of it, but I can never forget the day we came within one swing of the crowbar of losing everything. Vandals are probably much smarter now: They know to smash the backup disks as well as the computers themselves. Being prepared for disasters entails much more than just doing regular backups.

Nowadays, the trendy term for disaster planning is *business continuity planning* (BCP). I suppose the term *disaster planning* sounded too negative, like we were planning for disasters to happen. The new term refocuses attention on the more positive aspect of preparing a plan that will enable a business to carry on with as little interruption as possible in the event of a disaster.

Assessing Different Types of Disasters

Disasters come in many shapes and sizes. Some types of disasters are more likely than others. For example, your building is more likely to be struck by lightning than to be hit by a comet. In some cases, the likelihood of a particular type of disaster depends on where you're located. For example, crippling snowstorms are more likely in New York than in Florida.

In addition, the impact of each type of disaster varies from company to company. What may be a disaster for one company may only be a mere inconvenience for another. For example, a law firm may tolerate a disruption in telephone service for a day or two. Loss of communication via phone would be a major inconvenience, but not a disaster. To a telemarketing firm, however, a day or two with the phones down is a more severe problem because the company's revenue depends on the phones.

One of the first steps in developing a business continuity plan is assessing the risk of the various types of disasters that may affect your organization. To assess risk, you weigh the likelihood of a disaster happening with the severity of the impact that the disaster would have. For example, the impact of a meteor crashing into your building is probably pretty severe, but the odds of that happening are miniscule. On the other hand, the odds of your building being destroyed by fire are much higher, and the impact of a devastating fire would be about the same as the impact of a meteor.

The following sections describe the most common types of risks that most companies face. Notice throughout this discussion that although many of these risks are related to computers and network technology, some are not. The scope of business continuity planning is much larger than just computer technology.

Environmental disasters

Environmental disasters are what most people think of first when they think of disaster recovery. Some types of environmental disasters are regional. Others can happen pretty much anywhere.

✦ Fire is probably the first disaster that most people think of when they consider disaster planning. Fires can be caused by unsafe conditions, by carelessness, such as electrical wiring that isn't up to code, by natural causes, such as lightning strikes, or by arson.

✦ Earthquakes can cause not only structural damage to your building, but they can also disrupt the delivery of key services and utilities, such as water and power to your company. Serious earthquakes are rare and unpredictable, but some areas experience them with more regularity

than others. If your business is located in an area known for earthquakes, your BCP should consider how your company would deal with a
devastating earthquake.

✦ Weather disasters can cause major disruption to your business.
Moderate weather may close transportation systems so that your
employees can't get to work. Severe weather may damage your building
or interrupt delivery of services, such as electricity and water.

✦ Flooding can wreak havoc with electrical equipment, such as computers. If floodwaters get into your computer room, chances are good that
the computer equipment will be totally destroyed. Note that flooding
can be caused not only by bad weather, but also by burst pipes or malfunctioning sprinklers.

✦ Lightning storms can cause electrical damage to your computer and
other electronic equipment if lightning strikes your building or causes
surges in the local power supply.

Deliberate disasters

Some disasters are the result of deliberate actions by others. For example:

✦ Vandalism or arson may damage or destroy your facilities or your computer systems. The vandalism or arson may be targeted at you specifically by a disgruntled employee or customer, or it may be random.
Either way, the effect is the same.

✦ Theft is always a possibility. You may come to work someday to find
that your servers or other computer equipment have been stolen.

✦ Don't neglect the possibility of sabotage. A disgruntled employee who
gets a hold of an administrator's account and password can do all sorts
of nasty things to your network.

✦ Terrorism used to be something that most Americans weren't concerned about, but September 11, 2001, changed all that. No matter
where you live in the world, the possibility of a terrorist attack is real.

Disruption of services

You may not realize just how much your business depends on the delivery
of services and utilities. A business continuity plan should take into consideration how you will deal with the loss of certain services.

✦ Electrical power is crucial for computers and other types of equipment.
During a power failure once (I live in California, so I'm used to it), I discovered that I can't even work with pencil and paper because all my
pencil sharpeners are electric. Electrical outages are not uncommon,

but fortunately, the technology to deal with them is readily available. UPS (uninterruptible power supply) equipment is reliable and inexpensive.

✦ Communication connections can be disrupted by many causes. About a year ago, a railroad overpass was constructed across the street from my office. One day a backhoe cut through the phone lines, completely cutting off our phone service — including our Internet connection — for a day and a half.

✦ An interruption in the water supply may not shut down your computers, but it can disrupt your business by forcing you to close your facility until the water supply is reestablished.

Equipment failure

Modern companies depend on many different types of equipment for their daily operations. The failure of any of these key systems can disrupt business until the systems are repaired.

✦ Computer equipment failure can obviously affect business operations.

✦ Air-conditioning systems are crucial to regulate temperatures, especially in computer rooms. Computer equipment can be damaged if the temperature climbs too high.

✦ Elevators, automatic doors, and other equipment may also be necessary for your business.

Other disasters

You should assess many other potential disasters. Here are just a few:

✦ Labor disputes.

✦ Loss of key staff due to resignation, injury, sickness, or death.

✦ Workplace violence.

✦ Public health issues, such as epidemics, mold infestations, and so on.

✦ Loss of a key supplier.

✦ Nearby disaster, such as a fire or police action across the street that results in your business being temporary blocked off.

Analyzing the Impact of a Disaster

With a good understanding of the types of disasters that can affect your business, you can turn your attention to the impact that these disasters can have on your business. The first step is to identify the key business processes that can be impacted by different types of disasters. These business processes are different for each company. For example, here are a few of the key business processes for a small publishing company:

✦ Editorial processes, such as managing projects through the process of technical editing, copyediting, and production.

✦ Acquisition processes, such as determining product development strategies, recruiting authors, and signing projects.

✦ Human resource processes, such as payroll, hiring, employee review, and recruiting.

✦ Marketing processes, including sales tracking, developing marketing materials, sponsoring sales conferences, exhibiting at trade events, and so on.

✦ Sales and billing processes, such as filling customer orders, maintaining the company Web site, managing inventory, and handling payments.

✦ Executive and financial processes, such as managing cash flow, securing credit, raising capital, deciding when to go public, and deciding when to buy a smaller publisher or sell out to a bigger publisher.

The impact of a disruption to each of these processes will vary. One common way to assess the impact of business process loss is to rate the impact of various degrees of loss for each process. For example, you may rate the loss of each process for the following time frames:

✦ 0 to 2 hours

✦ 2 to 24 hours

✦ 1 to 2 days

✦ 2 days to 1 week

✦ More than one week

For some business processes, an interruption of two hours or even one day may be minor. For other processes, even the loss of a few hours may be very costly.

Developing a Business Continuity Plan

A *business continuity plan* is simply a plan for how you will continue operation of your key business processes should the normal operation of the process fail. For example, if your primary office location is shut down for a week because of a major fire across the street, you won't have to suspend operations if you have a business continuity plan in place.

The key to a business continuity plan is redundancy of each component that is essential to your business processes. These components include

✦ **Facilities:** If your company already has multiple office locations, you may be able to temporarily squeeze into one of the other locations for the duration of the disaster. If not, you should secure arrangements in advance with a real-estate broker so that you can quickly secure an alternate location. By having an arrangement made in advance, you can move into an emergency location on a moment's notice.

✦ **Computer equipment:** It doesn't hurt to have a set of spare computers in storage somewhere so that you can dig them out to use in an emergency. Preferably these computers would already have your critical software installed. The next best thing would be to have detailed plans available so that your IT staff can quickly install key software on new equipment to get your business up and running.

It goes without saying that you should also keep a current set of backup tapes at an alternate location.

✦ **Phones:** Discuss emergency phone services in advance with your phone company. If you're forced to move to another location on 24-hour notice, how quickly can you get your phones up and running? And can you arrange to have your incoming toll-free calls forwarded to the new location?

✦ **Staff:** Unless you're a government agency, you probably don't have redundant employees. However, you can make arrangements in advance with a temp agency to provide clerical and administrative help on short notice.

✦ **Stationery:** This sounds like a small detail, but you should store a supply of all your key stationery products, such as letterhead, envelopes, invoices, statements, and so on, in a safe location. That way, if your main location is suddenly unavailable, you don't have to wait a week to get new letterhead or invoices printed.

✦ **Hard copy files:** Keep a backup copy of important printed material, such as customer billing files, sales records, and so on, at an alternate location.

Holding a Fire Drill

Remember in grade school when the fire alarm would go off and your teacher would tell the kids to calmly put down their work and walk out to the designated safe zone in an orderly fashion? Drills are important so that when and if a real fire occurs, you don't run and scream and climb all over each other in order to be the first one to get out.

Any disaster recovery plan is incomplete unless you test it to see whether it works. Testing doesn't mean that you should burn your building down one day to see how long it takes you to get back up and running. It does mean, however, that you should periodically simulate a disaster in order to prove to yourself and your staff that you can recover.

The most basic type of disaster recovery drill is a simple test of your network backup procedures. You should periodically attempt to restore key files from your backup tapes just to make sure that you can. You achieve several benefits by restoring files on a regular basis:

✦ Tapes are unreliable. The only way to be sure that your tapes are working is to periodically restore files from them.

✦ Backup programs are confusing to configure. I've seen people run backup jobs for years that don't include all the data they think they're backing up. Only when disaster strikes and they need to recover a key file do they discover that the file isn't included in the backup.

✦ Restoring files can be a little confusing, especially when you use a combination of normal and incremental or differential backups. Add to that the pressure of having the head of the company watching over your shoulder while you try to recover a lost file. If you regularly conduct file restore drills, you'll familiarize yourself with the restore features of your backup software in a low-pressure situation. Then, you can easily restore files for real when the pressure's on.

You can also conduct walk-throughs of more serious disaster scenarios. For example, you can set aside a day to walk though the process of moving your entire staff to an alternate location. During the walk-through, you can double-check that all the backup equipment, documents, and data are available as planned. If something is missing, it's better to find out now rather than while the fire department is still putting water on the last remaining hot spots in what used to be your office.

Chapter 5: Dealing with Dysfunctional E-Mail

E-mail is a vital function of most computer networks. Unfortunately, e-mail is also one of the most troublesome aspects of networking. Why? Because the very nature of e-mail requires your network to communicate with other networks in order to send and receive messages. Opportunities for this communication to go wrong are endless.

That most mail gets through to its intended recipient is a testament to the quality of the Internet's e-mail system, which is based on standards that have endured for more than 20 years. Once in awhile, though, something goes wrong, and an outgoing e-mail message gets returned with an error message. When that happens, the user who sent the mail often picks up the phone and calls the network administrator. Then it's time for you to go to work.

In this chapter, you discover how to diagnose and correct the most common problems that lead to undeliverable e-mail. Unfortunately, delivery problems are often a result of errors on the recipient's end of the communication, so you can't do a whole lot besides contacting the recipient so that he can correct the problem. Of course, that's not always easy to do because you can't just e-mail someone to tell him that his e-mail isn't working.

Coping with the Dreaded Nondelivery Report

The software that routes e-mail through the Internet is almost as diligent as the real post office in the efforts that it makes to deliver mail. However, the e-mail system isn't perfect, and sometimes the mail just doesn't get through.

When an e-mail can't be delivered, the person who originally sent the undeliverable mail receives a report in his or her inbox called a *nondelivery report,* also known as an *NDR.* Figure 5-1 shows a typical nondelivery report.

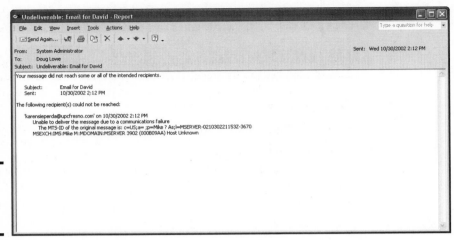

Figure 5-1:
A nondelivery report.

The nondelivery report should give you a clue as to why the mail could not be delivered. The most common causes of undeliverable mail are

✦ **The e-mail address is incorrect.** The wrong address results in one of two types of errors, depending on which portion of the e-mail address is wrong. If you get the domain name wrong, the nondelivery report indicates an error, such as *destination not found* or *bad destination system address*. If the recipient's name is incorrect, the nondelivery report indicates an error, such as *recipient not found* or *no such user*.

For example, if you try to send mail to me@mydomain.cmo instead of me@mydomain.com, the delivery will fail because the domain is incorrect. However, if you try to send the mail to em@mydomain.com instead of me@mydomain.com, the delivery will fail because the recipient is incorrect.

✦ **The recipient's domain MX records may be configured incorrectly.** In this case, you've sent the mail to the correct address, but the mail system can't find the recipient's mail server because of the incorrect MX record.

Some mail gateways are more tolerant of MX errors than others. As a result, a minor error in the MX configuration may not be noticed because the recipient receives most of his or her mail. (*MX records* are how system administrators specify the location of an organization's mail servers. For more information about MX records, refer to Chapter 4 of Book 5.)

✦ **The recipient's mail server is down.** If a downed server is the case, hopefully the recipient's system administrator will get the server back up soon so that the mail can be delivered.

✦ **Your mail gateway is unable to reach the recipient's mail gateway due to communication failures.** This usually means that your mail server's Internet connection is down. After the connection has been reestablished, the mail can be resent.

✦ **The recipient's mail server rejects the mail because it doesn't trust you.** In many cases, this happens if your mail gateway has been listed at one of the Internet's many blacklist sites because of a spam problem or other abuse problem. For information about how to get off a blacklist, see the section "Help! I've Been Blacklisted!" later in this chapter.

Viewing the Mail Server's Error Logs

Sometimes, you can garner additional information about the reason a mail message didn't get through by examining your e-mail server's error logs. For example, if your mail delivery fails because of a communication error, the mail server's error logs may help you pinpoint the cause of the communication failure.

If you're using a Windows server with Exchange Server as your e-mail gateway, you can find the e-mail by opening the Event Viewer. E-mail events are logged in the Application log. Other mail gateways have similar logs.

Checking Out a Remote Mail System

One way to diagnose undeliverable e-mail problems is to attempt to manually connect to the remote mail server to see if it responds. To do this, you must first determine the host name for the remote mail server. Then, you can manually connect to the server to see whether it responds. The following sections describe procedures that you can follow to complete these tasks.

Discovering the mail server for a domain

The mail server for a domain, such as `mydomain.com`, is assigned its own host name, such as `mail.mydomain.com`. You can discover the name of the mail server for a given domain by using the `NSLOOKUP` command to display the appropriate DNS records for the domain. Here are the steps:

1. Open a command prompt window.

To do that, choose Start⇨Run from the Start menu, then type **command,** and press Enter.

2. Enter the command nslookup.

The NSLOOKUP command responds with a display similar to this:

```
G:\DOCUME~1\DOUGLO~1>nslookup
Default Server:  ns7.attbi.com
Address:  204.127.198.19

>
```

3. Enter the command set type=mx.

This command configures NSLOOKUP to look for MX records, which list the mail servers for the domain.

4. Type the domain for the undeliverable e-mail.

For example, type **LoweWriter.com** if you can't send mail to the domain LoweWriter.com. NSLOOKUP responds by displaying the mail server information for the domain, like this:

```
> set type=mx
> lowewriter.com
Server:  ns7.attbi.com
Address:  204.127.198.19

lowewriter.com  MX preference = 50, mail exchanger =
    sasi.pair.com
lowewriter.com  nameserver = NS000.NS0.com
lowewriter.com  nameserver = NS207.pair.com
NS000.NS0.com   internet address = 216.92.61.61
NS207.pair.com  internet address = 209.68.2.52
>
```

The mail server is listed on the MX line; in this case, it's sasi.pair.com.

5. Type Exit **to end the** NSLOOKUP **program.**

You're returned to the normal MS-DOS command prompt.

Many domains have more than one mail server. In that case, each mail server will be listed on a separate MX line. Usually, the preference values are different for each server. Use the one with the lowest preference value. If the preference values are the same for all the servers, you can use any of the servers listed.

Another way to determine the mail server for an e-mail address is to use a Web-based nslookup tool. My favorite is `www.dnsreport.com`. Just go to `www.dnsreport.com` in any browser, type the domain portion of the e-mail address into the DNS Report text box, and then click the DNS Report button. This action displays a page that shows a variety of information about the domain's DNS configuration and points out possible errors in the DNS records. Scroll down the page to find the MX section, where you can find the mail servers listed.

For example, Figure 5-2 shows a portion of a DNS report from `www.dnsreport.com` for the `wiley.com` domain. As you can see, three mail servers are listed: `xmail.wiley.com`, `xmail2.wiley.com`, and `xmail3.wiley.com`.

Verifying a mail server

After you've determined the name of the mail server, you can use the `TELNET` command to log on to the mail server in order to determine whether the server is working correctly. Depending on how the mail server is configured, you may also be able to verify that the recipient name portion of your undeliverable mail is recognized.

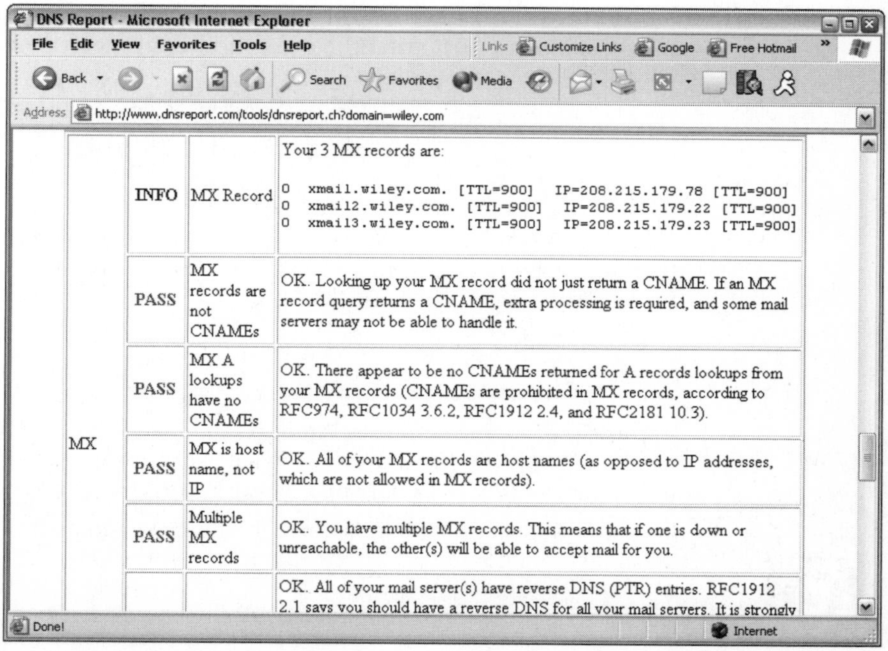

Figure 5-2: You can use `www.dnsreport.com` to determine the mail servers for a domain.

To log on to a mail server and verify an address, follow these steps:

1. **Open a command prompt window.**

   To do that, choose Start⇨Run from the Start menu, then type **command,** and press Enter.

   (You can skip this step if the command window is still open from the procedure described in the previous section.)

2. **Type** telnet *mail server* 25.

   For example, if the server you're trying to reach is LoweWriter.com, type **telnet LoweWriter.com 25**.

   Port 25 is the TCP/IP port that e-mail servers use.

   If the connection is successful, you receive a message such as:

   ```
   220 sasi.pair.com ESMTP
   ```

   The display may include additional information, but the 220 message is the only one that's important. It's the message that indicates you've successfully reached a mail server on port 25 at the specified host address.

3. **Type** vrfy *user@domain.com* **to verify the recipient's e-mail address.**

   For example, if the undeliverable e-mail address is BigBoss@LoweWriter.com, type **vrfy BigBoss@LoweWriter.com**. If the mail server is able to verify that the e-mail address is correct, it will respond with a 250 message, such as:

   ```
   250 Doug Lowe <BigBoss@LoweWriter.com>
   ```

   If the user doesn't exist, you'll get a 550 message, such as:

   ```
   550 String does not match anything
   ```

   Unfortunately, many (if not most) mail servers are configured so that they won't verify addresses. You may get back any of the following messages:

   ```
   252 Cannot verify user
   252 Send some mail, I'll try my best
   500 Command unrecognized
   ```

   In this case, you've confirmed that the domain portion of the e-mail address is correct and that the mail server is working, but you aren't able to verify that the recipient's name is correct.

   To verify that the recipient is correct, you can send mail to the domain's postmaster account to ask. For example, send mail to postmaster@LoweWriter.com to ask the postmaster at the LoweWriter.com domain if a particular user exists.

4. **Type** quit **to break the connection and exit the Telnet program and then type** Exit **to close the command window.**

    That's it; you're done.

Viewing Message Headers

To make e-mail more user-friendly, modern e-mail clients hide nasty details, such as the e-mail message headers that accompany messages. Sometimes, however, these headers can help track down the cause of e-mail delivery problems. E-mail headers are especially useful if you suspect that a message you receive isn't from whom it claims to be from. If you reply to a message and your reply comes back as nondeliverable, you can look into the message headers to find out the actual e-mail address of the person who sent you the original message.

To display e-mail headers in Microsoft Outlook, open the message and then choose View⇨Options to display the Message Options dialog box, as shown in Figure 5-3. The message headers are shown in a scrollable text box at the bottom of this dialog box.

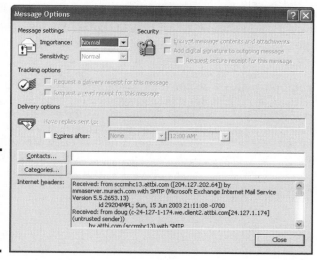

Figure 5-3: How message headers are displayed in Outlook.

Help! I've Been Blacklisted!

In recent years, a number of antispam sites have sprung up on the Internet to help network administrators keep spam out of their e-mail systems. One of the most popular antispam techniques is the use of *blacklists*. A blacklist is simply a list of known senders of spam. E-mail gateways can be configured so that when incoming mail arrives, the mail is checked against one of these blacklists. If the mail originates from a server that has been blacklisted, the message is either rejected or simply ignored.

Unfortunately, this system is not perfect. Sometimes, legitimate mail servers find themselves blacklisted even though they're not spammers. In some cases, this is because the administrators of those systems have left security holes that can lead to spamming unplugged. The most common of these holes is called an *open relay*. If your mail server is an open relay, it can be hijacked by spammers and used to deliver their mail anonymously. Because open relays are a major source of spam, many blacklists automatically blacklist servers that are configured as open relays.

Some blacklists are complaint-driven. You get listed in the blacklist if someone complains that you have been sending spam to that person. Unfortunately, it's possible to be falsely accused, so you may find yourself blacklisted even if you've done nothing wrong.

If you discover that you are blacklisted, the first step is to find out which blacklists you're on and why. Then, correct the problems that caused you to be blacklisted and ask the lists to retest your server so that you can be removed from the lists.

Unfortunately, it's much easier to get on a blacklist than it is to get off of one. Once you've been blacklisted, it can easily take several weeks to get off the lists after you've corrected the problem.

The most comprehensive Web site for solving blacklist problems is `relays.osirusoft.com`. From this page, you can enter your domain name to discover whether you have been listed on any of the major blacklists. If this site reports that you are on any blacklists, you have to correct the problem that caused you to be blacklisted and then ask each of the blacklists to retest your site and remove you from their lists. Then, recheck your domain at `relays.osirusoft.com` to make sure that you've been removed. Don't be surprised if it takes several weeks to get removed from all the blacklists.

Book V

TCP/IP and the Internet

The 5th Wave   By Rich Tennant

"The divorce was amicable. She got the Jetta, the sailboat, and the recumbent bike. I got the servers and the domain name."

Contents at a Glance

Chapter 1: Introduction to TCP/IP and the Internet

In This Chapter

✔ Introducing the Internet

✔ Familiarizing yourself with TCP/IP standards

✔ Figuring out how TCP/IP lines up with the OSI reference model

✔ Discovering important TCP/IP applications

*J*ust a few short years ago, TCP/IP was known primarily as the protocol of the Internet, and the biggest challenge of getting a local area network (LAN) connected to the Internet was figuring out how to mesh TCP/IP with the proprietary protocols that were the basis of the LANs — most notably IPX/SPX and NetBEUI. A few years ago, network administrators realized that they could save the trouble of meshing TCP/IP with IPX/SPX and NetBEUI by eliminating IPX/SPX and NetBEUI from the equation altogether. As a result, TCP/IP is not just the protocol of the Internet now, but it's also the protocol on which many — if not most — local area networks are based.

This chapter is a gentle introduction to the Internet in general and the TCP/IP suite of protocols in particular. After I get the introductions out of the way, you'll be able to focus more in-depth on the detailed TCP/IP information given in the remaining chapters of this book.

What Is the Internet?

The Goliath of all computer networks, the Internet links tens of millions of computer users throughout the world. Strictly speaking, the Internet is a network of networks. It consists of tens of thousands of separate computer networks, all interlinked, so that a user on any of those networks can reach out and touch a user on any of the other networks. This network of networks connects nearly 5 million computers to each other.

One of the official documents of the Internet Engineering Task Force (RFC 2026) defines the Internet as "a loosely-organized international collaboration of autonomous, interconnected networks." Broken down piece-by-piece, this definition encompasses several key aspects of what the Internet is:

✦ **Loosely organized:** No single organization has authority over the Internet. As a result, the Internet is not highly organized. Online services, such as America Online or The Microsoft Network, are owned and operated by individual companies that control exactly what content appears on the service and what software can be used with the service. No one exercises that kind of control over the Internet. As a result, you can find just about any kind of material imaginable on the Internet. No one guarantees the accuracy of information that you find on the Internet, so you have to be careful as you work your way through the labyrinth.

✦ **International:** More than 100 countries are represented on the Internet.

✦ **Collaboration:** The Internet exists only because many different organizations cooperate to provide the services and support needed to sustain it. For example, much of the software that drives the Internet is open-source software that is developed collaboratively by programmers throughout the world, who constantly work to improve the code.

✦ **Autonomous:** The Internet community respects that organizations that join the Internet are free to make their own decisions about how they configure and operate their networks. Although legal issues sometimes boil up, for the most part, each player on the Internet operates independently.

✦ **Interconnected:** The whole key to the Internet is the concept of *interconnection,* which is using standard protocols that enable networks to communicate with each other. Without the interconnection provided by the TCP/IP protocol, the Internet would not exist.

✦ **Networks:** The Internet would be completely unmanageable if it consisted of 171 million individual users, all interconnected. That's why the Internet is often described as a *network of networks*. Most of the individual users who are on the Internet don't access the Internet directly. Instead, they access the Internet indirectly through another network, which may be a LAN in a business or academic environment or a dialup or broadband network provided by an Internet service provider (ISP). In each case, however, the users of the local network access the Internet via a gateway IP router.

The Internet is composed of several distinct types of networks: Government agencies, such as the Library of Congress and the White House; military sites (did you ever see *War Games?*); educational institutions, such as universities and colleges (and their libraries); businesses, such as Microsoft and IBM; Internet service providers, which allow individuals to access the Internet; and commercial online services, such as America Online and The Microsoft Network.

TECHNICAL STUFF

Just how big is the Internet?

Because the Internet is not owned or controlled by any one organization, no one knows how big the Internet really is. Several organizations do attempt to periodically determine the size of the Internet. One such organization is the Internet Software Consortium (ISC), which completed its last survey in January 2003. ISC found that more than 171 million host computers are connected to the Internet. The same survey showed a mere 72 million hosts in January 2000, so the size of the Internet has grown considerably in just a few years. If you go back ten years (to 1993), the survey found only 1.7 million host computers.

Unfortunately, no one knows how many actual users are on the Internet. Each host can support a single user, or — in the case of domains such as `aol.com` (America Online), or `msn.com` (The Microsoft Network) — hundreds of thousands or perhaps even millions of users. So no one really knows. Still, the indisputable point is that the Internet is big, and it's getting bigger every day.

(If you're already on the Net and are interested, you can check up on the latest Internet statistics from the Internet Software Consortium by visiting its Web site at `www.isc.org/ds`.)

A Little Internet History

The Internet has a fascinating history, if such things interest you. There's no particular reason why you should be interested in such things, of course, except that a superficial understanding of how the Internet got started may help you to understand and cope with the way this massive computer network exists today. So here goes.

The Internet traces its beginnings back to a small network called ARPANET, built by the Department of Defense in 1969 to link defense installations. ARPANET soon expanded to include not only defense installations, but universities as well. In the 1970s, ARPANET was split into two networks, one for military use (which was renamed MILNET) and the original ARPANET for nonmilitary use. The two networks were connected by a networking link called IP, the *Internet protocol* — so called because it allowed communication between two networks.

The good folks who designed IP had the foresight to realize that soon, more than two networks would want to be connected. In fact, they left room for tens of thousands of networks to join the game, which is a good thing because it wasn't long before the Internet began to take off.

By the mid-1980s, ARPANET was beginning to reach the limits of what it could do. Enter the National Science Foundation (NSF), which set up a nationwide network designed to provide access to huge *supercomputers,* those monolithic computers used to discover new prime numbers and calculate the orbits of distant galaxies. The supercomputers were never put to much use, but the network that was put together to support the supercomputers, called NSFNET, was used. In fact, NSFNET replaced ARPANET as the new backbone for the Internet.

Then, out of the blue, it seemed as if the whole world became interested in the Internet. Stories about it appeared in *Time* and *Newsweek.* Any company that had "dot com" in its name practically doubled in value every month. Al Gore claimed he invented it. The Net began to grow so fast that even NSFNET couldn't keep up, so private commercial networks got into the game. The size of the Internet nearly doubled every year for most of the 1990s. Then, in the first few years of the millennium, the growth rate slowed a bit. However, the Internet still seems to be growing at the phenomenal rate of about 30 to 50 percent per year, and who knows how long this dizzying rate of growth will continue.

TCP/IP Standards and RFCs

The TCP/IP protocol standards that define how the Internet works are managed by an organization called the *Internet Engineering Task Force,* or IETF. However, the IETF doesn't impose standards. Instead, it simply oversees the process by which ideas are developed into agreed-upon standards.

An Internet standard is published in a document known as a *Request for Comments*, or RFC. When a document is accepted for publication, it is assigned an RFC number by the IETF. The RFC is then published. After it's published, an RFC is never changed. If a standard is enhanced, the enhancement is covered in a separate RFC.

At the time of this writing, more than 3,500 RFCs were available from IETF's Web site (www.ietf.org). The oldest RFC is RFC 0001, published in 1969. It describes how the host computers communicated with each other in the original ARPANET. The most recent RFC (as of June 2003) is RFC 3559, a proposed standard entitled "Multicast Address Allocation MIB."

Not all RFCs represent Internet standards. The following paragraphs summarize the various types of RFC documents:

✦ **Internet Standards Track:** An RCF that represents an Internet standard. Standard Track RFCs have one of three maturity levels, as described in Table 1-1. An RFC enters circulation with Proposed Standard status, but may be elevated to Draft Standard status and ultimately, to Internet Standard status.

Table 1-1	Maturity Levels for Internet Standards Track RFCs
Maturity Level	*Description*
Proposed Standard	Proposed standards are generally stable, have resolved known design choices, are believed to be well understood, have received significant community review, and appear to enjoy enough community interest to be considered valuable.
Draft Standard	Draft standards are well understood and known to be quite stable. At least two interoperable implementations must exist, developed independently from separate code bases. The specification is believed to be mature and useful.
Internet Standard	Internet Standards have been fully accepted by the Internet community as highly mature and useful standards.

+ **Experimental specifications:** A result of research or development efforts. They're not intended to be standards, but it's felt that the information they contain may be of use to the Internet community.

+ **Informational specifications:** Simply provide general information for the Internet community.

+ **Historic specifications:** RFCs that have been superceded by a more recent RFC and are considered obsolete.

+ **Best Current Practice (BCP):** RFCs are documents that summarize the consensus of the Internet community's opinion on the best way to perform an operation or procedure. BCPs are guidelines, not standards.

Table 1-2 summarizes the RFCs that apply to the key Internet standards described in this book.

Table 1-2		RFCs for Key Internet Standards
RFC	*Date*	*Description*
768	August 1980	User Datagram Protocol (UDP)
791	September 1981	Internet Protocol (IP)
792	September 1981	Internet Control Message Protocol (ICMP)
793	September 1981	Transmission Control Protocol (TCP)
826	November 1982	Ethernet Address Resolution Protocol (ARP)
950	August 1985	Internet Standard Subnetting Procedure
959	October 1985	File Transfer Protocol (FTP)
1034	November 1987	Domain Names — Concepts and Facilities (DNS)

(continued)

Table 1-2 *(continued)*

RFC	Date	Description
1035	November 1987	Domain Names — Implementation and Specification (DNS)
1939	May 1996	Post Office Protocol Version 3 (POP3)
2131	March 1997	Dynamic Host Configuration Protocol (DHCP)
2236	November 1997	Internet Group Management Protocol (IGMP) (Updates RFC 1112)
2616	June 1999	Hypertext Transfer Protocol — HTTP/1.1
2821	April 2001	Simple Mail Transfer Protocol (SMTP)

The TCP/IP Protocol Framework

Like the seven-layer OSI Reference Model, TCP/IP protocols are based on a layered framework. TCP/IP has four layers, as shown in Figure 1-1. These layers are described in the following sections.

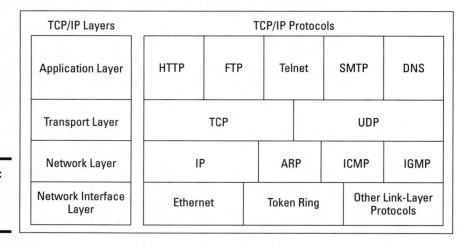

Figure 1-1: The four layers of TCP/IP.

Network Interface layer

The lowest level of the TCP/IP architecture is the Network Interface layer. It corresponds to the OSI's Physical and Data Link layers. You can use many different TCP/IP protocols at the Network Interface layer, including Ethernet and Token Ring for local area networks and protocols such as X.25, Frame Relay, and ATM for wide-area networks.

The Network Interface layer is assumed to be unreliable.

Network layer

The Network layer is where data is addressed, packaged, and routed among networks. Several important Internet protocols operate at the Network layer:

✦ **Internet Protocol (IP):** A routable protocol that uses IP addresses to deliver packets to network devices. IP is an intentionally unreliable protocol, so it doesn't guarantee delivery of information.

✦ **Address Resolution Protocol (ARP):** Resolves IP addresses to hardware MAC addresses.

✦ **Internet Control Message Protocol (ICMP):** Sends and receives diagnostic messages. ICMP is the basis of the ubiquitous Ping command.

✦ **Internet Group Management Protocol (IGMP):** Used to multicast messages to multiple IP addresses at once.

Transport layer

The Transport layer is where sessions are established and data packets are exchanged between hosts. Two core protocols are found at this layer:

✦ **Transmission Control Protocol (TCP):** Provides reliable connection-oriented transmission between two hosts. TCP establishes a session between hosts, and then ensures delivery of packets between the hosts.

✦ **User Datagram Protocol (UDP):** Provides connectionless, non-reliable, one-to-one or one-to-many delivery

Application layer

The Application layer of the TCP/IP model corresponds to the Session, Presentation, and Application layers of the OSI Reference Model. A few of the most popular Application layer protocols are

✦ **Hypertext Transfer Protocol (HTTP):** The core protocol of the World Wide Web.

✦ **File Transfer Protocol (FTP):** A protocol that enables a client to send and receive complete files from a server.

✦ **Telnet:** The protocol that lets you connect to another computer on the Internet in a terminal emulation mode.

✦ **SMTP:** One of several key protocols that are used to provide e-mail services.

✦ **Domain Name System:** The protocol that allows you to refer to other host computers by using names rather than numbers.

Chapter 2: Understanding IP Addresses

*O*ne of the most basic components of TCP/IP is IP addressing. Every device on a TCP/IP network must have a unique IP address. In this chapter, I explore the ins and outs of these IP addresses. Enjoy!

Understanding Binary

Before you can understand the details of how IP addressing works, you need to understand how the binary numbering system works because binary is the basis of IP addressing. If you already understand binary, please skip right over this section to the section "Introducing IP Addresses." I don't want to bore you with stuff that's too basic.

Counting by ones

Binary is a counting system that uses only two numerals: 0 and 1. In the decimal system to which most people are accustomed, you use 10 numerals: 0 through 9. In an ordinary decimal number, such as 3,482, the rightmost digit represents ones; the next digit to the left, tens; the next, hundreds; the next, thousands; and so on. These digits represent powers of ten: first 10^0 (which is 1); next, 10^1 (10); then 10^2 (100); then 10^3 (1,000); and so on.

In binary, you have only two numerals rather than ten, which is why binary numbers look somewhat monotonous, as in 110011, 101111, and 100001.

The positions in a binary number (called *bits* rather than *digits*) represent powers of two rather than powers of ten: 1, 2, 4, 8, 16, 32, and so on. To figure the decimal value of a binary number, you multiply each bit by its corresponding power of two and then add the results. The decimal value of binary 10101, for example, is calculated as follows:

$$
\begin{array}{rcrcrcr}
 & 1 \times 2^0 & = & 1 \times & 1 & = & 1 \\
+ & 0 \times 2^1 & = & 0 \times & 2 & = & 0 \\
+ & 1 \times 2^2 & = & 1 \times & 4 & = & 4 \\
+ & 0 \times 2^3 & = & 0 \times & 8 & = & 0 \\
+ & 1 \times 2^4 & = & 1 \times & 16 & = & \underline{16} \\
 & & & & & & 21
\end{array}
$$

Fortunately, converting a number between binary and decimal is something a computer is good at — so good, in fact, that you're unlikely ever to need to do any conversions yourself. The point of learning binary is not to be able to look at a number such as 1110110110110 and say instantly, "Ah! Decimal 7,606!" (If you could do that, Barbara Walters would probably interview you, and they would even make a movie about you — starring Dustin Hoffman.)

Instead, the point is to have a basic understanding of how computers store information and — most important — to understand how the hexadecimal counting system works (which is described in the following section).

Here are some of the more interesting characteristics of binary and how the system is similar to and differs from the decimal system:

✦ In decimal, the number of decimal places allotted for a number determines how large the number can be. If you allot six digits, for example, the largest number possible is 999,999. Because 0 is itself a number, however, a six-digit number can have any of 1 million different values.

   Similarly, the number of bits allotted for a binary number determines how large that number can be. If you allot eight bits, the largest value that number can store is 11111111, which happens to be 255 in decimal.

✦ To quickly figure how many different values you can store in a binary number of a given length, use the number of bits as an exponent of two. An eight-bit binary number, for example, can hold 2^8 values. Because 2^8 is 256, an eight-bit number can have any of 256 different values — which is why a byte, which is eight bits, can have 256 different values.

✦ This "powers of two" thing is why computers don't use nice, even, round numbers in measuring such values as memory or disk space. A value of 1K, for example, is not an even 1,000 bytes — it's 1,024 bytes because 1,024 is 2^{10}. Similarly, 1MB is not an even 1,000,000 bytes, but rather is 1,048,576 bytes, which happens to be 2^{20}.

✦ One basic test of computer nerddom is knowing your powers of two because they play such an important role in binary numbers. Just for the fun of it, but not because you really need to know, Table 2-1 lists the powers of two up to 32.

✦ Table 2-1 also shows the common shorthand notation for various powers of two. The abbreviation *K* represents 2^{10} (1,024). The *M* in *MB* stands for 2^{20}, or 1,024K, and the *G* in *GB* represents 2^{30}, which is 1,024M. These shorthand notations don't have anything to do with TCP/IP, but they're commonly used for measuring computer disk and memory capacities, so I thought I'd throw them in at no charge because the table had extra room.

Table 2-1			Powers of Two		
Power	*Bytes*	*Kilobytes*	*Power*	*Bytes*	*K, MB, or GB*
2^1	2		2^{17}	131,072	128K
2^2	4		2^{18}	262,144	256K
2^3	8		2^{19}	524,288	512K
2^4	16		2^{20}	1,048,576	1MB
2^5	32		2^{21}	2,097,152	2MB
2^6	64		2^{22}	4,194,304	4MB
2^7	128		2^{23}	8,388,608	8MB
2^8	256		2^{24}	16,777,216	16MB
2^9	512		2^{25}	33,554,432	32MB
2^{10}	1,024	1K	2^{26}	67,108,864	64MB
2^{11}	2,048	2K	2^{27}	134,217,728	128MB
2^{12}	4,096	4K	2^{28}	268,435,456	256MB
2^{13}	8,192	8K	2^{29}	536,870,912	512MB
2^{14}	16,384	16K	2^{30}	1,073,741,824	1GB
2^{15}	32,768	32K	2^{31}	2,147,483,648	2GB
2^{16}	65,536	64K	2^{32}	4,294,967,296	4GB

Doing the logic thing

One of the great things about binary is that it's very efficient at handling special operations called *logical operations*. Four basic logical operations exist, though additional operations are derived from the basic four operations. Three of the operations — AND, OR, and XOR — compare two binary digits (bits). The fourth (NOT) works on just a single bit.

The following list summarizes the basic logical operations:

◆ **AND:** An AND operation compares two binary values. If both values are 1, the result of the AND operation is 1. If one or both of the values are 0, the result is 0.

◆ **OR:** An OR operation compares two binary values. If at least one of the values is 1, the result of the OR operation is 1. If both values are 0, the result is 0.

◆ **XOR:** An XOR operation compares two binary values. If exactly one of them is 1, the result is 1. If both values are 0 or if both values are 1, the result is 0.

◆ **NOT:** The NOT operation doesn't compare two values. Instead, it simply changes the value of a single binary value. If the original value is 1, NOT returns 0. If the original value is 0, NOT returns 1.

Table 2-2 summarizes how AND, OR, and XOR work.

Table 2-2		Logical Operations for Binary Values		
First value	*Second value*	*AND*	*OR*	*XOR*
0	0	0	0	0
0	1	0	1	1
1	0	0	1	1
1	1	1	1	0

Logical operations are applied to binary numbers that have more than one binary digit by applying the operation one bit at a time. The easiest way to do this manually is to line the two binary numbers on top of one another and then write the result of the operation beneath each binary digit. The following example shows how you would calculate 10010100 AND 11011101:

```
      10010100
AND   11011101
      10010100
```

As you can see, the result is 10010100.

Working with the binary Windows Calculator

The Calculator program that comes with all versions of Windows has a special Scientific mode that many users don't know about. When you flip the Calculator into this mode, you can do instant binary and decimal conversions, which can occasionally come in handy when you're working with IP addresses.

To use the Windows Calculator in Scientific mode, launch the Calculator by choosing Start➪All Programs➪Accessories➪Calculator. Then, choose the View➪Scientific command from the Calculator's menu. The Calculator changes to a fancy scientific model — the kind I paid $200 for when I was in college. All kinds of buttons appear, as shown in Figure 2-1.

Figure 2-1:
The
Scientific
mode of the
Calculator
lets you
convert
between
decimal and
binary.

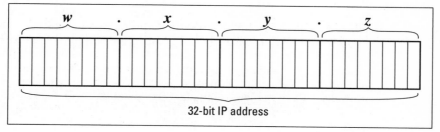

You can click the Bin and Dec radio buttons to convert values between decimal and binary. For example, to find the binary equivalent of decimal 155, enter **155** and click the Bin radio button. The value in the display changes to 10111011.

Here are a few other things to note about the Scientific mode of the Calculator:

✦ Although you can convert decimal values to binary values with the scientific Calculator, the Calculator can't handle the dotted-decimal IP address format that's described later in this chapter. To convert a dotted-decimal address to binary, just convert each octet separately. For example, to convert 172.65.48.120 to binary, first convert 172; then convert 65; then convert 48; and finally, convert 120.

✦ The scientific Calculator has several features that are designed specifically for binary calculations, such as AND, XOR, NOT, NOR, and so on.

✦ The scientific Calculator can also handle hexadecimal conversions. Hexadecimal doesn't come into play when dealing with IP addresses, but it is used for other types of binary numbers, so this feature sometimes proves to be useful.

Introducing IP Addresses

An *IP address* is a number that uniquely identifies every host on an IP network. IP addresses operate at the Network layer of the TCP/IP protocol stack, so they are independent of lower-level Data Link layer MAC addresses, such as Ethernet MAC addresses.

IP addresses are 32-bit binary numbers, which means that theoretically, a maximum of something in the neighborhood of 4 billion unique host addresses can exist throughout the Internet. You'd think that would be enough, but TCP/IP places certain restrictions on how IP addresses are allocated. These restrictions severely limit the total number of usable IP addresses, and today, about half of the total available IP addresses have already been assigned. However, new techniques for working with IP addresses have helped to alleviate this problem, and a new standard for 128-bit IP addresses (known as *IPv6*) is on the verge of winning acceptance.

Networks and hosts

IP stands for *Internet Protocol,* and its primary purpose is to enable communications between networks. As a result, a 32-bit IP address actually consists of two parts:

✦ The *network ID* (or *network address*): Identifies the network on which a host computer can be found.

✦ The *host ID* (or *host address*): Identifies a specific device on the network indicated by the network ID.

Most of the complexity of working with IP addresses has to do with figuring out which part of the complete 32-bit IP address is the network ID and which part is the host ID. The original IP specification uses a system called *address classes* to determine which part of the IP address is the network ID and which part is the host ID. A newer system, known as *classless IP addresses,* is rapidly taking over the address classes system.

As I examine the details of how host IDs are assigned, you may notice that two host addresses seem to be unaccounted for. For example, the Class C addressing scheme, which uses eight bits for the host ID, allows only 254 hosts — not the 256 hosts you'd expect. That's because host 0 (the host ID is all zeros) is always reserved to represent the network itself. The host ID can't be 255 (the host ID is all ones) because that host ID is reserved for use as a broadcast request that's intended for all hosts on the network.

The dotted-decimal dance

IP addresses are usually represented in a format known as *dotted-decimal notation*. In dotted-decimal notation, each group of eight bits, known as an *octet*, is represented by its decimal equivalent. For example, consider the following binary IP address:

11000000101010001000100000011100

To convert this value to dotted-decimal notation, first divide it into four octets, as follows:

11000000 10101000 10001000 00011100

Then, convert each of the octets to its decimal equivalent:

11000000 10101000 10001000 00011100
192   168   136   28

Then, use periods to separate the four decimal numbers, like this:

192.168.136.28

This is the format in which you'll usually see IP addresses represented.

Figure 5-2 shows how the 32 bits of an IP address are broken down into four octets of eight bits each. As you can see, the four octets of an IP address are often referred to as w, x, y, and z.

Classifying IP Addresses

When the original designers of the IP protocol created the IP addressing scheme, they could have assigned an arbitrary number of IP address bits for the network ID. The remaining bits would then be used for the host ID. For example, suppose that the designers decided that half of the address (16 bits) would be used for the network, and the remaining 16 bits would be used for the host ID. The result of that scheme would be that the Internet could have a total of 65,536 networks, and each of those networks could have 65,536 hosts.

In the early days of the Internet, this scheme probably seemed like several orders of magnitude more than would ever be needed. However, the IP designers realized from the start that few networks would actually have tens of thousands of hosts. Suppose that a network of 1,000 computers joins the

Internet and is assigned one of these hypothetical network IDs. Because that network will use only 1,000 of its 65,536 host addresses, more than 64,000 IP addresses would be wasted.

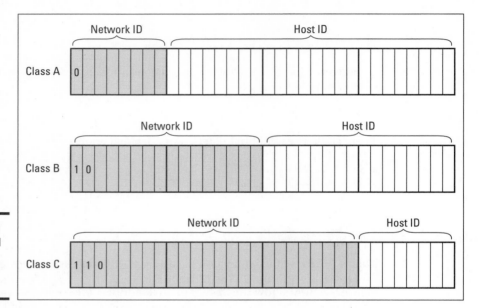

Figure 2-2:
Octets and dotted-decimal notation.

As a solution to this problem, the idea of IP address *classes* was introduced. The IP protocol defines five different address classes: A, B, C, D, and E. The first three classes, A through C, each use a different size for the network ID and host ID portion of the address. Class D is for a special type of address called a *multicast address*. Class E is an experimental address class that isn't used.

The first four bits of the IP address are used to determine into which class a particular address fits, as follows:

✦ If the first bit is a zero, the address is a Class A address.

✦ If the first bit is one and if the second bit is zero, the address is a Class B address.

✦ If the first two bits are both one and if the third bit is zero, the address is a Class C address.

✦ If the first three bits are all one and if the fourth bit is zero, the address is a Class D address.

✦ If the first four bits are all one, the address is a Class E address.

Because Class D and E addresses are reserved for special purposes, I focus the rest of the discussion here on Class A, B, and C addresses. Table 2-3 summarizes the details of each address class.

Table 2-3			IP Address Classes		
Class	Address Number Range	Starting Bits	Length of Network ID	Number of Networks	Hosts
A	1-126.x.y.z	0	8	126	16,777,214
B	128-191.x.y.z	10	16	16,384	65,534
C	192-223.x.y.z	110	24	2,097,152	254

Class A addresses

Class A addresses are designed for very large networks. In a Class A address, the first octet of the address is the network ID, and the remaining three octets are the host ID. Because only eight bits are allocated to the network ID and the first of these bits is used to indicate that the address is a Class A address, only 126 Class A networks can exist in the entire Internet. However, each Class A network can accommodate more than 16 million hosts.

Only about 40 Class A addresses are actually assigned to companies or organizations. The rest are either reserved for use by the IANA (*Internet Assigned Numbers Authority*) or are assigned to organizations that manage IP assignments for geographic regions such as Europe, Asia, and Latin America.

Just for fun, Table 2-4 lists some of the better-known Class A networks. You'll probably recognize many of them. In case you're interested, you can find a complete list of all the Class A address assignments at www.iana.org/assignments/ipv4-address-space.

You may have noticed in Table 2-3 that Class A addresses end with 126.x.y.z, and Class B addresses begin with 128.x.y.z. What happened to 127.x.y.z? This special range of addresses is reserved for loopback testing, so these addresses aren't assigned to public networks.

Table 2-4		Some Well-Known Class A Networks	
Net	*Description*	*Net*	*Description*
3	General Electric Company	32	Norsk Informasjonsteknology
4	Bolt Beranek and Newman Inc.	33	DLA Systems Automation Center
6	Army Information Systems Center	35	MERIT Computer Network
8	Bolt Beranek and Newman Inc.	38	Performance Systems International
9	IBM	40	Eli Lilly and Company
11	DoD Intel Information Systems	43	Japan Inet
12	AT&T Bell Laboratories	44	Amateur Radio Digital Communications
13	Xerox Corporation	45	Interop Show Network
15	Hewlett-Packard Company	46	Bolt Beranek and Newman Inc.
16	Digital Equipment Corporation	47	Bell-Northern Research
17	Apple Computer Inc.	48	Prudential Securities Inc.
18	MIT	51	Department of Social Security of UK
19	Ford Motor Company	52	E.I. duPont de Nemours and Co., Inc.
20	Computer Sciences Corporation	53	Cap Debis CCS (Germany)
22	Defense Information Systems Agency	54	Merck and Co., Inc.
25	Royal Signals and Radar Establishment	55	Boeing Computer Services
26	Defense Information Systems Agency	56	U.S. Postal Service
28	Decision Sciences Institute (North)	57	SITA
29-30	Defense Information Systems Agency		

Class B addresses

In a Class B address, the first two octets of the IP address are used as the network ID, and the second two octets are used as the host ID. Thus, a Class B address comes close to my hypothetical scheme of splitting the address down the middle, using half for the network ID and half for the host ID. It

What about IPv6?

Most of the current Internet is based on version 4 of the Internet Protocol, also known as IPv4. IPv4 has served the Internet well for more than 20 years. However, the growth of the Internet has put a lot of pressure on IPv4's limited 32-bit address space. This chapter describes how IPv4 has evolved to make the best possible use of 32-bit addresses, but eventually all the addresses will be assigned and the IPv4 address space will be filled to capacity. When that happens, the Internet will have to migrate to the next version of IP, known as IPv6.

IPv6 is also called *IP next generation,* or *IPng,* in honor of the favorite television show of most Internet gurus, *Star Trek: The Next Generation.*

IPv6 offers several advantages over IPv4, but the most important is that it uses 128 bits for Internet addresses rather than 32 bits. The number of host addresses possible with 128 bits is a number so large that it would make Carl Sagan proud. It doesn't just double or triple the number of available addresses. Just for the fun of it, here is the number of unique Internet addresses provided by IPv6:

340,282,366,920,938,463,463,374,607,431,768,211,456

This number is so large it defies understanding. If the IANA were around at the creation of the universe and started handing out IPv6 addresses at a rate of one per millisecond, they would now, 15 billion years later, have not yet allocated even 1 percent of the available addresses.

Unfortunately, the transition from IPv4 to IPv6 has been a slow one. Thus, the Internet will continue to be driven by IPv4 for at least a few more years.

isn't identical to this scheme, however, because the first two bits of the first octet are required to be 10, in order to indicate that the address is a Class B address. As a result, a total of 16,384 Class B networks can exist. All Class B addresses fall within the range 128.x.y.z to 191.x.y.z. Each Class B address can accommodate more than 65,000 hosts.

The problem with Class B networks is that even though they are much smaller than Class A networks, they still allocate far too many host IDs. Very few networks have tens of thousands of hosts. Thus, careless assignment of Class B addresses can lead to a large percentage of the available host addresses being wasted on organizations that don't need them.

Class C addresses

In a Class C address, the first three octets are used for the network ID, and the fourth octet is used for the host ID. With only eight bits for the host ID, each Class C network can accommodate only 254 hosts. However, with 24 network ID bits, Class C addresses allow for more than 2 million networks.

The problem with Class C networks is that they're too small. Although few organizations need the tens of thousands of host addresses provided by a Class B address, many organizations need more than a few hundred. The large discrepancy between Class B networks and Class C networks is what led to the development of *subnetting*, which is described in the next section.

Subnetting

Subnetting is a technique that lets network administrators use the 32 bits available in an IP address more efficiently by creating networks that aren't limited to the scales provided by Class A, B, and C IP addresses. With subnetting, you can create networks with more realistic host limits.

Subnetting provides a more flexible way to designate which portion of an IP address represents the network ID and which portion represents the host ID. With standard IP address classes, only three possible network ID sizes exist: 8 bits for Class A, 16 bits for Class B, and 24 bits for Class C. Subnetting lets you select an arbitrary number of bits to use for the network ID.

Two reasons compel people to use subnetting. The first is to allocate the limited IP address space more efficiently. If the Internet was limited to Class A, B, or C addresses, every network would be allocated 254, 65 thousand, or 16 million IP addresses for host devices. Although many networks with more than 254 devices exist, few (if any) exist with 65 thousand, let alone 16 million. Unfortunately, any network with more than 254 devices would need a Class B allocation and probably waste tens of thousands of IP addresses.

The second reason for subnetting is that even if a single organization has thousands of network devices, operating all those devices with the same network ID would slow the network down to a crawl. The way TCP/IP works dictates that all the computers with the same network ID must be on the same physical network. The physical network comprises a single *broadcast domain*, which means that a single network medium must carry all the traffic for the network. For performance reasons, networks are usually segmented into broadcast domains that are smaller than even Class C addresses provide.

Subnets

A *subnet* is a network that falls within a Class A, B, or C network. Subnets are created by using one or more of the Class A, B, or C host bits to extend the network ID. Thus, instead of the standard 8-, 16-, or 24-bit network ID, subnets can have network IDs of any length.

Figure 2-3 shows an example of a network before and after subnetting has been applied. In the unsubnetted network, the network has been assigned the Class B address 144.28.0.0. All the devices on this network must share the same broadcast domain.

In the second network, the first four bits of the host ID are used to divide the network into two small networks, identified as subnets 16 and 32. To the outside world (that is, on the other side of the router), these two networks still appear to be a single network identified as 144.28.0.0. For example, the outside world considers the device at 144.28.16.22 to belong to the 144.28.0.0 network. As a result, a packet sent to this device will be delivered to the router at 144.28.0.0. The router then considers the subnet portion of the host ID to decide whether to route the packet to subnet 16 or subnet 32.

Subnet masks

In order for subnetting to work, the router must be told which portion of the host ID should be used for the subnet network ID. This little sleight of hand is accomplished by using another 32-bit number, known as a *subnet mask*. Those IP address bits that represent the network ID are represented by a 1 in the mask, and those bits that represent the host ID appear as a 0 in the mask. As a result, a subnet mask always has a consecutive string of ones on the left, followed by a string of zeros.

For example, the subnet mask for the subnet shown in Figure 2-3, where the network ID consists of the 16-bit network ID plus an additional 4-bit subnet ID, would look like this:

```
11111111 11111111 11110000 00000000
```

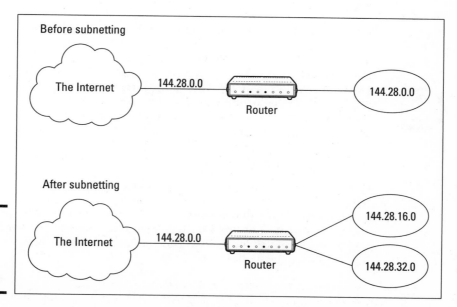

Figure 2-3:
A network before and after subnetting.

In other words, the first 20 bits are ones, the remaining 12 bits are zeros. Thus, the complete network ID is 20 bits in length, and the actual host ID portion of the subnetted address is 12 bits in length.

To determine the network ID of an IP address, the router must have both the IP address and the subnet mask. The router then performs a bitwise operation called a *logical AND* on the IP address in order to extract the network ID. To perform a logical AND, each bit in the IP address is compared to the corresponding bit in the subnet mask. If both bits are 1, the resulting bit in the network ID is set to 1. If either of the bits are 0, the resulting bit is set to 0.

For example, here's how the network address is extracted from an IP address using the 20-bit subnet mask from the previous example:

```
                    144  .   28  .   16  .   17
IP address:   10010000 00011100 00100000 00001001
Subnet mask:  11111111 11111111 11110000 00000000
Network ID:   10010000 00011100 00100000 00000000
                    144  .   28  .   16  .    0
```

Thus, the network ID for this subnet is 144.28.16.0.

The subnet mask itself is usually represented in dotted-decimal notation. As a result, the 20-bit subnet mask used in the previous example would be represented as 255.255.240.0:

```
Subnet mask:  11111111 11111111 11111111 11111111
                  255  .   255  .   240  .    0
```

Don't confuse a subnet mask with an IP address. A subnet mask doesn't represent any device or network on the Internet. It's just a way of indicating which portion of an IP address should be used to determine the network ID. (You can spot a subnet mask right away because the first octet is always 255, and 255 is not a valid first octet for any class of IP address.)

Network prefix notation

Because a subnet mask always begins with a consecutive sequence of ones to indicate which bits to use for the network ID, you can use a shorthand notation known as a *network prefix* to indicate how many bits of an IP address represent the network ID. The network prefix is indicated with a slash immediately after the IP address, followed by the number of network

ID bits to use. For example, the IP address 144.28.16.17 with the subnet mask 255.255.240.0 can be represented as 144.28.16.17/20, because the subnet mask 255.255.240.0 has 20 network ID bits.

Network prefix notation is also called *classless interdomain routing* notation, or just *CIDR* for short, because it provides a way of indicating which portion of an address is the network ID and which is the host ID without relying on standard address classes.

Default subnets

The *default subnet masks* are three subnet masks that correspond to the standard Class A, B, and C address assignments. These default masks are summarized in Table 2-5.

Table 2-5	The Default Subnet Masks		
Class	Binary	Dotted-Decimal	Network Prefix
A	11111111 00000000 00000000 00000000	255.0.0.0	/8
B	11111111 11111111 00000000 00000000	255.255.0.0	/16
C	11111111 11111111 11111111 00000000	255.255.255.0	/24

Keep in mind that a subnet mask is not actually required in order to use one of these defaults. That's because the IP address class can be determined by examining the first three bits of the IP address. If the first bit is 0, the address is Class A, and the subnet mask 255.0.0 is applied. If the first two bits are 10, the address is Class B, and 255.255.0.0 is used. If the first three bits are 110, the Class C default mask 255.255.255.0 is used.

The great subnet roundup

You should know about a few additional restrictions that are placed on subnet masks. In particular:

✦ The minimum number of network ID bits is eight. As a result, the first octet of a subnet mask is always 255.

✦ The maximum number of network ID bits is 30. You have to leave at least two bits for the host ID portion of the address to allow for at least two hosts. If you used all 32 bits for the network ID, that would leave no bits for the host ID. Obviously, that won't work. Leaving just one bit for the host ID won't work, either. That's because a host ID of all ones is reserved for a broadcast address and all zeros refers to the network itself. Thus, if you used 31 bits for the network ID and left only one for the host ID, host ID 1 would be used for the broadcast address and host ID 0 would be the network itself, leaving no room for actual hosts. That's why the maximum network ID size is 30 bits.

✦ Because the network ID is always composed of consecutive bits set to 1, only nine values are possible for each octet of a subnet mask (including 0). For your reference, these values are listed in Table 2-6.

Table 2-6	The Subnet Octet Values
Binary octet	*Decimal*
00000000	0
10000000	128
11000000	192
11100000	224
11110000	240
11111000	248
11111100	252
11111110	254
11111111	255

Table 2-7 lists the possible subnet masks that you can use for a Class A address.

Table 2-7		Class A Subnet Masks		
Subnet Bits	*CIDR*	*Dotted-Decimal*	*Number of Subnets*	*Number of Hosts*
0	/8	255.0.0.0	0	16,777,214
1	/9	255.128.0.0	2	8,388,606
2	/10	255.192.0.0	4	4,194,302
3	/11	255.224.0.0	8	2,097,150
4	/12	255.240.0.0	16	1,048,574
5	/13	255.248.0.0	32	524,286
6	/14	255.252.0.0	64	262,142

Subnet Bits	CIDR	Dotted-Decimal	Number of Subnets	Number of Hosts
7	/15	255.254.0.0	128	131,070
8	/16	255.255.0.0	256	65,534
9	/17	255.255.128.0	512	32,766
10	/18	255.255.192.0	1,024	16,382
11	/19	255.255.224.0	2,048	8,190
12	/20	255.255.240.0	4,096	4,094
13	/21	255.255.248.0	8,192	2,046
14	/22	255.255.252.0	16,384	1,022
15	/23	255.255.254.0	32,768	510
16	/24	255.255.255.0	65,536	254
17	/25	255.255.255.128	131,072	126
18	/26	255.255.255.192	262,144	62
19	/27	255.255.255.224	524,288	30
20	/28	255.255.255.240	1,048,576	14
21	/29	255.255.255.248	2,097,152	6
22	/30	255.255.255.252	4,194,304	2

Table 2-8 lists the possible subnet masks that you can use for a Class B address.

Table 2-8		Class B Subnet Masks		
Subnet Bits	CIDR	Dotted-Decimal	Number of Subnets	Number of Hosts
1	/17	255.255.128.0	2	32,766
2	/18	255.255.192.0	4	16,382
3	/19	255.255.224.0	8	8,190
4	/20	255.255.240.0	16	4,094
5	/21	255.255.248.0	32	2,046
6	/22	255.255.252.0	64	1,022
7	/23	255.255.254.0	128	510
8	/24	255.255.255.0	256	254
9	/25	255.255.255.128	512	126

(continued)

Table 2-8 (continued)

Subnet Bits	CIDR	Dotted-Decimal	Number of Subnets	Number of Hosts
10	/26	255.255.255.192	1,024	62
11	/27	255.255.255.224	2,048	30
12	/28	255.255.255.240	4,096	14
13	/29	255.255.255.248	8,192	6
14	/30	255.255.255.252	16,384	2

Table 2-9 lists the possible subnet masks that you can use for a Class C address.

Table 2-9   **Class C Subnet Masks**

Subnet Bits	CIDR	Dotted-Decimal	Number of Subnets	Number of Hosts
1	/25	255.255.255.128	1	126
2	/26	255.255.255.192	2	62
3	/27	255.255.255.224	4	30
4	/28	255.255.255.240	8	14
5	/29	255.255.255.248	16	6
6	/30	255.255.255.252	32	2

IP block parties

A subnet can be thought of as a range or block of IP addresses that have a common network ID. For example, the CIDR 192.168.1.0/28 represents the following block of 14 IP addresses:

```
192.168.1.1     192.168.1.2     192.168.1.3     192.168.1.4
192.168.1.5     192.168.1.6     192.168.1.7     192.168.1.8
192.168.1.9     192.168.1.10    192.168.1.11    192.168.1.12
192.168.1.13    192.168.1.14
```

Given an IP address in CIDR notation, it's useful to be able to determine the range of actual IP addresses that the CIDR represents. This matter is straightforward when the octet within which the network ID mask ends happens to be 0, as in the preceding example. You just determine how many host IDs are allowed based on the size of the network ID and count them off.

However, what if the octet where the network ID mask ends is not 0? For example, what are the valid IP addresses for 192.168.1.100/28? In that case, the calculation is a little harder. The first step is to determine the actual network ID. You can do that by converting both the IP address and the subnet mask to binary and then extracting the network ID as in this example:

```
                192  .  168  .    1  .   100
IP address:   11000000 10101000 00000001 01100100
Subnet mask:  11111111 11111111 11111111 11110000
Network ID:   11000000 10101000 00000001 01100000
                192  .  168  .    1  .   96
```

As a result, the network ID for 192.168.1.100/28 is 192.168.1.96.

Next, determine the number of allowable hosts in the subnet based on the network prefix. You can look up this number in Table 2-7. For a 28-bit network prefix, the number of hosts is 14.

To determine the first IP address in the block, add 1 to the network ID. Thus, the first IP address in my example is 192.168.1.97. To determine the last IP address in the block, add the number of hosts to the network ID. In my example, the last IP address is 192.168.1.110. As a result, the CIDR 192.168.1.100/28 designates the following block of IP addresses:

```
192.168.1.97    192.168.1.98    192.168.1.99    192.168.1.100
192.168.1.101   192.168.1.102   192.168.1.103   192.168.1.104
192.168.1.105   192.168.1.106   192.168.1.107   192.168.1.108
192.168.1.109   192.168.1.110
```

Variable-length subnet masking

Subnet masking lets you divide a network into two or more equal-sized subnets. For example, you can use the subnet mask 255.255.255.224 to divide a Class C address into four subnets with 30 hosts each. The subnet mask 255.255.255.240 creates 16 subnets that can have 14 hosts each. These subnet masks will work if you need to divide your network into subnets of roughly equal size. Most networks, however, don't divide up so evenly. You may have one network that needs 30 hosts and two networks that need 14 hosts each.

Variable-length subnet masking — also known as *VLSM* — lets you carve up an IP address space into subnets of unequal size. You can arrange the subnets in whatever way works best for you, provided that each of the subnets has a valid subnet mask and you don't allow the subnets to overlap.

For example, suppose that you are given the Class C address 206.68.100.0, and you need one subnet that can have up to 62 hosts, one subnet that can accommodate up to 30 hosts, and two subnets that can have up to 14 hosts. The subnet masks for the subnets are listed here:

✦ Subnet 1 with 62 hosts: 255.255.255.192

✦ Subnet 2 with 62 hosts: 255.255.255.224

✦ Subnets 3 and 4 with 62 hosts: 255.255.255.240

To create subnets using VLSM, you simply carve up the total address space that you have available to you into the subnets you need. One way to do that is to make a table that lists four addresses for each subnet: the subnet address, the first host address, the last host address, and the broadcast address. In this way, you can account for every address in the address space you're trying to carve up. For example, Table 2-10 shows one way you can create four subnets from the 206.68.100.0 Class C address.

Table 2-10	A Class C Address with Variable-Length Subnets			
Subnet	*Description*	*Address*	*Subnet mask*	*CIDR*
Subnet 1 (62 hosts)	Subnet	206.68.100.0	255.255.255.192	/26
	First host	206.68.100.1	255.255.255.192	/26
	Last host	206.68.100.62	255.255.255.192	/26
	Broadcast	206.68.100.63	255.255.255.192	/26
Subnet 2 (30 hosts)	Subnet	206.68.100.64	255.255.255.224	/27
	First host	206.68.100.65	255.255.255.224	/27
	Last host	206.68.100.94	255.255.255.224	/27
	Broadcast	206.68.100.95	255.255.255.224	/27
Subnet 3 (14 hosts)	Subnet	206.68.100.96	255.255.255.240	/28
	First host	206.68.100.97	255.255.255.240	/28
	Last host	206.68.100.110	255.255.255.240	/28
	Broadcast	206.68.100.111	255.255.255.240	/28
Subnet 4 (14 hosts)	Subnet	206.68.100.112	255.255.255.240	/28
	First host	206.68.100.113	255.255.255.240	/28
	Last host	206.68.100.126	255.255.255.240	/28
	Broadcast	206.68.100.127	255.255.255.240	/28

Note that these four subnets don't use up the entire range of addresses available to the Class C address. Because the four subnets will use a total of only 120 hosts, it will use only half of the available address space. The addresses from 206.68.100.128 to 206.68.100.255 are available for future use.

If you had used equal-length subnet masks to split this Class C address into four equal subnets, these addresses would not be available. In effect, half of the addresses would be wasted.

Supernetting

Supernetting is the opposite of subnetting. It allows you to combine two or more networks of the same class into a single network. For example, suppose that your network requires about 500 host IDs. Your ISP could assign you a Class B network, but that would waste thousands of host addresses. Instead, your ISP could assign you two Class C addresses. That would give you enough total host addresses, but you'd have two separate networks.

With supernetting, your ISP can assign you two adjacent Class C addresses, for a total of 512 addresses. Then, by specifying 255.255.254.0 as the subnet mask rather than using the default Class C mask (255.255.255.0), the two Class C addresses will be treated as a single network.

You have to follow two rules in order to combine addresses with supernetting:

✦ The addresses must be adjacent to each other. For Class C addresses, that means that the third octets are consecutive numbers. For example, 206.100.128.0 and 206.100.129.0 are adjacent Class C addresses, but 206.100.128.0 and 206.100.144.0 are not.

✦ The third octet of the first address to be subnetted must be divisible by two. As a result, you can supernet the address blocks 206.100.128.0 and 206.100.129.0 because the address blocks are adjacent and the third octet of the first address (128) is divisible by two. However, you can't supernet 206.100.129.0 and 206.100.130.0 because the third octet of the first address is not an even number.

Private and public addresses

Any host with a direct connection to the Internet must have a globally unique IP address. However, not all hosts are connected directly to the Internet. Some are on networks that are not connected to the Internet. Some hosts are hidden behind firewalls, so their Internet connection is indirect.

Several blocks of IP addresses are set aside just for this purpose, for use on private networks that are not connected to the Internet or to use on networks that are hidden behind a firewall. Three such ranges of addresses exist, summarized in Table 2-11. Whenever you create a private TCP/IP network, you should use IP addresses from one of these ranges.

Table 2-11	Private Address Spaces	
CIDR	*Subnet Mask*	*Address Range*
10.0.0.0/8	255.0.0.0	10.0.0.1 – 10.255.255.254
172.16.0.0/12	255.255.240.0	172.16.1.1 – 172.31.255.254
192.168.0.0/16	255.255.0.0	192.168.0.1 – 192.168.255.254

Network Address Translation

Many firewalls use a technique called *network address translation* (or *NAT*) to hide the actual IP address of a host from the outside world. When that's the case, the NAT device must use a globally unique IP to represent the host to the Internet, but behind the firewall, the host can use any IP address it wants. As packets cross the firewall, the NAT device translates the private IP address to the public IP address and vice versa.

One of the benefits of NAT is that it helps to slow down the rate at which the IP address space is assigned. That's because a NAT device can use a single public IP address for more than one host. It does so by keeping track of outgoing packets so that it can match up incoming packets with the correct host. To understand how this works, consider the following sequence of steps:

1. A host whose private address is 192.168.1.100 sends a request to 216.239.57.99, which happens to be `www.google.com`. The NAT device changes the source IP address of the packet to 208.23.110.22, the IP address of the firewall. That way, Google will send its reply back to the firewall router. The NAT records that 192.168.1.100 sent a request to 216.239.57.99.

2. Now another host, at address 192.168.1.107, sends a request to 207.46.134.190, which happens to be `www.microsoft.com`. The NAT device changes the source of this request to 208.23.110.22 so that Microsoft will reply to the firewall router. The NAT records that 192.168.1.107 sent a request to 207.46.134.190.

3. A few seconds later, the firewall receives a reply from 216.239.57.99. The destination address in the reply is 208.23.110.22, the address of the firewall. To determine to whom to forward the reply, the firewall checks its records to see who is waiting for a reply from 216.239.57.99. It discovers that 192.168.1.100 is waiting for that reply, so it changes the destination address to 192.168.1.100 and sends the packet on.

Actually, the process is a little more complicated than that, because it's very likely that two or more users may have pending requests from the same public IP. In that case, the NAT device uses other techniques to figure out to which user each incoming packet should be delivered.

Chapter 3: Using DHCP

In This Chapter

✔ **Discovering the basics of DHCP**

✔ **Exploring scopes**

✔ **Configuring a DHCP server**

✔ **Setting up a DHCP client**

*E*very host on a TCP/IP network must have a unique IP address. Each host must be properly configured so that it knows its IP address. When a new host comes online, it must be assigned an IP address that is within the correct range of addresses for the subnet and is not already in use. Although you can manually assign IP addresses to each computer on your network, that task quickly becomes overwhelming if the network has more than a few computers.

That's where *DHCP*, the *Dynamic Host Configuration Protocol*, comes into play. DHCP automatically configures the IP address for every host on a network, thus assuring that each host has a valid unique IP address. DHCP even automatically reconfigures IP addresses as hosts come and go. As you can imagine, DHCP can save a network administrator many hours of tedious configuration work.

In this chapter, you discover the ins and outs of DHCP: what it is, how it works, and how to set it up.

Understanding DHCP

DHCP allows individual computers on a TCP/IP network to obtain their configuration information — in particular, their IP address — from a server. The DHCP server keeps track of which IP addresses have already been assigned so that when a computer requests an IP address, the DHCP server will offer it an IP address that is not already in use.

Configuration information provided by DHCP

Although the primary job of DHCP is to dole out IP addresses and subnet masks, DHCP actually provides more configuration information than just the IP address to its clients. The additional configuration information is referred to as *DHCP options*. The following is a list of some common DHCP options that can be configured by the server:

✦ The router address, also known as the Default Gateway address.

✦ The expiration time for the configuration information.

✦ Domain name.

✦ DNS server address.

✦ WINS server address.

DHCP servers

A DHCP server can be a server computer located on the TCP/IP network. All modern server operating systems have a built-in DHCP server. To set up DHCP on a network server, all you have to do is enable the server's DHCP function and configure its settings. In the section "Working with a DHCP Server," later in this chapter, I show you how to configure a DHCP server for Windows 2003.

A server computer running DHCP doesn't have to be devoted entirely to DHCP unless the network is very large. For most networks, a file server can share duty as a DHCP server. This is especially true if you provide long leases for your IP addresses. (I explain the idea of leases later in this chapter.)

Many multifunction routers also have built-in DHCP servers. So if you don't want to burden one of your network servers with the DHCP function, you can enable the router's built-in DHCP server. An advantage of allowing the router to be your network's DHCP server is that you rarely need to power down a router. In contrast, you occasionally need to restart or power down a file server to perform system maintenance, to apply upgrades, or to perform troubleshooting.

Most networks require only one DHCP server. Setting up two or more servers on the same network requires that you carefully coordinate the IP address ranges (known as *scopes*) for which each server is responsible. If you accidentally set up two DHCP servers for the same scope, you may end up with duplicate address assignments if the servers attempt to assign the same IP address to two different hosts. To prevent this from happening, it's best to set up just one DHCP server unless your network is so large that one server can't handle the workload.

How DHCP actually works

You can configure and use DHCP without knowing the details of how DHCP client configuration actually works. However, a basic understanding of the process can help you to understand what DHCP is actually doing. This understanding is not only enlightening, it can be downright handy when you're troubleshooting DHCP problems.

The following paragraphs are a blow-by-blow account of how DHCP configures TCP/IP hosts. This procedure happens every time you boot up a host computer. It also happens when you release an IP lease and request a fresh lease.

1. When a host computer starts up, the DHCP client software sends a special broadcast packet, known as a *DHCPDiscover message.* This message uses the subnet's broadcast address (all host ID bits set to one) as the destination address and 0.0.0.0 as the source address.

   The client has to specify 0.0.0.0 as the source address because it doesn't yet have an IP address, and it specifies the broadcast address as the destination address because it doesn't know the address of any DHCP servers. In effect, the DHCPDiscover message is saying, "Hey! I'm new here. Are there any DHCP servers out there?"

2. The DHCP server receives the broadcast DHCPDiscover message and responds by sending a *DHCPOffer message.* The DHCPOffer message includes an IP address that the client can use.

   Like the DHCPDiscover message, the DHCPOffer message is sent to the broadcast address. This makes sense because the client to which the message is being sent doesn't yet have an IP address and won't have one until it accepts the offer. In effect, the DHCPOffer message is saying, "Hello there, whoever you are. Here's an IP address you can use, if you want it. Let me know."

   What if the client never receives a DHCPOffer message from a DHCP server? In that case, the client waits for a few seconds and tries again. The client will try four times — at 2, 4, 8, and 16 seconds. If it still doesn't get an offer, it will try again after five minutes.

3. The client receives the DHCPOffer message and sends back a message known as a *DHCPRequest message*. At this point, the client doesn't actually own the IP address. It's simply indicating that it's ready to accept the IP address that was offered by the server. In effect, the DHCPRequest message says, "Yes, that IP address would be good for me. Can I have it, please?"

4. When the server receives the DHCPRequest message, it marks the IP address as assigned to the client and broadcasts a *DHCPAck message*. The DHCPAck message says, in effect, "Okay, it's all yours. Here's the rest of the information you need to use it."

5. When the client receives the DHCPAck message, it configures its TCP/IP stack by using the address it accepted from the server.

Understanding Scopes

A *scope* is simply a range of IP addresses that a DHCP server is configured to distribute. In the simplest case, where a single DHCP server oversees IP configuration for an entire subnet, the scope corresponds to the subnet. However, if you set up two DHCP servers for a subnet, you can configure each with a scope that allocates only one part of the complete subnet range. In addition, a single DHCP server can serve more than one scope.

You must create a scope before you can enable a DHCP server. When you create a scope, you can provide it with the following properties:

✦ A scope name, which helps you to identify the scope and its purpose.

✦ A scope description, which lets you provide additional details about the scope and its purpose.

✦ A starting IP address for the scope.

✦ An ending IP address for the scope.

✦ A subnet mask for the scope. You can specify the subnet mask with dotted decimal notation or with CIDR notation.

✦ One or more ranges of excluded addresses. These addresses won't be assigned to clients. For more information, see the section "Feeling excluded?" later in this chapter.

✦ One or more reserved addresses. These are addresses that will always be assigned to particular host devices. For more information, see the section "Reservations suggested," later in this chapter.

✦ The lease duration, which indicates how long the host will be allowed to use the IP address. The client will attempt to renew the lease when half of the lease duration has elapsed. For example, if you specify a lease duration of eight days, the client will attempt to renew the lease after four days have passed. This allows the host plenty of time to renew the lease before the address is reassigned to some other host.

✦ The router address for the subnet. This value is also known as the Default Gateway address.

✦ The domain name and the IP address of the network's DNS servers and WINS servers.

Feeling excluded?

Everyone feels excluded once in awhile. With a wife, three daughters, and a female dog, I know how it feels. Sometimes, however, being excluded is a good thing. In the case of DHCP scopes, exclusions can help you to prevent IP address conflicts and can enable you to divide the DHCP workload for a single subnet among two or more DHCP servers.

An *exclusion* is a range of addresses that are not included in a scope. The exclusion range falls within the range of the scope's starting and ending addresses. In effect, an exclusion range lets you punch a hole in a scope. The IP addresses that fall within the hole won't be assigned.

The following are several reasons for excluding IP addresses from a scope:

✦ The computer that runs the DHCP service itself must usually have a static IP address assignment. As a result, the address of the DHCP server should be listed as an exclusion.

✦ Some hosts may not be able to support DHCP. In that case, the host will require a static IP address. For example, you may have a really old MS-DOS computer that doesn't have a DHCP client. By excluding its IP address from the scope, you can prevent that address from being assigned to any other host on the network.

Reservations suggested

In some cases, you may want to assign a particular IP address to a particular host. One way to do this is to configure the host with a static IP address so that the host doesn't use DHCP to obtain its IP configuration. However, two major disadvantages to that approach exist:

✦ TCP/IP configuration supplies more than just the IP address. If you use static configuration, you must manually specify the subnet mask, Default Gateway address, DNS server address, and other configuration information required by the host. If this information changes, you have to change it not only at the DHCP server, but also at each host that you've configured statically.

✦ You must remember to exclude the static IP address from the DHCP server's scope. Otherwise, the DHCP server won't know about the static address and may assign it to another host. Then, you'll have two hosts with the same address on your network.

A better way to assign a fixed IP address to a particular host is to create a DHCP reservation. A *reservation* simply indicates that whenever a particular host requests an IP address from the DHCP server, the server should provide it the address that you specify in the reservation. The host won't receive the IP address until the host requests it from the DHCP server, but whenever the host does request IP configuration, it will always receive the same address.

To create a reservation, you associate the IP address that you want assigned to the host with the host's MAC address. As a result, you need to get the MAC address from the host before you create the reservation. You can get the MAC address by running the command `ipconfig /all` from a command prompt. (If that fails because TCP/IP has not yet been configured on the computer, you can also get the MAC address by running the System Information command, which is Start⇨All Programs⇨Accessories⇨System Tools⇨System Information.)

What about BootP?

BootP, which stands for *Bootstrap Protocol*, is an Internet protocol that enables diskless workstations to boot themselves over the Internet. Like DHCP, BootP allows a computer to receive an IP address assigned from a server. However, unlike DHCP, BootP also enables the computer to download a *boot image file*, which the computer can then use to boot itself from. A significant difference between BootP and DHCP is that BootP comes into play before the computer actually loads an operating system. In contrast, DHCP is used after an operating system has been loaded, during the configuration of network devices.

Most DHCP servers can also support the BootP protocol. So if your network has diskless workstations, you can use the DHCP server's BootP support to boot those computers. At one time, diskless workstations were all the rage because network administrators thought they'd be easier to manage. Users hated them, however. So most diskless workstations are now beehives, and the BootP protocol isn't used much.

If you set up more than one DHCP server, be sure to specify the same reservations on each server. If you forget to repeat a reservation on one of the servers, that server may assign the address to another host.

How long to lease?

One of the most important decisions that you'll make when you configure a DHCP server is the length of time to specify for the lease duration. The default value is eight days, which is appropriate in many cases. However, you may encounter situations in which a longer or shorter interval may be appropriate.

✦ The more stable your network, the longer the lease duration can safely exist. If you only periodically add new computers to the network or replace existing computers, you can safely increase the lease duration past eight days.

✦ The more volatile the network, the shorter the lease duration should be. For example, a wireless network in a university library is used by students who bring their laptop computers into the library to work for a few hours at a time. For this network, a duration such as one hour may be appropriate.

Don't configure your network to allow infinite duration leases. Some administrators feel that this cuts down the workload for the DHCP server on stable networks. However, no network is permanently stable. Whenever you find a DHCP server that's configured with infinite leases, look at the active leases. I guarantee you'll find IP leases assigned to computers that no longer exist.

Working with a DHCP Server

The exact steps that you should follow when configuring and managing a DHCP server depend on the network operating system that you're using. The following procedures show you how to work with a DHCP server in Windows Server 2003. The procedures for other operating systems are similar.

Installing and configuring a DHCP server

To install the DHCP server role on Windows Server 2003, follow these steps:

1. **Choose Start⇨Administrative Tools⇨Manage Your Server.**

The Manage Your Server application appears.

2. **Click the Add or Remove a Role link.**

   The Configure Your Server Wizard appears.

3. **Select DHCP Server from the list of roles and then click Next.**

   The Configure Your Server Wizard lists the changes it is about to make.

4. **Click Next.**

   The Wizard calls up the Windows Setup program to install the DHCP server components. This can take a few minutes, so be patient. When the components are installed, the Windows Setup program automatically ends and is replaced by the New Scope Wizard dialog box, as shown in Figure 3-1. The New Scope Wizard guides you through the process of creating the first scope for the DHCP server.

Figure 3-1:
The New
Scope
Wizard
comes to
life.

5. **Click the Next button.**

   The wizard asks for a name and description for the new scope.

6. **Type the name and description for the scope.**

   The name can be anything you want. I suggest that you use a generic name such as "Office" or your company name unless you're creating two or more scopes. Then, the names should indicate the function of each scope.

7. **Click Next.**

   The wizard asks for the scope range, as shown in Figure 3-2.

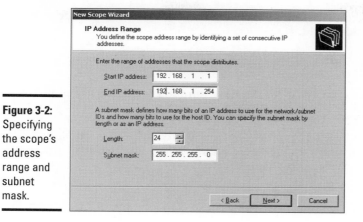

Figure 3-2:
Specifying
the scope's
address
range and
subnet
mask.

8. Enter the start and end IP address and the subnet mask.

You can enter the subnet mask by either selecting its length from the
Length spin button or by entering the complete subnet mask into the
Subnet Mask text box. In this example, I've entered the range 192.168.1.1
through 192.168.1.254, with a subnet mask of 255.255.255.0.

9. Click Next.

The next screen of the wizard lets you create exclusions, as shown in
Figure 3-3.

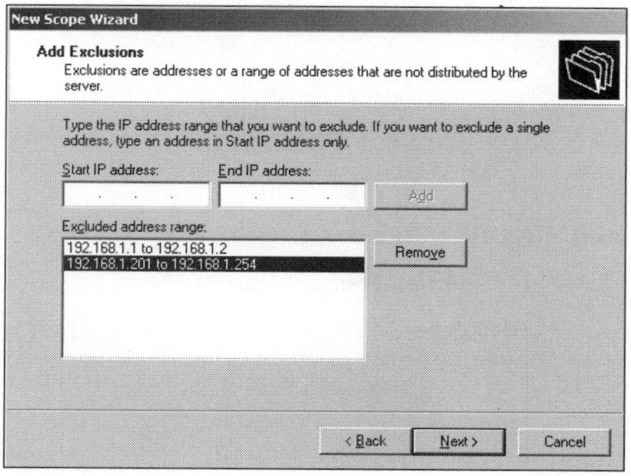

Figure 3-3:
Specifying
exclusions.

10. **Enter each exclusion by entering the start and end IP address and then clicking Add.**

    In Figure 3-3, I've entered two exclusions.

11. **Click Next.**

    Next, the wizard asks for the lease duration, as shown in Figure 3-4.

12. **Use the spin boxes to specify the lease duration.**

    The default setting is eight days. For more information about how to choose an appropriate lease duration, refer to the section "How long to lease?" earlier in this chapter.

13. **Click Next.**

    The wizard asks whether you want to configure the DHCP options now or later.

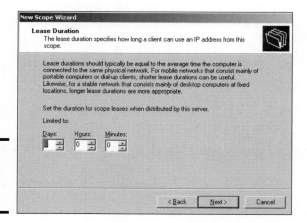

Figure 3-4:
Specifying
the lease
duration.

14. **Check Yes and then click Next.**

    The wizard asks for the IP address of the router.

15. **Enter the router's IP address, click Add, and then click Next.**

    Next, the wizard asks for the DNS configuration information, as shown in Figure 3-5.

16. **Enter the domain name and DNS servers.**

    To enter a DNS server, type its address in the IP address text box and click Add. You typically have more than one DNS server. In Figure 3-5, I specified `LoweWriter.com` for the domain name and provided IP addresses for three DNS servers.

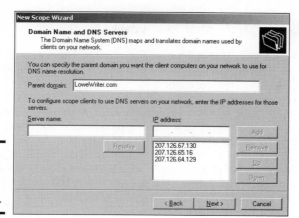

Figure 3-5:
Specifying
the DNS
information.

17. **Click Next.**

The wizard next asks for the WINS configuration information.

18. **Enter the WINS server configuration and then click Next.**

To specify a WINS server, enter the server's IP address and click Add. You can add multiple IP addresses if your network has more than one WINS server.

When you click Next, the wizard displays a screen asking whether you want to activate the scope now or later.

19. **Choose Yes or No to activate the scope now or wait until later and then click Next.**

If you need to do some more configuration work before the DHCP server is ready to go live, choose No here. For example, if you need to first configure another scope, choose No. Otherwise, choose Yes to activate the scope as soon as the wizard finishes.

When you click Next, a final screen appears, congratulating you on your hard work.

20. **Click Finish to close the New Scope Wizard.**

You're returned to the Configure Your Server Wizard, with a message that indicates the server has been configured for DHCP.

21. **Click Finish to close the Configure Your Server Wizard.**

You're returned to the Manage Your Server application.

Managing a DHCP server

You can bring up the DHCP management console by choosing Start➪
Administrative Tools➪DHCP or by clicking Manage This DHCP Server from
the Manage Your Server application. Either way, the DHCP management console appears, as shown in Figure 3-6.

From the DHCP console, you have complete control over the DHCP server's
configuration and operation. The following paragraphs summarize some of
the things that you can do from the DHCP console:

✦ You can *authorize* the DHCP server, which allows it to begin assigning
  client IP addresses. To authorize a server, select the server, choose
  Action➪Manage Authorized Servers, and click Authorize.

✦ To add another scope, right-click the server in the tree and choose the
  New Scope command from the menu that appears. This brings up the
  New Scope Wizard. You can follow Steps 5 through 20 in the previous
  section to complete the wizard.

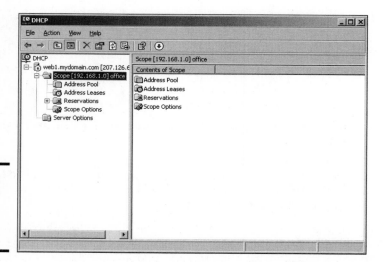

Figure 3-6:
The DHCP
manage-
ment
console.

✦ To activate or deactivate a scope, right-click the scope in the tree and
  choose the Activate or Deactivate command.

✦ To change scope settings, right-click the scope and choose the Properties
  command. This brings up the Scope Properties dialog box, as shown in
  Figure 3-7. From this dialog box, you can change the scope's start and
  end IP addresses, subnet mask, and DNS configuration.

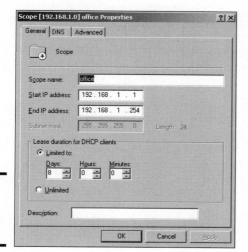

Figure 3-7:
The Scope
Properties
dialog box.

✦ To change the scope exclusions, click Address Pool under the scope in the tree. This will list each range of addresses that's included in the scope. You can add or delete a range by right-clicking the range and choosing the Delete command from the menu that appears. You can also add a new exclusion range by right-clicking Address Pool in the tree and choosing Add New Exclusion from the pop-up menu.

✦ To view or change reservations, click Reservations in the tree.

✦ To view a list of the addresses that are currently assigned, click Address Leases in the tree.

How to Configure a Windows DHCP Client

Configuring a Windows client for DHCP is easy. The DHCP client is automatically included when you install the TCP/IP protocol, so all you have to do is configure TCP/IP to use DHCP. To do this, bring up the Network Properties dialog box by choosing Network or Network Connections in the Control Panel (depending on which version of Windows the client is running). Then, select the TCP/IP protocol and click the Properties button. This brings up the TCP/IP Properties dialog box, as shown in Figure 3-8. To configure the computer to use DHCP, check Obtain An IP Address Automatically and Obtain DNS Server Address Automatically.

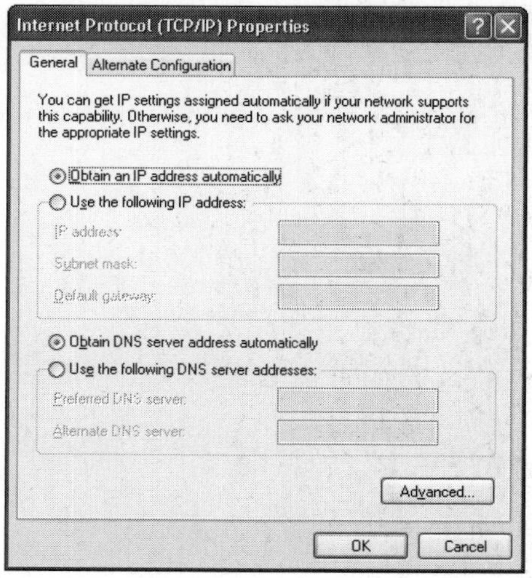

Figure 3-8:
Configuring
a Windows
client to use
DHCP.

Automatic Private IP Addressing

If a Windows computer is configured to use DHCP but the computer can't obtain an IP address from a DHCP server, the computer automatically assigns itself a private address by using a feature called *Automatic Private IP Addressing,* or *APIPA* for short. APIPA assigns a private address from the 169.254.*x.x* range and uses a special algorithm to ensure that the address is unique on the network. As soon as the DHCP server becomes available, the computer requests a new address, so the APIPA address is used only while the DHCP server is unavailable.

Renewing and releasing leases

Normally, a DHCP client attempts to renew its lease when the lease is halfway to the point of being expired. For example, if a client obtains an eight-day lease, it attempts to renew the lease after four days. However, you can renew a lease sooner by issuing the `ipconfig /renew` command at a command prompt. You may want to do this if you've changed the scope's configuration or if the client's IP configuration isn't working correctly.

You can also release a DHCP lease by issuing the `ipconfig /release` command at a command prompt. When you release a lease, the client computer no longer has a valid IP address. This is shown in the output from the `ipconfig /release` command:

```
C:\>ipconfig /release

Windows IP Configuration

Ethernet adapter Local Area Connection:

        Connection-specific DNS Suffix  . :
        IP Address. . . . . . . . . . . : 0.0.0.0
        Subnet Mask . . . . . . . . . . : 0.0.0.0
        Default Gateway . . . . . . . . :
```

Here, you can see that the IP address and subnet masks are set to 0.0.0.0
and the Default Gateway address is blank. When you release an IP lease, you
can't communicate with the network by using TCP/IP until you issue an
`ipconfig /renew` command to renew the IP configuration or restart the
computer.

Chapter 4: Using DNS

In This Chapter

✔ **Discovering the basics of DNS**

✔ **Exploring zones**

✔ **Examining resource records**

✔ **Configuring a DNS server**

✔ **Setting up a DNS client**

*D*NS, which stands for *domain name system,* is the TCP/IP facility that lets you use names rather than numbers to refer to host computers. Without DNS, you'd buy books from 207.171.182.16 instead of from www. amazon.com, you'd sell your used furniture at 66.135.192.87 instead of on www.ebay.com, and you'd search the Web at 216.239.51.100 instead of at www.google.com.

Understanding how DNS works and how to set up a DNS server is crucial to setting up and administering a TCP/IP network. This chapter introduces you to the basics of DNS, including how the DNS naming system works and how to set up a DNS server.

If you want to review the complete official specifications for DNS, look up RFC 1034 and 1035 at www.ietf.org/rfc/rfc1034.txt and www.ietf/rfc/rfc1035.txt.

Understanding DNS Names

DNS is a *name service* that provides a standardized system for providing names to identify TCP/IP hosts and a way to look up the IP address of a host given the host's DNS name. For example, if you use DNS to look up the name www.ebay.com, you get the IP address of Ebay's Web host: 66.135.192.87. Thus, DNS allows you to access Ebay's Web site using the DNS name www.ebay.com rather than the site's IP address.

The following sections describe the basic concepts of DNS.

Domains and domain names

To provide a unique DNS name for every host computer on the Internet, DNS uses a time-tested technique: divide and conquer. DNS uses a hierarchical naming system that's similar to the way folders are organized hierarchically on a Windows computer. Instead of folders, however, DNS organizes its names into *domains*. Each domain includes all the names that appear directly beneath it in the DNS hierarchy.

For example, Figure 4-1 shows a small portion of the DNS domain tree. At the very top of the tree is the *root domain,* which is the anchor point for all domains. Directly beneath the root domain are four *top-level domains,* named edu, com, org, and gov.

In reality, many more top-level domains than this exist in the Internet's root domain; for more information, see the section "Top level domains," later in this chapter.

Beneath the com domain is another domain called LoweWriter, which happens to be my own personal domain (pretty clever, eh?). To completely identify this domain, you have to combine it with the name of its *parent domain* (in this case, com) to create the complete domain name: `LoweWriter.com`. Notice that the parts of the domain name are separated from each other with periods, which are pronounced "dot." As a result, when you read this domain name, you should pronounce it "LoweWriter dot com."

Beneath the LoweWriter node are four host nodes, named `doug`, `debbie`, `server1`, and `printer1`. These correspond to three computers and a printer on my home network. You can combine the host name with the domain name to get the complete DNS name for each of my network's hosts. For example, the complete DNS name for my server is `server1.LoweWriter.com`. Likewise, my printer is `printer1.LoweWriter.com`.

Here are a few additional details that you need to remember about DNS names:

✦ DNS names are not case-sensitive. As a result, LoweWriter and Lowewriter are treated as the same name, as are LOWEWRITER, LOWEwriter, and LoWeWrItEr. When you use a domain name, you can use capitalization to make the name easier to read, but DNS ignores the difference between capital and lowercase letters.

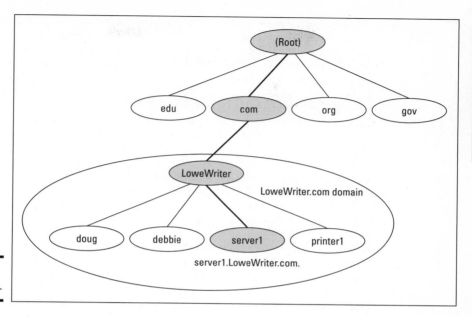

Figure 4-1:
DNS names.

✦ The name of each DNS node can be up to 63 characters long (not includ-ing the dot) and can include letters, numbers, and hyphens. No other special characters are allowed.

✦ A *subdomain* is a domain that's beneath an existing domain. For exam-ple, the com domain is actually a subdomain of the root domain. Likewise, LoweWriter is a subdomain of the com domain.

✦ DNS is a hierarchical naming system that's similar to the hierarchical folder system used by Windows. However, one crucial difference exists between DNS and the Windows naming convention. When you construct a complete DNS name, you start at the bottom of the tree and work your way up to the root. Thus, doug is the lowest node in the name doug.LoweWriter.com. In contrast, Windows paths are the opposite: They start at the root and work their way down. For example, in the path \Windows\System32\dns, dns is the lowest node.

✦ The DNS tree can be up to 127 levels deep. However, in practice, the DNS tree is pretty shallow. Most DNS names have just three levels (not counting the root), and although you'll sometimes see names with four or five levels, you'll rarely see more levels than that.

✦ Although the DNS tree is shallow, it's very broad. In other words, each of the top-level domains has a huge number of second-level domains immediately beneath it. For example, at the time of this writing, the com domain had more than 1.7 million second-level domains beneath it.

Fully qualified domain names

If a domain name ends with a trailing dot, that trailing dot represents the root domain, and the domain name is said to be a *fully qualified domain name* (also known as an *FQDN*). A fully qualified domain name is also called an *absolute name*. A fully qualified domain name is unambiguous because it identifies itself all the way back to the root domain. In contrast, if a domain name doesn't end with a trailing dot, the name may be interpreted in the context of some other domain. Thus, DNS names that don't end with a trailing dot are called *relative names*.

This is similar to the way relative and absolute paths work in Windows. For example, if a path begins with a backslash, such as \Windows\System32\dns, the path is absolute. However, a path that doesn't begin with a backslash, such as System32\dns, uses the current directory as its starting point. If the current directory happens to be \Windows, then \Windows\System32\dns and System32\dns refer to the same location.

In many cases, relative and fully qualified domain names are interchangeable because the software that interprets them always interprets relative names in the context of the root domain. That's why, for example, you can type www.wiley.com — without the trailing dot — rather than www.wiley.com. to go to Wiley's home page in a Web browser. Some applications, such as DNS servers, may interpret relative names in the context of a domain other than the root.

Top-Level Domains

A *top-level domain* is a domain that appears immediately beneath the root domain. Top-level domains come in two categories: generic domains and geographic domains. These categories are described in the following sections. (Actually, a third type of top-level domain exists; it's used for reverse lookups. I describe it later in this chapter, in the section "Reverse Lookup Zones.")

Generic domains

Generic domains are the popular top-level domains that you see most often on the Internet. Originally, seven top-level organizational domains existed. In 2002, seven more were added to help ease the congestion of the original seven — in particular, the com domain.

Table 4-1 summarizes the original seven generic top-level domains. Of these, you can see that the `com` domain is far and away the most populated, with more than 1.7 million second-level domains beneath it.

The Size column in this table indicates approximately how many second-level domains existed under each top-level domain as of June 2003, according to the Internet Software Consortium's survey, found at `www.isc.org`.

Table 4-1	The Original Seven Top-Level Domains	
Domain	*Description*	*Size*
com	Commercial organizations	1,716,051
edu	Educational institutions	3,994
gov	U.S. government institutions	566
int	International treaty organizations	60
mil	U.S. military institutions	93
net	Network providers	181,746
org	Noncommercial organizations	176,736

Because the `com` domain ballooned to an almost unmanageable size in the late 1990s, the Internet authorities approved seven new top-level domains in an effort to take some of the heat off of the `com` domain. Most of these domains, listed in Table 4-2, became available in 2002. As you can see, they haven't really caught on yet. They're still pretty new, so they still may take off after they've been around for awhile.

Table 4-2	The New Seven Top-Level Domains	
Domain	*Description*	*Size*
aero	Aerospace industry	60
biz	Business	6,506
coop	Cooperatives	100
info	Informational sites	6,134
museum	Museums	7
name	Individual users	144
pro	Professional organizations	2

Geographic domains

Although the top-level domains are open to anyone, U.S. companies and organizations dominate them. An additional set of top-level domains corresponds to international country designations. Organizations outside of the United States often use these top-level domains to avoid the congestion of the generic domains.

Table 4-3 lists those geographic top-level domains that had more than 200 registered subdomains at the time of this writing. In all, about 150 geographic top-level domains exist. The exact number varies from time to time as political circumstances change.

Table 4-3	**Geographic Top-Level Domains with More Than 200 Subdomains**		
Domain	*Description*	*Domain*	*Description*
ac	Ascension Island	ie	Ireland
am	Armenia	is	Iceland
as	American Samoa	it	Italy
at	Austria	jp	Japan
be	Belgium	kz	Kazakhstan
bg	Bulgaria	li	Liechtenstein
bm	Bermuda	lt	Lithuania
br	Brazil	lu	Luxembourg
bz	Belize	lv	Latvia
ca	Canada	md	Moldova, Republic Of
cc	Cocos (Keeling) Islands	nl	Netherlands
ch	Switzerland	no	Norway
cl	Chile	nu	Niue
cx	Christmas Island	pl	Poland
cz	Czech Republic	pt	Portugal
de	Germany	ro	Romania
dk	Denmark	ru	Russian Federation
ee	Estonia	se	Sweden
es	Spain	si	Slovenia
fi	Finland	sk	Slovakia (Slovak Republic)

Domain	Description	Domain	Description
fm	Micronesia, Federated States Of	st	Sao Tome And Principe
fo	Faroe Islands	to	Tonga
fr	France	tv	Tuvalu
gr	Greece	us	United States
hr	Croatia (local name: Hrvatska)	ws	Samoa
hu	Hungary		

The Hosts File

Long ago, in a network far away, the entire Internet was small enough that network administrators could keep track of it all in a simple text file. This file, called the *Hosts file,* simply listed the name and IP address of every host on the network. Each computer had its own copy of the Hosts file. The trick was keeping all those Hosts files up-to-date. Whenever a new host was added to the Internet, each network administrator would manually update his or her copy of the Hosts file to add the new host's name and IP address.

As the Internet grew, so did the Hosts file. In the mid-1980s, it became obvious that a better solution was needed. Imagine trying to track the entire Internet today using a single text file to record the name and IP address of the millions of hosts on the Internet! DNS was invented to solve this problem.

Understanding the Hosts file is important for two reasons:

✦ The Hosts file is not dead. For small networks, a Hosts file may still be the easiest way to provide name resolution for the network's computers. In addition, a Hosts file can coexist with DNS. The Hosts file is always checked before DNS is used, so you can even use a Hosts file to override DNS if you want.

✦ The Hosts file is the precursor to DNS. DNS was devised to circumvent the limitations of the Hosts file. You'll be in a better position to appreciate the benefits of DNS when you understand how the Hosts file works.

The Hosts file is a simple text file that contains lines that match IP addresses with host names. You can edit the Hosts file with any text editor, including Notepad or the MS-DOS EDIT command. The exact location of the Hosts file depends on the client operating system, as listed in Table 4-4.

Table 4-4	Location of the Hosts File
Operating System	*Location of Hosts file*
Windows 9*x*	c:\windows\hosts
Windows NT/2000	c:\winnt\system32\drivers\etc\hosts
Windows XP	c:\windows\system32\drivers\etc\hosts
Unix/Linux	/etc/hosts

All TCP/IP implementations are installed with a starter Hosts file. For example, Listing 4-1 shows a sample Windows TCP/IP Hosts file. As you can see, the starter file begins with some comments that explain the purpose of the file. It also includes a host mapping for the host name `localhost`, mapped to the IP address 127.0.0.1. The IP address 127.0.0.1 is the standard loopback address. As a result, this entry allows a computer to refer to itself by using the name `localhost`.

Listing 4-1   A Sample Hosts File

```
# Copyright (c) 1993-1999 Microsoft Corp.
#
# This is a sample HOSTS file used by Microsoft TCP/IP for Windows.
#
# This file contains the mappings of IP addresses to host names. Each
# entry should be kept on an individual line. The IP address should
# be placed in the first column followed by the corresponding host name.
# The IP address and the host name should be separated by at least one
# space.
#
# Additionally, comments (such as these) may be inserted on individual
# lines or following the machine name denoted by a '#' symbol.
#
# For example:
#
#      102.54.94.97     rhino.acme.com          # source server
#       38.25.63.10     x.acme.com              # x client host
#
127.0.0.1       localhost
```

To add an entry to the Hosts file, simply edit the file using any text editor. Then, add a line at the bottom of the file, after the localhost entry. Each line that you add should list the IP address and the host name that you want to use for the address. For example, to associate the host name `server1.LoweWriter.com` with the IP address 192.168.168.201, you add this line to the Hosts file:

```
192.168.168.201 server1.LoweWriter.com
```

Then, whenever an application requests the IP address of the host name
`server1`, the IP address 192.168.168.201 is returned.

You can also add an alias to a host mapping. This enables users to access a
host by using the alias as an alternate name. For example, consider the following line:

```
192.168.168.201 server1.LoweWriter.com s1
```

Here, the device at address 192.168.168.201 can be accessed as
`server1.LoweWriter.com` or just `s1`.

Listing 4-2 shows a Hosts file with several hosts defined.

Listing 4-2   A Hosts File with Several Hosts Defined

```
# Copyright (c) 1993-1999 Microsoft Corp.
#
# This is a sample HOSTS file used by Microsoft TCP/IP for Windows.
#
# This file contains the mappings of IP addresses to host names. Each
# entry should be kept on an individual line. The IP address should
# be placed in the first column followed by the corresponding host name.
# The IP address and the host name should be separated by at least one
# space.
#
# Additionally, comments (such as these) may be inserted on individual
# lines or following the machine name denoted by a '#' symbol.
#
# For example:
#
#      102.54.94.97      rhino.acme.com        # source server
#       38.25.63.10      x.acme.com            # x client host
#
127.0.0.1         localhost
#
192.168.168.200 doug.LoweWriter.com           #Doug's computer
192.168.168.201 server1.LoweWriter.com s1     #Main server
192.168.168.202 debbie.LoweWriter.com         #Debbie's computer
192.168.168.203 printer1.LoweWriter.com p1    #HP Laser Printer
```

Even if your network uses DNS, every client still has a Hosts file that defines
at least localhost.

Understanding DNS Servers and Zones

A *DNS server* is a computer that runs DNS server software, helps to maintain the DNS database, and responds to DNS name resolution requests from other computers. Although many DNS server implementations are available, the two most popular are Bind and the Windows DNS service. Bind runs on UNIX-based computers (including Linux computers), while Windows DNS (naturally) runs on Windows computers. Both provide essentially the same services and can interoperate with each other.

The key to understanding how DNS servers work is to realize that the DNS database — that is, the list of all the domains, subdomains, and host mappings — is a massively distributed database. No single DNS server contains the entire DNS database. Instead, authority over different parts of the database is delegated to different servers throughout the Internet.

For example, suppose that I set up a DNS server to handle name resolutions for my `LoweWriter.com` domain. Then, when someone requests the IP address of `doug.LoweWriter.com`, my DNS server can provide the answer. However, my DNS server wouldn't be responsible for the rest of the Internet. Instead, if someone asks my DNS server for the IP address of some other computer, such as `coyote.acme.com`, my DNS server will have to pass the request on to another DNS server that knows the answer.

Zones

To simplify the management of the DNS database, the entire DNS namespace is divided into *zones,* and the responsibility for each zone is delegated to a particular DNS server. In many cases, zones correspond directly to domains. For example, if I set up a domain named `LoweWriter.com`, I can also set up a DNS zone called `LoweWriter.com` that will be responsible for the entire `LoweWriter.com` domain.

However, the subdomains that make up a domain can be parceled out to separate zones, as shown in Figure 4-2. Here, a domain named `LoweWriter.com` has been divided into two zones. One zone, `us.LoweWriter.com`, is responsible for the entire `us.LoweWriter.com`. subdomain. The other zone, `LoweWriter.com`, is responsible for the entire `LoweWriter.com` domain except the `us.LoweWriter.com` subdomain.

Why would you do that? The main reason is to delegate authority for the zone to separate servers. For example, Figure 4-2 suggests that part of the `LoweWriter.com` domain is administered in the United States, and part of it is administered in France. The two zones in the figure allow one server to be completely responsible for the U.S. portion of the domain, while the other server handles the rest of the domain.

The old phony Hosts file trick

The Hosts file can be the basis of a fun practical joke. Of course, neither I nor my editors or publishers recommend that you actually do this. So if it gets you into trouble, don't send your lawyers to me. This sidebar is here only to let you know what to do if it happens to you.

The idea is to edit your poor victim's Hosts file so that whenever the user tries to access his or her favorite Web site, a site of your choosing comes up instead. For example, if you're trying to get your husband to take you on a cruise, add a line to his Hosts file that replaces his favorite Web site with the Web site for a cruise line. For example, this line should do the trick:

151.124.250.181 www.espn.com

Now, whenever your husband tries to call up the ESPN Web site, he'll get the Carnival Cruise Lines home page instead.

Of course, to actually pull a stunt like this would be completely irresponsible. Especially if you didn't first make a backup copy of the Hosts file, just in case it somehow gets messed up.

But be warned: If the wrong Web sites suddenly start coming up, check your Hosts file to see whether it's been tampered with.

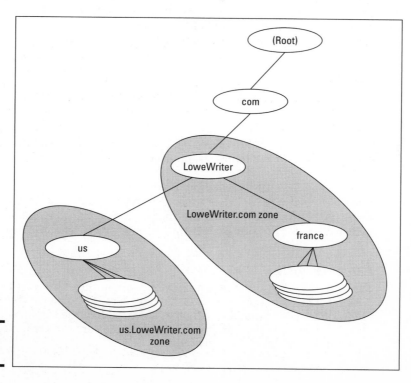

Figure 4-2:
DNS zones.

The following are the two basic types of zones:

✦ A *primary zone* is the master copy of a zone. The data for a primary zone is stored in the local database of the DNS server that hosts the primary zone. Only one DNS server can host a particular primary zone. Any updates to the zone must be made to the primary zone.

✦ A *secondary zone* is a read-only copy of a zone. When a server hosts a secondary zone, the server doesn't store a local copy of the zone data. Instead, it obtains its copy of the zone from the zone's primary server by using a process called *zone transfer.* Secondary servers must periodically check primary servers to see whether their secondary zone data is still current. If not, a zone transfer is initiated to update the secondary zone.

Primary and secondary servers

Each DNS server is responsible for one or more zones. The following are several different roles that a DNS server can take.

✦ Primary server for a zone, which means that the DNS server hosts a primary zone. The data for the zone is stored in files on the DNS server. Every zone must have one primary server.

✦ Secondary server for a zone, which means that the DNS server obtains the data for a secondary zone from a primary server. Every zone should have at least one secondary server. That way, if the primary server goes down, the domain defined by the zone can be accessed via the secondary server or servers.

A secondary server should be on a different subnet than the zone's primary server. If the primary and secondary servers are on the same subnet, both servers will be unavailable if the router that controls the subnet goes down.

Note that a single DNS server can be the primary server for some zones and a secondary server for other zones. A server is said to be *authoritative* for the primary and secondary zones that it hosts because it can provide definitive answers for queries against those zones.

Root servers

The core of DNS is the *root servers,* which are authoritative for the entire Internet. The main function of the root servers is to provide the address of the DNS servers that are responsible for each of the top-level domains. These servers, in turn, can provide the DNS server address for subdomains beneath the top-level domains.

The root servers are a major part of the glue that holds the Internet together. As you can imagine, they're swamped with requests day and night. A total of 13 root servers are located throughout the world. Table 4-5 lists the IP address and location of each of the 13 root servers.

Table 4-5		The 13 Root Servers	
Server	*IP Address*	*Operator*	*Location*
A	198.41.0.4	VeriSign Global Registry Services	Dulles, VA
B	128.9.0.107	Information Sciences Institute	Marina Del Rey, CA
C	192.33.4.12	Cogent Communications	Herndon, VA & Los Angeles
D	128.8.10.90	University of Maryland	College Park, MD
E	192.203.230.10	NASA Ames Research Center	Mountain View, CA
F	192.5.5.241	Internet Software Consortium	Palo Alto, CA; San Jose, CA; New York City; San Francisco; Madrid; Hong Kong; Los Angeles
G	192.112.36.4	U.S. DOD Network Information Center	Vienna, VA
H	128.63.2.53	U.S. Army Research Lab	Aberdeen, MD
I	192.36.148.17	Autonomica	Stockholm
J	192.58.128.30	VeriSign Global Registry Services	Dulles, VA; Mountain View CA; Sterling, VA (2 locations); Seattle, WA; Amsterdam, NL; Atlanta, GA; Los Angeles
K	193.0.14.129	Reseaux IP Europeens Network Coordination Centre	London
L	198.32.64.12	IANA	Los Angeles
M	202.12.27.33	WIDE Project	Tokyo

DNS servers learn how to reach the root servers by consulting a *root hints* file that's located on the server. In the UNIX/Linux world, this file is known as `named.root` and can be found at `/etc/named.root`. For Windows DNS servers, the file is called `cache.dns` and can be found in `\windows\system32\dns\` or `\winnt\system32\dns\`, depending on the Windows version. Listing 4-3 shows the file itself.

Listing 4-3   The Named.Root File

```
;       This file holds the information on root name servers needed to
;       initialize cache of Internet domain name servers
;       (e.g. reference this file in the "cache  .  <file>"
;       configuration file of BIND domain name servers).
;
;       This file is made available by InterNIC registration services
;       under anonymous FTP as
;           file                /domain/named.root
;           on server           FTP.RS.INTERNIC.NET
;       -OR- under Gopher at    RS.INTERNIC.NET
;           under menu          InterNIC Registration Services (NSI)
;             submenu           InterNIC Registration Archives
;           file                named.root
;
;       last update:    Aug 22, 1997
;       related version of root zone:   1997082200
;
;
; formerly NS.INTERNIC.NET
;
.                           3600000   IN  NS    A.ROOT-SERVERS.NET.
A.ROOT-SERVERS.NET.         3600000       A     198.41.0.4
; formerly NS1.ISI.EDU
;
.                           3600000       NS    B.ROOT-SERVERS.NET.
B.ROOT-SERVERS.NET.         3600000       A     128.9.0.107
; formerly C.PSI.NET
;
.                           3600000       NS    C.ROOT-SERVERS.NET.
C.ROOT-SERVERS.NET.         3600000       A     192.33.4.12
; formerly TERP.UMD.EDU
;
.                           3600000       NS    D.ROOT-SERVERS.NET.
D.ROOT-SERVERS.NET.         3600000       A     128.8.10.90
; formerly NS.NASA.GOV
;
.                           3600000       NS    E.ROOT-SERVERS.NET.
E.ROOT-SERVERS.NET.         3600000       A     192.203.230.10
; formerly NS.ISC.ORG
;
.                           3600000       NS    F.ROOT-SERVERS.NET.
F.ROOT-SERVERS.NET.         3600000       A     192.5.5.241
; formerly NS.NIC.DDN.MIL
;
.                           3600000       NS    G.ROOT-SERVERS.NET.
G.ROOT-SERVERS.NET.         3600000       A     192.112.36.4
; formerly AOS.ARL.ARMY.MIL
```

```
;
.                       3600000     NS      H.ROOT-SERVERS.NET.
H.ROOT-SERVERS.NET.     3600000     A       128.63.2.53
;
; formerly NIC.NORDU.NET
;
.                       3600000     NS      I.ROOT-SERVERS.NET.
I.ROOT-SERVERS.NET.     3600000     A       192.36.148.17
;
; temporarily housed at NSI (InterNIC)
;
.                       3600000     NS      J.ROOT-SERVERS.NET.
J.ROOT-SERVERS.NET.     3600000     A       198.41.0.10
;
; housed in LINX, operated by RIPE NCC
;
.                       3600000     NS      K.ROOT-SERVERS.NET.
K.ROOT-SERVERS.NET.     3600000     A       193.0.14.129
;
; temporarily housed at ISI (IANA)
;
.                       3600000     NS      L.ROOT-SERVERS.NET.
L.ROOT-SERVERS.NET.     3600000     A       198.32.64.12
;
; housed in Japan, operated by WIDE
;
.                       3600000     NS      M.ROOT-SERVERS.NET.
M.ROOT-SERVERS.NET.     3600000     A       202.12.27.33
; End of File
```

Caching

DNS servers don't really like doing all that work to resolve DNS names. But they're not stupid. They know that if a user visits www.wiley.com today, he'll probably do it again tomorrow. As a result, name servers keep a cache of query results. The next time the user visits www.wiley.com, the name server is able to resolve this name without having to query all those other name servers.

The Internet is constantly changing, however, so cached data can quickly become obsolete. For example, suppose that Wiley Publishing, Inc., switches its Web site to a different server? It can update its name servers to reflect the new IP address, but any name servers that have a cached copy of the query will be out-of-date.

To prevent this from being a major problem, DNS data is given a relatively short expiration time. The expiration value for DNS data is called the *TTL*, which stands for *time to live*. TTL is specified in seconds. To help you decipher them, Table 4-6 lists some of the most common TTL values.

Table 4-6	Common TTL values
TTL Value	*Duration*
60	1 minute
600	10 minutes
3600	1 hour
36000	10 hours
86400	24 hours
172800	48 hours
604800	7 days
3600000	1,000 hours (41+ days)

Understanding DNS Queries

When a DNS client needs to resolve a DNS name to an IP address, it uses a library routine called a *resolver* to handle the query. The resolver takes care of sending the query message over the network to the DNS server, receiving and interpreting the response, and informing the client of the results of the query.

A DNS client can make two basic types of queries: recursive and iterative. The following paragraphs describe the difference between these two query types. (The following discussion assumes that the client is asking the server for the IP address of a host name, which is the most common type of DNS query. You find out about other types of queries later; they, too, can be either recursive or iterative.)

✦ **Recursive queries:** When a client issues a *recursive DNS query,* the server must reply with either the IP address of the requested host name or an error message indicating that the host name doesn't exist. If the server doesn't have the information, it asks another DNS server for the IP address. When the first server finally gets the IP address, it sends it back to the client. If the server determines that the information doesn't exist, it returns an error message.

✦ **Iterative queries:** When a server receives an iterative query, it returns the IP address of the requested host name if it knows the address. If the server doesn't know the address, it returns a *referral,* which is simply the address of a DNS server that should know. The client can then issue an iterative query to the server to which it was referred.

Normally, DNS clients issue recursive queries to DNS servers. If the server knows the answer to the query, it replies directly to the client. If not, the server issues an iterative query to a DNS server that it thinks should know the answer. If the original server gets an answer from the second server, it returns the answer to the client. If the original server gets a referral to a third server, the original server issues an iterative query to the third server. The original server keeps issuing iterative queries until it either gets the answer or an error occurs. It then returns the answer or the error to the client.

A real-life example

Confused? I can understand why. An example may help to clear things up. Suppose that a user wants to view the Web page www.wiley.com. The following sequence of steps occurs to resolve this address:

1. The browser asks the client computer's resolver to find the IP address of www.wiley.com.

2. The resolver issues a recursive DNS query to its name server. In this case, I'll call the name server ns1.LoweWriter.com.

3. The name server ns1LoweWriter.com checks to see whether it knows the IP address of www.wiley.com. It doesn't, so the name server issues an iterative query to one of the root name servers to see whether it knows the IP address of www.wiley.com.

4. The root name server doesn't know the IP address of www.wiley.com, so it returns a list of the name servers that are authoritative for the com domain.

5. The ns1.LoweWriter.com name server picks one of the com domain name servers and sends it an iterative query for www.wiley.com.

6. The com name server doesn't know the IP address of www.wiley.com, so it returns a list of the name servers that are authoritative for the wiley.com domain.

7. The ns1.LoweWriter.com name server picks one of the name servers for the wiley.com domain and sends it an iterative query for www.wiley.com.

8. The wiley.com name server knows the IP address for www.wiley.com, so the name server returns it.

9. The ns1.LoweWriter.com name server shouts with joy for having finally found the IP address for www.wiley.com. It gleefully returns this address to the client. It also caches the answer so that the next time the user looks for www.wiley.com, the name server won't have to contact other name servers to resolve the name.

10. The client also caches the results of the query. Then, the next time the client needs to look for www.wiley.com, the client can resolve the name without troubling the name server.

Zone Files and Resource Records

Each DNS zone is defined by a *zone file* (also known as a *DNS database* or a *master file*). For Windows DNS servers, the name of the zone file is *domain*.zone. For example, the zone file for the LoweWriter.com zone is named LoweWriter.com.zone. For BIND DNS servers, the zone files are named db.*domain*. Thus, the zone file for the LoweWriter.com domain would be db.LoweWriter.com. The format of the zone file contents is the same for both systems, however.

A zone file consists of one or more *resource records*. Creating and updating the resource records that compose the zone files is one of the primary tasks of a DNS administrator. The Windows DNS server provides a friendly graphical interface to the resource records. However, you should still be familiar with the details of how to construct resource records.

Resource records are written as simple text lines, with the following fields:

```
Owner    TTL    Class    Type    RDATA
```

These fields must be separated from each other by one or more spaces. The following paragraphs describes the five resource record fields:

✦ **Owner:** The name of the DNS domain or the host that the record applies to. This is usually specified as a fully qualified domain name (with a trailing dot) or as a simple host name (without a trailing dot), which is then interpreted in the context of the current domain.

You can also specify a single @ symbol as the owner name. In that case, the current domain is used.

✦ **TTL:** Also known as *time to live;* the number of seconds that the record should be retained in a server's cache before it's invalidated. If you omit the TTL value for a resource record, a default TTL is obtained from the SOA record. (For your reference, Table 4-6 lists commonly used TTL values.)

✦ **Class:** Defines the protocol to which the record applies. You should always specify IN, for the Internet protocol. If you omit the class field, the last class field that you specified explicitly is used. As a result, you'll sometimes see zone files that specify IN only on the first resource record (which must be an SOA record) and then allow it to default to IN on all subsequent records.

✦ **Type:** The resource record type. The most commonly used resource types are summarized in Table 4-7 and are described separately later in this section. Like the Class field, you can also omit the Type field and allow it to default to the last specified value.

✦ **RDATA:** Resource record data that is specific to each record type.

Table 4-7	Common Resource Record Types	
Type	*Name*	*Description*
SOA	Start Of Authority	Identifies a zone.
NS	Name Server	Identifies a name server that is authoritative for the zone.
A	Address	Maps a fully qualified domain name to an IP address.
CNAME	Canonical Name	Creates an alias for a fully qualified domain name.
MX	Mail Exchange	Identifies the mail server for a domain.
PTR	Pointer	Maps an IP address to a fully qualified domain name for reverse lookups.

Most resource records fit on one line. If a record requires more than one line, you must enclose the data that spans multiple lines in parentheses.

You can include comments to clarify the details of a zone file. A comment begins with a semicolon and continues to the end of the line. If a line begins with a semicolon, the entire line is a comment. You can also add a comment to the end of a resource record. You see examples of both types of comments later in this chapter.

SOA records

Every zone must begin with a *start of authority* (SOA) record, which names the zone and provides default information for the zone. Table 4-8 lists the fields that appear in the RDATA section of an SOA record. Note that these fields are positional, so you should include a value for all of them and list them in the order specified. Because the SOA record has so many RDATA fields, you'll probably need to use parentheses to continue the SOA record onto multiple lines.

Table 4-8	RDATA Fields for an SOA Record
Name	*Description*
MNAME	The domain name of the name server that is authoritative for the zone.
RNAME	A e-mail address (specified in domain name format; not regular e-mail format) of the person responsible for this zone.
SERIAL	The serial number of the zone. Secondary zones use this value to determine whether they need to initiate a zone transfer to update their copy of the zone.
REFRESH	A time interval that specifies how often a secondary server should check to see whether the zone needs to be refreshed. A typical value is 3600 (one hour).
RETRY	A time interval that specifies how long a secondary server should wait after requesting a zone transfer before trying again. A typical value is 600 (ten minutes).
EXPIRE	A time interval that specifies how long a secondary server should keep the zone data before discarding it. A typical value is 86400 (one day).
MINIMUM	A time interval that specifies the TTL value to use for zone resource records that omit the TTL field. A typical value is 3600 (one hour).

Note two things about the SOA fields:

✦ The e-mail address of the person responsible for the zone is given in DNS format; not in normal e-mail format. Thus, you separate the user from the mail domain with a dot rather than an @ symbol. For example, doug@LoweWriter.com would be listed as doug.lowewriter.com.

✦ The serial number should be incremented every time you change the zone file. If you edit the file using the graphic interface provided by Windows DNS, the serial number is incremented automatically. However, if you edit the zone file using a simple text editor, you have to manually increment the serial number.

Here's a typical example of an SOA record, with judicious comments to identify each field:

```
lowewriter.com. IN  SOA (
    ns1.lowewriter.com                        ; authoritative name
    server
    doug.lowewriter.com                       ; responsible person
    148                                       ; version number
    3600                                      ; refresh (1 hour)
```

```
600                            ; retry (10 minutes)
86400                          ; expire (1 day)
3600 )                         ; minimum TTL (1 hour)
```

NS records

Name server (NS) records identify the name servers that are authoritative for the zone. Every zone must have at least one NS record and should have at least two so that if the first name server is unavailable, the zone will still be accessible.

The owner field should either be the fully qualified domain name for the zone, with a trailing dot, or an @ symbol. The RDATA consists of just one field: the fully qualified domain name of the name server.

The following examples show two NS records that serve the lowewriter.com domain:

```
lowewriter.com.   IN  NS   ns1.lowewriter.com.
lowewriter.com.   IN  NS   ns2.lowewriter.com.
```

A records

Address (A) records are the meat of the zone file: They provide the IP addresses for each of the hosts that you want to make accessible via DNS. In an A record, you usually list just the host name in the owner field, thus allowing DNS to add the domain name to derive the fully qualified domain name for the host. The RDATA field for the A record is the IP address of the host.

The following lines define various hosts for the LoweWriter.com domain:

```
doug        IN  A   192.168.168.200
server1     IN  A   192.168.168.201
debbie      IN  A   192.168.168.202
printer1    IN  A   192.168.168.203
router1     IN  A   207.126.127.129
www         IN  A   64.71.129.102
```

Notice that for these lines, I didn't specify the fully qualified domain names for each host. Instead, I just provided the host name. DNS will add the name of the zone's domain to these host names in order to create the fully qualified domain names.

If I wanted to be more explicit, I could have listed these A records like this:

```
doug.lowewriter.com.       IN  A  192.168.168.200
server1.lowewriter.com.    IN  A  192.168.168.201
debbie.lowewriter.com.     IN  A  192.168.168.202
printer1.lowewriter.com.   IN  A  192.168.168.203
router1.lowewriter.com     IN  A  207.126.127.129
www.lowewriter.com.        IN  A  64.71.129.102
```

However, all this does is increase the chance for error. Plus, it creates more work for yourself later if you decide to change your network's domain.

CNAME records

A *canonical name* (CNAME) record creates an alias for a fully qualified domain name. When a user attempts to access a domain name that is actually an alias, the DNS system substitutes the real domain name — known as the *canonical name* — for the alias. The owner field in the CNAME record provides the name of the alias that you want to create. Then, the RDATA field provides the canonical name — that is, the real name of the host.

For example, consider these resource records:

```
ftp.lowewriter.com.    IN  A      207.126.127.132
files.lowewriter.com.  IN  CNAME  www1.lowewriter.com.
```

Here, the host name of an FTP server at 207.126.127.132 is `ftp.lowewriter.com`. The CNAME record allows users to access this host as `files.lowewriter.com` if they prefer.

PTR records

A *pointer* (PTR) record is the opposite of an address record: It provides the fully qualified domain name for a given address. The owner field should specify the reverse lookup domain name and the RDATA field specifies the fully qualified domain name. For example, the following record maps the address 64.71.129.102 to `www.lowewriter.com`:

```
102.129.71.64.in-addr.arpa.  IN  PTR  www.lowewriter.com.
```

PTR records don't usually appear in normal domain zones. Instead, they appear in special reverse lookup zones. For more information, see the section "Reverse Lookup Zones," later in this chapter.

MX records

Mail exchange (MX) records identify the mail server for a domain. The owner field provides the domain name that users address mail to. The

RDATA section of the record has two fields. The first is a priority number used to determine which mail servers to use when several are available. The second is the fully qualified domain name of the mail server itself.

For example, consider the following MX records:

```
lowewriter.com.    IN  MX  0   mail1.lowewriter.com.
lowewriter.com.    IN  MX  10  mail2.lowewriter.com.
```

In this example, the lowewriter.com domain has two mail servers, named mail1.lowewriter.com and mail2.lowewriter.com. The priority numbers for these servers are 0 and 10. Because it has a lower priority number, mail will be delivered to mail1.lowewriter.com first. The mail2.lowewriter.com server will be used only if mail1.lowewriter.com isn't available.

The server name specified in the RDATA section should be an actual host name, not an alias created by a CNAME record. Although some mail servers can handle MX records that point to CNAMEs, not all of them can. As a result, you shouldn't specify an alias in an MX record.

You should also be sure to create a reverse lookup record (PTR, described in the next section) for your mail servers. Some mail servers won't accept mail from a server that doesn't have valid reverse lookup entries.

Reverse Lookup Zones

Normal DNS queries ask a name server to provide the IP address that corresponds to a fully qualified domain name. This kind of query is called a *forward lookup*. A *reverse lookup* is the opposite of a forward lookup: It returns the fully qualified domain name of a host based on its IP.

Reverse lookups are possible because of a special domain called the *in-addr.arpa* domain. The in-addr.arpa domain provides a separate fully qualified domain name for every possible IP address on the Internet. To enable a reverse lookup for a particular IP address, all you have to do is create a PTR record in a reverse lookup zone (a zone that is authoritative for a portion of the in-addr.arpa domain). The PTR record maps the in-addr.arpa domain name for the address to the host's actual domain name.

The technique used to create the reverse domain name for a given IP address is pretty clever. It creates subdomains beneath the in-addr.arpa domain by using the octets of the IP address, listing them in reverse order. For example, the reverse domain name for the IP address 207.126.67.129 is 129.67.126.207.in-addr.arpa.

Why list the octets in reverse order? Because that correlates the network portions of the IP address, which work from left to right, with the subdomain structure of DNS names, which works from right to left. The following description should clear this up:

✦ The 255 possible values for the first octet of an IP address each have a subdomain beneath the `in-addr.arpa` domain. For example, any IP address that begins with 207 can be found in the `207.in-addr.arpa` domain.

✦ Within this domain, each of the possible values for the second octet can be found as a subdomain of the first octet's domain. Thus, any address that begins with 207.126 can be found in the `126.207.in-addr.arpa` domain.

✦ The same holds true for the third octet, so any address that begins with 207.126.67 can be found in the `67.126.207.in-addr.arpa` domain.

✦ By the time you get to the fourth octet, you've pinpointed a specific host. So the fourth octet completes the fully qualified reverse domain name. Thus, 207.126.67.129 is mapped to `129.67.126.207.in-addr.arpa`.

As a result, to determine the fully qualified domain name for the computer at 207.126.67.129, the client queries its DNS server for the FQDN that corresponds to `129.67.126.207.in-addr.arpa`.

Working with the Windows DNS Server

The procedure for installing and managing a DNS server depends on the network operating system that you're using. The following sections are specified to working with a DNS server in Windows 2003. Working with BIND in a Linux/UNIX environment is similar, but without the help of a graphical user interface.

You can install the DNS server on Windows Server 2003 from the Manage Your Server application. (Choose Start➪Administrative Tools➪Manage Your Server.) Click the Add Or Remove A Role link, select DNS Server from the list of server roles, and then click Next to install the DNS server. The Configure A DNS Server Wizard appears, as shown in Figure 4-3. This wizard guides you through the process of configuring the first zone for your DNS server.

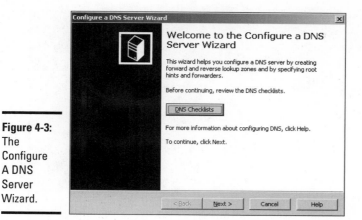

Figure 4-3:
The
Configure
A DNS
Server
Wizard.

After you've set up a DNS server, you can manage the DNS server from the DNS management console, shown in Figure 4-4. Here, you can perform common administrative tasks such as adding additional zones, changing zone settings, adding A or MX records to an existing zone, and so on. The DNS management console hides the details of the actual resource records from you, thus allowing you to work with a friendly graphical user interface instead.

To add a new host (that is, an A record) to a zone, right-click the zone in the DNS management console and choose the Add New Host command. This brings up the New Host dialog box, as shown in Figure 4-5. This dialog box lets you specify the following information:

✦ **Name:** The host name for the new host.

✦ **IP Address:** The host's IP address.

✦ **Create associated pointer (PTR) record:** Automatically creates a PTR record in the reverse lookup zone file. Select this option if you want to allow reverse lookups for the host.

✦ **Allow any authenticated user to update:** Select this option if you want to allow other users to update this record or other records with the same host name. You should usually leave this option unchecked.

✦ **Time to live:** The TTL value for this record.

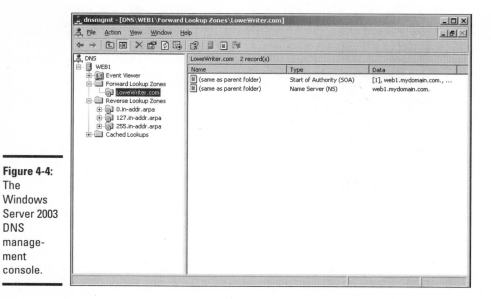

Figure 4-4:
The Windows Server 2003 DNS management console.

You can add other records, such as MX or CNAME records, in the same way.

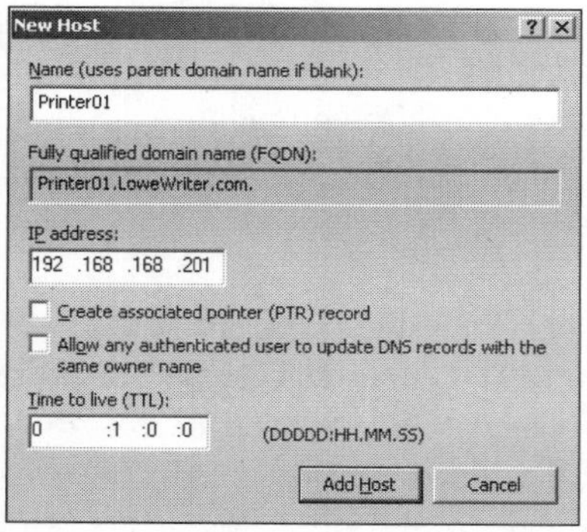

Figure 4-5:
The New Host dialog box.

How to Configure a Windows DNS Client

Client computers don't need much configuration in order to work properly with DNS. The client must have the address of at least one DNS server. Usually, this address is supplied by DHCP, so if the client is configured to obtain its IP address from a DHCP server, it will also obtain the DNS server address from DHCP.

To configure a client computer to obtain the DNS server location from DHCP bring up the Network Properties dialog box by choosing Network or Network Connections in Control Panel (depending on which version of Windows the client is running). Then, select the TCP/IP protocol and click the Properties button. This summons the TCP/IP Properties dialog box, as shown in Figure 4-6. To configure the computer to use DHCP, check Obtain An IP Address Automatically and Obtain DNS Server Address Automatically.

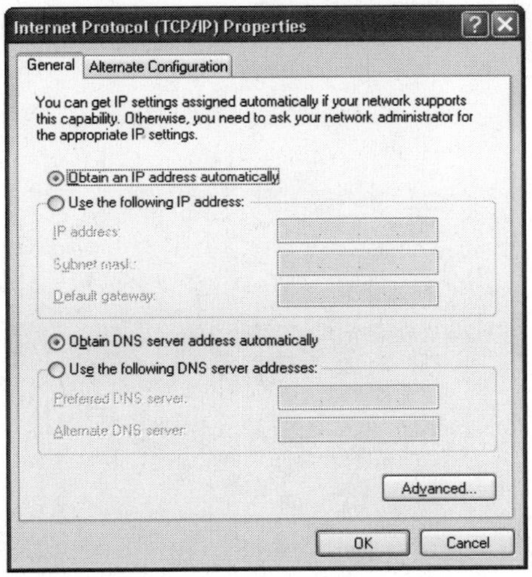

Figure 4-6:
Configuring a Windows client to obtain its DNS address from DHCP.

If the computer doesn't use DHCP, you can use this same dialog box to manually enter the IP address of your DNS server.

Chapter 5: Using FTP

In This Chapter

- Figuring out the basics of FTP
- Setting up an FTP server
- Retrieving files from an FTP server
- Using FTP commands

FTP is the basic method for exchanging files over the Internet. If you need to access files from someone's FTP site, this chapter shows you how to do so by using a Web browser or a command-line FTP client. If you need to set up your own FTP server to share files with other users, this chapter shows you how to do that, too.

Introducing FTP

FTP, which stands for *File Transfer Protocol,* is as old as the Internet itself. The first versions of FTP date back to the early 1970s, and even the current FTP standard (RFC 959) dates back to 1985. You can use FTP with the command-line FTP client, which has a decidedly 1980s feel to it, or you can access FTP sites with most modern Web browsers if you prefer a graphic interface. Old computer hounds prefer the FTP command-line client — probably for nostalgic reasons.

In spite of its age, FTP is still commonly used on the Internet. In Chapter 4 of this book, I mention that InterNIC maintains an FTP site at `ftp.rs.internic.net`, from which you can download important files such as `named.root`, which provides the current location of the Internet's root name servers. Many other companies maintain FTP sites from which you can download software, device drivers, documentation, reports, and so on. FTP is also one of the most common ways to publish HTML files to a Web server. Because FTP is still so widely used, it pays to know how to use it from both the command line and from a browser.

In the Windows world, an FTP server is integrated with Microsoft's Web server, Internet Information Services, or IIS. As a result, you can manage FTP from the IIS management console along with other IIS features. Note that the FTP component is an optional part of IIS, so you may need to install it separately if you opted to not include it when you first installed IIS.

On UNIX and Linux systems, FTP isn't usually integrated with a Web server. Instead, the FTP server is installed as a separate program. You're usually given the option to install FTP when you install the operating system. If you choose not to, you can always install it later.

When you run an FTP server, you expose a portion of your file system to the outside world. As a result, you need to be careful about how you set up your FTP server so that you don't accidentally allow hackers access to the bowels of your file server. Fortunately, the default configuration of FTP is pretty secure. You shouldn't tinker much with the default configuration unless you know what you're doing.

Configuring an FTP Server

In this section, I show you how to configure FTP services in Microsoft IIS. The examples show IIS version 6 running on Windows Server 2003, but the procedures are essentially the same for other IIS versions.

Installing FTP

Although FTP is integrated with IIS, FTP is not installed by default when you install IIS. As a result, if you didn't specifically select FTP when you installed IIS, you'll need to install FTP before you can set up an FTP site. You can install the FTP protocol by choosing Control Panel⇨Add Or Remove Programs⇨Add/Remove Windows Components. Then, select Application Server from the list of components, click Details, and choose Internet Information Services (IIS). Click Details again and then select File Transfer Protocol (FTP) from the list of IIS subcomponents. Finally, click OK to install FTP. If asked, you'll need to insert the Windows Server 2003 setup disk.

When you first install FTP, a default FTP site is created automatically. To manage the default site, open the Internet Information Services Manager by choosing Start⇨Administrative Programs⇨Internet Information Services. Then, select the default FTP site, as shown in Figure 5-1.

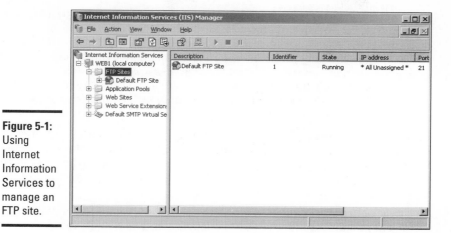

Figure 5-1:
Using
Internet
Information
Services to
manage an
FTP site.

Changing the FTP site properties

You can change the properties for an FTP site by right-clicking the site in the Internet Information Services Manager and choosing the Properties command. This brings up the FTP Site Properties dialog box, as shown in Figure 5-2.

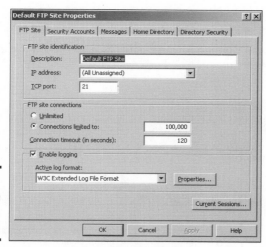

Figure 5-2:
The FTP Site
Properties
dialog box.

The FTP Site Properties dialog box contains the following tabs that let you configure the properties of your FTP site:

✦ **FTP Site:** The only item that you're likely to change on the main FTP Site tab is the name of the FTP site. You can also specify the IP address and port number for the site, but you'll usually leave these items set to their default values. You can also limit the number of connections allowed and disable logging.

✦ **Security Accounts:** The Security Accounts tab lets you specify whether you want to allow anonymous logons for the FTP site. If the site is open to the general public to download files, you'll want to enable anonymous logons. If you want to control access to the site, you should use this tab to disable anonymous logons.

The Security Accounts tab also lets you specify under which Windows account anonymous users will be logged on. The default value, IUSR_*computername,* is usually appropriate.

✦ **Messages:** This tab, shown in Figure 5-3, lets you create four customized messages that appear when users access the site:

  • The Banner message appears when a user first accesses the site, before he or she has logged on. If the site allows anonymous logons, you may mention that in the Banner message.

  • The Welcome message appears after the user has successfully logged on to your site.

  • The Exit message appears when the user leaves the site.

  • The Maximum Connections message appears when the connection limit has been exceeded.

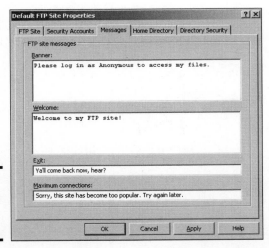

Figure 5-3:
Customizing
the site's
messages.

✦ **Home Directory:** This tab lets you specify the location of the site's home directory. This directory can be a folder on the server's hard drive, or it can be a shared folder on another server. To the user, this directory appears to be the FTP site's root directory. As a result, the user is able to access any child folders that appear beneath the home directory. However, the user won't be able to access any other directories on the server's hard drive.

✦ **Directory Security:** This tab lets you limit access to your FTP site based on the client computer's IP address. You can either deny access to all computers except the ones you specifically list or grant access to all computers except the ones you specifically list.

Adding content to your FTP site

When you set up an FTP site, Internet Information Services creates an empty home directory for the site. Then it's up to you to add to this directory whatever files you want to make available on the site. The easiest way to do that is to simply open a My Computer window and copy the files to the site's home directory. If you're not sure where the site's home directory is located, you can find it by right-clicking the site in the IIS Manager, choosing Properties, and then choosing the Home Directory tab.

The following paragraphs offer some useful tips for setting up FTP site content:

✦ Create a `readme.txt` file in the FTP site's home directory that describes the content and rules for your site. Hopefully, users will view this file when they visit your site. There's no guarantee that they will, but you can always hope.

✦ If your site has a lot of files, organize them into subdirectories beneath the home directory.

✦ Stick to short filenames. Users working with command-line clients appreciate brevity because they'll have to type the filenames accurately in order to retrieve your files.

✦ Don't use spaces in filenames. Some clients balk at names that include spaces.

Adding an additional FTP site

IIS can host more than an FTP site on the same computer. If you need to host multiple sites, you can add additional sites by using the FTP Site Creation Wizard. To start this wizard, right-click the FTP Sites folder in IIS Manager and choose New➪Ftp Site.

Accessing an FTP Site with a Browser

Modern Web browsers include built-in support for FTP. Internet Explorer lets you access an FTP site almost as if it were a local disk. You can even drag and drop files to and from an FTP site.

To access an FTP site in a Web browser, just type the name of the site in the address bar. If you want, you can explicitly specify the FTP protocol by typing **ftp://** before the FTP site name, but that's usually not necessary. The browser determines that the name you type is an FTP site and invokes the FTP protocol automatically.

Figure 5-4 shows you how a typical FTP site appears when accessed with Internet Explorer 6. As you can see, the files and folders appear as if they were on a local disk. You can double-click a folder to display the files contained in that folder, and you can download files by dragging them from the browser window to the desktop or to another window. You can also upload files by dragging them from the desktop or another window into the FTP browser window.

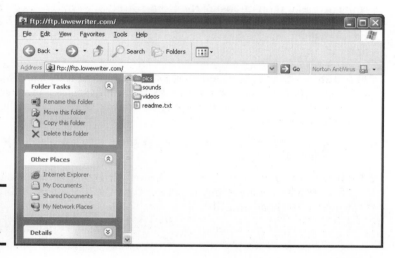

Figure 5-4: Browsing an FTP site.

If the contents of an FTP site don't appear in the browser window, you may need to log on to the site. Choose the File⇨Login As command to display the Log On As dialog box, shown in Figure 5-5. If the site administrator has given you a name and password, you can enter it here to access the site. Otherwise, check the Log On Anonymously check box and click Log On.

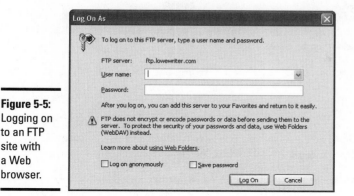

Figure 5-5:
Logging on
to an FTP
site with
a Web
browser.

Using an FTP Command-Line Client

If you're a command-line junkie, you'll appreciate the FTP command that comes with Windows. It isn't pretty, but it gets the job done. At the end of this chapter, you can find a command reference that details all the subcommands you can use with the FTP command. In this section, I just show you a typical session in which I sign on to an FTP server named ftp.lowewriter. com, switch to a directory named Pics, download a file, and then log off.

First, open a command window; to do so, choose Start➪Run, type **Command** in the text box, and click OK. Then, navigate to the directory to where you want to download files. This step is important because although you can change the local working directory from within the FTP command, it's much easier to just start FTP from the right directory.

To start FTP, type **ftp** with the name of the FTP server as the parameter, like this:

```
C:\>ftp ftp.lowewriter.com
```

Assuming that you typed the site name correctly, the FTP command connects to the site, displays the banner message, and prompts you to log on:

```
Connected to ftp.lowewriter.com.
220-Microsoft FTP Service
220 We have 999 spooks here, but there's always room for one
    more! To volunteer, log in as Anonymous.
User (ftp.lowewriter.com:(none)):
```

To log on anonymously, type **Anonymous** and press Enter. The server responds by telling you that Anonymous access is allowed and asks for your e-mail address as a password:

```
331 Anonymous access allowed, send identity (e-mail name) as
    password.
Password:
```

Type your e-mail address as the password, and then press Enter. The Welcome message appears, followed by the ftp> prompt:

```
230-Welcome to my FTP site! For spooky Halloween pictures,
    check out the Pics folder.
230 Anonymous user logged in.
ftp>
```

Whenever you see the ftp> prompt, the FTP command is waiting for you to enter a subcommand. Start by entering **dir** to see a directory listing.

```
200 PORT command successful.
150 Opening ASCII mode data connection for /bin/ls.
06-30-03  08:05PM       <DIR>          pics
06-30-03  07:55PM                 2365 readme.txt
06-30-03  07:55PM       <DIR>          sounds
06-30-03  07:56PM       <DIR>          videos
226 Transfer complete.
ftp: 190 bytes received in 0.00Seconds 190000.00Kbytes/sec.
ftp>
```

As you can see, the response from the dir command is not quite as clean as the display from an MS-DOS command. Still, you can pick out that the directory includes three subdirectories named pics, sounds, and videos, and a single file named readme.txt. The size of the file is 2,365 bytes.

Here's a good question: If you enter a dir command, why does the response say, "200 PORT command successful?" The answer has to do with the way the FTP protocol works. When you enter a dir command, the FTP client forwards a PORT command to the server that opens a data transfer port that is then used to return the resulting directory listing. The server replies that the PORT command has successfully opened a data transfer port. Then, it sends the directory listing back. Finally, it sends two more lines: one to indicate that the transfer is complete (that is, that the dir output has been successfully sent); the other to summarize the number of bytes of data that were sent and the data transfer rate.

The files that I want to download are located in the pics subdirectory, so the next command to issue is cd pics. This results in the following output:

```
250 CWD command successful.
ftp>
```

Once again, the command's output isn't exactly what you'd expect. The FTP protocol doesn't actually have a CD command. Instead, it uses a command named CWD, which stands for *change working directory,* to change the directory. The Windows FTP client uses command CD instead of CWD to be more consistent with the Windows/MS-DOS user interface, which uses the command CD to change directories. When you type a CD command at the ftp> prompt, the FTP client sends a CWD command to the FTP server. The server then replies with the message "CWD command successful" to indicate that the directory has been changed.

Next, type **dir** again. The FTP server displays the directory listing for the Pics directory:

```
200 PORT command successful.
150 Opening ASCII mode data connection for /bin/ls.
06-27-03  10:04PM              123126 door.jpg
06-27-03  10:06PM              112457 echair.jpg
06-27-03  10:06PM               81610 fence.jpg
06-27-03  10:09PM              138102 fog.jpg
06-27-03  10:09PM               83712 gallows.jpg
06-27-03  10:10PM              166741 ghost.jpg
06-27-03  09:58PM              119859 skel01.jpg
06-27-03  10:05PM               87720 wall.jpg
226 Transfer complete.
ftp: 400 bytes received in 0.00Seconds 400000.00Kbytes/sec.
ftp>
```

Here, you can see that the Pics directory contains eight files. To download a file, you use the GET command, specifying the name of the file that you want to download. For example, to download the door.jpg file, type **get door.jpg.** The FTP server transfers the file to your computer and displays the following response:

```
200 PORT command successful.
150 Opening ASCII mode data connection for door.jpg(123126
    bytes).
226 Transfer complete.
ftp: 123126 bytes received in 0.13Seconds 985.01Kbytes/sec.
ftp>
```

Notice again that the response indicates that the command actually processed by the server is a PORT command. The file is transferred in ASCII mode. The entire transfer takes 0.13 seconds, which works out to a transfer rate of about 985KB per second.

Now that you've downloaded the file, you can end the session by typing **bye**. FTP responds by displaying the site's goodbye message; then it returns you to the MS-DOS command prompt:

```
221 Hurry back...

C:\>
```

Of course, FTP is a lot more involved than this simple session suggests. Still, the most common use of FTP is to download files, and most downloads are no more complicated than this example.

FTP Command and Subcommand Reference

The rest of this chapter is an FTP command reference. In the following sections, you can find complete reference information for the FTP command and all its subcommands. The first command in this section is the FTP command itself. After that, all the FTP command's subcommands are listed in alphabetical order.

The FTP command

What it does:	Starts the FTP client so that you can transfer files to and from an FTP server.
Syntax:	**ftp** [**-v**] [**-d**] [**-i**] [**-n**] [**-g**] [**-s:***filename*] [**-a**] [**-w:***windowsize*] [**-A**] [*host*]
Parameters:	**-v** Turns off Verbose mode.
	-d Turns on Debug mode.
	-i Turns off Prompt mode.
	-n Forces manual logon.
	-g Turns off Glob mode.

-s	Specifies a script file that contains FTP commands.
-a	Specifies that any network interface can be used to bind the data connection.
-w	Specifies the size of the transmission buffer. The default is 4K.
-A	Automatically logs on as Anonymous.
Host	The FTP server to which you want to connect. This can be the server's DNS name or an IP address.

Examples:	**ftp ftp.lowewriter.com** **ftp ftp.lowewriter.com -A**
More info:	Unlike most Windows commands, the switches for this command begin with a hyphen, not a slash.
	If you want to script subcommands, use the -s switch. Input redirection doesn't work with FTP.
	When FTP is running, the prompt `ftp>` appears. When this prompt is displayed, you can enter any of the FTP subcommands described in the rest of this section.

Summary of FTP subcommands

To give you a quick overview of what FTP subcommands are available, Table 5-1 lists each of the subcommands along with a brief description of each subcommand's function.

Table 5-1	FTP Subcommands
Command	*Description*
!	Escape to the shell
?	Print local help information
Append	Append to a file
ASCII	Set ASCII transfer type
Bell	Beep when command completed

(continued)

Table 5-1 *(continued)*

Command	Description
Binary	Set binary transfer type
Bye	Terminate ftp session and exit
Cd	Change remote working directory
Close	Terminate ftp session
Debug	Toggle debugging mode
Delete	Delete remote file
Dir	List contents of remote directory
Disconnect	Terminate ftp session
Get	Receive file
Glob	Toggle metacharacter expansion of local file names
Hash	Toggle printing `#' for each buffer transferred
Help	Print local help information
Lcd	Change local working directory
Literal	Send arbitrary ftp command
Ls	List contents of remote directory
Mdelete	Delete multiple files
Mdir	List contents of multiple remote directories
Mget	Get multiple files
Mkdir	Make directory on the remote machine
Mls	List contents of multiple remote directories
Mput	Send multiple files
Open	Connect to remote ftp
Prompt	Force interactive prompting on multiple commands
Put	Send one file
Pwd	Print working directory on remote machine
Quit	Terminate ftp session and exit
Quote	Send arbitrary ftp command
Recv	Receive file
Remotehelp	Get help from remote server
Rename	Rename file
Rmdir	Remove directory on the remote machine
Send	Send one file

Command	Description
Status	Show current status
Trace	Toggle packet tracing
Type	Set file transfer type
User	Send new user information
Verbose	Toggle verbose mode

! (Escape)

What it does: Escape to a command shell.

Syntax: **!**

More info: This command brings up a temporary command prompt so that you can enter commands. To return to the ftp> prompt, type **exit**.

? (Help)

What it does: Displays help information.

Syntax: **?** [*command*]

     help [*command*]

Example: **help mput**

More info: **?** and **help** are interchangeable. If you enter **?** or **help** by itself, a list of FTP commands appears. If you enter **?** or **help** followed by a command name, a summary of that command's function appears.

Append

What it does: Uploads a file and appends it to the end of an existing file on the remote system.

Syntax: **append** *localfile* [*remotefile*]

Example: **append extra.txt start.txt**

More info: If you omit the *remotefile* parameter, the remote file is assumed to have the same name as the local file.

ASCII

What it does: Sets the ASCII transfer mode.

Syntax: **ascii**

More info: This command sets the transfer type of ASCII, which is best suited for text files. ASCII is the default transfer type.

Bell

What it does: Causes the FTP client to beep when each transfer is complete.

Syntax: **bell**

More info: This command is useful when you're downloading long files and want to take a nap during the download. Unfortunately, it doesn't beep when it sees your boss approaching your office, so you'll need some other alarm system to cover that contingency.

Binary

What it does: Sets the binary transfer type.

Syntax: **binary**

More info: The binary file type is best for executable files and other nontext files.

Bye

What it does: Ends the FTP session and exits the FTP client.

Syntax: **bye**

More info: This is the command to use when you're done. It's the same as the `quit` command.

Cd

What it does: Changes the working directory on the remote computer.

Syntax: **cd** *remotedirectory*

Example:	**cd pics**
More info:	Use this to change to the directory that contains the files you want to download or the directory you want to upload files to.
	Use **cd ** to go to the root directory.

Close

What it does:	Closes the session with the remote computer but doesn't leave the FTP program.
Syntax:	**close**
More info:	You can use this command if you want to switch to another FTP server without leaving and restarting the FTP program. This command is the same as the Disconnect command.

Debug

What it does:	Toggles debug mode.
Syntax:	**debug**
More info:	When debug mode is on, the FTP client displays the actual FTP commands that are sent to the FTP server. This can be useful if you're an FTP guru trying to diagnose a problem with a server or a client, but it can also be fun if you just want to see how FTP client commands (like CD) get translated into FTP server commands (like CWD).

Delete

What it does:	Deletes the specified file on the remote computer.
Syntax:	**delete** *remotefile*
Example:	**delete fright.txt**
More info:	You can delete only one file at a time with this command. To delete more than one file in a single command, use the mdelete command.

Dir

What it does:	List contents of remote directory.
Syntax:	**dir** [*remotedirectory*] [*localfile*]
Examples:	**dir** **dir \pics** **dir \pics picdir.txt**
More info:	The first parameter lets you list a directory other than the current working directory. The second parameter lets you capture the output to a file on the local computer.

Disconnect

What it does:	Disconnects from the remote computer but doesn't leave the FTP program.
Syntax:	**disconnect**
More info:	You can use this command if you want to switch to another FTP server without leaving and restarting the FTP program. This command is the same as the Close command.

Get

What it does:	Downloads a file from the remote computer.
Syntax:	**get** *remotefile* [*localfile*]
Examples:	**get boo.exe** **get boo.exe bar.exe**
More info:	This command downloads the specified file from the current working directory on the remote system to the current directory on the local system. The second parameter lets you save the file using a different name than the name used on the remote system.
	You can use this command to download only one file at a time. To download multiple files, use the mget command.
	This command is the same as the get command.

Glob

What it does: Toggles the use of wildcards for local filenames.

Syntax: **glob**

More info: If globbing is on, you can use * and ? characters in local filenames. Globbing is on by default.

Hash

What it does: Toggles the display of hash marks (#) to indicate transfer progress.

Syntax: **hash**

More info: Hash is off by default. If you turn it on by issuing the hash command, a hash mark (#) appears each time a 2K data block is transferred. This helps you track the progress of transfers.

Help

What it does: Displays help information.

Syntax: **?** [*command*]

help [*command*]

Example: **help mput**

More info: **?** and **help** are interchangeable. If you enter **?** or **help** by itself, a list of FTP commands appears. If you enter **?** or **help** followed by a command name, a summary of that command's function appears.

Lcd

What it does: Changes the working directory on the local computer.

Syntax: **lcd** *localdirectory*

Example: **lcd \docs**

More info: Use this to change to the directory you want to download files to or that contains files you want to upload.

Literal

What it does:	Sends a native FTP command directly to the server.
Syntax:	**literal** *arguments...*
Example:	**literal cwd pics**
More info:	Use this command if you're an FTP guru and you want to send a native FTP command to the server. It's the same as the quote command.

Ls

What it does:	List contents of remote directory.
Syntax:	**ls** [*remotedirectory*] [*localfile*]
Examples:	**ls** **ls \pics** **ls \pics picdir.txt**
More info:	The first parameter lets you list a directory other than the current working directory. The second parameter lets you capture the output to a file on the local computer.

Mdelete

What it does:	Delete multiple files.
Syntax:	**mdelete** *remotefile...*
Examples:	**mdelete file1.txt** **mdelete file1.txt file2.txt file3.txt**
More info:	This command deletes one or more files from the current working directory on the remote system.

Mdir

What it does:	Lists the contents of multiple remote directories.
Syntax:	**mdir** *remotedirectory...* [*localfile*]
Examples:	**mdir pics videos -**

More info:	Specify a hyphen as the last parameter to display the output on the screen. Otherwise, the last parameter will be interpreted as the name of the local file you want the directory listing captured to.

Mget

What it does:	Downloads multiple files.
Syntax:	**mget** *remotefile...*
Examples:	**mget file1.txt** **mget file1.txt file2.txt file3.txt**
More info:	This command downloads one or more files from the current working directory on the remote system to the current directory on the local computer.

Mkdir

What it does:	Creates a directory on the remote system.
Syntax:	**mkdir** *remotedirectory*
Examples:	**mdir plans**
More info:	The new subdirectory is created in the current working directory on the remote system.

Mls

What it does:	Lists the contents of multiple remote directories.
Syntax:	**mls** *remotedirectory...* [*localfile*]
Examples:	**mls pics videos -**
More info:	Specify a hyphen as the last parameter to display the output on the screen. Otherwise, the last parameter will be interpreted as the name of the local file you want the directory listing captured to.

Mput

What it does:	Uploads multiple files.
Syntax:	**mput** *localfile...*

Examples: **mput file1.txt**
                   mput file1.txt file2.txt file3.txt

More info: This command uploads one or more files from the
                   current directory on the local system to the current
                   working directory on the remote system.

Open

What it does: Connects to an FTP server.

Syntax: **open** *remotesystem* [*port*]

Examples: **open ftp.microsoft.com**
                   open ftp.weirdport.com 1499

More info: Specify the port number only if the remote system
                   does not use the standard FTP ports (20 and 21).

Prompt

What it does: Toggles prompting for multiple transfers.

Syntax: **prompt**

More info: When prompt mode is on, you're prompted for each
                   file before the file is transferred. Prompt mode is on
                   by default.

Put

What it does: Uploads a file to the remote computer.

Syntax: **put** *localfile* [*remotefile*]

Examples: **put boo.exe**
                   put boo.exe bar.exe

More info: This command uploads the specified file from the
                   current directory on the local system to the current
                   working directory on the remote system. The second
                   parameter lets you save the file using a different name
                   than the name used on the local system.

                   You can use this command to upload only one file at a
                   time. To upload multiple files, use the `mput` command.

                   This command is the same as the `send` command.

Pwd

What it does: Displays the current working directory on the remote computer.

Syntax: **pwd**

More info: If you aren't sure what the current directory is on the remote system, use this command to find out.

Quit

What it does: Ends the FTP session and quits the FTP program.

Syntax: **quit**

More info: This is the command to use when you're done. It's the same as the bye command.

Quote

What it does: Sends a native FTP command directly to the server.

Syntax: **quote** *arguments...*

Example: **quote cwd pics**

More info: Use this command if you're an FTP guru and you want to send a native FTP command to the server. It's the same as the literal command.

Recv

What it does: Downloads a file from the remote computer.

Syntax: **recv** *remotefile* [*localfile*]

Examples: **recv boo.exe**
recv boo.exe bar.exe

More info: This command downloads the specified file from the current working directory on the remote system to the current directory on the local system. The second parameter lets you save the file using a different name than the name used on the remote system.

You can use this command to download only one file at a time. To download multiple files, use the mget command.

This command is the same as the get command.

Remotehelp

What it does: Displays help for remote commands.

Syntax: **remotehelp** [*command*]

Example: **remotehelp cwd**

More info: If you enter remotehelp by itself, a list of FTP commands is displayed. If you enter remotehelp followed by a command name, a summary of that command's function appears.

Rename

What it does: Renames a file on the remote system.

Syntax: **rename** *filename newfilename*

Example: **rename door.jpg doorway.jpg**

More info: Use this command to change the name of a file on the remote system.

Rmdir

What it does: Removes a directory on the remote system.

Syntax: **rmdir** directoryname

Example: **rmdir oldpics**

More info: This command removes a directory and all the files in it, so use it with caution!

Send

What it does: Uploads a file to the remote computer.

Syntax: **send** *localfile* [*remotefile*]

Examples:	**send boo.exe** **send boo.exe bar.exe**
More info:	This command uploads the specified file from the current directory on the local system to the current working directory on the remote system. The second parameter lets you save the file using a different name than the name used on the local system.
	You can use this command to upload only one file at a time. To upload multiple files, use the mput command.
	This command is the same as the put command.

Status

What it does:	Displays the current status of the FTP client.
Syntax:	**status**
More info:	Use this command to display the current settings of options, such as Bell, Prompt, and Verbose, as well as the current connection status.

Trace

What it does:	Activates trace mode.
Syntax:	**trace**
More info:	When trace mode is on, detailed information about each packet transmission is displayed. Trace is off by default and should be left off unless you're digging deep into the bowels of FTP or just want to show off.

Type

What it does:	Sets the transfer type to ASCII or Binary or displays the current mode.
Syntax:	**type** [**ascii** *or* **binary**]
Examples:	**type ascii** **type binary** **type**

More info: Use ASCII transfers for text files and binary transfers for nontext files.

If you don't specify a type, the current transfer type appears.

You can also use the `ascii` or `binary` commands to switch the transfer type.

User

What it does: Logs you on to a remote system.

Syntax: **user** *username* [*password*]

Examples: **user doug**
user doug notmypw

More info: This command logs you on to the remote system using the user name and password you provide. If you omit the password, you're prompted to enter it.

Verbose

What it does: Toggles verbose mode.

Syntax: **verbose**

More info: When verbose mode is on, FTP responses appear. Verbose mode is on by default.

Chapter 6: TCP/IP Tools and Commands

In This Chapter

✔ Recognizing tools and commands

✔ Making all your hosts sing with IPConfig and Ping

Most client and server operating systems that support TCP/IP come with a suite of commands and tools that are designed to let you examine TCP/IP configuration information and diagnose and correct problems. Although the exact form of these commands varies between Windows and UNIX/Linux, most are surprisingly similar. This chapter is a reference to the most commonly used TCP/IP commands.

Arp

The `arp` command lets you display and modify the ARP cache. (ARP stands for *address resolution protocol*.) The ARP cache is a simple mapping of IP addresses to MAC addresses. Each time a computer's TCP/IP stack uses ARP to determine the MAC address for an IP address, it records the mapping in the ARP cache so that future ARP lookups will go faster.

If you use the `arp` command without any parameters, you get a list of the command's parameters. To display the ARP cache entry for a specific IP address, use the `-a` switch followed by the IP address. For example:

```
C:\>arp -a 192.168.168.22

Interface: 192.168.168.21 --- 0x10004
  Internet Address        Physical Address        Type
  192.168.168.22          00-60-08-39-e5-a1       dynamic

C:\>
```

You can display the complete ARP cache by using `-a` without specifying an IP address, like this:

```
C:\>arp -a

Interface: 192.168.168.21 --- 0x10004
  Internet Address      Physical Address      Type
  192.168.168.9         00-02-e3-16-e4-5d     dynamic
  192.168.168.10        00-50-04-17-66-90     dynamic
  192.168.168.22        00-60-08-39-e5-a1     dynamic
  192.168.168.254       00-40-10-18-42-49     dynamic

C:\>
```

ARP is sometimes useful when diagnosing duplicate IP assignment problems. For example, suppose that you can't access a computer that has an IP address of 192.168.168.100. You try to ping the computer, expecting the ping to fail, but lo and behold, the ping succeeds. One possible cause for this problem may be that two computers on the network have been assigned the address 192.168.168,100, and your ARP cache is pointing to the wrong one. The way to find out is to go to the 192.168.168.100 computer that you want to access, run ipconfig /all, and make a note of the physical address. Then return to the computer that's having trouble reaching the 192.168.168.100 computer, run arp -a, and compare the physical address with the one you noted. If they're different, it means that two computers have been assigned the same IP address. You can then check the DHCP or static TCP/IP configuration of the computers involved to find out why.

Hostname

The Hostname command is the simplest of all the TCP/IP commands presented in this chapter. It simply displays the computer's host name. For example:

```
C:\>hostname
doug

C:\>
```

Here, the host name for the computer is doug. The Windows version of the Hostname command has no parameters. However, the UNIX/Linux versions of Hostname let you set the computer's host name as well as display it. You do that by specifying the new hostname as an argument.

IPConfig

The IPConfig command displays information about a computer's TCP/IP configuration. It can also be used to update DHCP and DNS settings.

Displaying basic IP configuration

To display the basic IP configuration for a computer, use the IPConfig command without any parameters, like this:

```
C:\>ipconfig

Windows IP Configuration

Ethernet adapter Local Area Connection:

        Connection-specific DNS Suffix  . :
        IP Address. . . . . . . . . . . : 192.168.1.100
        Subnet Mask . . . . . . . . . . : 255.255.255.0
        Default Gateway . . . . . . . . : 192.168.1.1

C:\>
```

When you use IPConfig without parameters, the command displays the name of the adapter, domain name used for the adapter, the IP address, subnet mask, and default gateway configuration for the adapter. This is the easiest way to determine a computer's IP address.

If your computer indicates an IP address in the 169.254.*x.x*, odds are good that the DHCP server is not working. 169.254.*x.x* is the Class B address block that Windows uses when it resorts to IP Autoconfiguration. This usually happens only when the DHCP server can't be reached or isn't working.

Displaying detailed configuration information

You can display detailed IP configuration information by using the /all switch with the IPConfig command, like this:

```
C:\>ipconfig /all

Windows IP Configuration

        Host Name . . . . . . . . . . . : doug
        Primary DNS Suffix  . . . . . . :
        Node Type . . . . . . . . . . . : Unknown
        IP Routing Enabled. . . . . . . : No
        WINS Proxy Enabled. . . . . . . : No

Ethernet adapter Local Area Connection:

        Connection-specific DNS Suffix  . :
        Description . . . . . . . . . . : D-Link DFE-530TX+
  PCI Adapter
        Physical Address. . . . . . . . : 00-50-BA-84-39-11
        Dhcp Enabled. . . . . . . . . . : Yes
```

```
        Autoconfiguration Enabled . . . . : Yes
        IP Address. . . . . . . . . . . . : 192.168.1.100
        Subnet Mask . . . . . . . . . . . : 255.255.255.0
        Default Gateway . . . . . . . . . : 192.168.1.1
        DHCP Server . . . . . . . . . . . : 192.168.1.1
        DNS Servers . . . . . . . . . . . : 204.127.198.19
                                            63.240.76.19
        Lease Obtained. . . . . . . . . : Wednesday, July
02, 2003 3:27:09 PM
        Lease Expires . . . . . . . . . : Thursday, July
03, 2003 3:27:09 PM

C:\>
```

You can determine a lot of information about the computer from the
IPConfig /all command. For example:

+ The computer's host name is doug.

+ The computer's IP address is 192.168.1.100, and the subnet mask is
  255.255.255.0.

+ The default gateway is a router located at 192.168.1.1.

+ This router is also the network's DHCP server.

+ The DNS servers are at 204.127.198.19 and 63.240.76.19.

+ The computer obtained its IP address from the DHCP server on
  Wednesday, July 2, 2003 at 3:27:09 p.m., and the lease expires 24 hours
  later.

Renewing an IP lease

If you're having an IP configuration problem, you can often solve it by
renewing the computer's IP lease. To do that, use the /renew switch, like
this:

```
C:\>ipconfig /renew

Windows IP Configuration

Ethernet adapter Local Area Connection:

        Connection-specific DNS Suffix  . :
        IP Address. . . . . . . . . . . . : 192.168.1.100
        Subnet Mask . . . . . . . . . . . : 255.255.255.0
        Default Gateway . . . . . . . . . : 192.168.1.1

C:\>
```

When you renew an IP lease, the IPConfig command displays the new lease information.

This command won't work if you've configured the computer to use a static IP address.

Releasing an IP lease

You can release an IP lease by using the IPConfig command with the /release parameter, like this:

```
C:\>ipconfig /release

Windows IP Configuration


Ethernet adapter Local Area Connection:

        Connection-specific DNS Suffix  . :
        IP Address. . . . . . . . . . . . : 0.0.0.0
        Subnet Mask . . . . . . . . . . . : 0.0.0.0
        Default Gateway . . . . . . . . . :

C:\>
```

As you can see, the DNS suffix and default gateway for the computer are blank, and the IP address and subnet mask are set to 0.0.0.0.

After you've released the DHCP lease, you can use the ipconfig /renew command to obtain a new DHCP lease for the computer.

Flushing the local DNS cache

You probably won't need to do this unless you're having DNS troubles. If you've been tinkering with your network's DNS configuration, you may need to flush the cache on your DNS clients so that they'll be forced to reacquire information from the DNS server. You can do that by using the /flushdns switch:

```
C:\>ipconfig /flushdns

Windows IP Configuration

Successfully flushed the DNS Resolver Cache.

C:\>
```

Even if you don't need to do this, it's fun just to see the computer say "flushed." If I worked at Microsoft, you'd be able to upgrade Windows Me computers to Windows XP by using the /flushME switch.

Nbtstat

Nbtstat is a Windows-only command that can help solve problems with NetBIOS name resolution. (*Nbt* stands for *NetBIOS over TCP/IP.*) You can use any of the switches listed in Table 6-1 to specify what Nbtstat output you want to display. For example, you can use the -a switch to display the cached name table for a specified computer, like this:

```
C:\>nbtstat -a doug

Local Area Connection:
Node IpAddress: [192.168.168.21] Scope Id: []

          NetBIOS Remote Machine Name Table

     Name              Type         Status
   ---------------------------------------------
     DOUG        <00>  UNIQUE       Registered
     DOUG        <20>  UNIQUE       Registered
     MMADOMAIN   <00>  GROUP        Registered
     MMADOMAIN   <1E>  GROUP        Registered
     DOUG        <01>  UNIQUE       Registered

     MAC Address = 00-02-B3-98-40-D1

C:\>
```

Table 6-1 lists the switches that you can use with Nbtstat and explains the function of each switch.

Table 6-1	Nbtstat Command Switches
Switch	**What It Does**
-a name	Lists the specified computer's name table given the computer's name.
-A IP-address	Lists the specified computer's name table given the computer's IP address.
-c	Lists the contents of the NetBIOS cache.
-n	Lists locally registered NetBIOS names.

Switch	What It Does
-r	Displays a count of the names resolved by broadcast and via WINS.
-R	Purges and reloads the cached name table from the LMHOSTS file.
-RR (ReleaseRefresh)	Releases and then reregisters all names.
-S	Displays the sessions table using IP addresses.
-s	Displays the sessions table and converts destination IP addresses to computer NETBIOS names.

Netdiag

Netdiag is a powerful, network-testing utility that performs a variety of network diagnostic tests that can help you to pinpoint a networking problem. Listing 6-1 shows the output from a typical execution of the Netdiag command. (I've taken the liberty of editing it down somewhat to make it more compact.) You can scan this listing to see the types of tests that the Netdiag command performs.

Unfortunately, the Netdiag command isn't available for Windows *9x* computers (including Windows Me), and it isn't installed by default in Windows XP. However, you can install it in Windows XP by inserting your Windows XP installation CD in your computer's CD drive. If you're asked to reinstall Windows, say no. Instead, choose to browse the CD. Navigate your way down to the \Support\Tools folder on the CD and then double-click the Setup.exe icon in the \Support\Tools folder.

The Netdiag command has several switches that let you control the output generated by the command:

✦ **/q:** Lists only those tests that fail.

✦ **/v:** Generates verbose output, (even more verbose than usual).

✦ **/debug:** Generates extremely verbose output — way more than when you use /v.

✦ **/l:** Stores the output from the command in a file named NetDiag.log.

✦ **/fix:** Attempts to fix DNS problems that are discovered.

Listing 6-1   Output from the Netdiag command

```
. . . . . . . . . . . . . . . . . . . . . . . . . . . . .
     Computer Name: DOUG
     DNS Host Name: Doug
     System info : Windows 2000 Professional (Build 2600)
     Processor : x86 Family 15 Model 2 Stepping 4,
     GenuineIntel
     List of installed hotfixes :
          Q147222
          Q308677
          Q308678
          Q310601
          Q311889
          Q315000

Netcard queries test . . . . . . . : Passed

Per interface results:
     Adapter : Local Area Connection
          Netcard queries test . . . : Passed

          Host Name. . . . . . . . . : Doug
          IP Address . . . . . . . . : 192.168.168.21
          Subnet Mask. . . . . . . . : 255.255.255.0
          Default Gateway. . . . . . : 192.168.168.254
          DNS Servers. . . . . . . . : 192.168.168.10
                                       168.215.210.50
                                       192.9.9.3

          AutoConfiguration results. . . . . . : Passed

          Default gateway test . . . : Passed

          NetBT name test. . . . . . : Passed

          WINS service test. . . . . : Skipped
               There are no WINS servers configured for this
          interface.

Global results:

Domain membership test . . . . . . : Passed
     DNS domain name is not specified.
     DNS forest name is not specified.

NetBT transports test. . . . . . . : Passed
     List of NetBt transports currently configured:
          NetBT_Tcpip_{4A526104-BAEB-44F0-A2F6-A804FE31BBAA}
```

        1 NetBt transport currently configured.

Autonet address test . . . . : Passed

IP loopback ping test. . . . . . . : Passed

Default gateway test . . . . : Passed

NetBT name test. . . . . : Passed

Winsock test . . . . : Passed

DNS test . . . . : Passed

Redir and Browser test . . . . . . : Passed
      List of NetBt transports currently bound to the Redir
          NetBT_Tcpip_{4A526104-BAEB-44F0-A2F6-A804FE31BBAA}
      The redir is bound to 1 NetBt transport.

      List of NetBt transports currently bound to the browser
          NetBT_Tcpip_{4A526104-BAEB-44F0-A2F6-A804FE31BBAA}
      The browser is bound to 1 NetBt transport.

DC discovery test. . . . . : Skipped

DC list test . . . . : Skipped

Trust relationship test. . . . . . : Skipped

Kerberos test. . . . . : Skipped

LDAP test. . . . . : Skipped

Bindings test. . . . . : Passed

WAN configuration test . . . . . . : Skipped
      No active remote access connections.

Modem diagnostics test . . . . . . : Passed

IP Security test . . . . : Passed
      Service status is: Started
      Service startup is: Automatic
      IPSec service is available, but no policy is assigned or
      active
      Note: run "ipseccmd /?" for more detailed information

The command completed successfully.

Netstat

The `Netstat` command displays a variety of statistics about a computer's active TCP/IP connections. It's a useful tool to use when you're having trouble with TCP/IP applications, such as FTP, HTTP, and so on.

Displaying connections

If you run `netstat` without specifying any parameters, you get a list of active connections, something like this:

```
C:\>netstat

Active Connections

    Proto  Local Address    Foreign Address
      State
    TCP     Doug:1463        192.168.168.10:1053
      ESTABLISHED
    TCP     Doug:1582        192.168.168.9:netbios-ssn
      ESTABLISHED
    TCP     Doug:3630        192.168.168.30:9100
      SYN_SENT
    TCP     Doug:3716        192.168.168.10:4678
      ESTABLISHED
    TCP     Doug:3940        192.168.168.10:netbios-ssn
      ESTABLISHED

C:\>
```

This list shows all the active connections on the computer and indicates the local port used by the connection, as well as the IP address and port number for the remote computer.

You can specify the `-n` switch to display both local and foreign addresses in numeric IP form:

```
C:\>netstat -n

Active Connections

    Proto  Local Address          Foreign Address          State
    TCP     192.168.168.21:1463    192.168.168.10:1053
      ESTABLISHED
    TCP     192.168.168.21:1582    192.168.168.9:139
      ESTABLISHED
    TCP     192.168.168.21:3658    192.168.168.30:9100
      SYN_SENT
```

```
TCP      192.168.168.21:3716    192.168.168.10:4678
   ESTABLISHED
TCP      192.168.168.21:3904    207.46.106.78:1863
   ESTABLISHED
TCP      192.168.168.21:3940    192.168.168.10:139
   ESTABLISHED

C:\>
```

Finally, you can specify the -a switch to display all TCP/IP connections and ports that are being listened to. I won't list the output from that command here because it would run several pages and I want to do my part for the rainforest. Suffice it to say that it looks a lot like the netstat output shown previously, but a lot longer.

Displaying interface statistics

If you use the -e switch, Netstat displays various protocol statistics, like this:

```
C:\>netstat -e
Interface Statistics
```

	Received	Sent
Bytes	672932849	417963911
Unicast packets	1981755	1972374
Non-unicast packets	251869	34585
Discards	0	0
Errors	0	0
Unknown protocols	1829	

```
C:\>
```

The items to pay attention to in this output are the Discards and Errors. These numbers should be zero, or at least close to it. If they're not, the network may be carrying too much traffic or the connection may have a physical problem. If no physical problem exists with the connection, try segmenting the network to see whether the error and discard rate drops.

You can display additional statistics by using the -s switch, like this:

```
C:\>netstat -s

IPv4 Statistics

   Packets Received            = 2135249
   Received Header Errors      = 0
```

```
                Received Address Errors             = 10319
                Datagrams Forwarded                 = 0
                Unknown Protocols Received          = 0
                Received Packets Discarded          = 0
                Received Packets Delivered          = 2125141
                Output Requests                     = 1999963
                Routing Discards                    = 0
                Discarded Output Packets            = 0
                Output Packet No Route              = 0
                Reassembly Required                 = 0
                Reassembly Successful               = 0
                Reassembly Failures                 = 0
                Datagrams Successfully Fragmented   = 0
                Datagrams Failing Fragmentation     = 0
                Fragments Created                   = 0

        ICMPv4 Statistics
                                        Received        Sent
                Messages                2364            2254
                Errors                  0               0
                Destination Unreachable 295             27
                Time Exceeded           108             0
                Parameter Problems      0               0
                Source Quenches         0               0
                Redirects               0               0
                Echos                   48              2179
                Echo Replies            1913            48
                Timestamps              0               0
                Timestamp Replies       0               0
                Address Masks           0               0
                Address Mask Replies    0               0

        TCP Statistics for IPv4

                Active Opens                        = 23625
                Passive Opens                       = 1074
                Failed Connection Attempts          = 5283
                Reset Connections                   = 6572
                Current Connections                 = 5
                Segments Received                   = 1791463
                Segments Sent                       = 1784391
                Segments Retransmitted              = 11100

        UDP Statistics for IPv4

                Datagrams Received      = 330669
                No Ports                = 2909
                Receive Errors          = 0
                Datagrams Sent          = 202142


        C:\>
```

Nslookup

The Nslookup command is a powerful tool for diagnosing DNS problems. You know you're experiencing a DNS problem when you can access a resource by specifying its IP address but not its DNS name. For example, if you can get to ebay.com by typing 66.135.192.87 in your browser's address bar but not by typing ebay.com, you have a DNS problem.

Looking up an IP address

The simplest use of Nslookup is to look up the IP address for a given DNS name. For example, how did I know that 66.135.192.87 was the IP address for ebay.com? I used Nslookup to find out:

```
C:\>nslookup ebay.com
Server:  ns1.orng.twtelecom.net
Address:  168.215.210.50

Non-authoritative answer:
Name:    ebay.com
Address:  66.135.192.87

C:\>
```

As you can see, I typed nslookup followed by the DNS name I wanted to look up. Nslookup issued a DNS query to find out. The DNS query was sent to the name server named ns1.orng.twtelecom.net at 168.215.210.50. It then displayed the IP address that's associated with ebay.com: 66.135.192.87.

In some cases, you may find that the Nslookup command gives you the wrong IP address for a host name. To know that for sure, of course, you have to know with certainty what the host IP address *should* be. For example, if you know that your server is 203.172.182.10, but Nslookup returns a completely different IP address for your server when you query the server's host name, something is probably wrong with one of the DNS records.

Using Nslookup subcommands

If you type Nslookup without any arguments, the Nslookup command enters a subcommand mode. It displays a prompt character (>) to let you know that you're in Nslookup's subcommand mode rather than at a normal Windows command prompt. In subcommand mode, you can enter various subcommands to set options or to perform queries. You can type a question mark (?) to get a list of these commands. Table 6-2 lists the subcommands you'll use most.

Get me out of here!

One of my pet peeves is that it seems as if every program that uses subcommands chooses a different command to quit the application. I can never remember whether the command to get out of Nslookup is quit, bye, or exit. So I usually end up trying them all. And no matter what program I'm using, I always seem to choose the one that works for some other program first. When I'm in Nslookup, I use Bye first. When I'm in FTP, I try Exit first. Arghh! If I were King of the Computer Hill, every program that had subcommands would respond to the following commands by exiting the program and returning to a command prompt:

- ✔ Quit
- ✔ Exit
- ✔ Bye
- ✔ Leave
- ✔ Sayonara
- ✔ Manana
- ✔ Makelikeatree
- ✔ Andgetouttahere (in honor of Biff from the *Back to the Future* movies, of course)

Table 6-2	The Most Commonly Used Nslookup Subcommands
Subcommand	*What It Does*
name	Queries the current name server for the specified name.
server name	Sets the current name server to the server you specify.
root	Sets the root server as the current server.
set type=x	Specifies the type of records to be displayed, such as A, CNAME, MX, NS, PTR, or SOA. Specify ANY to display all records.
set debug	Turns on debug mode, which displays detailed information about each query.
set nodebug	Turns off debug mode.
set recurse	Enables recursive searches.
set norecurse	Disables recursive searches.
exit	Exits the Nslookup program and returns you to a command prompt.

Displaying DNS records

One of the main uses of Nslookup is to examine your DNS configuration to make sure that it's set up properly. To do that, follow these steps:

1. **At a command prompt, type** nslookup **without any parameters.**

Nslookup displays the name of the default name server and displays the > prompt.

```
C:\>nslookup
Default Server:  ns1.orng.twtelecom.net
Address:  168.215.210.50
>
```

2. **Type the subcommand** set type=any.

   Nslookup silently obeys your command and displays another prompt:

   ```
   > set type=any
   >
   ```

3. **Type your domain name.**

   Nslookup responds by displaying the name servers for your domain:

   ```
   > lowewriter.com
   Server:  ns1.orng.twtelecom.net
   Address:  168.215.210.50

   Non-authoritative answer:
   lowewriter.com   nameserver = NS000.NS0.com
   lowewriter.com   nameserver = NS207.PAIR.com

   lowewriter.com   nameserver = NS000.NS0.com
   lowewriter.com   nameserver = NS207.PAIR.com
   >
   ```

4. **Use a server command to switch to one of the domain's name servers.**

   For example, to switch to the first name server listed above, type **server
   NS000.NS0.com**. Nslookup replies with a message that indicates the
   new default server:

   ```
   > server ns000.ns0.com
   Default Server:  ns000.ns0.com
   Address:  216.92.61.61

   >
   ```

5. **Type your domain name again.**

   This time, Nslookup responds by displaying the DNS information for
   your domain:

   ```
   > lowewriter.com
   Server:  ns000.ns0.com
   Address:  216.92.61.61

   lowewriter.com
           primary name server = ns207.pair.com
           responsible mail addr = root.pair.com
           serial  = 2001121009
           refresh = 3600 (1 hour)
           retry   = 300 (5 mins)
           expire  = 604800 (7 days)
   ```

```
                 default TTL = 3600 (1 hour)
lowewriter.com  nameserver = ns000.ns0.com
lowewriter.com  nameserver = ns207.pair.com
lowewriter.com  MX preference = 50, mail exchanger =
    sasi.pair.com
lowewriter.com  internet address = 209.68.34.15
>
```

6. Type Exit to leave the `Nslookup` **program.**

You're returned to a command prompt.

```
> exit

C:\>
```

Wasn't that fun?

Locating the mail server for an e-mail address

If you're having trouble delivering mail to someone, you can use `Nslookup` to determine the IP address of the user's mail server. Then, you can use the `Ping` command to see whether you can contact the user's mail server. If not, you can use the `Tracert` command to find out where the communication breaks down.

To find a user's mail server, start `Nslookup` and enter the command **set type=MX**. Then, enter the domain portion of the user's e-mail address. For example, if the user's address is Doug@LoweWriter.com, enter LoweWriter.com. `Nslookup` displays the MX information for the domain, like this:

```
C:\>nslookup
Default Server: ns7.attbi.com
Address:  204.127.198.19

> set type=mx
> lowewriter.com
Server:  ns7.attbi.com
Address:  204.127.198.19

lowewriter.com  MX preference = 50, mail exchanger =
    sasi.pair.com
lowewriter.com  nameserver = ns000.ns0.com
lowewriter.com  nameserver = ns207.pair.com
ns000.ns0.com   internet address = 216.92.61.61
ns207.pair.com  internet address = 209.68.2.52
>
```

Here, you can see that the name of the mail server for the `LoweWriter.com` domain is `sasi.pair.com`.

Taking a ride through DNS-Land

Ever find yourself wondering how DNS really works? I mean, how is it that you can type a DNS name like `www.disneyland.com` into a Web browser, and you're almost instantly transported to the Magic Kingdom? Is it really magic?

Nope. It isn't magic; it's DNS. Chapter 4 of this book presented a somewhat dry and theoretical overview of DNS. Now that you have the `Nslookup` command in your trusty TCP/IP toolbox, let's take a little trip through the Internet's maze of DNS servers to find out how DNS gets from `www.disneyland.com` to an IP address in just a matter of milliseconds.

DNS does its whole name resolution thing so fast, it's easy to take it for granted. If you follow this little procedure, you'll gain a deeper appreciation for what DNS does literally tens of thousands of times every second of every day.

1. **At a command prompt, type** nslookup **without any parameters.**

    `Nslookup` displays the name of the default name server and displays the > prompt.

    ```
    C:\>nslookup
    Default Server:  ns1.orng.twtelecom.net
    Address:  168.215.210.50
    >
    ```

2. **Type** root **to switch to one of the Internet's root servers.**

    `Nslookup` switches to one of the Internet's 13 root servers and then displays the > prompt.

    ```
    > root
    Default Server:  A.ROOT-SERVERS.NET
    Address:  198.41.0.4
    ```

3. **Type** www.disneyland.com.

    `Nslookup` sends a query to the root server to ask whether it knows the IP address of `www.disneyland.com`. The root server answers with a referral, meaning that it doesn't know about `www.disneyland.com`, but you should try one of these servers because they know all about the `com` domain.

```
> www.disneyland.com
Server:   A.ROOT-SERVERS.NET
Address:  198.41.0.4

Name:     www.disneyland.com
Served by:
- A.GTLD-SERVERS.NET
         192.5.6.30
         com
- G.GTLD-SERVERS.NET
         192.42.93.30
         com
- H.GTLD-SERVERS.NET
         192.54.112.30
         com
- C.GTLD-SERVERS.NET
         192.26.92.30
         com
- I.GTLD-SERVERS.NET
         192.43.172.30
         com
- B.GTLD-SERVERS.NET
         192.33.14.30
         com
- D.GTLD-SERVERS.NET
         192.31.80.30
         com
- L.GTLD-SERVERS.NET
         192.41.162.30
         com
- F.GTLD-SERVERS.NET
         192.35.51.30
         com
- J.GTLD-SERVERS.NET
         192.48.79.30
         com

>
```

4. **Type** server **followed by the name or IP address of one of the** com
domain name servers.

It doesn't really matter which one you pick. Nslookup switches to that
server. (The server may spit out some other information besides what
I've shown here; I left it out for clarity.)

```
> server 192.48.79.30

Default Server:  [192.48.79.30]
Address:  192.48.79.30

>
```

5. **Type** www.disneyland.com **again.**

   Nslookup sends a query to the com server to ask whether it knows where the Magic Kingdom is. The com server's reply indicates that it doesn't know where www.disneyland.com is, but it does know which server is responsible for disneyland.com.

   ```
   > www.disneyland.com
   Server:  [192.48.79.30]
   Address:  192.48.79.30

   Name:     www.disneyland.com
   Served by:
   - huey.disney.com
             204.128.192.10
             disneyland.com
   - noc.unt.edu

             disneyland.com
   - ns3-auth.sprintlink.net
             144.228.255.10
             disneyland.com
   - ns2-auth.sprintlink.net
             144.228.254.10
             disneyland.com

   >
   ```

   Isn't it just like Disney to name their nameserver huey.disney.com?

6. **Type** server **followed by the name or IP address of the second-level domain name server.**

   Nslookup switches to that server:

   ```
   > server huey.disney.com
   Default Server:  huey.disney.com
   Address:  204.128.192.10

   >
   ```

7. **Type** www.disneyland.com **again.**

   Once again, Nslookup sends a query to the name server to find out whether it knows where the Magic Kingdom is. Of course, huey. disney.com *does* know, so it tells you the answer:

   ```
   > www.disneyland.com
   Server:  huey.disney.com
   Address:  204.128.192.10

   Name:     disneyland.com
   ```

```
Address:   199.181.135.201
Aliases:   www.disneyland.com

>
```

8. **Type** Exit **and then shout like Tigger in amazement at how DNS queries work.**

   And be glad that your DNS resolver and primary name server do all this querying for you automatically.

Okay, maybe that wasn't an e-ticket ride. But it never ceases to amaze me that the DNS system can look up any DNS name hosted anywhere in the world almost instantly.

PathPing

PathPing is an interesting command that's unique to Windows. It's sort of a cross between the Ping command and the Tracert command, combining the features of both into one tool. When you run PathPing, it first traces the route to the destination address much the way Tracert does. Then, it launches into a 25-second test of each router along the way, gathering statistics on the rate of data loss to each hop. If the route has a lot of hops, this can take a long time. However, it can help you to spot potentially unreliable hops. If you're having intermittent trouble reaching a particular destination, PathPing may help you pinpoint the problem.

The following command output is typical of the PathPing command. (The -n switch causes the display to use numeric IP numbers only instead of DNS host names. Although fully qualified host names are convenient, they tend to be very long for network routers, which makes the PathPing output very difficult to decipher.)

```
C:\>pathping -n www.lowewriter.com

Tracing route to lowewriter.com [209.68.34.15]
over a maximum of 30 hops:
  0  192.168.168.21
  1  66.193.195.81
  2  66.193.200.5
  3  168.215.55.173
  4  168.215.55.101
  5  168.215.55.77
  6  66.192.250.38
  7  66.192.252.22
  8  208.51.224.141
  9  206.132.111.118
```

```
10    206.132.111.162
11    64.214.174.178
12    192.168.1.191
13    209.68.34.15

Computing statistics for 325 seconds...
              Source to Here    This Node/Link
Hop   RTT  Lost/Sent = Pct    Lost/Sent = Pct   Address
  0                                               192.168.168.21
                                0/ 100 =   0%       |
  1   1ms   0/ 100 =   0%       0/ 100 =   0%     66.193.195.81]
                                0/ 100 =   0%       |
  2   14ms  0/ 100 =   0%       0/ 100 =   0%     66.193.200.5
                                0/ 100 =   0%       |
  3   10ms  0/ 100 =   0%       0/ 100 =   0%     168.215.55.173
                                0/ 100 =   0%       |
  4   10ms  0/ 100 =   0%       0/ 100 =   0%     168.215.55.101
                                0/ 100 =   0%       |
  5   12ms  0/ 100 =   0%       0/ 100 =   0%     168.215.55.77
                                0/ 100 =   0%       |
  6   14ms  0/ 100 =   0%       0/ 100 =   0%     66.192.250.38
                                0/ 100 =   0%       |
  7   14ms  0/ 100 =   0%       0/ 100 =   0%     66.192.252.22
                                0/ 100 =   0%       |
  8   14ms  0/ 100 =   0%       0/ 100 =   0%     208.51.224.141
                                0/ 100 =   0%       |
  9   81ms  0/ 100 =   0%       0/ 100 =   0%     206.132.111.118
                                0/ 100 =   0%       |
 10   81ms  0/ 100 =   0%       0/ 100 =   0%     206.132.111.162]
                                0/ 100 =   0%       |
 11   84ms  0/ 100 =   0%       0/ 100 =   0%     64.214.174.178]
                                0/ 100 =   0%       |
 12   --- 100/ 100 =100%      100/ 100 =100%     192.168.1.191
                                0/ 100 =   0%       |
 13   85ms  0/ 100 =   0%       0/ 100 =   0%     209.68.34.15

Trace complete.
```

Ping

Ping is probably the most basic TCP/IP command line tool. Its main purpose is to determine whether you can reach another computer from your computer. It uses the ICMP protocol to send mandatory ECHO_REQUEST datagrams to the specified host computer. When the reply is received back from the host, the Ping command displays how long it took to receive the response.

You can specify the host to ping using an IP address, as in this example:

```
C:\>ping 192.168.168.10

Pinging 192.168.168.10 with 32 bytes of data:

Reply from 192.168.168.10: bytes=32 time<1ms TTL=128
Reply from 192.168.168.10: bytes=32 time<1ms TTL=128
Reply from 192.168.168.10: bytes=32 time<1ms TTL=128
Reply from 192.168.168.10: bytes=32 time<1ms TTL=128

Ping statistics for 192.168.168.10:
    Packets: Sent = 4, Received = 4, Lost = 0 (0% loss),
Approximate round trip times in milli-seconds:
    Minimum = 0ms, Maximum = 0ms, Average = 0ms

C:\>
```

By default, the Ping command sends four packets to the specified host. It displays the result of each packet sent and then displays summary statistics: how many packets were sent, how many replies were received, the error loss rate, and the approximate round-trip time.

You can also ping using a DNS name, as in this example:

```
C:\>ping www.lowewriter.com

Pinging lowewriter.com [209.68.34.15] with 32 bytes of data:

Reply from 209.68.34.15: bytes=32 time=84ms TTL=53
Reply from 209.68.34.15: bytes=32 time=84ms TTL=53
Reply from 209.68.34.15: bytes=32 time=84ms TTL=53
Reply from 209.68.34.15: bytes=32 time=84ms TTL=53

Ping statistics for 209.68.34.15:
    Packets: Sent = 4, Received = 4, Lost = 0 (0% loss),
Approximate round trip times in milli-seconds:
    Minimum = 84ms, Maximum = 84ms, Average = 84ms

C:\>
```

The Ping command uses a DNS query to determine the IP address for the specified host and then pings the host based on its IP address.

The Ping command has a number of other switches that you'll use rarely, if ever. Some of these switches are available only for some operating systems. To find out which switches are available for your version of Ping, type **ping /?** (Windows) or **man ping** (UNIX/Linux).

You can find a very interesting story about the creation of the `Ping` command written by the command's author, Mike Muus, at his Web site at `http://ftp.arl.mil/~mike/ping.html`. (Sadly, Mr. Muus was killed in an automobile accident in November 2000.)

Route

The `Route` command displays or modifies the computer's routing table. For a typical computer that has a single network interface and is connected to a LAN that has a router, the Route table is pretty simple and isn't often the source of network problems. Still, if you're having trouble accessing other computers or other networks, you can use the `Route` command to make sure that a bad entry in the computer's routing table isn't the culprit.

For a computer with more than one interface and that is configured to work as a router, the routing table is often a major source of trouble. Setting up the routing table properly is a key part of configuring a router to work.

Displaying the routing table

To display the routing table in Windows, use the route print command. In UNIX/Linux, you can just use route without any command-line switches. The output displayed by the Windows and UNIX/Linux commands are similar. Here's an example from a typical Windows client computer:

```
C:\>route print
===========================================================
 ==============
Interface List
0x1 ........................... MS TCP Loopback interface
0x2 ...00 50 ba 84 39 11 ...... D-Link DFE-530TX+ PCI Adapter
===========================================================
 ==============
===========================================================
 ==============
Active Routes:
Network Destination        Netmask          Gateway       Interface  Metric
          0.0.0.0          0.0.0.0      192.168.1.1   192.168.1.100     20
        127.0.0.0        255.0.0.0        127.0.0.1       127.0.0.1      1
      192.168.1.0    255.255.255.0    192.168.1.100   192.168.1.100     20
    192.168.1.100  255.255.255.255        127.0.0.1       127.0.0.1     20
    192.168.1.255  255.255.255.255    192.168.1.100   192.168.1.100     20
    255.255.255.255  255.255.255.255  192.168.1.100   192.168.1.100      1
Default Gateway:       192.168.1.1
===========================================================
 ==============
```

```
Persistent Routes:
  None

C:\>
```

For each entry in the routing table, five items of information are listed:

✦ The destination IP address — actually, this is the address of the destination subnet and must be interpreted in the context of the subnet mask.

✦ The subnet mask that must be applied to the destination address to determine the destination subnet.

✦ The IP address of the gateway to which traffic intended for the destination subnet will be sent.

✦ The IP address of the interface through which the traffic will be sent to the destination subnet.

✦ The *metric,* which indicates the number of hops required to reach destinations via the gateway.

Each packet that's processed by the computer is evaluated against the rules in the routing table. If the packet's destination address matches the destination subnet for the rule, the packet is sent to the specified gateway via the specified network interface. If not, the next rule is applied.

The computer I ran the route command on in this example is on a private 192.168.1.0 subnet. The computer's IP address is 192.168.1.100, and the default gateway is a router at 192.168.1.1.

Here's how the rules shown in this example are used. Notice that you have to read the entries from the bottom up:

✦ The first rule is for packets sent to 255.255.255.255, with subnet mask 255.255.255.255. This special IP address is for broadcast packets. The rule specifies that these broadcast packets should be delivered to the local network interface (192.168.1.100).

✦ The next rule is for packets sent to 192.168.1.255, again with subnet mask 255.255.255.255. These are also broadcast packets and are sent to the local network interface.

✦ The next rule is for packets sent to 192.168.1.100, again with subnet mask 255.255.255.255. This is for packets that the computer is sending to itself via its own IP address. This rule specifies that these packets will be sent to the local loopback interface on 127.0.0.1.

✦ The next rule is for packets sent to 192.168.1.0 with subnet mask 255.255.255.0. These are packets intended for the local subnet. They're sent to the subnet via the local interface at 192.169.1.100.

✦ The next rule is for packets sent to the loopback address (127.0.0.1, subnet mask 255.0.0.0). These packets are sent straight through to the loopback interface, 127.0.0.1.

✦ The last rule is for everything else. All IP addresses will match the destination IP address 0.0.0.0 with subnet mask 0.0.0.0 and will be sent to the default gateway router at 192.168.1.1 via the computer's network interface at 192.168.1.100.

One major difference between the Windows version of Route and the UNIX/Linux version is the order in which they list the routing table. The Windows Route command lists the table starting with the most general entry and working toward the most specific. The UNIX/Linux version is the other way around: It starts with the most specific and works toward the more general. The UNIX/Linux order makes more sense — the Windows Route command displays the routing list upside down.

Modifying the routing table

Besides displaying the routing table, the Route command also lets you modify it by adding, deleting, or changing entries.

You shouldn't modify the routing table unless you know what you're doing. If you mess up the routing table, your computer may not be able to communicate with anyone.

The syntax for the route command for adding, deleting, or changing a route entry is

```
route [-p] command dest [mask subnet] gateway [-if interface]
```

The following paragraphs describe each of the Route command's parameters:

✦ **–p:** Makes the entry persistent. If you omit -p, the entry will be deleted the next time you reboot. (Used only with Add commands.)

✦ *command:* Either add, delete, or change.

✦ *destination:* The IP address of the destination subnet.

✦ **mask** *subnet*: The subnet mask. If you omit the subnet mask, the default is 255.255.255.255, meaning that the entry will apply only to a single host rather than a subnet. So you'll usually want to include the mask.

✦ *gateway*: The IP address of the gateway to which packets will be sent.

✦ **if** *interface*: The IP address of the interface through which packets will be sent. If your computer has only one network interface, you can omit this.

Suppose that your network has a second router that serves as a link to another private subnet, 192.168.2.0 (subnet mask 255.255.255.0). The interface on the local side of this router is at 192.168.1.200. To add a static route entry that sends packets intended for the 192.168.2.0 subnet to this router, use a command like this:

```
C:\>route -p add 192.168.2.0 mask 255.255.255.0 192.168.1.200
```

Now, suppose that you later change the IP address of the router to 192.168.1.222. You can update this route with the following command:

```
C:\>route change 192.168.2.0 mask 255.255.255.0 192.168.1.222
```

Notice that I specified the mask again. If you omit the mask from a route change command, the command changes the mask to 255.255.255.255!

Finally, suppose that you realize that setting up a second router on this network wasn't such a good idea after all, so you want to just delete the entry. The following command will do the trick:

```
C:\>route delete 192.168.2.0
```

Tracert

The Tracert command (spelled *traceroute* in UNIX/Linux implementations) is one of the key diagnostic tools for TCP/IP. It displays a list of all the routers that a packet must go through to get from the computer where Tracert is run to any other computer on the Internet. Each one of these routers is called a *hop*, presumably because the original designers of the IP protocol played a lot of hopscotch when they were young. If you're unable to connect to another computer, you can use Tracert to find out exactly where the problem is occurring.

Tracert makes three attempts to contact the router at each hop and displays the response time for each of these attempts. Then, it displays the DNS name of the router (if available) and the router's IP address.

To use `Tracert`, type the `Tracert` command followed by the host name of the computer to which you want to trace the route. For example, suppose that you're having trouble sending mail to a recipient at `wiley.com`. You've used `Nslookup` to determine that the mail server for `wiley.com` is `xmail.wiley.com`, so now you can use `Tracert` to trace the routers along the patch from your computer to `xmail.wiley.com`:

```
C:\>tracert xmail.wiley.com

Tracing route to xmail.wiley.com [208.215.179.78]
over a maximum of 30 hops:

  1    27 ms    14 ms    10 ms  10.242.144.1
  2    11 ms    43 ms    10 ms  bar01-p5-0-
0.frsnhe4.ca.attbb.net [24.130.64.125]
  3     9 ms    14 ms    12 ms  bar01-p4-0-
0.frsnhe1.ca.attbb.net [24.130.0.5]
  4    25 ms    30 ms    29 ms  bic01-
p6-0.elsgrdc1.ca.attbb.net [24.130.0.49]
  5    25 ms    29 ms    43 ms  bic02-
d4-0.elsgrdc1.ca.attbb.net [24.130.0.162]
  6    21 ms    19 ms    20 ms  bar01-
p2-0.lsanhe4.ca.attbb.net [24.130.0.197]
  7    37 ms    38 ms    19 ms  bic01-
p2-0.lsanhe3.ca.attbb.net [24.130.0.193]
  8    20 ms    22 ms    21 ms  12.119.9.5
  9    21 ms    21 ms    22 ms  tbr2-p012702.la2ca.ip.att.net
[12.123.199.241]
 10    71 ms   101 ms    62 ms  tbr2-p013801.sl9mo.ip.att.net
[12.122.10.13]
 11    68 ms    77 ms    71 ms  tbr1-p012401.sl9mo.ip.att.net
[12.122.9.141]
 12    79 ms    81 ms    83 ms  tbr1-cl4.wswdc.ip.att.net
[12.122.10.29]
 13    83 ms   107 ms   103 ms  tbr1-p012201.n54ny.ip.att.net
[12.122.10.17]
 14   106 ms    85 ms   105 ms  gbr6-p30.n54ny.ip.att.net
[12.122.11.14]
 15   104 ms    96 ms    88 ms  gar3-p370.n54ny.ip.att.net
[12.123.1.189]
 16    98 ms    86 ms    83 ms  12.125.50.162
 17    85 ms    90 ms    87 ms  xmail.wiley.com
[208.215.179.78]

Trace complete.
```

Wow, when I send mail to my editors at Wiley, the mail travels through 17 routers along the way. No wonder I'm always missing deadlines!

Understanding how Tracert works

Understanding how Tracert works can provide some insight that may help you interpret the results it provides. Plus, you can use this knowledge to impress your friends, who probably don't know how it works.

The key to Tracert is a field that's a standard part of all IP packets called TTL, which stands for *time to live.* In most other circumstances, a value called TTL would be a time value — not in IP packets, however. In an IP packet, the TTL value indicates how many routers a packet can travel through on its way to its destination. Every time a router forwards an IP packet, it subtracts one from the packet's TTL value. When the TTL value reaches zero, the router refuses to forward the packet.

The Tracert command sends a series of special messages called ICMP Echo Requests to the destination computer. The first time it sends this message, it sets the TTL value of the packet to 1. When the packet arrives at the first router along the path to the destination, that router subtracts one from the TTL value and sees that the TTL value has become 0, so it sends a Time Exceeded message back to the original host. When the Tracert command receives this Time Exceeded message, it extracts the IP address of the router from it, calculates the time it took for the message to return, and displays the first hop.

Then the Tracert command sends another Echo Request message, this time with the TTL value set to 2. This message goes through the first router to the second router, which sees that the TTL value has been decremented to zero and sends back a Time Exceeded message. When Tracert receives the Time Exceeded message from the second router, it displays the line for the second hop. This process continues, each time with a greater TTL value, until the Echo Request finally reaches the destination.

Pretty clever, eh?

(Note that the UNIX/Linux traceroute command uses a slightly different set of TCP/IP messages and responses to accomplish the same result.)

The most likely problem that you'll encounter when you use Tracert is a timeout during one of the hops. Timeouts are indicated by asterisks where you'd expect to see a time. For example, the following Tracert output shows the fourth hop timing out on all three attempts:

```
C:\>tracert xmail.wiley.com

Tracing route to xmail.wiley.com [208.215.179.78]
over a maximum of 30 hops:

  1    27 ms    14 ms    10 ms  10.242.144.1
  2    11 ms    43 ms    10 ms  bar01-p5-0-
  0.frsnhe4.ca.attbb.net [24.130.64.125]
  3     9 ms    14 ms    12 ms  bar01-p4-0-
  0.frsnhe1.ca.attbb.net [24.130.0.5]
  4     *         *         *     Request timed out.
```

Sometimes timeouts are caused by temporary problems, so you should try the Tracert again to see whether the problem persists. If you keep getting timeouts at the same router, the router may be having a genuine problem.

Winipcfg

Windows 9*x* computers have a graphical version of the `ipconfig` command called `winipcfg`. When you enter the command `winipcfg` at a command prompt, the dialog box shown in Figure 6-1 appears. This dialog box displays the adapter's MAC address and the basic IP configuration details: the IP address, subnet mask, and default gateway. For computers that have more than one network adapter, a drop-down list lets you select the adapter to display.

Figure 6-1:
The
`Winipcfg`
command
displays
the IP
Configura-
tion dialog
box.

The IP Configuration dialog box offers the following buttons:

✦ **OK:** Dismisses the dialog box.

✦ **Release:** Releases the DHCP lease for the current adapter.

✦ **Renew:** Renews the DHCP lease or obtains a new lease for the current adapter.

✦ **Release All:** Releases the DHCP leases for all adapters.

✦ **Renew All:** Renews the DHCP leases for all adapters.

✦ **More Info**: Expands the dialog box to display additional IP configuration information, as shown in Figure 6-2.

Here's a little-known trick: You can right-click the title bar of the IP configuration dialog box and choose the Copy command to copy the IP configuration to the clipboard. You can then paste the configuration information into another program, such as Notepad or Word, so that you can save it for future reference. The output that results from this trick depends on whether you've clicked the More Info button. If you don't click More Info, the output resembles the output from the `ipconfig` command without parameters. If you do click More Info, the output resembles the output from the `ipconfig /all` command.

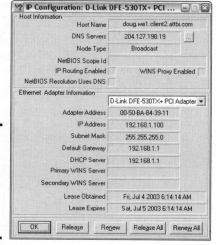

Figure 6-2:
The `Winipcfg` command can display more information.

The `Winipcfg` command is only available on Windows 95, 98, and Me computers. However, Microsoft offers a version called `wntipcfg.exe` that runs on Windows NT/2000/XP. You can download `wntipcfg.exe` free of charge from Microsoft's Web site at the following address:

```
www.microsoft.com/windows2000/techinfo/reskit/tools/
    existing/wntipcfg-o.asp
```

Because Microsoft periodically reorganizes its Web site, you may not find `wntipcfg.exe` at that address. If not, go to a search site such as Google (`www.google.com`) and search for "wntipcfg.exe download."

Book VI

Wireless and Home Networking

The 5th Wave   By Rich Tennant

"Okay – did you get that?"

Contents at a Glance

Chapter 1: Networking Your Home

In This Chapter

- ✔ Finding out why you should network at home
- ✔ Discovering the different ways to network your home
- ✔ Finding out about other devices you can connect
- ✔ Seeing an example of a home network

These days, more and more people have more than one computer in their homes, and more and more people are linking them together with networks. A home network can be as simple as a single desktop computer networked with a notebook computer to share files and a printer. However, I've seen home networks that include a dozen or more computers. I know of one computer enthusiast who has at least one computer in every room of his house and a couple of Linux server computers in his garage.

In this chapter, I show you how to network the computers in your home so that you can share a printer, hard drive, CD-ROM drive, and an Internet connection. Nothing fancy here — just the bare necessities that you need to get a network up and running.

Deciding Why You Need a Network

If you have two or more computers in your home, you should network them. Why? Because you're a family, and families share everything, and the best way to share computers is to network them. Besides, it's fun, it will impress your neighbors, and it isn't that expensive.

Before you go to the trouble of setting up a network, though, you should identify the reasons why you want to create a network and then set some goals. The following paragraphs describe some of the specific benefits achieved by setting up a network at home.

- ✦ **Sharing an Internet connection.** This is especially useful if you have a high-speed broadband Internet connection. By sharing the connection over the Internet, you'll be able to access the Internet from any computer in your home. For example, the kids can do their homework on the computer in the den while you check your stock portfolio from the computer in the master bedroom. If you have a wireless network, you can read your e-mail on your notebook computer while relaxing poolside in the back yard.

For many families, sharing an Internet connection is *the* reason to set up a network. In fact, some industry prognosticators have said that networking for the purpose of sharing an Internet connection at home is the hottest growth segment in the computer business today.

Naturally, you have to have a working Internet connection before you can share it over a network. If your main purpose for setting up a network is to share an Internet connection and you don't already have an Internet connection, I suggest that you get the Internet connection up and running on one of your computers first. Then you can install a network to share the connection. If Internet connection sharing is just one of several goals for your network, however, you may opt for the opposite approach: getting your network up and running first and then getting your Internet connection.

This is a networking book — not a parenting book. Because I'm a parent of teenagers myself, though, I'd be remiss if I didn't point out one of the potential drawbacks of sharing an Internet connection over a home network: It can make monitoring your children's Internet experience more difficult. If you put networked computers in your kids' rooms, it won't be easy to look over their shoulders while they use the Internet to make sure that they aren't wandering into trouble.

✦ **Sharing a printer.** Because the price of printers is so cheap these days, it's tempting to buy a printer for every room in your house. However, the truth is that there's no such thing as a free lunch when it comes to printers. You're much better off spending a few hundred dollars on one decent printer that you can share over a network than buying a $50 printer for each person in your family.

When you set up a shared printer, anyone on the network can send a document directly to the printer without having to visit the computer to which the printer is physically connected. However, the computer to which the printer is connected does have to be turned on in order for this type of printer sharing to work. As an alternative to connecting a shared printer to one of the computers on the network, you may want to get a printer that has a built-in networking port so that you can connect the printer directly to the network. Then, anyone on the network can use the printer without worrying about whether some other computer is turned on.

✦ **Sharing hard drive storage.** If you work together on projects with other family members, shared hard drive storage is an invaluable network resource. Instead of having everyone save their own copies of their documents on their own computers, you can set up a common storage area on one of the computers and have everyone save their files in that location. Then, anyone can access the files.

Obviously, this arrangement raises security and privacy issues. Make sure that everyone knows that the public storage area is just that: public. If they want anything to remain private, they shouldn't put it there.

One benefit of using shared hard drive storage is that it lets you back up everyone's files all at once. That way, each family member doesn't have to back up his or her own files. Be sure to make it clear to everyone that only the files on the shared network hard drive are being backed up, however. If they create any files on their own computers, they have to be responsible for backing them up.

✦ **Breathing new life into old computers.** If you have an old computer that doesn't have much hard drive space, you can extend its usefulness by connecting it to a network. For example, suppose that you have an old 200MHz Pentium computer running Windows 95, with a 250MB hard drive — barely large enough to hold Windows, let alone any real data. With a network, you can connect to your brand-new computer with its 60GB hard drive and store your files there. You're not going to turn an old dog into a racehorse, but you may find that the old dog can still learn a few new tricks.

If you're computer savvy, you can also put old computers to use by setting them up as dedicated network servers. For example, I have a friend who had two ancient 100MHz Pentium computers that were destined for the beehive factory. He installed Linux on both of them and uses one as a firewall to protect his network from hackers and the other as a print server for an old but still serviceable HP laser printer.

Choosing How to Network Your Home

Although nearly all business and office networks use Ethernet to connect their computers, several simpler alternatives are available for home networks. The following sections describe five ways to network the computers in your home.

Phone line networks

Phone line networks let you network your computers by using your home's existing phone lines. If you already have phone jacks near the locations where you want to put your computers, a phone line network may be the easiest way to get a network up and running.

Phone line networks are based on a specification developed by an organization called the *Home Phone Networking Alliance,* which is also known as *HomePNA*, or sometimes just *HPNA*. The original HPNA standard was too slow to be useful for any significant networking, with a maximum data transmission rate of only 1Mbps (as opposed to Ethernet's 10 or 100Mbps). The newer HPNA 2.0 standard, however, runs at 10Mbps — the same as old-style Ethernet. 10Mbps isn't lightning fast, but it's more than fast enough to share an Internet connection and light-duty file and printer sharing. The only real limitation is that each computer must be located near a phone jack.

You may think that using your home phone wiring to network your computers would tie up your phone lines, but that's not the case. Phone line networks don't interfere with normal phone use, so you can talk on the phone and exchange information over your phone line network at the same time.

Each computer on the phone line network needs a phone line adapter. Phone line adapters come in two basic varieties:

✦ **Internal adapters:** PCI or ISA cards, which you must install inside your computer, much like an Ethernet adapter card. Make sure that your computer has a free PCI or ISA slot before purchasing an internal adapter.

✦ **External adapters:** These are little boxes that sit next to your computer, which you plug into an available port on your computer. The most popular external adapters plug into a USB port, but you can also get adapters that plug into a parallel printer port, and you can even get adapters that plug into Ethernet ports for computers that have built-in Ethernet adapters (such as Macintosh computers).

After you install an Internet adapter or plug an external adapter into the appropriate port, you just plug the adapter into the nearest phone jack and you're ready to start networking.

In theory, the HomePNA standard means that you should be able to mix and match phone line network adapters from different companies on a single network. I wouldn't try it, though. Phone line adapters tend to work best with their own kind, so use the same brand adapters for all your computers.

Besides HPNA network adapters, you can also get HPNA/Ethernet bridges that let you connect a phone line network to a cabled Ethernet network. For example, Linksys makes a product (HBP200) that links an Ethernet network to a HPNA 2.0 network. To use this device, you use a phone cord to connect the bridge's HPNA port to any phone jack in your home. Then, you use a twisted-pair patch cable to connect the bridge's 10BaseT port to a 10BaseT or 10/100BaseT hub or switch or a wireless access point. This simple connection enables any computers connected to the phone line network to communicate with computers connected on an Ethernet network.

Another handy device made by Linksys is HPRO200, which combines the bridging function of the HBP200 with a Cable/DSL router so that you can share an Internet connection.

For more information about HPNA and HPNA products, check out these Web sites:

✦ `www.homepna.org`: The home page of the Home Phone Networking Aliance.

✦ `www.linksys.com`: Makes HPNA network interface cards and bridges.

✦ `www.netgear.com`: Makes an HPNA Cable/DSL router.

Power line networks

Another way to connect your home computers without having to string wire through your house is to use networks that work over your home's electrical power system. In most homes, just about every wall has a power outlet, so power line networks are more flexible than phone line networks in terms of where you can locate your computers.

The first generation of power line networks were slow, sending data at just a few hundred Kbps. However, recent advances have led to a new standard, promoted by the HomePlug Powerline Alliance, which has a theoretical maximum of 14Mbps. In most environments, the actual throughput is about 6Mbps, but that's more than enough for most home network uses.

To set up a PowerLine network, all you have to do is purchase a PowerLine USB adapter for each computer in your home. You plug the PowerLine adapter into any electrical outlet in your home. Then, use a USB cable to connect the PowerLine adapter to a USB port on your computer. You then install the driver that comes with the PowerLine adapter, and you're ready to network.

You can mix a PowerLine network with an Ethernet network by using a PowerLine/Ethernet bridge. This device plugs into an electrical outlet and has a single RJ-45 jack into which you can plug a patch cable. Plug the other end of the patch cable into an Ethernet hub or switch and *voilà!*, you've bridged your networks.

USB networks

Most newer computers have one or more *USB ports* that enable you to connect devices such as keyboards, mice, printers, scanners, cameras, and so on. USB, which stands for *universal serial bus*, was designed to be a universal connecting point for adding extraneous devices to your computer. Prior to USB, each device had its own unique style of connector. With USB, everything that plugs into your computer, except the monitor and the speakers, uses the standardized USB bus. (You can even get USB speakers, but most computers still use old-fashioned audio connectors for sound.)

You can also use USB to create a simple network — provided that the computers are located close to each other. If you want to network just two computers, you can purchase a special USB network connection cable that lets you connect the two computers directly. Note that you have to use a special cable to do this; you can't simply connect two computers to each other by using a standard USB cable.

To connect more than two computers, you can get an inexpensive USB hub. Then, you use a USB networking cable to connect each of the computers to the hub.

Although USB networks are fairly easy to set up and use, they have three significant drawbacks:

✦ USB networks are slower than Ethernet networks, unless you use more expensive USB 2.0 devices.

✦ The total cable length for a USB network can't be longer than 16 feet unless you use a special booster cable. This makes sense when you consider that USB's original purpose was to connect peripheral devices such as keyboards and mice to a computer.

✦ USB network devices are actually more expensive than Ethernet devices. For example, USB network connection cables are about $70 each. You can get USB Ethernet adapters for about $25.

Wireless networks

The most flexible of all home-networking technologies is wireless, which sends network data through the air by using radio signals. With a wireless network, you don't have to string any wire anywhere in your house, and you don't have to locate your computers near an existing phone or power outlet. In fact, you can roam around the house with a laptop computer and connect to the network anywhere — even out by the pool!

Wireless networking devices come in two flavors, depending on which version of the IEEE wireless networking standards they support:

✦ **IEEE 802.11b:** This is the older and slower version. The maximum data rate is 11Mbps.

✦ **IEEE 802.11a:** Although you would think *a* comes before *b,* it doesn't when it comes to wireless networking standards. 802.11a is a newer and faster standard than 802.11b. 802.11a devices operate at 54Mbps.

✦ **IEEE 802.11g:** This is the latest version of wireless Ethernet. Like 802.11a, 802.11g can operate as fast as 54Mbps. However, it's also backward-compatible with 802.11b. As a result, an 802.11g device can communicate with an existing 802.11b network, and vice-versa.

To set up a wireless network, you need a wireless network adapter for each computer. The network adapter can be an internal adapter card that you install in the computer or an external card that you connect to the computer via a USB port. External adapters are better than internal adapters because you can easily move an external adapter around, if necessary, to get the best antenna placement.

If some of your computers are connected via a cabled Ethernet network, you can get a *wireless access point* (called a *WAP*) that bridges the wireless network with the cabled Ethernet network. You can also get wireless access points that include built-in cable/DSL routers to share a broadband Internet connection.

Wireless is the most expensive way to network your home computers. You can buy Ethernet adapter cards for as little as $20 and phone line network adapters for about $60, but a wireless network will cost you about $100 per computer.

You can find out more about setting up a wireless network in Chapter 4 of this book.

Wireless networks are especially useful for notebook computers because notebooks are inherently mobile. If you have a wireless network, you can use your notebook computer anywhere within range of the network, which will include any room in your house, the back yard, and may even include the neighbor's yard.

**Book VI
Chapter 1**

**Networking
Your Home**

Wireless networks present a bit of a security risk that you should at least be aware of. Unless you take steps to secure your wireless network, anyone who can get within range of your radio signals can sneak into your network. For more information about securing a wireless network, see Chapter 5 of this book.

Cabled Ethernet

Although phone line, power line, and wireless networks are easier to set up than an Ethernet network, Ethernet is still the fastest and most flexible choice for networking your home. If you decide to use Ethernet to build your home network, you will need the following Ethernet components:

✦ **A 10/100baseT Ethernet network card for each computer.** You have no need to spend big money on the networking cards. If you can find them for $20 each, buy them.

Make sure to get a card that fits one of the available expansion slots inside your computer. You need to know what type of available expansion slots your computer has. Most newer computers have PCI slots. If you have an older computer, you may have a different type of slot — most likely an ISA slot. Check the manual that came with your computer to find out for sure.

If you don't want to crack the case off your computer to install a network adapter, you can get an external USB network adapter instead. A USB Ethernet adapter costs about $30 and is a lot easier to install than an internal adapter. If your computer has a USB 2.0 port, make sure to get a USB 2.0 Ethernet adapter. That way, you won't lose any speed when connecting to a 100Mbps Ethernet network. The original USB 1.0 standard operated at only 14Mbps, so it effectively limits a USB 1.0 Ethernet connection to 10Mbps.

Most newer computers have 10/100BaseT Ethernet ports already built-in. If this is the case with your computer, you don't have to buy one.

✦ **A 10/100baseT hub or switch with enough ports for all your computers.** You can get four- or five-port switches for about $50. You may be able to find an eight-port 10BaseT hub at a thrift store for a buck or two.

✦ **A twisted-pair cable with RJ-45 connectors on both ends for each computer.** A 25-foot cable costs about $10.

Do *not* buy phone cable. The twisted-pair cable used for 10baseT networks looks like phone cable, but it isn't the same.

Stupid stuff about printer switches

If your only reason for networking is to share a printer, you may want to go a cheaper route: Buy a switch box instead of a network. Switch boxes enable two or more computers to share a single printer. Instead of running a cable directly from one computer to the printer, you run cables from each computer to the switch box and then run one cable from the switch box to the printer. Only one of the computers has access to the printer at a time; the switch decides which one.

You can find two kinds of printer switches:

- **Manual printer switches:** These have a knob on the front that enables you to select which computer is connected to the printer. When you use a manual switch, you must first make sure that the knob is set to your computer before you try to print. Turning the knob while someone else is printing will probably cost you a bag of doughnuts.

- **Automatic printer switches:** These have a built-in electronic ear that listens to each computer. When it hears one of the computers trying to talk to the printer, the electronic ear automatically connects that computer to the printer. The switch also has an electronic holding pen called a *buffer* that can hold printer output from one computer if another computer is using the printer. Automatic switches aren't foolproof, but they work most of the time.

Naturally, a good automatic switch costs more than a manual switch. For example, a manual switch that can enable four computers to share one printer costs about $20. A decent automatic switch to enable four computers to share a printer can set you back about $75. Still, that's a lot cheaper and easier to set up than a full-blown network.

You can probably find an inexpensive starter kit that includes everything that you need to network two computers together: two twisted-pair network cards, a hub, and two cables. If you have more than two computers, you can buy an add-on kit for each additional computer.

Strange Things to Add To Your Network

Most home networks exist for the sake of sharing an Internet connection as well as hard drive storage and printers. However, a surprising collection of other devices can be added to a network to create the ultimate Gee-Whiz home network. The following paragraphs describe some of the more unusual gadgets you can incorporate into a home network:

✦ **TiVo:** In case you haven't heard, TiVo is a television device that automatically records your favorite programs onto a built-in hard drive so that you can play them back later. It's like a digital VCR, but much more intelligent. For example, you can tell it to record every episode of your favorite series, and it will automatically schedule the recordings. If the show changes time slots, the schedule is updated automatically. TiVo can also automatically skip reruns.

The latest version of TiVo includes the Home Media Option, which is a network connection that lets you incorporate TiVo into your home computer network. This effectively ties your television set and stereo system to your network, as well. For example, you can play MP3 files from your computer on your stereo system. Or you can use your TV to view slide shows automatically created from pictures on your computer.

✦ **Video games:** Both the Sony PlayStation 2 and the Xbox game consoles include Ethernet ports so that you can connect them to the network. If the network then has a broadband Internet connection, you can play Xbox or PlayStation games against other gamers via the Internet.

✦ **Cameras:** You've probably seen the Internet pop-up ads for inexpensive wireless video cameras that tie right into your network. These devices let you monitor your front yard, swimming pool, or the baby's nursery from any computer on the network.

✦ **Home automation:** The ultimate in home network geekdom is the ability to turn your lights on or off over the network. Even higher on the geek factor is the ability to turn your lights on from anywhere on the Internet. All you need to accomplish this feat is a home automation system based on the popular X-10 home automation system. X-10 is actually an old power line networking technology that's slow, but reliable and inexpensive. The core of an X-10 system is one or more inexpensive appliance modules that plug into the wall and respond to X-10 signals received over the power lines. The appliance module enables you to remotely turn on or off a light or any other electrical device. You can control X-10 appliances by using an inexpensive controller/timer device, or you can buy a computer interface that lets you control an X-10 appliance from your computer. If you install an X-10 computer interface into a networked computer, you can control your home's lights and appliances over the network. With the right software, you can dim your lights from an Internet connection anywhere in the world.

A Home Network Example

Submitted for your approval, please find enclosed a sample networking plan for the home of one Wally and June Cleaver, typical residents in a suburb of Mayfield, state unknown. The Cleavers are a typical American family, with two boys and four computers:

✦ Ward Cleaver's computer is a fairly new 2.2 GHz Pentium 4 with 512MB of RAM and an 80GB hard drive. Ward runs Microsoft Windows XP Professional and Office XP for spreadsheet analysis (Excel) and occasional word processing (Word). He also has a high-speed laser printer. He uses the computer mostly for work that he brings home from the office. However, his computer is also connected to a cable Internet connection. Because Ward's computer is the only one with Internet access, the rest of the family is always trying to trick him into leaving the house so that they can get on the Net. (Ward's computer has a built-in Ethernet port, which is currently being used for the cable Internet connection.)

✦ June Cleaver's computer is an older 1.2GHz Pentium 4 with 128MB of RAM and a 20GB hard drive. June runs Windows 98 Second Edition and uses her computer mostly to store her favorite recipes. She also publishes a monthly newsletter for her bridge club. She has a little inkjet printer that she bought at a garage sale for $20, but it doesn't work well, so she would like to use Ward's laser printer to print her recipes and newsletter.

✦ Wally's computer is a 200MHz Pentium with 32MB of RAM, a 300MB hard drive, and Windows 95. Fortunately, Wally has been saving up his allowance since 1957 and now has enough to buy a new computer. He wants to move the computer out to the garage, where he can use it to control their annual Christmas light display.

✦ The Beaver has a 3.0GHz Intel Pentium 4 notebook computer with 1GB of RAM, a 60GB hard drive, and a built-in 10/100BaseT Ethernet port worth about $2,500. The computer originally belonged to Eddie Haskell, but Beave traded a Joe DiMaggio, a Barry Bonds, and a Sammy Sosa for it. The Beaver uses his computer to do homework and to keep an inventory of his extensive baseball card collection using a database program that he created himself by using Java.

The Cleavers want to network their computers for two simple reasons:

✦ So that everyone can access the laser printer.

✦ So that everyone can access the Internet via a high-speed cable connection.

Because Ward's and June's computers are located downstairs in the den, they will use a wired Ethernet connection to connect them. Rather than tear up the house to run cable up to the kids' room, they'll use wireless to connect to Beaver's computer and the one Wally plans on buying soon. Ward has given Wally permission to purchase any computer he wants, provided he can pay for it with the allowance money he's saved up, with just one stipulation: The computer must have a built-in wireless adapter.

Ward calls a family meeting, and they put together the following shopping list for their network:

✦ A combination DSL/cable router, four-port 10/100Mbps switch, and a wireless access point similar to the Linksys BEFW11S4. Cost: about $80.

✦ A 10/100BaseT Ethernet internal network adapter card for June's computer. Cost: about $20.

✦ A 20-foot Cat-5e patch cable to connect June's computer to the switch and a 10-foot Cat 5e patch cable to connect Wally's computer. Cost: about $15.

✦ A wireless USB adapter for Beaver's notebook computer. Cost: about $80. At first, the Cleavers thought they could get a device that would plug into the Ethernet port that's built into Beaver's notebook. After searching the Web, however, they learned that what they would need to do that is a wireless Ethernet bridge. Unfortunately, the cheapest one they could find was $130. So they decided to save $50 by using a USB wireless adapter.

✦ Wally wanted to get a wireless adapter for his old Pentium clunker so he could control the annual holiday display from the Internet, but Ward said absolutely not. After the family meeting, however, Beaver told Wally that the other day he and Lumpy found a pile of stuff behind one of Mayfield's many failed dot-com businesses and got 1,000 feet of brand new Cat-5e cable. So this weekend, while Ward's golfing, they plan on running the cable out their window, over the roof, and into the garage where the computer will be stored. Beaver suggests they hang some towels on the cable so Ward will think it's a clothesline.

The total estimated cost for the new network is $195.

Chapter 2: Connecting to the Internet with Internet Explorer

In This Chapter

✔ Finding out whether you're already connected to the Internet

✔ Getting connected if you aren't so lucky

✔ Comparing various Internet pricing plans to get the best deal

✔ Setting up your Internet connection with the Internet Connection Wizard

The main reason many people set up a home network is to share an Internet connection. As it turns out, setting up the Internet connection that you want to share may actually be harder than setting up a network to share it!

This chapter explores the various options for connecting your computer to the Internet using Internet Explorer, which is far and away the most popular program used today for accessing the Internet. If you're already connected to the Internet, you can skip this chapter and go directly to the next chapter, where you can find out how to set up a network to share that connection.

Some General Tips

Before I dive into the many technical details, here are a few general tips for setting up an Internet connection:

✦ Upgrade to the latest and greatest version of Windows: Windows XP. If you can afford it, get Windows XP Professional Edition rather than Home Edition. Professional Edition has more support for networks than Home Edition provides. All versions of Windows include a version of Internet Explorer and built-in support for Windows, but the newer versions are much easier to set up.

✦ If you have several computers, set up the Internet connection on the newest, best, and fastest of your computers.

✦ If you plan on connecting to the Internet over the phone, either with a simple dialup connection or with a high-speed DSL connection, make sure that your computer is located near a telephone outlet.

✦ If you have a friend who already has access to the Internet, treat him to lunch and pick his brain (well, not literally). Find out what kind of modem he has, who his Internet Service Provider (ISP) is, how much he is paying for it, what he likes best about it, what he hates about it, what he would do differently, and whether he thinks John Travolta should go back to playing nice guys.

✦ If a friend happens to be a computer expert, see whether you can bribe her into helping you set up your Internet access. Don't offer cash; bartering is better. Offer to mow her lawn or wash her car.

Deciding How to Connect

Just a few years ago, you really had only one way to connect to the Internet from home: with a modem and a dialup phone connection. So the only choice you had was choosing the dialup service. Nowadays, you must make choices.

The first choice is whether to stick with a slower but less expensive *dialup connection* that uses a modem and works over a standard telephone line or to switch to a *broadband connection* that is faster but more expensive. If the only reason you want to use the Internet is for e-mail or online chatting, you may be satisfied with a dialup connection. However, if you want to surf the Web, watch online media, or play online games, you won't be happy with anything but a broadband connection.

If you opt for broadband, you then have to choose which of several different broadband options to pick. The choices are cable, DSL, and satellite.

The following sections explore the ins and outs of dialup connections and various broadband options.

Choosing dialup

The oldest and still one of the most popular methods of connecting to the Internet is with a *modem*. If your computer is relatively new, you may be lucky: It probably already has a modem in it. In that case, all you have to do is plug the modem into the telephone jack by using a phone cord, and you're ready to go.

If your computer doesn't have a modem, you need to purchase and install one yourself. Fortunately, you can stroll right down to your nearest electronics superstore, computer superstore, or office-supply superstore and buy one off the shelf for less than $50. If you shop around, you can probably find one for as little as $15.

Modems come in a variety of speeds. The speed of a modem determines how fast the modem can pump data through the phone line. Modem speed is measured in units called *bps,* which stands for *bits per second.* When you buy a modem, make sure that you get a 56,000bps modem, usually called a 56K modem. (The term *baud* is sometimes used as a substitute for bps. Both have pretty much the same meaning.)

If your computer has an older modem in it, watch out. Older modems may not be fast enough to access the Internet efficiently. If you're working with an older, 14400bps modem or — heaven forbid — a 2400bps modem, you should definitely replace it with a faster model. If you have a newer, 28.8K or 33.6K modem, you can continue to use it. However, your Internet access will be noticeably faster if you upgrade to a 56K modem.

Your modem must be connected to a phone line so that your computer can access the outside world. Unfortunately, whenever you use the Internet, the modem ties up your phone line. Anyone calling your number gets a busy signal, and you can't use the phone to call out for pizza. If being deprived of telephone privileges while you're online proves to be a problem, you can always have the phone company install a separate phone line for your modem. (Or you can use your cell phone to order pizza.)

If the thought of installing a modem nauseates you, pack up your computer and take it to your friendly local computer shop. The folks there can sell you a modem and install it for you for a small charge.

The following paragraphs summarize the pros and cons of using a dialup connection:

✦ **Pro:** Dialup is the least expensive way to connect to the Internet. Dialup providers, such as AOL or MSN, charge about $25 per month for access. You can probably find a local provider who charges $15 or less.

✦ **Con:** Dialup ties up a phone line while you're online. If you can't live with that, you'll need a second phone line dedicated to the dialup connection. Assuming that the phone line costs you $15 to $20 per month, your total cost for the Internet connection is now $30 to $45, which isn't much cheaper than DSL or cable.

✦ **Pro:** Your computer probably already has a modem built-in, so you don't have to buy or install any extra equipment.

✦ **Con:** Dialup is slow. When you see a broadband connection at your neighbor's house, you'll be embarrassed to admit that you still use dialup. You may as well admit that you still drive a Pinto.

✦ **Con:** You have to dial in to make a connection. The computer does the dialing for you, but the whole process takes a few minutes. You get to stare at the screen or play a quick hand of solitaire while you wait.

✦ **Con:** Busy signals! Some ISPs oversell their dialup capacity. When that happens, you get a busy signal when you dial in. You then get to play more solitaire while your computer automatically dials and redials and reredials until you finally get in.

✦ **Con:** Unreliable connections are a common problem. Sure enough, right in the middle of an hour-long download (which would have taken three minutes with a broadband connection), your dialup connection will inexplicably disconnect.

Choosing cable

If you plan on using the Internet frequently and don't mind spending a few extra dollars for Internet access, you may want to consider connecting to the Internet with a cable provider. Cable brings you the Internet on the same line that brings 40 billion TV channels into your home.

To find out what cable Internet offerings are available to you, visit your local cable television provider's Web page. A typical cable Internet service costs $40 to $45 per month. However, some providers give you a discount if you also subscribe to cable television.

Cable Internet connections require a special *cable modem* that is similar in function to a dialup modem. The Internet data itself is sent over the cable TV network using a portion of the channel space available to the cable provider on their cable network. Usually, more channel space is devoted to downstream transmission (data sent to your home) than for upstream traffic (data sent from your home to the Internet) because most users download far more data from the Internet than they upload.

You can either purchase your own cable modem or lease the modem from your cable provider. If you choose to purchase your own cable modem, be sure to find out from your provider what type of modems they support. They may recommend a particular modem brand and model. If so, get the one that they recommend.

The cable modem can connect to your computer through either a 10BaseT Ethernet connection or a USB connection. Because it is faster and more flexible, I recommend that you get a cable modem with an Ethernet connection.

Most newer cable Internet systems work with a industry modem standard called *docsis*. Docsis stands for *data over cable service interface specification,* but that won't be on the test. If your cable provider supports docsis, you should be able to use any docsis-compliant cable modem. However, you should still check with the cable company before you buy a cable modem, just to make sure that they'll support the modem you want to purchase.

Note that because the data is carried on just a few channels devoted to the Internet, using the Internet with a cable connection doesn't disrupt normal TV. In other words, you can still watch the History Channel while your kids are chatting online with their friends.

So just how fast is cable? The answer depends on several factors. Most cable service is rated at 1.5Mbps for downstream traffic, which is about 25 times faster than a 56Kbps dialup connection. To put that into perspective, a large media file that may take an hour to download with a dialup connection will take two or three minutes to download with a cable connection.

However, cable connections don't always reach their maximum potential speed. The main reason for slowdowns is that you may be sharing your cable connection with your neighbors. Most cable networks use very fast fiber-optic cables to transmit signals from their central office to neighborhoods. From there, the signal is carried on a shared coaxial cable from house to house. As a result, each household that connects to the Internet shares the cable with all other households in the neighborhood.

This doesn't really slow the Internet connection down as much as you may think. For example, if 50 homes share a single 1.5Mbps connection, does that mean that each home gets only 30Kbps? Not at all. That would happen only if all 50 users decided to download data at the exact same instant. In actual practice, most users download data for just a fraction of a second and then spend a few minutes looking at the data they just downloaded. So at any given moment, only a few users are actually sending or receiving data. And even if the cable connection does slow noticeably during peak hours, it will still be much faster than a dialup connection.

The following paragraphs summarize the main pros and cons of broadband cable Internet:

✦ **Pro:** The connection is about 25 times faster than dialup. Web pages that took 30 seconds to appear with a dialup connection now seem to appear instantly. Downloads that took hours with dialup take minutes with cable.

✦ **Pro:** The connection is always on, so you don't have to wait for a dialup connection to be established before using the Internet.

✦ **Pro:** The connection doesn't tie up a phone line.

✦ **Pro:** The connection is reliable.

✦ **Con:** Cable is more expensive than dialup. A typical cable subscription is about $40 to $45 per month.

✦ **Con:** You have to use a special cable modem, which you can either purchase yourself or lease from the cable company.

✦ **Con:** Although the connection is pretty reliable, if it does go down, you get to contend with typical cable company service. For example, the last time my cable service went down, it was on a Monday. I called the cable company and was told that the earliest a technician could come out was Thursday. Also, the appointment was one of those "the technician will be there sometime between 8 a.m. and Memorial Day" appointments. Fortunately, the cable connection mysteriously fixed itself the next day, so I cancelled the appointment.

✦ **Con:** If you go with cable, you're computer-nerd friends will tell you that you should have gone with DSL instead.

Choosing DSL

DSL is the most popular alternative to cable for broadband internet access. *DSL,* which stands for *digital subscriber line,* is a digital phone service that works over POTS (*plain old telephone service*) lines. In other words, DSL runs on the phone lines that you already have installed in your home.

DSL speeds are comparable to cable modem speeds. Typically, 1.5Mbps is the maximum you can expect for downloads. Uploads are usually considerably slower, but Internet users download much more than they upload, so the difference is not usually noticeable.

One disadvantage of DSL is that the cable length between your home and the phone company's central office is limited to a maximum of 18,000 feet (about 3.4 miles). That's the length of the cable — not the physical distance between you and the central office. Phone companies tend to route cables in very circuitous routes in order to accommodate a variety of factors. So even though you may be just a mile away from a central office, the actual cable distance may be much more.

Even if you're within the maximum 18,000 feet, if you're at the edge of the limit, your actual speed may be slower than the maximum. In fact, the only way to find out how much speed you'll actually get from a DSL connection is to hook it up and find out. So when you choose an ISP provider, make sure that they offer a money-back guarantee if the connection doesn't work or works too slowly.

If you're more than 18,000 feet from a central office, you may still be able to use a slower version of DSL called *IDSL*. IDSL is a cross between ISDN and DSL. It runs at the same speed as ISDN, but offers the always-on connection of DSL and is much less expensive than ISDN. (Given a choice between IDSL and cable, however, cable is the hands-down winner.)

Like cable, DSL is always connected to the Internet, so you don't have to wait for a connection to be established when you need to access the Internet. Unlike a dialup connection, however, DSL doesn't interrupt normal phone service. You can talk on the phone and use DSL on the same line at the same time. A special filter called a *low pass filter* (*LPF*) is installed on each telephone to prevent the voice and data signals from interfering with each other.

DSL uses a device that's similar to a cable modem, called a *DSL transceiver* (commonly referred to as a *DSL modem*). Unlike cable modems, you can't buy a DSL transceiver at the corner 7-11. You need to use the transceiver provided by your ISP.

Another difference between cable and DSL is that while cable companies have monopolies, the government broke up the phone company monopoly many years ago. As a result, if DSL is available in your area, you can probably choose from several different DSL providers. This isn't necessarily an advantage, however. Having too many ISPs to pick from can make choosing one very difficult. The fact that the ISP doesn't own the actual phone lines can also lead to finger-pointing when something goes wrong.

To find out whether DSL is available in your area and to get a list of providers, go to www.dslreports.com. This great Web site asks for your phone number and address to estimate your distance from the central office and displays a list of ISPs that can provide service for your location. It also includes loads of other information about DSL and other broadband connections.

The following paragraphs summarize the pros and cons of DSL:

+ **Pro:** The connection is about the same as cable — as much as 25 times faster than dialup.

+ **Pro:** The connection is always on.

+ **Pro:** You can talk on the phone without interfering with the DSL connection.

+ **Pro:** The connection is reliable.

+ **Con:** DSL is more expensive than dialup and a little more expensive than cable. A typical DSL subscription is about $45 to $60 per month.

What about ISDN?

ISDN, which stands for *integrated services digital network,* is a digital phone service that was popular a few years ago as an alternative to dialup connections. ISDN allows data to be sent about twice as fast as a conventional phone line — up to 128 Kbps (kilobits per second) rather than 56 Kbps. As an added plus, a single ISDN line can be logically split into two separate channels, so you can carry on a voice conversation while your computer is connected to the Internet.

However, ISDN is inferior to cable and DSL connections in many ways. For starters, it's slower. ISDN may be twice as fast as a regular dialup connection, but a cable modem or DSL connection is at least ten times as fast and often

even faster than that. Plus, ISDN is not an always-on connection like cable or DSL. With ISDN, you must dial and connect to the Internet each time you want to use it, much as you do with a regular dialup connection. Also, ISDN is actually more expensive than cable or DSL.

In short, ISDN is fast becoming a thing of the past. It was a good idea for its time, but its time has passed. If you're using ISDN for your Internet access, you may want to consider switching to cable or DSL.

Note that you can run DSL over an ISDN line by using a technique called IDSL. IDSL isn't any faster than ISDN, but it is an always-on connection, and it's much cheaper than ISDN.

✦ **Con:** You have to use a special DSL transceivers, and you have to install LPF filters on each phone.

✦ **Con:** Finger-pointing can occur because the phone line and the ISP are two separate companies.

✦ **Con:** If you go with DSL, your computer-nerd friends will tell you that you should have gone with cable instead.

Choosing a Provider

An *Internet service provider,* or ISP, is a company that charges you, usually on a monthly basis, for access to the Internet. The ISP has a bunch of modems connected to phone lines that you can dial into. These modems are connected to a computer system, which is, in turn, connected to the Internet via a high-speed data link. The ISP's computer acts as a liaison between your computer and the Internet.

Typically, an ISP provides you with the following services in exchange for your hard-earned money:

✦ **Access to the World Wide Web:** Most ISPs let you access any Web site on the Internet from your computer. Some ISPs provide built-in filtering software that automatically blocks access to pornography and other objectionable Web sites.

✦ **Electronic mail:** The ISP assigns you an e-mail address that anyone on the Internet can use to send you mail. You can use Microsoft Outlook Express, which comes with Internet Explorer, to access your e-mail.

✦ **Access to Internet newsgroups:** In newsgroups, you can follow ongoing discussions about your favorite topics.

✦ **Software to access the Internet:** In many cases, this software includes Microsoft Internet Explorer. Alternatively, it may include a different Web browser, such as Netscape Navigator. (If your ISP doesn't provide Internet Explorer, you can obtain it for free from Microsoft after you set up your Internet connection. Find out how to do so later in this chapter, in the section "Getting Internet Explorer.")

✦ **Technical support, the quality of which varies greatly:** If you have trouble with your Internet connection, try calling your ISP's technical support line. If you're lucky, an actual human being who knows something about computers will pick up the phone and help you solve your problem. Next best: You're put on hold, but someone eventually answers and helps you. Not so good: The technical support line is always busy. Worse: You get a recording that says, "All our support engineers are busy. Please leave a message, and we'll get back to you." Yeah, right.

Basically, two types of companies provide access to the Internet: national providers, such as AOL and MSN, and local providers. The following sections describe the pros and cons of both types of providers and the Internet access they provide.

Online services

Online services are nationwide (or even global) providers that not only connect you to the Internet, but also provide exclusive content services that are available only to members. The three biggest online services are America Online (AOL), CompuServe, and The Microsoft Network (MSN). On the plus side, you gain access to unique content that's available only to members of the online service. On the minus side, you pay for this extra service. The following are the pricing plans of the three major online services:

✦ **America Online (AOL):** The most popular online service, AOL has more than 35 million subscribers. AOL has several pricing plans. The standard monthly plan gives you unlimited access to AOL and the Internet for $23.90 per month; if you prepay 12 months, the rate drops to $19.95 per month. The light usage plan gives you three hours per month for

$4.95, with each additional hour costing $2.50. And the limited usage plan gives you five hours for $9.95 per month, with each additional hour costing $2.95. You can find information about the current pricing plan for AOL at `www.aol.com/info/pricing.adp`. (Or search Google for "AOL price plan."

✦ **CompuServe:** Running second in online service popularity is CompuServe, which claims more than 2.2 million users. CompuServe has two pricing plans. The best-value plan gives you 20 hours per month for $9.95, with each additional hour costing $2.95. The unlimited plan gives you unlimited access for $19.95 per month. You can lower this amount to $17 per month if you pay an entire year in advance.

America Online owns CompuServe, but at least for now, AOL and CompuServe continue to operate as separate online services.

✦ **The Microsoft Network (MSN):** MSN is the Microsoft attempt to challenge America Online and CompuServe. MSN offers unlimited access for $21.95 per month. MSN also offers an hourly plan that's $9.95 per month for up to 20 hours and $1.50 per hour for each additional hour.

If you opt to use an online service as your Internet service provider, you need to carefully select the correct pricing plan for the number of hours that you intend to use the service. To make this point, Table 2-1 shows the monthly cost for each of the preceding plans for monthly usages of 10, 20, 40, and 60 hours. As you can see, the actual monthly cost varies tremendously, depending on which plan you select.

Table 2-1	Pricing Plans Compared			
	Number of Hours			
Price Plan	10	20	40	60
America Online, standard	$23.90	$23.90	$23.90	$23.90
America Online, light usage	$22.45	$47.45	$97.45	$147.45
America Online, limited usage	$24.70	$54.20	$113.20	$172.20
CompuServe, unlimited	$19.95	$19.95	$19.95	$19.95
CompuServe, best value	$9.95	$9.95	$68.98	$127.95
The Microsoft Network, unlimited	$21.95	$21.95	$39.95	$69.95
The Microsoft Network, hourly	$9.95	$9.95	$21.95	$21.95

I hear too many horror stories about families who have signed up for America Online, expecting the monthly bill to be only $9.95, only to discover a $200 bill the first month. The problem is that the kids discover the Internet one evening and end up spending four or five hours online every night for two weeks before the parents catch on.

Are the online services worth it?

Because you can access the Internet in less expensive ways, this question naturally comes up: "Are the extra features you get with an online service worth the extra cost?" This may sound like a cop-out, but that question has no right or wrong answer. The answer depends on whether you use and benefit from the additional features provided by online services.

One major advantage of online services is their organization. The Internet is a sprawling mess, and sometimes it's hard to find what you want. In contrast, online services are well organized. Information in online services is neatly arranged according to topic. Not so on the Internet.

Another benefit you can probably expect from your online service is customer service support.

CompuServe and America Online both have large support staffs that can help make sure that you get on and stay on the Internet without lots of technical headaches. The quality of technical support that comes with an ISP varies greatly from one ISP to the next.

Still, if you subscribe to an online service and then discover that you use it only to access the Internet, you may be better off canceling your online service subscription and signing up with a simple Internet service provider instead.

Also, most online services have a "bring your own access" plan that lets you use their software and access their content. AOL, CompuServe, and MSN charge $9.95 per month for this service.

My advice: If you sign up for an online service, always start off with an unlimited-access plan. This type of plan may cost you $10 or $15 more if you end up not using it as much as you expect, but that's better than paying $50 to $100 more for exceeding the limited-usage plan. Also, make sure that all family members, including the kids, understand how the pricing works.

Basic Internet service providers

The alternative to using a commercial online service is to sign up with a basic Internet service provider, or ISP. ISPs provide the same Internet access that online services do, but they don't provide their own additional content. ISPs are invariably less expensive than commercial online services because they don't have the added expense that results from providing their own proprietary services.

Technically, any company that provides you with Internet access is an ISP, including commercial online services. However, I prefer to use the term *ISP* to refer to a company that specializes in providing only Internet access without providing a separate online service of its own.

The changing role of online services

The sudden growth of the Internet has had a profound impact on established online services like MSN and America Online. In the past, online services required you to use software provided by the online service to access the information available at the service. For example, to access America Online, you must use special software provided by America Online. MSN and CompuServe work the same way.

All that is changing, however. Online services are discovering that users prefer to choose access software — so the providers are slowly but surely moving their services to a format that provides users with online access by means of standard Internet Web browsers, such as Netscape Navigator and Internet Explorer.

These developments don't mean that online services are becoming part of the World Wide Web or that you can look forward to free CompuServe or America Online access. The online services will continue to offer distinctive subscriber-only features, such as discussion forums, file libraries, stock-quote services, and reference databases.

The gradual change indicates a move toward using the same software to access an online service and the World Wide Web and picking which browser program you prefer to use to access your online service.

These changes are evolving slowly. You can't change the software used by millions of subscribers all at once. The change is certain, however, and within a few years all the major online services will let you use Internet Explorer or any other Web browser to access their content.

In fact, MSN is already at that point. The latest version of MSN is Web-based so that you can move seamlessly between Internet Web sites and The Microsoft Network without changing browsers.

You can choose from nationally known service providers, such as EarthLink or AT&T WorldNet Service, or you can select a local ISP. To find the ISPs in your area, check the *Yellow Pages* under Computers — Online Services and Internet (or a similar heading).

Most ISPs offer unlimited access for $15 to $20 per month. Some offer a limited-hours plan for slightly less (for example, 40 hours for $10). Either way, the cost of using an ISP is likely to be less than the cost of using a commercial online service, unless you end up using the Internet for only a few hours each month.

America Online, CompuServe, and MSN let you access their services for $9.95 per month, if you use your own Internet service provider. In other words, you can access the online service by dialing into your own ISP rather than by dialing one of the online service's numbers. Or, you can use a broadband connection to access your online service.

Getting Internet Explorer

Naturally, before you can begin to use Internet Explorer, you must install it on your computer. This section explains how.

As you may know, Internet Explorer is free. It comes with Windows, so you already have a version of it on your computer. You can download the current version from Microsoft's Web site, provided that you have a current enough operating system. (Internet Explorer 6 requires at least Windows 98 Second Edition or Windows NT 4.0.)

Here are some of the ways you can obtain Internet Explorer 6:

✦ If you already have Internet access and are using another program (such as Netscape Navigator or an earlier version of Internet Explorer), you can download Internet Explorer 6 from Microsoft's Web site at `www.microsoft.com/ie`. Note that the download for Internet Explorer can take several hours if you don't have a cable or DSL connection. Better go to the local video store and rent a movie before proceeding. Or start the download just before you go to bed. The download should be finished by morning.

✦ If your computer runs the latest version of Windows, known as Windows XP, you already have Internet Explorer 6.

✦ If you sign up with an Internet service provider that uses Internet Explorer as its default browser, you may get a CD with Internet Explorer on it. However, make sure that the service uses the latest version of Internet Explorer; some ISPs offer only older versions of Internet Explorer.

Internet Explorer has been through several major revisions. The current version, Internet Explorer 6, is among the more powerful Web browsers available. If you have an earlier version (5.5, 5, 4, 3, 2, or 1), be sure to upgrade to Version 6 as soon as possible. You can find Internet Explorer 6 available for download at `www.microsoft.com`.

If your computer already has Internet Explorer, but you're not sure what version, you can easily find out. Start Internet Explorer by clicking the Internet Explorer icon on your desktop or on the Windows taskbar. Then choose Help➪About Internet Explorer. This action summons a dialog box that tells you which version of Internet Explorer is installed on your computer.

After you download the Internet Explorer file, exit from your Web browser, open the folder into which you downloaded the file, and double-click the file's icon. The Internet Explorer setup program then installs Internet Explorer for you. (Depending on the browser you use, Internet Explorer may automatically install itself after the download finishes. If so, just sit back and enjoy the ride.)

If you don't want to contend with an hours-long download, you can get Internet Explorer 6 on CD from Microsoft in the U.S. by calling 800-458-2048.

To install the downloaded Internet Explorer 6 on your computer, just follow the instructions that appear when you go to the Internet Explorer download page. If you get Internet Explorer 6 on a CD, insert the CD in your CD-ROM drive and follow the instructions that appear on-screen.

The Internet Explorer 6 Setup program asks you several questions before it installs Internet Explorer on your computer. For starters, the Setup program asks whether you want to install all of Internet Explorer or just part of it. You have two choices:

✦ **Typical Set Of Components:** Installs just those parts of Internet Explorer that you'll probably use, in Microsoft's opinion. This is the easiest and fastest way to install Internet Explorer.

✦ **Customize Your Installation:** Lets you pick exactly which parts of Internet Explorer you want to install. Use this option if you're choosey.

If you have plenty of hard drive space on your computer and don't mind a long download (as in several hours long, unless you have a DSL or cable connection), I suggest that you opt for the Customize Your Installation option and then select any of the Internet Explorer components that you think you may need. If you select the typical installation, you can always return to the download page later and pick up the components you didn't install the first time.

If you have a working Internet Connection, you can also upgrade to Internet Explorer 6 by clicking the Start button and then choosing Settings⇨Windows Update. Performing these steps takes you to the Windows Update site, which automatically offers to install new Windows features, including Internet Explorer 6.

Setting Up Your Internet Connection

In the old days, setting up a connection to the Internet was a complicated affair best handled by computer experts with pocket protectors and tape on their glasses. With Internet Explorer 6 and newer versions of Windows, however, configuring your computer to connect to the Internet is a simple, straightforward process. All you have to do is run a special connection wizard that handles all the configuration details for you.

Depending on the version of Windows you are using, the connection wizard is called either the Internet Connection Wizard or the New Connection Wizard. Either wizard will help you get connected to the Internet.

To set up an Internet connection in Windows XP, you use the New Connection Wizard, as described in the following steps:

1. **Gather the information that you need to configure your Internet connection.**

Book VI
Chapter 2

You need the following information, which your Internet service provider should be able to supply:

- The name of your Internet service provider.

- The telephone number you dial to connect to the Internet.

- The name and password you must use to access the system.

- Your IP address, unless an IP address is assigned automatically each time you log on.

- The DNS server address.

- Your e-mail address and the address of your e-mail server.

- The address of your Internet news server.

2. **Fetch your Windows installation disks or CD.**

You may not need these, but the New Connection Wizard sometimes asks for them. Better keep your disks handy just in case.

3. **Start the New Connection Wizard.**

Click the Start button on the taskbar and choose All Programs⇨ Accessories⇨Communications⇨New Connection Wizard. The New Connection Wizard comes to life.

Another way to start the New Connection Wizard is to double-click the Internet Explorer icon on your desktop. If you don't have an Intenet connection already set up, Internet Explorer will automatically start the New Connection Wizard for you.

4. **Click Next.**

The next screen of the New Connection Wizard appears. This screen lists the various types of connections that the New Connection Wizard can help you make.

5. Select the Connect To The Internet option and then click Next.

The New Connection Wizard displays the screen shown in Figure 2-1, which describes three different ways it can help you set up an Internet connection:

- The first option enables you to set up a new Internet connection. Choose this option if you don't already have any type of Internet connection or an account with an Internet service provider. The Internet Connection Wizard uses your modem to dial in to a Microsoft computer that maintains a list of Internet service providers. A list of ISPs in your area appears, and you are granted the privilege of signing up with one of these providers and having your connection configured automatically.

- The second option lets you manually configure your Internet account.

- The third option lets you use a CD that you have obtained from an Internet service provider to set up your connection.

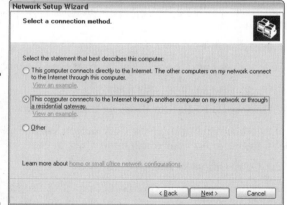

Figure 2-1: The Internet Connection Wizard is ready to set up an Internet connection.

6. Choose the second option (assuming that you already have an Internet account) and then click Next.

The Internet Connection Wizard displays a dialog box asking whether you plan to connect to the Internet via an ISP with a modem and phone line or with a broadband connection.

7. Check the appropriate connection option and then click Next.

Assuming that you're connecting to an ISP via a telephone connection and a modem, the wizard displays a dialog box similar to the one shown in Figure 2-2.

Figure 2-2:
Type a name for your connection.

8. **Type a name for your connection and then click Next.**

A dialog box asking for your ISP's phone number appears.

9. **Type the phone number for your service provider and then click Next.**

The Internet Connection Wizard wants to know your name and password.

10. **Type your name and password and then click Next.**

Your password isn't displayed when you type it, so you don't need to worry about anyone watching over your shoulder. If you click Next, the Internet Connection Wizard displays the dialog box shown in Figure 2-3.

Figure 2-3:
The New Connection Wizard has done its job.

11. **Click Finish.**

You're done with the New Connection Wizard. Now all that's left to do is to tell Outlook Express how to read your e-mail and newsgroups.

12. **Start Outlook Express by clicking the Start button on the Windows taskbar and then choosing E-mail: Outlook Express on the Start menu.**

Outlook Express appears.

13. **Choose the Tools⇨Accounts command.**

Accounts dialog box appears. This dialog box lets you add mail and news accounts to Outlook Express.

14. **Click Add⇨Mail and configure your e-mail account.**

This summons a wizard that asks you for the information needed to set up your e-mail account. When asked, type your e-mail account information, clicking Next to move from one screen to the next and Finish when the wizard reaches its last screen.

15. **Click Add⇨News and configure your news account.**

The wizard appears again, this time asking for information about your news account.

16. **Click Close to dismiss the Accounts dialog box.**

You're done!

Now you can access the Internet by double-clicking the Internet Explorer icon that appears on your desktop. (If you opted to install the Active Desktop option when you installed Internet Explorer, you don't have to double-click the icon; a single click does the trick.) When the Connection Manager dialog box appears, click Connect and start exploring!

Chapter 3: Home Networking with Windows XP

In This Chapter

✔ Using the Windows XP Network Setup Wizard

✔ Manually configuring network settings

✔ Sharing folders and printers

✔ Sharing an Internet connection

✔ Managing your home network

*A*fter you've purchased and installed the hardware for your home network, it's time to configure the software to get your network up and running. In this chapter, you find out how to use the Windows Network Setup Wizard to automatically configure a home network. If you're allergic to wizards, you also discover how to manually configure settings for a home network. Then, you see how to share files, printers, and Internet connections on your network.

Using the Windows XP Network Setup Wizard

Windows Millennium Edition and Windows XP come with a special Network Setup Wizard that is designed to simplify the task of setting up a network for your home or small office. Before you run the Network Setup Wizard, though, you should first install your network hardware:

✦ For a cabled network, you should install a network adapter in any computer that doesn't already have one, and then you should install a hub or switch and connect all the computers to the hub or switch with twisted-pair cable. If you want to share a broadband Internet connection, you should get a cable/DSL router rather than a basic hub or switch.

✦ For a wireless network, install a wireless adapter for each computer. If you want to provide a shared wireless connection, you should also set up a wireless DSL/cable router.

Deciding on computer names

Before you run the wizard, you should decide on the names that you want to use for your computers. In particular:

✦ You need to come up with a unique name for each computer on the network. You can use the name of the person who uses the computer the most or the room where the computer is located, or you can make up random names like Herbie or Gertrude.

Write the name that you want to use for each of your computers here:

Computer 1: _____

Computer 2: _____

Computer 3: _____

Computer 4: _____

Computer 5: _____

✦ You also need to come up with a unique workgroup name for your network. Every computer on the network must specify the name of the workgroup to which it belongs. In order for your computers to talk to each other, they should specify the same workgroup. The default for Windows XP is MSHOME. MSHOME is okay, but Skynet would be more timely.

Write the name that you want to use for your workgroup here:

Workgroup: _____

Running the wizard

The Windows XP Network Setup Wizard gathers information about your network and then automatically configures your computer's network settings. It also can create a diskette that you can use to automatically configure your other computers for the network.

If you're using Windows Millennium Edition, the wizard is called the Home Network Wizard. It is similar, but not identical, to the Windows XP Network Setup Wizard. So expect to deviate just a bit from the following procedure.

Before you begin, get a blank diskette that you can use to create the Network Setup Disk. The wizard prompts you to insert the disk when it's needed.

To run the Network Setup Wizard, just follow these steps:

1. **Open My Network Places from your desktop or the Start menu and then click Set Up A Home Or Small Office Network.**

   Or, if you prefer, you can start the Home Networking Wizard by choosing Start⇨All Programs⇨Accessories⇨Communications⇨Network Setup Wizard. Either way, the Network Setup Wizard comes to life, as shown in Figure 3-1.

Figure 3-1:
The
Network
Setup
Wizard.

2. **Click Next.**

   The Network Setup Wizard displays a screen that lists some things you should do before you start, such as installing network cards in each of the computers that you want to network, connecting cables, and so on.

3. **Click Next.**

   The Network Setup Wizard now asks how your computer is connected to the Internet.

4. **Select the Internet option that you want to use for the computer.**

   Choose the first option if your computer has a direct connection to the Internet and you want to share that connection with other network users. Choose the second option if one of the other computers on your network has an Internet connection you want to use, or if you have a cable or DSL router that connects to the Internet.

   If neither of these options applies, choose Other and click Next. The wizard then displays some additional choices, including an option to not connect to the Internet at all.

5. Click Next.

The wizard asks for a name for the computer.

6. Type a description and name for your computer and then click Next.

Use the name that you wrote down for this computer in the section "Deciding on computer names," earlier in this chapter.

For dramatic effect, take the computer's mouse outside on a starry night, hold it up toward the sky with both hands, and shout the computer's name three times.

When you click Next, the Wizard asks for a name for your network workgroup.

7. Type a name for your network workgroup.

Use the workgroup name that you wrote down in the section "Deciding on computer names," earlier in this chapter.

All the computers on your network should use the same workgroup name. Otherwise, the computers aren't able to access each other.

8. Click Next.

The Network Setup Wizard displays a list of the network settings that it is about to apply. On this screen, the wizard offers to create a network setup disk for you. You'll want to create this disk if your network will include any computers that don't run Windows XP.

9. Click Next.

Your computer grinds and whirs for a few minutes while the wizard adjusts your network settings. After it finishes, the screen shown in Figure 3-2 appears.

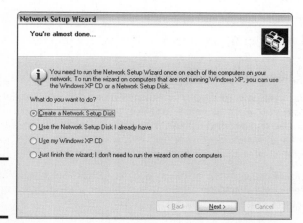

Figure 3-2:
Almost
done. . . .

10. **If all the computers on your network run Windows XP, choose Just Finish The Wizard, click Next, and move on to Step 12.**

    Otherwise, choose Create A Network Setup Disk and click Next.

    The wizard instructs you to insert a blank formatted diskette in your diskette drive.

11. **Insert a blank formatted disk in your diskette drive and click Next.**

    The Home Network Wizard writes a bunch of files to the disk. When it finishes, the wizard displays a final screen, which politely congratulates you on your ingenuity for making it all the way through the wizard's many steps.

12. **Click Finish to end the wizard.**

    The wizard is finished.

13. **Now run the wizard on the other computers in your network.**

    For Windows XP computers, you can just repeat this procedure. For computers that run earlier versions of Windows, insert the disk that you created in Step 10. Then, click the Start button, choose Run, type **a:setup,** and click OK. The Network Setup Wizard magically appears.

If you want to change any of the settings that you made when you ran the wizard, just run the wizard again.

Setting Up a Network without the Wizard

If using wizards is against your religion, don't despair. You can still set up a home network just as good as the one the Network Setup Wizard creates. You just have to trudge your way through the network settings yourself.

Windows automatically detects the presence of a network adapter and configures it for basic networking. However, you may need to manually change the configuration of a network connection. This section shows you how to do that.

Configuring the network connection

To configure a network connection in Windows XP Home Edition, follow these steps:

1. **Click Start➪Control Panel to open the Control Panel.**

    The Control Panel appears.

2. **Double-click the Network Connections icon.**

   The Network Connections folder appears, as shown in Figure 3-3.

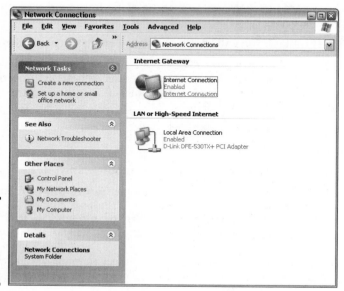

Figure 3-3:
The
Network
Connections
folder.

3. **Right-click the connection that you want to configure and then choose Properties from the menu that appears.**

   The Properties dialog box for the network connection appears, as shown in Figure 3-4.

4. **Make sure that the network items the computer needs are listed in the network connection Properties dialog box.**

   Make sure that at least the following three items are listed in the Properties dialog box:

   - **Client For Microsoft Networks:** This item is required to access a Microsoft Windows network. It should always be present.

   - **File And Printer Sharing For Microsoft Networks:** This item allows your computer to share its files or printers with other computers on the network.

   - **Internet Protocol (TCP/IP):** This item enables the client computer to communicate via the TCP/IP protocol, which allows the computer to access the Internet and other computers on your home network.

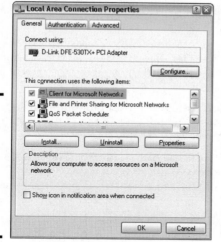

Figure 3-4:
The
Properties
dialog box
for a
network
connection
(Windows
XP).

5. **If you need to add an item, click the Install button and install the missing item.**

When you click the Install button, a dialog box appears, asking whether you want to add a network client, adapter, protocol, or service, as shown in Figure 3-5. Depending on which item you're missing, click Client, Service, or Protocol and then click Add. A list of available networking items appears. Select the item that you want to install and then click OK.

Figure 3-5:
Adding a
protocol.

6. **To configure TCP/IP settings, click Internet Protocol (TCP/IP) and click Properties to display the TCP/IP Properties dialog box; adjust the settings and then click OK.**

This brings up the TCP/IP Properties dialog box, which lets you choose from the following options:

- **Obtain An IP Address Automatically:** Choose this option if your network has a DHCP server that assigns IP addresses automatically. Choosing this option will drastically simplify the task of administering TCP/IP on your network.

- **Use The Following IP Address:** If your computer must have a specific IP address, choose this option and then type the computer's IP address, subnet mask, and default gateway address.

- **Obtain DNS Server Address Automatically:** The DHCP server can also provide the address of the Domain Name System (DNS) server that the computer should use. Choose this option if your network has a DHCP server.

- **Use The Following DNS Server Addresses:** Choose this option if a DHCP server is not available. Then, type the IP address of the primary and secondary DNS servers.

7. Click OK to close the Properties dialog box.

You can now move on to the task of setting up your computer's identification.

Here are a few variations for earlier Windows versions:

✦ To display the Network Properties dialog box in Windows 9*x*, right-click Network Neighborhood on the Desktop and choose Properties. Or, simply open the Control Panel and double-click Network.

✦ After you add a network client, service, or protocol to the Network Properties dialog box in Windows 9*x*, you must bind it to the adapter you want to use it with. To do that, bring up the Properties dialog box for the client, service, or protocol that you want to bind, click the Bindings tab, and add the network adapter you want to bind to.

Identifying your computer

Every computer on a network must have a unique name. In addition, each computer must specify the name of the workgroup to which it belongs. Each computer should specify the same workgroup name.

To set the computer name in Windows XP, follow these steps:

1. Open the Control Panel and double-click the System icon to bring up the System Properties dialog box.

2. Click the Computer Name tab.

The computer identification information is displayed, as shown in Figure 3-6.

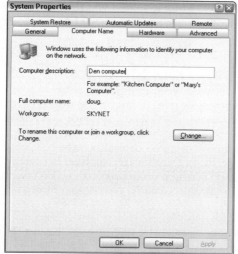

**Book VI
Chapter 3**

**Home Networking
with Windows XP**

Figure 3-6:
The
Computer
Name tab of
the System
Properties
dialog box.

3. **Click the Change button.**

   The Computer Name Changes dialog box appears.

4. **Type the new computer and workgroup names.**

   Remember, each computer on your network should specify the same workgroup name.

5. **Click OK.**

6. **When a dialog box appears, informing you that you need to restart the computer, click OK and then restart the computer.**

   You're done!

The procedure for changing the computer identification on Windows 98 or 95 is similar. Start by right-clicking the Network Places icon on the desktop and choosing Properties. Then, click the Identification tab, type the computer name, description, and workgroup name, and click OK.

Sharing Hard Drive Files

Sharing hard drive files is one of the main reasons for setting up a home network. The following sections describe the basics of hard drive sharing, the benefits of hard drive sharing, how to set up a shared hard drive, and how to access a shared hard drive.

If you've read this entire book start to finish, you probably already know a lot about hard drive sharing. In that case, you can review or even skip these topics.

Understanding hard drive sharing

Before you set up your network, your computer probably had just one hard drive, known as C: drive (maybe two, C: and D:). In any case, these drives are physically located inside your PC. They are your local drives.

Now that you've set up a network, you probably have access to drives that aren't located inside your PC but are located instead in one of the other computers on the network. These network drives can be located on a dedicated server computer or, in the case of a peer-to-peer network, on another client computer.

In some cases, you can access an entire network drive over the network. In most cases, though, you can't access the entire drive. Instead, you can access only certain folders (*directories* in old MS-DOS lingo) on the network drives. Either way, the shared drives or folders are known in Windows terminology as *shared folders*.

Shared folders can be set up with restrictions on how you may use them. For example, you may be granted full access to some shared folders so that you can copy files to or from them, delete files on them, create or remove folders on them, and so on. On other shared folders, your access may be limited in certain ways. For example, you may be able to copy files to or from the shared folder, but not delete files, edit files, or create new folders. You may also be asked to enter a password before you can access a protected folder. The amount of hard drive space that you're allowed to use on a shared folder may also be limited.

Keep in mind that in addition to accessing shared folders that reside on other people's computers, you can also designate your computer as a server to enable other network users to access folders that you share.

Four good uses for a shared folder

After you know which shared network folders are available, you may wonder what you're supposed to do with them. Here are four good uses for a network folder.

✦ **Use it to store files that everybody needs:** A shared network folder is a good place to store files that more than one user needs to access.

Without a network, you have to store a copy of the file on everyone's computer, and you have to worry about keeping the copies synchronized (which you can't do, no matter how hard you try). Or you can keep the file on a disk and pass it around. Or you can keep the file on one computer and play musical chairs — whenever someone needs to use the file, he or she goes to the computer that contains it.

With a network, you can keep one copy of the file in a shared folder on the network, and everyone can access it.

✦ **Use it to store your own files:** You can also use a shared network folder as an extension of your own hard drive storage. For example, if you've filled up all the free space on your hard drive with pictures, sounds, and movies that you've downloaded from the Internet, but Ward's computer has billions and billions of gigabytes of free space, you have all the drive space you need. Just store your files on Ward's computer!

✦ **Use it as a pit stop for files on their way to other users:** "Hey, Wally, could you send me a copy of last month's baseball stats?"

"Sure, Beave." But how? If the baseball stats file resides on Wally's local drive, how does Wally send a copy of the file to Beaver's computer? Wally can do this by copying the file to a network folder. Then Beaver can copy the file to his local hard drive.

Note that most e-mail programs also let you deliver files to other users. This is called "sending a file attachment." The advantage of sending a file via e-mail is that you don't have to worry about details, such as where to leave the file on the server and who's responsible for deleting the file.

✦ **Use it to back up your local hard drive:** If enough drive space is available on the file server, you can use it to store backup copies of the files on your hard drive. Just copy the files that you want to back up to a shared network folder.

Obviously, copying all your data files to the network drive can quickly fill up the network drive. So you have to make sure that the network drive has plenty of spare room.

Designating a shared drive or folder

To enable other network users to access files that reside on your hard drive, you must designate either the entire drive or a folder on the drive as a shared drive or folder. If you share an entire drive, other network users can access all the files and folders on the drive. If you share a folder, network users can access only those files that reside in the folder you share. (If the folder that you share contains other folders, network users can access files in those folders, too.)

I recommend against sharing an entire hard drive, unless you want to grant everyone on the network the freedom to sneak a peek at every file on your hard drive. Instead, you should share just the folder or folders that contain the specific documents that you want others to be able to access. For example, if you store all your Word documents in the My Documents folder, you can share your My Documents folder so that other network users can access your Word documents.

To share a folder on a Windows XP computer, follow these steps:

1. Double-click the My Computer icon on your desktop.

The My Computer window comes to center stage.

2. Select the folder that you want to share.

Click the icon for the drive that contains the folder that you want to share and then find the folder itself and click it.

3. Choose the File⇨Sharing And Security command.

The Properties dialog box for the folder that you want to share appears. Notice that the sharing options are grayed out.

4. Click the Share This Folder On The Network option.

After you click this option, the rest of the sharing options come alive, as shown in Figure 3-7.

If you prefer, you can skip Steps 2 through 4. Instead, just right-click the folder that you want to share and then choose Sharing And Security from the pop-up menu that appears.

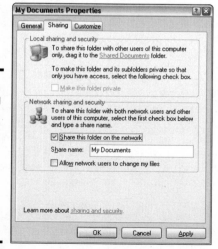

Figure 3-7: The Sharing options come to life when you click the Share This Folder On The Network option.

5. **Change the share name if you don't like the name that Windows proposes.**

   The *share name* is the name that other network users use to access the shared folder. You can use any name you want, but the name can be no more than 12 characters in length. Uppercase and lowercase letters are treated the same in a share name, so the name My Documents is the same as MY DOCUMENTS.

   Windows proposes a share name for you, based on the actual folder name. If the folder name is 12 or fewer characters, the proposed share name is the same as the folder name. If the folder name is longer than 12 characters, then Windows abbreviates it. For example, the name Multimedia Files becomes MULTIMEDIA F.

   If the name that Windows chooses doesn't make sense to you or seems cryptic, you can change the share name to something better. For example, I would probably use MEDIA FILES instead of MULTIMEDIA F.

6. **If you want to allow other network users to change the files in this folder, check the Allow Network Users To Change My Files option.**

   If you leave this option unchecked, other network users will be able to open your files, but they won't be able to save any changes they make.

7. **Click OK.**

   The Properties dialog box vanishes, and a hand is added to the icon for the folder to show that the folder is shared.

If you change your mind and decide that you want to stop sharing a folder, double-click the My Computer icon, select the folder or drive that you want to stop sharing, and choose File⇨Sharing to summon the Properties dialog box. Uncheck the Share This Folder On The Network option and then click OK.

The procedure for sharing folders in previous versions of Windows is similar, but the command is called Sharing instead of Sharing And Security.

Oh, the Network Places You'll Go

Windows enables you to access network resources, such as shared folders, by opening the My Network Places icon that resides on your desktop. When you first open My Network Places, you're greeted by icons that represent the shared resources that you can access from your computer, as shown in Figure 3-8.

**Book VI
Chapter 3**

**Home Networking
with Windows XP**

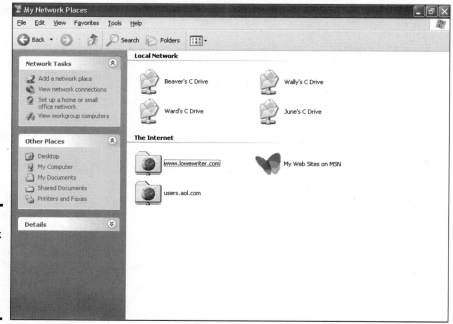

Figure 3-8:
My Network Places lists the shared resources on your network.

As you can see from Figure 3-8, each of the four computers on the network has been set up as a shared drive. You can open any of these shared drives and access the files that they contain as if they were on your local computer.

You can summon a list of all the computers that are available on your network by clicking View Workgroup Computers in the Network Tasks section of the My Network Places window. This action displays an icon for each computer on your network.

You can also access My Network Places from any Windows application program. For example, suppose that you're working with Microsoft Word and want to open a document file that has been stored in a shared folder on your network. All you have to do is choose File⇨Open to bring up the Open dialog box. Near the top of the Open dialog box is a list box labeled *Look In*. From this list, choose the My Network Places icon to display a list of shared network resources that you can access, as shown in Figure 3-9. Then, locate the document file that you want to open on the network.

If you're using Windows 95 or 98, My Network Places is referred to as the Network Neighborhood. When you call up the Network Neighborhood in Windows 95 or 98, you're immediately greeted by a list of the computers available on your network. You can then click one of the computers to access its shared drives and folders.

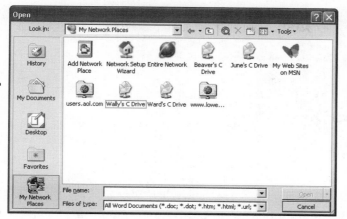

Figure 3-9:
You can access My Network Places from any Windows program.

Mapping network drives

If you find yourself accessing a particular shared folder frequently, you may want to use a special trick called *mapping* to access the shared folder more efficiently. Mapping assigns a drive letter to a shared folder. Then you can use the drive letter to access the shared folder as if it were a local drive. In this way, you can access the shared folder from any Windows program without having to navigate through the Network Neighborhood.

For example, you can map a shared folder named \Wal's Files to drive G: on your computer. Then, to access files stored in the shared \Wal's Files folder, you would look on drive G:. You'll be able to access drive G: from My Computer, as if drive G: were a local drive.

To map a shared folder to a drive letter, follow these steps:

1. **Use the Network Neighborhood to locate the shared folder that you want to map to a drive.**

2. **Right-click the shared folder and then choose the Map Network Drive command from the pop-up menu that appears.**

 This action summons the Map Network Drive dialog box, shown in Figure 3-10.

3. **Change the drive letter in the Drive drop-down list if you want to.**

 You probably don't have to change the drive letter that Windows selects (in Figure 3-10, drive Y:). If you're picky, you can select the drive letter from the Drive drop-down list.

4. **If you want this network drive to be automatically mapped each time you log on to the network, check the Reconnect At Logon option.**

   If you leave the Reconnect At Logon option unchecked, the drive letter is available only until you shut Windows down or log off the network. If you check this option, the network drive automatically reconnects each time you log on to the network.

   Be sure to check the Reconnect At Logon option if you use the network drive often.

5. **Click OK.**

   That's it! You're done.

Here are a few points to ponder as you lay awake tonight thinking about network drive mapping:

✦ Assigning a drive letter to a network drive is called *mapping the drive,* or *linking the drive,* as network nerds call it. "Drive H: is mapped to a network drive," they say.

✦ Network drive letters don't have to be assigned the same way for every computer on the network. For example, a shared folder that is assigned drive letter H: on your computer may be assigned drive letter Q: on someone else's computer. In that case, your drive H: and the other computer's drive Q: are really the same shared folder. This can be very confusing. So when you set up your drive mappings, try to use the same drive letters on everyone's computer.

✦ Accessing a shared network folder through a mapped network drive is much faster than accessing the same folder via the My Network Places. That's because Windows has to browse the entire network in order to list all available computers whenever you open the My Network Places window. In contrast, Windows doesn't have to browse the network at all in order to access a mapped network drive.

✦ If you choose the Reconnect At Logon option for a mapped drive, you receive a warning message if the drive is not available when you log on. In most cases, the problem is that the server computer isn't turned on. Sometimes, however, this message is caused by a broken network connection.

Sharing a Printer

Sharing a printer is much more traumatic than sharing a hard drive. When you share a hard drive, other network users access your files from time to time. When they do, you hear your drive click a few times, and your computer may hesitate for a half-second or so. The interruptions caused by other users accessing your drive are sometimes noticeable, but rarely annoying.

When you share a printer, however, your coworker down the hall is liable to send a 40-page report to your printer just moments before you try to print a 1-page memo that has to be on the boss's desk in two minutes. The printer may run out of paper or, worse yet, it may jam during someone else's print job — and you'll be expected to attend to the problem.

Although these interruptions can be annoying, sharing your printer makes a lot of sense in some situations. If you have the only decent printer in your office or workgroup, your coworkers will be bugging you to let them use it anyway. You may as well share the printer on the network. At least this way, they won't be lining up at your door asking you to print their documents for them.

Designating a shared printer

The following procedure shows you how to share a printer in Windows:

1. **From the Start menu, choose Control Panels and then choose Printers And Faxes.**

The Printers And Faxes folder appears.

2. **Select the printer that you want to share.**

Click the icon for the printer to select the printer.

3. **Choose File⇨Sharing.**

You're right: This doesn't make sense. You're sharing a printer — not a file — but the Sharing command is found under the File menu. Go figure.

When you choose File⇨Sharing, the Properties dialog box for the printer appears.

4. Click the Share This Printer option.

Figure 3-11 shows the Printer Properties dialog box that appears after you click the Shared As option.

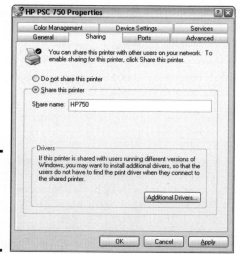

Figure 3-11:
The
Properties
dialog box
for a shared
printer.

5. Change the Share Name if you don't like the name suggested by Windows.

Other computers use the share name to identify the shared printer, so choose a meaningful or descriptive name.

6. Click OK.

You return to the Printers folder, where a hand is added to the printer icon to show that the printer is now a shared network printer.

To take your shared printer off the network so that other network users can't access it, follow the preceding procedure through Step 3 to call up the Printer Properties dialog box. Check Do Not Share This Printer and then click OK. The hand disappears from the printer icon to indicate that the printer is no longer shared.

Adding a network printer

Now that you've shared one of your computer's printers, you have to set up your other computers so that they have access to the shared printer. To do that, open the Control Panel and choose Printers And Faxes. Then click the

Add A Printer link in the Printer Tasks taskbar. This starts the Add Printer Wizard. When the wizard asks whether you want to add a local or a network printer, choose network. Then, when the wizard asks you to specify a printer, choose the Browse option and click Next. A dialog box similar to the one shown in Figure 3-12 appears, showing the computers and shared resources available in My Network Places.

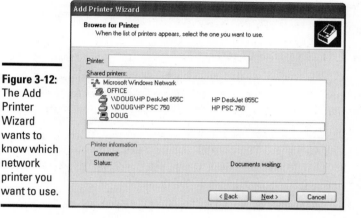

Figure 3-12: The Add Printer Wizard wants to know which network printer you want to use.

Sniff around in this dialog box until you find the printer that you want to use from your computer. Click this printer and then click OK to return to the Add Printer Wizard.

Next, the wizard copies the correct printer driver for the network printer to your computer. Depending on the operating system that your computer uses and the Windows version that you use, you may be asked to insert your Windows CD-ROM so that Windows can locate the driver files, or you may have to insert the driver disk that came with the printer. In many cases, however, Windows copies the driver files directly from the server computer to which the printer is attached, so you won't have to bother with the Windows CD or the printer's driver disks.

Finally, the Add Printer Wizard asks whether you want to designate the printer as your default printer. Check Yes if this is the printer you will use most of the time. If you have a local printer that you use most of the time and are just creating a connection to a network printer that you will use only on special occasions, check No. Then click Next to continue and finish the wizard.

Using a network printer

After you have installed the network printer in Windows, printing to the network printer is a snap. You can print to the network printer from any Windows program by using the File⇨Print command to summon the Print dialog box. Near the top of this dialog box is a drop-down list titled Name, which lists all the printers that are installed on your computer. Choose the network printer from this list and then click OK to print your document. That's all there is to it!

Sharing an Internet Connection

One of the main reasons for setting up a home network is to share an Internet connection. One way to do that is to use a Windows feature known as ICS, which stands for *Internet connection sharing*. ICS comes with all versions of Windows since Windows 98 Second Edition. With ICS, only one computer, known as the *gateway computer*, has a direct connection to the Internet, such as a dialup modem connection or a DSL connection. The other computers on your network connect to the Internet through the gateway computer.

Here are some key points to know about Internet connection sharing:

✦ ICS uses a technique called *network address translation*, or *NAT*, to fool the Internet into thinking that your entire network is really just one computer with a single IP address. Whenever one of the computers on your network requests information from the Internet, ICS replaces that computer's IP address with the gateway computer's IP address before sending the request to the Internet. Then, when the requested information returns from the Internet, ICS figures out which computer on your network actually requested the information and sends the information to the correct computer. In this way, all interaction with the Internet is funneled through the gateway computer.

✦ ICS allows several network users to share an Internet connection simultaneously. As a result, multiple users can browse the Web, read their e-mail, or play online games all at the same time.

✦ Unfortunately, ICS can share only one Internet connection. If your network is large enough that a single Internet connection — even a high-speed cable or DSL connection — is not enough to satisfy your users' Internet demands, you have to use the more advanced communication features of a Windows or NetWare server instead of ICS.

✦ The gateway computer must be on before other computers can connect to the Internet through ICS.

✦ Windows XP simplifies the task of setting up Internet connection sharing by configuring it automatically for you when you run the Network Setup Wizard. So if you've run the Network Configuration Wizard, you don't have to take any extra steps to configure ICS.

To activate Internet connection sharing, follow this procedure on the computer that has the Internet connection that you want to share:

1. Choose Start⇨Control Panel.

The Control Panel appears.

2. Click the Network Connections link.

If Control Panel appears in Classic view rather than Category view, you won't see a Network Connections link. Instead, just double-click the Network Connections icon.

3. Double-click the Local Area Connection icon.

A dialog box appears, showing the connection's status.

4. Click the Properties button.

The Connection Properties dialog box appears.

5. Click the Advanced Tab and then check the Allow Other Network Users To Connect Through This Computer's Internet Connection check box.

This option enables Internet connection sharing.

6. Click OK.

You're done!

After you've enabled Internet connection sharing for the computer that actually hosts the Internet connection, you can then configure the other computers on your network to access the shared Internet connection. To do that, first make sure that each client computer has TCP/IP installed properly and is configured to obtain its IP address from DHCP. Then, run the Internet Connection Wizard on each computer. When asked, choose the Set Up My Connection Manually option and then choose the Connect To A Broadband Connection That Is Always On option. That should do it! (For more information about the Internet Connection Wizard, refer to Chapter 2 of this book.)

Internet Connection Sharing dynamically assigns IP addresses to the computers that use the shared Internet connection. These addresses are assigned from the subnet 192.168.0.0, subnet mask 255.255.255.0.

Setting up a firewall

A *firewall* is a security-conscious router that sits between the outside world and your network in an effort to prevent *them* from getting to *you*. The firewall acts as a security guard between the Internet and your LAN. All network traffic into and out of the LAN must pass through the firewall, which prevents unauthorized users from accessing the LAN.

Some type of firewall is a must if you host a Web site on a server computer that's connected to your LAN. Without a firewall, anyone who visits your Web site can potentially break into your LAN and steal your top-secret files, read your private e-mail, or — worse yet — reformat your hard drive.

Firewalls can also work the other way, preventing your network users from accessing Internet sites that you designate as off-limits.

You can set up a firewall in several ways. One is to purchase a hardware firewall, which is basically a router with built-in firewall features. Most hardware firewalls include a Web-based management program that enables you to connect to the firewall from any computer on your network by using a Web browser. You can then customize the firewall settings to suit your needs. For more information, see the section "Using a broadband router," later in this chapter.

If you are sharing an Internet connection via a Windows XP computer, you already have a built-in firewall. All you have to do is turn it on. Just follow these steps:

1. **Choose Start➪Control Panel.**

   The Control Panel appears.

2. **Click the Network Connections link.**

   If Control Panel appears in Classic view rather than Category view, you won't see a Network Connections link. Instead, just double-click the Network Connections icon.

3. **Double-click the Local Area Connection icon.**

   A dialog box appears, showing the connection's status.

4. **Click the Properties button.**

   The Connection Properties dialog box appears.

5. **Click the Advanced Tab and then check the Protect My Computer option.**

   This option enables the firewall.

6. **Click OK.**

That's all there is to it.

If you use a broadband router with a built-in firewall, do *not* activate the Windows firewall. At best, it will needlessly duplicate the work of the router. At worst, it will block all network access to the computer, so other users won't be able to access your shared folders or printers.

Using a broadband router

The best way to share an Internet connection on a home network is to purchase a broadband router. This is a small device (about the size of a clock radio) that automatically handles the task of sharing your Internet connection. When you use a broadband router, you don't have to configure one of your network's computers to share the Internet connection.

Most broadband routers will work with either cable Internet or DSL. Most also double as a small Ethernet hub or switch (typically offering four ports), and some even do triple duty as a wireless access point for a wireless network.

For example, Linksys makes a product called the EtherFast Cable/DSL Router, which you can purchase for under $100. As its name suggests, the EtherFast Cable/DSL Router includes a router that creates a link between your LAN and a cable or DSL modem. In addition, the EtherFast Cable/DSL Router provides a four-port 10/100Mbps Ethernet switch, which enables you to connect four computers (or more if you cascade additional hubs or switches).

The EtherFast Cable/DSL Router provides network address translation, so that anyone on the LAN can access the Internet through the cable or DSL connection and also acts as a firewall by preventing unauthorized users from accessing your LAN via the Internet connection.

Managing Your Home Network

After you network the computers in your home, you — or whoever is the most computer-savvy in your household — must become the home network manager. Unfortunately, all the concerns that arise when using a network in a business situation apply to home networks as well. In particular, the following list highlights some of the things to stay on top of regarding your home network:

✦ **Make sure that everyone knows how to access the network and use the shared drives and printers.** Hold a family meeting to go over the do's and don'ts of the network.

✦ **Think about whether you really want to grant full access to everyone's documents over the network.** What if your teenager gets mad at you because you won't let him borrow the car, so he decides to delete a bunch of your important files from the privacy of his bedroom? Maybe you should think about security — giving each user a user ID and password and then password-protecting folders that contain private information.

✦ **Make sure that everyone knows that the task of backing up is his or her own responsibility.** Don't let your kid blame you when he or she loses a 30-page term paper because of the "stupid network." The epitome of parenting for the new millennium may be to add "backing up the network" to the kids' list of Saturday chores, right after mowing the lawn and cleaning the bathrooms.

✦ **Keep an eye on disk space.** With the whole family using the network, you may be amazed at how quickly the gigabytes fill up.

Chapter 4: Setting Up a Wireless Network

In This Chapter

✔ Looking at wireless network standards

✔ Reviewing some basic radio terms

✔ Considering infrastructure and ad-hoc networks

✔ Working with a wireless access point

✔ Configuring Windows for wireless networking

Since the beginning of Ethernet networking, cable has been getting smaller and easier to work with. The original Ethernet cable was about as thick as your thumb, weighed a ton, and was difficult to bend around tight corners. Then came coaxial cable, which was lighter and easier to work with. Coaxial cable was supplanted by unshielded twisted-pair (UTP) cable, which is the cable used for most networks today. Coaxial and UTP cable is still *cable,* though, which means that you have to drill holes and pull cable through walls and ceilings in order to wire your entire home or office.

That's why wireless networking has become so popular. With wireless networking, you don't need cables to connect your computers. Instead, wireless networks use radio waves to send and receive network signals. As a result, a computer can connect to a wireless network at any location in your home or office.

Wireless networks are especially useful for notebook computers. After all, the main benefit of a notebook computer is that you can carry it around with you wherever you go. At work, you can use your notebook computer at your desk, in the conference room, in the break room, or even out in the parking lot. At home, you can use it in the bedroom, kitchen, den, game room, or out by the pool. With wireless networking, your notebook computer can be connected to the network, no matter where you take it.

This chapter introduces you to the ins and outs of setting up a wireless network. I tell you what you need to know about wireless networking standards, how to plan a wireless network, how to install and configure wireless network components, and how to create a network that mixes both wireless and cabled components.

Diving into Wireless Networking

A *wireless network* is a network that uses radio signals rather than direct cable connections to exchange information. A computer with a wireless network connection is like a cell phone. Just as you don't have to be connected to a phone line to use a cell phone, you don't have to be connected to a network cable to use a wireless networked computer.

The following paragraphs summarize some of the key concepts and terms that you need to understand in order to set up and use a basic wireless network:

✦ A wireless network is often referred to as a *WLAN*, for *wireless local area network*. Some people prefer to switch the acronym around to *local area wireless network*, or *LAWN*. The term *Wi-Fi* is often used to describe wireless networks, although it technically refers to just one form of wireless networks: the 802.11b standard. (See the section "Eight-Oh-Two-Dot-Eleventy Something?," later in this chapter, for more information.)

✦ A wireless network has a name, known as a *SSID*. SSID stands for *service set identifier* — wouldn't that make a great *Jeopardy!* question? (I'll take obscure four-letter acronyms for $400, please!) Each of the computers that belong to a single wireless network must have the same SSID.

✦ Wireless networks can transmit over any of several channels. In order for computers to talk to each other, they must be configured to transmit on the same channel.

✦ The simplest type of wireless network consists of two or more computers with wireless network adapters. This type of network is called an *ad-hoc mode network*.

✦ A more complex type of network is an *infrastructure mode network*. All this really means is that a group of wireless computers can be connected not only to each other, but also to an existing cabled network via a device called a *wireless access point,* or WAP. (I tell you more about ad-hoc and infrastructure networks later in this chapter.)

A Little High School Electronics

I was a real nerd in high school: I took three years of electronics. The electronics class at my school was right next door to the auto shop. Of course, all the cool kids took auto shop and only nerds like me took electronics. We hung in there, though, and learned all about capacitors and diodes while the cool kids were learning how to raise their cars and install 2 Gigawatt stereo systems.

It turns out that a little of that high school electronics information proves useful when it comes to wireless networking. Not much, mind you. But you'll understand wireless networking much better if you know the meanings of some basic radio terms.

Waves and frequencies

For starters, *radio* consists of electromagnetic waves that are sent through the atmosphere. You can't see or hear them, but radio receivers can pick them up and convert them into sounds, images, or — in the case of wireless networks — data.

Radio waves are actually cyclical waves of electromagnetic energy that repeat at a particular rate, called the *frequency*. Figure 4-1 shows two frequencies of radio waves: the first is one cycle per second; the second is two cycles per second. (Real radio doesn't operate at that low of a frequency, but I figured one and two cycles per second would be easier to draw than 680,000 cycles per second or 2.4 million cycles per second.)

The measure of a frequency is *cycles per second,* which indicates how many complete cycles the wave makes in one second (duh). In honor of Heinrich Hertz, the first person to successfully send and receive radio waves (it happened in the 1880s), *cycles per second* is usually referred to as *Hertz,* abbreviated Hz. Thus, 1 Hz is one cycle per second. Incidentally, when the prefix *K* (for Kilo, or 1,000), *M* (for Mega, 1 million), or *G* (for Giga, 1 billion) is added to the front of Hz, the *H* is still capitalized. Thus, 2.4MHz is correct (not 2.4Mhz).

The beauty of radio frequencies is that transmitters can be tuned to broadcast radio waves at a precise frequency. Likewise, receivers can be tuned to receive radio waves at a precise frequency, ignoring waves at other frequencies. That's why you can tune the radio in your car to listen to dozens of different radio stations: Each station broadcasts at its own frequency.

Wavelength and antennas

A term related to frequency is *wavelength*. Radio waves travel at the speed of light. The term *wavelength* refers to how far the radio signal travels with each cycle. For example, since the speed of light is roughly 300,000,000 meters per second, the wavelength of a 1Hz radio wave is about 300,000,000 meters. The wavelength of a 2Hz signal is about 150,000,000 meters.

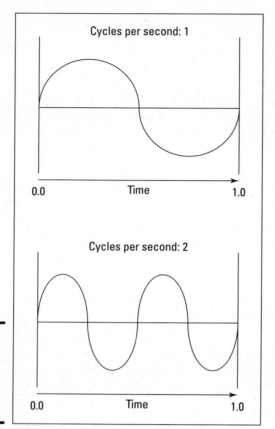

Figure 4-1:
Radio
waves
frequently
have
frequency.

As you can see, the wavelength decreases as the frequency increases. The wavelength of a typical AM radio station broadcasting at 580KHz is about 500 meters. For a TV station broadcasting at 100MHz, it's about 3 meters. For a wireless network broadcasting at 2.4GHz, the wavelength is about 12 centimeters.

It turns out that the shorter the wavelength, the smaller the antenna needs to be in order to adequately receive the signal. As a result, higher frequency transmissions need smaller antennas. You may have noticed that AM radio stations usually have huge antennas mounted on top of tall towers, but cell phone transmitters are much smaller and their towers aren't nearly as tall. That's because cell phones operate on a higher frequency than do AM radio stations. So who decides what type of radio gets to use specific frequencies? That's where spectrums and the FCC come in.

Spectrums and the FCC

The term *spectrum* refers to a continuous range of frequencies on which radio can operate. In the United States, the Federal Communications Commission (FCC) regulates how various portions of the radio spectrum can be used. Essentially, the FCC has divided the radio spectrum into dozens of small ranges called *bands* and restricted certain uses to certain bands. For example, AM radio operates in the band from 535KHz to 1,700KHz.

Table 4-1 lists some of the most popular bands. Note that some of these bands are wide — for example, UHF television begins at 470MHz and ends at 806MHz, but other bands are restricted to a specific frequency. The difference between the lowest and highest frequency within a band is called the *bandwidth*.

Table 4-1	Popular Bands of the Radio Spectrum
Band	*Use*
535KHz – 1,700KHz	AM radio
5.9MHz – 26.1MHz	Short wave radio
26.96MHz – 27.41MHz	Citizens Band (CB) radio
54MHz – 88MHz	Television (VHF channels 2 through 6)
88MHz – 108MHz	FM radio
174MHz – 220MHz	Television (VHF channels 7 through 13)
470MHz – 806MHz	Television (UHF channels)
806MHz – 890MHz	Cellular networks
900MHz	Cordless phones
1850MHz – 1990MHz	PCS Cellular
2.4GHz – 2.4835GHz	Cordless phones and wireless networks (802.11b and 802.11g)
4GHz – 5GHz	Large dish satellite TV
5GHz	Wireless networks (802.11a)
11.7GHz – 12.7GHz	Small disk satellite TV

Two of the bands in the spectrum are allocated for use by wireless networks: 2.4GHz and 5GHz. Note that these bands aren't devoted exclusively to wireless networks. In particular, the 2.4GHz band shares its space with cordless phones. As a result, cordless phones can sometimes interfere with wireless networks.

And now a word from the irony department

I was an English literature major in college, so I like to use literary devices such as irony. Of course, irony doesn't come up much in computer books. So when it does, I like to jump on it like a hog out of the water.

So here's my juicy bit of irony for today: The very first Ethernet system was actually a wireless network. Ethernet traces its roots back to a network developed at the University of Hawaii in 1970, called the Alohanet. This network transmitted its data by using small radios. If two computers tried to broadcast data at the same time, the computers detected the collision and tried again after a short, random delay. This technique was the inspiration for the basic technique of Ethernet, now called *carrier sense multiple access with collision detection,* or CSMA/CD. The wireless Alohanet was the network that inspired Robert Metcalfe to develop his cabled network, which he called *Ethernet,* as his doctoral thesis at Harvard in 1973.

For the next 20 years or so, Ethernet was pretty much a cable-only network. It wasn't until the mid-1990s that Ethernet finally returned to its wireless roots.

Eight-Oh-Two-Dot-Eleventy Something? (Or, Understanding Wireless Standards)

The most popular standards for wireless networks are the IEEE 802.11 standards. These standards are essential wireless Ethernet standards and use many of the same networking techniques that the cabled Ethernet standards (in other words, 802.3) use. Most notably, 802.11 networks use the same CSMA/CD technique as cabled Ethernet to recover from network collisions.

The 802.11 standards address the bottom two layers of the IEEE seven-layer model: The Physical layer and the Media Access Control (MAC) layer. Note that TCP/IP protocols apply to higher layers of the model. As a result, TCP/IP runs just fine on 802.11 networks.

The original 802.11 standard was adopted in 1997. Two additions to the standard, 802.11a and 802.11b, were adopted in 1999. At the time of this writing, an additional extension to the standard called 802.11g was on the verge of being adopted.

Table 4-2 summarizes the basic characteristics of the three variants of 802.11.

Table 4-2		802.11 Variations	
Standard	*Speeds*	*Frequency*	*Typical Range (Indoors)*
802.11a	Up to 54Mbps	5GHz	150 feet
802.11b	Up to 11Mbps	2.4GHz	300 feet
802.11g	Up to 54Mbps	2.4GHz	300 feet

Currently, most wireless networks are based on the 802.11b standard. Although 802.11a is faster than 802.11b, it is considerably more expensive and has less range. In addition, 802.11a and 802.11b aren't compatible with each other because 802.11a transmits at 5GHz and 802.11b transmits at 2.4GHz. As a result, 802.11a and 802.11b devices can't receive each other's signals.

The new standard, 802.11g, solves this problem by enabling high-speed connections at 2.4GHz. As a result, 802.11g devices are compatible with existing 802.11b networks.

802.11b networks operate on the same radio frequency as many cordless phones: 2.4GMHz. If you set up an 802.11b network in your home and you also have a 2.4GHz cordless phone, you may find that the network and phone occasionally interfere with each other. The only way to completely avoid the interference is to switch to a 900MHz phone or use more expensive 802.11a network components, which transmit at 5GHz rather than 2.4GHz.

Home on the Range

The maximum range of an 802.11b wireless device indoors is about 300 feet. This can have an interesting effect when you get a bunch of wireless computers together — such that some of them are in range of each other, but others are not. For example, suppose that Wally, Ward, and the Beaver all have wireless notebooks. Wally's computer is 200 feet away from Ward's computer, and Ward's computer is 200 feet away from Beaver's in the opposite direction (see Figure 4-2). In this case, Ward is able to access both Wally's computer and Beaver's computer, but Wally can access only Ward's computer, and Beaver can access only Ward's computer. In other words, Wally and Beaver won't be able to access each other's computers, because they're outside of the 300-feet range limit. (This is starting to sound suspiciously like an algebra problem. Now suppose that Wally starts walking toward Ward at 2 miles per hour, and Beaver starts running toward Ward at 4 miles per hour . . .)

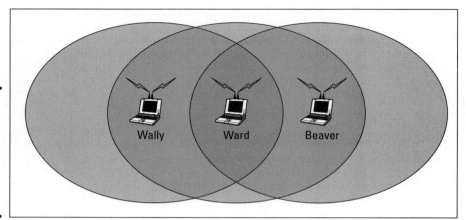

Figure 4-2:
Ward,
Wally, and
the Beaver
playing with
their
wireless
network.

Although the normal range for 802.11b is 300 feet, the range may be less in actual practice. Obstacles such as solid walls, bad weather, cordless phones, microwave ovens, backyard nuclear reactors, and so on can all conspire together to reduce the effective range of a wireless adapter. If you're having trouble connecting to the network, sometimes just adjusting the antenna helps.

Also, wireless networks tend to slow down when the distance increases. 802.11b network devices claim to operate at 11Mbps, but they usually achieve that speed only at ranges of 100 feet or less. At 300 feet, they often slow down to 1Mbps. You should also realize that when you're at the edge of the wireless device's range, you're more likely to suddenly lose your connection due to bad weather.

Wireless Network Adapters

Each computer that will connect to your wireless network needs a *wireless network adapter*. The wireless network adapter is similar to the network interface card (NIC) that is used for a standard Ethernet connection. However, instead of having a cable connector on the back, a wireless network adapter has an antenna.

You can get several basic types of wireless network adapters, depending on your needs and the type of computer you will use it with:

✦ A wireless PCI card is a wireless network adapter that you install into an available slot inside a desktop computer. In order to install this type of card, you need to take your computer apart. So use this type of card only if you have the expertise and the nerves to dig into your computer's guts.

✦ A wireless USB adapter is a separate box that plugs into a USB port on your computer. Because the USB adapter is a separate device, it takes up extra desk space. However, you can install it without taking your computer apart.

✦ A wireless PC card is designed to slide into the PC card slot found in most notebook computers. This is the type of card to get if you want to network your notebook.

You can purchase an 802.11b wireless PCI adapter for about $50. USB 802.11b adapters cost about $60, as do PC card 802.11 adapters for notebooks. You can expect to pay about $25 more for an equivalent 802.11g adapter.

**Book VI
Chapter 4**

**Setting Up a
Wireless Network**

TIP

At first, you may think that wireless network adapters are prohibitively expensive. After all, you can buy a regular Ethernet adapter for as little as $20. However, when you consider that you don't have to purchase and install cable to use a wireless adapter, the price of wireless networking becomes more palatable.

Figure 4-3 shows a typical wireless network adapter. This one is a Linksys WUSB11, which sells for about $60. To install this device, you simply connect it to one of your computer's USB ports with the included USB connector. You then install the driver software that comes on the CD, and you're ready to network. The device is relatively small. You'll find a little strip of Velcro on the back, which you can use to mount it on the side of your computer or desk if you want. The adapter gets its power from the USB port itself, so there's no separate power cord to plug in.

Wireless Access Points

Unlike cabled networks, wireless networks don't need a hub or switch. If all you want to do is network a group of wireless computers, you just purchase a wireless adapter for each computer, put them all within 300 feet of each other, and *voilà!* — instant network.

But what if you already have an existing cabled network? For example, suppose that you work at an office with 15 computers all cabled up nicely, and you just want to add a couple of wireless notebook computers to the network. Or suppose that you have two computers in your den connected to each other with network cable, but you want to link up a computer in your bedroom without pulling cable through the attic.

Figure 4-3:
A Linksys
WUSB11
USB 802.11b
Wireless
networking
adapter.

That's where a *wireless access point,* also known as a *WAP,* comes in. A WAP actually performs two functions. First, it acts as a central connection point for all your computers that have wireless network adapters. In effect, the WAP performs essentially the same function as a hub or switch performs for a wired network.

Second, the WAP links your wireless network to your existing wired network so that your wired computer and your wireless computers get along like one big happy family. Sounds like the makings of a Dr. Seuss story. ("Now the wireless sneeches had hubs without wires. But the twisted-pair sneeches had cables to thires. . . .")

Wireless access points are sometimes just called *access points,* or *APs.* An access point is a box that has an antenna (or often a pair of antennae) and an RJ-45 Ethernet port. You just plug the access point into a network cable and then plug the other end of the cable into a hub or switch, and your wireless network should be able to connect to your cabled network.

Figure 4-4 shows how an access point acts as a central connection point for wireless computers and how it bridges your wireless network to your wired network.

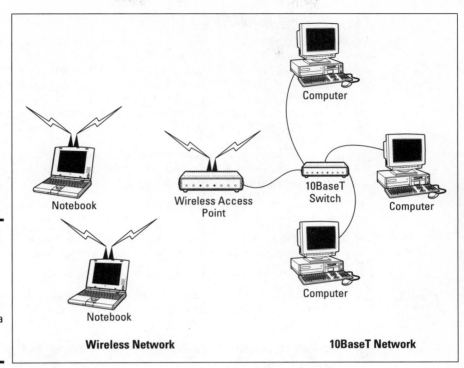

Figure 4-4:
A wireless
access
point
connects a
wireless
network to a
cabled
network.

Infrastructure mode

When you set up a wireless network with an access point, you are creating an *infrastructure mode* network. It's called *infrastructure mode* because the access point provides a permanent infrastructure for the network. The access points are installed at fixed physical locations, so the network has relatively stable boundaries. Whenever a mobile computer wanders into the range of one of the access points, it has come into the sphere of the network and can connect.

An access point and all the wireless computers that are connected to it are referred to as a *Basic Service Set,* or *BSS*. Each BSS is identified by a *Service Set Identifier,* or *SSID*. When you configure an access point, you specify the SSID that you want to use. The SSID is often a generic name such as *wireless,* or it can be a name that you create. Some access points use the MAC address of the WAP as the SSID.

Multifunction WAPs

Wireless access points often include other built-in features. For example, some access points double as Ethernet hubs or switches. In that case, the access point will have more than one RJ-45 port. In addition, some access points include broadband cable or DSL firewall routers that enable you to connect to the Internet. For example, Figure 4-5 shows a Linksys BEFW11S4 wireless access point router. I have one of these little guys in my home. This inexpensive (about $80) device includes the following features:

✦ An 802.11b wireless access point that lets me connect a notebook computer and a computer located on the other side of the house because I didn't want to run cable through the attic.

✦ A four-port 10/100MHz switch that I can connect up to four computers to via twisted-pair cable.

✦ A DSL/cable router that I connect to my cable modem. This enables all the computers on the network (cabled and wireless) to access the Internet.

A multifunction access point that's designed to serve as an Internet gateway for home networks is sometimes called a *residential gateway*.

Figure 4-5:
A Linksys
BEFW11S4
wireless
access
point router.

Roaming

You can use two or more wireless access points to create a large wireless network in which computer users can roam from area to area and still be connected to the wireless network. As the user moves out of the range of one access point, another access point automatically picks up the user and takes over without interrupting the user's network service.

To set up two or more access points for roaming, you must carefully place the WAPs so that all areas of the office or building that are being networked are in range of at least one of the WAPs. Then, just make sure that all the computers and access points use the same SSID and channel.

Two or more access points joined for the purposes of roaming, along with all the wireless computers connected to any of the access points, form what's called an *Extended Service Set,* or *ESS*. The access points in the ESS are usually connected to a wired network.

One of the current limitations of roaming is that each access point in an ESS must be on the same TCP/IP subnet. That way, a computer that roams from one access point to another within the ESS retains the same IP address. If the access points had a different subnet, a roaming computer would have to change IP addresses when it moved from one access point to another.

Wireless bridging

Another use for wireless access points is to bridge separate subnets that can't easily be connected by cable. For example, suppose that you have two office buildings that are only about 50 feet apart. To run cable from one building to the other, you'd have to bury conduit — a potentially expensive job. Because the buildings are so close, though, you can probably connect them with a pair of wireless access points that function as a *wireless bridge* between the two networks. Connect one of the access points to the first network and the other access point to the second network. Then, configure both access points to use the same SSID and channel.

Ad-hoc networks

A wireless access point is not necessary to set up a wireless network. Any time two or more wireless devices come within range of each other, they can link up to form an *ad-hoc network*. For example, if you and a few of your friends all have notebook computers with 802.11b wireless network adapters, you can meet anywhere and form an ad-hoc network.

All of the computers within range of each other in an ad-hoc network are called an *Independent Basic Service Set*, or *IBSS*.

Configuring a Wireless Access Point

The physical setup for a wireless access point is pretty simple: You take it out of the box, put it on a shelf or on top of a bookcase near a network jack and a power outlet, plug in the power cable, and plug in the network cable.

The software configuration for an access point is a little more involved, but still not very complicated. It's usually done via a Web interface. To get to the configuration page for the access point, you need to know the access point's IP address. Then, you just type that address into the address bar of a browser from any computer on the network.

Multifunction access points usually provide DHCP and NAT services for the networks and double as the network's gateway router. As a result, they typically have a private IP address that's at the beginning of one of the Internet's private IP address ranges, such as 192.168.0.1 or 10.0.0.1. Consult the documentation that came with the access point to find out more.

If you use a multifunction access point that is both your wireless access point and your Internet router and you can't remember the IP address, run the IPCONFIG command at a command prompt from any computer on the network. The Default Gateway IP address should be the IP address of the access point.

Basic configuration options

Figure 4-6 shows the main configuration screen for a Linksys BEFW11S4 wireless access point router that was pictured in Figure 4-5. I called up this configuration page by entering 192.168.1.1 in the address bar of a Web browser and then supplying the login password when prompted.

This configuration page offers the following configuration options that are related to the wireless access point functions of the device. Although these options are specific to this particular device, most access points have similar configuration options.

✦ **Enable/Disable:** Enables or disables the device's wireless access point functions.

✦ **SSID:** The Service Set Identifier used to identify the network. Most access points have well-known defaults. You can talk yourself into thinking that your network is more secure by changing the SSID from the default to something more obscure, but in reality, that only protects you from first-grade hackers. By the time most hackers get into the second grade, they learn that even the most obscure SSID is easy to get around. So I recommend that you leave the SSID at the default and apply better security measures, as described in the next chapter.

✦ **Allow broadcast SSID to associate?** Disables the access point's periodic broadcast of the SSID. Normally, the access point regularly broadcasts its SSID so that wireless devices that come within range can detect the network and join in. For a more secure network, you can disable this function. Then, a wireless client must already know the network's SSID in order to join the network.

✦ **Channel:** Lets you select one of 11 channels on which to broadcast. All the access points and computers in the wireless network should use the same channel. If you find that your network is frequently losing connections, try switching to another channel. You may be experiencing interference from a cordless phone or other wireless device operating on the same channel.

Switching channels is also a friendly way for neighbors with wireless networks to stay out of each other's way. For example, if you share a building with another tenant who also has a wireless network, you can agree to use separate channels so that your wireless networks won't interfere with each other. Keep in mind that this doesn't give you any real measure of security because your neighbor could secretly switch back to your channel and listen in on your network. So you still need to secure your network as described in the next chapter.

**Book VI
Chapter 4**

Setting Up a
Wireless Network

Figure 4-6:
The main config-
uration
page for a
Linksys
wireless
access
point router.

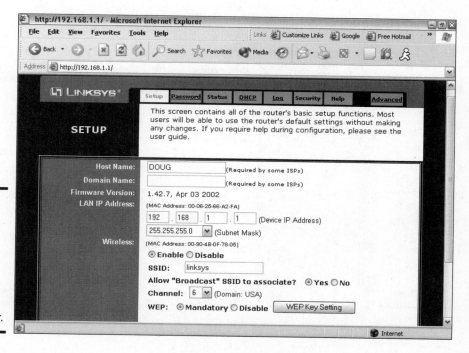

✦ **WEP — Mandatory or Disable:** Lets you use a security protocol called *wired equivalent privacy.* I have more to say about this in the next chapter.

DHCP configuration

You can configure most multifunction access points to operate as a DHCP server. For small networks, it's common for the access point to also be the DHCP server for the entire network. In that case, you need to configure the access point's DHCP server. Figure 4-7 shows the DHCP configuration page for the Linksys WAP router. To enable DHCP, you check the Enable option and then specify the other configuration options to use for the DHCP server.

Larger networks that have more demanding DHCP requirements are likely to have a separate DHCP server running on another computer. In that case, you can defer to the existing server by disabling the DHCP server in the access point.

For more information on configuring a DHCP server, please refer to Book V, Chapter 3.

Figure 4-7: Configuring DHCP for a Linksys wireless access point router.

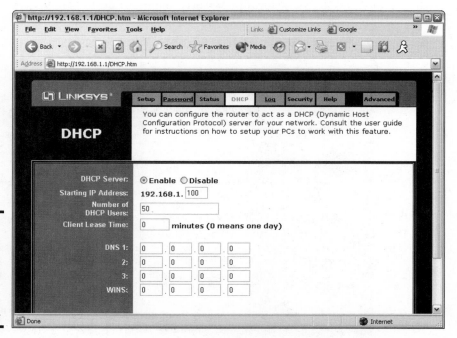

Configuring Windows XP for Wireless Networking

The first step in configuring Windows XP for wireless networking is to install the appropriate device driver for your wireless network adapter. To do that, you need the installation CD that came with the adapter. Follow the instructions that came with the adapter to install the drivers.

Windows XP has some nice built-in features for working with wireless networks. You can configure these features by opening the Network Connections folder. (Choose Start➪Control Panel and then double-click the Network Connections icon.) Right-click the wireless network connection and then choose Properties to bring up the Properties dialog box. Then, click the Wireless Networks tab to display the wireless networking options shown in Figure 4-8.

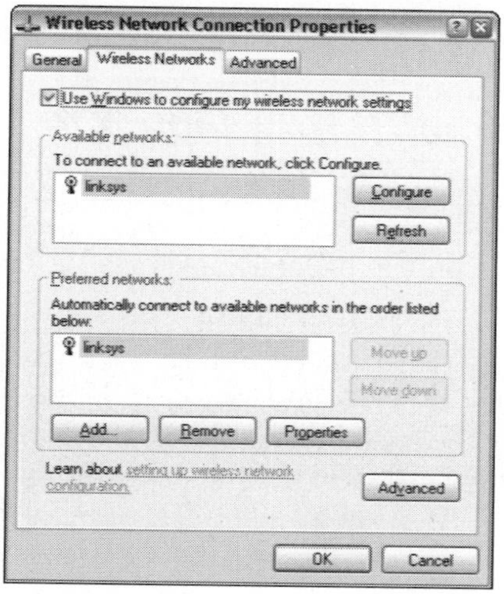

**Book VI
Chapter 4**

**Setting Up a
Wireless Network**

Figure 4-8:
Configuring
wireless
networking
in Windows
XP.

Each time you connect to a wireless network, Windows XP adds that network to this dialog box. Then, you can juggle the order of the networks in the Preferred Networks section to indicate which network you'd prefer to join if you find yourself within range of two or more networks at the same time. You can use the Move Up and Move Down buttons next to the Preferred Networks list to change your preferences.

To add a network that you haven't yet actually joined, click the Add button. This brings up the dialog box shown in Figure 4-9. Here, you can type the SSID value for the network that you want to add. You can also specify other information, such as whether to use data encryption, how to authenticate yourself, and whether the network is an ad-hoc rather than an infrastructure network.

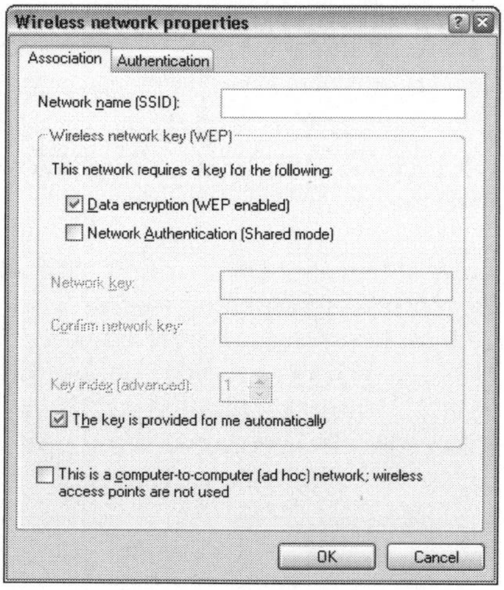

Figure 4-9:
Configuring wireless networking in Windows XP.

Using a Wireless Network with Windows XP

Windows XP also has some nice built-in features that simplify the task of using a wireless network. For example, when your computer comes within range of a wireless network, a pop-up balloon appears in the taskbar, indicating that a network is available.

If one of your preferred networks is within range, clicking the balloon automatically connects you to that network. If Windows XP doesn't recognize any of the networks, clicking the balloon displays the dialog box shown in Figure 4-10. With this dialog box, you can choose the network that you want to join (if more than one network is listed) and then click Connect to join the selected network.

Figure 4-10:
Joining a network.

After you've joined a wireless network, a network status icon appears in the notification area of the taskbar. You can quickly see the network status by hovering the mouse over this icon; a balloon appears to indicate the state of the connection. For more detailed information, you can click the status icon to display the Wireless Network Connection Status dialog box, shown in Figure 4-11.

Figure 4-11: The Wireless Network Connection Status dialog box.

This dialog box provides the following items of information:

✦ **Status:** Indicates whether you are connected.

✦ **Duration:** Indicates how long you've been connected.

✦ **Speed:** Indicates the current network speed. Ideally, this should say 11Mbps for an 802.11b network, or 54Mbps for an 802.11a or 802.11g network. However, if the network connection is not of the highest quality, the speed may drop to a lower value.

✦ **Signal Strength:** Displays a graphic representation of the quality of the signal.

✦ **Packets Sent & Received:** Indicates how many packets of data you've sent and received over the network.

You can click the Properties button to bring up the Connection Properties dialog box for the wireless connection.

Chapter 5: Securing a Wireless Network

In This Chapter

✓ Reviewing the threats posed by wireless networks

✓ Examining the strange world of wardriving and warchalking

✓ Enabling the security features of your wireless access point

Before you dive headfirst into the deep end of the wireless networking pool, you should first consider the inherent security risks in setting up a wireless network. With a cabled network, the best security tool that you have is the lock on the front door of your office. Unless someone can physically get to one of the computers on your network, he or she can't get into your network. (Well, I'm sort of ignoring your wide-open broadband Internet connection for the sake of argument.)

If you go wireless, an intruder doesn't have to get into your office to hack into your network. He or she can do it from the office next door. Or the lobby. Or the parking garage beneath your office. Or the sidewalk outside. In short, when you introduce wireless devices into your network, you usher in a whole new set of security issues to deal with.

This chapter explores some of the basic security issues that come with the territory when you go wireless.

Understanding Wireless Security Threats

Wireless networks have the same basic security considerations as wired networks. As a network administrator, you need to balance the need of legitimate users to access network resources against the risk of illegitimate users breaking into your network. That's the basic dilemma of network security. Whether the network uses cables, wireless devices, kite strings and tin cans, or smoke signals, the basic issues are the same.

On one extreme of the wireless network security spectrum is the totally open network, in which anyone within range of your wireless transmissions can log in as an administrator and gain full access to every detail of your network. On the other end is what I call the "cone-of-silence syndrome," in which the network is so secure that no one can gain access to the network — not even legitimate users.

The goal of securing a wireless network is to find the happy medium between these two extremes that meets the access and risk-management needs of your organization.

The following sections describe the most likely types of security threats that wireless networks encounter. You should take each of these kinds of threats into consideration when you plan your network's security.

Intruders

With a wired network, an intruder must usually gain access to your facility to physically connect to your network. Not so with a wireless network — in fact, with wireless, anyone with a notebook that has wireless network capability can gain access to your network if they can place themselves physically within range of your network's radio signals. Consider these possibilities:

✦ If you share a building with other tenants, the other tenants' offices may be within range.

✦ If you're in a multifloor building, the floor immediately above or below you may be in range.

✦ The lobby outside your office may be within range of your network.

✦ The parking lot outside or the parking garage in the basement may be in range.

If a would-be intruder can't get within normal broadcast range, he or she may try one of several tricks to increase the range:

✦ A would-be intruder can switch to a bigger antenna to extend the range of his or her wireless computer. Some experiments have shown that big antennas can receive signals from wireless networks that are miles away. In fact, I once read of someone who listened in on wireless networks based on San Francisco from the Berkeley hills, which is across the San Francisco Bay.

✦ If a would-be intruder is serious about breaking into your network, he or she may smuggle a wireless repeater device into your facility — or near it — to extend the range of your wireless network to a location that he or she *can* get to.

Of course, a *physical* connection to your network is not the only way an intruder can gain access. You must still take steps to prevent an intruder from sneaking into your network through your Internet gateway. In most cases, this means that you need to set up a firewall to block unwanted and unauthorized traffic.

Freeloaders

Freeloaders are intruders who want to piggyback on your wireless network to get free access to the Internet. If they manage to gain access to your wireless network, they probably won't do anything malicious: They'll just fire up their Web browsers and surf the Internet. These are folks who are too cheap to spend $45 per month on their own broadband connection at home, so they'd rather drive into your parking lot and steal yours.

Even though freeloaders may be relatively benign, they can be a potential source of trouble. In particular:

✦ Freeloaders use bandwidth that you're paying for. As a result, their mere presence can slow down Internet access for your legitimate users.

✦ After freeloaders gain Internet access through your network, they can potentially cause trouble for you or your organization. For example, they may use your network to download illegal pornography. Or they may try to send spam via your mail server. Most ISPs will cut you off cold if they catch you sending spam, and they won't believe you when you tell them the spam came from a kid parked in a Pinto out in your parking lot.

✦ If you're in the business of *selling* access to your wireless network, freeloaders are obviously a problem.

✦ If freeloaders can get in, so can more malicious intruders.

Eavesdroppers

Eavesdroppers just like to listen to your network traffic. They don't actually try to gain access via your wireless network — at least, not at first. They just listen.

Unfortunately, wireless networks give them plenty to listen to. For example:

✦ Most wireless access points regularly broadcast their SSID for anyone who's listening to hear.

✦ When a legitimate wireless network user joins the network, an exchange of packets occurs as the network authenticates the user. An eavesdropper can capture these packets and, if security isn't set up right, determine the user's logon name and password.

✦ An eavesdropper can steal files that are opened from a network server. For example, if a wireless user opens a confidential sales report that's saved on the network, the sales report document is broken into packets that are sent over the wireless network to the user. A skilled eavesdropper can copy those packets and reconstruct the file.

✦ When a wireless user connects to the Internet, an eavesdropper can see any packets that the user sends to or receives from the Internet. If the user purchases something online, the transaction may include credit card and other personal information. (Hopefully, these packets will be encrypted so the eavesdropper won't be able to decipher the data.)

Jamming

A *spoiler* is a hacker who gets kicks from jamming networks so that they become unusable. A spoiler usually accomplishes this by flooding the network with meaningless traffic so that legitimate traffic gets lost in the flow. Spoilers may also try to place viruses or worm programs on your network via an unsecured wireless connection.

Rogue access points

One of the biggest problems that network administrators have to deal with is the problem of rogue access points. A *rogue access point* is an access point that suddenly appears out of nowhere on your network. What usually happens is that an employee decides to connect a notebook computer to the network via a wireless computer. So the user stops at Computers-R-Us on the way home from work one day and buys a Fischer-Price wireless access port for $75 and plugs it into the network, without asking permission.

Now, in spite of all the elaborate security precautions you've taken to fence in your network, this well-meaning user has opened the barn door. It's *very* unlikely that the user will enable the security features of the wireless access point; in fact, he or she probably isn't even aware of the security implications of setting up an unprotected access point.

Unless you take some kind of action to find it, a rogue access point can operate undetected on your network for months or even years. You may not discover it until you report to work one day and find that your network has been trashed by an intruder who found his or her way into your network via an unprotected wireless access point that you didn't even know existed.

Here are some steps you can take to reduce the risk of rogue access points appearing on your system:

✦ Establish a policy prohibiting users from installing wireless access points on their own. Then, make sure that you inform all network users of the policy and let them know why installing an access point on their own can be such a major problem.

✦ If possible, establish a program that quickly and inexpensively grants wireless access to users who want it. The reasons rogue access points show up in the first place are (1) users need it, and (2) it's hard to get through channels. If you make it easier for users to get legitimate wireless access, you're less likely to find wireless access points hidden behind file cabinets or in flower pots.

✦ Once in awhile, take a walk through the premises looking for rogue access points. Take a look at every network outlet in the building and see what's connected to it.

✦ Turn off all your wireless access points and then walk around the premises with a wireless-equipped notebook computer that has scanning software, such as Network Stumbler (www.netstumbler.com), looking for wireless access. (Of course, just because you detect a wireless network doesn't mean you have found a rogue access point — you may have stumbled onto a wireless network from a nearby office or home.)

✦ If your network is large, consider using a software tool such as AirWave (www.airwave.com) to snoop for unauthorized access points.

What About Wardrivers and Warchalkers?

The recent explosion of wireless networking has led to a few new terms, including *wardriving* and *warchalking*. Whether wardriving and warchalking actually represent security threats is a question that's subject to a lot of debate.

Wardriving

Wardriving refers to the practice of driving around town with notebook computers looking for open access to wireless networks just to see what networks are out there. Some wardrivers even make maps and put them on the Internet.

The basic intent of wardriving is to discover open wireless networks that can be accessed from public places. A side benefit is that it can help network administrators discover holes in their network security. If your network shows up on a wardriving map, be grateful for the wardrivers who discovered your vulnerability. And by publishing it, they've given you incentive to plug the hole!

The downside of wardriving is that intruders can check the wardriving maps posted on the Internet to find potential targets.

The origins of war

Where does the term *wardriving* come from? Although the term has nothing to do with actual combat, I've heard two plausible explanations for its origin:

✔ It derives from the popular hacker word *warez* (pronounced *wayrz*), which refers to pirated software. Thus, wardriving refers to looking for pirated wireless network access.

✔ It derives from the movie *Wargames*, in which a very young Matthew Broderick hacks his way into the Pentagon's top-secret nuclear defense network by setting up his computer to dial numbers sequentially until it finds a computer worth hacking into. This practice was called *wardialing*.

Wardrivers arm themselves with the following equipment:

✦ A car.

✦ A notebook computer with a wireless adapter.

✦ An external antenna isn't a must, but it helps.

✦ Software that can scan for open wireless networks.

✦ A GPS, or *global positioning system,* a device that can automatically track where you are.

✦ Software that correlates the discovery of open networks with location data obtained from the GPS device.

✦ Free time.

For more information about wardriving, check out the Web site www. wardriving.com.

Warchalking

Warchalking refers to marking the location of open access points with special chalk symbols on the sidewalk. The chalk symbols indicate that a network is nearby. So if you're wandering around in downtown San Francisco and you spot a warchalk symbol on the curb, you can sit down at the nearest park bench, fire up your notebook computer, and start surfing the Internet.

Figure 5-1 shows the common warchalking symbol for an open (unprotected) wireless network. The SSID of the open network is listed above the symbol. You may also find other information written, such as the bandwidth of the Internet connection available through the access point.

Warchalking Web sites like to relate that the practice of warchalking dates back to the Great Depression in the United States, when homeless people used chalk or coal to write symbols on sidewalks, fences, or railroad trestles to provide information or warnings to their fellow travelers. For example, some symbols represented food, water, or safe places to camp, while other symbols represented dangerous areas or aggressive police. I leave it up to you to decide whether college kids wandering the streets looking for free Internet access is the same as the unemployed and homeless of the Great Depression looking for food.

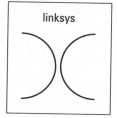

Figure 5-1:
A war-
chalking
symbol.

Securing Your Wireless Network

Hopefully, you're convinced that wireless networks do indeed pose many security risks. In the following sections, I describe some steps that you can take to help secure your wireless network.

Changing the password

Probably the first thing you should do when you install a wireless access point is to change its administrative password. Most access points have a built-in, Web-based setup page that you can access from any Web browser to configure the access point's configuration settings. The setup page is protected by a username and password. However, the username and password are initially set to default values that are easy to guess.

For example, the default username for Linksys access points is blank, and the password is "admin." If you leave the username and password set to their default values, anyone can access the access point and change its configuration settings, thus bypassing any other security features that you enable for the access point.

So, the first step in securing your wireless access point is changing the setup password to a value that can't be guessed. I suggest that you use a random combination of numerals and both uppercase and lowercase letters. Be sure to store the password in a secure location; if you forget it, you won't be able to reconfigure your router.

Securing the SSID

The next step is to secure the SSID that identifies the network. A client must know the access point's SSID in order to join the wireless network. If you can prevent unauthorized clients from discovering the SSID, you can prevent them from accessing your network.

Securing the SSID is not a complete security solution, so you shouldn't rely on it as your only security mechanism. SSID security can slow down casual intruders and wardrivers who are just looking for easy and free Internet access, but it isn't possible to prevent serious hackers from discovering your SSID.

You can do three things to secure your SSID:

✦ **Change the SSID from the default.** Most access points come preconfigured with well-known default SSIDs. For example, Table 5-1 lists some well-known default SSIDs. By changing your access point's SSID, you can make it more difficult for an intruder to determine your SSID and gain access.

Table 5-1	Common Default SSID Values
SSID	*Manufacturer*
3com	3Com
Compaq	Compaq
linksys	Linksys
tsunami	Cicso
Wireless	NetGear
WLAN	DLink
WLAN	SMC

✦ **Disable SSID broadcast.** Most access points frequently broadcast their SSIDs so that clients can discover the network when they come within range. Clients that receive this SSID broadcast can then use the SSID to join the network.

You can increase network security somewhat by disabling the SSID broadcast feature. That way, clients won't automatically learn the access point's SSID. To join the network, a client computer must figure out the SSID on its own. You can then tell your wireless network users the SSID to use when they configure their clients.

Unfortunately, when a client computer connects to a wireless network, it sends the SSID to the access point in an unencrypted packet. So a sophisticated intruder who's using a packet sniffer to eavesdrop on your wireless network can determine your SSID as soon as any legitimate computer joins the network.

✦ **Disable guest mode:** Many access points have a guest mode feature that enables client computers to specify a blank SSID or to specify "any" as the SSID. If you want to ensure that only clients that know the SSID can join the network, you must disable this feature.

Enabling WEP

WEP stands for *Wired Equivalent Privacy* and is designed to make wireless transmission as secure as transmission over a network cable. WEP encrypts your data by using either a 40-bit key or a 128-bit key. 40-bit encryption is faster than 128-bit encryption and is adequate for most purposes. So I suggest that you enable 40-bit encryption unless you work for the CIA.

Note that in order to use WEP, both the client and the server must know the encryption keys being used. So a client that doesn't know the access point's encryption keys won't be able to join the network.

You can specify encryption keys for WEP in two ways. The first is to create the 10-digit key manually by making up a random number. The second method, which I prefer, is to use a *passphrase,* which can be any word or combination of numerals and letters that you want. WEP automatically converts the passphrase to the numeric key used to encrypt data. If the client knows the passphrase used to generate the keys on the access point, the client will be able to access the network.

As it turns out, security experts have identified a number of flaws with WEP that compromise its effectiveness. As a result, with the right tools, a sophisticated intruder can get past WEP. So although it's a good idea to enable WEP, you shouldn't count on it for complete security.

Besides just enabling WEP, you should take two steps to increase its effectiveness:

✦ **Make WEP mandatory:** Some access points have a configuration setting that enables WEP but makes it optional. This may prevent eavesdroppers from viewing the data transmitted on WEP connections, but it doesn't prevent clients that don't know your WEP keys from accessing your network.

✦ **Change the encryption keys:** Most access points come preconfigured with default encryption keys that make it easy for even casual hackers to defeat your WEP security. You should change the default keys either by using a passphrase or by specifying your own keys. Figure 5-2 shows the WEP key configuration page for a typical access point (in this case, a Linksys BEFW11).

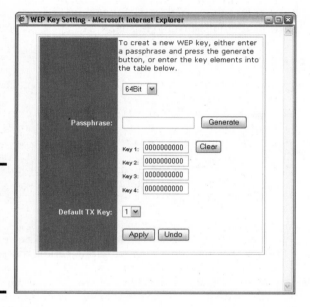

Figure 5-2:
Changing
WEP
settings on
a Linksys
wireless
access
point.

Using MAC address filtering

MAC address filtering allows you to specify a list of MAC addresses for the devices that are allowed to access the network. If a computer with a different MAC address tries to join the network via the access point, the access point will deny access.

MAC address filtering is a great idea for wireless networks with a fixed number of clients. For example, if you set up a wireless network at your office so that a few workers can connect their notebook computers, you can specify the MAC addresses of those computers in the MAC filtering table. Then, other computers won't be able to access the network via the access point.

Don't neglect the basics

The security techniques described in this chapter are specific to wireless networks. They should be used alongside the basic security techniques that are presented in Book III. In other words, don't forget the basics, such as:

✔ Use strong passwords for your user accounts

✔ Apply security patches to your servers

✔ Change default server account information (especially the administrator password)

✔ Disable unnecessary services

✔ Regularly check your server logs

✔ Install virus protection

✔ Back up!

Unfortunately, it isn't difficult to configure a computer to lie about its MAC address. Thus, after a potential intruder determines that MAC filtering is being used, he or she can just sniff packets to determine an authorized MAC address and then configure his or her computer to use that address. (This is called *MAC spoofing.*) So you shouldn't rely on MAC address filtering as your only means of security.

Figure 5-3 shows the screen used to edit the MAC address table for a Linksys wireless access point.

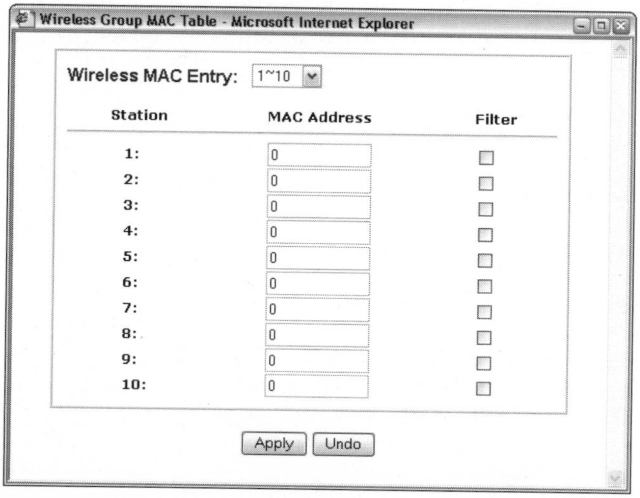

Figure 5-3: A MAC address table for a Linksys wireless access point.

Wireless Group MAC Table - Microsoft Internet Explorer

Wireless MAC Entry: 1~10

Station	MAC Address	Filter
1:	0	☐
2:	0	☐
3:	0	☐
4:	0	☐
5:	0	☐
6:	0	☐
7:	0	☐
8:	0	☐
9:	0	☐
10:	0	☐

Apply   Undo

Placing your access points outside the firewall

The most effective security technique for wireless networking is to place all your wireless access points *outside* of your firewall. That way, all network traffic from wireless users will have to travel through the firewall to access the network.

As you can imagine, doing this can significantly limit network access for wireless users. To get around those limitations, you can enable a virtual private network (VPN) connection for your wireless users. The VPN will allow full network access to authorized wireless users.

Obviously, this solution requires a bit of work to set up and can be a little inconvenient for your users. However, it's the only way to completely secure your wireless access points.

Book VII

Windows 2000 and 2003 Server Reference

The 5th Wave   By Rich Tennant

"Sure, at first it sounded great — an intuitive network adapter that helps people write memos by finishing their thoughts for them."

Contents at a Glance

Chapter 1: Installing and Configuring Windows 2000 and 2003 Server

In This Chapter

✓ Getting ready for the installation

✓ Installing a network operating system

✓ Figuring out what to do after you install the network operating system

*T*his chapter presents the procedures that you need to follow in order to install Windows 2000 Server or Windows Server 2003. The specific details provided are for Windows Server 2003. However, installing Windows 2000 Server is very similar, so you won't have any trouble adapting these procedures if you're installing Windows 2000 Server.

Planning a Windows Server Installation

Before you begin the Setup program to actually install a Windows Server operating system, you need to make a number of preliminary decisions. The following sections describe the decisions that you need to make before you install a Windows Server operating system.

Checking system requirements

Before you install a Windows Server operating system, you should make sure that the computer meets the minimum requirements. Table 1-1 lists the official minimum requirements for Windows Server 2003. (The minimums for Windows 2000 Server are slightly less.) Table 1-1 also lists what I consider to be more realistic minimums if you expect to get satisfactory performance from the server as a moderately used file server.

Table 1-1	Minimum Hardware Requirements for Windows Server 2003	
Item	*Official Minimum*	*A More Realistic Minimum*
CPU	133MHz Pentium	1GHz Pentium 4
RAM	128MB	512MB
Free disk space	1GB	5GB

Besides meeting the minimum requirements, you should also check to make sure that your specific hardware has been checked out and approved for use with Windows Server 2003. Microsoft publishes an official list of supported hardware, called the *Hardware Compatibility List*, or *HCL*. You can find the HCL at www.microsoft.com/whdc/hcl/default.mspx.

The Windows Server 2003 distribution CD-ROM includes a feature called the Check System Compatibility option that automatically checks your hardware against the HCL.

Reading the release notes

The Windows Server 2003 distribution CD-ROM includes a file called Relnotes.asp, located in the Docs file. It's pictured in Figure 1-1. You should read this file before you start Setup, just to check whether any of the specific procedures or warnings it contains applies to your situation.

One of the major new features of Windows Server 2003 is that it supports Microsoft's new software development platform, called *.NET* (pronounced *dot-net.*) A major component of .NET is ASP.NET, Microsoft's new facility for developing Web-based applications. ASP.NET replaces ASP (which is sometimes now called *ASP Classic*). Old-style ASP Classic files have the extension .asp, and the newer ASP.NET files use the extension .aspx.

So why I am telling you this now? Only because I can't figure out why the release notes file for the brand-new Windows Server 2003 is an old-style ASP file. Go figure.

Deciding whether to upgrade or install

Windows offers two installation modes that you should choose from before you begin setup: full installation or upgrade installation.

A *full installation* deletes any existing operating system it finds on the computer and configures the new operating system from scratch. If you do a full installation onto a disk that already has an operating system installed, the full installation offers to keep any existing data files that it finds on the disk.

Here are some points to ponder before you perform an upgrade installation:

✦ You can upgrade Windows Server 2003 over an existing Windows NT Server 4.0, provided that you've installed Service Pack 5. You can also upgrade Windows 2000 Server.

✦ You can't upgrade a client version of Windows to a server version.

✦ With an upgrade installation, you don't have to reinstall any applications that were previously installed on the disk.

✦ Always perform a full backup before doing an upgrade installation!

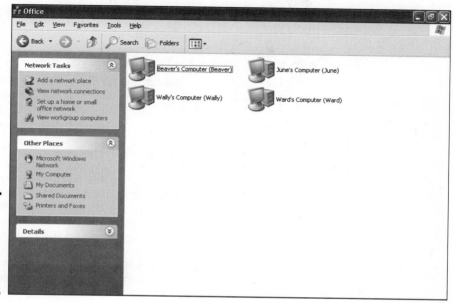

**Book VII
Chapter 1**

Installing and
Configuring
Windows 2000 and
2003 Server

Figure 1-1:
The relnotes.asp file for Windows Server 2003.

Considering your licensing options

You can purchase Microsoft operating systems on a per-server or a per-user basis. You need to know which plan you have when you install the operating system.

+ **Per-user licensing:** In this licensing mode, each client that accesses the server must have a Windows Server license. If your network has 25 users, you'd need a license that allows for 25 users — one for each client.

+ **Per-server licensing:** In per-server licensing, the server itself has a license that allows a specific number of concurrent client connections. This is a good choice if you have a large number of users, but only a small number of them use the computer at any given time. For example, if you have a large number of dialup or VPN users, you may want to opt for per-server licensing.

Thinking about multiboot

Windows includes a *multiboot* feature that lets you set up the computer so that it has more than one operating system. Then, when you boot up the computer, you can select which operating system that you want to boot up from a menu.

If you're a software developer or a network manager who needs to make sure that software is compatible with multiple operating systems, the multiboot feature can be useful. For most servers, however, you'll want to install just one operating system.

Choosing a file system

Windows servers provide three choices for the file system to format the server's disk: FAT, FAT32, and NTFS. In most cases, you should elect to use NTFS. Well, actually, you should use NTFS in almost all cases. Come to think of it, you should *always* use NTFS.

The name *FAT* refers to the *file allocation table* that was used in the original version of MS-DOS back when disco was still popular. FAT was a simple but effective way to track disk space allocated to files on diskettes and on small hard drives. The original FAT system used 16-bit disk addresses to divide the total space on a disk into 65,526 units called *clusters*, each of which could be allocated to any file on the disk. The size of each cluster could vary from as little as 2K to as much as 256K, depending on the size of the drive.

When disk drives started to get bigger than 512MB (can you remember when 512MB was a *huge* disk?), FAT was upgraded to FAT32, which used 32-bit addresses for clusters. That allowed a maximum of 524,208 clusters on the disk with the size of each cluster ranging from 4K to 32K, depending on the size of the drive.

FAT32 was a huge improvement over FAT, but both suffer from several inherent problems:

✦ Even with 32-bit addresses, FAT32 is stretched by today's 100GB+ disk drives.

✦ Neither FAT nor FAT32 have built-in security features.

✦ FAT and FAT32 are inherently unreliable. Most users, at one time or another, lose files due to the unreliability of FAT/FAT32.

✦ FAT and FAT32 allocate space inefficiently on large volumes because the smallest unit of space that they can allocate must be large — as much as 256K in some cases.

Here are just a few of the reasons that choosing NTFS for Windows servers is a no-brainer:

✦ NTFS has built-in security features that track security information for individual files and directories.

✦ NTFS tracks clusters with 64-bit disk addresses rather than 32-bit addresses (FAT32) or 16-bit addresses (FAT). As a result, an NTFS volume can theoretically have something in the neighborhood of 18 million billion disk clusters, which should keep you going for a while.

✦ The benefit of having so many clusters available is that the size of each cluster can be kept small. NTFS can efficiently use 4KB clusters for even the largest drives available today.

✦ NTFS drives are more reliable because NTFS keeps duplicate copies of important information, such as the location of each file on the hard drive. If a problem develops on an NTFS drive, Windows can usually correct the problem automatically without losing any data. In contrast, FAT drives are prone to losing data.

✦ The system that FAT uses to keep track of which disk clusters belong to a given file is prone to errors. In contrast, NTFS has more redundancy built in to its record keeping, so it's less likely to scramble up your files.

✦ NTFS has better support for large drives and large files. Table 1-2 compares some of the maximums of the FAT, FAT32, and NTFS file systems.

Table 1-2	File System Limits		
Limit	*FAT*	*FAT32*	*NTFS*
Maximum volume size	4GB	32GB	16TB
Maximum file size	2GB	4GB	16TB
Maximum files per folder	512	65,534	4,294,967,295
Maximum files per volume	65,526	524,208	Too many to count.

Planning your partitions

Partitioning enables you to divide a physical disk into one or more separate units called *partitions*. Each disk can have up to four partitions. All four of the partitions can be *primary partitions*, each of which can be formatted with a file system, such as NTFS or FAT32. Or, you can create up to three primary partitions and one *extended partition*, which can then be subdivided into one or more *logical drives*. Then, each logical drive can be formatted with a file system.

Although you can set up partitions for a Windows server in many ways, the following two approaches are the most common:

✦ Allocate the entire disk as a single partition that will be formatted with NTFS. The operating system will be installed into this partition, and disk space that isn't needed by the operating system or other network applications can be shared.

✦ Divide the disk into two partitions. Install the operating system and any other related software (such as Exchange Server or a backup utility) on the first partition. If the first partition will contain just the operating system, 10GB is a reasonable size, although you can get by with as little as 4GB if space is at a premium. Then, use the second partition for application data or network file shares.

**Book VII
Chapter 1**

Installing and
Configuring
Windows 2000 and
2003 Server

Deciding your TCP/IP configuration

Before you install the operating system, you should have a plan for how you will implement TCP/IP on the network. Here are some of the things you need to decide or find out:

What is the IP subnet address and mask for your network?

- ✦ What is the domain name for the network?
- ✦ What is the host name for the server?
- ✦ Will the server obtain its address from DHCP?
- ✦ Will the server have a static IP address? If so, what?
- ✦ Will the server be a DHCP server?
- ✦ What is the default gateway for the server? (That is, what is the IP address of the network's Internet router?)
- ✦ Will the server be a DNS server?

If the server will host TCP/IP services (such as DHCP or DNS), you'll probably want to assign the server a static IP address.

For more information about planning your TCP/IP configuration, see Book V.

Choosing workgroups or domains

A *domain* is a method of placing user accounts and various network resources under the control of a single directory database. Domains ensure that security policies are consistently applied throughout a network and greatly simplify the task of managing user accounts on large networks.

A *workgroup* is a simple association of computers on a network that makes it easy to locate shared files and printers. Workgroups don't have a sophisticated directory database, so they can't enforce strict security.

Microsoft says that workgroups should be used only for very small networks with just a few users. In fact, any network that is large enough to have a dedicated server computer running Windows 2000 Server or Windows Server 2003 is too large to use workgroups. As a result, if you're installing a Windows server, I recommend that you should always opt for domains.

After you decide to use domains, you have to make two basic decisions:

- ✦ **What will the domain name be?** If you have a registered Internet domain name, such as mydomain.com, you may want to use it for your network's domain name. Otherwise, you can make up any name you want.

✦ **What computer or computers will be the domain controllers for the domain?** If this is the first server in a domain, you must designate it as a domain controller. If you already have a server acting as a domain controller, you can either add this computer as an additional domain controller, or designate it as a *member server*.

You can always change the role of a server from a domain controller to a member server and vice versa if the needs of your network change. For small networks, I suggest that you use just one domain controller and designate the other servers as member servers. For larger networks, you may want to create several domain controllers to spread the work around.

Before You Install . . .

After you've made the key planning decisions for your Windows server installation, you should take a few precautionary steps before you actually start the Setup program. The following sections describe the steps that you should take before you perform an upgrade installation. Note that all these steps except the last one apply only to upgrades. If you're installing a Windows server on a new system, you can skip the first steps.

Backing up

Do a complete backup of the server before you begin. Although Windows Setup is reliable, sometimes something serious goes wrong that results in lost data.

Note that you don't have to back up the drive to external media, such as tape. If you can find a network disk share with enough free space, back up to it.

Checking the event logs

Look at the event logs of the existing server computer to check for recurring errors. You may discover that you have a problem with a SCSI device or your current TCP/IP configuration. Better to find out now rather than in the middle of Setup.

Uncompressing data

If you've used DriveSpace or any other disk compression software to compress a drive, you'll have to uncompress the drive before you run Setup. Neither Windows 2000 Server nor Windows Server 2003 support DriveSpace or other disk compression programs.

**Book VII
Chapter 1**

**Installing and
Configuring
Windows 2000 and
2003 Server**

Disconnect UPS devices

If you have installed an Uninterruptible Power Supply (UPS) device on the server and connected it to your computer via a serial cable, you should temporarily disconnect the serial cable before you run Setup. After Setup is complete, you can reconnect the serial cable.

Running Setup

Now that you've planned your installation and prepared the computer, you're ready to run the Setup program. The following procedure describes the steps that you must follow in order to install Windows Server 2003 on a new computer that has a bootable CD-ROM drive. The procedure for installing Windows 2000 Server is similar.

1. **Insert the distribution CD in the CD-ROM drive and restart the computer.**

   After a few moments, the Windows Setup Wizard fires up. It begins by asking what type of setup you'd like, as shown in Figure 1-2. The options are New Installation or Upgrade.

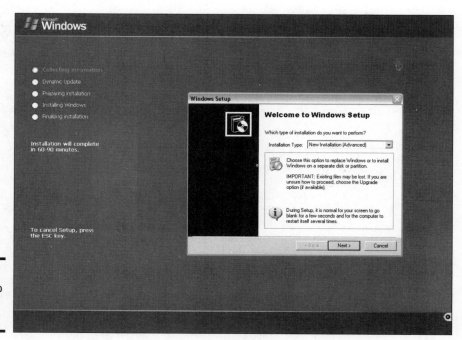

Figure 1-2:
Welcome to
Windows
Setup!

2. Choose New Installation (Advanced) and then click Next.

The Setup Wizard displays the License Agreement information. Read it if you enjoy legalese.

3. Click I Accept This Agreement and then click Next.

The wizard next asks for the Product Key, which is printed on a sticker attached to the CD case.

4. Enter the 25-character product key and then click Next.

Because the key is so long, it's easy to make a mistake. If Setup complains that the product key is invalid, don't panic. Just try again.

Next, the Setup Options screen appears.

5. Choose the Setup Options that you want and then click Next.

If you need to use accessibility features, such as the Magnifier, during Setup, click Accessibility Options and enable the features that you need. If you want to change the language setting, click Primary Language and make your selections.

When you click Next, the next phase of Setup begins: Dynamic Update. Setup offers to connect to Microsoft's Web site to see whether it should retrieve any late-breaking changes to Windows.

6. If you have a working Internet connection, click Yes and then click Next. If you don't, click No and then click Next.

If you clicked Yes, your computer connects to the Internet and retrieves any updates.

Next, your computer restarts and enters the third phase of Setup, which runs in text mode. A message appears, inviting you to press Enter to continue the Windows Setup process.

7. Press Enter.

Setup continues by displaying the computer's current partition information. Here, you can select the partition that you want to use for the installation. If necessary, you can reconfigure your partitions from this screen by deleting existing partitions or creating new ones. I assume here that you want to create a single partition that uses all available space on the drive.

8. Select the partition on which you want to install Windows and then press Enter.

Setup next asks what file system to install into the selected partition.

9. Choose NTFS and then press Enter.

Setup now formats the drive and then copies files to the newly format-ted drive. This step usually takes awhile. Because the computer is in text

Book VII
Chapter 1

Installing and Configuring Windows 2000 and 2003 Server

mode, you can't play Solitaire while you wait. I suggest you bring along your favorite book. Start on Chapter 1.

After all the files have been copied, Setup reboots your computer again and returns you to the more attractive GUI Setup program. Then, Setup examines all the devices on the computer and installs any necessary device drivers. You can read Chapter 2 of your book during this time.

When Setup finishes installing drivers, it displays a screen asking you to enter information about your region and language.

10. **Specify the correct region and language settings and then click Next.**

Setup now asks you to enter your name and your company name. Your name is required, but the company name is optional. (This is kind of funny, because most companies would prefer that you configure the server with the company name and leave your name out of it. Go figure.)

11. **Enter your name and company name and then click Next.**

Next, Setup asks you to select your licensing mode. When in doubt, choose Per Server.

12. **Choose the correct licensing mode and then click Next.**

Setup asks for the computer name and Administrator account password.

13. **Type the computer name and the Administrator account password and then click Next.**

Write down the Administrator password and store it in a secure location. If you lose it, you'll be in trouble.

When you click Next, Setup asks you what date and time it is.

14. **Type the correct date and time, specify your time zone, and then click Next.**

Next, Setup displays a screen that lists various network options.

15. **If the Typical network settings are appropriate, click Next and skip ahead. Otherwise, customize your network settings.**

If the server will use DHCP to obtain its IP address, the typical settings option is fine. Otherwise, you can choose Custom Settings, click Next, and then work your way through the network configuration pages.

After the network settings are configured, Setup asks whether the server will be part of a workgroup or a domain.

16. **Indicate whether you'll be joining a domain or workgroup and then type the domain or workgroup information and click Next.**

You're almost done! Setup starts another long process of copying files, during which you can read Chapter 3 of your favorite book.

After all the files are copied, the computer reboots one final time.

Now What?

Setup gets a working Windows operating system up and running on your server. However, you still have plenty of configuration information to specify before you can say your server is installed. Follow these steps to complete the installation and configuration of your server:

1. **Log on to Windows.**

To log on to Windows, press Ctrl+Alt+Delete. When the Log On To Windows dialog box appears, type the Administrator password and click OK.

2. **Activate Windows.**

The Product Activation feature is annoying to be sure, but Microsoft claims that it helps to reduce piracy. You have 30 days to activate Windows, but you may as well do it now.

Windows displays a pop-up reminder in the bottom-right corner of the desktop. When you click the reminder, the Activation Wizard appears, as shown in Figure 1-3. Follow the steps to activate Windows.

For more information about activation, see Book II, Chapter 3.

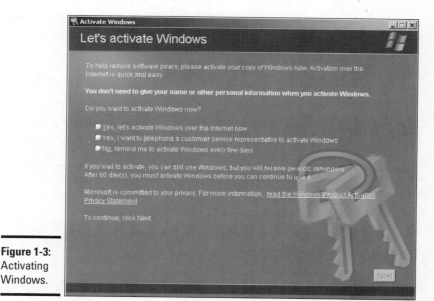

Figure 1-3:
Activating
Windows.

**Book VII
Chapter 1**

**Installing and
Configuring
Windows 2000 and
2003 Server**

3. Configure your server roles.

The first time your new Windows server boots up, the Configure Your Server Wizard appears automatically, as shown in Figure 1-4. Table 1-3 lists the roles that you can configure for the server by using this wizard.

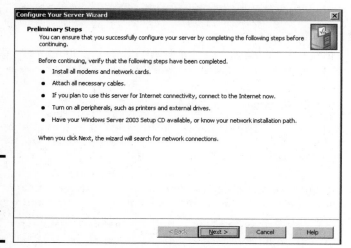

Figure 1-4: The Configure Your Server Wizard.

Table 1-3	Windows Server 2003 Roles
Role	*Description*
File Server	Lets you share disk folders that can be accessed over the network.
Print Server	Lets you share printers over the network.
Application Server	Installs Microsoft's Web server, Internet Information Service (also known as IIS).
Mail Server	Installs a basic POP3 and SMTP server for e-mail.
Terminal Server	Allows other users to run applications on the server via the network.
Remove Access/VPN Server	Enables dialup and VPN connections.
Domain Controller	Enables Active Directory and designates the server as a domain controller.
DNS Server	Enables the DNS server for DNS name resolution.
DHCP Server	Enables the DHCP server to dynamically assign IP addresses to client computers.
Streaming Media Server	Enables the Streaming Media Server.
WINS Server	Enables the WINS server for Windows-based name resolution.

Chapter 2: Managing User Accounts

In This Chapter

✔ **Understanding user accounts**

✔ **Creating user accounts**

✔ **Setting account options**

✔ **Working with groups**

✔ **Creating a roaming profile**

*E*very user who accesses a network must have a *user account*. User accounts let you control who can access the network and who can't. In addition, user accounts let you specify what network resources each user can use. Without user accounts, all your resources would be open to anyone who casually dropped by your network.

Understanding Windows User Accounts

User accounts are one of the basic tools for managing a Windows server. As a network administrator, you'll spend a large percentage of your time dealing with user accounts — creating new ones, deleting expired accounts, resetting passwords for forgetful users, granting new access rights, and so on. Before I get into the specific procedures of creating and managing user accounts, this section presents an overview of user accounts and how they work.

Local accounts versus domain accounts

A *local account* is a user account that's stored on a particular computer and applies only to that computer. Typically, each computer on your network will have a local account for each person that uses that computer.

In contrast, a *domain account* is a user account that's stored by Active Directory and can be accessed from any computer that's a part of the domain. Domain accounts are centrally managed. This chapter deals primarily with setting up and maintaining domain accounts.

User account properties

Every user account has a number of important *account properties* that specify the characteristics of the account. The three most important account properties are

- ✦ **Username:** A unique name that identifies the account. The user must enter the username when logging on to the network. The username is public information. In other words, other network users can (and often should) find out your username.

- ✦ **Password:** A secret word that must be entered in order to gain access to the account. You can set up Windows so that it enforces password policies, such as the minimum length of the password, whether the password must contain a mixture of letters and numerals, and how long the password remains current before the user must change it.

- ✦ **Group membership:** Indicates which group or groups to which the user account belongs. Group memberships are the key to granting access rights to users so that they can access various network resources, such as file shares or printers, or to perform certain network tasks, such as creating new user accounts or backing up the server.

Many other account properties record information about the user, such as the user's contact information, whether the user is allowed to access the system only at certain times or from certain computers, and so on. I describe some of these features in later sections of this chapter, and some are described in more detail in Chapter 4 of this book.

The Administrator account

Windows comes with a built-in account named Administrator that has complete access to all the features of the server. As a network administrator, you'll frequently log on using the Administrator account to perform maintenance chores.

Because the Administrator account is so powerful, you should always enforce good password practices for it. In other words, don't use your dog's name as the Administrator account password. Instead, pick a random combination of letters and numbers. Then, change the password periodically.

Write down the Administrator account password and keep it in a secure location. Note that by "secure location," I don't mean taped to the front of the monitor. Keep it in a safe place where you can retrieve it if you forget it, but where it won't easily fall into the hands of someone looking to break into your network.

Creating a New User

To create a new domain user account in Windows Server 2003, follow these steps:

1. **Choose Start⇨Administrative Tools⇨Active Directory Users And Computers.**

This fires up the Active Directory Users And Computer management console, as shown in Figure 2-1.

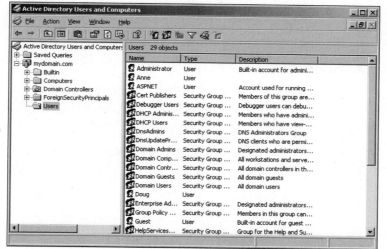

Figure 2-1:
The Active Directory Users and Computer management console.

Book VII
Chapter 2

Managing User
Accounts

2. **Right-click the domain that you want to add the user to and then choose New⇨User.**

This summons the New User Wizard, as shown in Figure 2-2.

3. **Type the user's first name, middle initial, and last name.**

As you type the name, the New User Wizard automatically fills in the Full Name field.

4. **Change the Full Name field if you want it to appear differently than proposed.**

For example, you may want to reverse the first and last names so the last name appears first.

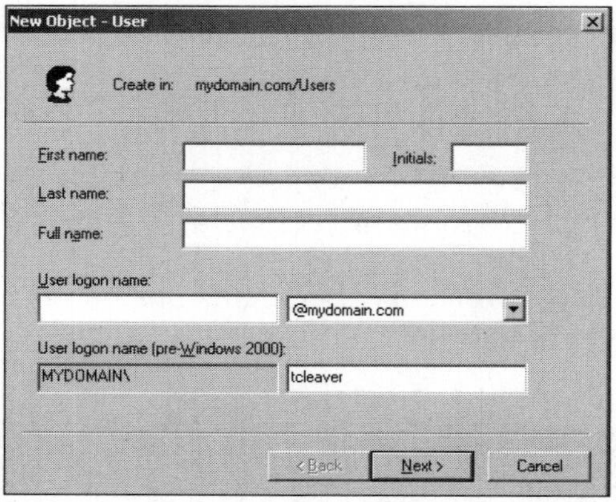

Figure 2-2:
Creating a
new user.

5. Type the user logon name.

This name must be unique within the domain.

Pick a naming scheme to follow when creating user logon names. For example, use the first letter of the first name followed by the complete last name, the complete first name followed by the first letter of the last name, or any other scheme that suits your fancy.

6. Click Next.

The second page of the New User Wizard appears, as shown in Figure 2-3.

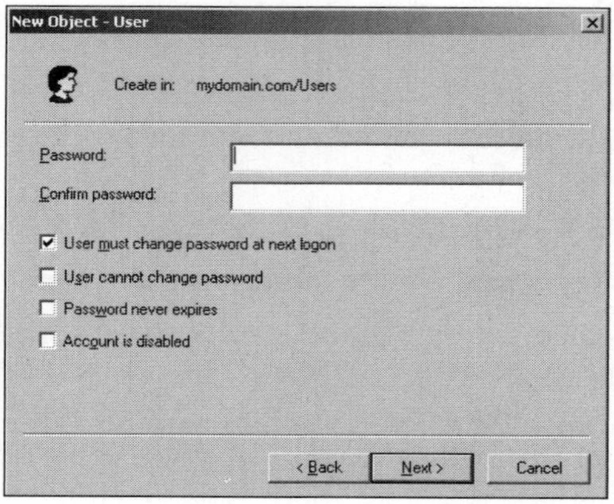

Figure 2-3:
Setting the
user's
password.

7. Type the password twice.

You're asked to type the password twice, so type it correctly. If you don't type it identically in both boxes, you're asked to correct your mistake.

8. Specify the password options that you want to apply.

The following password options are available:

- **User must change password at next logon.**
- **User cannot change password.**
- **Password never expires.**
- **Account is disabled.**

For more information about these options, see the section "Setting account options," later in this chapter.

9. Click Next.

You're taken to the final page of the New User Wizard, as shown in Figure 2-4.

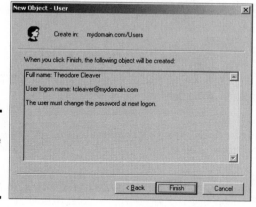

Figure 2-4: Verifying the user account information.

10. Verify that the information is correct and then click Finish to create the account.

If the account information is not correct, click the Back button and correct the error.

You're done! Now you can customize the user's account settings. At a minimum, you'll probably want to add the user to one or more groups. You may also want to add contact information for the user or set up other account options.

Setting User Properties

After you've created a user account, you can set additional properties for the user by right-clicking the new user and choosing Properties. This brings up the User Properties dialog box, which has about a million tabs that you can use to set various properties for the user. Figure 2-5 shows the General tab, which lists basic information about the user, such as the user's name, office location, phone number, and so on.

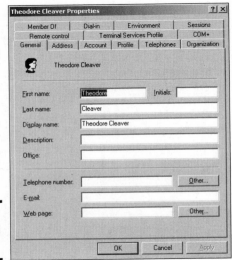

Figure 2-5:
The General
tab.

The following sections describe some of the administrative tasks that you can perform via the various tabs of the User Properties dialog box.

Changing the user's contact information

Several tabs of the User Properties dialog box contain contact information for the user. In particular:

✦ **Address:** Lets you change the user's street address, post-office box, city, state, ZIP code, and so on.

✦ **Telephones:** Lets you specify the user's phone numbers.

✦ **Organization:** Lets you record the user's job title and the name of his or her boss.

Setting account options

The Account tab of the User Properties dialog box, as shown in Figure 2-6, features a variety of interesting options that you can set for the user. From this dialog box, you can change the user's logon name. In addition, you can change the password options that you set when you created the account and set an expiration date for the account.

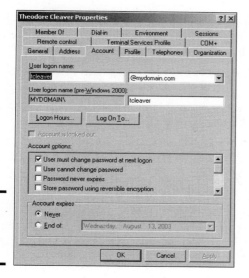

Figure 2-6:
The
Account
tab.

The following account options are available in the Account Options listbox:

✦ **User must change password at next logon:** This option, which is selected by default, allows you to create a one-time-only password that can get the user started with the network. The first time the user logs on to the network, he or she is asked to change the password.

✦ **User cannot change password:** Use this option if you don't want to allow users to change their passwords. (Obviously, you can't use this option and the previous one at the same time.)

✦ **Password never expires:** Use this option if you want to bypass the password expiration policy for this user so that the user will never have to change his or her password.

✦ **Store password using reversible encryption:** This option stores passwords using an encryption scheme that hackers can easily break, so you should avoid it like the plague.

✦ **Account is disabled:** This option allows you to create an account that you don't yet need. As long as the account remains disabled, the user won't be able to log on. See the section "Disabling and Enabling User Accounts," later in this chapter, to find out how to enable a disabled account.

✦ **Smart card is required for interactive logon:** If the user's computer has a smart card reader to automatically read security cards, check this option to require the user to use it.

✦ **Account is trusted for delegation:** This option indicates that the account is trustworthy and can set up delegations. This is an advanced feature that's usually reserved for Administrator accounts.

✦ **Account is sensitive and cannot be delegated:** Prevents other users from impersonating this account.

✦ **Use DES encryption types for this account:** Beefs up the encryption for applications that require extra security.

✦ **Do not require Kerberos preauthentication:** Select this option if you use a different implementation of the Kerberos protocol.

Specifying logon hours

You can restrict the hours during which the user is allowed to log on to the system by clicking the Logon Hours button from the Account tab of the User Properties dialog box. This brings up the dialog box shown in Figure 2-7.

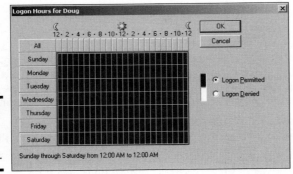

Figure 2-7:
Restricting
the user's
logon hours.

Initially, the Logon Hours dialog box is set to allow the user to log on at any time of day or night. To change the hours that you want the user to have access, click a day and time or a range of days and times and choose either Logon Permitted or Logon Denied.

Restricting access to certain computers

Normally, a user can use his or her user account to log on to any computer that's a part of the user's domain. However, you can restrict a user to certain computers by clicking the Logon To button in the Account tab of the User Properties dialog box. This brings up the Logon Workstations dialog box, as shown in Figure 2-8.

To restrict the user to certain computers, select the radio button labeled "The following computers." Then, for each computer you want to allow the user to log on from, type the computer's name in the text box and click Add.

If you make a mistake, you can select the incorrect computer name and click Edit to change the name or click Remove to delete the name.

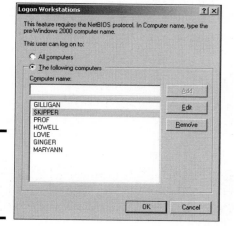

Figure 2-8:
Restricting
the user to
certain
computers.

Setting the user's profile information

The Profile tab, shown in Figure 2-9, lets you configure the user's profile information. This dialog box lets you configure three bits of information related to the user's profile:

✦ **Profile path:** This field specifies the location of the user's roaming profile. For more information, see the section "User Profiles," later in this chapter.

✦ **Logon script:** The name of the user's logon script. Logon scripts are a carryover from the early versions of Windows NT server, which relied on logon scripts to configure the user's computer when the user logged on. You can still use logon scripts, but profiles are the preferred way to specify the user's logon configuration.

✦ **Home folder:** This is where you specify the default storage location for the user.

The Profile tab lets you specify the location of an existing profile for the user, but it doesn't actually let you set up the profile. For more information about setting up a profile, see the section "User Profiles," later in this chapter.

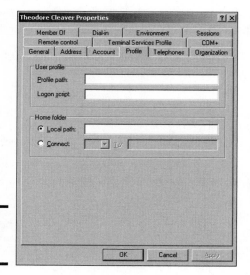

Figure 2-9:
The Profile tab.

Resetting User Passwords

By some estimates, the single most time-consuming task of most network administrators is resetting user passwords. It's easy to just think users are forgetful idiots, but put yourself in their shoes. We insist that they set their password to something incomprehensible, such as 94kD82leL384K, that they change it a week later to something more unmemorable, such as dJUQ63DWd8331, and that they don't write it down. Then we get mad when they forget their passwords.

So when a user calls and says he or she forgot his or her password, the least we can do is be cheerful when we reset if for them. After all, they've probably already spent 15 minutes trying to remember it before they finally gave up and admitted failure.

Here's the procedure to reset the password for a user domain account:

1. **Log on as an administrator.**

   You have to have administrator privileges in order to perform this procedure.

2. **Choose Start⇨Administrative Tools⇨Active Directory Users And Computers.**

   The Active Directory Users and Computer management console appears.

3. **Click Users in the console tree.**

4. **In the Details pane, right-click the user who forgot his or her password and choose Reset Password.**

5. **Type the new password in both password boxes.**

   You have to type the password twice to ensure that you type it correctly.

6. **If desired, check the User Must Change Password At Next Logon option.**

   If you check this option, the password that you assign will work for only one logon. As soon as the user logs on, he or she will be required to change the password.

7. **Click OK.**

   That's all there is to it! The user's password is now reset.

Disabling and Enabling User Accounts

If you want to temporarily prevent a user from accessing the network, you can disable his or her account. Then, you can enable the account later, when you're ready to restore the user to full access.

Here's the procedure:

1. **Log on as an administrator.**

   You have to have administrator privileges to perform this procedure.

2. **Choose Start⇨Administrative Tools⇨Active Directory Users And Computers.**

   The Active Directory Users And Computer management console appears.

3. **Click Users in the console tree.**

4. **In the Details pane, right-click the user that you want to enable or disable. Then, choose either Enable Account or Disable Account to enable or disable the user.**

Deleting a User

Deleting a user account is surprisingly easy. Just follow these steps:

1. **Log on as an administrator.**

   You have to have administrator privileges in order to perform this procedure.

2. **Choose Start⇨Administrative Tools⇨Active Directory Users And Computers.**

   The Active Directory Users And Computer management console appears.

3. **Click Users in the console tree.**

4. **In the details pane, right-click the user that you want to delete and choose Delete.**

   Windows will ask whether you really want to delete the user, just in case you're kidding.

5. **Click Yes.**

   Poof! The user is history.

Working with Groups

A *group* is a special type of account that represents a set of users who have common network access needs. Groups can dramatically simplify the task of assigning network access rights to users. Rather than assigning access rights to each user individually, groups let you assign rights to the group itself. Then, those rights automatically extend to any user that you add to the group.

The following sections describe some of the key concepts that you need to understand in order to use groups and some of the most common procedures you'll employ when setting up groups for your server.

Group types

Two distinct types of groups exist:

✦ **Security groups:** Most groups are security groups, which extend access rights to members of the group. For example, if you want to allow a group of users to access your high-speed color laser printer, you can create a group called ColorPrintUsers. Then, you can grant permission to use the printer to the ColorPrintUsers group. Finally, you can add individual users to the ColorPrintUsers group.

✦ **Distribution groups:** Distribution groups aren't used as much as security groups. They're designed as a way to send e-mail to a group of users by specifying the group as the recipient.

Group scope

Three distinct group scopes exist:

✦ **Domain local:** A group with *domain local scope* can have members from any domain. However, the group can be granted permissions only from the domain in which the group is defined.

✦ **Global:** A group with *global scope* can have members only from the domain in which the group is defined. However, the group can be granted permissions in any domain in the forest.

✦ **Universal scope:** Groups with *universal scope* are available in all domains that belong to the same forest.

As you can probably guess, universal scope groups are usually found only on very large networks.

One common way to use domain local and global groups is like this:

✦ Use domain local groups to assign access rights for network resources. For example, to control access to a high-speed color printer, create a domain local group for the printer. Grant the group access to the printer, but don't add any users to the group.

✦ Use global groups to associate users with common network access needs. For example, create a global group for users who need to access color printers. Then, add each user who needs access to a color printer membership in the group.

✦ Finally, add the global group to the domain local group. That way, access to the printer will be extended to all members of the global group.

This technique gives you the most flexibility when your network grows.

Book VII Chapter 2

Managing User Accounts

Default groups

Both Windows 2000 Server and Window Server 2003 come with a number of predefined groups that you can use. Although you shouldn't be afraid to create your own groups when you need them, there's no reason to create your own group if you find a default group that meets your needs.

Some of these groups are listed in the Builtin container in the Active Directory Users And Computers management console. Others are found in the Users container. Table 2-1 lists the more useful default groups found in Builtin, while Table 2-2 lists the default groups found in the Users container.

Table 2-1	Default Groups Located in the Builtin Container
Group	*Description*
Account Operators	This group is for users who should be allowed to create, edit, or delete user accounts, but shouldn't be granted full administrator status.
Administrators	These are the system administrators who have full control over the domain. The Administrator account is a default member of this group. You should create only a limited number of accounts that belong to this group.
Backup Operators	This group is for users who need to perform backup operations. Because this group must have access to the files that are backed up, it presents a security risk. So you should limit the number of users that you add to this group.
Guests	This group allows members to log on but little else. The default Guest account is a member of this group.
Network Configuration Operators	This group is allowed to twiddle with network configuration settings, including releasing and renewing DHCP leases.
Print Operators	This group grants users access to printers, including the ability to create and share new printers and to manage print queues. Allow logon locally; shut down the system.
Remote Desktop Users	This group can remotely log on to domain controllers in the domain.
Replicator	This group is required to support directory replication. Don't add users to this group.
Server Operators	These users can log on locally to a domain controller.
Users	These users can perform common tasks, such as running applications and using local and network printers.

Table 2-2	Default Groups Located in the Users Container
Group	*Description*
Cert Publishers	These users can publish security certificates for users and computers.
DnsAdmins	This group is installed if you install DNS. It grants administrative access to the DNS Server service.
DnsUpdateProxy	This group is installed if you install DNS. It allows DNS clients to perform dynamic updates on behalf of other clients, such as DHCP servers.
Domain Admins	These users have complete control of the domain. By default, this group is a member of the Administrators group on all domain controllers, and the Administrator account is a member of this group.
Domain Computers	This group contains all computers that belong to the domain. Any computer account created becomes a member of this group automatically.
Domain Controllers	This group contains all domain controllers in the domain.
Domain Guests	This group contains all domain guests.
Domain Users	This group contains all domain users. Any user account created in the domain is added to this group automatically.
Group Policy Creator Owners	These users can modify Group Policy for the domain.
IIS_WPG	This group is created if you install IIS. It is required in order for IIS to operate properly.
RAS and IAS Servers	This group is required in order for RAS and IAS servers to work properly.

Creating a group

If none of the built-in groups meet your needs, you can create your own group by following these steps:

1. **Log on as an administrator.**

You have to have administrator privileges to perform this procedure.

2. **Choose Start➪Administrative Tools➪Active Directory Users And Computers.**

The Active Directory Users And Computer management console appears.

3. **Right-click the domain to which you want to add the group and then choose New➪Group.**

The New Group dialog box appears, as shown in Figure 2-10.

Figure 2-10:
Creating a
new group.

4. **Type the name for the new group.**

5. **Choose the group scope.**

   The choices are Domain Local, Global, or Universal. For groups that will
   be granted access rights to network resources, use Domain Local. Use
   Global for groups to which you'll add users and Domain Local groups. Use
   Universal groups only if you have a large network with multiple domains.

6. **Choose the group type.**

   The choices are Security and Distribution. In most cases, you'll specify
   Security.

7. **Click OK.**

   The group is created.

Adding a member to a group

Groups are collections of objects, called *members*. The members of a group
can be user accounts or other groups. When you create a group, it has no
members. As a result, the group isn't very useful until you add at least
one member.

Follow these steps to add a member to a group:

1. **Log on as an administrator.**

   You have to have administrator privileges in order to perform this
   procedure.

2. **Choose Start⇨Administrative Tools⇨Active Directory Users And Computers.**

   The Active Directory Users and Computer management console appears.

3. **Open the folder that contains the group to which you want to add members and then double-click the group.**

   The Group Properties dialog box appears.

4. **Click the Members tab.**

   The members of the group are displayed, as shown in Figure 2-11.

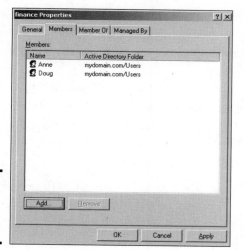

Figure 2-11: Adding members to a group.

5. **Type the name of a user or other group that you want to add to this group and then click Add.**

   The member is added to the list.

6. **Repeat Step 5 for each user or group that you want to add.**

   Keep going until you've added everyone!

7. **Click OK.**

That's all there is to it.

The Group Properties dialog box also has a Member Of tab that lists each group that the current group is a member of.

Adding members to a group is only half of the process of making a group useful. The other half is adding access rights to the group so that the members of the group can actually *do* something. The procedures for doing that are covered in the next chapter.

User Profiles

User profiles automatically maintain desktop settings for Windows users. By default, user profiles are stored on each user's local computer. The following items are just some of the settings that are stored as part of the user profile:

- ✦ Desktop settings in the Display Properties dialog box, including wallpaper, screen savers, and color schemes.
- ✦ Start menu programs and Windows toolbar options.
- ✦ Favorites, which provide easy access to the files and folders that the user accesses frequently.
- ✦ Application Data, such as option settings, custom dictionaries, and so on.
- ✦ Cookies, used for Internet browsing.
- ✦ My Recent Documents, which keeps shortcuts to the documents most recently accessed by the user.
- ✦ Templates, which stores user templates.
- ✦ Network Neighborhood, which keeps shortcuts to the user's network locations.
- ✦ Send To, which keeps shortcuts to document-handling utilities.
- ✦ Local Settings, such as history and temporary files.
- ✦ Printers, which keeps shortcuts to the user's printers.
- ✦ My Documents.

Types of user profiles

Four types of user profiles exist:

- ✦ **Local user profile:** A *local user profile* is stored on the user's local computer and is applied only when the user logs on to that computer. A local user profile is created automatically when a new user logs on.
- ✦ **Roaming user profile:** A *roaming user profile* is created on a network share. That way, the user can access the roaming profile when he or she logs on to any computer on the network.

✦ **Mandatory user profile:** A *mandatory user profile* is a roaming user profile that the user is not allowed to change. One benefit of mandatory user profiles is that users can't mess up their desktop settings. Another is that you can create a single mandatory profile that can be used by multiple users.

✦ **Temporary user profile:** If a roaming or mandatory profile is not available for some reason, a *temporary user profile* is automatically created for the user. The temporary profile is deleted when the user logs off, so any changes that the user makes while using a temporary profile are lost at the end of the session.

Creating a roaming profile

A roaming user profile is simply a user profile that has been copied to a network share so that it can be accessed from any computer on the network.

Before you can create roaming user profiles, you should create a shared folder on the server to hold the profiles. You can name the shared folder anything you like, but most administrators call it Users. For information on the procedure to create a shared folder, see Chapter 3 of this book.

After you've created the shared Users folder, you can copy the profile to the server by following these steps at the user's local computer:

1. **Log on to the computer by using an account other than the one you want to make a user account.**

Windows won't let you copy the profile that you're logged on with.

2. **Open the Control Panel and then double-click the System icon.**

3. **Click the Advanced tab and then click the Settings button in the User Profile section.**

This step brings up the dialog box shown in Figure 2-12.

4. **Select the profile that you want to copy and then click Copy To.**

A Copy To dialog box appears.

5. **Type the path and name for the roaming profile Copy Profile To box.**

For example, to copy a profile named Doug to the User share on a server named Server01, type **\\Server01\Users\Doug**.

6. **Click OK.**

The profile is copied.

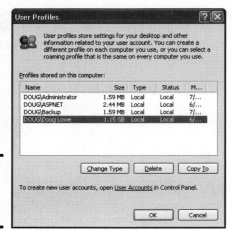

Now, you can go back to the server, log on as an administrator, and follow these steps to designate a roaming profile for the user's domain account:

1. **Choose Start⇨Administrative Tools⇨Active Directory Users And Computers**.

The Active Directory Users And Computer management console appears.

2. **Right-click the user account and choose Properties.**

The User Properties dialog box appears.

3. **Click the Profile tab.**

The Profile tab appears. This tab was shown in Figure 2-9, so I won't repeat it again here.

4. **Type the path and name of the profile in the Profile Path text box.**

The path and name that you type here should be the same path and name that you used to copy the profile to the server.

5. **Click OK.**

Chapter 3: Managing a File Server

In This Chapter

✔ **Configuring a file server**

✔ **Sharing folders**

✔ **Setting permissions**

✔ **Configuring offline storage options**

✔ **Setting up shadow copies**

✔ **Kicking users off your file server**

*1*n this chapter, you discover how to set up and manage file and print servers in Windows 2000 Server and Windows Server 2003. Because the features for file and print servers are essentially the same for both operating systems, the techniques presented in this chapter should work for either system.

Understanding Permissions

Before I get into the details of setting up a file server, you need to have a solid understanding of the concept of permissions. *Permissions* are what allow users to access shared resources on a network. Simply sharing a resource such as a disk folder or a printer doesn't guarantee that a given user will be able to access that resource. Windows makes this decision based on the permissions that have been assigned to various groups for the resource and group memberships of the user. If the user belongs to a group that has been granted permission to access the resource, the access will be allowed. If not, access will be denied.

In theory, permissions sound pretty simple. In practice, however, it can get pretty complicated. The following paragraphs explain some of the nuances of how access control and permissions work:

✦ Every object — that is, every file and folder — on an NTFS volume has a set of permissions called the *Access Control List,* or *ACL,* associated with it.

✦ The ACL identifies the users and groups who can access the object and specify what level of access that the user or group has. For example, a folder's ACL may specify that one group of users can read files in the folder, while another group can read and write files in the folder, and a third group is denied access to the folder altogether.

✦ Container objects — files and volumes — allow their ACLs to be inherited by the objects that they contain. As a result, if you specify permissions for a folder, those permissions extend to the files and child folders that appear within it.

✦ Table 3-1 lists the six permissions that can be applied to files and folders on an NTFS volume.

✦ Actually, the six file and folder permissions are composed of various combinations of *special permissions* that grant more detailed access to files or folders. Table 3-2 lists the special permissions that apply to each of the six file and folder permissions.

✦ It's best to assign permissions to groups rather than to individual users. Then, if a particular user needs access to a particular resource, add that user to a group that has permission to use the resource.

Table 3-1	File and Folder Permissions
Permission	*Description*
Full control	The user has unrestricted access to the file or folder.
Modify	The user can change the file or folder's contents, delete the file or folder, read the file or folder, or change the attributes of the file or folder. For a folder, this permission allows you to create new files or subfolders within the folder.
Read & Execute	For a file, this permission grants the right to read or execute the file. For a folder, this permission grants the right to list the contents of the folder or to read or execute any of the files in the folder.
List Folder Contents	This permission applies only to folders; it grants the right to list the contents of the folder.
Write	Grants the right to change the contents of a file or its attributes. For a folder, grants the right to create new files and subfolders within the folder.
Read	Grants the right to read the contents of a file or folder.

Table 3-2	Special Permissions					
Special Permission	*Full Control*	*Modify*	*Read & Execute*	*List Folder Contents*	*Read*	*Write*
Traverse Folder/Execute File	*	*	*	*		
List Folder/Read Data	*	*	*	*	*	
Read Extended Attributes	*	*	*	*	*	
Create Files/Write Data	*	*				*
Create Folders/Append Data	*	*				*

Special Permission	Full Control	Modify	Read & Execute	List Folder Contents	Read	Write
Write Attributes	*	*				*
Write Extended Attributes	*	*				*
Delete Subfolders and Files	*					
Delete	*	*				
Read Permissions	*	*	*	*	*	*
Change Permissions	*					
Take Ownership	*					
Synchronize	*	*	*	*	*	*

Understanding Shares

A *share* is simply a folder that is made available to other users via the network. Each share has the following elements:

+ **Share name:** The name by which the share is known over the network. To be compatible with older computers, you should stick to eight-character share names whenever possible.

+ **Path:** The path to the folder on the local computer that's being shared, such as C:\Accounting.

+ **Description:** A one-line description of the share.

+ **Permissions:** A list of users or groups who have been granted access to the share.

When you install Windows and configure various server roles, special shared resources are created to support those roles. You shouldn't disturb these special shares unless you know what you're doing. Table 3-3 lists some of the more common special shares.

Notice that some of the special shares end with a dollar sign ($). These shares are *hidden shares* that aren't visible to users. However, you can still access them by typing the complete share name (including the dollar sign) when the share is needed. For example, the special share C$ is created to allow you to connect to the root directory of the C: drive from a network client. You wouldn't want your users to see this share, would you? (Of course, shares such as C$ are also protected by privileges so that if an ordinary user finds out that C$ is the root directory of the server's C: drive, he or she still can't access it.)

Table 3-3	Special Shares
Share Name	*Description*
drive$	The root directory of a drive.
ADMIN$	Used for remote administration of a computer. This share points to the operating system folder (usually, `C: \Windows`).
IPC$	Used by named pipes, a programming feature that lets processes communicate with one another.
NETLOGON	Required in order for domain controllers to function.
SYSVOL	Another required domain controller share.
PRINT$	Used for remote administration of printers.
FAX$	Used by fax clients.

Configuring the File Server Role

Windows Server 2003 includes a handy wizard that automatically configures the computer as a file server. The following procedure shows you how to use this wizard.

1. **Log on as an administrator.**

You need administrator rights in order to make the changes called for by this wizard.

2. **Choose Start⇨Administrative Tools⇨Manage Your Server.**

The Manage Your Server screen appears, as shown in Figure 3-1. This screen shows the various roles that you've configured for the server. If the File Server role already appears, you can skip the rest of this procedure — you've already configured the computer to be a file server.

3. **Choose Add Or Remove A Role.**

A screen appears, suggesting that you take some preliminary steps, such as connecting network cables and installing modems. Read this list just to make sure that you've done it all already.

4. **Click Next until you get to the Server Role page.**

The Server Role page, shown in Figure 3-2, lists the various roles that can be configured for the server.

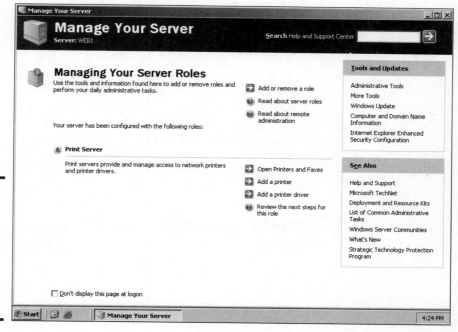

Figure 3-1:
The
Manage
Your Server
screen lets
you
configure
roles for
your server.

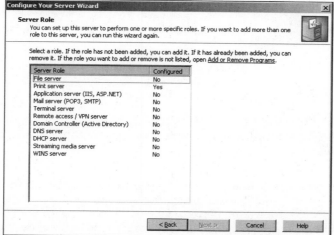

Figure 3-2:
The Server
Role page.

5. Select File Server and then click Next.

The File Server Disk Quotas page appears, as shown in Figure 3-3. This page lets you set up disk quotas to track and limit the amount of disk space used by each user. The default setting is to limit each user to a paltry 5MB of disk space. Microsoft recommends that you set this limit low and then change it for users who need more space.

This page also lets you specify the consequences that will occur if a user exceeds the quota. By default, no consequences are specified, so the quota is just a tracking device. If you want, you can tell Windows to refuse to let the user have more space than the quota specifies, or you can specify that an event should be logged to let you know that a user has exceeded the quota.

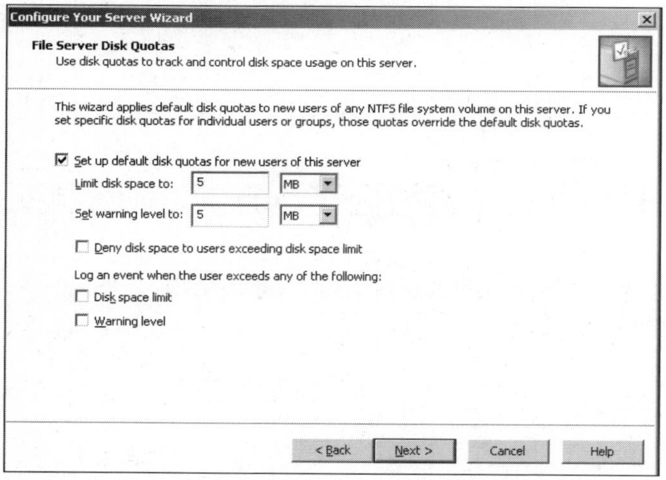

Figure 3-3:
The File Server Disk Quotas page.

6. Specify the disk quota settings that you want to use and then click Next.

The Indexing Service page appears. This page lets you indicate whether you want to activate the Windows Indexing Service for the file server. In most cases, activating this service is a bad idea because it can dramatically slow down the performance of the server. Few users take advantage of the Indexing Service, but if you need it, it's available here.

7. Check Yes if you want to use the Indexing Service or leave No checked to disable Indexing and then click Next.

A summary page appears, listing the options that you've selected.

8. Click Next.

The computer grinds and whirs for a moment as it configures the file server. In a moment, the Share A Folder Wizard appears. This wizard allows you to set up the initial file shares for the server.

9. Use the Share A Folder Wizard to share one or more folders.

For the complete procedure for using this wizard, see the section "Sharing a folder from the File Server Manager," later in this chapter.

After you're finished with the Share A Folder Wizard, the screen shown in Figure 3-4 is displayed.

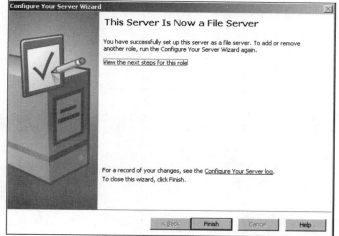

Figure 3-4: Congratulations! You have successfully created a file server.

10. Click Finish.

You're returned to the Manage Your Server page, which now lists the File Server role as active.

That's it. You have now configured the computer to be a file server.

Managing Your File Server

Windows Server 2003 also includes a handy File Server Manager console, as shown in Figure 3-5. From this console, you can easily create new shares, set up the permissions for a share, delete a share, and so on. To summon the File Server Manager, choose Start⇨Administrative Tools⇨Manage Your Server and then choose Manage File Server.

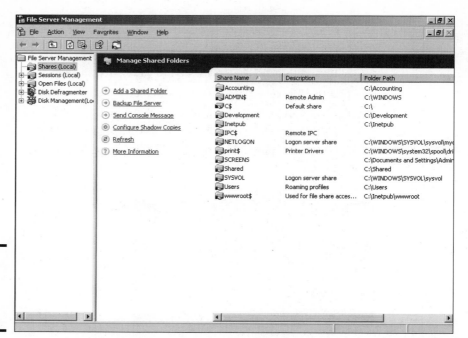

Figure 3-5:
The File
Server
Manager
console.

The following sections describe some of the more common procedures that you'll use when managing your file server.

Sharing a folder from the File Server Manager

To be useful, a file server should offer one or more *shares* — folders that have been designated as publicly accessible via the network. You can see a list of the current shares available from a file server by firing up the File Server Manager and clicking Shares in the console tree. The File Server Manager displays the share name, description, and network path for each share that you've already created.

To create additional shares, use the Share A Folder Wizard, as described in the following procedure.

1. **Select Shares from the console tree and then choose Action⇨New Share.**

   The Share A Folder Wizard comes to life, as shown in Figure 3-6.

Figure 3-6:
The Share
A Folder
Wizard.

2. Click Next.

The wizard asks you what folder you want to share, as shown in Figure 3-7.

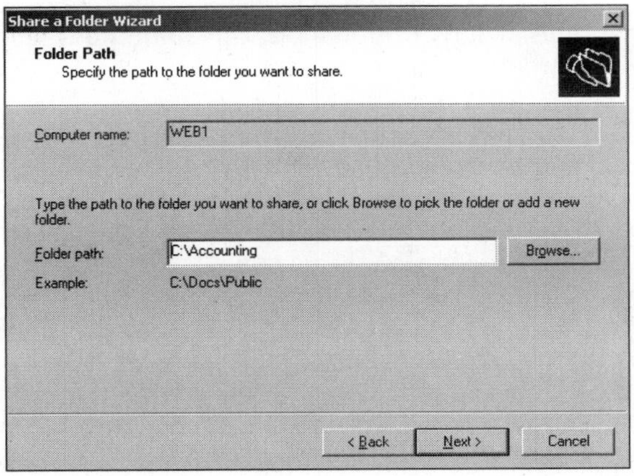

Figure 3-7:
Specifying
the folder to
share.

3. Type the path of the folder that you want to share over the network and then click Next.

If you aren't sure of the path, you can click Browse. This action calls up a dialog box that lets you search the server's hard drive for a folder to share. You can also create a new folder from this dialog box if the folder that you want to share doesn't yet exist. After you've selected or created the folder to share, click OK to return to the wizard.

Next, the dialog box shown in Figure 3-8 appears.

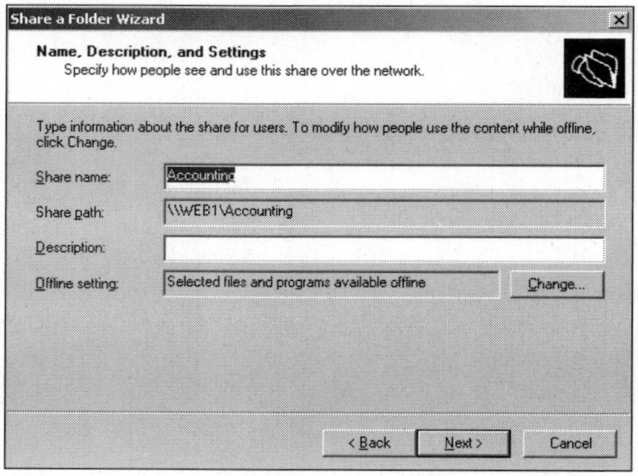

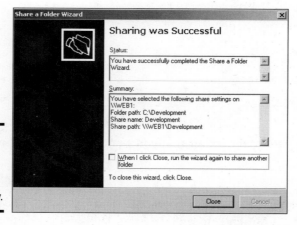

Figure 3-8:
Giving your
share a
name.

4. **Type the name that you want to use for the share in the Share Name box and a description of the share in the Description box.**

   The default name is the name of the folder being shared. If the folder name is long, you can use a more succinct name here.

   The description is strictly optional but can sometimes help users to determine the intended contents of the folder.

5. **Click Next.**

   The dialog box shown in Figure 3-9 appears.

Figure 3-9:
The share
was
completed
successfully.

6. **If you want to create another share, check the Run The Wizard Again checkbox, click Finish, and return to Step 3; otherwise, click Finish to dismiss the wizard.**

If you click Finish, you're returned to the File Server Management console. The share or shares that you created will now appear in the list.

Sharing a folder without the wizard

If you think wizards should be confined to Harry Potter movies, you can set up a share without bothering the wizard. Just follow these steps:

1. **Open the My Computer window and navigate to the folder that you want to share.**

2. **Right-click the folder and choose Sharing And Security.**

This action brings up the Properties dialog box for the folder, with the Sharing tab already selected, as shown in Figure 3-10.

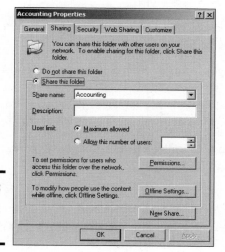

Figure 3-10: Manually sharing a folder.

3. **Select the Share This Folder option to designate the folder as shared.**

The rest of the controls on this dialog box will be unavailable until you check this box.

4. **Type the name that you want to use for the share in the Share Name box and a description of the share in the Description box.**

The default name is the name of the folder being shared. If the folder name is long, you can use a more succinct name here.

The description is strictly optional but can sometimes help users to determine the intended contents of the folder.

5. **Change the user limit if you want.**

   In most cases, it's best to leave this set at Maximum Allowed.

6. **If you want to specify permissions now, click Permissions.**

   This brings up a dialog box that lets you create permissions for the share. For more information, see the next section, "Granting permissions."

7. **Click OK.**

   The folder is now shared.

Granting permissions

When you first create a file share, all users are granted read-only access to the share. If you want to allow users to modify files in the share or allow them to create new files, you need to add additional permissions. Here's how to do this via the File Server Manager:

1. **Click Shares in the console tree.**

   A list of all the server's shares appears.

2. **Right-click the share you want to set permissions for, choose Properties, and then click the Share Permissions tab.**

   The dialog box shown in Figure 3-11 appears. This dialog box lists all the users and groups to whom you've granted permission for the folder. When you select a user or group from the list, the check boxes at the bottom of the list change to indicate which specific permissions you've assigned to each user or group.

3. **Click Add.**

   The dialog box shown in Figure 3-12 appears.

4. **Type the name of the user or group to whom you want to grant permission and then click OK.**

   You're returned to the Share Permissions tab, with the new user or group added.

If you're not sure of the name, click Advanced. This action brings up the dialog box shown in Figure 3-13. Here, you can click the Find Now button to display a list of all users and groups in the domain.

Alternatively, you can enter the first part of the name that you're looking for before you click Find Now to search more specifically. When you find the user or group that you're looking for, click OK.

5. **Check the appropriate Allow or Deny check boxes to specify which permissions to allow for the user or group.**

6. **Repeat Steps 3 through 5 for any other permissions that you want to add.**

7. **When you're done, click OK.**

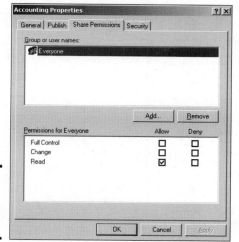

Figure 3-11: The Share Permissions tab.

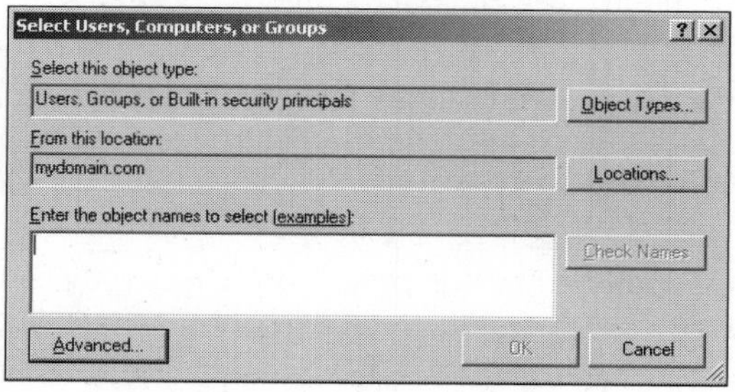

Figure 3-12: The Select Users, Computers, or Groups dialog box.

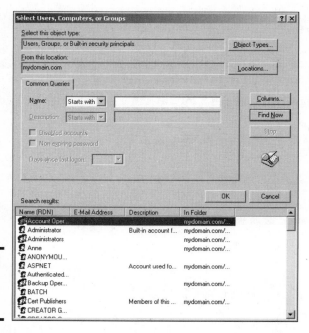

Figure 3-13:
Looking up
users and
groups.

Here are a few other thoughts to ponder concerning adding permissions:

✦ If you want to just grant full access to everyone for this folder, don't bother adding another permission. Instead, click the Everyone group to select it and then check the Allow box for each permission type.

✦ You can remove a permission by selecting the permission and then clicking Remove.

✦ If you'd rather not fuss with the File Server Manager, you can set the permissions from My Computer. Right-click the shared folder and choose Sharing And Security and then click Permissions. You can then follow the preceding procedure, picking up at Step 3.

✦ The permissions assigned in this procedure apply only to the share itself. The underlying folder can also have permissions assigned to it. If that's the case, whichever of the restrictions is more restrictive will always apply. For example, if the Share Permissions grant a user Full Control permission, but the folder permission grants the user only Read permission, the user will be given Read permission for the folder.

Advanced Features for Managing File Servers

After you've configured the server's File Server role, created shares, and granted permissions, you can usually let a file server run along pretty much unattended except for the occasional need to check the amount of free disk space remaining on the server, and regularly backing up the server. However, you may need to use a few other options and features in some circumstances.

Configuring offline settings

The *offline files* feature allows a user to maintain a copy of shared files on his or her computer so that the user can access the files when not connected to the network. This feature is most useful for notebook computer users who want to take their computers home with them or to travel with them. Windows saves a local copy of the user's network files on the client computer and automatically synchronizes the copies.

To control the offline settings for a share, right-click the share and choose Properties. Then, click the Offline Settings button. This brings up the dialog box shown in Figure 3-14. Here, you can choose one of three options for saving local copies of files in the share:

✦ **Only the files and programs that users specify will be available offline:** This option puts the responsibility for specifying which files should be saved for offline use on the user. This is the option to use if only a portion of the files in the shared folder need to be available for offline use.

✦ **All files and programs that users open from the share will be automatically saved offline:** This option automates offline storage by automatically saving a local copy of any file that the user retrieves from the share. You should use this option only for folders whose entire contents should be available to offline users.

✦ **Files or programs from the share will not be available offline:** Use this option to disable offline storage for the shared folder.

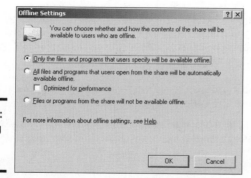

Figure 3-14:
Configuring
offline
settings.

Each user who wants to use offline files must configure his or her computer for offline work. To do that, the user can open My Computer, choose Tools⇨Folder Options, and select the Offline Files tab.

Setting up shadow copies

Shadow copies is a new feature for Windows Server 2003 that makes back-ups of a shared resource easy to get to on a scheduled basis. The user can access the shadow copies to retrieve files that were accidentally deleted or modified. When you enable shadow copies, you can set up a schedule to dictate how often the shadow copy should be made and the amount of storage to allocate to shadow copies.

To enable shadow copies, select the share and choose Configure Shadow Copies. The dialog box shown in Figure 3-15 appears. Click Enable to activate shadowing using the default schedule, which creates two shadow copies every day: one at 7 a.m. and the other at noon. To change this schedule, click Settings and set up the schedule however you want.

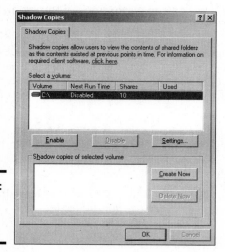

Figure 3-15:
Enabling shadow copies.

The following paragraphs describe some additional things that you need to know about using shadow copies:

✦ Shadow copies can retain up to 64 versions of the shadowed data. When this limit is reached, the oldest copy is deleted.

✦ The shadow copy feature doesn't copy all the files in the shared folder — only those that have changed since the last shadow copy was created.

✦ To access shadow copies, each user must install special client software on his or her computer. This software is automatically installed in the `\%systemroot%\System32\clients\twclient` folder on the server. You should copy the contents of this folder to a shared folder. Then, you can install the software on client computers by opening the shared folder and running `twclient.msi`.

✦ Shadow copies are not a substitute for regular backups!

Dealing with users

In the File Server Manager, you can click the Sessions folder in the console tree to display a list of all the users who are currently accessing the file server, as shown in Figure 3-16. This information may be useful if you're considering shutting down the server, or if you're just nosey and want to know who's using the server.

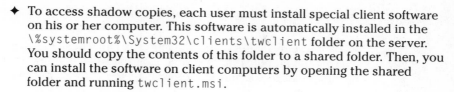

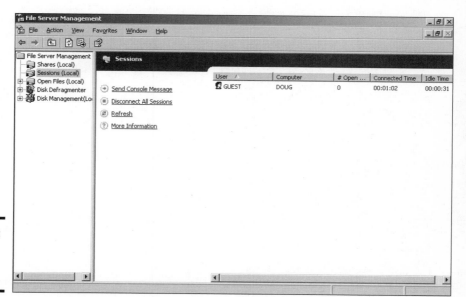

**Book VII
Chapter 3**

**Managing a
File Server**

Figure 3-16:
Finding out
who's on
first.

The following are some of the more interesting things you can do to your file server's users:

✦ You can force a user off your file server by right-clicking the user and choosing Disconnect.

✦ You can blow everyone off the server by clicking the Disconnect All Sessions link. This action is something you should do only in drastic circumstances.

✦ You can send a message to a user by clicking the Send Console Message link.

✦ If you're really nosy, you can click the Open Files folder in the console tree to find out what files each user has open. If you want to gain an appreciation for how hard your file server works, do this sometime on a busy day.

Chapter 4: Managing Security

In This Chapter

- ✔ Establishing password policies
- ✔ Using encrypted files and folders
- ✔ Auditing security events

*O*ne of the most important tasks assigned to any network administrator is the planning, implementing, and managing of the network's security policy. Much of Book III dealt with the general techniques of network security management. In this chapter, you find out the specifics of setting up security in a Windows 2000 Server and Windows Server 2003 environment.

Earlier chapters cover some of the basic Windows security features, such as setting up user and group accounts and granting rights. This chapter supplements that basic information and presents some additional security techniques, such as working with encryption, setting up a certificate server, and creating a virtual private network (VPN).

Configuring Account Policies

Accounts are the front door to your network. Although hackers love to break into your network through the back door, that usually requires some work on their part. It's much easier to come in through the front door if they discover that you've left it wide open.

To guard the front door, Windows lets you set *account policies* that enforce good security practices for user accounts. These account policies fall into three categories: password policies, account lockout policies, and Kerberos policies. After I describe these policy categories, I show you how to set them.

Password policies

Passwords are the keys to your network. No matter what other security measures you put in place, if you let your users leave their passwords blank, set their password to password, or use their last names as their passwords, your network may as well be an open book.

Fortunately, Windows' password policies let you enforce certain rules that compel your users to use strong passwords. You won't make many friends by setting these policies, but you'll sleep better.

The following list summarizes the various password policies that you can set.

✦ **Enforce password history:** This policy forces the user to use a certain number of distinct passwords before he or she is allowed to reuse a password. The minimum is zero, which disables this policy. The maximum is 24, which is probably overkill. A more realistic setting is about five.

✦ **Maximum password age:** This policy determines how long the user can keep a password before being required to change it. Typical settings are 30, 45, or 60 days.

✦ **Minimum password age:** This policy determines how long the user has to wait after changing the password before he or she can change it again. You should set this policy to at least one day. Otherwise, clever users can circumvent the Enforce Password History policy by cycling through multiple passwords all in one sitting just to get back to his or her favorite password.

✦ **Minimum password length:** This policy prevents the use of short passwords. The default setting of zero is ridiculous! That effectively lets your users not use passwords. I suggest a minimum of six or seven characters.

✦ **Passwords must meet complexity requirements:** This policy will probably make you very unpopular, but I suggest that you enable it. When this policy is enabled, all passwords must meet the following requirements:

  • The password may not contain all or part of the user's account name.

  • The password must be at least six characters long.

  • The password must contain at least three different types of characters. You can pick from uppercase letters, lowercase letters, numerals, and special symbols, such as $, %, #, and @.

✦ **Store passwords using reversible encryption for all users in the domain:** This policy sounds like it increases security, but actually it decreases security because reversible encryption is a type of encryption that's very easy to break. As a result, you should leave this policy disabled.

Account lockout policy

The next set of account policies is the *account lockout policies*. These policies determine what to do when Windows determines that someone is trying to guess their way into the network by repeatedly trying to log on with different passwords. When Windows decides that someone is trying to break in, it temporarily locks out the account. Hopefully, this action nips the would-be intruder's plans in the bud.

The following account lockout policies are available:

✦ **Account lockout threshold:** This policy determines how many times a user can unsuccessfully attempt to log on before the system decides to lock out the user. The default is zero, but that's a little draconian. After all, we all make mistakes. And if we're going to insist that users have passwords like `KR4dk26xsa92`, we'd better allow for a mistake or two as they try to type the password. A more reasonable threshold is from three to five mistakes.

✦ **Account lockout duration:** This policy determines how long the user will be locked out when the number of unsuccessful logon attempts exceeds the threshold. The default is Not Defined, which means that the user won't be locked out. I suggest a duration of at least 15 minutes.

✦ **Reset account lockout counter after:** This policy lets you cut the user some slack if the user waits awhile between invalid attempts. If a hacker is trying to gain entrance to your network by trying random passwords, he or she will probably keep trying different passwords one right after the other, without much delay in between. If a user makes two or three mistakes entering his or her password, then takes a few minutes off (during which time the user rifles through his or her desk drawers looking for that sticky note on which the password is written), and then tries again, the system should reset the invalid logon attempt count to give the user a fresh start. I suggest a setting of about 10 minutes for this policy.

Kerberos policy

Kerberos policy is a network security protocol that authenticates clients once when they log on and then grants the client a ticket that can be used throughout the session to access restricted resources. Some amusement parks work this way: You can purchase a wristband that grants you access to all rides in the park. If you're not wearing a wristband, you can't get on any of the rides.

The following Kerberos policies are available:

✦ **Enforce user logon restrictions:** This policy causes Kerberos to check the user's rights before granting a Kerberos ticket.

✦ **Maximum lifetime for service ticket:** Specifies how long a service ticket should be considered valid. The default is 600 minutes (10 hours).

✦ **Maximum lifetime for user ticket:** Specifies how long a user ticket should be considered valid. The default is 600 minutes (10 hours).

✦ **Maximum lifetime for user ticket renewal:** Specifies how long a user ticket should be considered renewable. When a ticket expires, the user can renew the ticket as long as the ticket's renewal lifetime hasn't expired. The default is seven days.

✦ **Maximum tolerance for computer clock synchronization:** Kerberos relies on time stamps as part of its protocol for repelling certain kinds of attacks. In order for this to work, the clocks on the client and server computers must be relatively close to each other. The default setting of five minutes is usually appropriate.

Setting account policies

The following procedure shows you how to change account policies:

1. **Log on as an administrator.**

You need administrator access in order to perform this procedure.

2. **Choose Start➪Administrative Tools➪Domain Security Policies.**

The Domain Controller Security Policy console appears.

3. **Expand Account Policies.**

The account policies are shown.

4. **Select the policy category that you want to change from the console tree.**

For example, Figure 4-1 shows the Password Policies screen.

5. **Double-click the policy that you want to change.**

The policy dialog box appears. For example, Figure 4-2 shows the dialog box for the Maximum Password Age policy.

6. **Set the value that you want for the policy and then click OK.**

You're returned to the policy console.

7. **Repeat Steps 4 through 6 for any other policies that you want to change.**

8. **Close the Group Policy Object Editor.**

You're done!

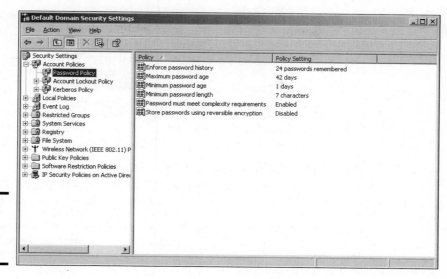

Book VII
Chapter 4

Managing
Security

Figure 4-1:
Editing the
password
policies.

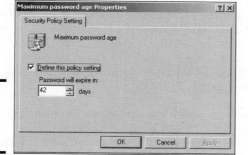

Figure 4-2:
Changing a
security
policy.

Encrypting Files and Folders

Encryption refers to the process of translating plain text information into a
secret code so that unauthorized users can't read the data. Encryption is
not new. Secret agents have long used codebooks to encode messages, and
breaking the code has always been one of the top priorities of counter-intel-
ligence. As it turns out, code-breaking during World War II was one of the
main reasons that electronic computers were invented.

Both Windows 2000 Server and Windows Server 2003 have a feature called
Encrypted File System, or *EFS* for short, that lets you save data on disk in an
encrypted form. This prevents others from reading your data even if they
manage to get their hands on your files.

Encryption is especially useful in environments where the server can't be physically secured. If a thief can steal the server computer (or just its hard drive), he or she may be able to crack through the Windows security features and gain access to the data on the hard drive by using low-level disk diagnostic tools. If the files are stored in encrypted form, however, the thief's efforts will be wasted because the files will be unreadable.

The following sections describe some basic concepts of data encryption; then I show you how to use the Encrypted File System to save encrypted data.

Understanding public key encryption

All forms of encryption use some sort of *key* to encrypt and decrypt the data. In World War II and Cold War spy movies, the key is a codebook that has a list of code words or phrases that match up to real words or phrases. The most basic type of data encryption, called *synchronous data encryption,* uses numeric keys that are used to apply complex mathematical operations to the source data in order to translate the data into encrypted form. These operations are reversible, so if you know the key, you can reverse the process and decrypt the data.

For example, suppose that the encryption technique is as simple as shifting every letter of the alphabet up by the value of the key. Thus, if the key is 3, then A becomes D, B becomes E, C becomes F, and so on. The message "Elementary, my dear Watson" becomes "Hohphqwdua, pa ghdu Zdwvrq." This message is incomprehensible, unless you know the key. Then, reconstructing the original message is easy.

Of course, the actual keys and algorithms used for cryptography are much more complicated. Keys are typically binary numbers of 40 or 128 bits, and the actual calculations used to render the data in encrypted form are complicated enough that they're patented. The basic idea is the same, though.

The classic dilemma of cryptography is this: How can I securely send the key to the person with whom I want to exchange secret messages? The answer is you can't. You can't encrypt the key, because the other person would need to know the key in order to decrypt it.

That's where *public key encryption* comes into play. Public key encryption is a technique that was developed in the 1970s in which two keys are used: a *private key* and a *public key*. The keys are related to each other mathematically. Either of the keys can be used to encrypt the data, but the encryption process isn't completely reversible: You have to have the private key in order to decrypt the data.

As a result, if you want to exchange encrypted data with someone, you can generate a private and public key and then send the public key to the other person, have that person use the key to encrypt the data, and have him or her send the encrypted data back to you. You can then use the private key to decrypt the data.

The key to public key encryption is that you can't decrypt the data with the public key alone. Thus, no one but you can decrypt a message after it's been encrypted with a public key. In fact, the person who encrypted the message in the first place can't even decrypt it.

Understanding EFS

EFS is a public key encryption system that lets users automatically encrypt files on an NTFS volume. To encrypt a file with EFS, two types of keys are required. First, each user is issued a public and private key pair. The server uses the public key to encrypt data. The user uses the private key to decrypt data.

The public/private key pair doesn't encrypt the data itself, however. Instead, when a user requests that a file be encrypted, EFS generates a random key called the *bulk symmetric encryption key*. This is a simple symmetric key that's used to both encrypt and decrypt the file. Then, the symmetric encryption key is encrypted using the user's public key and recorded with the file. As a result, the user's private key is required to decrypt the symmetric encryption key, which can then be used to decrypt the file itself.

EFS is installed automatically with Windows Server 2003 and Windows 2000 Server, so you don't have to do anything special to configure or install it. The keys are also managed automatically, so you don't have to do anything special to create keys or give them to users. In fact, end users handle most of the details of using EFS, as described in the next section.

Encrypting a folder

Although you can encrypt individual files, Microsoft recommends that you always use encryption at the folder level to encrypt all the files within a folder. That's important for the sake of security because many applications create temporary files that otherwise wouldn't be encrypted.

To designate that a folder should be encrypted, follow these steps:

1. **Locate the folder in My Computer or My Network Places**.

2. **Right-click the folder and choose Properties**.

The Properties dialog box appears.

3. **Click the Advanced button**.

The Advanced Attributes dialog box appears, as shown in Figure 4-3.

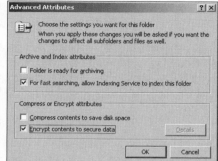

Figure 4-3:
Encrypting a
file or folder.

4. **Check Encrypt Contents To Secure Data and then click OK.**

   If you encrypt a file, an Encryption Warning dialog box appears to ask whether you want to encrypt just the file or the file and the folder that contains it. If you encrypt a folder, a Confirm Attribute Changes dialog box appears to ask whether you want to apply the change to just the folder, or also to all the files and subfolders contained in the folder.

5. **Select the option that you want to use in the Encryption Warning Or Confirm Attribute Changes dialog box and then click OK.**

   That's all there is to it.

You can't both encrypt and compress data. If you encrypt a folder that is compressed, Windows automatically uncompresses the folder. If you compress a folder that is encrypted, Windows automatically removes the encryption.

After you have designated a folder as being encrypted, any files that you save in the folder will be automatically encrypted. When you open the files, they will be automatically decrypted so you can work with them as if they weren't encrypted.

Sharing an encrypted folder with other users

For each encrypted file or folder, EFS maintains a list of users who are authorized to decrypt the file or folder. If you want to allow another user to access the file or folder, you can add that user to the list. Here are the steps:

1. **Locate the folder in My Computer or My Network Places.**

2. **Right-click the folder and choose Properties.**

   The Properties dialog box appears.

3. **Click the Advanced button.**

The Advanced Attributes dialog box appears. (Refer to Figure 4-2.)

4. **Click the Details button.**

   This calls up the Encryption Details dialog box, as shown in Figure 4-4.

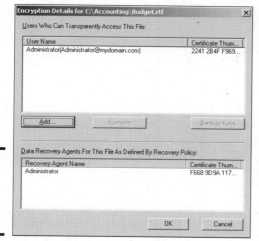

Figure 4-4:
The
Encryption
Details
dialog box.

Book VII
Chapter 4

Managing
Security

5. **Click the Add button.**

   The Select User dialog box appears, listing the users that you can add.

6. **Select the user that you want to add and then click OK.**

   If you can't find the user you're looking for, click Find User. This button allows you to search Active Directory for the user.

7. **Repeat Steps 5 and 6 to add other users.**

   You can add as many as you want.

8. **Click OK.**

   You're returned to the Properties dialog box.

9. **Click OK again.**

   Now you're done!

Auditing Security Events

An important part of any network's security is monitoring security events to determine when security problems have occurred or when security policy has been changed.

Security-related events are recorded in the Windows event log. You can view this log by choosing Start⇨Administrative Tools⇨Event Viewer. Then click Security in the console tree. The Event Viewer appears, as shown in Figure 4-5.

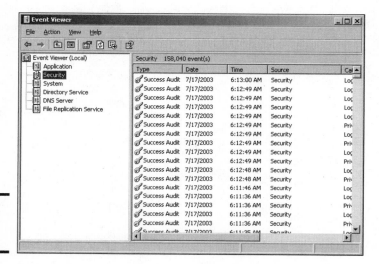

Figure 4-5:
The Event
Viewer.

You can control what types of security-related events are added to the log by adjusting the Audit Policy settings. Here's the procedure:

1. **Log on as an administrator.**

   You need administrator access in order to perform this procedure.

2. **Choose Start⇨Administrative Tasks⇨Domain Controller Security Policies.**

   The Domain Control Security Policies console appears. (If you want a refresher on its appearance, refer back to Figure 4-1.)

3. **Expand Local Policies and then click Audit Policy.**

   The Audit Policy settings appear, as shown in Figure 4-6.

4. **To change an audit policy, double-click the security event that you want to change and then select Success or Failure.**

   Choose Success to audit successful attempts and Failure to audit failed attempts. Table 4-1 describes the security events that you can audit.

5. **Repeat Step 4 for any other events that you want to change.**

6. **Close the Group Policy Object Editor.**

   You're done!

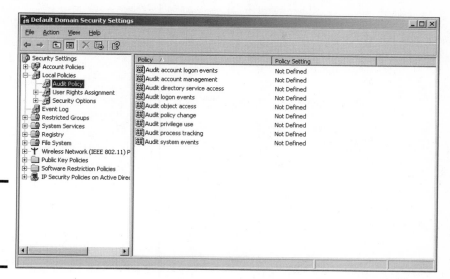

Book VII
Chapter 4

Managing Security

Figure 4-6:
Setting the security audit policies.

Table 4-1	Audit Policies
Policy	*Description*
Audit account logon events	Audits all attempts to log on to a domain using a user account. If you specify Success, your event log will fill up quickly as users log on to the system. If you specify Failure, you'll get an event in the log every time a user types the wrong password.
Audit account management	Audits account management events, such as creating or changing a user or group account, resetting a password, and so on.
Audit directory service access	Audits user access to active directory objects.
Audit logon events	Audits local computer logon attempts.
Audit object access	Audits all access to objects, such as files, folders, registry keys, printers, and so on.
Audit policy change	Audits changes to account policies.
Audit privilege use	Audits all instances of a user exercising one of his or her rights.
Audit process tracking	Generates detailed audit events that track the process of events, such as program activation, process exits, and so on.
Audit system events	Audits user restarts and shutdowns.

Chapter 5: Troubleshooting

In This Chapter

✔ **Examining the Event Viewer**

✔ **Perusing the Performance Console**

✔ **Checking out the Computer Management console**

✔ **Saluting the Services console**

*B*oth Windows 2000 Server and Windows Server 2003 are extremely reliable. Get them configured right in the first place, and they'll chug along without incident. That is, at least until something goes wrong. Which is inevitable.

In this chapter, I review some of the tools that Windows provides to help you diagnose trouble. Before I start, however, I want to point you to a few other chapters that also have troubleshooting information in them. This chapter deals only with those tools that apply specifically to Windows servers. You can find other information in these chapters:

✦ Book II, Chapter 6 gives you some guidance on verifying that the network is functioning.

✦ Book IV, Chapter 1 gives some basic network troubleshooting tips.

✦ Book IV, Chapter 2 gives some basic performance management tips.

✦ Book V, Chapter 6 explains how to use the TCP/IP troubleshooting tools (such as `Ping` and `Ipconfig`).

Working with the Event Viewer

Windows has a built-in event-tracking feature that automatically logs a variety of interesting system events. Usually, when something goes wrong with your server, you can find at least one and maybe dozens of events in one of the logs. All you have to do is open the Event Viewer and check the logs for suspicious-looking entries.

Using the Event Viewer

To display the event logs, choose Start⇨Administrative Tools⇨Event Viewer. This brings up the Event Viewer, as shown in Figure 5-1. The tree on the left side of the Event Viewer lists the five categories of events that are tracked:

✦ **Application:** Lists events that were generated by application programs. In most cases, these are events that the application's developers purposely wrote to the event log in order to inform you of error conditions or developing trouble.

✦ **Security:** Lists security-related events, such as unsuccessful logon attempts, changes to security policy, and so on. For information about how to change the events that are written to the security log, see Chapter 4 of this book.

✦ **System:** This is where you find events related to hardware or operating system failures. For example, if you're having trouble with a hard drive, you should check here for events related to the hard drive.

✦ **Directory Service:** Active Directory events are recorded here.

✦ **DNS Server:** If you're having trouble with your DNS service, look at this log to find the details.

✦ **File Replication Service:** Here is where you find events logged by File Replication Service.

Select one of these options to see the log that you want to view. In Figure 5-1, I clicked the System Events log and scrolled down the list a little to find some messages related to a DHCP problem.

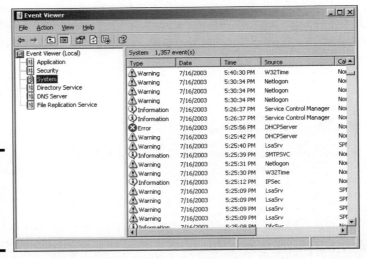

Figure 5-1:
The Event Viewer lets you examine events.

Notice the cute little icons next to each item in the log. Table 5-1 summarizes the meaning of these icons.

Table 5-1		Icons Used in the Event Log
Icon	*Name*	*Description*
ⓘ Information	Information	This message simply indicates that some noteworthy operation completed successfully.
⚠ Warning	Warning	An event developed a problem that wasn't fatal, but it may indicate a problem looming on the horizon.
✖ Error	Error	This message indicates that something has gone wrong.

To see the details for a particular event, double-click the event to bring up the Event Properties dialog box, shown in Figure 5-2. Here you can see the details of the event. In some cases, you may be able to diagnose a problem just by reading the error message displayed in this dialog box. In other cases, this information just points you in the right direction — it tells you *what* went wrong, but you still have to figure out *why*.

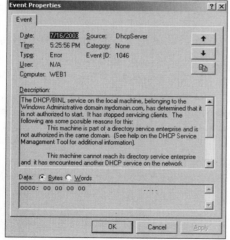

Figure 5-2:
Viewing an
event.

Setting event log policies

You can set default policies that affect how application, security, and system event logs are kept by opening the Default Domain Controller Security Settings console (Choose Start⇨Administrative Tools⇨Default Domain

Security Settings) and clicking Event Log in the console tree. This displays the event log policies, as shown in Figure 5-3.

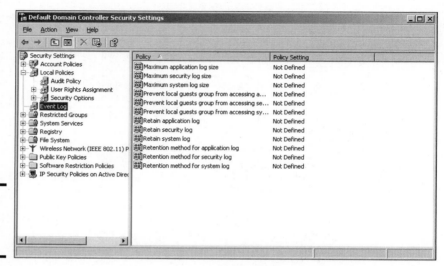

Figure 5-3:
Setting the event log policies.

You can use these policies to specify the following options:

✦ **Maximum log size:** Lets you specify the maximum size of the log in KB.

✦ **Prevent local guests from accessing log:** Prevents users who are logged on using a guest account from viewing the logs. This is a good security precaution.

✦ **Retain log:** This policy sounds like it may let you disable the log, but it doesn't. Instead, it specifies the number of days that log data should be kept if you specify By Days as the Retention Method policy.

✦ **Retention method for log:** Specifies how log events should be overwritten when the log becomes full. Options are By Days, As Needed, or Do Not Overwrite.

Monitoring Performance

Performance Console is a troubleshooting tool that can help you track down nasty and elusive problems — particularly the type that don't cause the server to crash, but just cause it to run slowly. With Performance Console, you can look at many different aspects of system performance to figure out why your system is dragging.

Using the Performance Console

To run the Performance Console, choose Start⇨Administrative Tools⇨ Performance. The Performance Console comes to life, as shown in Figure 5-4.

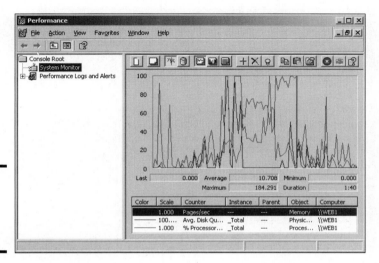

**Book VII
Chapter 5**

Troubleshooting

Figure 5-4:
Using
Perform-
ance
Console.

The display in Figure 5-4 shows performance data in the form of a graph. Although it isn't apparent from the figure, the display constantly updates itself as it gathers new data.

Performance Console lets you keep track of several different aspects of system performance at once. You track each performance aspect by setting up a *counter*. You can choose from hundreds of different counters. Table 5-2 describes some of the most commonly used counters. Notice that each counter refers to a server object, such as physical disk, memory, or the processor.

Table 5-2		Commonly Used Performance Counters
Object	*Counter*	*Description*
Physical Disk	% Free Space	The percentage of free space on the server's physical disks. Should be at least 15%.
Physical Disk	Average Queue Length	Indicates how many disk operations are waiting while the disk is busy servicing other disk operations. Should be two or less.
Memory	Pages/second	The number of pages retrieved from the virtual memory page files per second. A typical threshold is about 2,500.
Processor	% Processor Time	Indicates the percentage of the processor's time that it is busy doing work rather than sitting idle. Should be 85% or less.

To add a counter, click the Add button to bring up the Add Counters dialog box, as shown in Figure 5-5. Then select the object that you want from the Performance Object drop-down list, choose the counter that you want to add from the list, and click Add. You can add more than one counter from this dialog box; when you're finished adding counters, click Close to dismiss the Add Counters dialog box.

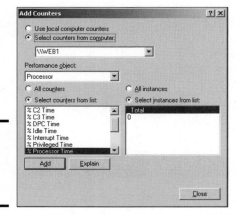

Figure 5-5:
Adding perform-ance counters.

You can switch the display to a histogram, as shown in Figure 5-6, by click-ing the View Histogram button. This displays your performance counters as bar graphs, which can sometimes make it easier to spot which counter is causing the most activity.

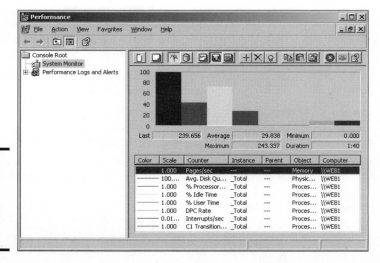

Figure 5-6:
Perform-ance Monitor in Histogram mode.

You can also switch the display to Report mode by clicking the View Report button, as shown in Figure 5-7. Here, the performance data is displayed in numeric form.

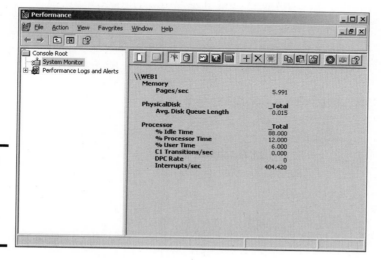

Book VII
Chapter 5

Troubleshooting

Figure 5-7:
Perform-
ance
Monitor in
Report
mode.

The act of gathering performance data slows down your server, so don't leave performance logging on all the time. Use it only occasionally to gather baseline data or when you're experiencing a performance problem.

Creating performance logs

Instead of staring at the Performance Console for hours on end waiting for a performance glitch to occur, Performance Console lets you set up logs that can track performance data over time. When the network is running well, you can collect log data to act as a baseline, so you'll know if performance has slipped. When the network is not acting well, you can collect log data to help isolate the problem.

Performance Console can create two types of logs:

✦ **Counter logs:** Simply accumulate performance counter data that you can display in summarized form later.

✦ **Trace logs:** Measure the performance of certain types of memory and resource events.

To set up a counter log, follow these steps:

1. **Right-click Counter Logs in the console tree and choose New Log Settings.**

   This action brings up a dialog box that asks for the name of the counter log.

2. **Type a name for your log and then click OK.**

   A dialog box similar to the one shown in Figure 5-8 appears.

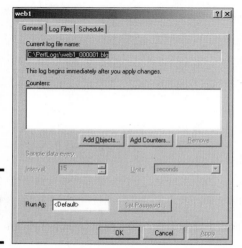

Figure 5-8:
Setting up a perform-
ance log.

3. **Click Add Counters to add a counter to the log.**

   This action brings up the Add Counters dialog box, which you can see in Figure 5-5.

4. **Select the object that you want from the Performance Object drop-down list, choose the counter you want to add from the list, and click Add.**

   The counter is added to the Counters list.

5. **Repeat Step 4 for each counter that you want to track.**

   You can track as many counters as you want.

6. **Click Close.**

   The Add Counters dialog box closes.

7. **If you want to schedule the log to run automatically, click the Schedule tab and set up the schedule.**

   The tab allows you to specify an automatic start and stop time so the log will run automatically.

8. **Click OK.**

   You're returned to the Performance Monitor console.

If you didn't schedule the monitor to start and stop automatically, you can start the log manually by selecting the log and then clicking the Start button in the toolbar. When you want to stop the log, select the log and click the Stop button.

To display the data accumulated by a performance log, click the System Monitor in the console tree and then click the View Log Data button in the toolbar. This brings up the System Monitor Properties dialog box with the Source tab selected, as shown in Figure 5-9. You can then select the log file that you want to display and click OK. If the log file doesn't appear in the list, click the Add button, select the file, and click OK.

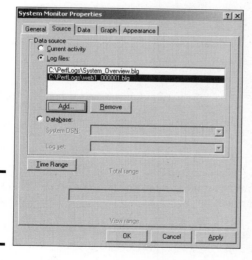

Figure 5-9:
Choosing a
log to
display.

Using the Computer Management Console

The Start➪Administrative Tools➪Computer Management command leads you to the Computer Management Console, which is a tool that's often useful when tracking down problems in a Windows Server 2003 system. Poke around the console tree in Computer Management, and you'll find

✦ **Event Viewer:** Refer to the section "Using the Event Viewer," earlier in this chapter, for more information.

✦ **Shared Folders:** Here you can manage your shared folders, current sessions, and open files. For more information, see Chapter 4 of this book.

✦ **Performance Logs and Alerts:** Refer to the section "Using the Performance Console," earlier in this chapter, for more information.

✦ **Device Manager:** A handy tool for diagnosing problems with hardware devices. Device Manager lists all the hardware devices currently installed on the computer, as shown in Figure 5-10. You can double-click a device to bring up a Properties dialog box that displays information about the status of the device and lets you change drivers or configuration settings.

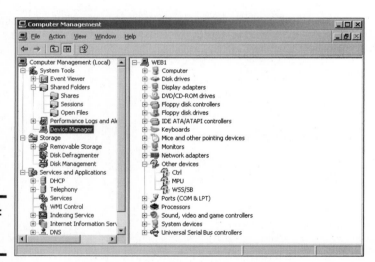

Figure 5-10:
Device
Manager.

✦ **Removable Storage:** Lets you track removable storage media, such as tapes and CDs, and manage tape and CD libraries.

✦ **Disk Defragmenter:** Lets you optimize the way data is stored on your disks.

✦ **Disk Management:** Lets you work with disk partitions, format disks, create mirror sets, and perform other disk operations.

✦ **Services and Applications:** Lets you manage services and applications that you've installed on the computer, such as DHCP, DNS, IIS, and so on.

Working with Services

The last troubleshooting tool I want to describe in this chapter is the Services console, which you can access by choosing Start➪Administrative Tools➪Services. As Figure 5-11 shows, the Services console displays a list of all the services that are currently running on your system.

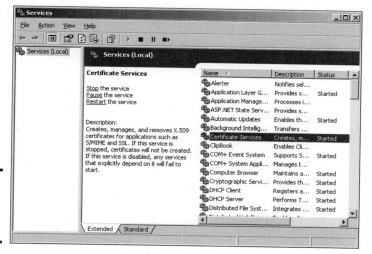

Figure 5-11: The Services console.

If a Windows server feature isn't working properly, the problem is often that something has caused one of the services associated with the feature to stop. You can often correct the problem by calling up the Services console and restarting the service. To do that, just select the service and then click the Start The Service link.

Of course, this action doesn't correct the underlying cause of the problem. If the service stopped because of a one-time error, simply restarting the service may be all that you need to do. In many cases, though, the problem that caused the service to start will resurface and cause the service to stop again.

Chapter 6: Windows Commands

In This Chapter

✔ Getting started with a command window

✔ Taking advantage of command tricks and techniques

✔ Looking at batch files

✔ Using the amazing Net commands

*A*lthough Windows sports a fancy graphical interface that makes it possible to perform most network management tasks by pointing and clicking, you can also do almost any network management task from a command prompt. Whether you choose to do so is largely a matter of personal style. Some network administrators pride themselves in being able to type Windows commands blindfolded and with two fingers from each hand tied behind their backs. Others have fully embraced the graphical user interface and think the command line is for administrators with UNIX envy.

So the choice is yours. Skip this chapter if the thought of typing commands causes you to lose sleep. For those of you who are willing to venture forth, this chapter begins with an overview of working from the command prompt. Then, it describes some of the more useful Windows commands. Finally, this chapter introduces the fine (and almost lost) art of writing batch files.

Using a Command Window

Command prompts are even older than video monitors. The first computer I worked on used a teletype machine as its terminal, so the command prompt was printed on paper rather than displayed on-screen. Surprisingly, though, the concept of the command prompt hasn't changed much since those days. The system displays a prompt to let you know it's waiting for a command. When you type the command and press the Enter key, the system reads your command, interprets it, executes it, displays the results, and then displays the prompt again so that you can enter another command.

Opening and closing a command window

To get to a command prompt on a Windows server, follow these steps:

1. Choose Start⇨Run.

The Run dialog box appears.

2. Type cmd.

Cmd.exe is the name of the command processor for Windows NT and Windows Server.

If you type **Command** instead, you get Command.com, the old MS-DOS command processor, which is considerably less powerful than cmd.exe.

3. Click OK.

The command prompt window appears, as shown in Figure 6-1.

Figure 6-1:
The command prompt window.

You can now type any commands that you want in the window.

To exit the command prompt, type **Exit** and press Enter. This properly terminates cmd.exe and closes the command prompt window. If you try to close the command prompt window by clicking its Close button, Windows is forced to shut down cmd.exe. The process will work, but you'll have to click your way through an intervening dialog box and wait a few seconds while Windows terminates cmd.exe. Entering the Exit command is a much faster method.

Editing commands

Most of the time, you'll just type commands by using the keyboard. If you make a mistake, you'll just retype the command again, being careful not to repeat the mistake. However, cmd.exe has several built-in editing features that can simplify the task of correcting a mistaken command or entering a sequence of similar commands:

✦ Press the right arrow key to recall the text of the last command that you entered, one letter at a time. When you get to the spot where the new command should differ from the previous command, start typing.

✦ Press F3 to recall all of the previous command, from the current cursor position to the end of the line.

✦ If you want to repeat a command that you've used recently, press the up arrow key. This recalls up to 50 of the most recently executed commands. You can press Enter to execute a command as is, or you can edit the command before you execute it.

Using the Control menu

Although the command window has no menu bar, it does have a menu that you can access via the control box at the top-left corner of the window. Besides the commands found on this menu for all windows (such as Move, Size, and Minimize), this menu includes three additional commands:

✦ **Edit:** The Edit command leads to a submenu with several choices. Several of these commands work together so that you can copy information from the command window to the Clipboard and vice versa. If you choose Edit⇨Mark, you're placed in a special editing mode that lets you highlight text in the command window with the mouse. (Normally, the mouse doesn't do anything in the command window.) You can then choose Edit⇨Copy or just press Enter to copy the text that you selected to the Clipboard.

You can also use the Edit menu to paste text from the Clipboard, to scroll the window, and to search the window for text.

✦ **Default:** Lets you set default properties for the command window.

✦ **Properties:** Displays a Properties dialog box that you can use to change the appearance of the window. You can change the font size, choose background colors, and make other adjustments to make the command window look good on your computer.

Special Command Tricks

Before I get into the details of using specific commands, I want to describe some techniques you should familiarize yourself with. In many cases, these techniques can let you accomplish in a single command what would otherwise take dozens of separate commands.

Wildcards

Wildcards are one of the most compelling reasons to use the command prompt. With wildcards, you can process all the files that match a particular naming pattern with a single command. For example, suppose that you have a folder containing 500 files, and you want to delete all the files that contain the letters *Y2K* and end with the extension .doc, which happens to be 50 files. If you open a My Documents window, you'll spend ten minutes picking these files out from the list. From a command window, you can delete them all with the single command Del *Y2K*.doc.

You can use two wildcard characters: an asterisk stands for any number of characters, including zero, and an exclamation mark stands for just one character. Thus, !Text.doc would match files with names like aText.doc, xText.doc, and 4Text.doc, but not abcText.doc or just Text.doc. However, *Text.doc would match any of the names mentioned in the previous sentence.

Wildcards work differently than they did in MS-DOS. In MS-DOS, anything you typed after an asterisk was ignored. Thus, ab*cd.doc was the same as ab*.doc. In Windows, the asterisk wildcard can come before static text, so ab*cd.doc and ab*.doc are *not* the same.

Chaining commands

You can enter two or more commands on the same line by separating the commands with an ampersand, like this:

```
C:>copy *.doc a: & del *.doc
```

Here, the Copy command copies all the .doc files to the A: drive. Then, the Del command deletes the .doc files.

Although that may be convenient, it's also dangerous. What if the A: drive fills up so that all the files can't be copied? In that case, the Del command executes anyway, deleting the files that didn't get copied.

A safer alternative is to use two ampersands, which says to execute the second command only if the first command finishes successfully. Thus:

```
C:>copy *.doc a: && del *.doc
```

Now, the Del command will be executed only if the Copy command succeeds.

You can also use two pipe characters (the *pipe* is the vertical bar character that's above the backslash on the keyboard) to execute the second command only if the first command fails. Thus,

```
C:>copy *.doc a: || echo Oops!
```

displays the message "Oops!" if the Copy command fails.

Finally, you can use parentheses to group commands. Then, you can use the other symbols in combination. For example:

```
C:>(copy *.doc a: && del *.doc) || echo Oops!
```

Here, the files are copied and then deleted if the copy was successful. If either command fails, the message is displayed.

Redirection and Piping

Redirection and piping are related techniques. *Redirection* lets you specify an alternate destination for output that will be displayed by a command or an alternate source for input that should be fed into a command. For example, you can save the results of an ipconfig /all command to a file named myconfig.txt like this:

```
C:>ipconfig /all > myconfig.txt
```

Here, the greater-than sign (>) is used to redirect the command's console output.

If a command accepts input from the keyboard, you can use input redirection to specify a file that contains the input you want to feed to the command. For example, you can create a text file named lookup.txt with subcommands for a command such as nslookup. Then, you can feed those scripted subcommands to the nslookup command, like this:

```
C:>nslookup <lookup.txt
```

Piping is a similar technique. It takes the console output from one command and feeds it into the next command as input. Piping is often used with special commands called *filters,* which are designed to read input from the console, modify the data in some way, and then write it to the console.

For example, suppose that you want to display the contents of a file named users.txt sorted into alphabetical order. You can use the Type command, which displays a file on the console, and then pipe the output into the Sort command, a filter that sorts its input and displays the sorted output on the console. The resulting command would look like this:

```
C:>type users.txt | sort
```

The vertical bar is often called the *pipe character* because it's the symbol used to indicate piping.

Environment variables

The command shell makes several *environment variables* available to commands. Environment variables all begin and end with percent signs. You can use an environment variable anywhere in a command. For example:

```
C:>echo %OS% running on a %PROCESSOR_IDENTIFIER%
```

displays a line such as:

```
Windows_NT running on an x86 Family 15 Model 2 Stepping 4,
    GenuineIntel
```

Interestingly, Windows NT, Windows 2000 Server, and Windows Server 2003 all display "Windows_NT" for the operating system name.

If the environment variable represents a path, you may need to enclose it in quotation marks, like this:

```
C:>dir "%HOMEPATH%"
```

This command displays the contents of the user's home directory. The quotation marks are required here because the environment variable expands to a pathname that may include spaces, and the command shell requires that long filenames that include spaces must be enclosed in quotation marks.

Table 6-1 lists the environment variables that are available to you and your commands.

Table 6-1	Environment Variables
Variable	*Description*
%ALLUSERSPROFILE%	The location of the All Users profile.
%APPDATA%	The path where applications store data by default.
%CD%	The path to the current directory.
%CMDCMDLINE%	The command line that was used to start the command shell.
%CMDEXTVERSION%	The version number of the command shell.
%COMPUTERNAME%	The computer's name.
%COMSPEC%	The path to the command shell executable (cmd.exe).
%DATE%	The current date in the format generated by the date /t command.
%ERRORLEVEL%	The error returned by the most recent command.
%HOMEDRIVE%	The drive letter of the user's home directory.
%HOMEPATH%	The path to the user's home directory.

Variable	Description
%HOMESHARE%	The network path to the user's shared home directory.
%LOGONSERVER%	The name of the domain contoller the user logged on to.
%NUMBER_OF_PROCESSORS%	The number of processors on the computer.
%OS%	The name of the operating system.
%PATH%	The current search path.
%PATHEXT%"	A list of the extensions the operating system treats as executable files.
%PROCESSOR_ARCHITECTURE%	The chip architecture of the processor.
%PROCESSOR_IDENTIFIER%	A description of the processor.
%PROCESSOR_REVISION%	The revision level of the processor.
%PROMPT%	The current prompt string.
%RANDOM%	A random number between 1 and 32,767.
%SYSTEMDRIVE%	The drive containing the operating system.
%SYSTEMROOT%	The path to the operating system.
%TEMP%	The path to a temporary folder for temporary files.
%TMP%	Same as %TEMP%.
%TIME%	The time in the format produced by the time /t command.
%USERDOMAIN%	The name of the user's domain.
%USERNAME%	The user's account name.
%USERPROFILE%	The path to the user's profile.
%WINDIR%	The path to the operating system directory.

**Book VII
Chapter 6**

**Windows
Commands**

Batch files

A *batch file* is simply a text file that contains one or more commands. Batch files are given the extension .bat and can be run from a command prompt as if they were commands or programs. You can also run a batch file from the Start menu by choosing Start➪Run, typing the name of the batch file, and clicking OK.

As a network administrator, you'll find plenty of uses for batch files. Most of them won't be very complicated. For example, here are some examples of very simple batch files I've used:

✦ I once used a one-liner file to copy the entire contents of a key shared network drive to a user's computer every night at 10 p.m. The user had just purchased a new Dell computer with a 100GB drive, and the server had only a 20GB drive. The user wanted a quick-and-dirty backup solution that would complement the regular tape backups that run every night.

✦ I've also used a pair of short batch files to stop and then restart Exchange server before and after nightly backups for backup software that didn't have an Exchange plug-in that could back up the mail store while it was open.

✦ If I frequently need to work with several related folders at once, I create a short batch file that opens Explorer windows for each of the folders. (You can open an Explorer window from a batch file simply by typing the path to the folder that you want to open as a command.) Then, I place the batch file on my desktop so I can get to it quickly.

You can also use batch files to create logon scripts that are executed whenever a user logs on. Microsoft keeps trying to get users to use profiles instead of logon scripts, but many networks still use logon scripts.

You can use Notepad to create batch files, but I prefer the text-mode `Edit` command. Just type **Edit filename** at a command prompt to bring up the text editor, as shown in Figure 6-2.

Figure 6-2:
The Edit command.

Using Windows Net Commands

Among the more useful commands for Network administrators are the `Net Services` commands. These commands are all two-word commands, beginning with Net — such as `Net Use` and `Net Start`. In the following sections, I present each of the `Net` commands, in alphabetical order for handy reference. First, though, I want to point out a few details about the `Net` commands:

✦ You can get a quick list of the available `Net` commands by typing **net /?** at a command prompt.

✦ You can get brief help for any net command by typing **net help command.** For example, to display help for the `Net Use` command, type **net help use**. (Yes, we all could use some help.)

✦ Many of the Net commands prompt you for confirmation before completing an operation. For these commands, you can specify /Y or /N to bypass the confirmation prompt. You'll want to do that if you include these commands in a batch file that runs unattended. Note that you can use /Y or /N on any Net command, even if it doesn't prompt you for confirmation. So I suggest that you place /Y on every Net command in a batch file that you intend on running unattended.

The Net Accounts command

This command updates user account policies for password requirements. Here's the command syntax:

```
net accounts [/forcelogoff:{minutes | no}]
             [/minpwlen:length]
             [/maxpwage:{days | unlimited}]
             [/minpwage:days]
             [/uniquepw:number]
             [/domain]
```

The following paragraphs describe the parameters for the Net Accounts command:

✦ **Forcelogoff:** Specifies how long to wait before forcing a user off the system when the user's logon time expires. The default value, no, prevents users from being forced to log off. If you specify a number, the user will be warned a few minutes before being forcibly logged off.

✦ **Minpwlen:** Specifies the minimum length for the user's password. *Number* can be from 0 through 127. The default is 6.

✦ **Maxpwlen:** Specifies the number of days a user's password is considered valid. *Unlimited* means the password will never expire. *Days* can be from 1 through 49,710, which is about 135 years. The default is 90.

✦ **Minpwage:** Specifies the minimum number of days after a user changes a password before the user can change it again. The default value is 0. You should usually set this value to 1 day in order to prevent users from bypassing the Uniquepw policy.

✦ **Uniquepw:** Indicates how many different passwords the user must use before he or she is allowed to reuse the same password again. The default setting is 5. The range is from 0 to 24.

✦ **Domain:** Specifies that the operation should be performed on the primary domain controller rather than on the local computer.

If you enter Net Accounts without any parameters, the command simply displays the current policy settings.

**Book VII
Chapter 6**

**Windows
Commands**

Here's an example that sets the minimum and maximum password ages:

```
C:>net accounts /minpwage:7 /maxpwage:30
```

The Net Computer command

This command creates or deletes a computer account. Here's the syntax:

```
net computer \\computername {/add | /del}
```

The following paragraphs describe the parameters for the Net Computer command:

+ ***Computername***: The name of the computer to add or delete.

+ **Add:** Create a computer account for the specified computer.

+ **Delete:** Deletes the specified computer account.

Here's an example that adds a computer named *theodore:*

```
C:>net computer \\theodore /add
```

The Net Config command

This command lets you view or configure various network services. Here's the syntax:

```
net config [{server|workstation}]
```

To configure server settings, use this syntax:

```
net config server [/autodisconnect:time]
                  [/srvcomment:"text"]
                  [/hidden:{yes | no}]
```

The following paragraphs describe the parameters for the Net Config command:

+ **Server:** Lets you display and configure the Server service while it's running.

+ **Workstation:** Lets you display and configure the Workstation service while it's running.

+ **Autodisconnect:** Specifies how long user's session can be inactive before it's disconnected. Specify -1 to never disconnect. The range is -1 to 65535 minutes, which is about 45 days. The default is 15 minutes.

✦ **Srvcomment:** Specifies a description of the server. The comment can be up to 48 characters long and should be enclosed in quotation marks.

✦ **Hidden:** Specifies whether the server appears in screens that display available servers. Hiding a server doesn't make the server unavailable; it just means that the user will have to know the name of the server in order to access it. The default is No.

Here's an example that set's a server's descriptive comment:

```
C:>net config server /srvcomment:"DHCP Server"
```

The Net Continue command

This command continues a service you've suspended with the Net Pause command. Here's the syntax:

```
net continue service
```

Here are some typical services that you can pause and continue.

✦ **Netlogon:** The Net Logon service.

✦ **Schedule:** The Task Scheduler service.

✦ **Server:** The Server service.

✦ **Workstation:** The Workstation service.

Here's an example that continues the Workstation service:

```
CL>net continue workstation
```

If the service name has embedded spaces, enclose the service name in quotation marks. For example, this command continues the NT LM Security Support Provider Service:

```
C:>net continue "nt lm security support provider"
```

The Net File command

This command lists all open shared files and the number of file locks placed on each file. You can also use this command to close files and remove locks, which is a useful procedure when a user manages to accidentally leave a file open or locked. Here's the syntax:

```
C:>net file [id [/close]]
```

The following paragraphs describe the `Net File` command's parameters:

+ **ID:** The file's identification number.

+ **Close:** Closes an open file and releases any locks that were placed on the file.

To close a file, you must issue the command from the server where the file is shared.

`Net Files` works, too.

To close an open file, first run `Net Files` without any parameters to list the open files. Here's a sample of the output that you can expect from `Net File`:

```
File       Path              Username    #locks
------------------------------------------------
0          C:\BUDGET.DOC     WARD        0

1          C:\RECIPE.MDF     JUNE        4
```

Next, run `Net Files` again, specifying the file number displayed for the file that you want to close. For example, to close the `RECIPE.MDF` file, use this command:

```
C:>net file 1 /close
```

The Net Group command

This command lets you add, display, or change global groups. This command has a number of different syntaxes, depending on how you intend to use it.

To display information about a group or to change a group's comment, use this syntax:

```
net group groupname [/comment:"text"] [/domain]
```

To create a new group, use this syntax:

```
net group groupname /add [/comment:"text"] [/domain]
```

To delete a group, use this syntax:

```
net group groupname /delete [/domain]
```

Finally, to add or remove users from a group, use this syntax:

```
net group groupname username[ ...] {/add | /delete} [/domain]
```

The following paragraphs describe the parameters that you can use with the Net Group command:

✦ **Groupname:** The name of the group to add, change, or delete. If you specify this parameter and no others, a list of users in the group appears.

✦ **Comment:** Specifies a comment for the group. The comment be up to 48 characters in length and should be enclosed in quotation marks.

✦ **Domain:** Specifies that the operation should be performed on the primary domain controller rather than on the local computer.

✦ **Add:** Creates a new group or adds users to an existing group. Before you add a user to a group, you must first create a user account for the user.

✦ **Delete:** Removes a group or removes users from the group.

✦ **Username:** One or more usernames to be added to or removed from the group. If you list more than one name, separate the names with spaces.

Windows isn't picky: You can specify Net Groups rather than Net Group if you want.

This example lists all the groups on a server:

```
C:>net group
```

This example adds a group named Admin:

```
C:>net group Admin /add
```

This example adds three users to the Admin group:

```
C:>net group Admin Ward Wally June /add
```

This example lists the users in the Admin group:

```
C:>net group Admin
```

The Net Help command

This command displays help for the Net command or for a specific Net subcommand. Here's the basic syntax:

```
net help [command]
```

The *command* parameter can be any of the following commands:

ACCOUNTS	HELP	SHARE
COMPUTER	HELPMSG	START
CONFIG	LOCALGROUP	STATISTICS
CONFIG SERVER	NAME	STOP
CONFIG WORKSTATION	PAUSE	TIME
CONTINUE	PRINT	USE
FILE	SEND	USER
GROUP	SESSION	VIEW

You can type **net help services** to display a list of services that you can start via the Net Start command.

The Net Helpmsg command

Displays an explanation of network error codes. Here's the syntax:

```
net helpmsg message#
```

The *message#* parameter should be the four-digit number displayed when the error occurred. For example, if you get an error with message 2180, use this command to see an explanation of the error:

```
C:>net helpmsg 2180

The service database is locked.

EXPLANATION

Another program is holding the service database lock.

ACTION

Wait for the lock to be released and try again later.  If it
    is possible to determine which program is holding the
    lock, then end that program.
```

The Net Localgroup command

This command lets you add, display, or change local groups. This command has a number of different syntaxes, depending on how you intend to use it.

To display information about a local group or to change a local group's comment, use this syntax:

```
net localgroup groupname [/comment:"text"] [/domain]
```

To create a new group, use this syntax:

```
net localgroup groupname /add [/comment:"text"] [/domain]
```

To delete a group, use this syntax:

```
net localgroup groupname /delete [/domain]
```

Finally, to add or remove users from a group, use this syntax:

```
net localgroup groupname username[ ...] {/add | /delete}
               [/domain]
```

The following paragraphs describe the parameters that you can use with the Net Localgroup command:

✦ ***Groupname:*** The name of the group to add, change, or delete. If you specify this parameter and no others, a list of users in the group appears.

✦ **Comment:** Specifies a comment for the group. The comment can be up to 48 characters in length and should be enclosed in quotation marks.

✦ **Domain:** Specifies that the operation should be performed on the primary domain controller rather than on the local computer.

✦ **Add:** Creates a new group or adds users to an existing group. Before you add a user to a group, you must first create a user account for the user.

✦ **Delete:** Removes a group or removes users from the group.

✦ **Username:** One or more usernames to be added to or removed from the group. If you list more than one name, separate the names with spaces.

This example lists all the local groups:

```
C:>net localgroup
```

This example adds a local group named Admin:

```
C:>net localgroup Admin /add
```

This example adds three users to the Admin local group:

```
C:>net localgroup Admin Ward Wally June /add
```

This example lists the users in the Admin group:

```
C:>net localgroup Admin
```

**Book VII
Chapter 6**

**Windows
Commands**

The Net Name command

This command creates or removes an alias that can be used to send messages to the computer, or lists any existing aliases. Here's the syntax:

```
net name [name {/add|/delete}]
```

You can use the following parameters with the Net Name command:

+ **Name:** The name of the alias to create or remove.
+ **Add:** Creates the alias.
+ **Delete:** Removes the alias.

Use net name to specify a name for receiving messages. You must start the Messenger service before you can use net name. Each messaging name must be unique on the network. Names created with net name are strictly for messaging — not for group names. Windows XP uses three name types.

To list the current names for a computer, use the Net Name command like this:

```
C:\>net name

Name
-------------------------------------------------------
DOUG
DOUG LOWE
The command completed successfully.
```

To add the name T1000 to your computer, use this command:

```
C:>net name T1000 /add
```

To delete the name, use this command:

```
C:>net name T1000 /delete
```

The Net Pause command

This command temporarily pauses a service. It's a good idea to pause a service for a while before you stop the service altogether. That gives users who are currently using the service a chance to finish up any pending tasks, while at the same time preventing other users from beginning new sessions with the service. To reactivate the service later, use the Net Continue command.

The syntax to pause a service is:

```
net pause service
```

Here are some typical services you can pause:

✦ **Netlogon:** The Net Logon service.

✦ **Schedule:** The Task Scheduler service.

✦ **Server:** The Server service.

✦ **Workstation:** The Workstation service.

Here's an example that pauses the Workstation service:

```
CL>net pause workstation
```

If the service name has embedded spaces, enclose the service name in quotation marks. For example, this command pauses the NT LM Security Support Provider Service:

```
C:>net pause "nt lm security support provider"
```

The Net Print command

This command displays information about print jobs and shared print queues. To display information about a print queue, use this syntax:

```
net print \\computername\sharename
```

To display information about a specific print job or to change the status of a print job, use this syntax:

```
net print [\\computername] job# [/HOLD | /RELEASE | /DELETE]
```

The following paragraphs describe the parameters of the Net Print command:

✦ ***computername*:** The name of the computer sharing the printer.

✦ **Sharename:** The name of the shared printer.

✦ **job#:** The identification number for the print job.

✦ **Hold:** Prevents a job in a queue from printing. The job remains in the queue but is not printed until released.

✦ **Release:** Releases a job that was held.

✦ **Delete:** Removes a job from the print queue.

To display the status of the print queue for a printer named LASER1 on a computer named PSERVER, use this command:

```
C:>net print \\PSERVER\LASER1

Printers at \\PSERVER
Name                 Job #       Size       Status

------------------------------------------------------------

LASER1Queue         3 jobs                 *Printer Active*

      Ward          54         43546       Printing
      Wally         55         13565       Waiting
      Beaver        56         18321       Waiting
```

Now suppose that you happen to be user Beaver, and you want to crowd ahead of Wally's print job. All you have to do is issue this command:

```
C:>net print \\PSERVER 55 /hold
```

The Net Send command

This command lets you send messages to other users on the network. The message pops up, interrupting whatever the user is doing. Use this command sparingly, or you'll lose friends quickly. Here's the syntax:

```
net send {name | * | /domain[:name] | /users} message
```

Here's what each of the parameters do:

- ✦ *Name:* Provides the name of the user or computer to whom you want to send the message. (This can also be an alias created by the Net Name command.) If the name includes spaces, enclose it in quotes.

- ✦ *:* Sends the message to all computers in the domain or workgroup.

- ✦ **Domain:** Sends the message to everyone in the computer's domain or workgroup. If you specify a domain name, the message is sent to all users in the specified domain or workgroup.

- ✦ **Users:** Sends the message to all users who are currently connected to the server.

- ✦ *Message:* The message to be sent. Interestingly, you don't have to enclose the message in quotes even if it contains spaces.

To send the message "I'm shutting down the server in 10 minutes" to everyone on the network, use this command:

```
C:>net send * I'm shutting down the server in 10 minutes
```

To send the message "How about lunch?" to a user named Pooh, use this command:

```
C:>net send pooh How about lunch?
```

The Net Session command

This command lets you view current server connections and kick users off if you feel inclined. Here's the syntax:

```
net session [\\ComputerName] [/delete]
```

Here's what the parameters do:

✦ **ComputerName:** Indicates which computer whose session you want to view or disconnect. If you omit this parameter, all sessions are listed.

✦ **Delete:** Disconnects the computer's session. Any open files are immediately closed. If you use this parameter without specifying a computer name, all computers currently connected to the server are disconnected.

This is an obviously dangerous command. If you disconnect users while they're updating files or before they have a chance to save their work, they will be hopping mad.

To find out who is connected to a computer, use this command:

```
C:>net session
Computer     User name       Client type    Opens  Idle time
---------------------------------------------------------------
\\DEN        Ward            Windows XP     1      00:00:4
\\BEDROOM    Administrator   Windows 2003   0      02:15:17
```

The Net Share command

This command lets you manage shared resources. To display information about all shares or a specific share, use this syntax:

```
net share [ShareName]
```

To create a new share, use this syntax:

```
net share ShareName=path
          [{/users:number|/unlimited}]
          [/remark:"text"]
          [/cache: {manual|automatic|no}]
```

To change the properties of an existing share, use this syntax:

```
net share ShareName [{/users:number|unlimited}]
                [/remark:"text"]
                [/cache: {manual|automatic|no}]
```

To delete an existing share, use this syntax:

```
net share {ShareName|drive:path} /delete
```

Here's what each of the parameters do:

+ ***ShareName:*** Specifies the share name. Use this parameter by itself to display information about the share.

+ ***Path:*** Specifies the path to the folder to be shared. The path should include a drive letter. If the path includes spaces, enclose it in quotation marks.

+ **Users:** Specifies how many users can access the share concurrently.

+ **Unlimited:** Specifies that an unlimited number of users can access the share concurrently.

+ **Remark:** Creates a descriptive comment for the share. The comment should be enclosed in quotation marks.

+ **Cache:** Specifies the caching option for the share.

+ **Delete:** Stops sharing the folder.

If you use `Net Share` without any parameters, all the current shares are listed, as shown in this example:

```
C:>net share

Sharename    Resource                        Remark
-------------------------------------------------------------
ADMIN$       C:\WINNT                        Remote Admin
C$           C:\                             Default Share
print$       C:\WINNT\SYSTEM\SPOOL
IPC$                                         Remote IPC
LASER        LPT1                            Spooled Laser printer
```

The following example creates a share named Docs:

```
C:>net share Docs=C:\SharedDocs /remark:"Shared documents"
```

The Net Start command

This command lets you start a networking service or display a list of all the services that are currently running. The syntax is

```
net start [service]
```

In most cases, you'll use this command to start a service that you've previously stopped with the Net Stop command. In that case, you should first run the Net Start command without any parameters to find the name of the service that you want to stop. Make a note of the exact spelling of the service that you want to stop. Then, use the Net Stop command to stop the service. When you want to restart the service, use the Net Start command again — this time specifying the service to start.

For example, suppose that you need to stop your DNS server. Using Net Start, you discover that the name of the service is "DNS Server," so you use the following command to stop it:

```
C:>net stop "DNS Server"
```

Then, you can later use this command to restart the service:

```
C:>net start "DNS Server"
```

The Net Statistics command

This command lists the statistics log for the local Workstation or Server service. The syntax is

```
net statistics [{workstation | server}]
```

You can specify Workstation or Server to indicate for which service you'd like to view statistics.

If you use Net Statistics Workstation, the following information appears:

✦ The computer name.

✦ The date and time the statistics were last updated.

✦ The number of bytes and server message blocks (SMB) received and transmitted.

✦ The number of read and write operations that succeeded or failed.

✦ The number of network errors.

✦ The number of sessions that failed, disconnected, or were reconnected.

✦ The number of connections to shared resources that succeeded or failed.

**Book VII
Chapter 6**

**Windows
Commands**

If you use Net Statistics Server, the following information is listed.

+ The computer name.

+ The date and time the statistics were last updated.

+ The number of sessions that have been started, disconnected automatically, and disconnected because of errors.

+ The number of kilobytes sent and received, and the average response time.

+ The number of password and permission errors and violations.

+ The number of times the shared files, printers, and communication devices were used.

+ The number of times the size of the memory buffer was exceeded.

The Net Stop command

This command lets you stop a networking service. The syntax is

```
net stop service
```

To use this command, first run the Net Start command to determine the exact spelling of the service that you want to stop. If the service name includes spaces, enclose it in quotation marks.

You can restart the service later using the Net Start command.

The following example stops the DNS Server service:

```
C:>net stop "DNS Server"
```

The Net Time command

This command synchronizes the computer's clock with the clock on another computer. To access a clock on another computer in the same domain or workgroup, use this form:

```
net time \\ComputerName [/set]
```

To synchronize time with a domain, use this form:

```
net time /domain[:DomainName] [/set]
```

To use an RTS time server, use this syntax:

```
net time /rtsdomain[:DomainName] [/set]
```

To specify the computer to use for Network Time Protocol, use this syntax:

```
net time [\\ComputerName] [/querysntp]
    [/setsntp[:NTPServerList]]
```

For example, to set the computer's clock to match the Server01, use this command:

```
C:>net time \\Server01 /set
```

The Net Use command

This command connects or disconnects to a shared resource on another computer and maps the resource to a drive letter. Here's the complete syntax:

```
net use [{drive | *}]
        [{\\ComputerName\ShareName]
        [{Password | *}]]
        [/user:[DomainName\]UserName]
        [/savecred]
        [/smartcard]
        [{/delete | /persistent:{yes | no}}]
```

To set up a home directory, use this syntax:

```
net use [drive [/home[{password | *}]
        [/delete:{yes | no}]]
```

And to control whether connections should be persistent, use this:

```
net use [/persistent:{yes | no}]
```

Here's what the parameters do:

**Book VII
Chapter 6**

**Windows
Commands**

✦ *DeviceName*: Specifies the drive letter. (Note that for a printer, you should specify a printer device such as LPT1: here instead of a drive letter.) If you specify an asterisk, Windows will determine what drive letter to use.

✦ *\\ComputerName\ShareName*: The server and share name to connect to.

✦ *Password*: The password needed to access the shared resource. If you use an asterisk, you're prompted for the password.

✦ **User:** Specifies the username to use for the connection.

✦ **Savecred:** Saves the credentials for reuse later if the user is prompted for a password.

✦ **Smartcard:** Specifies that the connection should use a smart card for authorization.

✦ **Delete:** Deletes the specified connection. If you specify an asterisk (*), all network connections are canceled.

✦ **Persistent:** Specifies whether connections should be persistent.

✦ **Home:** Connects to the home directory.

To display all current connections, type **net use** with no parameters.

The following example shows how to create a persistent connection to a drive named Acct on a server named Server01, using drive K:

```
C:>net use k: \\Server01\Acct /persistent: yes
```

The following example drops the connection:

```
C:>net use k: /delete
```

The Net User command

This command creates or changes user accounts. To display a user's information, use this form:

```
net user username
```

To update user information, use this form:

```
net user [username [password | *] [options]] [/domain]
```

To add a new user, use this form:

```
net user username [password | *] /add [options] [/domain]
```

To delete a user, use this form:

```
net user username /delete [/domain]
```

Most of the parameters for this command are straightforward. However, the *options* parameters can have a variety of different settings. Table 6-2 lists the descriptions of these options as presented by the Net Help Users command:

Table 6-2	The Options Parameters
Options	*Description*
/ACTIVE:{YES | NO}	Activates or deactivates the account. If the account is not active, the user can't access the server. The default is YES.
/COMMENT:"text"	Provides a descriptive comment about the user's account (maximum of 48 characters). Enclose the text in quotation marks.
/COUNTRYCODE:nnn	Uses the operating system country code to implement the specified language files for a user's help and error messages. A value of 0 signifies the default country code.
/EXPIRES:{date | NEVER}	Causes the account to expire if date is set. NEVER sets no time limit on the account. An expiration date is in the form mm/dd/yy or dd/mm/yy, depending on the country code. Months can be a number, spelled out, or abbreviated with three letters. Year can be two or four numbers. Use slashes(/) (no spaces) to separate parts of the date.
/FULLNAME:"name"	Is a user's full name (rather than a username). Enclose the name in quotation marks.
/HOMEDIR:pathname	Sets the path for the user's home directory. The path must exist.
/PASSWORDCHG:{YES | NO}	Specifies whether users can change their own password. The default is YES.
/PASSWORDREQ:{YES | NO}	Specifies whether a user account must have a password. The default is YES.
/PROFILEPATH[:path]	Sets a path for the user's logon profile.
/SCRIPTPATH:pathname	Is the location of the user's logon script.
/TIMES:{times | ALL}	Is the logon hours. TIMES is expressed as day[-day][,day[-day]],time[-time][,time[-time]], limited to 1-hour increments. Days can be spelled out or abbreviated. Hours can be 12- or 24-hour notation. For 12-hour notation, use am, pm, a.m., or p.m. ALL means a user can always log on, and a blank value means a user can never log on. Separate day and time entries with a comma, and separate multiple day and time entries with a semicolon.
/USERCOMMENT:"text"	Lets an administrator add or change the User Comment for the account.
/WORKSTATIONS: {computername[,...] | *}	Lists as many as eight computers from which a user can log on to the network. If /WORKSTATIONS has no list or if the list is *, the user can log on from any computer.

Book VII
Chapter 6

Windows
Commands

To display information for a particular user, use the command like this:

```
C:>net user Doug
```

To add a user account for Theodore Cleaver with the username Beaver, use this command:

```
C:>net user Beaver /add /fullname:"Theodore Cleaver"
```

The Net View command

This command displays information about your network. If you use it without parameters, it displays a list of the computers in your domain. You can use parameters to display resources that are being shared by a particular computer. Here's the syntax:

```
net view [\\ComputerName] [/domain[:DomainName]]
net view /network:nw [\\ComputerName]
```

Here's what the parameters do:

✦ *ComputerName:* The computer whose shared resources you want to view.

✦ **Domain:** The domain you want to view if other than the current domain.

Here's typical output from a New View command:

```
C:>net view

Server Name          Remark
-------------------------------------------------
\\Server01           Main file server
\\Print01            Main print server
```

Book VIII

NetWare 6 Reference

The 5th Wave

By Rich Tennant

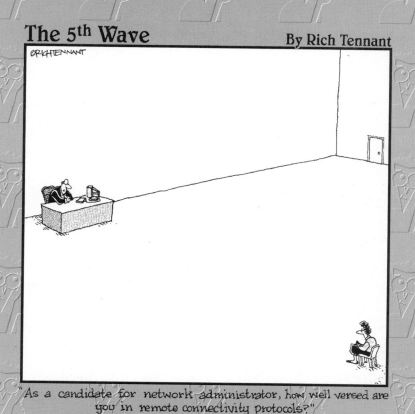

"As a candidate for network administrator, how well versed are you in remote connectivity protocols?"

Contents at a Glance

Chapter 1: Installing and Managing NetWare 6

In This Chapter

✔ **Getting ready to install NetWare**

✔ **Installing a network operating system**

✔ **Setting up the client software**

✔ **Looking at Novell's management tools**

This chapter presents the procedures you need to follow to install NetWare Version 6. The specific details provided are for the evaluation version of NetWare 6.0. However, the procedures for other versions of NetWare are similar, so you won't have any trouble adapting these procedures if you're installing a different version of NetWare.

Planning a NetWare Installation

Before you begin the Setup program to actually install a NetWare operating system, you need to make a number of preliminary decisions. The following sections describe the decisions that you need to make before you install a NetWare operating system.

Checking system requirements

Before you install a NetWare operating system, you should make sure that the computer meets the minimum requirements. Table 1-1 lists the official minimum requirements for NetWare 6. Table 1-1 also lists what I consider to be more realistic minimums if you expect to get satisfactory performance from the server as a moderately used file server.

Table 1-1	Minimum Hardware Requirements for NetWare 6	
Item	*Official Minimum*	*A More Realistic Minimum*
CPU	Pentium II, any speed	Pentium III, at least 700MHz
RAM	256MB	512MB
Free disk space	2.2GB	5GB

(continued)

Table 1-1 *(continued)*

Item	Official Minimum	A More Realistic Minimum
Video	Super VGA	Super VGA is good enough
Network	Any network board	100BaseT bus mastering PCI card
CD	Any CD-ROM drive	Any drive is sufficient
Mouse	Recommended	Definitely recommended

Figuring out how you'll boot during installation

Installing NetWare raises several classic rock-and-a-hard-place issues. The first issue that you're likely to encounter is that you have to have an operating system in place in order to run the operating system's installation program. So, which comes first — the OS chicken or the OS egg? Fortunately, you don't have to answer philosophy questions. You just have to figure out how to boot the computer so that you can run the NetWare installation program.

DOS boot!

If your computer is unable to boot from its CD-ROM drive, you have to set up a small DOS partition from which you can boot the computer in order to install NetWare. This partition must be at least 200MB, but 400MB is better. It doesn't need much of an operating system — just barebones DOS will do fine. However, the partition does need to have the drivers for your CD-ROM drive. Otherwise, you won't be able to access the NetWare installation CD.

Fortunately, NetWare comes with everything that you need to make a bootable DOS partition except the DOS drivers for your CD drive. Dig up the driver diskettes that came with the CD drive (you still have them, right?) or go to the CD drive manufacturer's Web site and download the latest DOS drivers.

To create the DOS partition, first boot the computer from the NetWare 6 License and Cryptography diskette, which has a bootable Caldera DOS on it. Next, use the FDISK command to repartition the hard drive, creating a 200MB–400MB primary partition, and reboot the computer. Then, run Format c: /S to format the DOS partition and copy the operating system to it.

Now remove the diskette and reboot. Copy the CD-ROM drivers from the driver diskette onto the C: drive and then edit the AUTOEXEC.BAT and CONFIG.SYS files to load the drivers. You'll have to check the manufacturer's documentation to find out what commands are required. While you're at it, put a FILES=50 and BUFFERS=30 command in CONFIG.SYS. You should now be able to reboot and access the CD drive.

Whew. See why it's better to just boot from the CD?

You can use one of the two common ways to boot during installation:

✦ If the computer has a bootable CD-ROM drive, you can boot the computer from the NetWare installation CD. This is the easiest way to go. To find out whether it'll work, just put the installation CD-ROM in the drive and restart the computer. If the computer starts the NetWare installation program, you're in business. If not, don't give up: It may be that the computer can boot from the CD-ROM, but the BIOS configuration isn't set to allow it. Check the BIOS configuration to see.

✦ If the computer can't boot from the CD-ROM drive, you'll need to set aside a bootable DOS partition on the hard drive. Sounds like a job for FDISK! For the details on how to do so, see the sidebar, "DOS Boot!"

Reading the Readme file

The `Readme` file for NetWare is available online at the following address:

`www.novell.com/documentation/lg/nw6p/`

You should read this file before you start Setup just to make sure that any of the specific procedures or warnings that it contains does not apply to your situation.

Deciding whether to upgrade or install

NetWare offers two installation modes from which you should choose before you begin setup: full installation or upgrade installation.

A *full installation* deletes any existing operating system that it finds on the computer and configures the new operating system from scratch. If you do a full installation onto a disk that already has an operating system installed, the full installation offers to keep any existing data files it finds on the disk.

You can upgrade the following previous NetWare versions to NetWare 6:

✦ NetWare 5.1 with Support Pack 2 or later

✦ NetWare 5 with Support Pack 6 or later

✦ NetWare 4.2 with Support Pack 8 or later

✦ NetWare 4.11 with Support Pack 8 or later

If you're stuck with an earlier version of NetWare, you may as well do a full installation.

Always do a complete backup before starting an upgrade installation!

Planning your partitions

Partitioning enables you to divide a physical disk into one or more separate units called *partitions*. NetWare requires at least two partitions to install:

✦ A bootable DOS partition, which must be at least 200MB. Give yourself a little breathing room and make it more like 400MB.

✦ The SYS partition, which is where NetWare will live. This partition must be at least 2.2GB, but 4GB is a more reasonable size for the SYS partition.

You'll usually create at least one additional partition on the server for application data, file server storage, and so on. It's best to create these additional partitions later, however. For now, you can concentrate on getting NetWare up and running.

Deciding your TCP/IP configuration

Before you install the operating system, you should have a plan for how you'll implement TCP/IP on the network. Here are some of the things that you need to decide or find out:

✦ What is the public IP subnet address and mask for your network?

✦ What is the domain name for the network?

✦ What is the host name for the server?

✦ Will the server obtain its address from DHCP?

✦ Will the server have a static IP address? If so, what?

✦ Will the server be a DHCP server?

✦ What is the default gateway for the server? (That is, what is the IP address of the network's Internet router?)

✦ Will the server be a DNS server?

If you intend the server to host TCP/IP services (such as DHCP or DNS), you'll probably want to assign the server a static IP address.

Planning your tree

NetWare has its own directory service called *eDirectory,* which is a direct descendant of *Novell Directory Services* (also known as *NDS*) from NetWare 5. When you install a NetWare server, you have to decide where the server will fit in the scheme of your existing NDS tree. If this is the first NetWare server on your network, you have to create a new NDS eDirectory tree.

Before you install the server, you should determine the following items of information for your NDS tree:

✦ The name of the NDS tree.

✦ The name of the organization, which is usually your company name.

✦ The name of the organizational unit, if any. NDS lets you subdivide your organization into units, such as divisions or regions. If your company is small, you may not need organizational units.

✦ The location within the NDS tree where the server will be located — either the organization or an organizational unit.

Running nwdeploy.exe

If your network already has at least one NetWare server, you should run a special program called NWDEPLOY.EXE to prepare your NDS directory for the new version of NetWare. To do so, insert the NetWare 6 installation CD into a Windows client computer and then run NWDEPLOY.EXE.

Installing NetWare

Now that you've planned your installation and prepared the computer, you're ready to begin the installation. The following procedure describes the steps that you must follow to install NetWare on a new computer that has an empty disk and a bootable CD-ROM drive:

1. **Insert the installation CD in the CD-ROM drive and restart the computer.**

After a few moments, the NetWare Setup Wizard fires up. It asks a few preliminary questions, such as what language you want to install in, and whether your CD-ROM drive is an IDE or a SCSI drive. Answer these questions, and you're rewarded with this message:

```
Welcome to NetWare Server installation. By continuing, you agree to
    accept all terms and conditions presented in the License Agreement.
```

You're then presented with three options: Read License Agreement, Accept License Agreement, or Exit.

2. **Read the license agreement and then choose Accept License Agreement.**

Assuming that you're starting with a clean disk, you see the following message:

```
No bootable partitions were found on the computer's hard disk. NetWare
    requires a 100MB boot (DOS) partition and recommends 200MB.
    Installation will create a boot partition.
```

Your options at this point are Create A New Boot Partition and Exit. You can also press F3 to view the drive's existing partitions.

3. Choose Create A New Boot Partition.

The following message now appears:

```
Specify the size of the boot partition to create.
```

The default size is 200MB. You can choose Modify to change the boot partition size or choose Continue to accept the proposed size.

4. Choose Continue.

Now this ominous message appears:

```
Are you sure? Creating a new boot partition will remove all data
    volumes, and partitions on the first hard disk.
```

Don't be afraid, Luke!

5. Choose Continue.

It doesn't take but a few seconds to completely wipe your disk clean. The following message almost immediately appears:

```
A new boot partition has been successfully created. To recognize the new
    boot partition, the computer will now reboot.
```

This is probably the last time the installation program does anything significant so quickly.

6. Choose Reboot and then wait while your computer boots.

When your computer starts back up, it formats the boot partition and begins to initialize itself. This process takes a few minutes, so be patient. Eventually, you see this message:

```
Welcome to the NetWare Server installation. A new installation will
    destroy existing data on NetWare partitions. To keep data, select
    Upgrade.

IMPORTANT: You must run NetWare Deployment Manager before installing
    into an existing network. If you have not, insert the NetWare 6 CD
    into a Windows workstation and run NWDEPLOY.EXE

Is this an express install or a custom install? Express

Is this a new server, upgrade, or pre-migration? New server
```

7. If this isn't the first NetWare server on your network and you haven't yet run NWDEPLOY.EXE, **do it now.**

Refer to the section "Running NWDEPLOY.EXE," earlier in this chapter.

8. Choose Express to perform an express install.

Express Install makes a number of installation decisions for you. Because the default choices are appropriate for most networks, I suggest that you use Express installation. If you prefer, you can choose Custom. Then, you have to provide additional information as installation proceeds.

9. Choose New Server and then choose Continue.

A confirmation message appears:

```
The Express installation will select the following defaults:
A 4GB volume SYS will be created.
LAN and disk drives will be auto discovered.
Country code: 1      Codepage: 437
Video: Super VGA Plug N Play
Keyboard: United States      Mouse: Auto
Default products will be installed: Native File Access, iManage, Novell
     Advanced Audit Service
```

10. Click Continue.

Now the installation program begins copying files. It copies *lots* of files. Now would be a good time to take a walk.

When all the files have been copied, the installation program switches to a more attractive graphical user interface, as shown in Figure 1-1. The first GUI screen asks for the name of the server.

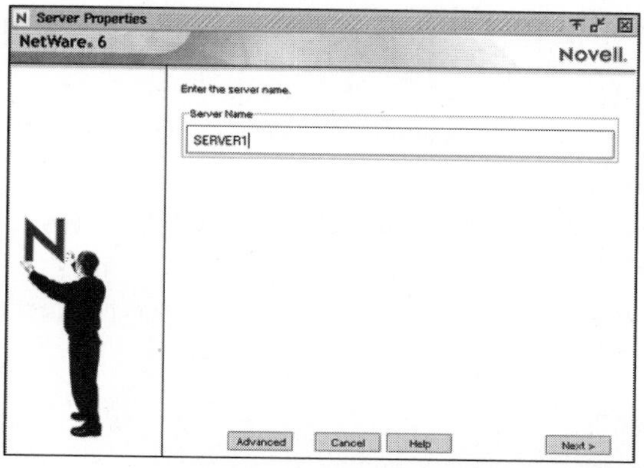

Figure 1-1: NetWare's installation program uses an attractive graphical user interface.

Screen shot courtesy Novell, Inc.

11. Enter the name of the server and then click Next.

Now the GUI installation program asks you to insert your Netware License and Cryptography diskette so that it can read your region-specific cryptography information.

If you're installing the free evaluation version of NetWare, you don't have a NetWare License and Cryptography diskette to insert. Instead, you should click Browse, navigate to Root➪Local Files➪NETWARE6➪LICENSE➪DEMO, and then click OK.

12. Insert your license diskette and click Next.

The installation program gets the information it needs from the diskette and then displays the screen shown in Figure 1-2, which asks for basic IP configuration information for each of your network cards.

Figure 1-2:
The installation program needs to know your IP information.

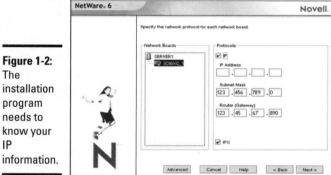

Screen shot courtesy Novell, Inc.

13. Enter the IP configuration information for each network card and then click Next.

For each network card, you can enter the following information:

- Whether the card supports the IP protocol
- The IP address
- The subnet mask
- The router (gateway) address
- Whether the card supports the IPX protocol

When you click Next, the installation program asks for the hostname for each network card.

14. **Enter the hostname for each network card and then click Next.**

Next, you're asked to enter DNS information, as shown in Figure 1-3.

15. **Enter the domain name and the address of up to three nameservers and then click Next.**

Now the installation program wants to know what time zone you're in.

16. **Choose the time zone and then click Next.**

The installation program now asks whether you want to create a new NDS tree or join an existing tree.

17. **If this is the first NetWare server on your network, choose New NDS Tree; otherwise, choose Existing NDS Tree.**

The next screen asks for the following NDS information, as shown in Figure 1-4.

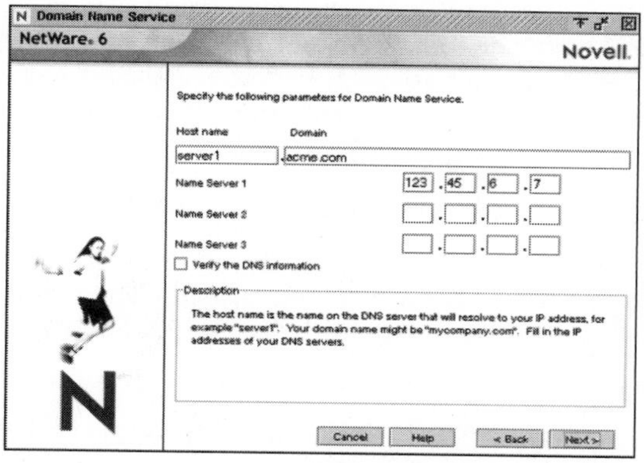

Figure 1-3:
NetWare's
installation
program
now asks
for your
DNS
information.

Screen shot courtesy Novell, Inc.

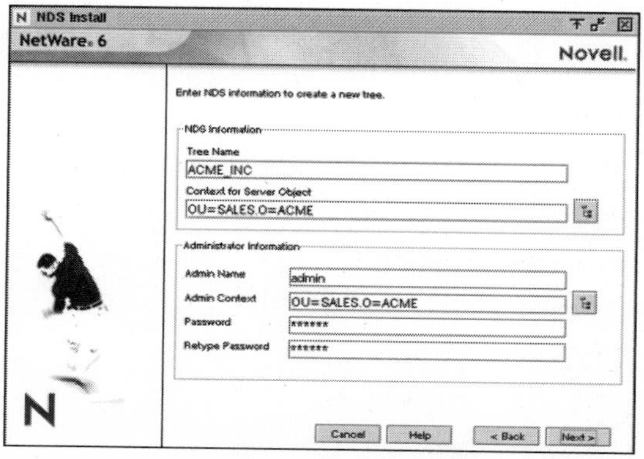

Figure 1-4:
Specifying
NDS
information.

Screen shot courtesy Novell, Inc.

**Book VIII
Chapter 1**

Installing
and Managing
NetWare 6

18. **Enter the NDS information and then click Next.**

You can enter the following NDS information on this screen:

- The name of the NDS tree
- The context for the server object
- The administrator's name
- The administrator's context
- The administrator's password

The context items need a little explanation. It specifies the organization and organization unit (if any) that the server or administrator is defined in. If the object is defined in the organization, specify O=*organization* — for example, O=Lowe. If the object is defined in an organizational unit, specify OU=*organizationalunit*.O=*organization* — for example, OU=Dev.O=Lowe.

When you click Next, the installation program creates your NDS information and then displays a summary screen that lists the NDS tree name, the server context, and the Administrator's name.

19. **Click Next.**

You're now asked to insert your license diskette.

If you're installing the free evaluation version of NetWare, you don't have a license diskette to insert. Instead, you should click Browse, navigate to Root⇨Local Files⇨NETWARE6⇨LICENSE⇨DEMO, and then click OK.

20. **Insert the Netware License and Cryptography diskette and click Next.**

The installation program gets what it needs from the diskette and then displays the summary page shown in Figure 1-5, which lists the products that are about to be installed. You're almost done. . . .

Figure 1-5:
The summary page lists the components that will be installed.

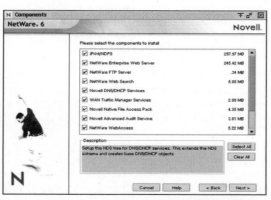

Screen shot courtesy Novell, Inc.

21. Click Finish.

The installation program copies all the remaining files, installs the services you've selected, and configures your server. This takes awhile, as a lot of files need to be copied. So this would be a good time to take a walk.

After it's done, the final installation screen appears, congratulating you on completing the installation and telling you to restart the computer.

22. Choose Yes.

Your computer reboots — only this time, a working NetWare server comes to life.

Installing Client Software

Now that you've set up a NetWare server, you also have to configure your client computers to access it. All versions of Windows include built-in support for NetWare servers, so you don't have to do anything special to access NetWare servers if you're happy with Microsoft's client files. However, Novell has a product called Novell Client that is a huge improvement over Windows' native NetWare support. If you're going to go to all the trouble of installing a NewWare server, you may as well get the best client support.

The easiest way to install the Novell client software is to insert the Novell Client CD in the client computer and open the `INSTALL.HTML` file in the CD drive's root directory. This launches an HTML-based installation routine that's easy enough to use.

If you don't have the Novell Client CD, you can download the Novell Client from Novell's Web site (`www.novell.com`). Then, you can place the Novell Client installation files on a network disk and install the Novell Client software on each client computer via the network.

Looking at Novell's Administration Tools

One of the best things about NetWare is that it has a lot of tools for administering the server. Unfortunately, many of these tools provide overlapping functions. With NetWare, if there's one way to do something, you can bet there are three or four others as well.

You can use many of the administration tools from either the server's console itself or remotely from any workstation on the network. This makes it possible to manage an entire network from the comfort of your own cubicle. You rarely have to venture into the computer room. You may want to go there once in awhile just to hear the hum of your servers and to remind yourself how much you appreciate remote management.

The following sections describe the major network administration tools you'll use as you manage a NetWare network.

ConsoleOne

ConsoleOne is an all-in-one client-based management program. You can install ConsoleOne on any workstation. It's Java-based, which means it can run on almost any workstation platform. However, Java is pretty demanding on your computer's resources, so you shouldn't try to run it on an older system. Use it only on newer systems that have plenty of RAM. Novell says the minimum is 64MB, but it recommends 128MB.

You can install ConsoleOne on a Windows computer from the CD, or you can download it from Novell's download site (download.novell.com). After you've installed it, you can start it by double-clicking the ConsoleOne icon on your desktop.

You can also install it on a NetWare or Windows server. To run ConsoleOne from a network location, map a drive to the directory where you installed ConsoleOne and then run consoleone.exe. You may want to create a desktop shortcut to this file so that you don't have to hunt and peck for it each time you need to use it.

Figure 1-6 shows ConsoleOne in action. When you first start ConsoleOne, it may not look this interesting. The tree pane on the left may contain just the Tree icon until you log on. You do that by clicking the NDS Authenticate button or by choosing File➪Authenticate. After you've logged on, the tree expands to resemble Figure 1-6.

Here are some additional thoughts to keep in mind as you ponder whether ConsoleOne is the tool for you:

✦ ConsoleOne has the same look and feel on whatever platform you run it, whether at the server, on your Windows 2000 or XP Professional desktop, or on a Linux or UNIX box.

✦ ConsoleOne has the best support for NDS.

✦ ConsoleOne is still pretty new, so it doesn't support every feature that's available in NetWare. Specifically, ConsoleOne lacks full support for print services and some older services.

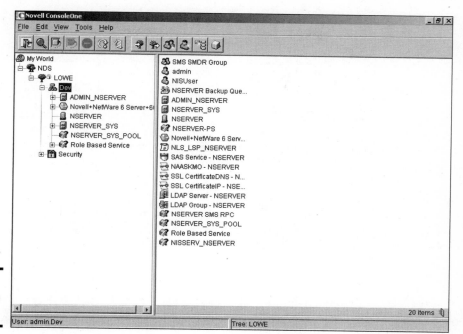

Figure 1-6:
ConsoleOne
in action.

The Welcome Brigade

If you open a Web browser on any client computer on your network and point it to a NetWare 6 server, you get the page shown in Figure 1-7. This page includes a variety of links to useful Web-based services. It's a good way to start exploring NetWare's Web features.

Web Manager

Web Manager is a portal to a series of Web-based management tools that you can access from any computer on the network that has a relatively current Web browser (at least Internet Explorer 5.0 or Netware 4.5). To access it, point your browser at port 2200 of the server on a secure connection by using the server's IP address or DNS name. For example, either of the following options call up the Web Manager page for my test NetWare server:

```
https//:192.168.1.60:2200
https//:Nserver.LoweWriter.com:2200
```

Figure 1-8 shows Web Manager in action. The next three sections describe three Web-based management tools that you can access from Web Manager: eDirectory, Remote Manager, and iManage.

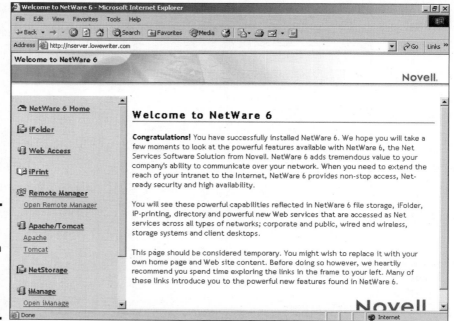

Figure 1-7:
Point your
browser at a
NetWare
server, and
here's what
you get.

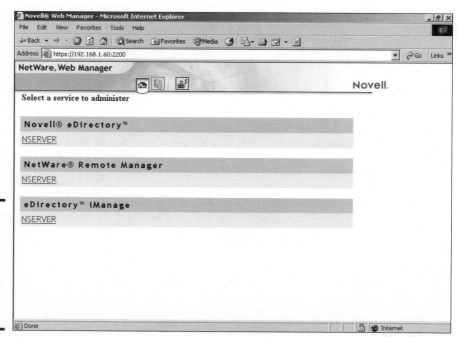

Figure 1-8:
Web
Manager
provides
links to
Web-based
manage-
ment tools.

eDirectory Administration

The Novell eDirectory Administration tool lets you manage eDirectory information remotely from a Web-based interface, as shown in Figure 1-9. Using this tool, you can create and modify basic eDirectory objects including users, groups, organizations, and organizational units.

Remote Manager

Remote Manager is a server-based Web tool that lets you manage a NetWare server's configuration. Figure 1-10 shows the Remote Manager Volume Management page, which lets you manage volumes on a remote server.

You can get to Remote Manager from the Web Manager page, or you can go there directly by pointing your browser to port 8008 of the server by using the server's DNSS name or IP address. After you get to Remote Manager, I suggest that you bookmark it to make it easier to come back again later.

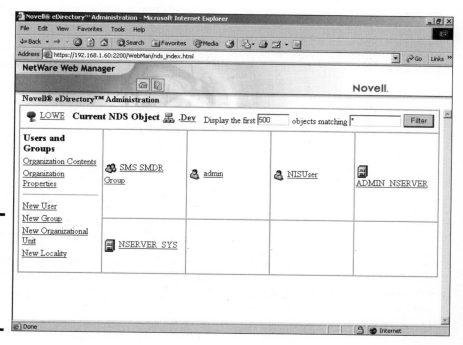

Figure 1-9: eDirectory Administrator lets you manage eDirectory objects.

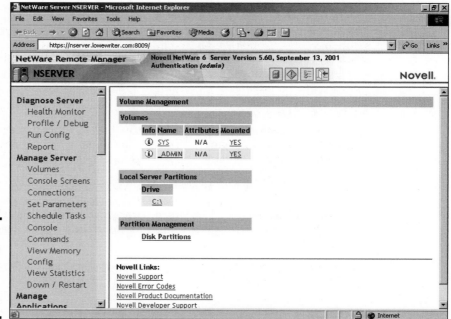

Figure 1-10:
The Remote
Manager
Volume
Manage-
ment page.

The left pane of the Remote Manager page is a menu that lets you access the following administration features:

✦ **Diagnose Server:** These tools let you diagnose problems with the server. The choices are Health Monitor, Profile/Debug, Run Config, and Report.

✦ **Manage Server:** These tools let you manage the server's configuration. The choices are Volumes, Console Screens, Connections, Set Parameters, Schedule Tasks, Console Commands, View Memory Config, View Statistics, and Down /Restart.

✦ **Manage Applications:** These tools let you manage server applications. The choices are List Modules, Protected Memory, System Resources, NetWare Registry, Winsock 2.0, Protocol Information, and Java Application Information.

✦ **Manage Hardware:** These tools let you manage the server's hardware. The choices are Processors, Disk /LAN Adapters, PCI Devices, and Other Resources.

✦ **Manage eDirectory:** These tools give you access to eDirectory. The choices are Access Tree Walker, View eDirectory Partitions, NDS iMonitor, DS Trace, NFAP Security, and NFAP Import Users.

✦ **User Server Groups:** These tools let you set up server groups to make servers easier to manage. The options are Build Group and Load Group File.

✦ **Access Other Servers:** These tools let you manage other servers. The choices are Managed Server List and Basic File Access.

✦ **NetWare Usage:** These tools let you capture and display server usage information. The options are Usage Information and Configuration.

iManage

Novell's iManage (which is sometimes referred to as iManager) is another Web-based tool. Because it's Web-based, you can use it from any computer on the network. iManage is shown in Figure 1-11.

You can get to iManage from the Web Manager, or you can call it up directly by using this address:

```
https://server's_IP_address:2200/eMFrame/iManage.html
```

After you get to iManage, I suggest that you bookmark it.

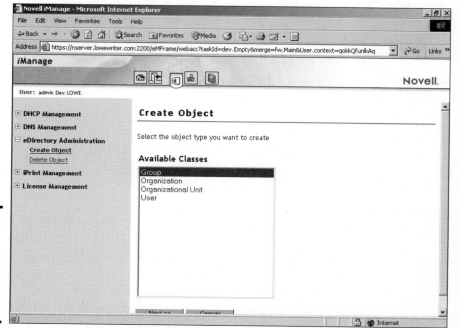

Figure 1-11: iManager lets you manage DHCP, DNS, eDirectory, and iPrint.

iManage provides the following administrative tools:

✦ **DHCP Management:** Lets you configure the DHCP server.

✦ **DNS Management:** Lets you configure the DNS server.

✦ **eDirectory Administration:** Lets you create or remove eDirectory user, group, organization, or organizational units.

✦ **iPrint Management:** Lets you manage network printing.

✦ **License Management:** Lets you manage Novell licensing.

RConsoleJ

RConsoleJ is a remote server console through which you can enter old-fashioned server commands from a remote workstation. This essentially gives you the power of a server console at your desktop.

To set up RConsoleJ, follow these steps:

1. **On the server, open a server console by choosing Novell⇨Utilities⇨Server Console.**

A server console window appears.

2. **Enter the command** RCONAG6.

You're prompted for a password.

3. **Type the password that you want remote administrators to use.**

Be careful! You don't get to type this twice, so if you make a mistake, you'll have to run RCONAG6 again.

4. **Respond to the rest of the prompts by pressing Enter to accept the defaults.**

When it's done, close the Server Console window.

5. **On the workstation from which you want to access RConsoleJ, map a drive to the root folder of SYS.**

This command will do the trick:

```
net use r: \\Nserver\SYS
```

6. **Click Start⇨Run and then run** \PUBLIC\MGMT\CONSOLEONE\1.2\ RCONJ.EXE **on the mapped drive.**

The Novell RConsoleJ dialog box appears, as shown in Figure 1-12.

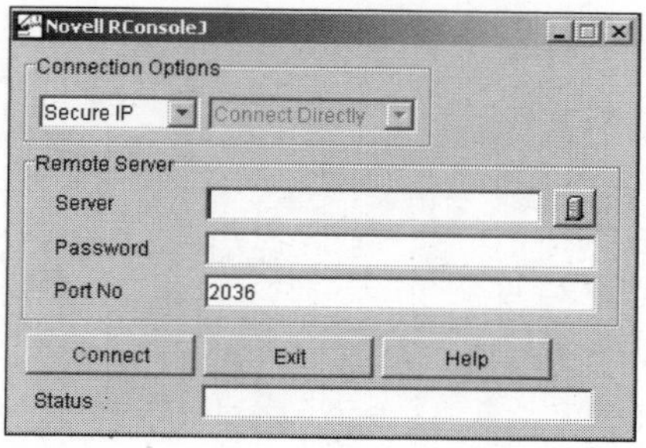

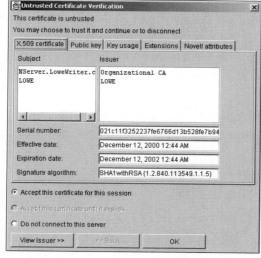

Figure 1-12:
RConsoleJ
asks what
server you
want to
connect to.

7. **Type the full name of the server and the remote password that you created in Step 3 and then press Connect.**

   The network whirs and spins for a moment. Then, the dialog box shown in Figure 1-13 appears. This dialog box asks you to accept the server's security certificate.

8. **Click OK.**

   The RConsoleJ window appears, as shown in Figure 1-14.

9. **Play with the console.**

   You can enter all sorts of commands here, which I won't get into now.

Figure 1-13:
RConsoleJ
asks
whether you
want to trust
the security
certificate.

Book VIII
Chapter 1

Installing
and Managing
NetWare 6

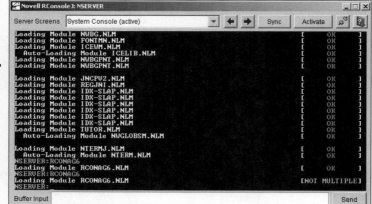

Figure 1-14:
RConsoleJ
lets you
enter server
console
commands
from a
remote
location.

10. **When you're done, close the window.**

You're disconnected from the server.

For more information about commands that you can use from the server console or from RConsoleJ, see Chapter 4 of this book.

Chapter 2: Managing User Objects

In This Chapter

✓ Understanding user objects

✓ Creating user objects

✓ Setting user properties

✓ Working with groups

*E*very user who accesses a NetWare server must have a *user object* defined in an NDS directory tree. User objects enable you to control who can access the network and who can't. In addition, user objects let you specify what network resources each user can use. Without user objects, all your resources would be open to anyone who casually dropped by your network.

Understanding NetWare User Accounts

Every user object has several important properties that specify the characteristics of the object. The three most important object properties are

+ **Username:** A unique name that identifies the user. The user must enter the username when logging on to the network. The username is public information. In other words, other network users can (and often should) find out your username.

+ **Password:** A secret word that must be entered in order to gain access to the object. You can set up NetWare so that it enforces password policies, such as the minimum length of the password and how long the password remains current before the user must change it.

+ **Group membership:** Indicates which group or groups to which the user object belongs. Group memberships are the key to granting access rights to users so that they can access various network resources, such as file shares or printers, or perform certain network tasks, such as creating new user objects or backing up the server.

Here are some additional user object properties to ponder:

✦ **Home directory:** A directory on a NetWare server where the user can store files. Usually, this directory is a subdirectory of a directory named Home or Users, and the subdirectory name is the same as the user-name. Thus, the home directory for a user named Wally would be `\Home\Wally` or `\Users\Wally`.

✦ **User restrictions:** These properties restrict how the user may access the network, such as what time of day the user can access the network or what types of passwords the user can create.

✦ **Security equal to:** You can specify that a user's security rights should be granted to another user.

✦ **Logon script:** You can use logon scripts to customize the user's network environment.

✦ **Trustee rights:** You can grant the user access to other objects.

✦ **File and folder rights:** You can grant the user access to specific files or folders.

The Admin Object

NetWare comes with a built-in object named *admin* that has complete access to all the features of the server. As a network administrator, you'll frequently log on as admin to perform maintenance chores.

Because the admin user is so powerful, you should always enforce good password practices for it. In other words, don't use your dog's name as the admin user's password. Instead, pick a random combination of letters and numbers. Then, change the password periodically.

 Write down the admin password and keep it in a secure location. Note that by "secure location," I don't mean taped to the front of the monitor. Keep it in a safe place where you can retrieve it if you forget it, but where it won't easily fall into the hands of someone looking to break into your network.

Creating a New User

You can create a new user object in many ways in NetWare 6. You can create new users with ConsoleOne, eDirectory Administrator, Remote Manager, and several other tools. In the following procedure, I show you how to do it by using ConsoleOne. The procedures for other tools are similar.

1. **Open ConsoleOne and log on if asked.**

The ConsoleOne screen appears, as shown in Figure 2-1.

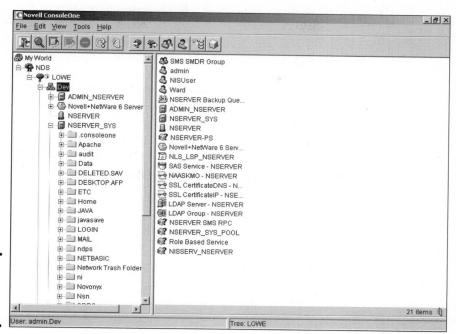

Figure 2-1:
ConsoleOne
awaits your
command.

2. **Right-click the organization that you want to add the user to and then choose New⇨User.**

   This summons the New User dialog box, as shown in Figure 2-2.

Book VIII
Chapter 2

Managing User Objects

Figure 2-2:
Creating a
new user.

3. **Type the username in the Name field and the user's last name in the Surname field.**

   These are the only two fields that are required. After you enter them, the OK button is enabled.

4. **If you want to create a home directory for the user, check the Create Home Directory checkbox and then enter the path where you want the directory to be created.**

   For example, enter **\SYS\Home** to create the home directory as a subdirectory of Home directory on the SYS volume.

5. **Select the password option that you want.**

   You can choose one of two ways to create the password:

   - **Prompt During Creation:** You are prompted for the password immediately after completing this dialog box.

   - **Prompt User On First Login:** The user is required to supply a password the first time that he or she uses the account.

6. **If you want to specify other user properties now, check the Define Additional Properties check box.**

   If you leave this box unchecked, you can easily set the additional properties later.

7. **If you want to create another user after you've finished with this user, check the Create Another User checkbox.**

   This option simplifies the task of creating multiple users.

8. **Click OK.**

   You're prompted for the password, as shown in Figure 2-3.

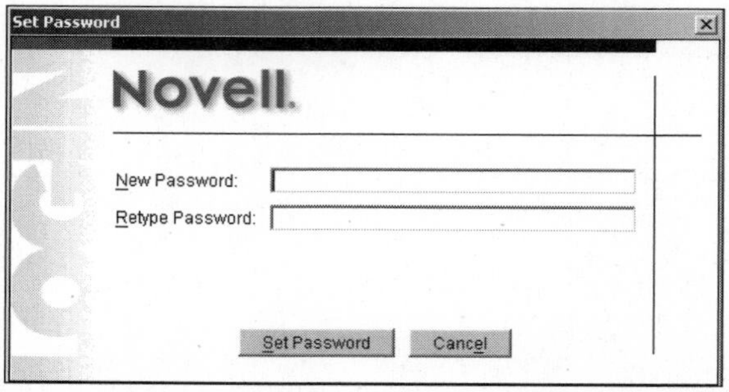

Figure 2-3:
Setting the user's password.

9. **Type the password twice.**

   You're asked to type the password twice to verify accuracy. If you don't type it identically in both boxes, you'll be asked to correct your mistake.

10. **Click Set Password.**

    The user is created. If you checked the Define Additional Properties check box, you're taken to the Properties page for the user as described in the next section. If you checked the Create Another User checkbox, the New User dialog box reappears so that you can create another user. Otherwise, you're returned to the main ConsoleOne window.

Now that you've created a user, you'll want to customize the user's properties. At the minimum, you'll probably want to add the user to one or more groups. You may also want to add restrictions or set other properties.

Setting User Properties

After you've created a user object, you can set additional properties for the user by right-clicking the new user and choosing Properties. This brings up the User Properties dialog box, which has about a million tabs that you can use to set various properties for the user. Figure 2-4 shows the General tab, which lists basic information about the user, such as the user's name, office location, phone number, and so on.

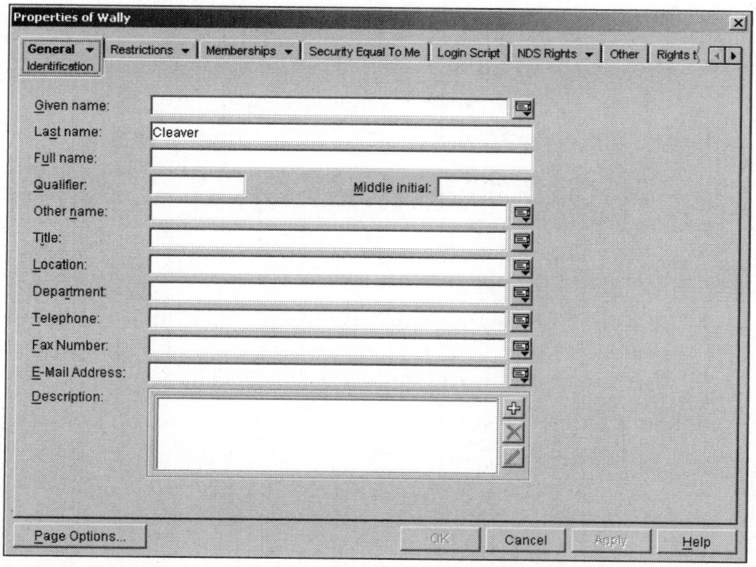

Figure 2-4: The General tab.

The following sections describe some of the administrative tasks that you can perform via the various tabs of the User Properties dialog box.

The tabs in the Properties dialog box work a little differently than most tabbed dialog boxes you've seen. Each tab is actually a menu that lets you select one of several options. For example, the General tab lets you choose four options: Identification, Postal Address, Environment, and See Also. To access the tab menu, just click the down-arrow at the right edge of each tab.

The General tab

The General tab has four options:

+ **Identification:** Provides basic identity information for the user, such as name, title, department, phone numbers, e-mail addresses, and so on.

+ **Postal Address:** Lets you specify the user's mailing address.

+ **Environment:** Lets you set several aspects of the user's environment, including the default logon server and the user's home directory.

+ **See Also:** Lets you list other objects that are related to this user.

The Restrictions tab

The Restrictions tab of the User Properties dialog box lets you set account restrictions for the user. For example, Figure 2-5 shows the Password Restrictions tab. Here, you can set the following restrictions on the user's password:

+ **Allow User To Change Password:** Select this to allow the user to change his or her password.

+ **Require A Password:** Check this to require a password for the account.

+ **Minimum Password Length:** Specify the shortest allowable password.

+ **Force Periodic Password Changes:** Requires that the user regularly change the password. You can specify an interval between forced changes and a specific expiration date for the password.

+ **Require Unique Passwords:** Requires that the last eight passwords used be unique. This prevents a user from reusing the same few passwords every time you force a password change.

+ **Limit Grace Logons:** Lets you specify how many times the user can log on with an expired password without changing the password.

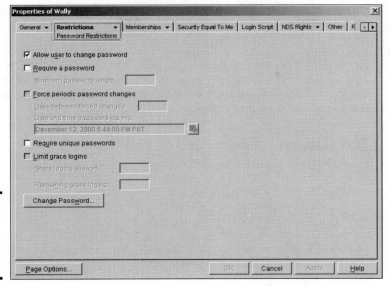

Figure 2-5:
The
Password
Restrictions
dialog box.

The other options on the Restrictions tab menu are as follows:

✦ **Logon Restrictions:** Lets you enable or disable an account, provide an expiration date for the account, and limit the number of concurrent sessions the user can have.

✦ **Time Restrictions:** Prevents the user from logging on at certain times of the day or on certain days. This is a great way to keep people from hacking into your network at 2 a.m., but it's also a great way to discourage people from working extra hours.

✦ **Address Restrictions:** Lets you specify that the user can log on only from certain computers.

✦ **Intruder Lockout:** If the system locks out a user because it thinks the account has been compromised, you can come to this page to reinstate the user.

✦ **Account Balance:** This tab lets you set up accounting for the user.

The Memberships tab

The Group Membership page under the Memberships tab lets you add the user to one or more groups. The user then inherits all the rights of the

Book VIII
Chapter 2

Managing User
Objects

group. To add the user to a group, click the Add button. For more information about using groups, see the section "Working with Groups," later in this chapter.

The other choice under the Memberships tab is the Security Equal To page. This page lets you assign this user the rights that have already been assigned to another user. This may sound like a useful feature, but groups are a much better way to handle such things.

The Security Equal To Me tab

This tab lets you grant the security rights of this user to other users. Again, groups are a better way to handle this need.

The Logon Script tab

On this tab, you can create or edit a logon script for the user. See Chapter 4 of this book for information about commands that you can use in logon scripts.

The NDS Rights tab

This tab has three options:

✦ **Trustees of this object:** Lists the trustees for this user.

✦ **Inherited rights filter:** Lists inherited rights filters, which let you limit how rights are inherited from trustees.

✦ **Effective rights:** Lists the effective rights for other objects to this user.

The Other tab

On this tab, you can find other properties that didn't seem to fit anywhere else. None of them are particularly important in most cases.

The Rights To Files And Folders tab

This tab, shown in Figure 2-6, lets you grant rights over various files and folders to a user. These rights are best managed by using groups, but you may occasionally need to grant them to a specific user. For example, you may grant greater rights to the manager of a team than to the rest of the team members.

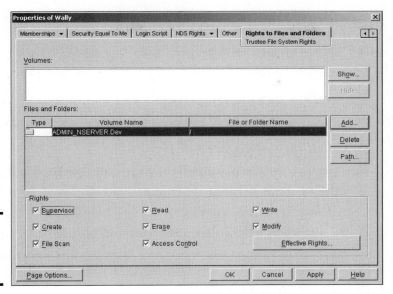

Figure 2-6:
The Rights
To Files And
Folders tab.

To grant rights to a file or folder, click the Add button. Then, navigate to the file or folder to which you want to grant the rights and click OK. Finally, select the rights that you want to grant by using the check boxes. NetWare lets you grant eight distinct rights:

✦ **Supervisor:** Grants all rights, including the ability to grant rights over the object to other users.

✦ **Read:** The user can open and read the file.

✦ **Write:** The user can open and write to the file.

✦ **Create:** The user can create a new file in this directory.

✦ **Erase:** The user can delete the file.

✦ **Modify:** The user can save changes to the file. This right also allows the user to rename the file or change its attributes.

✦ **File Scan:** The user can see this file in directory listings.

✦ **Access Control:** The user can change the file's trustee assignments.

Some Common User Maintenance Chores

The following sections describe a few of the most common tasks for managing NetWare user objects.

Resetting user passwords

Here's the quick procedure to reset a password from ConsoleOne:

1. **Call up the Properties page for the user.**
2. **Open the Password Restrictions page under the Restrictions tab.**
3. **Click the Change Password button.**

   A dialog box appears, asking for the new password.
4. **Type the new password in both password boxes.**

   You have to type the password twice to ensure that you type it correctly.
5. **Click OK.**

   That's all there is to it! The user's password is now reset.

Disabling and enabling user accounts

If you want to temporarily prevent a user from accessing the network, you can disable his or her object. Then, you can enable the object later, when you're ready to restore the user to full access.

1. **Call up the Properties page for the user.**
2. **Open the Logon Restrictions page under the Restrictions tab.**
3. **Check the Account Is Disabled option.**
4. **Click OK.**

Deleting a user

Deleting a user object is surprisingly easy. All you have to do is right-click the object and select Delete NDS object.

Working with Groups

A *group* is a special type of object that represents a set of users who have common network access needs. Groups can dramatically simplify the task of assigning network access rights to users. Rather than assign access rights to each user individually, groups let you assign rights to the group itself. Then, those rights automatically extend to any user you add to the group.

For example, suppose that your company has a team of four writers who are working on a series of books about your company's products. The files that these writers work with are all stored in a directory named \Books on the SYS volume. Rather than assign each of these four users access to the \Books directory, you can create a group named *Writers* and grant access to the \Books directory to the Writers group. Then, you can add each of the four users to the Writers group.

The following procedure shows you how to set up a group and add members to it:

1. **Right-click the organization to which you want to add the user and then choose New⇨Group.**

   This summons the New Group dialog box, as shown in Figure 2-7.

Figure 2-7:
The New
Group
dialog box.

2. **Type the name of the group in the Name field and then check the Define Additional Properties check box and click OK.**

   The Properties dialog box for the new group appears.

3. **Click the Rights To Files And Folders tab.**

   The Rights To Files And Folders tab appears. This looks just like the User object Rights To Files And Folders tab, which was shown in Figure 2-6.

4. **Click the Add button and add access to the network resources that the group will need.**

5. **After you've set up the rights you want, click the Members tab.**

   The Members tab appears.

6. **To add a member to the group, click Add and then select the member or members you want to add and click OK.**

   Figure 2-8 shows how the group looks with a couple of members added.

**Book VIII
Chapter 2**

**Managing User
Objects**

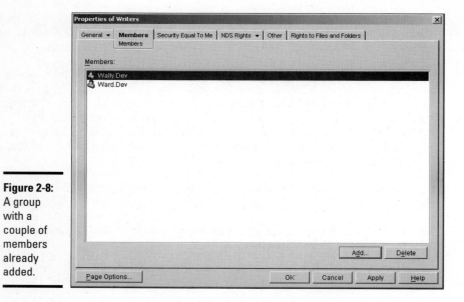

Figure 2-8:
A group
with a
couple of
members
already
added.

7. **Click OK.**

You're done. The group has been created.

Chapter 3: TCP/IP and NetWare 6

In This Chapter

✔ Configuring NetWare TCP/IP

✔ Setting up a DNS server

✔ Running a DHCP name server

As one of the pioneers of networking, Novell developed its own networking protocols years ago. In particular, the IPX protocol was for many years the de facto standard for PC-based networks. In recent years, however, the industry has made a shift to TCP/IP in order to simplify the task of connecting LANs to the Internet. On a modern network, TCP/IP is the only protocol needed — IPX has been all but eliminated.

Novell has reacted by endowing NetWare with a full suite of TCP/IP tools. In this chapter, you find out how to configure basic TCP/IP settings for your network interface cards. Then, you discover how to set up two basic TCP/IP services: DNS and DHCP.

Configuring TCP/IP with INETCFG

Thankfully, NetWare's installation program automatically handles most of the details of configuring your network. As a result, you'll probably need to mess with the network configuration if you add a network board to your computer after installing NetWare or if you decide to change a configuration setting, such as the computer's static IP address.

The primary tool for configuring TCP/IP in NetWare is Inetcfg, a text-mode program that you must run from a system console. You can run it on the server by choosing Novell⇨Utilities⇨System Console and entering **inetcfg** when the prompt finally appears. Or, you can run it from a remote computer by using RConsoleJ.

The first time you run Inetcfg, you'll be asked to transfer the network configuration information into the Inetcfg database. You can't use Inetcfg unless you do this, so you have little choice but to choose Yes.

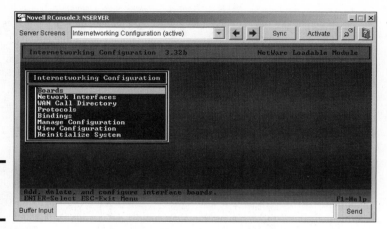

Figure 3-1:
Inetcfg's
main menu.

Figure 3-1 shows the Inetcfg main menu. This menu offers the following choices:

✦ **Boards:** Lets you add, delete, and configure network interface boards.

✦ **Network Interfaces:** Use this selection to configure the network interfaces for configured boards.

✦ **WAN Call Directory:** Lets you configure your WAN connections.

✦ **Protocols:** Lets you enable and configure network protocols.

✦ **Bindings:** Lets you bind protocols to network interfaces. This is where you set the TCP/IP configuration information for an interface.

✦ **Manage Configuration:** Lets you configure other settings.

✦ **View Configuration:** Displays the configuration commands that have been generated by Inetcfg.

✦ **Reinitialize System:** Restarts the network services to apply your changes.

The most common reason for using Inetcfg is to change the static IP address of a network interface. To do that, follow these steps:

1. **Start Inetcfg.**

The main menu appears.

2. **Choose Bindings.**

The Protocol To Interface/Group Bindings display appears, as shown in Figure 3-2.

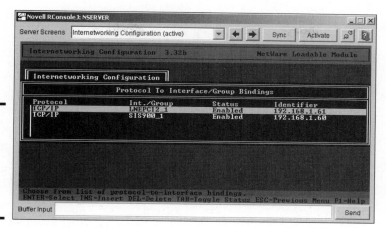

Figure 3-2:
The
Protocol To
Interface/
Group
Bindings
display.

3. **Select the interface whose IP address you want to change and press Enter.**

   The Binding TCP/IP To A LAN interface appears, as shown in Figure 3-3.

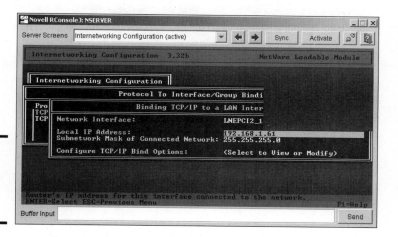

Figure 3-3:
Binding
TCP/IP To
A LAN
interface.

4. **Press Enter again.**

   A pop-up window appears so that you can enter a new IP address.

5. **Type the new IP address and press Enter.**

   The IP address is changed.

6. **If you need to change the subnet mask, select the subnet mask, press Enter, type a new subnet mask, and press Enter.**

   The subnet mask is changed.

7. **Press Esc twice to return to the main menu.**

8. **Select View Configuration, press Enter, select All INETCFG commands, and then press Enter again.**

   The configuration commands are displayed, as shown in Figure 3-4.

Figure 3-4:
The Inetcfg configuration commands.

9. **Press Esc twice to return to the main menu.**

10. **Select Reinitialize and press Enter.**

    A confirmation message appears to ask whether you really want to reinitialize the system.

11. **Select Yes and press Enter.**

    Another message box appears, warning you again.

12. **Press Enter.**

    The network system is restarted.

13. **Press Esc to quit Inetcfg.**

    A confirmation box appears to ask whether you really want to quit.

14. **Select Yes and press Enter to quit.**

    You're returned to a system console prompt.

15. **Close the console window.**

You're done!

Preparing for DNS and DHCP

When you install NetWare, you're asked whether you want to install DNS and DHCP. If you choose not to install DNS and DHCP when you install NetWare but then decide you want to set up a DNS or DHCP server, you'll need to prepare your eDirectory NDS tree for DNS and DHCP. Unfortunately, the only way to do that is from a console. Open a console window and enter the following command:

```
LOAD DNIPINST
```

You're prompted for a username and password; sign in with an Administrator account. The DNIPINST program then displays the dialog box shown in Figure 3-5. Here, DNIPINST is asking for the DNS context in which to install DNS and DHCP. Usually, you'll specify the organization or organizational unit that contains the server. In this case, I specified O=Dev as the context for each object. When you press Enter, a message appears, informing you that the NDS directory has been updated to make way for your DNS and DHCP information. You can now configure DNS and DHCP through iManage.

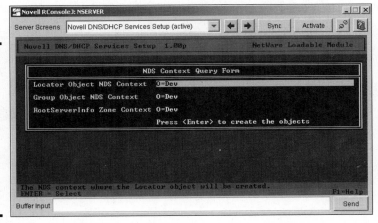

Figure 3-5:
The DNIPINST program asks for the NDS directory context for the DNS and DHCP information.

Configuring the DNS and DHCP Scope

Before you can create a DNS or DHCP server, you must first configure the DNS and DHCP scope. Here's the procedure:

1. **Start iManager and log on as an administrator.**

2. **Expand DNS Management in the menu pane and then choose DNS/DHCP Scope Settings.**

   The page shown in Figure 3-6 appears.

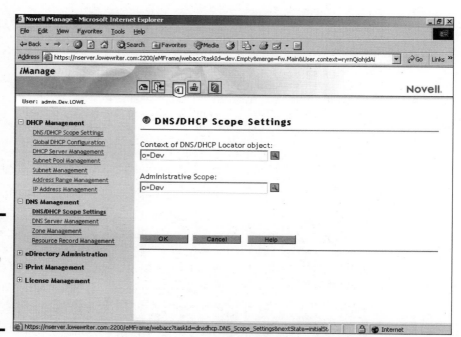

Figure 3-6: iManager asks for the scope for your DNS and DHCP servers.

3. **Enter the scope for the DNS and DCHP objects.**

   This should usually be the organization or organizational unit that contains the server. In this example, I specified O=Dev.

4. **Click OK twice.**

   The first OK configures the scope. The second OK returns you to the iManage greeting page.

Setting up a DNS Server

Before you set up a DNS server, you should carefully plan the server's authoritative zones. If you're not familiar with how DNS works or how zones are defined, read Book V, Chapter 4 before you begin this procedure.

The basic procedure for setting up a DNS server is this:

1. **Create a DNS server.**
2. **Create a zone for the domain that the DNS server will manage.**
3. **Create a reverse-lookup zone.**
4. **Create resource records for each host in the zone.**
5. **Start the DNS service.**

The following sections provide detailed procedures for each of these steps.

Step 1: Creating a DNS server

To create a DNS server, follow these steps:

1. **If you haven't already done so, prepare your NDS tree for DNS and DHCP and configure the DNS and DHCP scope.**

   The procedure for preparing the NDS tree for DNS is described earlier in this chapter, in the section "Preparing for DNS and DHCP."

   To set the DNS and DHCP scope, follow the steps in the section "Configuring the DNS and DHCP Scope," earlier in this chapter.

2. **Expand DNS Management in the iManage menu pane and then choose DNS Server Management.**

   This calls up DNS Server Management page, as shown in Figure 3-7.

3. **Choose Create Server from the drop-down menu and then click OK.**

   This brings up the Create DNS Server page, shown in Figure 3-8.

4. **Enter the server name, host name, and domain name.**

   The easiest way to enter the server name is to click Browse and locate the server in the NDS tree that's displayed. You must also enter the host name and the domain name for the DNS server.

5. **Click OK twice.**

   The first click creates the server and displays a configuration message. The second click returns you to the iManage home page.

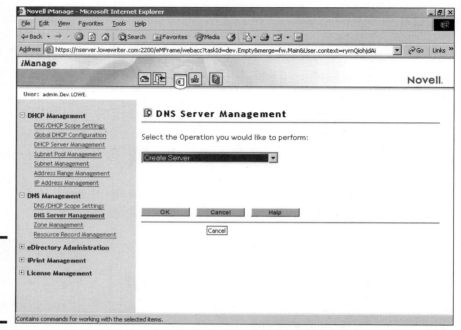

Figure 3-7:
The DNS
Server
Manage-
ment page.

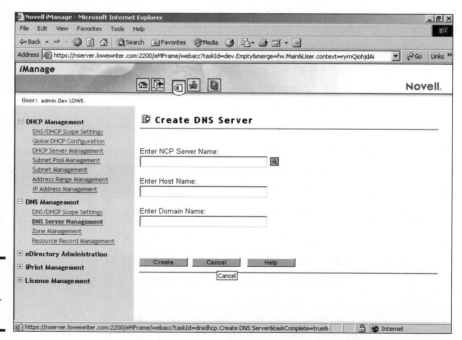

Figure 3-8:
The Create
DNS Server
page.

Step 2: Creating a zone

Now that you've created a DNS server, the next step is to create the DNS zone for which the server is authoritative. Follow these steps:

1. Choose Zone Management from the iManage menu pane.

This brings up the Zone Management page, which resembles the DNS Server Management page that was shown in Figure 3-7.

2. Choose Create Zone and click OK.

This brings up a page that asks you to select the DNS server that you want to modify.

3. Select the DNS server you just created and then click OK.

The Create Zone page appears, as shown in Figure 3-9.

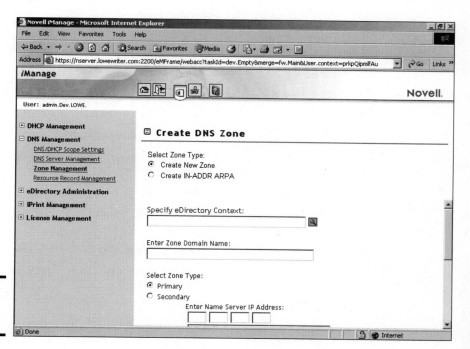

Figure 3-9:
The Create
Zone page.

4. Enter the information required for the zone.

You should enter the following fields:

- **eDirectory context:** The organization or organizational unit. If you want, you can click Browse and select this from a list.

- **Zone domain name:** The complete zone domain name, such as `LoweWriter.com`.

- **Zone type:** Primary.

- **Authoritative zone server:** The zone server you created earlier in this procedure.

5. **Click Create.**

   A confirmation page appears to let you know the zone was successfully created.

6. **Click OK.**

   You're returned to the iManage home page.

Step 3: Creating the reverse-lookup zone

The next step is to create a reverse-lookup zone that allows DNS to look up host names by IP addresses. A reverse-lookup zone uses the special `in-addr.arpa` domain and lists the octets of the IP address backwards to form the complete domain name. For example, the reverse-lookup zone for the subnet 207.126.67.129 is `129.67.126.207.in-addr.arpa`.

Fortunately, iManage handles most of the details of creating a reverse-lookup zone automatically. Here's the procedure:

1. **Choose Zone Management from the iManage menu pane.**

   This brings up the Zone Management page, which resembles the DNS Server Management page that was shown in Figure 3-7.

2. **Choose Create Zone and click OK.**

   This brings up a page that asks you to select the DNS server that you want to modify.

3. **Select the DNS server you just created and then click OK.**

   The Create Zone page appears. It was shown in Figure 3-9, so I won't repeat it here.

4. **Choose Create IN-ADDR ARPA.**

   This specifies that you want to create a reverse-lookup zone rather than a regular zone.

5. **Enter the information required for the reverse-lookup zone.**

   You should enter the following fields:

   - **eDirectory context:** The organization or organizational unit. If you want, you can click Browse and select this from a list.

- **Enter Zone Domain Name:** This field is a little misleading. What you really need to enter here is the IP address for the subnet for which this zone will provide reverse lookups. Leave the host portion of the subnet address set to zeros. NetWare will take care of reversing the octets for you when it creates the zone name, so you should enter the address here in the normal order.

- **Zone type:** Primary.

- **Authoritative zone server:** The zone server you created earlier in this procedure.

6. **Click Create.**

   A confirmation page appears to let you know the zone was successfully created.

7. **Click OK.**

   You're returned to the iManage home page.

Step 4: Creating resource records

After you've set up your zones, it's time to create the resource records for the zone. You'll probably need to create the following records:

✦ **NS:** Identifies a name server that is authoritative for the zone.

✦ **A:** Maps a fully qualified domain name to an IP address.

✦ **CNAME:** Creates an alias for a fully qualified domain name.

✦ **MX:** Identifies the mail server for a domain.

At the minimum, you'll want to create an A record for the server itself. You may also want to create CNAME records for server aliases, such as www or ft. If the zone receives e-mail, you'll need to create an MX record to name the mail servers.

Here's the general procedure for creating resource records:

1. **Choose Resource Record Management from the menu pane.**

   This brings up the Resource Record Management page, which resembles the DNS Server Management page that was shown in Figure 3-7.

2. **To add a resource record, choose Create Resource Record and click OK.**

   This brings up the Create Resource Record page, which asks you to select the domain name for the zone to which you want to add a resource record.

3. **Select the domain and then click Create.**

   The page shown in Figure 3-10 appears.

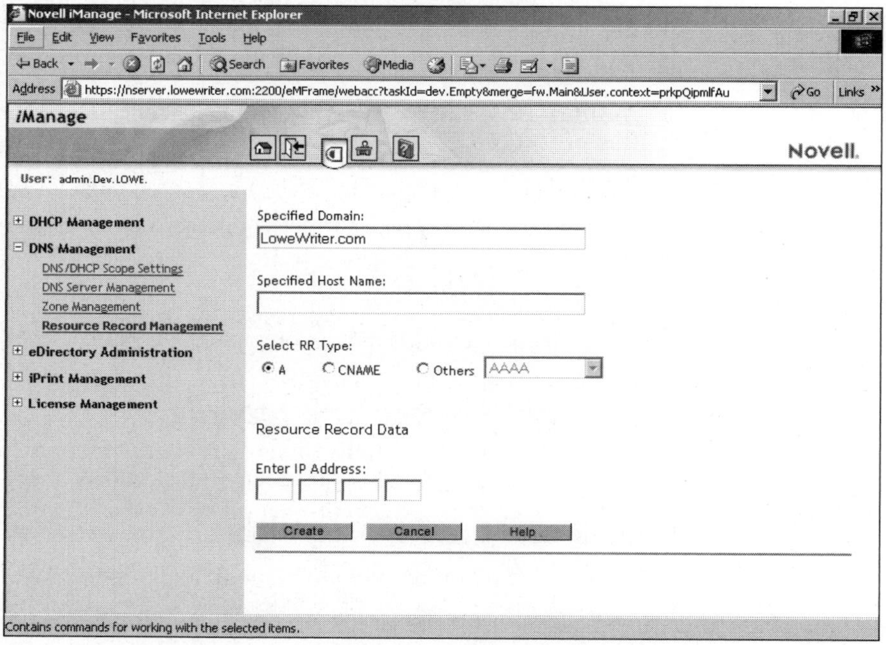

Figure 3-10:
Creating a
resource
record.

4. **Enter the resource record information.**

   You can specify the following information:

   - **Specified host name:** The host name that you want on the resource record.

   - **RR type:** The resource record type. Choose A to define the address of a host, CNAME to create an alias, or Other to create another record type.

   - **IP address:** The IP address to be associated with this record.

5. **Click Create.**

   The confirmation page appears to let you know the record was created.

6. **Click OK.**

   You're returned to the Create Resource Record page.

7. **Repeat Steps 3 through 6 to create additional resource records.**

   You can create as many resource records as the zone requires.

8. **When you're done, click Done and then click OK.**

   You're returned to the iManage home page. You're almost done, so hang in there.

Step 5: Starting the DNS service

The last step in setting up a DNS server is to actually start the DNS service. You can't do that from iManage; instead, you do it from a console window, like this:

1. **Open a server console.**

   Use RConsoleJ if you want to do this final step from a workstation rather than at the server.

2. **Enter the command NAMED.NLM.**

   This starts the DNS service. Now your DNS server is ready to work.

Out the NAMED.NLM line in your AUTOEXEC.NCF file to automatically run the DNS server every time you start your server.

After you've created a DNS server, you can use iManage at any time to modify the zone data or to add additional zones to the server. You can also use iManage to set up reverse-lookup zones as well as secondary and caching zones.

Setting Up a DHCP Server

DHCP is the TCP/IP protocol that automatically assigns IP addresses to hosts as they come on the network. For a very small network (say, fewer than 10 hosts), you don't really need DHCP: You can just configure each computer to have a static IP address. For larger networks, however, DHCP is almost a must. Without DHCP, you'll have to manually plan your entire IP address scheme and manually configure every computer with its IP information. Then, if a critical address such as your Internet gateway router or your DNS server address changes, you'll have to manually update each computer on the network. As you can imagine, DHCP can save you a lot of time.

For complete information about DHCP, please refer to Book V, Chapter 3. In the following sections, I show you how to set up a DHCP server on NetWare 6.

The basic procedure for setting up a DHCP server is this:

1. **Create a DHCP server.**
2. **Create a subnet pool.**
3. **Create a subnet in the subnet pool you created in Step 2.**
4. **Create an address range for the subnet.**
5. **Create IP address records for reserved addresses.**
6. **Start the DHCP server.**

The following sections provide detailed procedures for each of these steps.

Step 1: Creating a DHCP server

To create a DNS server, follow these steps:

1. **If you haven't already done so, prepare your NDS tree for DNS and DHCP and configure the DNS and DHCP scope.**

   The procedure for preparing the NDS tree for DNS is described earlier in this chapter, in the section "Preparing for DNS and DHCP."

   To set the DNS and DHCP scope, follow the steps in the section "Configuring the DNS and DHCP Scope," earlier in this chapter.

2. **Expand the DHCP Management option in the iManage menu pane and then choose DHCP Server Management.**

   This calls up DHCP Server Management page, as shown in Figure 3-11.

3. **Choose Create Server from the drop-down menu and then click OK.**

   This brings up the Create DHCP Server page, as shown in Figure 3-12.

4. **Enter the server name.**

   The easiest way to enter the server name is to click Browse and locate the server in the NDS tree that's displayed.

5. **Click OK twice.**

   The first click creates the server and displays a configuration message. The second click returns you to the iManage home page.

Figure 3-11:
The DHCP
Server
Manage-
ment page.

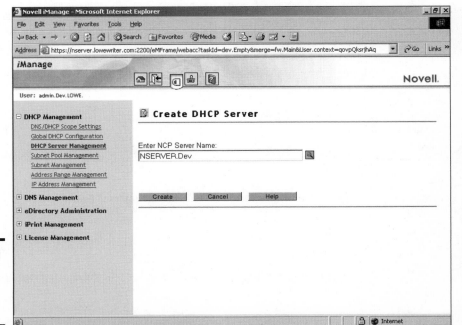

Figure 3-12:
The Create
DHCP
Server
page.

Step 2: Creating a subnet pool

Having created a DHCP server, the next step is to create a subnet pool. Here are the steps:

1. **Choose Subnet Pool Management from the iManage menu pane.**

   This brings up the Subnet Pool Management page, which resembles the DHCP Server Management page that was shown in Figure 3-11.

2. **Choose Create Subnet Pool and click OK.**

   The Create Subnet Pool page, as shown in Figure 3-13, appears.

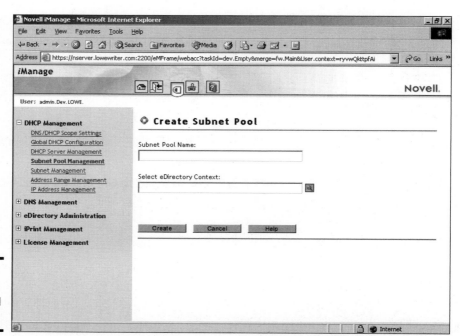

Figure 3-13:
The Create Subnet Pool page.

3. **Enter the name and context for the subnet pool.**

   The subnet pool name should be a name that uniquely identifies the subnet pool.

4. **Click Create.**

   A confirmation message appears to let you know the pool was successfully created.

5. Click OK.

You're returned to the iManage home page.

Step 3: Creating a subnet

After you've created a subnet pool, you should create a subnet record for each subnet that the DHCP server will administer. Follow these steps:

1. Choose Subnet Management from the iManage menu pane.

This brings up the Subnet Management page, which resembles the DHCP Server Management page that was shown in Figure 3-11.

2. Choose Create Subnet and click OK.

The Create Subnet page, as shown in Figure 3-14, appears.

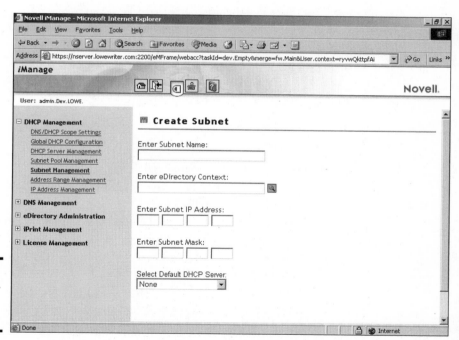

Figure 3-14: The Create Subnet page.

Book VIII
Chapter 3

TCP/IP and
NetWare 6

3. Enter the subnet record information.

You can specify the following information:

- **Subnet name:** A descriptive name for the subnet.
- **eDirectory context:** The context for the subnet.

- **Subnet IP address:** The IP address of the subnet. The host portion of this address should be zero — for example, 192.168.1.0.

- **Subnet mask:** The subnet mask for this subnet — for example, 255.255.255.0.

- **Default DHCP server:** Select the DHCP server from the drop-down list.

4. **Click Create.**

A confirmation message appears to let you know the subnet was successfully created.

5. **Click OK.**

You're returned to the iManage home page.

Step 4: Creating subnet address ranges

Having created a subnet, you now get to tell DHCP what range of addresses from the subnet the server should hand out. Follow these steps:

1. **Choose Address Range Management from the iManage menu pane.**

This brings up the Address Range Management page, which resembles the DHCP Server Management page that was shown in Figure 3-11.

2. **Choose Create Address Range and click OK.**

The Create Subnet page appears.

3. **Enter the address range information.**

You can specify the following information:

- **Subnet:** The subnets you define appear in this drop-down list. Choose the one you want to use.

- **Address range name:** Seems like you have to give a name to everything, doesn't it?

- **Start address:** The first IP address in the range. The host portion of this address can't be zero.

- **Last address:** The last IP address of the range. The host portion of this address can't be all ones (for example, 255 in a Class C address).

- **Default DHCP server:** Select the DHCP server from the drop-down list.

4. **Click Create.**

A confirmation message appears to let you know the address range was successfully created.

5. **Click OK.**

You're returned to the iManage home page.

Step 5: Creating IP address records

An IP address record lets you set up the server so that whenever a particular host requests an IP address from the DHCP server, the server should provide it the address that you specify in the IP address record. The host won't receive the IP address until it requests it from the DHCP server, but whenever it does request IP configuration, it will always receive the same address. In non-Novell versions of DHCP, this is called a *reservation*.

To reserve an IP address for a specific computer, you must know that computer's MAC address. As a result, you need to get the MAC address from the host before you create the reservation. You can get the MAC address by running the command `ipconfig /all` from a command prompt. (If that fails because TCP/IP has not yet been configured on the computer, you can also get the MAC address by running the System Information command (Start➪All Programs➪Accessories➪System Tools➪System Information).

To create an IP address record, follow these steps:

1. **Choose IP Address ManagementRange Management from the iManage menu pane.**

This brings up the IP Address Management page, which resembles the DHCP Server Management page that was shown in Figure 3-11.

2. **Choose Create IP Address and click OK.**

This brings up the Create IP Address page, as shown in Figure 3-15.

3. **Enter the IP address information.**

You can specify the following information:

- **Subnet:** The subnets you define appear in this drop-down list. Choose the one that you want to use.

- **IP address:** The IP address that you want to reserve.

- **Assignment type:** You can choose from two types of assignments. If you specify Exclude, the address will never be assigned to any computer. Use this option if you've used the IP address in a static assignment for a server computer or for a computer that can't work with DHCP. If you specify Manual, the IP address is reserved for a specific host.

- **Client identifier:** The MAC address of the computer to which you want to assign this IP address.

4. **Click Create.**

A confirmation message appears to let you know the IP address record was successfully created.

5. **Click OK.**

You're returned to the iManage home page.

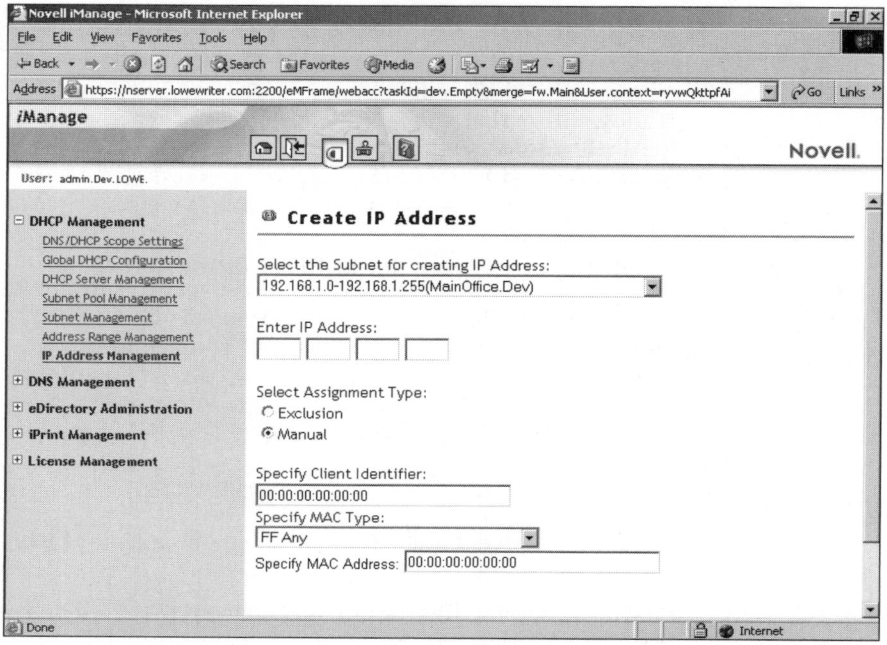

![Novell iManage - Microsoft Internet Explorer screenshot showing the Create IP Address page. The left navigation pane lists DHCP Management with subentries: DNS/DHCP Scope Settings, Global DHCP Configuration, DHCP Server Management, Subnet Pool Management, Subnet Management, Address Range Management, IP Address Management; and DNS Management, eDirectory Administration, iPrint Management, License Management. The main panel shows Create IP Address with fields: Select the Subnet for creating IP Address (192.168.1.0-192.168.1.255(MainOffice.Dev)), Enter IP Address, Select Assignment Type (Exclusion/Manual), Specify Client Identifier (00:00:00:00:00:00), Specify MAC Type (FF Any), Specify MAC Address (00:00:00:00:00:00).]

Figure 3-15:
The Create
IP Address
page.

Step 6: Starting the DHCP service

The last step in setting up a DHCP server is to actually start the DHCP service. You can't do that from iManage; instead, you do it from a console window, like this:

1. Open a server console.

Use RConsoleJ if you want to do this final step from a workstation rather than at the server.

2. Enter the command DHCPSRVR.NLM.

This starts the DHCP service. Now your DHCP server is ready to work.

After you get your DHCP server up and running, put the DHCPSVRVR.NLM line in your AUTOEXEC.NCF file. That way, the DHCP server will start automatically every time you start your server.

After you've created a DHCP server, you can use iManage at any time to modify the zone data or to add additional zones to the server. You can also use iManage to set up reverse-lookup zones, as well as secondary and caching zones.

Chapter 4: NetWare Login Scripts

In This Chapter

✓ Understanding the different types of login scripts

✓ Setting up login scripts

✓ Recognizing the most useful login script commands

*I*n a NetWare network, login scripts are the main way you set up each user's networking environment. With a login script, you can automatically map network drives, display messages, and execute programs. The beauty of login scripts is that you can create just a few login scripts and use them for all your users. In other words, using login scripts lets you automate much of your network setup.

Understanding Login Scripts

A *login script* is nothing more than a text file that contains a sequence of special login commands that are executed when a user logs in to a NetWare network. In most cases, the main job of the login script is to set up drive mappings that make it convenient for network users to access the applications and data that they need. For example, if all the users in a marketing department need access to the directory SYS:\DATA\MKTG, you can use login scripts to map this directory to drive M: for every marketing department user.

You can execute four types of login scripts when a user logs in:

✦ **Container script:** The container in which the user is defined (that is, the organization or organizational unit object) can have an associated login script. If so, this is the first script that is executed when any user defined in the organization or organizational unit logs on. This script lets you set up global drive mappings that you want to be common for all the users on your network.

✦ **Profile script:** Profiles can also have login scripts. If you've assigned a user to a profile, the profile's login script is executed after the container login script. Profiles are how you can create separate login scripts for different types of users within your network.

✦ **User script:** Users can have individualized login scripts. If a user has a login script, it's executed after the profile script is executed.

✦ **Default script:** If the user doesn't have a user script, the default script is run in its place after any container and profile scripts are executed.

To give you a feel for what a login script does, here's a simple example:

```
MAP DISPLAY OFF
MAP ERRORS OFF
MAP M:=SYS:\DATA\SALES
MAP N:=SYS:\DATA\MKTG
MAP O:=SYS:\DATA\FIN
```

This login file simply maps three subdirectories of the SYS volume to drives M:, N:, and O:. That way, the user can access sales data on drive N:, marketing data on drive O:, and financial data on drive P:.

In all likelihood, most users require access to only one of these drive mappings. You can create a more customized login script by adding IF statements to determine what groups the user is a member of and to map the drives accordingly:

```
MAP DISPLAY OFF
MAP ERRORS OFF
IF MEMBER OF ".SALES.Dev" THEN MAP M:=SYS:DATA\SALES
IF MEMBER OF ".MKTG.Dev" THEN MAP N:=SYS:DATA\MKTG
IF MEMBER OF ".FIN.Dev" THEN MAP O:=SYS:DATA\FIN
```

As you work more with login scripts, you'll discover many ways that you can customize them to automate your users' network configuration.

Creating Login Scripts

Login scripts are simple text files that reside on a server and are associated with container, profile, and user objects. The following procedure shows how to create a container, profile, or user script using ConsoleOne.

Creating a container or user script

Container and user scripts are the easiest types of scripts to create because you probably already have container and user objects defined in your NDS tree. To create a container or user script, follow these steps:

1. **Open ConsoleOne and log in as an administrator.**

   You need some authority to mess with people's login scripts.

2. **Expand the tree down to the organization or organizational unit where the user objects are defined.**

3. **Right-click the organization or organizational unit to create a container script or the user object for which you want to create a user script and select Properties.**

   The Properties dialog box for the container or the user appears.

4. **Click the Login Script tab.**

   The Login Script property page appears. Figure 4-1 shows what this page looks like for a container script. It's nearly identical for a user script.

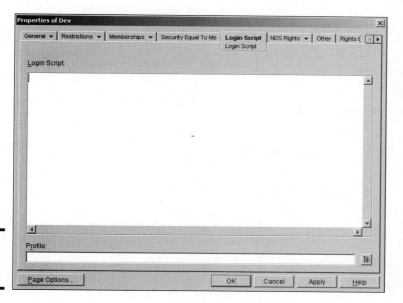

Figure 4-1:
Creating a
login script.

Book VIII
Chapter 4

NetWare Login
Scripts

5. **Type the login script in the text box.**

   You can use any of the commands described later in this chapter in your script.

6. **When you're done, click OK.**

   The login script is saved.

Creating a profile script

If you want to use profiles to manage login scripts, the procedure is a little more complicated because you have to create the profile, associate it with the user, and then grant the user the right to read the script. Here's the complete procedure:

1. Open ConsoleOne and log in as an administrator.

This procedure needs the administrator's authority.

2. Expand the tree down to the container where your user objects are defined.

3. Right-click the container and choose New⊏⊃Object.

The New Object dialog box appears, as shown in Figure 4-2.

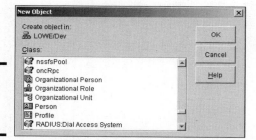

Figure 4-2:
The New
Object
dialog box.

4. Select Profile in the Class list and then click OK.

You have to scroll down the list to find Profile. When you click OK, the New Profile dialog box appears, as shown in Figure 4-3.

Figure 4-3:
The New
Profile
dialog box.

5. Enter the name of the profile that you want to create, check the Define Additional Properties check box, and then click OK.

The Properties box for the new profile appears.

6. **Click the Login Script tab.**

The Login Script page of the Properties dialog box appears. This dialog box looks almost exactly like the one shown in Figure 4-1, so I won't repeat it here.

7. **Type the login script in the text box.**

You can use any of the commands described later in this chapter in your script.

8. **When you're done, click the NDS Rights tab.**

The login script is saved, and you're taken to the NDS Rights page, shown in Figure 4-4. You use this page to grant users or groups the right to run the profile's login script.

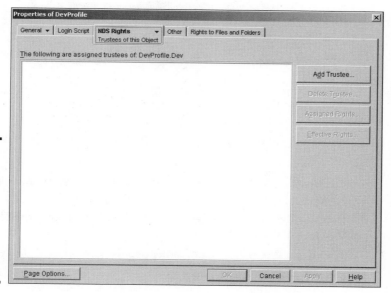

Figure 4-4:
The NDS Rights tab is where you grant users permission to run profile login scripts.

9. **Click Add Trustee.**

A Select Objects dialog box appears, listing all your users and groups.

10. **Choose the users or groups who will use the profile's login script and then click OK.**

It's best to choose one or more groups here rather than individual users. When you click OK, the Rights Assigned To Selected Objects dialog box appears, as shown in Figure 4-5.

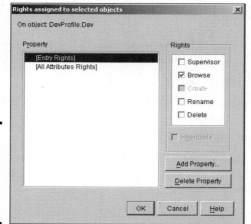

Figure 4-5:
The Rights
Assigned To
Selected
Objects
dialog box.

11. **Make sure that the Browse and Read rights are selected and then click OK.**

These rights should be selected by default, but double-check just to make sure. To see the Read right, you have to click All Attribute Rights in the Property list box.

When you click OK, you're returned to the profile's Properties page.

12. **Click OK.**

The profile is saved, and you're returned to the main ConsoleOne window.

13. **Double-click a user that you want to allow to use the profile script that you just created.**

The user's Properties dialog box appears.

14. **Click the Login Script tab.**

The Login Script page appears.

15. **Click the Browse button that's located to the right of the Profile text box at the bottom of the page.**

Another Select Object dialog box appears; this one lists all your profiles.

16. **Choose the profile you just created and then click OK.**

You're returned to the user's Property page.

17. **Click OK.**

You're done! You have successfully created a profile login script and attached it to a user.

Login Script Basics

The following sections describe the commands that you'll use most often when creating login scripts. Before I get into the details of each command, however, I want to point out a few nitty-gritty login script details:

+ Login scripts are not case-sensitive, except for text enclosed in parentheses.

+ Use only one command per line.

+ To create a comment, start the line with REM, an asterisk (*), or a semicolon (;).

+ To execute an external command, start the line with a hash mark (#).

+ Variables begin with a percent sign (%). For more information about variables, see the section "Identifier variables," later in this chapter.

+ You can also use DOS-style environment variables as described in the section "The Set command," later in this chapter.

+ The name of the NetWare server is available in the special parameters %0, and the name of the user is available as %1.

The Attach command

The Attach command connects you to an old-style, pre-NDS NetWare server. If your network still has NetWare 2.*x* or 3.*x* servers, you'll need to use this command. Otherwise, you can safely ignore this command.

The Display command

The Display command displays the contents of a file in the user's login window. Normally, the login text flies by so fast that users don't see it anyway, but you can add a Pause command to the login script to force the login script to stop so that the user has a chance to read the display.

One possible use of the Display command is to let you set up a message file that's displayed whenever users log on. For example, you can create a file named ANNOUNCE.TXT in SYS:\PUBLIC. Then, you can include this line in the container login script:

```
display SYS:PUBLIC\ANNOUNCE.TXT
```

Note that if the file doesn't exist, nothing is displayed.

The Exit command

The Exit command terminates the login script. You'll usually use it in combination with an IF command to terminate the login procedure if some unusual condition arises.

The Fire Phasers command

Being a Star Trek fan, this has always been my personal favorite login command, even though it's essentially useless. It sounds a beep or other sound and has the following syntax:

```
fire [phasers] [n] [soundfile]
```

Why do I say it's useless? Because usually Windows is playing its own symphonic startup sound right around the time your login procedure decides to fire its phasers. So the login beep is swallowed up in the Windows sound.

Identifier variables

Identifier variables are special variables that NetWare creates and are available to your login scripts. You can use an identifier variable just about anywhere you want in a login script. Table 4-1 lists the identifier variables that you're likely to use.

Table 4-1	Commonly Used Identifier Variables
Variable	*Description*
AM_PM	Either a.m. or p.m.
CN	The user's full eDirectory name
DAY	The day of the month (01 through 31)
DAY_OF_WEEK	The day of the week (Monday, Tuesday, and so on)
FILE_SERVER	The file server name
FULL_NAME	The user's unique username
GREETING_TIME	Morning, afternoon, or evening
HOUR	Hour (1 through 12)
HOUR24	Hour (1 through 24)
LAST_NAME	The surname from the user object
LOGIN_CONTEXT	The login context
LOGIN_NAME	The user's unique login name
MACHINE	The type of computer

Variable	Description
MEMBER OF "*group*"	True if the user is a member of the specified group
MINUTE	Minute (00 through 59)
MONTH	The month number (01 through 12)
MONTH_NAME	The name of the month (January, February, and so on)
NDAY_OF_WEEK	The weekday number (1 through 7, where Sunday is 1)
NOT MEMBER OF "*group*"	True if the user is not a member of the specified group
OS	A description of the client operating system
OS_VERSION	The version of the client operating system
PASSWORD_EXPIRES	The number of days until the user's password expires
PLATFORM	The user's operating system platform
SECOND	Second (00 through 59)
SHORT_YEAR	The last two digits of the year
SMACHINE	A short machine name
STATION	The computer's connection number
USER_ID	The user's numeric ID
WINVER	The Windows version

The If Command

The If command lets you include conditional logic in your login scripts. You can use it in two ways. The first is a single line IF, like this:

```
if condition then command
```

For example, this line maps a hard drive if the user is a member of the SALES group:

```
if member of ".SALES.DEV" then map m:=SYS:DATA\SALES
```

Or, for more complicated login scripts, you can use the multiline if-then-else statement with this syntax:

```
if condition then
    commands
[else
    commands ]
end
```

For example, here's an If that maps several drives and displays a flattering message if the administrator logs in:

```
if "%1"="ADMIN" then
    map W:=SYS:\SYSTEM
    map X:=SYS:\ETC
    write "Hello, boss. You look great today!"
else
    write "Hello ordinary non-administrator user!"
end
```

The condition test in an If statement can compare identifier variables, login parameters, environment variables, or literals. You can use any of the comparison operators listed in Table 4-2.

Table 4-2	Comparison Operators for If Statements
Operator	*Description*
=	Equal
<>	Not equal
>	Greater than
<	Less than
>=	Greater than or equal to
<=	Less than or equal to

The Include command

The Include statement lets you include another file or login script as a part of your login script. To include another file, use the Include command like this:

```
include SYS:PUBLIC\LOGINS\STDMAP.TXT
```

To include the login script of another object, use the command like this:

```
include .SalesProfile.Dev.LOWE
```

In this example, the login script for the SalesProfile object contained in the Dev organizational unit under the LOWE organization is included.

The Map command

The Map command is the main reason you need to create login scripts. It lets you associate an MS-DOS drive letter with a directory on a NetWare volume. The basic syntax is this:

```
map drive:=path
```

You have two ways to specify the drive:

+ As a drive letter, as in:

    ```
    map m:=SYS:Public
    ```

    Here, drive M: is mapped to SYS:Public.

+ A relative network drive, like this:

    ```
    map *1:=SYS:Public
    map *2:=SYS:Public\Data
    ```

    Here, the first network drive will be mapped to SYS:Public and the second network drive will be mapped to SYS:\Public\Data. When you use this notation, the drive letter depends on which drive letter is configured to be the first drive available for the network.

You can also use the Map command to set drive mapping options. Then, the syntax is

```
map [option]
```

The options can be

+ **display on | off**: Specifies whether messages should be displayed as the drives are mapped. You should usually include a map display off command near the start of every login script. When testing or debugging a login script, you can make this line a comment so that the text will be displayed.

+ **errors on | off**: Specifies whether error messages should be displayed as the drives are mapped. You should usually include a map errors off command near the start of every login script. When testing or debugging a login script, you can make this line a comment so that the text will be displayed.

+ **ins**: Inserts the drive mapping into the search mappings.

+ **del:** Deletes the drive mapping.

The No_Default command

This command causes the default login script to not run even if the user doesn't have a user login script.

The Pause command

The Pause command causes the login script to stop until the user presses a key. This is the only way to make sure that the user has time to read any messages created by the Display or Write commands.

The Set command

The Set command lets you create MS-DOS style environment variables. The syntax of the Set statement is this:

```
set variable=value
```

For example, this line creates an environment variable named messages, whose value is yes:

```
set messages="yes"
```

To use the value of an environment variable, enclose it in angle brackets (< >), like this:

```
if <messages>="yes" then pause
```

The Write command

The Write command displays a line in the login message dialog box. It has a simple syntax:

```
write "message"
```

If you want to include an identifier in the output, use a percent sign (%) before the identifier:

```
write %LAST_NAME
```

You can string together several identifiers and text strings by separating them with semicolons:

```
write "Hello ";%LAST_NAME
```

Chapter 5: NetWare Console Commands

In This Chapter

✔ Creating reference to the console commands that you're likely to use

✔ Reviewing some commands you won't often need but are nice to know just in case

✔ Getting familiar with a few commands you may never use but are still fun

*I*f you're a command line junkie, you'll love NetWare. NetWare has a nice collection of graphical tools for setting up and configuring a network. After you open a console window, you have access to more than 140 console commands that enable you to perform just about any network configuration task imaginable.

Not that you would want to use all 140 of them every day. Most of the functions that these commands perform are better done by the graphical management tools, such as ConsoleOne or Remote Manager. Still, you'll encounter situations when the quickest way to get something done is to pull up a console window and enter a command.

This chapter presents a collection of what I've found to be the most useful console commands, in alphabetical order. If you want to know more, you can find the complete NetWare 6 Utilities Reference online at Novell's Web site (`www.novell.com`). I'd give you the complete URL, but it's about two pages long. Instead, just go to Google or your favorite search engine and search for "NetWare 6 Utilities Reference." That should lead you right to the online manual.

Broadcast

The `Broadcast` command lets you send a message to all the users on your network or to a specific user or users. The syntax of the command is

```
broadcast "Message" [to users]
```

Actually, this command is identical to the SEND command described later in this chapter. I tend to use the Broadcast command for messages sent to all users and the Send command for messages sent to specific users. I'm just quirky, I guess.

Here's an example that sends a broadcast message warning that the server will be taken down soon:

```
broadcast "The server will self-destruct in five minutes."
```

This displays a dialog box, similar to the one shown in Figure 5-1, on every user's computer.

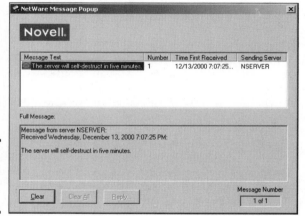

Figure 5-1:
A broadcast message dialog box.

Here's an example of a command sent to a specific user:

```
broadcast "How about lunch?" to Gilligan, Skipper
```

You can also broadcast a message to everyone from Remote Manager. Select Connections from the menu pane and then scroll down a bit to find the Broadcast Message To Everyone text box. Enter your message and then click Send.

Cls

The Cls command clears the console screen. If your console fills up with clutter, use this command to clean it up. You don't have any arguments; just enter cls and be done with it.

Config

The `Config` command displays interesting information about your server's configuration. The `Config` command may display several pages of information; you're prompted to press a key between pages. Here's a sample of the output created by this command:

```
NSERVER: config

File server name: NSERVER
Server Up Time:  4 Hours 5 Minutes 28 Seconds

SiS 900/7016 PCI Adapters NetWare ODI32 Driver
     Version 1.12    July 23, 2001
     Hardware setting: Slot 10004, I/O ports CC00h to CCFFh, Memory
CFFF7000h to CFFF7FFFh, Interrupt 5h
     Node address: 00D009811F5C
     Frame type: ETHERNET_II
     Board name: SIS900_1_EII
     LAN protocol: ARP
     LAN protocol: IP Addr:192.168.1.100 Mask:255.255.255.0

Linksys PCI II Ethernet Card Version 4.10(980310P)
     Version 7.01    March 10, 1998
     Hardware setting: Slot 2, I/O ports C800h to C81Fh, Interrupt 5
     Node address: 002078167C16
     Frame type: Ethernet_II
     Board name: LNEPCI2_1_EII
     LAN protocol: ARP
     LAN protocol: IP Addr:192.168.2.100 Mask:255.255.255.0

Tree Name: .LOWE.
Bindery Context(s):
     .Dev

NSERVER:
```

As you can see, this command gives you a quick summary of your computer's network configuration, including the adapter's type and name, as well as the protocols that are bound to each network board. You can also see the IP address assignments.

Disable Login

This command prevents users from logging in to the computer. The syntax is simple:

```
disable login
```

This command doesn't actually force anyone off the system, but it does prevent new users who aren't logged in already from logging in. It's usually used before downing a server. You can restore logins later by using the `Enable Login` command.

Dismount

The `Dismount` command takes a volume offline so that you can work on it or replace it. It has this syntax:

`dismount` *volume*

For example, the following command dismounts a volume named ARCHIVE:

`NSERVER: dismount archive`

It would be polite to broadcast a message first, just to let users know that the volume will be unavailable for a while.

Display Environment

The `Display Environment` command displays the current search path and the current settings for all settable server parameters. Here's a snipped sample of the output that it creates:

```
NSERVER: display environment
PATH=\\NSERVER\SYS\SYSTEM\;C:\NWSERVER;\\NSERVER\SYS\JAVA\NWGFX\;\\NSERVER\SYS\J
AVA\NJCLV2\BIN\;\\NSERVER\SYS\NI\BIN\;\\NSERVER\SYS\JAVA\BIN\;\\NSERVER\SYS\TOMC
AT\33\BIN\;\\NSERVER\SYS\APACHE\;\\NSERVER\sys\bi\update\bin;

Maximum Pending TCP Connection Requests:  128
BSD Socket default Buffer Size in Bytes:  32768
Discard Oversized Ping Packets:  ON
Largest Ping Packet Size:  10240
TCP Defend Land Attacks:  ON
IP Wan Client Validation:  OFF
TOS for IP packets:  0
Arp entry update time:  300
Arp entry expiry time:  300
ICMP Redirect Timeout:  3
Largest UDP Packet Size:  16384
Discard Oversized UDP Packets:  ON
TCP UDP Diagnostic Services:  OFF
TCP Path MTU Black Hole Detection and Recovery:  OFF
TCP Max Port Limit:  54999
TCP Sack Option:  ON

<Press ESC to terminate or any other key to continue>
```

It takes about a dozen screens like this to list all the server parameters.

Display Modified Environment

This command displays all the system parameters that have been changed from their default values. If you suspect that a rogue parameter setting is giving your server grief, this is the command to use to find out what parameters have been changed. Here's a sample of its output:

```
NSERVER: display modified environment

REPLY TO GET NEAREST SERVER:
     Current Setting: OFF
     Default Setting: ON

Maximum Packet Receive Buffers:
     Current Setting: 10000
     Default Setting: 5000

Minimum Packet Receive Buffers:
     Current Setting: 2000
     Default Setting: 500

Minimum Service Processes:
     Current Setting: 60
     Default Setting: 25

Maximum Service Processes:
     Current Setting: 570
     Default Setting: 500

Default Tree Name:
     Current Setting: LOWE
     Default Setting:
```

Down

This command is the NetWare executioner: It shuts the server down. Always use this command (or the graphical equivalent in Remote Manager) to properly shut down a server before you turn off its power. Down ensures that the system shuts down in an orderly fashion by closing files and cleanly terminating processes.

If you're going to immediately restart the server without actually powering it down, you can use the Reset Server or Restart Server commands instead.

The Down command has no parameters, so just hold your breath and type **down** to shut down a server.

It's polite to warn users with a Broadcast message a few minutes before downing a server.

Edit

The `Edit` command calls up a handy console editor that you can use to edit text files. The syntax of this command is

```
edit [file]
```

If the file doesn't already exist, `Edit` asks whether you want to create it. If you don't specify a file on the `Edit` command, you'll be asked to enter a filename.

Figure 5-2 shows the `Edit` command in action. `Edit` is pretty limited, but it's ideal for editing small text files. You can use a few special keys for basic editing functions:

+ **F1:** Displays a help screen.

+ **F5:** Toggles block mode. When block mode is on, you can select text to copy or delete.

+ **F6:** Copy blocked text to the buffer.

+ **Ins:** Paste copied text.

+ **Esc:** Exit.

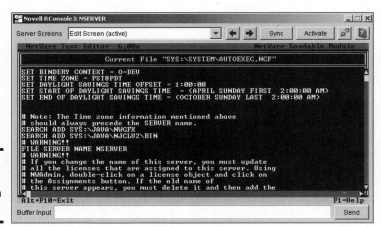

Figure 5-2: The `Edit` command in action.

Enable Login

This command allows users to log in to the computer. Use it after you disabled logins with `Disable Login`. The syntax is simple:

```
enable login
```

Help

This command displays help information for console commands. It has this syntax:

```
help [ command | all ]
```

You can use this command in one of three ways:

✦ If you enter Help without any parameters, a list of all commands appears.

✦ If you specify a command, a description of that command appears.

✦ If you enter help all, a description of all commands appears.

Load

The Load command loads a module. The basic syntax of the Load command is

```
[load] [ module ]
```

Notice that the keyword *load* is optional for this command. As a result, if you type just the name of a module at the console prompt, the module will be loaded.

You can load five types of modules:

✦ **NWPA drivers:** These files have .CDM and .HAM extensions. They are the drivers that support host adapters.

✦ **LAN drivers:** These files have the extension .LAN. They are the drivers that support network boards. Note that you can load and unload LAN drivers while the server is running and while users are logged in.

✦ **PSM modules:** These files have the extension .PSM. They are the modules that enable multiple processors to function in a coordinated way.

✦ **Utilities and applications:** These files have .NLM and .EXE extensions. They're the commands that you normally run from a console prompt. After you finish your tasks, you can unload the utility and free memory for other server functions.

✦ **Name space support:** These files have the extension .NAM. They're required to support non-DOS file and directory names.

**Book VIII
Chapter 5**

**NetWare Console
Commands**

Modules

The `Modules` command displays information about the modules that are loaded. The syntax is

```
modules [string]
```

You don't have to specify a string, but if you do, you'll be sitting at the console for a long time tapping the famous Any Key as information about hundreds of modules scrolls by. Better to use a string to limit your search. Here's an example that displays all modules that begin with `na`:

```
NSERVER:modules na*
NAWT.NLM
   Loaded from [SYS:\JAVA\BIN\]
   (Address Space = OS)
   NAWT - 1.1 Graphics
   Version 1.00a    October 5, 2001
   Copyright (c) 2001 Novell, Inc.
NAMED.NLM
   Loaded from [SYS:\SYSTEM\]
   (Address Space = OS)
   Novell DNS Server
   Version 5.10a    September 12, 2001
   Copyright 1997-2001, Novell inc.  All rights reserved.
```

If you're not sure that a service is working properly, run `Modules` to make sure that the service has been loaded.

Mount

The `Mount` command places a volume online so that users can access it. It has this syntax:

```
mount [ volume | all ]
```

For example, the following command mounts a volume named ARCHIVE:

```
NSERVER: mount archive
```

You can mount all currently unmounted volumes by entering `mount all`.

Scrsaver

The Scrsaver command adds a password-protected screen saver to the console. It has the following syntax:

```
Scrsaver [options]
```

Here are the options that you're most likely to use:

✦ **Activate:** Immediately activates the screen saver.

✦ **Delay:** Specifies how long the console must be inactive before the screen saver is activated. The default is delay=600, which works out to 10 minutes.

✦ **Disable:** Disables the screen saver.

✦ **Enable:** Enables the screen saver.

✦ **No password:** Allows the screen saver to be unlocked without entering a password.

Secure Console

The Secure Console command increases your server's security by preventing modules from being loaded from anywhere other than SYS:SYSTEM or C:\NWSERVER. It also disables the operating system debugger and prevents date and time changes.

The syntax is

```
secure console
```

After you've used the Secure Console command, the only way to get full access back is to down the server.

Set

The set command lets you set server parameters. Server parameters control the overall operation of a NetWare server. Most of the parameters are set automatically when the system starts up, but you may want to adjust the settings when you're installing new features or diagnosing problems.

The syntax is as follows:

```
set [parameter][=value]
```

**Book VIII
Chapter 5**

**NetWare Console
Commands**

The `Set` command can be used in three ways. If you specify `Set` without any parameters, a list of parameter categories is displayed. You can then choose one of the categories to display a list of all the parameters in that category along with an explanation of what the parameter does and its current setting.

If you know the name of a specific parameter, you can display its current setting by adding the parameter name to the `Set` statement, like this:

```
NSERVER:set time zone
Time zone is set to: EST5EDT
```

Now, suppose that you pack up your server and move to sunny California, so you want to change the `Time Zone` parameter to Pacific Standard Time. Then, you'd use this command:

```
NSERVER:set time zone=PST8PDT
Time zone is set to: PST8PDT
```

Send

The `Send` command lets you send a message to all the users on your network or to a specific user or users. The syntax of the command is

```
send "Message" [to users]
```

Actually, this command is identical to the `Broadcast` command described earlier in this chapter. I tend to use the `Broadcast` command for messages sent to all users and the `Send` command for messages sent to specific users. I'm just quirky, I guess.

Here's an example that sends a lunch invitation to a couple of friends:

```
send "How about lunch?" gilligan, skipper
```

This will display the message "How about lunch?" on Gilligan's and Skipper's computers.

Unload

The `Unload` command removes a module from memory. Its syntax is

```
unload module
```

You can use this command to disable a service that isn't working right. Sometimes simply unloading and reloading the service will correct a problem. You may also need to unload and then reload a service to make configuration changes effective.

Version

This command displays the NetWare version information. For example:

```
NSERVER:version
Novell NetWare 6
(C) Copyright 1983-2001 novell Inc. All Rights Reserved. Patent Pending.
Server Version 5.60 September 13, 2001
NDS Version 10110.20  September 6, 2001
```

Book IX

Linux Reference

The 5th Wave   By Rich Tennant

My job consists of working with the kernel all day.

Contents at a Glance

Chapter 1: Installing a Linux Server

In This Chapter

✔ Getting ready to install Linux

✔ Installing Linux

✔ Adding additional packages after installation

This chapter presents the procedures that you need to follow to install Linux on a server computer. The specific details provided are specifically for Red Hat Linux 9. However, installing other distributions of Linux is similar, so you won't have any trouble adapting these procedures if you're using a different distribution.

Planning a Linux Server Installation

Before you begin the installation program to actually install Linux, you need to make a number of preliminary decisions. The following sections describe the decisions that you need to make before you install Linux.

Checking system requirements

Before you install Linux, you should make sure that the computer meets the minimum requirements. Although the minimum requirements for Linux are considerably less than for the latest Windows or NetWare server operating systems, you can't run Linux on an abacus. The following paragraphs summarize the minimum capabilities you need.

✦ A Pentium-based computer. Even a slow 100MHz system will run Linux, but performance will be slow.

✦ 32MB of RAM or more. Actually, 128MB or more is better, but Linux can make do with less.

✦ A hard drive with enough free space to hold the packages that you need to install. The kernel itself needs about 850MB. If you choose not to install a graphical user interface, you can install a full-featured server in about 1.5GB. If you install everything, you'll need about 5GB.

✦ A CD-ROM drive is almost a must, and it's helpful if the computer can boot from the CD. If the computer doesn't have a CD, you can install over a network. If your computer can't boot from the CD, you can create a boot diskette from which to boot the computer.

✦ Just about any video card and monitor combination. You don't need anything fancy for a server.

✦ A mouse is very helpful. If you're converting an old junker computer to a Linux server and you've lost the mouse (that seems to happen a lot), pick one up at your local office supply store. A cheap one costs only about $15.

✦ A network card.

If you're concerned that some of your hardware may not be compatible because it's old or unusual, you can check the Hardware Compatibility List (HCL) for your distribution. The list for Red Hat is located at `http://hardware.redhat.com/hcl/`.

Choosing a distribution

Because the *kernel* (that is, the core operating functions) of the Linux operating system is free, several companies have created their own *distributions* of Linux, which include the Linux operating system along with a bundle of packages, such as administration tools, Web servers, and other useful utilities, as well as printed documentation. These distributions are inexpensive — ranging from $25 to $150 — and are well worth the small cost.

The following are some of the more popular Linux distributions:

✦ **Red Hat** is by most counts the most popular Linux distribution. Red Hat comes in two versions: Red Hat Linux ($39.95), which includes the basic Linux operating system and tools, and Red Hat Professional ($149.95), which adds a collection of workstation and server tools and comes with more printed documentation. Red Hat also has an Enterprise version, which includes a variety of professional support services for an annual licensing fee. For more information, see `www.redhat.com`.

All the examples in this book are based on Red Hat Linux.

✦ **Linux-Mandrake** is another popular Linux distribution, one that is often recommended as the easiest for first-time Linux users to install. Go to `www.linux-mandrake.com` for more information.

✦ **SuSE** (pronounced "Soo-zuh," like the famous composer of marches) is a popular Linux distribution that comes on six CD-ROMs and includes more than 1,500 Linux application programs and utilities, including everything you need to set up a network, Web, e-mail, or electronic commerce server. You can find more information at www.suse.com.

✦ **Slackware,** one of the oldest Linux distributions, is still popular — especially among Linux old-timers. A full installation of Slackware gives you all the tools that you need to set up a network or Internet server. See www.slackware.com for more information.

All distributions of Linux include the same core components — the Linux kernel, an X Server, popular windows managers such as GNOME and KDE, compilers, Internet programs such as Apache, Sendmail, and so on. However, not all Linux distributions are created equal. In particular, the manufacturer of each distribution creates its own installation and configuration programs to install and configure Linux.

The installation program is what makes or breaks a Linux distribution. All the distributions I list in this section have easy-to-use installation programs that automatically detect the hardware that is present on your computer and configure Linux to work with that hardware, thus eliminating most — if not all — manual configuration chores. The installation programs also let you select the Linux packages that you want to install and let you set up one or more user accounts besides the root account.

Figuring out how you'll boot during installation

Before you can install Linux, you must have a working operating system in place so that you can boot the Linux installation program. There are two common ways to boot your computer to install Linux:

✦ If the computer has a bootable CD-ROM drive, you can boot the computer from the Linux distribution CD. To find out whether this technique will work, just put the Linux distribution CD-ROM in the drive and restart the computer. If the computer doesn't boot from the CD-ROM, don't despair. The problem may be that the computer's BIOS configuration isn't set to allow the computer to boot from the CD-ROM drive. Check the computer's BIOS configuration to see whether this is the problem.

✦ If the computer can't boot from the CD-ROM drive, you can create a bootable floppy disk. To do that, insert the CD-ROM into the CD drive on a Windows computer and then run the program that creates a bootable Linux disk. For Red Hat Linux, this program is called rawrite.exe. If you have access to a working Linux system, you can also use it to create a boot disk.

Thinking about multiboot

Linux comes with a boot loader program called GRUB that lets you choose from several installed operating systems when you start your computer. GRUB makes it possible to keep your existing Windows system on a computer and install Linux into a separate partition. Then, each time you start the computer, you can decide whether to start Windows or Linux.

I'm not a big fan of having multiple operating systems on one computer. If the computer is going to be a production server, you're not going to need to reboot the computer into Windows anyway. However, installing Linux into a separate partition while keeping your Windows system intact may be a viable alternative if you want to experiment with Linux before you commit to it.

I can't see my C: drive!

Linux and Windows have a completely different method of referring to your computer's hard drives and partitions. The differences can take some getting used to for experienced Windows users.

Windows uses a separate letter for each drive and partition on your system. For example, if you have a single drive formatted into three partitions, Windows identifies the partitions as drives C:, D:, and E:. Each of these drives has its own root directory, which can, in turn, contain additional directories used to organize your files. As far as Windows is concerned, drives C:, D:, and E: are completely separate drives, even though the drives are actually just partitions on a single drive.

Linux doesn't use drive letters. Instead, Linux combines all the drives and partitions into a single directory hierarchy. In Linux, one of the partitions is designated as the *root* partition. The root partition is roughly analogous to the root directory of the C: drive on a Windows system. Then, the other partitions can be *mounted* on the root partition and treated as if they were directories on the root partition. For example, you may designate the first partition as the root partition and then mount the second partition as /user and the third partition as /var. Then, any files stored in the /user directory would actually be stored in the second partition, and files stored in the /var directory would be stored in the third partition.

The directory to which a drive mounts is called the drive's *mount point*.

Notice that Linux uses regular forward slash characters (/) to separate directory names rather than the backward slash characters (\) used by Windows. Typing backslashes instead of regular slashes is one of the most common mistakes made by new Linux users.

While I'm on the subject, Linux uses a different convention for naming files, too. In Windows, filenames end in a three-letter extension that is separated from the rest of the filename by a period. The extension is used to indicate the file type. For example, files that end in .exe are program files, but files that end in .doc are word-processing documents.

Linux doesn't use file extensions, but periods are often used in Linux filenames to separate different parts of the name and the last part often indicates the file type. For example, ldap.conf, and pine.conf are both configuration files.

Planning your partitions

Linux handles partitions a little differently than Windows. The Windows operating system installs itself into a single partition. However, Linux installations typically require three or more hard drive partitions:

✦ **A boot partition:** This should be small — 16MB is recommended. The boot partition contains the operating system kernel and is required to start Linux properly on some computers.

✦ **A swap partition:** This should be about twice the size of your computer's RAM. For example, if the computer has 256MB of RAM, allocate a 512MB swap partition. Linux uses this partition as an extension of your computer's RAM.

✦ **A root partition:** In most cases, this uses up the remaining free space on the drive. The root partition contains all the files and data used by your Linux system.

You can also create additional partitions if you want. The installation program includes a disk-partitioning feature that lets you set up your drive partitions and indicate the mount point for each partition. The installation program can make a recommendation for partitioning your drives that will be appropriate in most situations. (For more information about drive partitions, see the sidebar "I can't see my C: drive!" earlier in this chapter.)

Deciding your TCP/IP configuration

Before you install the operating system, you should have a plan for how you will implement TCP/IP on the network. Here are some of the things you need to decide or find out:

✦ What is the public IP subnet address and mask for your network?

✦ What is the domain name for the network?

✦ What is the host name for the server?

✦ Will the server obtain its address from DHCP?

✦ Will the server have a static IP address? If so, what?

✦ Will the server be a DHCP server?

✦ What is the default gateway for the server? (That is, what is the IP address of the network's Internet router?)

✦ Will the server be a DNS server?

If the server will host TCP/IP servers (such as DHCP or DNS), you'll probably want to assign the server a static IP address.

For more information about planning your TCP/IP configuration, see Book V.

Installing Red Hat Linux 9

Now that you've planned your installation and prepared the computer, you're ready to actually install Linux. The following procedure describes the steps you must follow to install Red Hat Linux 9 on a computer that has a bootable CD-ROM drive.

1. **Insert the Red Hat Installation CD 1 of 1 in the CD-ROM and restart the computer.**

The computer boots up from the CD drive and displays a Linux boot prompt, which looks like this:

```
Boot:
```

2. **Press Enter.**

The computer starts up Linux from the installation CD. A bunch of text mode messages are displayed, including a message indicating that Linux is starting Anaconda, the Red Hat installation program. The screen switches into graphics mode. Then, after a few minutes, the Welcome to Red Hat Linux screen is displayed.

Besides simply pressing Enter, you can start the installation program at the boot prompt in several other ways:

- Sometimes the native X server required by the installation program can't start up properly. If that happens to you, restart the computer and then enter **linux text** at the boot prompt. This runs the installation program in text mode.

- If the installation program fails because of a problem with automatic hardware detection, you can type **linux noprobe** at the boot prompt.

3. **Click Next.**

The Language Selection screen appears, offering quite a few language choices.

Virtual consoles and the installation program

Linux is inherently a command-line oriented operating system. Graphical user interfaces — including the installation program's GUI — are provided by an optional component called *X Window System*. However, while you're working with the graphical user interface of the installation program, Linux keeps several additional command-line consoles open. Normally, you don't need to use every one of these consoles during installation. However, if something goes wrong during installation, these consoles may be useful.

The following paragraphs describe the consoles:

✔ **Console 1: The Installation dialog.** This is the main installation console. You see it when Setup first starts. After the graphical user interface takes over, it's hidden in the background. You can call it up by pressing Ctrl+Alt+F1.

✔ **Console 2: Shell prompt.** This console provides you with a shell prompt, from which you can enter Linux commands. If you need to do something manually during installation, you can do it from this console. The keyboard shortcut is Ctrl+Alt+F2.

✔ **Console 3: Install log.** This console lists messages generated by the installation program. You can get to it by pressing Ctrl+Alt+F3.

✔ **Console 4: System log.** This console displays system-related messages. You can get to it by pressing Ctrl+Alt+F4.

✔ **Console 5: Other messages.** Still more messages may appear in this console, which you can open by pressing Ctrl+Alt+F5.

✔ **Console 6: X graphical display.** This is the console where the graphical user interface of the installation program is displayed. If you use a Ctrl+Alt keyboard combination to view any of the other logs, press Ctrl+Alt+F7 to return to the installation GUI.

4. **Choose your language and then click Next.**

The Keyboard Configuration screen appears. It lets you choose from about 55 different keyboard styles.

5. **Choose your keyboard type and then click Next.**

Next, the Mouse Configuration screen is displayed. The program makes a reasonable guess at what type of mouse you have, but it may guess wrong. So review the options on this screen and choose the correct mouse type.

6. **Choose your mouse type and then click Next.**

Next, the Installation Type screen is displayed, as shown in Figure 1-1. This screen gives you four installation type options:

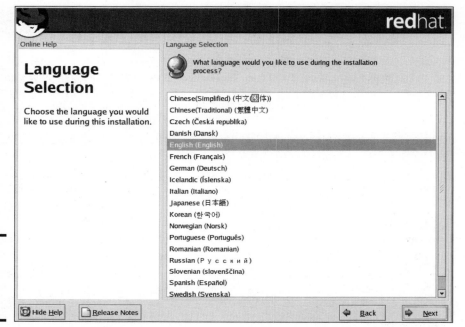

Figure 1-1:
The
Installation
Type
screen.

- **Personal Desktop:** For users who want to use Linux as an inexpensive replacement for Windows on desktop or notebook computers. This is the best option for users who aren't familiar with Linux.

- **Workstation:** For power users, such as software developers, who want a more powerful Linux environment.

- **Server:** Creates a basic Linux server environment with most of the tools typically used on network servers. This is the option I use in this chapter.

- **Custom:** For power users who want to pick and choose which Linux components to install.

7. **Choose Server and then click Next.**

   The Disk Partitioning Setup screen appears, as shown in Figure 1-2. Red Hat includes an Automatic partition option that simplifies the task of creating partitions for your Linux installation. Choose this option if your partitioning needs are pretty standard. If you want to customize the partition structure, choose Manually Partition With Disk Druid.

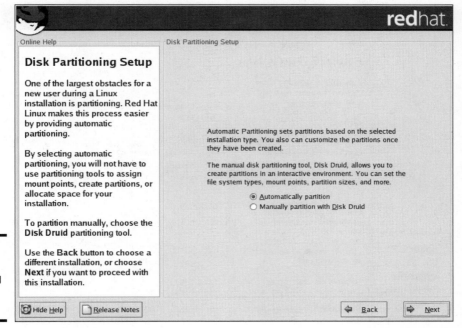

Figure 1-2:
The Disk
Partitioning
Setup
screen.

If you choose Automatic partition here, you still have some options on how to partition the drive in the next step. Plus, you get a chance to review the proposed partitioning to make sure that you like how the Installation program will partition your system. You can always back up and select Manually Partition With Disk Druid.

8. Choose Automatic Partition and then click Next.

The Automatic Partitioning screen is displayed, as shown in Figure 1-3. This screen gives you three options:

- **Remove All Linux Partitions On The System:** This option removes any existing Linux partitions, but leaves other partitions intact. This is the option to choose if you want to set up a dual-boot system that can run either Windows or Linux.

- **Remove All Partitions On This System:** This option wipes the hard drive completely clean and installs just the partitions needed to run Linux. This is the option to choose if you are converting an existing Windows computer to Linux and you don't want to keep the Windows configuration.

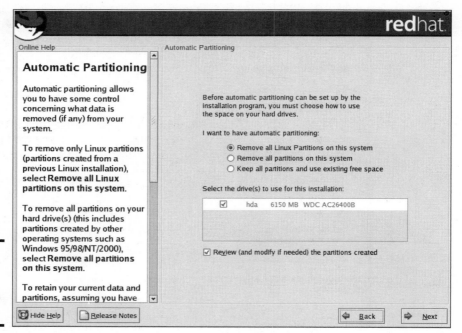

Figure 1-3:
The
Automatic
Partitioning
screen.

- **Keep All Partitions And Use Existing Free Space:** You can use this option if you have free unpartitioned space on the drive, and you want to use it for your Linux installation without deleting any existing partitions. If you've installed a new hard drive in the computer just for Linux, this is the option to choose.

The Automatic Partitioning screen also lists all the drives on your system and lets you select the drive to which you want to install Linux. If you have more than one drive, you need to choose to which drive to install Linux. If you have but one drive, it should be automatically selected.

This screen also has a check box titled Remove (And Modify If Needed) The Partitions Created. You should leave this box checked.

9. **Choose the partitioning options you want and then click Next.**

Assuming that you chose Remove All Partitions On This System, a dialog box with the following message appears:

```
You have selected to remove all partitions (ALL
DATA) on the following drives:

/dev/had

Are you sure you want to do this?
```

10. **Click Yes.**

The Disk Setup screen appears, as shown in Figure 1-4. Review the partitioning proposed on this screen carefully to make sure that it's what you want. You can use the following buttons on the Disk Setup screen to change the proposed partitioning:

- **New:** Creates a new partition.

- **Edit:** Displays a dialog box that lets you change the partition's mount point, size, and other properties for the selected partition.

- **Delete:** Removes the selected partition.

- **Reset:** Cancels any changes you've made and restores the partitioning structure to the original arrangement proposed by the installation program.

- **RAID:** Lets you configure software RAID partitions. Use this only if you know what you're doing.

- **LVM:** Lets you create LVM volumes. Don't use this unless you know what LVM volumes are and how to set them up.

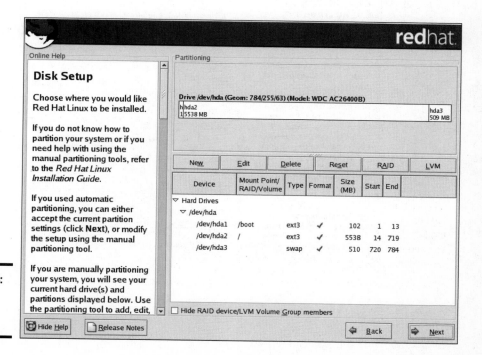

Figure 1-4:
The Disk
Setup
screen.

11. **Review the partition arrangement, make any changes necessary, and then click Next.**

This brings up the Boot Loader Configuration screen, as shown in Figure 1-5. This screen installs the GRUB boot loader and allows you to configure it to run multiple operating systems. By default, GRUB is configured to allow you to boot to any existing operating system that the installation program detects on your hard drive and defaults to the Linux installation you're creating now. You can change the GRUB settings if you want, but most of the time you'll use the defaults.

This screen also lets you specify a password for the boot loader program. This option provides an extra measure of security for your server. If you choose to use it, write down the password that you use and don't lose it!

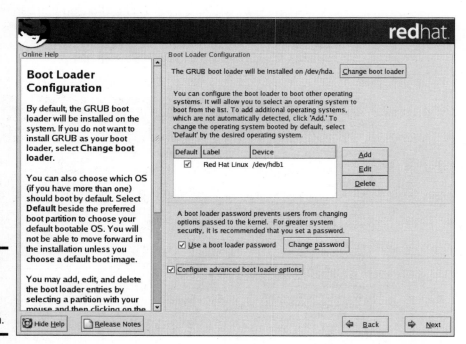

Figure 1-5: The Boot Loader Configuration screen.

12. **Click Next.**

Now the Network Configuration screen appears, as shown in Figure 1-6. This screen lists each network adapter detected in the server along with the adapter's configuration information. By default, the installation program assumes that this server will use DHCP to obtain its configuration information. If that's the case, skip ahead to Step 14.

13. **Click the Edit button and then manually configure the network information.**

When you click the Edit button, the dialog box shown in Figure 1-7 appears. To use this dialog box to configure the server's network information, first uncheck the Configure Using DHCP checkbox. Then, enter the IP address and netmask that you want to use for the server and click OK. When you're returned to the Network Configuration screen, you need to enter the following information:

- **Host name:** Enter the host name to use for the computer.

- **Gateway:** The IP address of the router that you connect to for your Internet connection.

- **DNS servers:** Up to three IP addresses for your DNS servers.

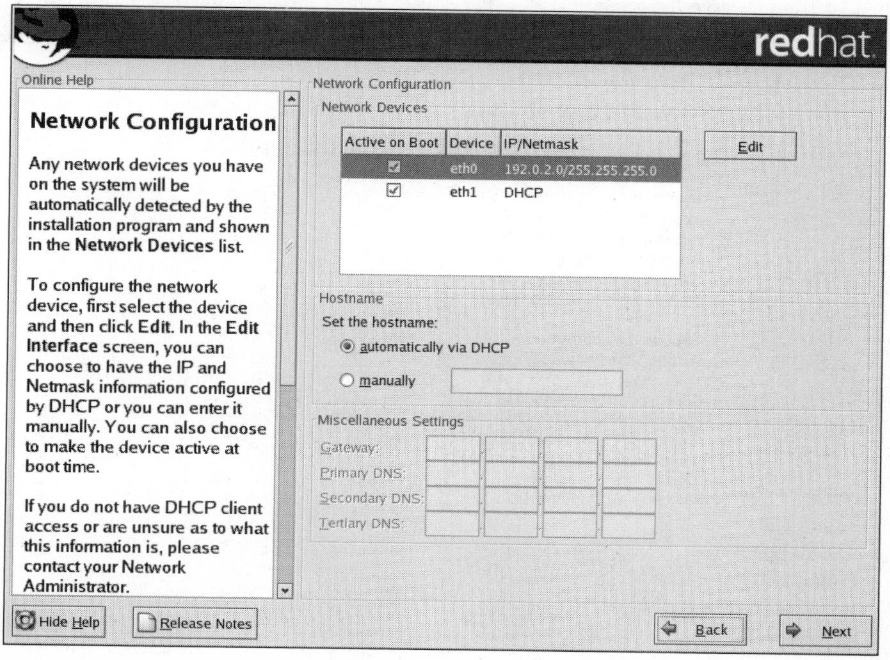

Figure 1-6:
The
Network
Configura-
tion screen.

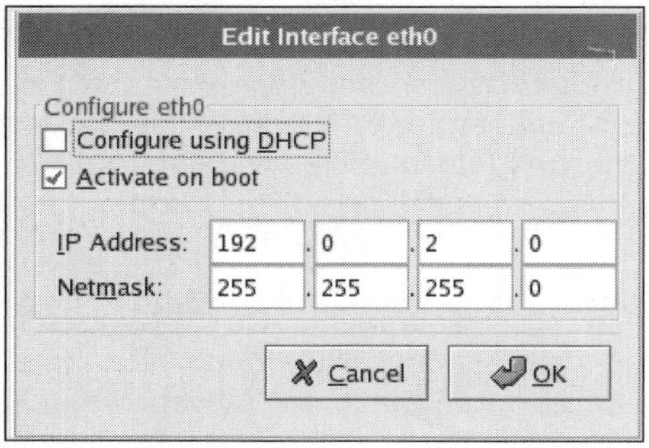

Figure 1-7:
The Edit
Interface
dialog box.

14. **Click Next.**

The Firewall Configuration screen is displayed, as shown in Figure 1-8. From this screen, you can choose to create a High Security firewall, a Medium Security firewall, or No Firewall. You can also customize the firewall rules that you want to use. You should play with these options only if you're familiar with how to set up a firewall. When in doubt, pick Medium.

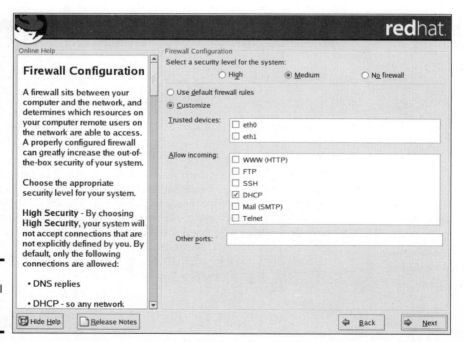

Figure 1-8:
The Firewall
Configura-
tion screen.

15. **Choose the firewall option that you want to use and then click Next.**

The Additional Language Support screen is displayed. On this screen, you can choose additional languages that Linux should support in addition to the default language.

16. **Choose any additional languages you want to support and then click Next.**

The Time Zone Selection screen appears. On this screen is a map of the world with dots representing about 500 different locations throughout the world.

17. **Click the location that's closest to you and then click Next.**

Next, the Set Root Password screen appears. This screen lets you enter the all-important Root account password. It's vital that this account be protected by a strong password, so choose a good one. Write it down somewhere and store it in a secure location away from the computer.

18. **Type the root account password twice and then click Next.**

Next, the Installation program displays the Package Group Selection screen, as shown in Figure 1-9. This screen offers a variety of packages that you can choose to install on your server. You have to make some important choices here:

- Do you want to outfit your Linux server with a graphical user interface, or will you be happy working at the command line? If you want a GUI, choose one now. The default for Red Hat Linux is GNOME.

    Although you can run a network server without a graphical user interface, the GUI gives you access to easy-to-use configuration tools. I suggest you install it unless you're a Linux guru.

- I recommend that you include the Editors group to get a good set of text editors. Much of Linux configuration involves editing configuration files, so you'll need a good text editor.

- What server packages do you want? Table 1-1 lists the Server package groups that are available and indicates which ones are selected by default when you choose a Server installation. I suggest that you include all these packages if you have the hard drive space, even if you don't think you need them all immediately. (The one likely exception is the SQL Database Server. If you won't be doing application development or installing application software that requires a SQL database server, you can omit this package.)

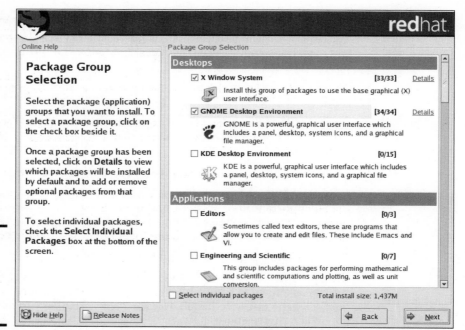

Figure 1-9:
The
Package
Group
Selection
screen.

- You may also want to include the System Tools group, which includes several useful system utilities.

- What good would a Linux server be without Linux games? The Games and Entertainment group will give you something to do when you grow tired of routine Linux administration chores.

Table 1-1	Server Package Groups	
Group	*Default?*	*Description*
Server Configuration Tools	Yes	Includes Red Hat tools for configuring network services such as DNS, Web servers, NFG server, Samba, and more.
Web Server	Yes	Includes packages that let you set up a Web server.
Mail Server	Yes	Includes packages that let you run a mail server.
Windows File Server	Yes	Includes Samba, which lets you run a file server for a Windows network.

Group	Default?	Description
DNS Name Server	No	Includes Bind, the most popular DNS name server.
FTP Server	No	Includes FTP server support.
SQL Database Server	No	The PostgreSQL and MySQL database servers.
News Server	No	Inn, the InterNetNews server.
Network Servers	No	Additional network servers, including DHCP, Finger, Telnet, and others.

19. **Select the package groups that you want to install and then click Next.**

When you click Next, the installation program does some double-checking to make sure that none of the packages you have chosen depend on other packages you have not chosen. If it finds such a dependency, it adds the dependent package so that your system will function properly.

Next, a screen ominously titled About To Install appears. You have now reached the moment of truth.

20. **Take a deep breath and click Next.**

The Installation program installs Linux on your system. This will take awhile — maybe a long while — so now would be a good time to grab a book or take a nap.

Make sure that you don't leave it alone for too long. You'll need to be there when the installation program prompts you to insert additional discs in the CD-ROM drive.

When the installation finishes, the Boot Disk Creation screen appears, asking whether you want to create a boot diskette. You'll need this diskette in case your hard drive becomes unbootable for any reason.

21. **Click Yes and then click Next.**

You're prompted to insert a blank disc.

22. **Insert a blank diskette in the diskette drive and then click Make Boot Disk.**

The boot disc is created. This will take a minute or so.

When the disc is finished, the installation program continues. If you didn't choose to install a graphical user interface, you can skip ahead to Step 26. Otherwise, a screen titled Graphical Interface (X) Configuration appears, asking you to specify the type of video card you have.

23. Select your video card type and then click Next.

Now a screen titled Monitor Configuration appears, asking you to specify what type of monitor you have.

24. Select your monitor type and click Next.

The screen shown in Figure 1-10 appears. In this screen, you configure the color depth and resolution of the monitor.

25. Choose the configuration settings you want and then click Next.

A screen titled Installation Complete appears.

26. Remove the floppy from the hard drive and the installation CD from the CD-ROM drive and then click Next.

The system is rebooted. Installation is done!

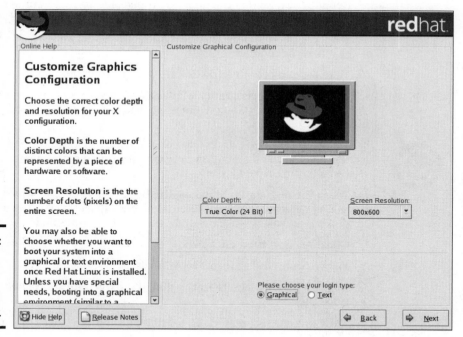

Figure 1-10: The Customize Graphics Configuration screen.

Using the Setup Agent

When Red Hat Linux restarts the first time after completing the installation program, it launches a handy feature called the Red Hat Setup Agent, provided you installed a GUI in which the Setup Agent can run. The Setup Agent resembles the installation program, but it asks a few questions that the installation program forgot to ask. When the Setup Agent starts, follow these steps to see it through to completion:

1. **On the Welcome screen, click Forward to get started.**

    The Setup Agent asks you to create a user account so that you don't have to access the system by using the root account, as shown in Figure 1-11.

2. **Type a name and password for the user account and then click Forward.**

    You'll have to type the password twice to verify that you typed it correctly. When it's done, the Setup Agent displays a page asking for the current date and time.

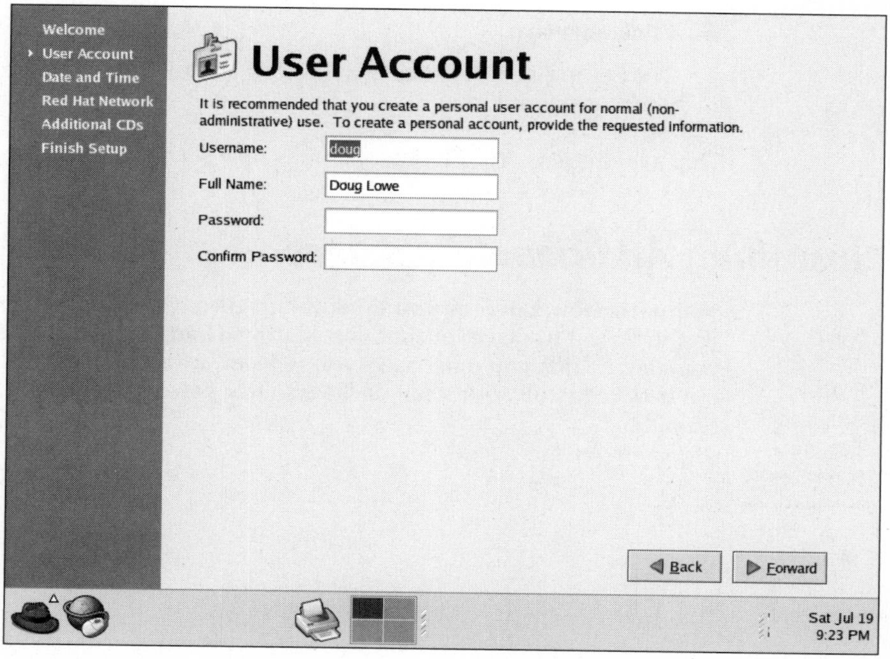

Figure 1-11:
Creating a
user
account.

3. **Select the correct date and time and then click Forward.**

   Now the Setup Agent wants to know whether you want to sign up for Red Hat Network, a service that informs you of updates to the packages you've installed and enables you to easily download and install the updates. You can do this now or later. If you opt to enroll now, you're prompted for the information necessary to sign up. Note that you need a working Internet connection to sign up now.

   Next, the Setup Agent asks whether you want to install software from the additional Red Hat installation CDs. You can install three items:

   - Red Hat Linux Documentation CD

   - Red Hat Linux Installation CD

   - Additional CDs

   To install one of these items, just click the item's Install button and follow the instructions.

4. **Click Forward.**

   The Setup Agent displays a page informing you that your system is now set up and ready to use. Aren't you proud?

5. **Click Forward.**

   The Setup Agent finishes, leaving you at a GNOME desktop, ready for you to explore Linux.

   That's all there is. Your Linux system is now set up and ready to go.

Installing Additional Packages

No matter how carefully you think things through when you install Linux, you're bound to discover that you wish you had installed some package that you didn't think you'd need. So you're faced with the prospect of figuring out how to install additional packages after you already have Linux up and running.

Although you can do so using shell commands, it's much easier to do it using the Red Hat installer. Just follow these steps:

1. **Insert disc 1 of the Red Hat Installation CDs into the CD-ROM drive.**

   After a few moments, a dialog box appears, asking whether you want to run the autorun program.

2. **Click Yes to run the autorun program.**

   The Package Management program comes to life and displays the window shown in Figure 1-12.

3. **Click Forward.**

   Package Management scans your computer to find out what packages are already installed and then displays the window shown in Figure 1-13. This should look familiar; it's essentially the same screen displayed during installation when the installer asks what packages you want to install.

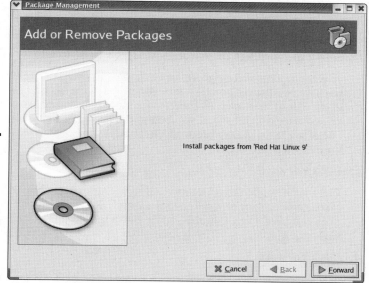

Figure 1-12:
The Package Management program lets you add or remove packages.

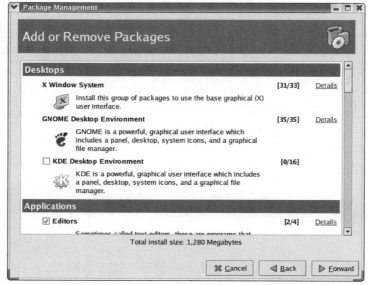

Figure 1-13:
You can pick
additional
packages to
install.

4. **Select the package or packages that you want to add.**

   You can add an entire group of packages or you can click the Details link to display a dialog box that lets you add selected packages from a group. Note that most of the groups include some packages that aren't selected by default when you select the group. As a result, you should click Details to make sure that the specific package in which you're interested is selected.

5. **Click Forward.**

   The Preparing System Update dialog box appears while the Package Management program determines which packages need to be upgraded. This can take a few minutes, so be patient. When it's done, the Package Manager displays a window listing the packages that will be installed.

6. **Click Forward.**

   The packages are installed. If asked, you may need to insert one of the distribution disks.

   When the packages have been installed, the Package Installation Complete page appears, announcing that the packages have been installed successfully.

7. Click Finish.

The Package Manager closes.

 Red Hat has an online service called the Red Hat Network that simplifies the task of downloading and installing updates to the packages you've installed on your system. You can sign up for this service when you install Red Hat Linux, or you can sign up later by going to the Red Hat Network's Web site at http://rhn.redhat.com.

Chapter 2: Getting Used to Linux

In This Chapter

✔ **Getting used to the Linux way of thinking**

✔ **Logging on and off Linux**

✔ **Using a GUI**

✔ **Working with commands**

✔ **Setting up user accounts**

*B*efore you can set up Linux to do serious networking, you need to discover the basics of getting around Linux. In this chapter, you find out those basics. You see how to log on and off Linux, how the Linux file system works, and how to use commands. I also introduce you to GNOME, the graphical user interface installed by default when you set up Red Hat Linux. Finally, I show you the basics of setting up a Linux user account.

In this chapter, I assume that you have plenty of experience with Windows, so I focus mostly on the differences between Linux and Windows — which, unfortunately, are many.

Linux: It Isn't Windows

Before I get into the details of actually using a Linux system, you need to understand some basic differences between Linux and Windows that will puzzle you at first. Linux looks a lot like Windows, but underneath it's very different. You won't have any trouble finding out how to point and click your way through the GNOME user interface, but before long, you'll run into Linux filenaming conventions, terminal windows, configuration files, and a host of other significant differences.

The following sections describe some of the more important differences between Linux and Windows.

X Window

Linux doesn't have a built-in graphical user interface (GUI) as Windows does. Instead, the GUI in Linux is provided by an optional component called *X Window System*. You can run Linux without X Window, in which case you interact with Linux by typing commands. If you prefer to use a GUI, you must install and run X Window.

X Window is split into two parts: a server component, called an *X server,* which handles the basic chores of managing multiple windows and providing graphics services for application programs, and a user interface component, called a *window manager,* which provides user interface features such as menus, buttons, toolbars, a taskbar, and so on. Several different window managers are available, each with a different look and feel. The most popular is GNOME. I describe it in more detail later in this chapter, in the section "Using GNOME."

Virtual consoles

Linux is a true multi-user operating system. This means that you can log on to Linux by using one user account and then log on by using a different account, so that you are logged on twice at the same time. You switch back and forth between the different user sessions, and actions that you take in one session don't affect any of your other sessions.

In addition to an X Window client such as GNOME, Linux provides a traditional text-based environment called a *console,* through which you can enter Linux commands to perform any function available in Linux. The more you work with Linux, the more you'll discover the limitations of even a sophisticated GUI such as GNOME. When that happens, you'll turn to a console where you can enter brute-force commands.

Because Linux is a multi-user system, it lets you work with more than one console. In fact, you actually have six virtual consoles at your disposal. You can switch to a particular virtual console by pressing Ctrl+Alt+F1 through F6. For example, to switch to virtual console 3, press Ctrl+Alt+F3.

When a GUI such as GNOME is running, you can switch to it by pressing Ctrl+Alt+F7.

Understanding the file system

The Linux file system is a bit different from the Windows file system. Two of the most obvious differences are actually superficial:

+ Linux uses forward slashes rather than backward slashes to separate directories. Thus, /home/doug is a valid path in Linux; \Windows\System32 is a valid path in Windows.

+ Linux names can contain more than one period. In Windows, a period is used to separate a filename from its extension. Linux doesn't have extensions, but lets you use periods to separate components of a name.

The fundamental difference between the Linux and Windows file system is that Linux treats everything in the entire system as a file, and it organizes everything into one gigantic tree that begins at a single root. When I say,

"Everything is treated as a file," I mean that hardware devices such as floppy drives, serial ports, and Ethernet adapters are treated as files.

The root of the Linux file system is the root partition from which the operating system boots. Additional partitions, including other devices that support file systems such as CD-ROM drives, floppy drives, or drives accessed over the network, can be grafted into the tree as directories called *mount points*. Thus, a directory in the Linux file system may actually be a separate hard drive.

Another important aspect of the Linux file system is that the directories that compose a Linux system are governed by a standard called the *Filesystem Hierarchy Standard* (FHS). This standard spells out which directories a Linux file system should have. Because most Linux systems conform to this standard, you can trust that key files will always be found in the same place.

Table 2-1 lists the top-level directories that are described in the FHS.

Table 2-1	Top-Level Directories in a Linux File System
Directory	*Description*
/bin	Essential command binaries
/boot	Static files of the boot loader
/dev	Devices
/etc	Configuration files for the local computer
/home	Home directories for users
/lib	Shared libraries and kernel modules
/mnt	Mount point for file systems mounted temporarily
/opt	Add-on applications and packages
/root	Home directory for the root user
/sbin	Essential system binaries
/tmp	Temporary files
/usr	Read-only, shared files such as binaries for user commands and libraries
/var	Variable data files

On Again, Off Again

Any user who accesses a Linux system, whether locally or over a network, must be authenticated by a valid user account on the system. In the following sections, you find out how to log on and off of a Linux system and how to shut down the system.

Logging on

When Linux boots up, it displays a series of startup messages as it starts the various services that compose a working Linux system. Assuming that you selected X Window when you installed Linux, you're eventually greeted by the screen shown in Figure 2-1. To log on to Linux, enter your user ID on this screen, press Enter, and then enter your password and press Enter again.

Figure 2-1:
Logging on
to Linux.

As a part of the installation process, the Setup Agent created a user account for you. You should use this user account rather than the root user account whenever possible. Use the root account only when you are making major changes to the system's configuration. When you're doing routine work, log on as an ordinary user in order to avoid accidentally corrupting your system.

When you log on, Linux grinds its gears for a moment and then displays the GNOME desktop, which I describe later in this chapter.

If you didn't install X server, you see a text-mode Login prompt that resembles this:

```
Red Hat Linux release 9 (Shrike)
Kernel 2.4.20-6 on an i586

LSERVER login:
```

The Login prompt displays the Linux version (Red Hat Linux release 9), the kernel version on which it's based (2.4.20-6), the CPU architecture (i586), and the server's hostname (LSERVER). To log in, type your user ID, press Enter, and then type the password and press Enter again.

After you've successfully logged on, you are greeted by a semi-friendly prompt similar to this:

```
Last login: Sun Jul 20 20:00:56 on :0
[doug@LSERVER doug]$
```

The prompt character in the standard Linux shell is a dollar sign ($) rather than a greater-than sign (>) as it is in MS-DOS or Windows. Also, notice that prompt indicates your username and server (doug@LSERVER), as well as the name of the current directory (doug).

Even if you've installed X server, you can still log on to a command shell by pressing Ctrl+Alt+F1. This switches you to a *virtual console,* which I describe in more detail in the section "Using virtual consoles," earlier in this chapter.

Logging off

After you've logged on, you'll probably want to know how to log off. If you logged on to GNOME, you can log off by clicking the main menu and choosing the Log Out command. A dialog box asks whether you're sure that you want to log out. Click OK.

In a command shell, you can log out in three ways:

✦ Enter the logout command.

✦ Enter the exit command.

✦ Press Ctrl+D.

Shutting down

As with any operating system, you should never turn off the power to a Linux server without first properly shutting down the system. You can shut down a Linux system by using one of these three techniques:

+ Press Ctrl+Alt+Delete.

+ From GNOME, click the main menu and choose Log Out. Then, when the confirmation dialog box appears, select Shut Down or Restart and click OK.

+ From a command shell, enter the `halt` command.

Using GNOME

Although you can do all your Linux configuration chores from the command line, Red Hat Linux includes a number of GNOME-based configuration tools for many configuration tasks. Although you can do most of your Linux configuration from GNOME, you will need to use a command shell once in awhile.

Figure 2-2 shows a typical GNOME desktop with the Text Editor application open. As you can see, the GNOME desktop looks a lot like Microsoft Windows. In fact, many of the basic skills for working with Windows — such as moving or resizing windows, minimizing or maximizing windows, and using drag-and-drop to move items between windows — work almost exactly the same in GNOME. So you should feel right at home.

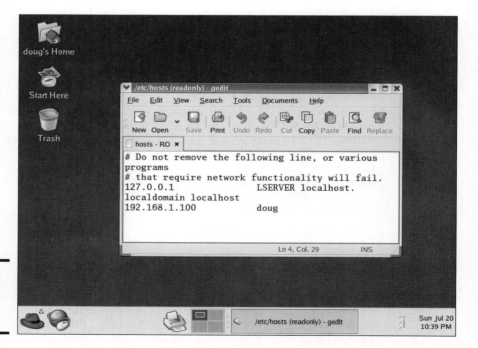

Figure 2-2:
A typical
GNOME
desktop.

The following paragraphs describe some of the key features of the GNOME desktop:

✦ On the desktop itself, you'll find several icons that let you access common features. The Home icon lets you access your home directory. The Start Here icon provides access to commonly used configuration utilities. The Trash icon is similar to the Recycle Bin in Windows.

✦ The area at the bottom of the desktop is called the *panel*. It works much like the taskbar in Windows. At the extreme left of the panel is a Red Hat icon. Click the hat to access the Main menu, which works like the Start menu in Windows. You can start an application by choosing the application in the Main menu.

✦ The down arrow at the top-left corner of each window reveals a menu of things that you can do with the window. Try the Roll Up command; it reduces a window to its title bar but leaves the window on the desktop. To restore the window, click the down arrow and choose Unroll. This menu also lets you move the window to a different workspace.

✦ *Workspaces,* you ask? A workspace is like a separate desktop where you can keep windows open in order to reduce the clutter on your screen. The panel contains a tool called the Workspace Switcher, which lets you switch active workspaces by clicking one of the rectangles in the grid.

Getting to a Command Shell

You can get to a command shell in one of two basic ways when you need to run Linux commands directly. The first is to press Ctrl+Alt+F*x* to switch to one of the virtual consoles. Then, you can log on and run commands to your heart's content. When you're done, press Ctrl+Alt+F7 to return to GNOME.

Alternatively, you can open a command shell directly in GNOME by choosing Main Menu⇨System Tools⇨Terminal. This opens a command shell in a window right on the GNOME desktop, as shown in Figure 2-3. Because this shell runs within the user account that GNOME is logged in as, you don't have to log on. You can just start typing commands. When you're done, type **Exit** to close the window.

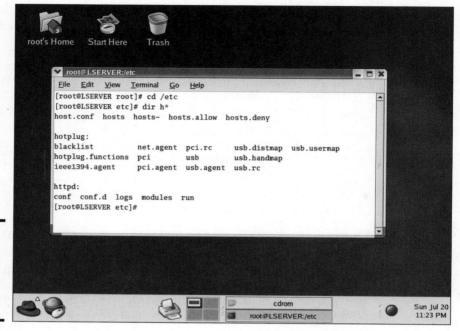

Figure 2-3:
Using a
Terminal
window to
run Linux
commands.

Managing User Accounts

One of the most common network administration tasks is adding a user account. The Setup Agent prompts you to create a user account the first time you start Linux after installing it. However, you'll probably need to create additional accounts.

Each Linux user account has the following information associated with it:

✦ **Username:** The name the user types to log on to the Linux system.

✦ **Full name:** The user's full name.

✦ **Home directory:** The directory that the user is placed in when he or she logs in. In Red Hat Linux, the default home directory is /home/username. For example, if the user name is blowe, the home directory will be /home/blowe.

✦ **Shell:** The program used to process Linux commands. Several shell programs are available. In most distributions, the default shell is /bin/bash.

✦ **Group:** You can create group accounts, which make it easy to apply identical access rights to groups of users.

✦ **User ID:** The internal identifier for the user.

You can add a new user by using the `useradd` command. For example, to create a user account named `slowe` and using default values for the other account information, open a Terminal window or switch to a virtual console and type this command:

```
# useradd slowe
```

The `useradd` command has many optional parameters that you can use to set account information, such as the user's home directory and shell.

Fortunately, most Linux distributions come with special programs that simplify routine system management tasks. Red Hat Linux is no exception. It comes with a program called Red Hat User Manager, shown in Figure 2-4. To start this program, choose Main Menu➪System Tools➪User And Groups.

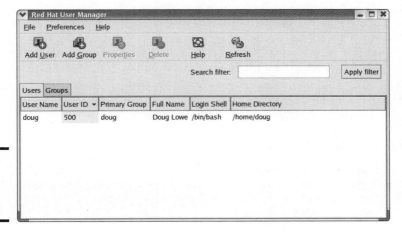

Figure 2-4:
Red Hat
User
Manager.

To create a user by using Red Hat User Manager, click the Add User button. This brings up a dialog box that asks for the user's name, password, and other information. Fill out this dialog box and then click OK.

The Red Hat User Manager also lets you create groups. You can simplify the task of administering users by applying access rights to groups rather than individual users. Then, when a user needs access to a resource, you can add the user to the group that has the needed access.

To create a group, click the Add Group button. A dialog box appears, asking for the name of the new group. Type the name you want and then click OK.

To add a user to a group, click the Groups tab in the Red Hat User Manager. Then, double-click the group to which you want to add users. This brings up the Group Properties dialog box. Click the Group Users tab and then check off the users that you want to belong to the group.

Chapter 3: Basic Linux Network Configuration

In This Chapter

✔ Configuring network interfaces with the Red Hat Network Configuration program

✔ Looking directly at network configuration files

✔ Using the `ifconfig` command to display network status

*I*n many cases, configuring a Linux server for networking is a snap. When you install Linux, the Installation program automatically detects your network adapters and installs the appropriate drivers. Then, you're prompted for basic network configuration information, such as the computer's IP address, host name, and so on.

However, you may need to manually change your network settings after installation. You may also need to configure advanced networking features that aren't configured during installation. In this chapter, you discover the basic procedures for configuring Linux networking services.

Using the Red Hat Network Configuration Program

Before you can use a network interface to access a network, you have to configure the interface's basic TCP/IP options, such as its IP address, host name, DNS servers, and so on. In this section, I show you how to do that by using Red Hat's Network Configuration program. You can access this program by choosing Main Menu⇨System Settings⇨Network.

If you prefer a more masochistic approach to configuring your network, see the section "Working with Network Configuration Files," later in this chapter.

The Network Configuration program lets you configure the basic TCP/IP settings for a network interface by pointing and clicking your way through tabbed windows. Here are the steps:

1. **Choose Main Menu⇨System Settings⇨Network.**

   The Network Configuration window appears, as shown in Figure 3-1.

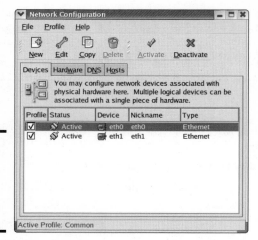

Figure 3-1:
Red Hat's
Network
Configura-
tion
program.

2. **Select the adapter that you want to configure and then click Edit.**

   The main window of the Network Configuration lists all the network interfaces installed in your computer. If your computer has more than one
   interface, make sure that you select the correct one before proceeding.

   When you click Edit, the Ethernet Device window appears, as shown in
   Figure 3-2.

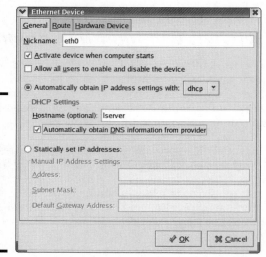

Figure 3-2:
The
Ethernet
Device
window is
where you
configure
basic
TCP/IP
settings.

3. **To configure the device to use DHCP, select the Automatically Obtain IP Address Settings with DHCP radio button, type the computer's name in the Hostname text box, and check the Automatically Obtain DNS Information From Provider option.**

If you plan on setting up this computer to be your network's DHCP or DNS server, you shouldn't check this box. Instead, you should assign a static IP address as described in Step 4.

Some DHCP servers can't provide DNS information. In that case, you shouldn't check the Automatically Obtain DNS Information From Provider option. Instead, you should manually configure your DNS information as described in Step 6.

4. **To configure the device by using a static IP address, select the Statically Set IP Addresses option and then enter the IP address, subnet mask, and default gateway that you want the adapter to use.**

The IP address is most likely located on one of the standard private subnets. You should almost always use a private address in the form 192.168.*x.x*.

If you are setting up this computer to be the gateway router that will manage traffic between your local network and the Internet, use a static address that is easy to remember, such as 192.168.1.1.

The subnet mask should be the mask that's appropriate for the IP address you choose. For a 192.168.*x.x* address, use 255.255.255.0.

The default gateway address should be the address of the gateway router that links your network to the Internet. If this computer *is* the gateway router, specify the gateway address provided to you by your ISP.

5. **Click OK.**

You're returned to the Network Configuration window.

6. **Click the DNS tab.**

The DNS configuration settings appear, as shown in Figure 3-3.

7. **Enter the IP addresses for the DNS servers that you want to use.**

If your network runs its own DNS server, you can specify its address here. Otherwise, you have to get the DNS server addresses from your ISP.

8. **Choose File⇨Save.**

Any changes that you've made to the network configuration are saved. Then, an informative dialog box appears with the following message:

```
Redhat-config-network:
Changes are saved.
You may want to restart
the network and network services
or restart the computer.
```

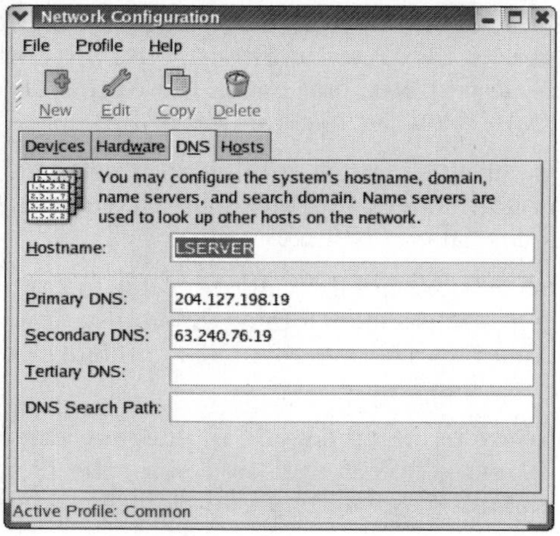

Figure 3-3:
Configuring
DNS.

9. **Click OK.**

You can now close the Network Configuration window.

10. **Restart the network services.**

To find out how to do restart, see the next section, "Restarting Your
Network."

Restarting Your Network

Whenever you make a configuration change to your network, you must
restart Linux networking services in order for the change to take effect. If
you find that to be annoying, just be thankful that you don't have to restart
the entire computer. Simply restarting the network services is sufficient.

You can restart the network services from a GNOME desktop by following
these steps:

1. **Choose Main Menu⇨System Settings⇨Server Settings⇨Services.**

The Service Configuration window appears, as shown in Figure 3-4.

2. **Select the Network service.**

You have to scroll down the list of services to find it.

3. **Click the Restart button.**

The service is stopped and then started again. When finished, a small
dialog box appears, displaying the message "Network restart successful."

Figure 3-4:
The Service
Configuration
window.

4. **Click OK.**

   You're returned to the Service Configuration program.

5. **Close the Service Configuration program.**

   That's all!

If you prefer working in a command shell, you can restart the network by entering the command `service network restart`. This results in a display similar to the following:

```
Shutting down interface eth0:                        [  OK  ]
Shutting down loopback interface:                    [  OK  ]
Setting network parameters:                          [  OK  ]
Bringing up loopback interface:                      [  OK  ]
Bringing up interface eth0:                          [  OK  ]
```

Working with Network Configuration Files

Like other operating system services, the Linux network is configured by settings that are specified in configuration files that you can find in the `/etc` directory or in one of its subdirectories. Graphical configuration programs such as Red Hat Network Configuration are actually little more than glorified text editors that enable you to select network configuration options from user-friendly screens and then save your configuration changes to the standard configuration files. If you prefer to do the grunt work yourself, you can open the configuration files in a text editor and make changes to them directly.

Any time you open up a configuration file in a text editor, you run the risk of messing up your system's configuration. So be careful!

Table 3-1 lists the main Linux network configuration files and describes what each file does. The details of these files are described in the sections that follow.

Table 3-1		Linux Network Configuration Files
File	*Location*	*Description*
network	/etc/sysconfig	Basic network configuration
hostname	/etc	Specifies the host name (obsolete, but should still be present)
ifcfg-eth0	/etc/sysconfig/ network-scripts	IP settings for the first Ethernet adapter
ifcfg-eth1	/etc/sysconfig/ network-scripts	IP settings for the second Ethernet adapter
hosts	/etc	Lists host address mappings
resolv.conf	/etc	Lists DNS nameservers
nsswitch.conf	/etc	Specifies the name search order
xinetd.conf	/etc	Specifies which network services are started automatically

The Network file

This file, which lives in /etc/sysconfig, specifies basic configuration settings for your network. Here's a typical Network file:

```
NETWORKING=yes
HOSTNAME=LSERVER
GATEWAY=192.168.1.1
```

This file specifies that networking is enabled, the computer's host name is LSERVER, and the default gateway address is 192.168.1.1.

The following paragraphs describe all the settings that are valid for this file:

✦ **NETWORKING:** Specifies YES or NO to enable or disable networking for the computer.

✦ **HOSTNAME:** Specifies the host name for this computer. You should also specify this name in /etc/hostname, although that file is considered obsolete and is used only by some old programs. Note that this can be a simple host name (like LSERVER) or a fully qualified domain name (like Lserver.LoweWriter.com).

✦ **FORWARD_IPV4:** Specifies YES or NO to enable or disable IP forwarding. Specify FORWARD_IPV4=YES to set up a router.

✦ **GATEWAY:** Specifies the IP address of the computer's default gateway. If the network has a gateway router, specify its address here. If this computer is the network's gateway router, specify the gateway IP address provided by your ISP.

✦ **GATEWAYDEV:** Specifies the interface (such as eth0) that should be used to reach the gateway.

The Hostname file

This file used to be where the computer's host name was specified. The host name is now specified in the /etc/sysconfig/network file, but some older programs still look for the host name in /etc/hostname. As a result, you should provide this file just in case.

The hostname file is simple: It contains just the computer's host name, like this:

```
LSERVER
```

Here, the computer's host name is LSERVER. You can also specify a fully qualified domain name such as Lserver.LoweWriter.com here.

The Ifcfg files

Each network interface has an ifcfg configuration file located in /etc/sysconfig/network-scripts. The device name is added to the end of the filename. So, for example, the configuration file for the first Ethernet interface is called ifcfg-eth0.

This file is created and updated by the Red Hat Network Configuration program, so you don't have to edit it directly (if you don't want to).

Here's a typical ifcfg file for an interface that has a static IP:

```
DEVICE=eth0
BOOTPROTO=none
ONBOOT=yes
USERCTL=no
IPADDR=192.168.1.200
NETMASK=255.255.255.0
BROADCAST=192.168.1.255
NETWORK=192.168.1.0
```

Here's an example for an interface that uses DHCP:

```
DEVICE=eth0
BOOTPROTO=dhcp
ONBOOT=yes
USERCTL=no
```

Here, the `ifcfg` file doesn't have to specify the IP address information because the interface gets that information from a DHCP server.

The following paragraphs describe the settings that you're most likely to see in this file:

+ **DEVICE:** The name of the device, such as eth0 or eth1.

+ **USERCTL:** Specifies YES or NO to indicate whether local users are allowed to start or stop the network.

+ **ONBOOT:** Specifies YES or NO to indicate whether the device should be enabled when Linux boots up.

+ **BOOTPROTO:** Specifies how the device gets its IP address. Possible values are NONE for static assignment, DHCP, or BOOTP.

+ **BROADCAST:** The broadcast address used to send packets to everyone on the subnet. For example: 192.168.1.255.

+ **NETWORK:** The network address. For example: 192.168.1.0.

+ **NETMASK:** The subnet mask. For example: 255.255.255.0.

+ **IPADDR:** The IP address for the adapter.

The Hosts file

The Hosts file is a simple list of IP addresses and the host names associated with each address. You can think of the Hosts file as a local DNS database of sorts. Whenever Linux needs to resolve a DNS name, it first looks for the name in the Hosts file. If Linux finds the name there, it doesn't have to do a DNS lookup; it simply uses the IP address found in the Hosts file.

For small networks, it's common to list the host name for each computer on the network in the Hosts file on each computer. Then, whenever you add a new computer to the network, you just update each computer's Hosts file to include the new computer. That's not so bad if the network has a just a few computers, but you wouldn't want to do it that way for a network with 1,000 hosts. That's why other name resolution systems are more popular for larger networks.

The default Linux Hosts file looks something like this:

```
# Do not remove the following line, or various programs
# that require network functionality will fail.
127.0.0.1  localhost.localdomain  localhost
```

Here, the names localhost.localdomain and localhost both resolve to 127.0.0.1, which is the standard local loopback address.

Here's an example of a Hosts file that has some additional entries:

```
# Do not remove the following line, or various programs
# that require network functionality will fail.
127.0.0.1  LServer localhost.localdomain  localhost
192.168.1.1      linksys
192.168.1.100    ward.cleaver.com ward
192.168.1.101    june.cleaver.com june
192.168.1.102    wally.cleaver.com wally
192.168.1.103    theodore.cleaver.com theodore beaver
```

Here, I've defined host names for each of the Cleaver family's four computers and their Linksys router. Each computer can be accessed by using two names (for example, ward.cleaver.com or just ward), except the last one, which has three names.

The resolv.conf file

The resolv.conf file lists the DNS nameservers that can be consulted to perform DNS lookups. A typical resolv.conf file may look like this:

```
Nameserver 192.168.1.110
nameserver 204.127.198.19
nameserver 63.249.76.19
```

If you have set up a name server on your own network, its IP address should be the first one listed.

The nsswitch.conf file

This configuration file controls how name resolution works when looking up various types of objects, such as host addresses and passwords. Listing 3-1 shows the sample nsswitch.conf file that comes with Red Hat Linux. As you can see, this file is loaded with comments that explain what the various settings do.

You can use the files, db, and dns keywords to specify how objects should be retrieved. Files specifies that the local file should be used. Db specifies a database lookup, and DNS specifies that a DNS server should be consulted.

The order in which you list these keywords determines the order in which the data sources are searched. Thus, if you want host names to be resolved first by the local Hosts file and then by DNS, you should include the following line in `nsswitch`:

```
hosts:  files dns
```

Listing 3-1   A Sample /etc/nsswitch.conf File

```
#
# /etc/nsswitch.conf
#
# An example Name Service Switch config file. This file should be
# sorted with the most-used services at the beginning.
#
# The entry '[NOTFOUND=return]' means that the search for an
# entry should stop if the search in the previous entry turned
# up nothing. Note that if the search failed due to some other reason
# (like no NIS server responding) then the search continues with the
# next entry.
#
# Legal entries are:
#
#       nisplus or nis+     Use NIS+ (NIS version 3)
#       nis or yp           Use NIS (NIS version 2), also called YP
#       dns                 Use DNS (Domain Name Service)
#       files               Use the local files
#       db                  Use the local database (.db) files
#       compat              Use NIS on compat mode
#       hesiod              Use Hesiod for user lookups
#       [NOTFOUND=return]   Stop searching if not found so far
#

# To use db, put the "db" in front of "files" for entries you want to be
# looked up first in the databases
#
# Example:
#passwd:    db files nisplus nis
#shadow:    db files nisplus nis
#group:     db files nisplus nis

passwd:     files
shadow:     files
group:      files

#hosts:     db files nisplus nis dns
hosts:      files dns

# Example - obey only what nisplus tells us...
#services:  nisplus [NOTFOUND=return] files
#networks:  nisplus [NOTFOUND=return] files
#protocols: nisplus [NOTFOUND=return] files
#rpc:       nisplus [NOTFOUND=return] files
#ethers:    nisplus [NOTFOUND=return] files
```

```
#netmasks:    nisplus [NOTFOUND=return] files

bootparams: nisplus [NOTFOUND=return] files

ethers:       files
netmasks:     files
networks:     files
protocols:    files
rpc:          files
services:     files

netgroup:     files

publickey:    nisplus

automount:    files
aliases:      files nisplus
```

The xinetd.conf file

Xinetd is a service that oversees a variety of networking services, such as Telnet or Finger. Xinetd listens for requests on the ports on which these services talk and automatically starts the service when a connection is made. Xinetd is controlled by the configuration file `xinetd.conf`, which is found in the `/etc` directory, and each of the services controlled by xinetd is in turn controlled by a configuration file found in the `/etc/xinet.d` directory.

You should leave most of the settings in these configuration files alone unless you've studied up on xinetd. (You can find out more about it at `www.xinetd.org`.) However, you may want to modify the configuration files in order to enable or disable specific services.

Each of the services controlled by xinetd has a configuration file in the `/etc/xinet.d` directory. Each of these configuration files ends with a line that enables or disables the service. For example, here's the configuration file for Telnet, `/etc/xinet.d/telnet`:

```
# default: on
# description: The telnet server serves telnet sessions; it uses \
#       unencrypted username/password pairs for authentication.
service telnet
{
    Flags              = REUSE
    socket_type        = stream
    wait               = no
    user               = root
    server             = /usr/sbin/in.telnetd
    log_on_failure    += USERID
    disable            = yes
}
```

Here, the last line disables Telnet. You can enable the Telnet service by changing the last line to `disable = no`.

Displaying Your Network Configuration with the ifconfig Command

Linux doesn't have an ipconfig command like Windows. Instead, the command that you use to display information about your network configuration is ifconfig. You can also use this command to set network configuration options, but in most cases, it's easier to use the Red Hat Network Configuration program or to directly edit the network configuration files.

If you enter ifconfig without any parameters, you'll get output similar to the following:

```
Eth0        Link encap:Ethernet  HWaddr 00:40:05:80:51:F3
            inet addr:192.168.1.200  Bcast:192.168.1.255  Mask:255.255.255.0
            UP BROADCAST RUNNING MULTICAST  MTU:1500  Metric:1
            RX packets:17293 errors:0 dropped:0 overruns:0 frame:0
            TX packets:334 errors:0 dropped:0 overruns:0 carrier:0
            collisions:0 txqueuelen:100
            RX bytes:1124153 (1.0 Mb)  TX bytes:45726 (44.6 Kb)
            Interrupt:3 Base address:0xc000

lo          Link encap:Local Loopback
            inet addr:127.0.0.1  Mask:255.0.0.0
            UP LOOPBACK RUNNING  MTU:16436  Metric:1
            RX packets:202939 errors:0 dropped:0 overruns:0 frame:0
            TX packets:202939 errors:0 dropped:0 overruns:0 carrier:0
            collisions:0 txqueuelen:0
            RX bytes:13856758 (13.2 Mb)  TX bytes:13856758 (13.2 Mb)
```

From this output, you can tell that the IP address of the Ethernet adapter (eth0) is 192.168.1.200, the broadcast address is 192.168.1.255, and the netmask is 255.255.255.0. You can also see transmit and receive statistics as well as information about the hardware configuration, such as the MAC address and the adapter's interrupt and memory base address assignments.

Linux offers many other commands that can help you to configure and troubleshoot a network. Many of these commands are described in detail in Chapter 6 of this book.

Chapter 4: Doing the Samba Dance

In This Chapter

✔ **Finding out what Samba does**

✔ **Installing Samba on your Linux computer**

✔ **Configuring Samba the easy way**

✔ **Tweaking the** `smb.conf` **file**

✔ **Using the Samba client**

*U*ntil now, you probably thought of Samba as a Brazilian dance with intricate steps and fun rhythms. In the Linux world, however, *Samba* refers to a file and printer-sharing program that allows Linux to mimic a Windows file and print server so that Windows computers can use shared Linux directories and printers. If you want to use Linux as a file or print server in a Windows network, you'll need to know how to dance the Samba.

Understanding Samba

Because Linux and Windows have such different file systems, you can't create a Linux file server simply by granting Windows users access to Linux directories. Windows client computers wouldn't be able to access files in the Linux directories. Too many differences exist between the file systems. For example:

◆ Linux filenames are case-sensitive whereas Windows filenames are not. For example, in Windows, `File1.txt` and `file1.txt` are the same file. In Linux, they are different files.

◆ Linux filenames can contain periods. In Windows, only one period is allowed — and it separates the filename from the file's extension.

◆ Windows has file attributes like read-only and archive. Linux doesn't have these.

More fundamentally, Windows networking uses a protocol called *SMB,* which stands for *server message block,* to manage the exchange of file data among file servers and clients. Linux doesn't have SMB support built in.

That's why Samba is required. Samba is a program that mimics the behavior of a Windows-based file server by implementing the SMB protocol. So when you run Samba on a Linux server, the Windows computers on your network see the Linux server as if it were a Windows server.

Like a Windows server, Samba works by designating certain directories as shares. A *share* is simply a directory that is made available to other users via the network. Each share has the following elements:

✦ **Share name:** The name by which the share is known over the network. Share names should be eight-character share names whenever possible.

✦ **Path:** The path to the directory on the Linux computer that's being shared, such as \Users\Doug.

✦ **Description:** A one-line description of the share.

✦ **Access:** A list of users or groups who have been granted access to the share.

Samba also includes a client program that lets a Linux computer access Windows file servers.

Why did Samba's developers choose to call their program *Samba?* Simply because the protocol that Windows file and print servers use to communicate with each other is called *SMB*, which stands for *server message block*. Add a couple of vowels to *SMB*, and you get *Samba*.

Installing Samba

If you didn't install Samba when you installed Linux, you'll have to install it now. You can do so in one of two basic ways. You can use Red Hat's GNOME-based package management tool to install Samba. Just insert the Red Hat distribution CD in the CD drive and click Yes when you're asked whether you want to run the autorun program. Then, when the Package Management window appears, select the Windows File Server group, which installs the Samba packages for you.

If you prefer to work from the command line, you can use the RPM command to install the Samba packages manually. Open a terminal window or log on to a virtual console. Insert the Linux distribution CD in the CD-ROM drive and then use this command:

```
Rpm -ivh /mnt/cdrom/RedHat/RPMS/samba*
```

This will install all the Samba packages from the distribution CD.

One sure way to render a Samba installation useless is to enable the default Linux firewall settings on the computer that runs Samba. The Linux firewall is designed to prevent users from accessing network services such as Samba. It's designed to be used between the Internet and your local network — not between Samba and your local network. Although it's possible to configure the firewall to allow access to Samba only to your internal network, a much better option is to run the firewall on a separate computer. That way, the firewall computer can concentrate on being a firewall, and the file server computer can concentrate on being a file server.

Starting and Stopping Samba

Before you can use Samba, you must start its two daemons, smbd and nmbd. Both can be started at once by starting the SMB service. From a command shell, use this command:

```
service smb start
```

Whenever you make a configuration change, such as adding a new share or creating a new Samba user, you should stop and restart the service with these commands:

```
service smb restart
```

If you prefer, you can stop and start the service with separate commands:

```
service smb stop
service smb start
```

If you're not sure if Samba is running, enter this command:

```
service smb status
```

You'll get a message indicating whether the smbd and nmbd daemons are running.

To configure Samba to start automatically when you start Linux, use this command:

```
chkconfig -level 35 smb on
```

To make sure that the chkconfig command worked right, enter this command:

```
chkconfig -list smb
```

You should see output similar to the following:

```
Smb        0:off  1:off  2:off  3:on   4:off  5:on   6:off
```

You can independently configure services to start automatically for each of the six *boot levels* of Linux. Boot level 3 is normal operation without an X server; level 5 is normal operation with an X server. So setting SMB to start for levels 3 and 5 makes SMB available — regardless of whether you're using a graphical user interface.

You can also start and stop Samba by using the Service Configuration tool, shown in Figure 4-1. Scroll down the list of services until you find the SMB service. You can use the three buttons in the toolbar at the top of the window to start, stop, or restart a service.

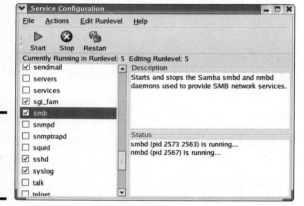

Figure 4-1: Using the Service Configuration tool.

You can also use the Service Configuration tool to start Samba automatically, although frankly, the `chkconfig` command is easier to use. To configure Samba to start automatically for levels 3 and 5, follow these steps:

1. **Choose Edit Runlevel⇨RunLevel 3.**

2. **Check the checkbox next to SMB in the list of services.**

3. **Choose File⇨Save Changes.**

4. **Choose Edit Runlevel⇨RunLevel 5.**

5. **Check the checkbox next to SMB in the list of services.**

6. **Choose File⇨Save Changes.**

Using the Red Hat Samba Server Configuration Tool

Red Hat Linux includes a handy GNOME-based configuration tool that simplifies the task of configuring Samba. To start it, choose Main Menu➪ System Settings➪Server Settings➪Samba Server. When you do so, the Samba Server Configuration window appears, as shown in Figure 4-2. This tool lets you configure basic server settings and manage shares.

Not all of Samba's configuration options are available from the Samba Server Configuration tool. For advanced Samba server configuration, you need to edit the `smb.conf` file directly, as described in the section "Editing the smb.conf File," later in this chapter.

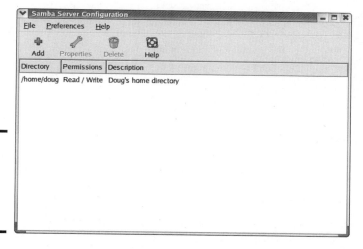

Figure 4-2:
Using the Samba Server Configuration tool.

Configuring server settings

To make your Samba server visible on the network, you need to configure its server settings. Follow these steps:

1. **Choose Preferences➪Server Settings.**

    The Server Settings dialog box springs to life, as shown in Figure 4-3.

2. **Enter the workgroup name and a description for your server.**

    The workgroup name must match the workgroup or domain name used by the computers that will be accessing the server.

3. **Click the Security tab.**

    The security settings appear, as shown in Figure 4-4.

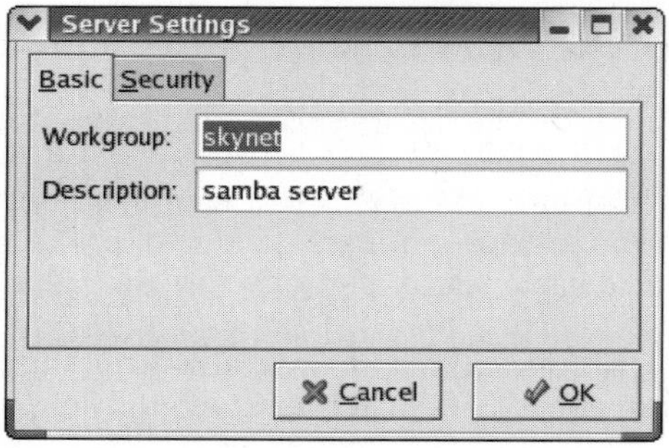

Figure 4-3:
Using the
Samba
Server
Configura-
tion tool.

Figure 4-4:
Setting
Samba's
security
options.

4. **Set the Authentication mode the way you want.**

The Authentication mode drop-down list offers four basic types of security:

- **Domain:** This mode configures the Samba server to use a Windows domain controller to verify the user. If you specify this option, you must provide the name of the domain controller in the Authentication Server field. Also, you must set Encrypted Passwords to Yes if you use Domain mode.

- **Server:** This mode configures Samba to use another Samba server to authenticate users. If you have more than one Samba server, this feature lets you set up user accounts on just one of the servers. Specify the name of the Samba server in which you want to perform the authentication in the Authentication Server field.

- **Share:** This mode authorizes users separately for each share that they attempt to access.

- **User:** This is the default mode. It requires that users provide a valid username and password when they first connect to a Samba server. That authentication then grants them access to all shares on the server, subject to the restrictions of the account under which they are authorized.

5. **Set Encrypt Passwords to Yes.**

   This option is required to allow users of Windows 98 or later versions to connect.

6. **Set the Guest Account to the account that you want anonymous users to access.**

   Normally, this account is set to Nobody, which is a user account that doesn't have access to anything. This essentially prevents anonymous users from access shares.

7. **Click OK.**

   The Server Settings dialog box is dismissed.

Configuring server users

You must create a separate Samba user account for each network user who needs to access the Samba server. In addition, you must first create a Linux user account for each user. The Samba user account maps to an existing Linux user account, so you must create the Linux user account first.

To create a Samba user account, follow these steps:

1. **From the Samba Server Configuration window, choose Preferences⇨Samba Users.**

   The Samba Users dialog box appears, as shown in Figure 4-5.

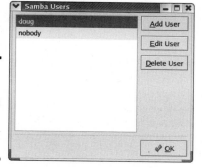

Figure 4-5:
The Samba Users dialog box lists your Samba users.

2. **Click Add User.**

   The dialog box in Figure 4-6 appears.

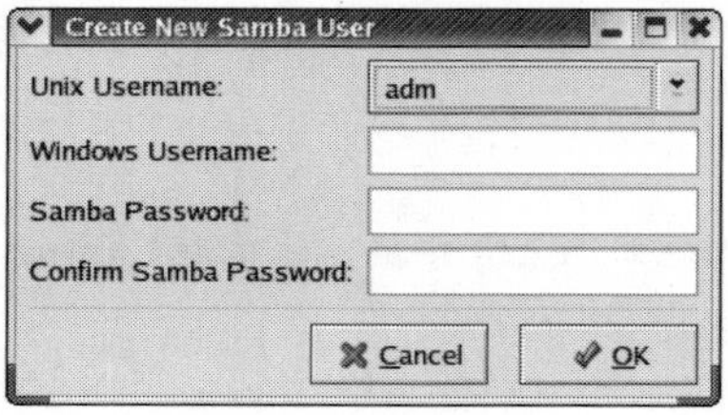

Figure 4-6:
Adding a
Samba user.

3. **From the Unix Username drop-down list, select the Linux user that you want this user to log in as.**

If you forgot to create the Linux user account for this user, choose Main Menu⇨System Settings⇨Users And Groups and create the account now.

4. **Enter the Windows username for the user.**

This is the name of the user's Windows user account.

5. **Type the user's password into the password fields.**

6. **Click OK.**

You're returned to the Samba Users dialog box, which should now list the user that you just created.

7. **Repeat Steps 2 through 6 for any other users you want to create.**

8. **After you're done, click OK.**

The Samba Users dialog box is dismissed.

Creating a share

To be useful, a file server should offer one or more *shares* — directories that have been designated as publicly accessible via the network. You can see a list of the current shares available from a file server by firing up the Samba Server Configuration program.

To create a new share, follow these steps:

1. **Click the Add button.**

The dialog box shown in Figure 4-7 appears.

2. **Type the path for the directory that you want to share in the Directory text box.**

If you aren't sure of the path, you can click Browse. This action calls up a dialog box that lets you search the server's file system for a directory folder to share. You can also create a new directory from this dialog box if the directory that you want to share doesn't yet exist. After you've selected or created the directory to share, click OK to return to the Create Samba Share dialog box.

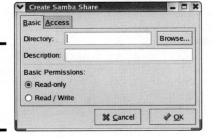

Figure 4-7:
The Create Samba Share dialog box.

3. **Type a description of the share in the Description box.**

   The description is strictly optional but can sometimes help users to determine the intended contents of the folder.

   You may be wondering why there's no text box labeled Share Name in the Create Samba Share dialog box. Unfortunately, the Samba Configuration program doesn't let you specify the share name for the share. Instead, it just uses the name of the directory being shared. If a share already exists by that name, the configuration program adds a number to the end of the directory name in order to make the share name unique.

   Don't despair, however. You can change the share name by editing the smb.conf file, as described later in this chapter.

4. **Specify whether you want the share to be read-only or read/write.**

   The default is read-only. If you want to let users save their files on your Samba server, you need to change this setting to read/write.

5. **Click the Access tab.**

   The Access Tab of the Create Samba Share dialog box appears, as shown in Figure 4-8.

Figure 4-8:
The Access tab of the Create Samba Share dialog box.

6. **If you want to limit access to the share, select the Only Allow Access To Specific Users checkbox and then select the users to whom you want to grant access.**

The Nobody user here is a little confusing. At first glance, you may think that checking Nobody would deny access to everyone, thus making the share completely inaccessible. However, that's not how it works. Instead, Nobody is a special user account that is used by default when a network user anonymously accesses a Samba server. As a result, enabling access for Nobody allows guest users to access the share.

7. **Click OK.**

You're returned to the Samba Configuration window, where the share that you just added appears in the list of shares.

When you create a new share by using the Samba Configuration program, the share should be immediately visible to other network users. If it's not, try restarting the Samba server as described in the section "Starting and Stopping Samba," earlier in this chapter.

Editing the smb.conf File

If you like the feeling of raw power that comes from editing configuration files, fire up your favorite text editor and play with the Samba configuration file. It's called `smb.conf` and is usually located in the `/etc/samba` directory, although some distributions may place this file in another location. Figure 4-9 shows you the `smb.conf` file being edited in the standard Text Editor program, which you can access by choosing Main Menu➪Accessories➪ Text Editor.

Any line in the `smb.conf` file that begins with a hash mark (#) or semicolon (;) is a comment. The default `smb.conf` file is loaded with comments that describe what each configuration line does. Plus, you can find many sample configuration entries that are commented out. The sample configuration lines are marked with a semicolon to distinguish them from explanatory text lines, which begin with a hash mark.

The overall structure of the `smb.conf` file is something like this:

```
[global]
    workgroup = workgroup
    server string = samba server
    security = USER
    encrypt passwords = yes
    smb passwd file = /etc/samba/smbpasswd
    guest ok = yes
```

```
        other global settings...

[sharename]
    comment = comment
    path = path
    writeable = yes
```

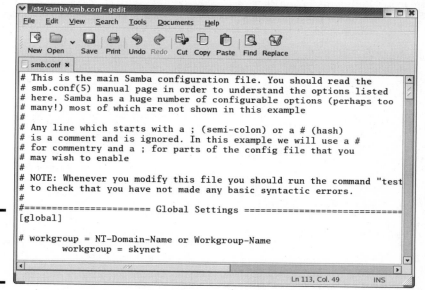

Figure 4-9:
Editing the
smb.conf
file.

The first section of the file, marked by the [global] line, contains options that apply to the entire server. These are the options that are set by the Preferences⇨Server Settings command in the GNOME Samba Server Configuration program. Table 4-1 lists a few of the more common settings that you can use in the global section.

Table 4-1	Common Global Settings for the smb.conf File
Setting	*Description*
workgroup	The name of the workgroup or domain.
server string	The comment that describes the server.
hosts allow	Lets you limit access to the Samba server to the IP addresses listed. If a partial IP address is listed (for example, 192.168.1), it is treated as a subnet.
guest ok	Specify Yes to allow guest access.
guest account	Specifies the Linux account to be used.
security	Specifies the security mode: Domain, Server, Share, or User.

Located after the global section is a section for each share that begins with the [*sharename*] line. The settings in these groups specify the details of a share, such as the comment and path. Table 4-2 lists the settings that you can specify for a share.

Table 4-2	Share Settings for the smb.conf File
Setting	*Description*
[*sharename*]	The name used by the share.
path=*path*	The path to the directory to be shared.
comment=*comment*	A description of the shared resource.
guest ok	Specify Yes to allow guest access.
writeonly	Specify Yes for read/write; No for read-only.
browseable	Specify Yes to make the share visible in My Network Places.
valid users	A list of users who can access the share.
hosts allow	Lets you limit access to the Samba server to the IP addresses listed. If a partial IP address is listed (for example, 192.168.1), it is treated as a subnet.

After you modify the smb.conf file and save your changes, you need to restart the SMB service in order for the changes to take effect. See the section "Starting and Stopping Samba," earlier in this chapter, for more information.

Using the Samba Client

Earlier in this chapter, I show you how to set up Samba's server program so that you can enable a Linux computer to operate as a file server in a Windows network, thus allowing Windows clients to access files in shared directories on the Linux computer. That's the most common reason for using Samba.

But Samba can also work the other way around: It includes a program called smbclient that lets you access Windows file servers from a Linux computer. The smbclient program works much like an FTP client, so if you've used FTP before, you'll have no trouble understanding how it works.

Smbclient is a command-line tool, so you need to log on to a virtual console or open a Terminal window. Then, enter the smbclient command, followed by the server and share name, like this:

```
smbclient //server01/share01
```

When the client successfully accesses the share, you are greeted by the friendly SMB prompt:

smb:\>

Then, you can enter smbclient commands to access the data in the shared directory. Table 4-3 summarizes the more common commands that are available at the smb:\> prompt.

Table 4-3	Commonly Used smbclient Commands
Command	*Description*
cd *directory*	Changes to the specified directory on the remote system.
del *filename*	Deletes the specified file or files on the remote system.
dir	Lists files in the current directory on the remote system.
exit	Terminates the session.
get *remote-file local-file*	Copies the specified remote file to the specified local file.
lcd *directory*	Changes the local current directory to the specified directory.
md *directory*	Creates a directory on the remote system.
mget *wildcard-mask*	Copies all files that match the wildcard mask from the remote system to the local system.
mput *wildcard-mask*	Copies all files that match the wildcard mask from the local system to the remote system.
put *local-file remote-file*	Copies the specified file from the local system to the remote system.
rd *directory*	Deletes the specified directory on the remote system.

Chapter 5: Running Internet Servers

In This Chapter

✔ Working with DHCP

✔ Running BIND

✔ Operating Sendmail

✔ Handling Apache

*O*ne of the main reasons that many network administrators add Linux servers to their networks is to run Internet services, such as DHCP, DNS, SMTP, and HTTP. Many of these services were originally developed for the UNIX environment, so they tend to run better under Linux than they do under Windows.

Well, that's the theory, at least. The most recent versions of Windows are probably just as good at running these services as Linux. Still, if you prefer to set up these services on a Linux server, this chapter is for you.

Running a DHCP Server

DHCP is the TCP/IP protocol that automatically assigns IP addresses to hosts as they come on the network. For a very small network (say, fewer than ten hosts), you don't really need DHCP: You can just configure each computer to have a static IP address. For larger networks, however, DHCP is almost a must. Without DHCP, you have to manually plan your entire IP address scheme and manually configure every computer with its IP information. Then, if a critical address such as your Internet gateway router or your DNS server address changes, you have to manually update each computer on the network. As you can imagine, DHCP can save you a lot of time.

Even for small networks, however, DHCP can be a timesaver. For example, suppose that you have a notebook computer that you take back and forth between home and office. If you don't set up a DHCP server at home, you have to change the computer's static IP address each time you move the computer. With DHCP, the computer can change IP addresses automatically.

For the complete lowdown on DHCP, please refer to Book V, Chapter 3. In the following sections, I show you how to install and configure a DHCP server on Red Hat Linux.

Installing DHCP

You can quickly find out whether DHCP is installed on your system by entering the following command from a shell prompt:

```
rpm -q dhcp
```

If DHCP has been installed, the package version is displayed. If not, the message `package dhcp is not installed` is displayed.

If DHCP isn't installed on your Linux server, you can install it by following these steps:

1. **Insert the Red Hat Linux distribution CD in your CD-ROM drive.**

2. **When prompted to run the** `Autorun` **file, click Yes.**

The Package Manager window opens.

3. **Click Forward.**

The Package Manager tallies up the packages that you've already installed on your computer. This may take a few moments. After it's done, the Package Manager displays a list of all the package groups that it can install.

4. **Scroll down the list, select Network Servers, and then click the Details link.**

This step brings up a list of specific packages in the Network Servers group.

5. **Select the DHCP package and then click Close.**

6. **Click Forward.**

Package Manager decides which packages it needs to install based on your selection. (This decision isn't as simple as it seems because many packages are dependent on other packages.)

7. **When Package Manager displays the list of packages that it proposes to install, click Forward.**

Package Manager updates your system. This step may also take awhile.

8. **When Package Manager program is done, click Finish.**

You're done! DHCP is now installed.

If you prefer to install DHCP manually, you can insert the distribution CD in the CD-ROM drive and then enter this command:

```
Rpm -ivh /mnt/cdrom/RedHat/RPMS/dhcp*
```

This command installs the DHCP package with a single command.

Configuring DHCP

You configure DHCP settings through a file called dhcpd.config that lives in the /etc directory. Red Hat provides you with a sample configuration file located in the directory /usr/share/doc/dhcp-*version*/dhcpd.conf. sample. Open this file in the text editor and then save it to the /etc directory, changing its name from dhcpd.conf.sample to just dhcpd.conf. Then, edit the file to reflect the settings that you want to use.

Listing 5-1 shows the sample configuration file that comes with Red Hat Linux.

Listing 5-1   A Sample dhcpd.conf File

```
ddns-update-style interim;
ignore client-updates;

subnet 192.168.0.0 netmask 255.255.255.0 {

# --- default gateway
    option routers              192.168.0.1;
    option subnet-mask          255.255.255.0;
    option nis-domain           "domain.org";
    option domain-name          "domain.org";
    option domain-name-servers  192.168.1.1;

option time-offset          -18000;    # Eastern Standard Time
#   option ntp-servers          192.168.1.1;
#   option netbios-name-servers 192.168.1.1;
# --- Selects point-to-point node (default is hybrid). Don't
# -- change this unless you understand Netbios very well
#   option netbios-node-type 2;

    range dynamic-bootp 192.168.0.128 192.168.0.255;
    default-lease-time 21600;
    max-lease-time 43200;

# we want the nameserver to appear at a fixed address
    host ns {
        next-server marvin.redhat.com;
        hardware ethernet 12:34:56:78:AB:CD;
        fixed-address 207.175.42.254;
        }
}
```

The following paragraphs describe some of the key points of this file:

+ **ddns-update-style:** The DHCP standards group is in the midst of deciding exactly how DCHP will handle changes to DNS data. This option specifies that the interim method should be used. This line is required — so don't mess with it.

+ **subnet:** This line specifies a subnet that's managed by this DHCP server. Following the subnet ID and netmask is an opening bracket; all the options that appear between this bracket and the closing bracket in the last line of the file belong to this subnet. In some cases, your DHCP server may dole out IP configuration information for two or more subnet groups. In that case, you'll need additional subnet groups in the configuration file.

+ **option routers:** This line provides the IP address of the default gateway.

+ **option subnet mask:** This line provides the subnet mask for the subnet.

+ **option nis-domain:** This line provides the NIS domain name. This line is important only if you've set up one or more NIS servers.

+ **option domain-name:** This line provides the domain name for the network.

+ **option domain-name-servers:** This line provides the IP addresses of your DNS servers.

+ **range:** This line specifies the range of addresses that the DHCP server will assign for this subnet.

+ **default-lease-time:** This line determines the default lease time in seconds.

+ **max-lease-time:** This line determines the maximum life of a lease.

+ **host:** This line specifies a reservation. The host group specifies the MAC address for the host and the fixed IP address to be assigned.

Starting DHCP

After you've set up the configuration file, you can start DHCP by opening a terminal window or virtual console and entering the following command:

```
dhcpd start
```

If an error exists in the configuration file, a message to that effect is displayed. You have to edit the file in order to correct the error and then start the DHCP service again.

You should also restart the service whenever you make a change to the configuration file. To restart DHCP, enter this command:

```
dhcpd restart
```

To automatically start DHCP whenever you start the computer, run this command:

```
Chkconfig -level 35 dhcpd on
```

Running a DNS Server

Linux comes with BIND, the best DNS server that money can buy. BIND is an extremely powerful program. Some people make entire careers of setting up and configuring BIND. In these few short pages, I just touch on the very basics of setting up a DNS server on your network.

You can find plenty of details about DNS in Book V, Chapter 4. Please review that chapter before playing with BIND on your Linux system.

Installing BIND

You can quickly find out whether BIND is installed on your system by entering the following command from a shell prompt:

```
rpm -q bind
```

If BIND has been installed, the package version is displayed. If not, the message `package bind is not installed` is displayed.

BIND is usually installed by default when you install Linux as a network server. If it isn't, you can easily install it by following these steps:

1. **Insert the Red Hat Linux distribution CD in your CD-ROM drive.**

2. **When prompted to run the** `Autorun` **file, click Yes.**

The Package Manager window opens.

3. **Click Forward.**

The Package Manager displays a list of all the package groups that it can install.

4. **Scroll down the list and select the DNS Name Server group.**

5. **Click Forward.**

The Package Management spends a few moments deciding which packages it needs to install based on your selection.

6. **When the Package Management program displays the list of packages it proposes to install, click Forward.**

The Package Management program updates your system. This step can take awhile, so be patient.

7. When the Package Management program is done, click Finish.

That's all there is. BIND is now installed and ready to configure.

If you prefer to install Bind manually, you can insert the distribution CD in the CD-ROM drive and then enter this command:

```
Rpm -ivh /mnt/cdrom/RedHat/RPMS/bind*
```

This command installs the BIND package with a single command.

Looking at BIND configuration files

Although Red Hat Linux includes a handy BIND configuration tool, you still need to know the location and purpose of each of BIND's basic configuration files. These files are described in the following sections.

named.conf

This file, found in the /etc directory, is the basic BIND configuration file. This file contains global properties and links to the other configuration files.

Because the Red Hat BIND configuration tool edits this file, you shouldn't edit this file directly. If you need to set your own configuration options, use named.custom instead.

Here's a typical named.conf file:

```
## named.conf - configuration for bind
#
# Generated automatically by redhat-config-bind, alchemist et al.
# Any changes not supported by redhat-config-bind should be put
# in /etc/named.custom
#
controls {
        inet 127.0.0.1 allow { localhost; } keys { rndckey; };
};

include "/etc/named.custom";

include "/etc/rndc.key";

zone  "0.0.127.in-addr.arpa" {
            type master;
            file  "0.0.127.in-addr.arpa.zone";
};

zone  "localhost" {
            type master;
            file  "localhost.zone";
};

zone  "lowewriter.com" {
```

```
                type master;
                file "lowewriter.com.zone";
    };
```

The line `include "/etc/named.custom";` is what causes the `named.custom` file to be read in. The `zone` lines name the zone files for each domain for which the server is responsible.

By default, this file always includes two zones: `0.0.127.in-addr.arpa`, which is the reverse-lookup zone for `localhost`, and localhost, the zone file for the local computer. Any other zones that you've added through the Red Hat BIND configuration tool appear in this file as well.

named.custom

This file, also found in `/etc`, lets you add additional information to the `named.conf` file. Here's a typical `named.custom` file:

```
## named.custom - custom configuration for bind
#
# Any changes not currently supported by redhat-config-bind should be put
# in this file.
#

zone "." {
    type hint;
    file "named.ca";
};

options {
        directory "/var/named/";
};
```

One reason to use this file is if you want to include zone files that you create yourself without the aid of the Red Hat BIND configuration program. If you want to include your own zone file, just add a zone statement that names the zone file. For example, suppose that you want to add a zone named `cleaver.com`, and you've manually created the `cleaver.com.zone`. To include this zone, add these lines to the `named.custom` file:

```
zone "cleaver.com" {
    type master;
    file "cleaver.com.zone";
};
```

named.ca

This file, located in the `/var/named` directory, lists the names and addresses of the Internet's root servers. It's a fascinating file to look at because it helps to unveil the mystery of how the Internet really works. You shouldn't change it, however, unless, of course, you happen to be the administrator of one of the Internet's root servers — in which case, I hope you're not reading this book to learn how BIND works.

Here's the `named.ca` file that ships with RedHat Linux 9:

```
;               This file holds the information on root name servers needed to
;               initialize cache of Internet domain name servers
;               (e.g. reference this file in the "cache  .  <file>"
;               configuration file of BIND domain name servers).
;
;               This file is made available by InterNIC
;               under anonymous FTP as
;                    file               /domain/named.cache
;                    on server          FTP.INTERNIC.NET
;
;               last update:   Nov 5, 2002
;               related version of root zone:   2002110501
;
;
; formerly NS.INTERNIC.NET
;
.                              3600000   IN  NS   A.ROOT-SERVERS.NET.
A.ROOT-SERVERS.NET.            3600000       A    198.41.0.4
;
; formerly NS1.ISI.EDU
;
.                              3600000       NS   B.ROOT-SERVERS.NET.
B.ROOT-SERVERS.NET.            3600000       A    128.9.0.107
;
; formerly C.PSI.NET
;
.                              3600000       NS   C.ROOT-SERVERS.NET.
C.ROOT-SERVERS.NET.            3600000       A    192.33.4.12
;
; formerly TERP.UMD.EDU
;
.                              3600000       NS   D.ROOT-SERVERS.NET.
D.ROOT-SERVERS.NET.            3600000       A    128.8.10.90
;
; formerly NS.NASA.GOV
;
.                              3600000       NS   E.ROOT-SERVERS.NET.
E.ROOT-SERVERS.NET.            3600000       A    192.203.230.10
;
; formerly NS.ISC.ORG
;
.                              3600000       NS   F.ROOT-SERVERS.NET.
F.ROOT-SERVERS.NET.            3600000       A    192.5.5.241
;
; formerly NS.NIC.DDN.MIL
;
.                              3600000       NS   G.ROOT-SERVERS.NET.
G.ROOT-SERVERS.NET.            3600000       A    192.112.36.4
;
```

```
; formerly AOS.ARL.ARMY.MIL
;
.                           3600000         NS      H.ROOT-SERVERS.NET.
H.ROOT-SERVERS.NET.         3600000         A       128.63.2.53
;
; formerly NIC.NORDU.NET
;
.                           3600000         NS      I.ROOT-SERVERS.NET.
I.ROOT-SERVERS.NET.         3600000         A       192.36.148.17
;
; operated by VeriSign, Inc.
;
.                           3600000         NS      J.ROOT-SERVERS.NET.
J.ROOT-SERVERS.NET.         3600000         A       192.58.128.30
;
; housed in LINX, operated by RIPE NCC
;
.                           3600000         NS      K.ROOT-SERVERS.NET.
K.ROOT-SERVERS.NET.         3600000         A       193.0.14.129
;
; operated by IANA
;
.                           3600000         NS      L.ROOT-SERVERS.NET.
L.ROOT-SERVERS.NET.         3600000         A       198.32.64.12
;
; housed in Japan, operated by WIDE
;
.                           3600000         NS      M.ROOT-SERVERS.NET.
M.ROOT-SERVERS.NET.         3600000         A       202.12.27.33
; End of File
```

An organization named Internic keeps the `named.ca` file up to date. You can download the most current version of `named.ca` from Internic's FTP site at `ftp.internic.net`. Every once in awhile, Internic publishes a new version of this file, so you should check now and then to make sure that your file is current.

named.local

This file, located in `/var/named`, is a zone file for your local computer — that is, for the localhost domain. Rarely (if ever) do you need to modify it. It typically looks like this:

```
$TTL 86400
@       IN      SOA     localhost. root.localhost. (
                        1997022700  ; Serial
                        28800       ; Refresh
                        14400       ; Retry
                        3600000     ; Expire
                        86400 )     ; Minimum
```

```
        IN    NS    localhost.

1       IN    PTR   localhost.
```

Zone files

Each zone for which your DNS server is authoritative should have a zone file, named *domain*.zone and located in the /var/named directory. If you like to edit DNS records directly, you can create this file yourself. Or, you can use the point-and-click interface of the Red Hat BIND configuration tool to automatically create the file.

Here's a typical zone file, named lowewriter.com.zone:

```
$TTL 86400
@    IN    SOA    ns207.pair.com.   root.localhost (
                  2 ; serial
                  28800 ; refresh
                  7200 ; retry
                  604800 ; expire
                  86400 ; ttl
                  )

     IN    NS    ns000.ns0.com.
     IN    NS    ns207.pair.com.

@    IN    MX    1    sasi.pair.com.

www  IN    A     209.68.34.15
```

Table 5-1 lists the most common types of records that appear in zone files. For a complete description of each of these record types, refer to Book V, Chapter 4.

Table 5-1	Common Resource Record Types	
Type	*Name*	*Description*
SOA	Start Of Authority	Identifies a zone.
NS	Name Server	Identifies a name server that is authoritative for the zone.
A	Address	Maps a fully qualified domain name to an IP address.
CNAME	Canonical Name	Creates an alias for a fully qualified domain name.
MX	Mail Exchange	Identifies the mail server for a domain.
PTR	Pointer	Maps an IP address to a fully qualified domain name for reverse lookups.

Creating a zone with the Red Hat BIND configuration tool

Red Hat Linux includes a program that lets you create BIND configuration files with an easy-to-use graphical interface. To start this program, choose Main Menu⇨System Settings⇨Server Settings⇨Domain Name Service. The Domain Name Service window, shown in Figure 5-1, appears.

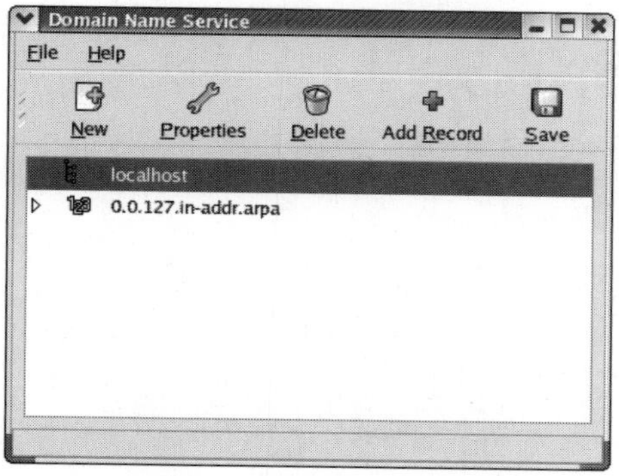

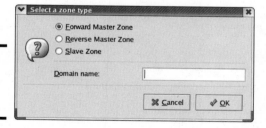

Figure 5-1:
Using the
Red Hat
BIND
configura-
tion
program.

The most common reason for using this configuration program is to create a zone file. To create a new zone file, follow these steps:

1. **Click the New button.**

The Select A Zone Type dialog box appears, as shown in Figure 5-2.

Figure 5-2:
Selecting
the zone
type.

2. **Choose Forward Master Zone, enter the zone's domain name in the text box, and click OK.**

When you enter the zone name, you usually want to enter just the top-level domain and the first-level domain, such as `LoweWriter.com` rather than `www.lowewriter.com`.

When you click OK, the Name To IP Translations dialog box appears, as shown in Figure 5-3.

Figure 5-3:
Specifying the name to IP trans-lations for the zone.

3. **Enter the name of the primary nameserver for the zone's SOA record in the Primary Nameserver box.**

   This name should end with a period.

4. **Click the Time Settings button.**

   This brings up the Zone Life Cycle Information dialog box, as shown in Figure 5-4.

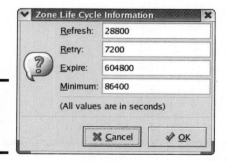

Figure 5-4:
Setting the zone's life cycle.

5. **Change the life cycle values if you want.**

   The following paragraphs explain the options on the Zone Life Cycle Information dialog box:

   - **Refresh:** A time interval that specifies how often a secondary server should check to see whether the zone needs to be refreshed. A typical value is 3,600 (one hour).

   - **Retry:** A time interval that specifies how long a secondary server should wait after requesting a zone transfer before trying again. A typical value is 600 (ten minutes).

   - **Expire:** A time interval that specifies how long a secondary server should keep the zone data before discarding it. A typical value is 86,400 (one day).

   - **Minimum:** A time interval that specifies the TTL value to use for zone resource records that omit the TTL field. A typical value is 3,600 (one hour).

6. **Click OK.**

   You're returned to the Name To IP Translations dialog box.

7. **Select the domain record in the Records list box and then click Edit.**

   The Settings dialog box appears, as shown in Figure 5-5.

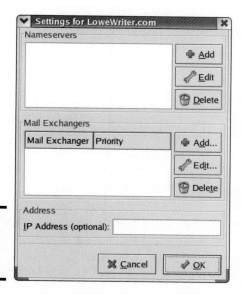

Figure 5-5:
The zone
Settings
dialog box.

8. **In the Nameservers section, click Add to create an NS record.**

The Nameserver Properties dialog box appears, as shown in Figure 5-6.

9. **Enter the DNS address of the nameserver and click OK.**

The name should end with a period. When you click OK, you're returned to the Settings dialog box. The nameserver that you added appears in the Nameserver list.

10. **Repeat Steps 8 and 9 to add additional nameservers.**

Every zone should have at least two nameservers so that if one goes down, the zone is still reachable via the second nameserver.

11. **In the Mail Exchangers section, click Add to create an MX record.**

The Add A Mail Exchanger dialog box, shown in Figure 5-7, appears.

12. **Type the Host Name and Priority for the mail exchanger and click OK.**

The host name should be the DNS name of your mail server. It should end with a period.

The priority number indicates which mail server should be used first. Priority numbers are like golf: lowest score wins.

When you click OK, you're returned to the Settings dialog box. The mail exchanger that you added appears in the nameserver list.

13. **Repeat Steps 11 and 12 to create additional MX records.**

Good DNS practice dictates that you should have two mail exchangers so that your mail will still be delivered if one is not available.

14. **Click OK.**

The Settings dialog box is dismissed, and you're returned to the Name To IP Translations dialog box.

15. **Click Add in the Records section to create a host (A) record.**

The Add A Record dialog box appears, as shown in Figure 5-8.

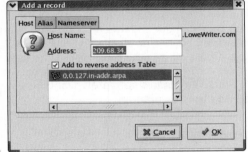

Figure 5-8:
Adding an A
record.

16. **Enter the Host Name and IP Address in the text boxes and then click OK.**

The host name is adzzded to the zone name to determine the fully qualified name that will be associated with the IP address you specify. For example, to associate `www.LoweWriter.com` with 64.71.129.102, type **www** in the Host Name box and **64.71.129.102** in the Address box.

17. **Repeat Step 16 for each A record that you want to create.**

18. **Click OK.**

You're almost done.

19. **Click the Save button to save your changes.**

This step writes the configuration changes that you made to the various BIND configuration files.

Restarting BIND

BIND runs as a service called `named`. As a result, when you make changes to your DNS configuration, you have to restart the `named` service to apply the changes. To do that, use this command:

```
service named restart
```

You can also restart the `named` service from the Service Configuration tool. Choose Main Menu⇨System Settings⇨Server Settings⇨Services. Then, scroll down the list to find `named` and click the Restart button.

Running Sendmail

Sendmail, which is a standard part of most Linux distributions, is one of the most popular mail server programs on the Internet. You can also use Sendmail as an alternative to expensive mail server programs, such as Microsoft Exchange Server, to provide e-mail services for your LAN.

Spam artists — unscrupulous marketers who clutter the Internet with millions of unsolicited e-mails — are constantly on the prowl for unprotected Sendmail servers, which they can use to launch their spam campaigns. If you don't protect your server, sooner or later a spammer will coax your computer into spending almost all its time sending out the spammer's e-mail. To protect your server from becoming an indentured spam servant, you can configure it to refuse any mail that merely wants to use your computer to relay messages to other computers.

Installing Sendmail

You can quickly find out whether Sendmail is installed on your system by entering the following command from a shell prompt:

```
rpm -q sendmail
```

If DHCP has been installed, the package version is displayed. If not, the message `package sendmail is not installed` is displayed.

While you're at it, you should check to make sure that `m4` is installed by running the command `rpm -q m4`. Then check to make sure that `sendmail-c4` is installed by running the command `rpm -q sendmail-c4`. `M4` and `sendmail-c4` are required if you want to make changes to your Sendmail configuration. They're installed by default when you install Sendmail, so they should be there if Sendmail is installed. It never hurts to check.

If Sendmail isn't installed, you can install it by following these steps:

1. **Insert the Red Hat Linux distribution CD in your CD-ROM drive.**

2. **When prompted to run the** `Autorun` **file, click Yes.**

    The Package Manager window opens.

3. **Click Forward.**

The Package Manager ushers forth a list of all the package groups that it can install.

4. **Scroll down the list and select Mail Server.**

5. **Click Forward.**

Be patient while the Package Manager decides which packages it needs to install based on your selection.

6. **When the Package Manager program displays the list of packages it proposes to install, click Forward.**

The Package Manager program updates your system. Be patient some more.

7. **When the Package Manager program is done, click Finish.**

You are now the proud owner of a computer with Sendmail.

If you prefer to install Sendmail manually, you can insert the distribution CD in the CD-ROM drive and then enter this command:

```
Rpm -ivh /mnt/cdrom/RedHat/RPMS/sendmail*
```

The DHCP package installs with a single command.

Modifying sendmail.mc

Sendmail is probably one of the most difficult programs to configure that you'll ever encounter. In fact, the basic configuration file, `sendmail.cf`, is well over 1,000 lines long. You don't want to mess with this file if you can possibly avoid it.

Fortunately, you don't have to. The `sendmail.cf` configuration file is generated automatically from a much shorter file called `sendmail.mc`. This file contains special macros that are processed by a program called m4. The m4 program reads the macros in the `sendmail.mc` file and expands them to create the actual `sendmail.cf` file.

Even so, the `sendmail.mc` file is a few hundred lines long. Configuring Sendmail isn't for the faint of heart.

You can find the `sendmail.mc` and `sendmail.cf` files in the `/etc/mail` directory. Before you edit these files, you should make backup copies of the current files. That way, if you mess up your mail configuration, you can quickly return to a working configuration by reinstating your backup copies.

After you've made backup copies, you can safely edit `sendmail.mc`. When you're finished, you can regenerate the `sendmail.cf` file by entering these commands:

```
cd /etc/mail
m4 sendmail.mc > sendmail.cf
service sendmail restart
```

The first command changes the current working directory to `/etc/mail`. Then, the second command compiles the `sendmail.mc` command into the `sendmail.cf` command. Finally, the third command restarts the Sendmail service so that the changes will take effect.

You need to be aware of two strange conventions used in the `sendmail.mc` file:

✦ Unlike most configuration files, comments don't begin with a hash mark (#). Instead, they begin with the letters `dnl`.

✦ Strings that are enclosed in quotation marks must begin with a backquote (`` ` ``), which is the located to the left of the numeral 1 on the keyboard, and end with an apostrophe ('), located to the right of the semicolon. So a properly quoted string looks like this:

```
MASQUERADE_AS(`mydomain.com')
```

Pretty strange, eh?

Here are two of the more common configuration changes that you may need to make to `sendmail.mc`:

✦ The default configuration allows connections only from localhost. If you want Sendmail to work as a server for other computers on your network, look for the following line in the `sendmail.mc` file:

```
DAEMON_OPTIONS(`Port-smtp,Addr=127.0.0.1, Name=MTA')dnl
```

Add `dnl #` to the beginning of this line to make it a comment.

✦ Masquerading allows all the mail being sent from your domain to appear as if it came from the domain (for example, `wally@cleaver.net`) rather than from the individual hosts (like `wally@wally.cleaver.net`). To enable masquerading, add lines similar to these:

```
MASQUERADE_AS(`cleaver.net')dnl
FEATURE(masquerade_envelope)dnl
FEATURE(masquerade_entire_domain)dnl
MASQUERADE_DOMAIN(`cleaver.net')dnl
```

Setting up aliases

An *alias* — also known as a *virtual user* — is an incoming e-mail address that is automatically routed to local users. For example, you may want to create a generic account such as sales@mydomain.com and have all mail sent to that account delivered to a user named *willie*. To do that, you edit the file /etc/mail/virtusers. This file starts out empty. To create a virtual user, just list the incoming e-mail address followed by the actual recipient.

For example, here's a virtusers file that defines several aliases:

```
sales@mydomain.com        willie
bob@mydomain.com          robert
marketing@mydomain.com    robert
```

After you make your changes, you should restart the Sendmail service.

Running a Web Server

All the popular Linux distributions come with Apache, the most popular Web server on the Internet today. In most cases, Apache is installed and configured automatically when you install Linux. Then, setting up a Web server for the Internet or an intranet is simply a matter of tweaking a few Apache configuration settings and copying your HTML document files to Apache's home directory.

Installing Apache

You can quickly find out whether Apache is installed on your system by entering the following command from a shell prompt:

```
rpm -q httpd
```

If Apache has been installed, the package version is displayed. If not, the message package httpd is not installed is displayed.

If Apache is not installed on your Linux server, you can install it by following these steps:

1. **Insert the Red Hat Linux distribution CD in your CD-ROM drive.**

2. **When prompted to run the** Autorun **file, click Yes.**

   The Package Manager window opens.

3. **Click Forward.**

   The Package Manager tallies up the packages that you've already installed on your computer. This may take a few moments. When it's done, it displays a list of all the package groups it can install.

4. **Scroll down the list and select Web Servers and then click Forward.**

   The Package Manager decides which packages it needs to install based on your selection.

5. **When the Package Manager program displays the list of packages it proposes to install, click Forward.**

   The Package Manager program updates your system. This step may also take awhile.

6. **When the Package Manager program is done, click Finish.**

   Apache is now installed.

If you prefer to install Apache manually, you can insert the distribution CD in the CD-ROM drive and then enter this command:

```
Rpm -ivh /mnt/cdrom/RedHat/RPMS/httpd*
```

This command installs Apache without muddling through the Package Manager screens.

You can test to see whether Apache is up and running by trying to display the default home page shipped with Apache from another computer on your network. You can do that by firing up a Web browser such as Internet Explorer and typing the IP address of your Linux server in the Address bar. If Apache is running on the server, a page such as the one shown in Figure 5-9 appears.

If this doesn't work, first make sure that you can ping your Linux server from the remote system. Then, check to see whether Apache is running on the Linux server by running the command `service httpd status`. If this command indicates that Apache is not running, enter the command `service httpd start` to get things going.

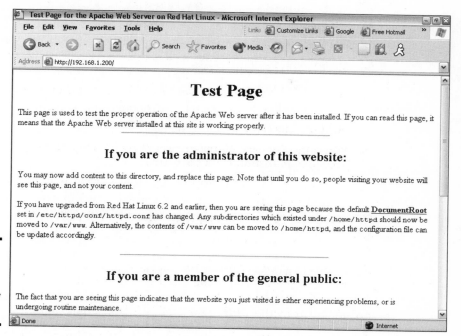

Figure 5-9:
The default
page
displayed by
Apache.

Configuring Apache

Apache should run fine using the default configuration settings made when you install it. However, you can change various configuration settings either by editing the Apache configuration files or by using Red Hat's Apache Configuration program, as shown in Figure 5-10.

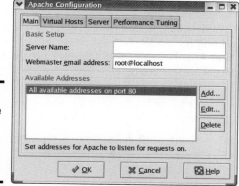

Figure 5-10:
The Apache
Configura-
tion
program
in action.

This program allows you to control a variety of Apache settings, including:

✦ The e-mail address of the server administrator

✦ The IP address of the server

✦ The server's name

✦ The location of the server's HTML documents

✦ The location of the server's log files

✦ CGI settings

✦ The TCP/IP port number

If you prefer, you can configure your Apache server by directly editing the configuration files. Apache's configuration settings are found in three separate configuration files, named `httpd.conf`, `srm.conf`, and `access.conf`. These files are located in `/etc/httpd/conf` in Red Hat Linux, but may be in a different location in other Linux distributions. Be sure to study the Apache documentation before you start messing with these files!

Whenever you make a configuration change to Apache, you should restart Apache by using the `service httpd restart` command.

Creating Web pages

This section is about how to create and edit HTML content for your Web site. Plenty of good books are available on how to do that, including my own *Creating Web Pages For Dummies Quick Reference*. Rather, I just want to point out a few key things that you need to know in order to set up a Web site using Apache:

✦ The default location for Web documents is `/var/www/html`. When you create Web pages for your site, save them in that directory.

✦ When a user visits your Web site by typing just the domain name without a filename (for example, `www.mydomain.com` instead of `www.mydomain.com/file1.html`), Apache displays the file named `index.html` or `index.htm`. You should give the home page for your Web site one of these two names.

✦ If the server will host two or more Web sites with separate domain names, you can set up a *virtual host* to handle each site.

✦ If you're a programmer, you can build complicated Web-based applications using PHP, which is installed along with Apache.

Chapter 6: Linux Commands

In This Chapter

✔ Discovering the basics of command shells

✔ Identifying file and directory commands

✔ Discovering commands that help with packages and services

✔ Figuring out commands for managing users and groups

✔ Becoming familiar with networking commands

*L*inux has several nice graphical user interfaces to choose from, and many of the more common Linux networking functions have graphical configuration utilities. Still, many Linux configuration tasks can only be done from a command shell. In many cases, the configuration utility provides access only to the most basic configuration parameters. So if you want to configure advanced features, you have to use commands. In fact, some network features don't have a graphical configuration utility, so you have no choice but to use commands.

Even when GNOME-based alternatives are available, you'll often resort to using commands because, frankly, that's what Linux was built to do. Unlike Windows, Linux relies on commands as its primary means of getting things done. So if you're going to work with Linux, knowing the basic commands presented in this chapter is a must.

Command Shell Basics

A *shell* is a program that accepts commands from a command prompt and executes them. The shell displays a prompt to let you know it's waiting for a command. When you type the command and press the Enter key, the system reads your command, interprets it, executes it, displays the results, and then displays the prompt again so that you can enter another command.

Getting to a shell

You can work with Linux commands directly from one of the six virtual consoles. If you like the responsiveness of text mode, virtual consoles are for you. To switch to a virtual console, press Ctrl+Alt+F*x*. For example, press Ctrl+Alt+F1 to switch to virtual console 1. After you're in a virtual console, you have to answer the logon prompt with a valid username and password. To return to GNOME, press Ctrl+Alt+F7.

The alternative is to work in a terminal window within the GNOME environment. If you have an older computer, you may find that the terminal window is a little unresponsive. If your computer is relatively new, however, the terminal window will be just as responsive as the text-mode virtual console. Plus, you'll have the benefit of a scroll bar that lets you scroll to see text that otherwise would have flown off the screen.

To open a terminal window, choose Main Menu⇨System Tools⇨Terminal. This opens a command shell in a window right on the GNOME desktop, as shown in Figure 6-1. Because this shell runs within the user account GNOME is logged in as, you don't have to log on. You can just start typing commands. When you're done, type **Exit** to close the window.

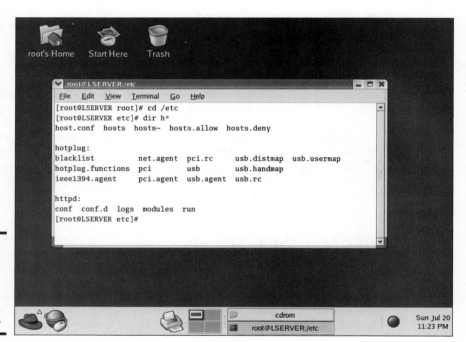

Figure 6-1:
Using a
Terminal
window
to enter
commands.

For normal Linux users, the command shell prompt character is a dollar sign ($). If you see a hash mark (#) as the prompt character, it means you're logged on as root. Whenever you see a hash prompt, you should be extra careful about what you do, because you can easily get yourself into trouble by deleting important files or otherwise corrupting the system.

Editing commands

Most of the time, you'll just type commands using the keyboard. If you make a mistake, you'll just retype the command again, being careful not to repeat the mistake. However, Linux shells have several built-in editing features that can simplify the task of correcting a mistaken command or entering a sequence of similar commands:

✦ If you want to repeat a command that you've used recently, press the Up Arrow key. This recalls your most recently executed commands. You can press Enter to execute a command as is, or you can edit the command before you execute it.

✦ The shell has a handy auto-complete feature that can finish partially spelled directory, file, or command names. Just type part of the name and then press the Tab key. If you've typed enough for the shell to figure out what you mean, the shell finishes the name for you. Otherwise, it just beeps, in which case you can type a few more letters and try again. In some cases, the shell displays a list of items that match what you've typed so far to help you know what to type next.

Wildcards

Wildcards are one of the most powerful features of command shells. With wildcards, you can process all the files that match a particular naming pattern with a single command. For example, suppose that you have a folder with 500 files in it, and you want to delete all the files that contain the letters Y2K and end with .doc, which happens to be 50 files. If you try to do this in GNOME, you'll spend ten minutes picking these files out from the list. From a shell, you can delete them all with the single command rm *Y2K*.doc.

You can use two basic wildcard characters. An asterisk (*) stands for any number of characters, including zero, while an exclamation mark (!) stands for just one character. Thus, !Text.doc matches files with names like aText.doc, xText.doc, and 4Text.doc, but not abcText.doc or just Text.doc. However, *Text.doc would match any of the names I mentioned.

You can also use brackets to indicate a range of characters to choose from. For example, report[123] matches the files report1, report2, or report3. You can also specify report[1-5] to match report1, report2, report3, report4, or report5. The wildcard r[aeiou]port matches files named raport, report, riport, roport, or ruport. As you can see, the possibilities are almost endless.

Redirection and piping

Redirection and piping are related techniques. *Redirection* lets you specify an alternate destination for output that will be displayed by a command or an alternate source for input that should be fed into a command. For example, you can save the results of an `ifconfig` command to `/home/doug/myconfig` like this:

```
$ ifconfig > /home/doug/myconfig
```

Here, the greater-than (>) sign is used to redirect the command's console output.

If a command accepts input from the keyboard, you can use input redirection to specify a file that contains the input that you want to feed to the command. For example, you can create a text file named `lookup.commands` with subcommands for a command such as `nslookup`. Then, you can feed those scripted subcommands to the `nslookup` command, like this:

```
$ nslookup < /home/doug/lookup.commands
```

Piping is a similar technique. It takes the console output from one command and feeds it into the next command as input. One of the most common uses of piping is to send the output of a command that displays a lot of information to the More program, which displays the output one page at a time. For example:

```
$ ifconfig | more
```

The vertical bar (|) is often called the *pipe character* because it's the symbol used to indicate piping.

Environment variables

The shell makes several *environment variables* available to commands. You can use an environment variable anywhere in a command by typing a dollar sign ($) followed by the environment variable name. For example:

```
$ echo This is $HOSTNAME running on an $HOSTTYPE
```

displays a line such as:

```
This is LSERVER running on an i386
```

Table 6-1 lists some of the more useful environment variables that are available to you and your commands.

Table 6-1	Environment Variables
Variable	*Description*
HOME	The current user's home directory.
HOSTNAME	The computer's hostname.

Variable	Description
HOSTTYPE	The host computer type.
OSTYPE	The operating system.
PATH	The search order for executable programs.
PROMPT_COMMAND	The command used to generate the prompt.
PWD	The present working directory.
SHELL	The shell being used.
USERNAME	The current username.

Shell scripts

A *shell script* is simply a text file that contains one or more commands. Shell scripts are similar to MS-DOS/Windows batch files, but can be much more complex. The simplest shell scripts are just lists of commands, but advanced shell scripts can include complicated scripting statements that border on a full-featured programming language.

You can create shell scripts by using any text editor. The easiest text editor to use is gedit, which you can access from the GNOME desktop by choosing Main Menu⇨Accessories⇨Text Editor. If you want your friends to think you're a Linux guru, however, take a few moments to learn how to use vi, a powerful text mode editor. To create or edit a file in vi, type the command vi followed by a filename. Then, type away. To use a vi command, press the Escape key and then type one of the commands listed in Table 6-2.

Table 6-2	Common vi Commands
Command	**Explanation**
i	Enters insert mode so that you can enter text at the cursor location. Move the cursor to the point where you want to enter the text first. When you're finished inserting text, press Esc to return to command mode.
:w	Saves the file (*w* stands for *write*).
:q	Quit.
:wq	Write and then quit.
:q!	Quit without saving.
/*string*	Search forward for *string*.
?*string*	Search backward for *string*.
n	Repeat the last search.
u	Undo the previous command.

After you've created a shell script, you have to grant yourself execute permission to run the script. To do that, use a command similar to this:

```
$ chmod 755 myscript
```

To run a shell script, you use the `sh` command and provide the name of the script file, like this:

```
$ sh myscript
```

Directory and File Handling Commands

Because much of Linux administration involves working with configuration files, you frequently need to use the basic directory and file handling commands presented in this section.

The pwd command

This command displays the current directory, which is called the *present working directory* — hence the command name `pwd`. Here's the syntax:

```
pwd
```

Enter this command, and you'll get output similar to the following:

```
$ pwd
/home/doug
```

The cd command

The `cd` command changes the current working directory. The syntax is as follows:

```
cd directory
```

You may want to follow the `cd` command up with a `pwd` command to make sure that you changed to the right directory. For example:

```
$ cd /etc/mail
$ pwd
/etc/mail
```

To change to a subdirectory of the current directory, omit the leading slash from the directory name. For example:

```
$ pwd
/home
```

```
$ cd doug
$ pwd
/home/doug
```

You can also use the double-dot (..) to represent the parent of the current directory. Thus, to move up one level, use the command cd ..:

```
$ pwd
/home/doug
$ cd ..
$ pwd
/home
```

The mkdir command

To create a new directory, you use the mkdir command. It has the following syntax:

```
mkdir directory
```

Here's an example that creates a subdirectory named images in the current directory:

```
$ mkdir images
```

This example creates a directory named /home/doug/images:

```
$ mkdir /home/doug/images
```

The rmdir command

The rmdir command removes a directory. It has the following syntax:

```
rmdir directory
```

Here's an example:

```
$ rmdir /home/doug/images
```

Here, the /home/doug/images directory is deleted. Note that the directory must be empty to be removed, so you have to first delete any files in the directory.

The ls command

The ls command lists the contents of the current directory. Here's the syntax:

```
ls [options] directory
```

The following paragraphs describe the more important options for the ls command:

✦ **-a:** Lists all the files in the directory, including files that start with a period.

✦ **-c:** Sorts entries by the time the files were last modified.

✦ **-d:** Lists only directory names.

✦ **-l:** Displays in long format.

✦ **-r:** Displays files in reverse order.

✦ **-R:** Lists the contents of all subdirectories, and subdirectories of subdirectories, and subdirectories of subdirectories of subdirectories . . . in other words, lists subdirectories recursively.

✦ **-s:** Displays file sizes.

✦ **-S:** Sorts files by size.

✦ **-t:** Sorts files by timestamp.

✦ **-u:** Sorts files by the time the files were last accessed.

✦ **-X:** Sorts files by their extensions.

Without arguments, the ls command lists all the files in the current directory, like this:

```
$ pwd
/etc/mail
$ ls
access          helpfile         Makefile       submit.cf       virtusertable
access.db       local-host-names sendmail.cf    submit.cf.bak   virtusertable.db
domaintable     mailertable      sendmail.mc    submit.mc
domaintable.db  mailertable.db   statistics     trusted-users
```

You can limit the display to certain files by typing a filename, which can include wildcards. For example:

```
$ ls a*
access          access.db
```

You can also specify the directory that you want to display, like this:

```
$ ls /etc/httpd
conf  conf.d  logs  modules  run
```

To display detailed information about the files in the directory, use the `-1` switch, as in this example:

```
$ ls /etc/mail/s* -l
-rw-r--r--   1 root     root      57427 Jul 19 16:35 sendmail.cf
-rw-r--r--   1 root     root       5798 Feb 24 16:15 sendmail.mc
-rw-------   1 root     root        628 Jul 24 17:21 statistics
-rw-r--r--   1 root     root      39028 Jul 19 17:28 submit.cf
-r--r--r--   1 root     root      39077 Feb 24 16:15 submit.cf.bak
-rw-r--r--   1 root     root        953 Feb 24 16:15 submit.mc
```

The cp command

The `cp` command copies files. Here's the basic syntax:

```
cp [options] source-file destination-file
```

The following paragraphs describe the more important options for the `ls` command:

✦ **-a:** The same as `-dpR`.

✦ **-b:** Makes backup copies of existing files before they are overwritten. Sounds like a good plan to me.

✦ **-d:** Copies links rather than the files the links point to.

✦ **-f:** Removes files that will be overwritten.

✦ **-i:** Interactively prompts for each file to be overwritten.

✦ **-l:** Creates links to files rather than actually copying file contents.

✦ **-p:** Preserves ownership and permissions.

✦ **-R:** Copies the contents of subdirectories recursively.

✦ **-s:** Creates symbolic links to files rather than actually copying file contents.

✦ **-u:** Replaces destination files only if the source file is newer.

To make a copy of a file within the same directory, use `cp` like this:

```
$ cp sendmail.cf sendmail.cf.backup
```

If you want to copy a file to another directory without changing the filename, use `cp` like this:

```
$ cp sendmail.cf /home/doug
```

You can use wildcards to copy multiple files:

```
$ cp send* /home/doug
```

To include files in subdirectories of the source file, use the -R switch, like this:

```
$ cp -R /etc/*.cf /home/doug
```

In this example, all files in the /etc directory or any of its subdirectories that end with .cf are copied to /home/doug.

The rm command

The rm command deletes files. The syntax is as follows:

```
rm [options] file
```

The options are described in the following paragraphs:

- ✦ **-f:** Removes files that will be overwritten.
- ✦ **-i:** Interactively prompts for each file to be overwritten.
- ✦ **-R:** Copies the contents of subdirectories recursively.

To delete a single file, use it like this:

```
$ rm any.old.file
```

To delete multiple files, use a wildcard:

```
$ rm any.*
```

To delete an entire directory, use the -r switch:

```
$ rm -r /doug/old.files
```

The mv command

The mv command moves files or renames them. In Linux, moving and renaming a file is essentially the same thing. Moving a file changes the file's directory location, but leaves its name the same. Renaming a file leaves the file in the same directory, but changes the file's name.

The syntax of the mv command is

```
mvp [options] source-file destination
```

The following paragraphs describe the options:

✦ **-b:** Makes backup copies of existing files before they are overwritten. Sounds like a good plan to me.

✦ **-f:** Removes files that will be overwritten.

✦ **-i:** Interactively prompts for each file to be overwritten.

✦ **-u:** Replaces destination files only if the source file is newer.

To move a file to another directory, provide a filename for the first argument and a directory for the second, like this:

```
$ mv monthly.report /home/Debbie/
```

To rename a file, provide filenames for both arguments:

```
$ mv monthly.report august.monthly.report
```

The touch command

The touch command is one of the more interesting Linux file management commands. Here's the syntax:

```
touch [options] file
```

Here are some of the options that you can use:

✦ **-a:** Changes the access time only.

✦ **-c:** Doesn't create files that don't exist.

✦ **-m:** Changes the modification time only.

The basic form of the touch command looks like this:

```
$ touch monthly.report
```

If you use touch on an existing file, the touch command changes the modification date of the file. If you use it on a command that doesn't exist, the touch command creates a new, empty file.

The cat command

The cat command displays the contents of a file. It has the following syntax:

```
cat [options] [filename...]
```

Notice that the filename is optional. If you omit the filename, the cat command obtains its input from the console, which you can redirect if you want.

Also notice that you can specify more than one filename. If you do, the files are combined to create a single output stream.

Here are some of the options you can use:

+ **-A:** Displays new line characters as $, tab characters as ^I, and control characters with a caret (^).

+ **-b:** Numbers all nonblank lines as they are displayed.

+ **-e:** Displays new line characters as $ and control characters with a caret (^).

+ **-E:** Displays new line characters as $.

+ **-n:** Numbers lines as they are displayed.

+ **-s:** Squeezes multiple spaces down to a single space.

+ **-t:** Displays tab characters as ^I and control characters with a caret (^).

+ **-T:** Displays tab characters as ^I.

+ **-v:** Shows nonprinting control characters with a caret (^).

Here's a basic example:

```
$ cat /etc/hosts
# Do not remove the following line, or various programs
# that require network functionality will fail.
127.0.0.1        LSERVER localhost.localdomain   localhost
$
```

If you don't provide any filename arguments, the `cat` command copies text from the keyboard and displays it on the console. You can use the `cat` command along with output redirection to quickly create a short text file, like this:

```
$ cat >mytext
This is line one.
This is line two.
This is line three.
<ctrl+D>
```

For the last line, press Ctrl+D. This signals the end of the input to the `cat` command.

Commands for Working with Packages and Services

As a Linux administrator, you'll frequently need to start and stop services and check the status of installed packages or install new packages. The following sections describe the Linux commands that help you to perform these tasks.

The service command

You use the `service` command to check the status of services and to start, stop, or restart services. You need to restart a service whenever you make a configuration change in order for your changes to take effect. Here's the basic syntax:

```
service [service] [ start | stop | restart ]
```

The following paragraphs describe some typical uses of the service command:

✦ To check the status of the `httpd` service (Apache), use this command:

```
$ service httpd status
```

✦ To stop the `httpd` service:

```
$ service httpd stop
```

✦ To start the `httpd` service:

```
$ service httpd start
```

✦ To restart the `httpd` service:

```
$ service httpd restart
```

The only trick to using the `service` command is that you have to know the name of the service. If you're not sure of the name, you can run the `service` command to display the status of all services, like this:

```
$ service --status-all
```

It will take a few moments to list all the services, but after the command is done, you can scroll through the list to find the service that you're looking for.

Table 6-3 lists some of the more common services.

Table 6-3	Common Linux Services
Service	*Description*
atd	Runs commands scheduled by the at command.
autof	Automatically mounts file systems.
crond	Runs programs at specified times.
dhcpd	The DHCP server.
finger	The Internet finger service.
httpd	The Apache Web server.

(continued)

Table 6-3 *(continued)*

Service	Description
imap	The IMAP mail protocol.
imaps	Secure IMAP service (SSL).
ipop3	The POP3 mail protocol.
iptables	Automatic packet filtering for firewalls.
isdn	ISDN services.
named	The Bind DNS server.
netf	The network file system.
network	Activates and deactivates all network interfaces.
nfs	Native UNIX/Linux network file sharing.
pop3s	Secure POP3 service (SSL).
sendmail	The Sendmail service.
smb	The Samba file and printer sharing service.
snmpd	Simple Network Management Protocol.
telnet	The Telnet server.

The rpm command

Rpm is the Red Hat Package Manager, a tool that simplifies the task of managing packages on your Linux system. Although rpm was originally developed for Red Hat Linux, it is now found on many Linux distributions.

Here's the basic syntax for querying the status of a package:

```
rpm -q [options] package
```

To install, upgrade, or remove a package, the basic syntax is more like this:

```
rpm [ -i | -u | -e ] [options] package-file
```

You can use quite a few options with the rpm command, but the most common are

✦ **-v:** Displays verbose output. You may as well know what rpm is doing while it chugs along.

✦ **-h:** Displays hash marks (#) periodically to reassure you that the program hasn't died.

You can use `rpm` to determine the status of installed packages on your system by using the `-q` switch. For example, to find out what version of Sendmail is installed, use this command:

```
$ rpm -q send*
Sendmail-8.12.8-4
```

Notice that you can use a wildcard with the package name. If you don't have a package whose name matches the package name you supply, you get the message `package not installed`.

To install a package, you use the `-i` switch and specify a wildcard filename that indicates the location of the package file. It's also a good idea to use the v and h switches. For example, to install Sendmail from a mounted CD-ROM drive, you'd use this command:

```
$ rpm -ivh /mnt/cdrom/RedHat/RPMS/sendmail*
```

If you want to update to a newer version of a package, you can use the `-u` switch instead of the `-i` switch:

```
$ rpm -uvh /mnt/cdrom/RedHat/RPMS/sendmail*
```

Finally, you can remove a package by using the `-e` switch:

```
$ rpm -e send*
```

Note that to use the `rpm` command, you should log in as root.

Commands for Administering Users

The following sections describe the Linux commands that you can use to create and manage user accounts from a command shell.

You should log on as root to perform these tasks.

The useradd command

The `useradd` command creates a user account. Here's the basic syntax for adding a new user:

```
useradd [options] user-name
```

You can also use this command to change the default options for new users. In that case, the syntax is more like this:

```
useradd -D [options]
```

The options are as follows:

- ✦ **c** *comment:* This should be the user's full name.
- ✦ **-d** *home-dir:* The home directory of the new user.
- ✦ **-e** *date:* The expiration date for the user.
- ✦ **-f** *time:* The number of days between logons before the user is considered expired.
- ✦ **-g** *group:* The initial logon group for the user.
- ✦ **-G** *groups:* Additional groups the user should belong to.
- ✦ **-m:** Creates the new user's home directory if it doesn't exist already.
- ✦ **-s** *shell-path:* Specifies the user's logon shell.

The following option is valid only with -D:

- ✦ **-b** *base-dir:* Provides the default base directory if a home directory is not specified.

Its most basic form, the useradd command creates a user with default option settings:

```
$ useradd theodore
```

This command creates a user named *theodore*.

Here's a command that specifies the user's full name in the comment option:

```
$ useradd -c 'Theodore Cleaver' theodore
```

The following command creates a temporary account named *ghost* that expires on Halloween of 2003:

```
$ useradd -e 2003-10-31 ghost
```

If you want to see what the default values are for account options, use the -D option without any other parameters:

```
$ useradd -D
GROUP=100
HOME=/home
INACTIVE=-1
EXPIRE=
SHELL=/bin/bash
SKEL=/etc/skel
```

The usermod command

The `usermod` command modifies an existing user. It has the following syntax:

```
usermod [options] user-name
```

The options are as follows:

- ✦ **c comment:** The user's full name.
- ✦ **-d home-dir:** The home directory of the new user.
- ✦ **-e date:** The expiration date for a logon.
- ✦ **-f time:** The number of days between logons before the user is considered expired.
- ✦ **-g group:** The initial logon group for the user.
- ✦ **-G groups:** Additional groups the user should belong to.
- ✦ **-m:** Creates the new user's home directory if it doesn't exist already.
- ✦ **-s shell-path:** Specifies the user's logon shell.
- ✦ **-l:** Locks an account.
- ✦ **-u:** Unlocks an account.

Here's an example that changes a user's full name:

```
$ usermod -c 'The Beave' theodore
```

The userdel command

The `userdel` command deletes a user. It has a simple syntax:

```
userdel [-r] user-name
```

If you specify `-r`, the user's home directory is deleted along with the account.

The chage command

The `chage` command modifies date policies for a user's passwords. It has the following syntax:

```
chage [options] user-name
```

The following paragraphs describe the options you can use:

✦ **-m** *days:* Specifies the minimum number of days allowed between password changes.

✦ **-M** *days:* Specifies the maximum number of days allowed between password changes.

✦ **-d** *date:* The date of the last password change.

✦ **-E** *date:* The date on which the account will expire.

✦ **-W** *days:* The number of days prior to the password expiring that the user will be warned the password is about to expire.

✦ **-I** *days:* The number of days of inactivity after the password has expired that the account is locked out. Specify 0 to disable this feature.

Here's an example that sets an account to expire on Halloween 2003:

```
$ chage -E 2003-10-31 ghost
```

If you specify a username but no other options, you are prompted to enter each option. This is a lot easier than trying to remember all the switches!

The passwd command

This command changes the password for a user account. Its syntax is

```
passwd [user]
```

If you don't supply a user, the password for the current user is changed.

The `passwd` prompts you to enter the new password twice in order to prevent the possibility of mistyping the password.

The newusers command

The `newusers` command provides an easy way to create a group of new user accounts. It reads a text file that contains one line for each new user, listing the user's name and password.

Here's the syntax of the `newusers` command:

```
newusers [filename]
```

If you omit the filename, `newusers` accepts input from the console.

Suppose that you have a file named /root/island.users that contains these lines:

```
gilligan     ml9jiedr
skipper      1hiecr8u
professor    dr0uxiaf
maryann      choe7rlu
ginger       jiuqled5
mrhowell     jlemoafl
lovie        zo2priak
```

You can then create these seven stranded user accounts by issuing this command:

```
$ newusers /root/island.users
```

Because the newusers file contains unencrypted passwords, you shouldn't leave it lying around. Require these new users to change their passwords immediately and delete the file you used to create the users.

The groupadd command

The groupadd command creates a new group. It has the following syntax:

```
groupadd [options] group
```

Although you have several possible options to use, the only one you're likely to need is -r, which creates a system group that has special privileges.

Here's an example that creates a group named castaways:

```
$ groupadd castaways
```

That's all you have to do to create a new group. To administer the group, you use the gpasswd command.

The groupdel command

The groupdel command deletes a group. It has the following syntax:

```
groupdel group
```

Here's an example that deletes a group named castaways:

```
$ groupdel castaways
```

Poof! The group is gone.

The gpasswd command

You use the gpasswd command to administer a group. This command has several different syntax options.

To change the group password:

```
gpasswd [ -r | -R ] group
```

To add a user:

```
gpasswd -a user group
```

To remove a user:

```
gpasswd -d user group
```

To create group administrators and/or members:

```
gpasswd [-A administrators...] [-M members... ] group
```

The options are as follows:

- **-r:** Removes the password from the group.
- **-R:** Disables access to the group via the newgrp command.
- **-a:** Adds the specified user to the group.
- **-d:** Deletes the specified user from the group.
- **-A:** Specifies one or more group administrators. Use commas with no intervening spaces to separate the administrators from each other. Each administrator must be an existing user.
- **-M:** Specifies one or more group members. Use commas with no intervening spaces to separate the members from each other. Each member must be an existing user.

The following example adds seven group members and one administrator to a group called castaways.

```
$ gpasswd -A skipper -M skipper,gilligan,professor,maryann,
ginger,mrhowell,lovie castaways
```

If the rest of the group finally decided to throw Gilligan off the island, they can remove him from the group with this command:

```
$ gpasswd -d gilligan castaways
```

Commands for Managing Ownership and Permissions

This section presents the details of the chown and chmod commands, which are the essential tools for assigning file system rights in the Linux environment.

You can view the ownership and permissions for a file using the ls command with the -l option.

The chown command

The chown command changes the owner of a file. Normally, the user who creates a file is the owner of the file. However, the owner can transfer the file to someone else via this command. The basic syntax of this command is

```
chown user file
```

For example, to change the owner of a file named rescue.plans to user professor, use this command:

```
$ chown professor rescue.plans
```

To change ownership of all the files in the directory named /home/island to professor, use this command:

```
$ chown professor /home/island
```

Issuing the following command would be a really bad idea:

```
$ chown gilligan rescue.plans
```

The chgrp command

Every file not only has an individual owner but also a group owner. You can change the group ownership using the chgrp command, which has the following basic syntax:

```
chgrp group file
```

For example, to grant the castaways group ownership of the file rescue.plans, use this command:

```
$ chgrp castaways rescue.plans
```

To change group ownership of all the files in the directory named /home/island to castaways, use this command:

```
$ chgrp castaways /home/island
```

The chmod command

The `chmod` command lets you change the permissions for a Linux file. Before explaining the syntax of the `chmod` command, you need to look at the cryptic way Linux reports file permissions. Linux grants three different types of permissions — read, write, and execute — for three different scopes: owner, group, and everyone. That's a total of nine permissions.

When you use the `ls` command with the `-l` option, the permissions are shown as a ten-character string that begins with a hyphen if the entry is for a file or a *d* if the entry is for a directory. Then, the next nine letters are the nine permissions, in this order:

+ Read, write, execute for the owner

+ Read, write, execute for the group

+ Read, write, execute for everyone

The letters *r, w,* or *x* appear if the permission has been granted. If the permission is denied, a hyphen appears.

For example, suppose the `ls  -l` command lists these permissions:

```
-rw-r--r--
```

You interpret this permission string like this:

+ The first hyphen indicates that this is a file, not a directory.

+ The next three positions are `rw-`. Therefore, the owner has read and write permissions on this file, but not execute permissions.

+ The next three positions are `r--`. That means the group owner has read permissions but not write or execute permission.

+ The last three positions are also `r--`. That means that everyone else has read permission but not write or execute permission.

The full syntax of the `chmod` command is pretty complex. However, you can do most of what you need to do with this form:

```
chmod specification file
```

Here, *specification* is in the form `u=rwx`, `g=rwx`, or `o=rwx` to set the permissions for the user (owner), group, and others (everyone). You don't have to specify *r, w,* and *x;* you just list the permissions that you want to grant. For example, to grant read and write permission for the user to a file named `rescue.plans`, use this command:

```
$ chmod u=rw rescue.plans
```

You can also combine specifications, like this:

```
$ chmod u=rw,g=rw,o=r rescue.plans
```

To revoke all rights for the user, group, or others, don't type anything after the equal sign. For example, this command revokes all rights for others:

```
$ chmod o= rescue.plans
```

Networking Commands

The following sections present Linux commands that are used to display information about the network or configure its settings.

You can find more detail about some of these commands in Book V, Chapter 5.

The hostname command

The `hostname` command simply displays the computer's host name. It has the following syntax:

```
hostname [name]
```

If you use this command without any parameters, the computer's host name is displayed. If you specify a name, the computer's host name is changed to the name you specify.

The ifconfig command

`Ifconfig` displays and sets configuration options for network interfaces. Although you can configure an Ethernet adapter using this command, you'll rarely have to. Linux does a pretty good job of automatically configuring network adapters, and the GNOME-based Network Configuration tool supplied with the Red Hat distribution should be able to handle most network configuration chores. So you'll use `ifconfig` mostly to display network configuration settings.

The basic syntax for `ifconfig` is

```
ifconfig interface [address] [netmask mask]
        [broadcast broadcast]
```

The following paragraphs describe the options that you can use on the ifconfig command:

✦ *Interface:* The symbolic name for your network adapter. It's typically eth0 for the first Ethernet adapter or eth1 for the second adapter.

✦ *Address:* The IP address you want to assign to the interface, such as 192.168.1.100.

✦ **netmask:** The subnet mask to use, such as 255.255.255.0.

✦ **broadcast:** The broadcast, which should be the highest address on the subnet. For example: 192.168.1.255.

If you enter ifconfig without any parameters, the ifconfig command displays the current status of your network adapters, like this:

```
eth0      Link encap:Ethernet  HWaddr 00:20:78:16:E0:6A
          UP BROADCAST RUNNING MULTICAST  MTU:1500  Metric:1
          RX packets:0 errors:0 dropped:0 overruns:0 frame:0
          TX packets:11 errors:0 dropped:0 overruns:0 carrier:0
          collisions:0 txqueuelen:100
          RX bytes:0 (0.0 b)  TX bytes:2916 (2.8 Kb)
          Interrupt:11 Base address:0xd000

eth1      Link encap:Ethernet  HWaddr 00:40:05:80:51:F3
          inet addr:192.168.3.100  Bcast:192.168.3.255  Mask:255.255.255.0
          UP BROADCAST RUNNING MULTICAST  MTU:1500  Metric:1
          RX packets:2358 errors:0 dropped:0 overruns:0 frame:0
          TX packets:1921 errors:0 dropped:0 overruns:0 carrier:0
          collisions:0 txqueuelen:100
          RX bytes:265194 (258.9 Kb)  TX bytes:424467 (414.5 Kb)
          Interrupt:3 Base address:0xc000

lo        Link encap:Local Loopback
          inet addr:127.0.0.1  Mask:255.0.0.0
          UP LOOPBACK RUNNING  MTU:16436  Metric:1
          RX packets:93707 errors:0 dropped:0 overruns:0 frame:0
          TX packets:93707 errors:0 dropped:0 overruns:0 carrier:0
          collisions:0 txqueuelen:0
          RX bytes:6393713 (6.0 Mb)  TX bytes:6393713 (6.0 Mb)
```

To change the IP address of an adapter, use ifconfig like this:

```
$ ifconfig eth0 192.168.1.200
```

The netstat command

The netstat command lets you monitor just about every aspect of a Linux server's network functions. This command can generate page after page of interesting information — if you know what it all means.

The two most common reasons to use netstat are to display the routing table and to display open TCP/IP connections. The syntax for displaying the routing table is

```
netstat -r
```

This results in a display similar to this:

```
Kernel IP routing table
Destination    Gateway        Genmask         Flags  MSS Window  irtt Iface
192.168.1.0    *              255.255.255.0   U        0 0          0 eth1
192.168.1.0    *              255.255.255.0   U        0 0          0 eth0
127.0.0.0      *              255.0.0.0       U        0 0          0 lo
```

To display TCP/IP connections, use this syntax:

```
netstat -l
```

This results in a display similar to the following:

```
Active Internet connections (only servers)
Proto Recv-Q Send-Q Local Address          Foreign Address     State
tcp        0      0 *:1024                  *:*                 LISTEN
tcp        0      0 LSERVER:1025            *:*                 LISTEN
tcp        0      0 *:netbios-ssn           *:*                 LISTEN
tcp        0      0 *:sunrpc                *:*                 LISTEN
tcp        0      0 *:http                  *:*                 LISTEN
tcp        0      0 *:x11                   *:*                 LISTEN
tcp        0      0 *:ssh                   *:*                 LISTEN
tcp        0      0 LSERVER:ipp             *:*                 LISTEN
tcp        0      0 LSERVER:smtp            *:*                 LISTEN
tcp        0      0 *:https                 *:*                 LISTEN
udp        0      0 *:1024                  *:*
udp        0      0 LSERVER:1026            *:*
udp        0      0 192.168.1.20:netbios-ns *:*
udp        0      0 192.168.1.20:netbios-ns *:*
udp        0      0 *:netbios-ns            *:*
udp        0      0 192.168.1.2:netbios-dgm *:*
udp        0      0 192.168.1.2:netbios-dgm *:*
udp        0      0 *:netbios-dgm           *:*
udp        0      0 *:940                   *:*
udp        0      0 *:sunrpc                *:*
udp        0      0 *:631                   *:*
Active UNIX domain sockets (only servers)
Proto RefCnt Flags       Type       State      I-Node Path
unix  2      [ ACC ]     STREAM     LISTENING  2663   /dev/gpmctl
unix  2      [ ACC ]     STREAM     LISTENING  2770   /tmp/.font-unix/fs7100
unix  2      [ ACC ]     STREAM     LISTENING  3144   /tmp/.ICE-unix/1953
.
.
.
```

From this display, you can tell which Linux services are actively listening on TCP/IP ports.

The ping command

Ping is the basic troubleshooting tool for TCP/IP. You use it to determine whether or not basic TCP/IP connectivity has been established between two computers. If you're having any kind of network trouble between two computers, the first troubleshooting step is almost always to see whether the computers can ping each other.

The basic syntax of `ping` is straightforward:

```
ping [options] address
```

The options can be

✦ **-c:** The number of packets to send. If you omit this, `ping` continues to send packets until you interrupt it.

✦ **-d:** Floods the network with packets, as many as 100 per second. Use with care!

✦ **i:** Specifies how many seconds to wait between sending packets. The default is one second. If you're having intermittent connection problems, you may try letting `ping` run for a while with this option set to a higher value, such as 60 a packet every minute.

✦ **R:** Displays the route the packets take to get to the destination computer.

`Ping` will continue to ping the destination computer until you interrupt it by pressing Ctrl+Z.

You can specify the host to ping using IP address, as in this example:

```
$ ping 192.168.1.100
PING 192.168.1.100 (192.168.1.100) 56(84) bytes of data.
64 bytes from 192.168.1.100: icmp_seq=1 ttl=128 time=0.382 ms
64 bytes from 192.168.1.100: icmp_seq=2 ttl=128 time=0.345 ms
64 bytes from 192.168.1.100: icmp_seq=3 ttl=128 time=0.320 ms
64 bytes from 192.168.1.100: icmp_seq=4 ttl=128 time=0.328 ms
```

You can also ping using a DNS name, as in this example:

```
$ ping www.lowewriter.com
PING www.lowewriter.com (209.68.34.15) 56(84) bytes of data.
64 bytes from www.lowewriter.com (209.68.34.15): icmp_seq=1 ttl=47 time=88.9 ms
64 bytes from www.lowewriter.com (209.68.34.15): icmp_seq=2 ttl=47 time=87.9 ms
64 bytes from www.lowewriter.com (209.68.34.15): icmp_seq=3 ttl=47 time=88.3 ms
64 bytes from www.lowewriter.com (209.68.34.15): icmp_seq=4 ttl=47 time=87.2 ms
```

The route command

The `route` command displays or modifies the computer's routing table. To display the routing table, use `route` without any parameters. To add an entry to the routing table, use this syntax:

```
route add [ -net | -host ] address [options]
```

To delete an entry, use this syntax:

```
route del [ -net | -host ] address [options]
```

The available options are:

+ **netmask** *mask:* Specifies the subnet mask for this entry.

+ **gw** *address:* Specifies the gateway address for this entry.

+ **dev** *if:* Specifies an interface (such as eth0 or eth1) for this entry.

If you enter `route` by itself, with no parameters, you'll see the routing table, as in this example:

```
$ route
Kernel IP routing table
Destination     Gateway        Genmask         Flags Metric Ref    Use Iface
192.168.1.0     *              255.255.255.0   U     0      0        0 eth1
192.168.1.0     *              255.255.255.0   U     0      0        0 eth1
169.254.0.0     *              255.255.0.0     U     0      0        0 eth1
127.0.0.0       *              255.0.0.0       U     0      0        0 lo
default         192.168.1.1    0.0.0.0         UG    0      0        0 eth1
```

Suppose that your network has a second router that serves as a link to another private subnet, 192.168.2.0 (subnet mask 255.255.255.0). The interface on the local side of this router is at 192.168.1.200. To add a static route entry that sends packets intended for the 192.168.2.0 subnet to this router, use a command like this:

```
$ route add 192.168.2.0 netmask 255.255.255.0 gw
    192.168.1.200
```

The traceroute command

The `traceroute` command displays a list of all the routers that a packet must go through in order to get from the local computer to a destination on the Internet. Each one of these routers is called a *hop*. If you're unable to connect to another computer, you can use `Tracert` to find out exactly where the problem is occurring.

Here's the syntax:

```
traceroute [-i interface] host
```

Although several options are available for the `traceroute` command, the one you're most likely to use is `-i`, which lets you specify an interface. This is useful if your computer has more than one network adapter.

Book X

Appendixes

The 5th Wave   By Rich Tennant

Contents at a Glance

Appendix A: Directory of Useful Web Sites

Throughout this book, I mention many Web sites you can visit to glean more information about various networking topics. This appendix gathers those sites into one convenient location and adds several more that are also worth visiting from time to time. Happy surfing!

Certification

Here are the sites to check out for official certification information.

- ✦ **www.microsoft.com/traincert:** Microsoft's certification headquarters.
- ✦ **www.comptia.org:** Independent certification including A+, Network+, and Security+.
- ✦ **www.novell.com/training/certinfo:** The home page for Novell certification.
- ✦ **www.ibm.com/certify:** IBM's certification home page.
- ✦ **www.cisco.com/certification:** Cisco's certification home page.
- ✦ **www.redhat.com/training/certification:** Red Hat's Linux certification home page.

Hardware

The following Web sites are general resources for researching computer hardware:

- ✦ **reviews.cnet.com:** CNET's reviews section offers reviews on all types of computer hardware, with a special section devoted to networking.
- ✦ **www.hardware.central:** Another good source for general computer hardware information, reviews, and advice.
- ✦ **www.tomshardware.com:** Tom's Hardware Guide is the place to go if you want detailed information about the latest in computer components.

The following manufacturers offer high-end networking products, including servers, routers, switches, and so on.

✦ **www.networking.ibm.com:** IBM's networking portal. A must-see.

✦ **servers.hp.com:** The home page for Hewlett Packard's server products.

✦ **www.dell.com/us/en/biz/products/line_servers.htm:** The home page for Dell's servers. (If you don't want to mess with such a long address, just go to `www.dell.com` and drill down to the servers page.)

✦ **www.gateway.com/work/servers.shtml:** Gateway's server home page.

✦ **www.sun.com/servers:** The home page for Sun servers.

✦ **www.tandem.com:** Tandem, a manufacturer of nonstop fault-tolerant servers, is now owned by Hewlett-Packard.

The best way to set up a multiboot system is to install each operating system into its own partition and use special partitioning software to manage the partitions. For example, programs such as Partition Magic (`www.powerquest.com`) or Paragon Partition Manager (`www.partition-manager.com`) are ideal for managing operating systems in multiple partitions.

Home Networking

The following Web sites have general information about home networking:

✦ **www.homenethelp.com:** An excellent Web site devoted to helping people get their home networks up and running, loaded with step-by-step procedures and flowcharts.

✦ **www.practicallynetworked.com:** This site is a great source of information for home networking, with general networking information, technology backgrounders, product reviews, troubleshooting advice, and more.

✦ **www.hometoys.com:** Information on all sorts of gadgets for the home, including networks.

✦ **www.microsoft.com/homenet:** A Microsoft Web site devoted to home and small office networking with Windows XP.

✦ **www.homenetnews.com:** Home Networking News, a newsletter devoted to home network.

✦ **www.homepna.org:** The home page of the Home Phone Networking Alliance.

◆ **www.homeplug.org:** The home page of the PowerLine Alliance, which promotes powerline networking.

◆ **www.linksys.com:** One of the most popular sources for networking devices for homes and small offices, including 10/100BaseT, wireless, and even phone and powerline devices.

◆ **www.netgear.com:** Makes home and small office networking devices, including 10/100BaseT adapters and switches, wireless devices, and phone-line systems.

Linux Sites

The following Web sites have general information about Linux:

◆ **www.linux.org:** One of the best overall Web sites for everything Linux. It's a central source of Linux information and news and many links to Linux distributions and downloadable applications.

◆ **www.justlinux.com:** This site includes a popular discussion forum where you can ask questions and, with luck, get answers.

Here are the home pages for some of the most popular distributions:

◆ **www.redhat.com:** The Web site of the most popular Linux distribution.

◆ **www.suse.com:** The SuSe distribution.

◆ **www.caldera.com:** The Caldera distribution from SCO.

◆ **www.linux-mandrake.com:** The Mandrake distribution.

◆ **www.slackware.com:** Slackware, one of the oldest Linux distributions.

Here are the home pages for some popular Linux networking software:

◆ **www.isc.org/products/BIND/:** The official page for BIND, the most popular DNS nameserver on the Internet.

◆ **www.sendmail.org:** Official site for Sendmail, the SMTP mail exchange server.

◆ **www.apache.org:** Official site for the Apache httpd server.

◆ **www.samba.org:** Official site for the Samba file and print server.

Magazines

Here are some links to various magazines on networking topics

+ **www.informationweek.com:** *InformationWeek*
+ **www.infoworld.com:** *InfoWorld*
+ **www.networkcomputing.com:** *Network Computing*
+ **www.networkmagazine.com:** *Network Magazine*
+ **www.winntmag.com:** *Windows & .NET Magazine*
+ **www.2600.com:** *2600 Magazine*

Microsoft

Microsoft's Web site is vast. Here are some links to a few useful areas within this huge Web site:

+ **www.microsoft.com/windows:** The home page for the Windows family of products.
+ **www.microsoft.com/windowsserver2003:** The home page for Windows Server 2003.
+ **www.microsoft.com/windows2000:** The home page for Windows 2000.
+ **www.microsoft.com/windowsserversystem:** The home page for Micrsoft server products.
+ **www.microsoft.com/technet:** TechNet, a great source for technical information on Microsoft technologies.
+ **support.microsoft.com:** Microsoft's general support site.

Network Standards Organizations

The following Web sites are useful when you're researching network standards.

+ **www.ansi.org:** The American National Standards Institute (ANSI), the official standards organization in the United States.
+ **www.ieee.org:** The Institute of Electrical and Electronic Engineers (IEEE), an international organization that publishes several key networking standards, including the official Ethernet standards (known as IEEE 802.3).
+ **www.iso.org:** The International Organization for Standardization (ISO), a federation of more than 100 standards organizations from throughout the world.

✦ **www.isoc.org:** The Internet Society, an international organization for global coordination and cooperation on the Internet.

✦ **www.ietf.org:** The Internet Engineering Task Force (IETF), responsible for the protocols that drive the Internet.

✦ **www.iana.org:** The Internet Assigned Numbers Authority, which has responsibility for the IP address space.

✦ **www.w3c.org:** The World Wide Web Consortium (W3C), an international organization that handles the development of standards for the World Wide Web.

✦ **www.rfc-editor.org:** This is the official repository of RFCs. It includes a search facility that lets you look up RFCs by name or keyword.

**Book X
Appendix A**

**Directory of Useful
Websites**

Reference Sites

A number of general-purpose and computer-specific reference sites provide encyclopedia-style articles or simple definitions of computer and networking terms. If you're not sure what some new technology is, start at one of these sites.

✦ **www.webopedia.com:** The Webopedia is a great online dictionary of computer and Internet terms. Not sure what direct sequence spread spectrum means? Look it up at the Webopedia!

✦ **www.whatis.com:** Another great dictionary of computer and networking terms.

✦ **www.howstuffworks.com:** This site has general information about many different types of technology: computers, automobiles, electronics, science, and more. The computer section provides good low-level introductions to various computer topics, including computer hardware, the Internet, and security.

Search Sites

Search engines are often the first place you turn to when you're trying to solve a network problem and you need information fast.

✦ **www.google.com:** Google is the most popular search site on the Internet today with a huge database of Web sites and newsgroup articles that's constantly updated. Google has powerful keyword search features that let you refine your search as you go.

✦ **www.altavista.com:** AltaVista, one of the top search sites on the Internet, with powerful advanced keyword features. AltaVista lets you search Web pages and newgroups.

✦ **www.yahoo.com:** Yahoo!, one of the original Web site catalogs, this site is still the best place to go if you want to browse through categories rather than search for keywords.

✦ **www.dogpile.com:** Dogpile is a meta-search tool that searches multiple search engines at the same time.

✦ **www.deja.com:** Deja News is the best place to go if you want to search Internet newsgroups.

TCP/IP and the Internet

The following sites have interesting information about the Internet:

✦ **www.internic.net:** The InterNIC Web site is a central point of information for domain registration. Check here for a list of accredited domain registrars.

✦ **www.networksolutions.com:** The home of Network Solutions, the most popular site for registering domain names.

✦ **www.register.com:** Register.com, another domain registration site.

✦ **www.isc.org:** The Internet Software Consortium, the folks who do the twice-a-year domain survey to try to estimate how big the Internet really is.

✦ **www.dslreports.com:** This site asks for your phone number and address to estimate your distance from the central office and displays a list of ISP's that can provide service for your location. It also includes loads of other information about DSL and other broadband connections.

For DNS information, try **www.dnsreport.com,** which lets you perform a variety of DNS lookups to make sure that your DNS zones are set up right.

For email blacklist issues, try **relays.osirusoft.com,** a comprehensive Web site for solving blacklist problems.

You can find information about commercial online services at:

✦ **www.aol.com:** America Online.

✦ **www.compuserve.com:** CompuServe.

✦ **www.msn.com:** The Microsoft Network.

You can find information about Web browsers at:

✦ **www.microsoft.com/ie:** The official home page for Internet Explorer.

✦ **www.netscape.com:** Netscape, the makers of Navigator.

✦ **www.mozilla.org:** The home of Mozilla, a popular alternative Web browser. Many users consider Mozilla to be the best Web browser around.

✦ **www.opera.com:** The home of Opera, another alternative to Internet Explorer.

Wireless Networking

Here are some Web sites with general information about wireless networking:

✦ **www.80211-planet.com:** 802.11 Planet, a large site devoted to news, information, and product reviews for wireless networking.

✦ **wifinetnews.com:** Wi-Fi Networking News, a source for daily news on wireless networking.

Here are the Web sites for the most popular manufacturers of wireless networking products:

✦ **www.linksys.com:** Linksys, a manufacturer of wireless network cards and access points.

✦ **www.netgear.com:** NETGEAR, another manufacturer of wireless components.

✦ **www.dlink.com:** DLINK, yet another manufacturer of inexpensive wireless products.

✦ **www.smc.com:** The home page for SMC, another manufacturer of wireless network products.

✦ **www.cisco.com:** Cisco is the place to go for high-end wireless networking.

✦ **www.3com.com:** 3Com is another good place to go for wireless networking components.

The following Web sites have interesting information about wireless network security:

✦ **www.netstumbler.com:** The makers of Network Stumbler, software that detects wireless network access and security problems.

✦ **www.airwave.com:** The makers of AirWave, a software-based tool that snoops for unauthorized access points.

✦ **www.wardriving.com:** An extensive site devoted to the practice of wardriving.

**Book X
Appendix A**

**Directory of Useful
Websites**

Appendix B: Glossary

10Base2: The type of coax cable most often used for Ethernet networks. Also known as *thinnet* or *cheapernet*. The maximum length of a single segment is 185 meters (600 feet).

10Base5: The original Ethernet coax cable, now used mostly as the backbone for larger networks. Also known as *yellow cable* or *thick cable*. The maximum length of a single segment is 500 meters (1,640 feet).

10BaseT: Twisted-pair cable, commonly used for Ethernet networks. Also known as *UTP, twisted pair,* or *twisted sister* (just kidding!). The maximum length of a single segment is 100 meters (330 feet). Of the three Ethernet cable types, this one is the easiest to work with.

100BaseFX: The Ethernet standard for high-speed fiber-optic connections.

100BaseTX: The leading standard for 100Mbps Ethernet, which uses two-pair Category-5 twisted-pair cable.

100BaseT4: An alternative standard for 100Mbps Ethernet using four-pair Category-3 cable.

100VG AnyLAN: A standard for 100Mbps Ethernet that isn't as popular as 100BaseT. Like 100BaseT, 100VG AnyLAN uses twisted-pair cable.

1000BaseT: A new standard for 1,000Mbps Ethernet using four-pair Category-5 unshielded twisted pair cable. 1000BaseT is also known as Gigabit Ethernet.

1000000000BaseT: Well, not really. But if current trends continue, we'll get there soon.

802.2: The forgotten IEEE standard. The more glamorous 802.3 standard relies upon 802.2 for moral support.

802.3: The IEEE standard known in the vernacular as *Ethernet*.

802.11: The IEEE standard for wireless networking. Two popular variants are 802.11a and 802.11b.

8088 processor: The microprocessor chip around which IBM designed its original PC, marking the transition from the Bronze Age to the Iron Age.

80286 processor: *Computo-habilis,* an ancient ancestor of today's modern computers.

80386 processor: The first 32-bit microprocessor chip used in personal computers, long since replaced by newer, better designs but still used by far too many people.

80486 processor: The last of Intel's CPU chips to have a number instead of a name. Replaced years ago by the Pentium processor.

AAUI: *Apple Attachment Unit Interface,* a type of connector used in some Apple Ethernet networks.

access rights: A list of rights that tell you what you can and can't do with network files or directories.

account: You can't get into the network without one of these. The network knows who you are and what rights you have on the network by virtue of your account.

acronym: An abbreviation made up of the first letters of a series of words.

Active Directory: The directory service in Windows 2000.

Active Server Pages: An Internet feature from Microsoft that enables you to create Web pages with scripts that run on the server rather than on the client. Also known as *ASP.* The newest version is called ASP.NET.

adapter card: An electronic card that you can plug into one of your computer's adapter slots to give it some new and fabulous capability, such as displaying 16 million colors, talking to other computers over the phone, or accessing a network.

address book: In an e-mail system, a list of users with whom you regularly correspond.

administrator: The big network cheese who is responsible for setting things up and keeping them running. Pray that it's not you. Also known as the *network manager.*

AFP: *Apple Filing Protocol,* a protocol for filing used by Apple. (That helps a lot, doesn't it?)

AGP: *Advanced Graphics Port,* a high-speed graphics interface used on most new computer motherboards.

allocation unit: Windows allocates space to files one allocation unit at a time; the allocation unit is typically 2,048 or 4,096 bytes, depending on the size of the disk. Also known as *cluster.* NetWare and Windows NT/2000/2003 Server can use allocation schemes that are more efficient than standard Windows.

antivirus program: A program that sniffs out viruses on your network and sends them into exile.

Apache: The most popular Web server on the Internet. It comes free with most versions of Linux.

AppleTalk: Apple's networking system for Macintoshes.

application layer: The highest layer of the OSI reference model, which governs how software communicates with the network.

archive bit: A flag that's kept for each file to indicate whether the file has been modified since it was last backed up.

ARCnet: A slow but steady network topology developed originally by Datapoint. ARCnet uses a token-passing scheme similar to Token Ring.

Athlon: A competitor to Intel's Pentium CPU chip manufactured by AMD.

attributes: Characteristics that are assigned to files. DOS alone provides four attributes: system, hidden, read-only, and archive. Network operating systems generally expand the list of file attributes.

AUI: *Attachment Unit Interface,* the big connector found on older network cards and hubs that's used to attach yellow cable via a transceiver.

AUTOEXEC.BAT: A batch file that DOS executes automatically every time you start your computer.

AUTOEXEC.NCF: A batch file that NetWare executes automatically every time you load the server software.

backbone: A trunk cable used to tie sections of a network together. The backbone is often 100Mbps Fast Ethernet.

BackOffice: A suite of Microsoft programs designed to run on a Windows server.

backup: A copy of your important files made for safekeeping in case something happens to the original files; something you should make every day.

banner: A fancy page that's printed between each print job so that you can easily separate jobs from one another.

batch file: In DOS, a file that contains one or more commands that are executed together as a set. You create the batch file by using a text editor (like the DOS `EDIT` command) and run the file by typing its name at the command prompt.

benchmark: A repeatable test you use to judge the performance of your network. The best benchmarks are the ones that closely duplicate the type of work you routinely do on your network.

BNC connector: The connector that's used with 10Base2 cable.

bottleneck: The slowest link in your network, which causes work to get jammed up. The first step in improving network performance is identifying the bottlenecks.

bridge: Not the popular card game, but a device that enables you to link two networks together. Bridges are smart enough to know which computers are on which side of the bridge, so they allow only those messages that need to get to the other side to cross the bridge. This device improves performance on both sides of the bridge.

broadband: A high-speed connection used for wide-area networking.

buffer: An area of memory that holds data en route to somewhere else. For example, a hard drive buffer holds data as it travels between your computer and the hard drive.

bus: A type of network topology in which network nodes are strung out along a single run of cable called a *segment.* 10Base2 and LocalTalk networks use a bus topology. *Bus* also refers to the row of expansion slots within your computer.

cache: A sophisticated form of buffering in which a large amount of memory is set aside to hold data so that it can be accessed quickly.

Category-3: An inexpensive form of unshielded twisted pair (UTP) that is suitable only for 10Mbps networks (10BaseT). Avoid using Category-3 cable for new networks.

Category-5: The higher grade of UPT cable that is suitable for 100Mbps networks (100BaseTX) and gigabit Ethernet (1000BaseT).

Category-6: An even higher grade of UTP cable that's more reliable than Category 5 cable for gigabit Ethernet.

CD-R drive: A CD drive that can read and write CDs.

CD-ROM: A high-capacity disc that uses optical technology to store data in a form that can be read but not written over.

CD-RW drive: A CD drive that can read, write, and then rewrite CDs.

Certified NetWare Engineer: Someone who has studied hard and passed the official exam offered by Novell. Also known as *CNE*.

Certified Network Dummy: Someone who knows nothing about networks but nevertheless gets the honor of installing one. Also known as *CND*.

chat: What you do on the network when you talk *live* with another network user.

Chaucer: A dead English dude.

cheapernet: See *10Base2*.

CHKDSK: A DOS command that checks the record-keeping structures of a DOS hard drive for errors.

click: What you do in Windows to get things done.

client: A computer that has access to the network but doesn't share any of its own resources with the network. See *server*.

client/server: A vague term meaning roughly that the work load is split between a client and server computer.

Clouseau: The most dangerous man in all of France. Some people say he only plays the fool.

cluster: See *allocation unit*.

coaxial cable: A type of cable that contains two conductors. The center conductor is surrounded by a layer of insulation, which is then wrapped by a braided-metal conductor and an outer layer of insulation.

Com1, Com2: The first two serial ports on a computer.

CompuServe: An online information network that you can access to talk with other users about issues such as NetWare, Windows NT/2000, politics, and the latest reality-based TV show.

computer name: A unique name assigned to each computer on a network.

CONFIG.SYS: A file on every DOS computer that contains configuration information. CONFIG.SYS is processed every time you start your computer.

console: In NetWare, the file server's keyboard and monitor. Console commands can be entered only at the server console.

console operator: In NetWare, a user working at the file server's console.

Control Panel: In Windows, an application that enables you to configure various aspects of the Windows operating system.

conventional memory: The first 640KB of memory on a DOS-based computer.

CPU: The *central processing unit,* or brains, of the computer.

crimp tool: A special tool used to attach connectors to cables. No network manager should be without one. Try not to get your fingers caught in it.

CSMA/CD: *Carrier Sense Multiple Access with Collision Detection,* the traffic management technique used by Ethernet.

daisy-chain: A way of connecting computer components in which the first component is connected to the second, which is connected to the third, and so on. In 10BaseT and 100BaseT Ethernet, you can daisy-chain hubs together.

DAT: *Digital audiotape,* a type of tape often used for network backup.

data-link layer: The second layer of the OSI model, responsible for transmitting bits of data over the network cable.

dedicated server: A computer used exclusively as a network server.

delayed write: A hard drive-caching technique in which data written to hard drive is placed in cache memory and actually written to hard drive later.

differential backup: A type of backup in which only the files that have changed since the last full backup are backed up.

DIP switch: A bank of switches used to configure an old-fashioned adapter card. Modern cards configure themselves automatically, so DIP switches aren't required. See *jumper block*.

directory hash: A popular breakfast food enjoyed by NetWare managers.

disk: Also known as a hard drive. A device that stores information magnetically on a hard drive. A hard drive is permanently sealed in an enclosure and has a capacity usually measured in thousands of megabytes. Also known as *gigabytes*. A *floppy disk* is removable and can have a capacity of 360KB, 720KB, 1.2MB, 1.44MB, or 2.88MB.

DMA channel: A direct pipeline for I/O that's faster than normal I/O. Network cards use DMA for fast network access.

DNS: See *Domain Name System*.

domain: (1) In a Windows NT/2000 network, one or more network servers that are managed by a single network directory. (2) In the Internet, a name assigned to a network.

Domain Name System (DNS): The naming system used on the Internet, in which a network is given a domain name and individual computers are given host names.

DOS: *Disk Operating System,* the original operating system for IBM and IBM-compatible computers. DOS isn't used as much now that Windows has taken over.

dot-matrix printer: A prehistoric type of printer that works by applying various-colored pigments to the walls of caves. Once the mainstay printer for PCs, dot-matrix printers have given way to laser printers and inkjet printers. High-speed matrix printers still have their place on the network, though, and matrix printers have the advantage of being able to print multipart forms.

DriveSpace: A disk compression feature of Windows 9x/Me (and MS-DOS 6.2). DriveSpace compresses file data so that files require less hard drive space. This compression increases the effective capacity of the hard drive, often by a factor of 2:1 or more.

dumb terminal: Back in the heyday of mainframe computers, a monitor and keyboard attached to the central mainframe. All the computing work occurred at the mainframe; the terminal only displayed the results and sent input typed at the keyboard back to the mainframe.

DVD drive: A new type of CD-ROM drive with much higher storage capacity than a standard CD-ROM drive — as much as 17GB on a single drive compared to the 600MB capacity of a standard CD.

Eddie Haskell: The kid who's always sneaking around, poking his nose into other people's business, and generally causing trouble. Every network has one.

editor: A program for creating and changing text files. DOS 5 and later versions come with a basic editor called EDIT. Other editors are available, but EDIT is good enough for most network needs.

EGA: The color monitor that was standard with IBM AT computers, based on 80286 processors. Now obsolete, but some are still in use.

EISA bus: *Extended Industry Standard Architecture,* an improved I/O bus that is compatible with the standard ISA bus but provides advanced features. Computers with an EISA bus were often used as file servers until the PCI bus became more popular. See *ISA bus* and *PCI.*

e-mail: Messages that are exchanged with other network users.

emoticon: A shorthand way of expressing emotions in e-mail and chats by combining symbols to create smiles, frowns, and so on.

enterprise computing: A trendy term that refers to a view of an organization's complete computing needs, rather than just a single department's or group's needs.

Ethernet: The World's Most Popular Network Standard.

EtherTalk: What you call Ethernet when you use it on a Macintosh.

ETLA: *Extended Three-Letter Acronym,* an acronym with four letters. See *TLA.*

Exchange Server: The software that handles e-mail services on a Windows NT or 2000 server.

Fast Ethernet: 100Mbps Ethernet. Also known as 100BaseT or 100BaseTX.

FAT: *File allocation table,* a record-keeping structure that DOS uses to keep track of the location of every file on a hard drive.

FAT32: An improved way of keeping track of hard drive files that can be used with Windows 98 and later.

FDDI: *Fiber Distributed Data Interface,* a 100Mbps network standard used with fiber-optic backbone. When FDDI is used, FDDI FDDI/Ethernet bridges connect Ethernet segments to the backbone.

ferrule: The outer metal tube that you crimp on to attach a BNC connector to the cable.

fiber-optic cable: A blazingly fast network cable that transmits data using light rather than electricity. Fiber-optic cable is often used as the backbone in large networks, especially where great distances are involved.

file rights: The ability of a particular network user to access specific files on a network server.

file server: A network computer containing hard drives that are available to network users.

firewall: A special type of router that connects a LAN to the Internet while preventing unauthorized Internet users from accessing the LAN.

FTP: *File Transfer Protocol,* a method for retrieving files from the Internet.

full backup: A backup of all the files on a hard drive, whether or not the files have been modified since the last backup. See *differential backup*.

gateway: A device that connects dissimilar networks. Gateways often connect Ethernet networks to mainframe computers or to the Internet.

GB: *Gigabyte,* roughly a billion bytes of hard drive storage (1,024MB to be precise). See *KB*, *MB*, and *TB*.

generation backup: A backup strategy in which several sets of backup disks or tapes are retained; sometimes called grandfather-father-son.

generation gap: What happens when you skip one of your backups.

glass house: The room where the mainframe computer is kept. Symbolic of the mainframe mentality, which stresses bureaucracy, inflexibility, and heavy iron.

group account: A grouping of user accounts that share common access rights.

groupware: A relatively new category of application programs that are designed with networks in mind to enable and even promote collaborative work.

guru: Anyone who knows more about computers than you do.

HTML: *Hypertext Markup Language,* the language used to compose pages that can be displayed via the World Wide Web.

HTTP: *Hypertext Transfer Protocol,* the protocol used by the World Wide Web for sending HTML pages from a server computer to a client computer.

HTTPS: A secure form of HTTP that is used to transmit sensitive data such as credit card numbers.

hub: In Ethernet, a device that is used with 10BaseT and 100BaseT cabling to connect computers to the network. Most hubs have from 5 to 24 ports. See also *switch*.

IACI: *International Association of the Computer Impaired.*

IDE: *Integrated Drive Electronics*, the most common type of hard drive interface in use today, popular because of its low cost and flexibility. For server computers, SCSI is the preferred drive interface. See **SCSI**.

IEEE: *Institute of Electrical and Electronic Engineers*, where they send computer geeks who've had a few too many parity errors.

incremental backup: A type of backup in which only the files that have changed since the last backup are backed up. Unlike a differential backup, an incremental backup resets each file's archive bit as it backs it up. See *archive bit*, *differential backup*, and *full backup*.

inkjet printer: A type of printer that creates full-color pages by spraying tiny jets of ink onto paper.

Internet: A humongous network of networks that spans the globe and gives you access to just about anything you could ever hope for, provided that you can figure out how to work it.

Internet Explorer: Microsoft's popular Web browser.

interoperability: Providing a level playing field for incompatible networks to work together, kind of like NAFTA.

intranet: A network that resembles the Internet but is accessible only within a company or organization. Most intranets use the familiar World Wide Web interface to distribute information to company employees.

intranetWare: A funny name that Novell used for NetWare when the term *intranet* was the hottest buzzword.

I/O port address: Every I/O device in a computer — including network interface cards — must be assigned a unique address. In the old days, you had to configure the port address using DIP switches or jumpers. Newer network cards automatically configure their own port addresses so that you don't have to mess with switches or jumper blocks.

IP address: A string of numbers used to address computers on the Internet. If you enable TCP/IP on your network, you must provide an IP address for each computer on the network.

IPX: A transport protocol used by NetWare.

IPX.COM: The program file that implements IPX.

IRQ: *Interrupt ReQuest*, network interface cards must be configured for the proper IRQ in order to work. In olden times, you had to use DIP switches or jumper blocks to set the IRQ. Nowadays, network cards configure themselves.

ISA bus: *Industry Standard Architecture,* a once popular type of expansion bus for accommodating adapter cards. Now replaced by PCI.

ISDN: A digital telephone connection that lets you connect to the Internet at about twice the speed of a regular phone connection.

ISO: *International Standards Organization,* whom we can thank for OSI.

ISP: *Internet service provider,* a company that provides access to the Internet for a fee.

Java: A programming language popular on the Internet.

JavaScript: A popular scripting language that can be used on Web pages.

JetDirect: A device made by Hewlett-Packard that enables printers to connect directly to the network without the need for a separate print server computer.

jumper block: A device used to configure an old-fashioned adapter card. To change the setting of a jumper block, you remove the jumper from one set of pins and place it on another.

KB: *Kilobytes,* roughly one thousand bytes (1,024 to be precise). See *GB*, *MB*, and *TB*.

LAN: *Local area network,* what this book is all about.

LAN Manager: An obsolete network operating system that Microsoft used to sell. Microsoft long ago put all its networking eggs in the Windows NT/2000 basket, so LAN Manager exists only on isolated islands along with soldiers who are still fighting World War II.

LAN Server: IBM's version of LAN Manager.

LANcache: The disk caching program that comes with LANtastic.

LANtastic: A peer-to-peer network operating system that was once the most popular choice for small networks. When the good folks at Microsoft saw how popular LANtastic was, they decided to add free networking features to Windows. As a result, not too many people use LANtastic anymore.

laser printer: A high-quality printer that uses lasers and photon torpedoes to produce beautiful output.

lemon-pudding layer: A layer near the middle of the OSI reference model that provides flavor and moistness to an otherwise dry and tasteless fruitcake.

Book X
Appendix B

Glossary

Linux: An almost-free version of the UNIX operating system that is becoming popular as a network server.

LLC sublayer: The *logical link sublayer* of layer 2 of the OSI model. The LLC is addressed by the IEEE 802.2 standard.

local area network: See *LAN*.

local bus: A fast expansion bus found on 486 and Pentium computers that operates at a higher speed than the old ISA bus and allows 32-bit data transfers. Two types are commonly found: VESA and PCI. Many 486 computers include several VESA local bus slots, but newer Pentium computers use PCI slots. For best network performance, all servers should have VESA or PCI disk I/O and network interface cards.

local resources: Disk drives, printers, and other devices that are attached directly to a workstation rather than accessed via the network.

LocalTalk: Apple's scheme for cabling Macintosh networks by using the Mac's printer ports. PhoneNET is a cabling scheme that's compatible with LocalTalk but less expensive.

log in: Same as *log on*.

log on: The process of identifying oneself to the network (or a specific network server) and gaining access to network resources.

log out: The process of leaving the network. When you log out, any network drives or printers you were connected to become unavailable to you.

LOGIN: The NetWare command used to log on to a NetWare network.

LOGIN **directory:** In NetWare, a network directory that's mapped to the workstation before the user has logged on. The LOGIN directory contains commands and programs that are accessible to every computer on the network, regardless of whether a user has logged on. Chief among these commands is the LOGIN command.

logon name: In a Windows network, the name that identifies a user uniquely to the network. Same as *user name* or *user ID*.

logon script: A file of NetWare commands that is executed when a user logs on.

LOGOUT: In NetWare, the command you use to log out.

LPT1: The first printer port on a PC. If a computer has a local printer, it more than likely is attached to this port. That's why you should set up printer redirections using LPT2 and LPT3.

Mac OS X: The latest and greatest operating system for Macintoshes.

Mac OS X Server: Apple's most powerful server operating system for Macintosh computers.

MAC sublayer: The *media access control* sublayer of layer 2 of the OSI model. The MAC is addressed by the IEEE 802.3 standard.

Macintosh: A cute little computer that draws great pictures and comes with built-in networking.

mail server: The server computer on which e-mail messages are stored. This same computer also may be used as a file and print server, or it may be dedicated as a mail server.

**Book X
Appendix B**

mainframe: A huge computer housed in a glass house on raised floors and cooled with liquid nitrogen. The cable that connects the hard drives to the CPU weighs more than most PCs.

Glossary

mapping: Assigning unused drive letters to network drives or unused printer ports to network printers. See *redirection*.

MB: *Megabytes,* roughly one million bytes (1,024K to be precise). See *GB*, *KB*, and *TB*.

memory: The electronic storage where your computer stores data that's being manipulated and programs that are running. See *RAM*.

metaphor: A literary construction suitable for Shakespeare and Steinbeck but a bit overused by writers of computer books.

modem: A device that converts signals the computer understands into signals that can be accurately transmitted over the phone to another modem, which converts the signals back into their original form. Computers use modems to talk to each other. *Modem* is a combination of *modulator-demodulator.*

mouse: The obligatory way to use Windows. When you grab it and move it around, the cursor moves on the screen. After you get the hand-eye coordination down, using it is a snap. *Hint:* Don't pick it up and talk into it like Scotty did in *Star Trek IV.* Very embarrassing, especially if you've traveled millions of miles to get here.

Mr. McFeeley: The nerdy-looking mailman on *Mr. Rogers' Neighborhood.* He'd make a great computer geek. Speedy delivery!

My Network Places: An icon on Windows XP, Windows 2000, and Window Millennium desktops that enables you to access network servers and resources. In Windows 95 and 98, this icon is known as *Network Neighborhood.*

.NET: A new Windows application environment that promises to simplify the task of creating and using applications for Windows and for the Web.

NETBIOS: *Network basic input output system,* a high-level networking standard developed by IBM and used by most peer-to-peer networks. It can be used with NetWare as well.

Netscape: The company that makes Navigator, a popular program for browsing the World Wide Web.

NetWare: A popular network operating system, the proud child of Novell, Inc.

NetWare Directory Services: A feature of NetWare first introduced with Version 4, in which the resources of the servers are pooled together to form a single entity.

NetWare Loadable Module: A program that's loaded at the file server. Also known as *NLM.* NLMs extend the functionality of NetWare by providing additional services. Btrieve runs as an NLM, as do various backup, antivirus, and other utilities.

network: What this book is about. For more information, see Books I through X.

network drive: A drive that resides somewhere out in the network rather than on your own computer.

network interface card: An adapter card that lets the computer attach to a network cable. Also known as *NIC.*

network layer: One of the layers somewhere near the middle of the OSI reference model. It addresses the interconnection of networks.

network manager: Hope that it's someone other than you.

Network Neighborhood: An icon on a Windows 95 or 98 desktop that enables you to access network servers and resources. In Windows 2000 and Windows Millennium, this icon is known as *My Network Places.*

network operating system: An operating system for networks, such as NetWare or Windows 2000 Server. Also known as *NOS.*

network resource: A disk drive, printer, or other device that's located in a server computer and shared with other users, in contrast with a *local resource,* which is located in a user's computer.

newsgroup: Internet discussion groups in which people leave messages that can be read and responded to by other Internet users.

NIC: See *network interface card*.

NLM: See *NetWare Loadable Module*.

node: A device on the network, typically a computer or printer. A router is also a node.

NOS: See *network operating system*.

Novell: The folks you can thank or blame for NetWare, depending on your mood.

NTFS: A special type of disk format that you can use on Windows NT/2000 Server and Windows XP hard drives for improved performance and security.

offline: Not available on the network.

online: Available on the network.

operator: A user who has control over operational aspects of the network, but doesn't necessarily have the power to grant or revoke access rights, create user accounts, and so on.

OSI: The agency Lee Majors worked for in *The Six Million Dollar Man*. Also, the *Open System Interconnection* reference model, a seven-layer fruitcake framework upon which networking standards are hung.

packets: Data is sent over the network in manageable chunks called *packets,* or *frames*. The size and makeup of a packet is determined by the protocol being used.

parallel port: A port normally used to connect printers, sometimes called a *printer port*. Parallel ports send data over eight "parallel" wires, one byte at a time. See *serial port*.

partition: A division of a single hard drives into several smaller units that are treated by the operating system as if they were separate drives.

password: The only thing protecting your files from an impostor masquerading as you. Keep your password secret, and you'll have a long and happy life.

Book X
Appendix B

Glossary

patch cable: A short cable used to connect a computer to a wall outlet, or one running from a patch panel to a hub.

PCI: *Peripheral Component Interconnect,* the high-speed bus design found in modern Pentium computers.

PCONSOLE: The NetWare command you use from a DOS command prompt to manage network printing.

peer-to-peer network: A network in which any computer can be a server if it wants to be. Kind of like the network version of the Great American Dream. You can easily construct peer-to-peer networks by using Windows.

permissions: Rights that have been granted to a particular user or group of users enabling them to access specific files.

PhoneNET: An alternative cabling scheme for Macintosh networks, cheaper than Apple's LocalTalk cables.

physical layer: The lowest layer of the OSI reference model (whatever that is). It refers to the parts of the network you can touch: cables, connectors, and so on.

pocket protector: A status symbol among computer geeks.

port: A connector on the back of your computer that you can use to connect a device such as a printer, modem, mouse, and so on.

PPP: *Point to Point Protocol,* the most common way of connecting to the Internet for World Wide Web access.

presentation layer: The sixth layer of the OSI reference model, which handles data conversions, compression, decompression, and other menial tasks.

print job: A report, letter, memo, or other document that has been sent to a network printer but hasn't printed yet. Print jobs wait patiently in the queue until a printer agrees to print them.

Print Manager: In old-style Windows (Windows 3.1 and Windows for Workgroups), the program that handles print spooling.

print queue: The line that print jobs wait in until a printer becomes available.

print server: A computer that handles network printing or a device such as a JetDirect, which enables the printer to attach directly to the network.

PRN: The DOS code name for the first parallel port. Also known as *LPT1.*

protocol: (1) The droid C-3PO's specialty. (2) The rules of the network game. Protocols define standardized formats for data packets, techniques for detecting and correcting errors, and so on.

punch-down block: A gadget for quickly connecting a bunch of wires, used in telephone and network wiring closets.

QIC: *Quarter-inch cartridge,* the most popular and least expensive form of tape backup. Now known as *Travan drives.* See **DAT** and ***Travan***.

queue: A list of items waiting to be processed. The term usually refers to the list of print jobs waiting to be printed, but networks have lots of other types of queues as well.

RAID: *Redundant Array of Inexpensive Disks,* a bunch of hard drives strung together and treated as if they were one drive. The data is spread out over several drives, and one of the drives keeps checking information so that if any one of the drives fails, the data can be reconstructed.

RAM: *Random access memory,* your computer's memory chips.

redirection: One of the basic concepts of networking, in which a device, such as a disk drive or printer, appears to be a local device but actually resides on the network. The networking software on your computer intercepts I/O requests for the device and redirects them to the network.

registry: The file where Windows keeps its configuration information.

repeater: A device that strengthens a signal so that it can travel on. Repeaters are used to lengthen the cable distance between two nodes. A *multiport repeater* is the same as a *hub*.

resource: A hard drive, hard drive directory, printer, modem, CD-ROM, or other device that can be shared on the network.

ring: A type of network topology in which computers are connected to one another in a way that forms a complete circle. Imagine the Waltons standing around the Thanksgiving table holding hands, and you have the idea of a ring topology.

RJ-45: The kind of plug used by 10BaseT and 100BaseT networks. It looks kind of like a modular phone plug, but it's bigger.

router: A device that works kind of like a bridge but can handle different protocols. For example, a router can link Ethernet to LocalTalk or a mainframe.

Samba: A program that runs on a Linux server, allowing the Linux computer to work as a file and print server in a Windows network.

Book X
Appendix B

Glossary

ScanDisk: A Windows command that examines your hard drive for physical defects.

scheduling software: Software that schedules meetings of network users. Works only if all network users keep their calendars up-to-date.

SCSI: *Small computer systems interface,* a connection used mostly for hard drives but also suitable for CD-ROM drives, tape drives, and just about anything else. Also winner of the Acronym Computer Geeks Love to Pronounce Most award.

segment: A single-run cable, which may connect more than two computers, with a terminator on each end.

serial port: A port normally used to connect a modem or mouse to a DOS-based computer, sometimes called a communications port. See *parallel port*.

server: A computer that's on the network and shares resources with other network users. The server may be dedicated, which means that its sole purpose in life is to provide service for network users, or it may be used as a client as well. See *client*.

session layer: A layer somewhere near the middle of the beloved OSI reference model that deals with sessions between network nodes.

SFT: *System Fault Tolerance,* a set of networking features designed to protect the network from faults, such as stepping on the line (known as a *foot fault*).

share name: A name that you assign to a network resource when you share it. Other network users use the share name to access the shared resource.

shared folder: A network server hard drive or a folder on a server hard drive that has been shared so that other computers on the network can access it.

shared resource: A resource, such as a hard drive or printer, that is made available to other network users.

shielded twisted pair: Twisted-pair cable with shielding, used mostly for Token Ring networks. Also known as *STP*. See *twisted pair*.

smiley: A face made from various keyboard characters; often used in e-mail messages to convey emotion. :-)

SNA: *Systems Network Architecture,* a networking standard developed by IBM that dates from the mid-Mainframerasic Period, approximately 65 million years ago. Used by fine IBM mainframe and AS/400 minicomputers everywhere.

sneakernet: The cheapest form of network, in which users exchange files by copying them to disks and walking them between computers.

SNMP: *Simple Network Management Protocol,* a standard for exchanging network management information between network devices that is anything but simple.

spooling: A printing trick in which data that is intended for a printer is actually written to a temporary hard drive file and later sent to the printer.

star: A type of network topology in which each node is connected to a central wiring hub. This gives the network a star-like appearance.

SUPERVISOR: The top-dog account in NetWare. Log on as SUPERVISOR, and you can do just about anything.

switch: An efficient type of hub that sends packets only to the port that is connected to the packet's recipient rather than sending packets to all of the ports, as a simple hub does.

SYS: The volume name of the system volume on most NetWare servers.

system fault tolerance: See *SFT.*

tape drive: The best way to back up a network server. Tape drives have become so inexpensive that even small networks should have one.

task: For a technically accurate description, enroll in a computer science graduate course. For a layperson's understanding of what a task is, picture the guy who used to spin plates on *The Ed Sullivan Show.* Each plate is a task. The poor guy had to frantically move from plate to plate to keep them all spinning. Computers work the same way. Each program task is like one of those spinning plates; the computer must service each one periodically to keep it going.

TB: *Terrazzo bytes,* imported from Italy. Approximately one trillion bytes (1,024GB to be precise). (Just kidding about *terrazzo bytes.* Actually, TB stands for *terabytes.* It won't be long before you can buy hard drives that can hold a terabyte or more.)

TCP/IP: *Transmission Control Protocol/Internet Protocol,* the protocol used by the Internet.

terminator: The little plug you have to use at each end of a segment of thin coax cable (10BaseT).

thinnet: See *10Base2.*

three-letter acronym: See *TLA*.

time sharing: A technique used on mainframe computers to enable several users to access the computer at the same time.

time-out: How long the print server waits while receiving print output before deciding that the print job has finished.

TLA: *Three-letter acronym,* such as FAT (File Allocation Table), DUM (Dirty Upper Memory), and HPY (Heuristic Private Yodel).

token: The thing that gets passed around the network in a Token Ring topology. See *Token Ring*.

Token Ring: A network that's cabled in a ring topology in which a special packet called a token is passed from computer to computer. A computer must wait until it receives the token before sending data over the network.

topology: The shape of the network; how its computers and cables are arranged. See *bus, star,* and *ring*.

transceiver: A doohickey that connects a network interface card (NIC) to a network cable. A transceiver is always required to connect a computer to the network, but 10Base2 and 10BaseT NICs have built-in transceivers. Transceivers were originally used with yellow cable. You can also get transceivers that convert an AUI port to 10BaseT.

transport layer: One of those layers somewhere near the middle of the OSI reference model that addresses the way data is escorted around the network.

Travan: A newer technology for inexpensive tape backup that can record up to 800MB on a single tape cartridge. See *QIC* and *DAT*.

trojan horse: A program that looks interesting but turns out to be something nasty, like a hard-drive reformatter.

trustee rights: In NetWare, rights that have been granted to a particular user or group of users enabling them to access specific files.

twisted pair: A type of cable that consists of one or more pairs of wires that are twisted in a certain way to improve the cable's electrical characteristics. See *unshielded twisted pair* and *shielded twisted pair*.

uninterruptible power supply: See *UPS*.

unshielded twisted pair: Twisted-pair cable that doesn't have a heavy metal shield around it. Used for 10BaseT networks. Also known as *UTP*. See *twisted pair*.

UPS: *Uninterruptible power supply,* a gizmo that switches to battery power whenever the power cuts out. The *Enterprise* didn't have one of these, which is why the lights always went out until Spock could switch to auxiliary power.

URL: *Uniform Resource Locator,* a fancy term for an Internet address. URLs are those familiar "dot" addresses, such as "www-dot-microsoft-dot-com" or "www-dot-dummies-dot-com."

USB: A high-speed serial interface that is found on most new computers. USB can be used to connect printers, scanners, mice, keyboards, network adapters, and other devices.

user ID: The name by which you're known to the network.

User Manager for Domains: The program you use on Windows NT to manage user accounts.

user profile: The way Windows keeps track of each user's desktop settings, such as window colors, wallpaper, screen savers, Start menu options, favorites, and so on.

user rights: Network actions that a particular network user is allowed to perform after he or she has logged on to the network. See *file rights*.

users' group: A local association of computer users, sometimes with a particular interest, such as networking.

UTP: *Unshielded twisted pair.* See *10BaseT*.

VBScript: A scripting language that can be used to add fancy features to Web pages or to create macros for Microsoft Office programs.

VGA: *Video Graphics Array,* the current standard in video monitors. Most VGA adapters these days are actually super VGA adapters, which are compatible with VGA adapters but have extra bells and whistles.

Vines: A network operating system made by Banyan, comparable to NetWare or Windows NT/2000 Server.

virus: An evil computer program that slips into your computer undetected, tries to spread itself to other computers, and may eventually do something bad like trash your hard drive.

volume name: In NetWare, each hard drive volume has a name. Most NetWare servers have a volume named SYS.

Web browser: A program that enables you to display information retrieved from the Internet's World Wide Web.

**Book X
Appendix B**

Glossary

Windows: The world's most popular operating system.

Windows 95: A version of Windows that became available in — you guessed it — 1995. Windows 95 was the first version of Windows that did not require DOS.

Windows 98: The successor to Windows 95 introduced in 1998. Windows 98 includes a new user interface that makes the Windows desktop resemble the World Wide Web.

Windows 2000 Server: The most popular Windows server operating system. Available in three editions: Windows 2000 Server, Windows 2000 Advanced Server, and Windows 2000 Datacenter Server for server computers.

Windows for Workgroups: Microsoft's first network-aware version of Windows, now pretty much defunct.

Windows Millennium Edition: The successor to Windows 98, designed especially for home users and featuring a Home Networking Wizard that simplifies the task of setting up a home network.

Windows NT: The predecessor to Windows 2000. Windows NT is available in two versions: Windows NT Client for desktop computers and Windows NT Server for server computers.

Windows Server 2003: The newest Windows server operating system version.

Windows XP: The newest version of Windows, designed for home or professional users.

wiring closet: Large networks need a place where cables can congregate. A closet is ideal.

workstation: See *client*.

World Wide Web: A graphical method of accessing information on the Internet.

WWW: See *World Wide Web*.

yellow cable: See *10Base5*.

Index